*"Journals is a treat to read, because it is the raw evidence of Ayn Rand's continuous growth across fifty years—her growth both as a philosopher and as an artist . . .*

*"We see the steps by which she [created her novels]—we are there when a dramatic event or scene first occurs to her, and we see what she finally does with it and why . . . We see how Ayn Rand uses (or deliberately does not use) her knowledge of real people. This last will answer such common questions as: Was Frank Lloyd Wright a model for Roark? Or William Randolph Hearst for Wynand? It will also answer some uncommon questions, such as: What female suggested Lois Cook? What scientist Robert Stadler? And what president Mr. Thompson?"*

—LEONARD PEIKOFF

LEONARD PEIKOFF is universally recognized as the world's premier Ayn Rand scholar. He worked closely with Rand for thirty years and was designated by her as heir to her estate. He has taught philosophy at Hunter College and New York University. Dr. Peikoff's books include *The Ominous Parallels* and *Objectivism: The Philosophy of Ayn Rand.* He is also co-editor of *The Ayn Rand Reader*, available in a Plume edition. For further information, you can go to his website, alshow.com.

DAVID HARRIMAN has M.S. degrees in both physics and philosophy. He has taught philosophy at California State University, San Bernardino, and is working on a book on the philosophy of physics. He has worked with Leonard Peikoff for several years.

# JOURNALS
# OF
# AYN RAND

## EDITED BY DAVID HARRIMAN

### FOREWORD BY LEONARD PEIKOFF

## A PLUME BOOK

PLUME
Published by the Penguin Group
Penguin Putnam Inc., 375 Hudson Street, New York, New York 10014, U.S.A.
Penguin Books Ltd, 27 Wrights Lane, London W8 5TZ, England
Penguin Books Australia Ltd, Ringwood, Victoria, Australia
Penguin Books Canada Ltd, 10 Alcorn Avenue, Toronto, Ontario, Canada M4V 3B2
Penguin Books (N.Z.) Ltd, 182–190 Wairau Road, Auckland 10, New Zealand

Penguin Books Ltd, Registered Offices: Harmondsworth, Middlesex, England

Published by Plume, a member of Penguin Putnam Inc.
Previously published in a Dutton edition.

First Plume Printing, August, 1999
10  9  8  7  6

 REGISTERED TRADEMARK—MARCA REGISTRADA

The Library of Congress has catalogued the Dutton edition as follows:
Rand, Ayn.
    Journals of Ayn Rand / edited by David Harriman ; foreword by Leonard Peikoff.
      p.   cm.
Includes index.
   ISBN 0-525-94370-6
       0-452-27887-2 (pbk.)
    1. Rand, Ayn—Diaries.   2. Women novelists, American—20th century—Diaries.
3. Women philosophers—United States—Diaries.   I. Harriman, David.
II. Peikoff, Leonard.   III. Title.
PS3535.A547Z476   1997
818'.5203—dc21
[B]                                                  97-12737
                                                    CIP

Printed in the United States of America
Set in Times New Roman

Information about other books by Ayn Rand and her philosophy, Objectivism, may be obtained by writing to OBJECTIVISM, Box 177, Murray Hill Station, New York, New York 10157 USA.

# CONTENTS

# FOREWORD
# BY LEONARD PEIKOFF

Ayn Rand's *Journals*—my name for her notes to herself through the decades—is the bulk of her still unpublished work, arranged chronologically. What remains to be published are two lecture courses on writing, presently being edited, and her old film scripts.

The *Journals* contains most of AR's notes for her three main novels—along with some early material, some notes made between *The Fountainhead* and *Atlas Shrugged*, and some notes from her final decades. The early material includes, among other things, AR's first philosophic musings on paper in English, written in her twenties. The middle section includes a fascinating transitional statement of her ethics, never finished, and also a vigorous essay on why the House Un-American Activities Committee in 1947 did *not* violate the civil rights of the Hollywood Communists. The final section includes the notes for AR's last projected novel, *To Lorne Dieterling*.

Some pieces important to this volume have been lost. I refer to eight or ten scenarios for the silent screen, written in the twenties. These stories, several pages apiece, featured strong heroes, a passionate love interest, and nonstop action, often set in exotic locales; they exemplified an extravagant romanticism bubbling over with the excitement of living. I first came upon these scenarios in the eighties, after AR's death. Had I been able to include them here, they would have brought a sorely needed balance to some other items, such as *The Little Street*, a bitter novelette from the same period. Mysteriously, these scenarios have disappeared from the Estate warehouse. If they should reappear, I promise to publish them.

Aside from occasional pieces, identified by the editor, the AR material in this book was written for herself, for her own clarity. No one, apart from her husband and a few associates, was ever shown any of this material, nor did AR intend to publish it. Obviously, therefore, nothing in the book may be taken as definitive of her ideas. On the contrary, most of these preliminary formulations were dropped, and a few were even contradicted, in her published works. In several cases, though hardly in all, the editor points out such discrepancies.

"The art of writing," AR wrote in a November 1944 note, "is the art of doing what you think you're doing. This is not as simple as it sounds. It implies a very difficult undertaking: the necessity to think. And it implies the requirement to think out three separate, very hard problems: What is it you want to say? How are you going to say it? Have you really said it?" It was to answer these questions that most of the *Journals* was written. In other words, the notes are nothing more than AR preparing herself to write by thinking aloud on paper—in random snatches, as and when she sought to clarify a point—without outline, structure, continuous theme, or editorial polish.

Despite its unedited character, however, the *Journals* is a treat to read, because it is the raw evidence of AR's continuous growth across fifty years—her growth both as a philosopher and as an artist.

One can see her growth as a philosopher in two ways: in her interests and in her ideas, i.e., in regard both to depth and to truth.

AR's mind moved systematically from politics (as a youth) to ethics (in her thirties and forties) to epistemology and metaphysics (in her fifties and later). This progression is not a mere change of interest, but a true organic development: the earlier stages increasingly exhibit the maturity of what is to come, which in turn always remains faithful in principle to its youthful origins. One great pleasure in reading the book is to see hints of later discoveries mentioned at first casually, even parenthetically. For instance, if you read AR's first philosophic musings with an eye to *Atlas Shrugged*, you will observe how much more you can see in her words now, thanks to her, than she herself could see at the time. Her distinctive ideas were present from her start as a thinker; they were implicit in her fundamental approach at least from the age of twelve. It was only a matter of time and logic until she was able to identify them explicitly.

The best evidence of AR's increasing depth is her unpublished manuscript *The Moral Basis of Individualism*. It is there that we see her evolution from *The Fountainhead*'s stress on independence to *Atlas Shrugged*'s recognition that the basic virtue is rationality, of which independence is but an aspect. We also see her taking the historic step from ethics to the base of philosophy. Traditionally, philosophers started their books on ethics by asking: What is the proper moral code? AR started there, too—until something occurred to her one day in mid-sentence: "Chapter 1 should *begin* by stating the [moral] axiom. Then define man's nature. Then ask [*these two words are deleted*] Or—begin by asking whether a moral code is necessary? Prove that it is—for a rational being. What is the rational? That which is true to *facts. . . .*" In regard to this passage I am tempted to paraphrase the mystics: To those who understand, no explanation is necessary; to those who do not, read Galt's speech.

In regard to the content of her ideas, AR also underwent an organic development as, step by step, she gained clarity about the full implications of her fundamental premises.

AR's first notes reveal an influence of Nietzsche, in the form of droplets of subjectivism, and of the idea that the heroes among men are innately great, as against the inherently corrupt masses, who deserve only bitterness and domination from their superiors. None of this is stated as a connected position, but such ideas do show up here and there.

· It is instructive to watch these droplets—every one of them—evaporate without residue, as AR's own principles emerge into the sunshine of explicit statement; it is a perfect example of science (reason) functioning as a self-corrective. After she comes to define "reason," subjectivism vanishes; after her analysis of individual rights, "domination" is gone; after she grasps the nature of volition, she says no more about "innate" stature.

By her early thirties, AR had thought herself out of every Nietzschean element. With *The Fountainhead*, the only trace left is in the characters of Dominique and Wynand, whose bitterness about the world Roark proves to be a cardinal error. After *The Fountainhead*, Nietzsche is not even an error to be refuted; there is nothing but pure Ayn Rand.

Although AR's vision of the ideal man remained constant through the decades, her view of his greatest enemy changed when the Nietzschean element was dropped. As a youngster, the first enemy of Man whom she could identify was Communism, the omnipotent State. Then, as she grew beyond politics, the enemy, for a short while, was taken to be the masses of average men as such, regardless of their political organization. One of the unique features of her mature hero-worship, by contrast, is her explicit benevolence towards the honest average man (as represented by Mike in *The Fountainhead* and Eddie Willers in *Atlas Shrugged*). By her early thirties, AR had discovered the real enemy of the ideal (which is also the real corrupter of politics and of the masses): the intellectuals of irrationalism. Thus, although AR's passionate values never changed, the early bitterness toward the commissars or the mob becomes in time the exposé of Ellsworth Toohey, and then the damnation of Kant.

One can see AR's growth as an artist in regard to every facet of writing a novel, with the emphasis on plot and characterization.

In regard to plot, we see the steps by which she learns to create it—we are there when a dramatic event or scene first occurs to her, and we see what she finally does with it and why. We see her continually restructure events so as to achieve an inexorable rise to a necessary but unpredictable climax. We see how several different lines of events (personal/emotional, economic, political, philosophical) are made to rise and climax at once, and how each of these lines helps reshape the others. And we see her carry on the plot struggles until she reaches the desired result: a seamless complexity that will enter the reader's mind with the simplicity of the inevitable.

In regard to characterization, we see her first concept of the cast (and her earliest names for the leads), then its simultaneous expansion and winnowing out. We see the sharpening focus on a character's distinctive attributes, and her decisions as to what kinds of actions and relationships will convey these objectively. We learn everything about the heroes and the villains that AR herself needs to know, even though she cannot always use the information in the final book. We are there when eloquent lines of dialogue occur to her, and sometimes see her move them from one mouth to another. And we see how AR uses (or deliberately does not use) her knowledge of real people. This last will answer such common questions as: Was Frank Lloyd Wright a model for Roark? Or William Randolph Hearst for Wynand? It will also answer some uncommon questions, such as: What female suggested Lois Cook? What scientist Robert Stadler? And what President Mr. Thompson?

In reading the *Journals*, we also see AR's methodical redefinition of a novel's theme so as to include the broader integrations she is always making and the concrete applications she is identifying. We see much of her research, from architecture to railroads to steel mills and copper mining, and how she uses it to aid her in the development of plot, character, and theme. And, sometimes—in regard both to fiction and to nonfiction—we see the first draft of a section, followed by her own ruthless critique and revision.

If the primary value of the *Journals* to us is the evidence it furnishes of AR's growth, a second value is the evidence that her growth was a product of *thinking*—in the art of which the *Journals* may serve as a textbook. The subtitle of this book really ought to be: How to Answer Your Own Questions.

Implicit in the countless examples of fruitful thinking which make up the book are dozens of practical guides to the art of *clear* thinking. Among other things, one can learn a great deal about the means of properly wording a question, the need for factual data (and at what point enough have been gathered), the roles of induction and deduction, the necessity and method of integration—then, as the final mopping up, the means of formulating a definitive proof of a conclusion.

On first reading (which is all I have done so far), three principles of clear thinking seemed, above all others, to leap out of the pages at me:

**1.** *The need for intellectual honesty.* For example, AR was troubled at one point by a seeming contradiction in her views—which she hastened not to evade, but to state forcefully. "[Now I shall consider] the hypothetical case of a monopoly (say, telephone) free to refuse services to an individual or a group of men or a branch of business. In this last case, it is obvious that the inventor's monopoly has such an absolute right. Does it mean, however, that individualism then degenerates into its opposite in practice, into collectivism? Has the size of an enterprise (made possible by the scope covered by modern inventions) anything to do with it? In other words, does invention such as the telephone give the individual who controls it a *collectivist's* power by the sheer size of his business? (*No,* I think.) . . ." (Sept. 30, 1944). AR raises, as a matter of course, every objection to her views that occurs to her—and then answers them all. This is one reason why, when she finally endorses a conclusion, she is certain of it.

**2.** *The need for precise formulation, even in private notes.* For example: "A possible definition of a *right*: a 'right' is that which it is morally permissible to defend by force. Here I have to be *very* careful. This might be totally wrong. If carelessly handled, it could be used as justification for the right of a communist to murder an employer who does not give him a job. Again, 'sins of omission' come in. This is only a hint, a possible clue to be thought out very carefully, from every possible angle and in every possible application. It is no good—*unless* a total *proof* of it can be given. . . ." (Oct. 26, 1944).

**3.** *The need for* fresh *writing.* To put this point negatively, there are no clichés in the *Journals*, no numbing restatements even of AR's own ideas. On the contrary, the notes are replete with new angles, new connections, new distinctions, new analogies, new wording— even in regard to issues which AR had discussed extensively in print. Most of this new material did not survive the *Journals*, despite its inherent interest; to her, it was merely steps on the road to clarity, the first birth pangs of the books still to come. My point, however, is that the freshness of the writing is a corollary of the process she is engaged in: not rationalistic deduction nor recitation of the known, but pioneering thought.

As a small example of the latter point, I offer the following note, never used in print, on the question of reason and emotion: "Man cannot, [some people] say, be called a rational being because his actions are not motivated by his mind; his mind is like his Sunday clothes, kept in a dark closet and donned reluctantly on rare occasions; and when donned, it makes him stiff, uncomfortable and unhappy, because it never fit him well in the first place. What man does on weekdays, they say, is to gallop about stark-naked, on all fours, because it reminds him of his mother who gave him a complex, and to whirl around catching his own tail which he hasn't got but feels he has; that is what he does because it makes him happy. Reason? Reason, they say, is just something he uses in such negligible, incidental matters as earning a living . . ." (July 30, 1945).

Too many of AR's professed admirers in print are academics of the scholastic persuasion. The *Journals* gives us the original, a purely Objectivist mind at work—mostly right, sometimes wrong, but always, from start to finish, reality-oriented.

In terms of cognitive value to the reader, the new material alone in this volume warrants the price. It is new to me also. No matter how clear Objectivism is in my mind, every time I read another Ayn Rand book, it becomes clearer. This book is no exception.

David Harriman has done an excellent editorial job. He has brought order to dozens of large cardboard cartons filled with scattered papers and mementos. He has selected the best of the notes, organized them chronologically, offered explanations when these were available and helpful, and edited the wording, especially for grammar, of the early pages, when AR had not yet fully grasped English. For all this work, I am grateful to David Harriman, as all fans of AR should be.

The final chapter of the *Journals* shows us AR near the end of her life. There is nothing to publish in regard to her work on mathematics or neurology, but some of her notes on psycho-epistemology have been included— along with every word she wrote for her last projected novel.

*To Lorne Dieterling* was to be "the story of a woman [a dancer] who is totally motivated by love for values—and how one maintains such a state when alone in an enemy world." (This formulation is from November 1957, a month after *Atlas Shrugged* was published.) The two basic "sense of life" music numbers to be danced by the heroine in the novel are the Overture to *La Traviata* and "Will O' the Wisp," one of AR's favorite "tiddly wink" pieces.

Verdi's *La Traviata* Overture, she writes, is to be "the dance of rising, without ever moving from one spot—done by means of her arms and body—ending on 'Dominique's statue' posture, as 'higher than raised arms,' as the achieved, as the total surrender to a vision and, simultaneously, 'This is I.' (The open, the naked, the 'without armor.')" As to "Will O' the Wisp," it represents "*the* triumph—the tap dance and ballet combined—*my* total sense of life. . . . (Probably danced in a low-grade dive, with Lorne [the hero] present. . . ."

Such was the sense of life not only of a young immigrant in her twenties who was brimming over with new ideas, but also of a philosopher in her seventies, who had lived consistently by every one of her ideas. Such was the sense of life of an artist "alone in an enemy world," who had already endured her greatest disappointments—and created her greatest achievements.

As David Harriman puts it in his eloquent conclusion:

"Ayn Rand has come full circle. She returned at the end to [the] problem [of irrational people] that had concerned her from the beginning. . . . At this stage, however, she knows the solution . . .

"It is fitting, therefore, that her last fiction notes are about a woman like herself, who maintains such a [joyous and lighthearted] view of life to the end, even while those around her do not."

She did it—how? In essence, by means of these *Journals* (and their equivalents through the decades). In other words, she did it in part through the knowledge she methodically struggled to gain, but above all through the intransigent will at the root of such a struggle: the will to think, in every issue and all her life long.

Whoever cares to match the price can reach the same result. As the first payment—I say this to those with their lives still ahead of them—I suggest that you read this book.

Leonard Peikoff
Irvine, California
October 1996

# EDITOR'S PREFACE

In a note to herself at the age of twenty-three, AR wrote: "From now on—no thought whatever about yourself, only about your work. You are only a writing engine. Don't stop, until you really and *honestly* know that you *cannot* go on." Throughout her long career, she remained true to this pledge—she was a "writing engine." With the publication of her journals, we can now see the "writing behind the writing" and appreciate fully the prodigious effort that went into her published work.

AR's notes, typically handwritten, were spread among the numerous boxes of papers she left behind at her death in 1982. My editing of this material has consisted of selection, organization, line editing, and insertion of explanatory comments.

*Selection.* This book presents AR's *working* journals—i.e., the notes in which she developed her literary and philosophical ideas. Notes of a personal nature will be included in a forthcoming authorized biography.

Approximately three-quarters of the working journals are presented here. I have included the material that I judge to be of interest to serious, philosophical admirers of AR's novels and ideas. This standard is, in effect, a middle ground between the scholar who wants every note, and the casual fan who might be satisfied with a selection of notes on fiction.

In most cases, I have described specific omissions in the chapter introductions. In general, notes have been omitted for the following reasons:

**1.** *Repetition with other notes.* AR sometimes rewrote her notes, often for the purpose of condensing and essentializing. I have included such later material only when it contains provocative new formulations.

**2.** *Repetition with published material.* Lengthy notes that merely state what the reader of her published work already knows, such as final outlines for novels, have been omitted.

**3.** *Quotes or paraphrases of other authors.* In her research, AR often

quoted or paraphrased material she had read. I have usually included
these notes only when she adds her own comments.

**4.** *Isolated, usually political, notes that are unrelated to the surrounding philosophic/literary material.* For example, AR's critique
of President Truman's decision to fire General MacArthur was
omitted because the only other notes from the period were on *Atlas
Shrugged*.

**5.** *Cryptic notes.* Some material was too cryptic to be intelligible.
Since AR typically wrote in complete sentences, such notes are rare.

I have taken this opportunity to publish a few pieces that are not from
AR's journals, but are closely related to her notes and of great interest to her
fans. In Chapter 10, for example, I have included AR's testimony before the
House Un-American Activities Committee, which is followed by her notes
on the hearings.

*Organization.* The journals are presented chronologically, so the reader
may follow the development of AR's ideas. However, for the purpose of
grouping together the notes on a particular topic, some departures from
chronological order have proved necessary. For example, the presentation of
her architectural research for *The Fountainhead* in a separate chapter
required minor violations of the chronology. Also, her notes from 1947
dealing with collectivist propaganda in the movies are presented before the
*Atlas Shrugged* notes, which begin in 1945. But in all such cases, the reason
for my order is obvious.

When a note is undated, I have made a guess at the approximate date,
and placed it next to related notes written at about that time.

The book divides naturally into five parts. As might be expected, the
two longest parts are the notes for *The Fountainhead* (Part 2) and *Atlas
Shrugged* (Part 4). Part 3 pertains to projects she worked on in the years
between these novels. Parts 1 and 5 are relatively short; they present respec-
tively her notes from the years prior to *The Fountainhead* and from the
post–*Atlas Shrugged* period. Within each part, the reasons for the chapter
divisions are either obvious or explained in my introductions.

*Line editing.* AR wrote her thoughts down as they occurred to her; she
did not outline material prior to writing the notes, and she did not edit the
wording afterwards.

Even so, not a great deal of line editing was required. I found few grammatical errors, except in the early notes of Part 1, which were written before
she had mastered English. Most of my line editing was done to facilitate

one's reading. I broke up paragraphs and sentences that were too long, occasionally supplied grammar that was merely implied, and eliminated the distracting overuse of parentheses, dashes and underlining. (Italics are used here to indicate her underlining; boldface type indicates words that she underlined twice.)

A certain amount of wordiness is endemic to journal writing. It is impossible—even for AR—consistently to find concise formulations while thinking aloud on paper. In many sentences, therefore, I have been able to eliminate words without affecting the meaning. However, I typically made such changes only when the original sentence was difficult to read. My restrained approach to the editing allows the journals to retain the spontaneous, informal character of notes to herself.

It was occasionally necessary to insert my word(s) into a sentence when the formulation was potentially confusing. My insertions are always enclosed in *square brackets* (not parentheses). When the editing of the book was complete, I double-checked all such changes against the original notes. I am confident that my insertions have not altered her intended meaning.

I have indicated my omission of passages within the notes by ellipsis points in square brackets; ellipsis points without the brackets are hers.

*Explanatory comments.* In general, I thought it best to leave the reader alone with the journals, and therefore I have kept my interruptions to a minimum. Many of my comments simply introduce the topic. When I could and where it was helpful, I have identified people, ideas or events unfamiliar to the general reader.

Sometimes it was necessary to comment on a philosophical passage that is clearly inconsistent with AR's mature views. In such cases, I do not attempt to explain the inconsistency; I simply cite the published work where the reader can find her definitive view.

In certain places, I could not resist calling the reader's attention to a striking aspect of a note. For example, I have identified a few notes in which she discusses a person or idea that later formed the basis for a character in *The Fountainhead* or *Atlas Shrugged*.

The only other comments inserted in the journals are some quotations from the biographical interviews given by AR in the early 1960s. During the interviews, she occasionally made remarks that offer special insight into the notes presented here.

My goal in all these changes has been to present the journals in a form that is easy to read, while intruding on her words as little as possible. I am satisfied with the result.

I wish to thank Leonard Peikoff for giving me access to the journals and for his continual editorial advice. Dr. Peikoff was particularly helpful in making my comments more concise and in suggesting to me additional comments. Thanks also to Catherine Dickerson and Diane LeMont for their careful, accurate typing of journals that were often difficult to read, and to Dina Garmong for translating the Russian passages in the earliest journals.

Finally, I owe a special debt to my wife, Barbara Belli, for her support and love throughout this lengthy project. Thank you, Barbara, for being my emotional fuel.

PART 1

# EARLY PROJECTS

# 1

# THE HOLLYWOOD YEARS

AR began her career in America by writing scenarios for the silent screen, work she could do despite having only a rudimentary knowledge of English. A little more than a year after coming to America, at the age of twenty-two, she was living at the Hollywood Studio Club and working as a junior screenwriter for Cecil B. DeMille.

This chapter begins with material found in two composition notebooks dating from the summer of 1927. The books contain two complete scenarios and one fragment. Although these scenarios are not explicitly philosophical, the reader will recognize in them characteristic features of AR. They are romantic adventure stories, which portray man as a heroic being capable of overcoming great obstacles to achieve his goals. It is easy to recognize the author of The Fountainhead when, at the age of twenty-two, she writes: "Life is achievement.... Give yourself an aim, something you want to do, then go after it, breaking through everything, with nothing in mind but your aim, all will, all concentration—and get it."

It is fascinating to see the seeds of her later work in these stories. In the first scenario, The Skyscraper, the hero is an architect named Howard Kane who—despite being charged with a serious crime and threatened with a lengthy prison sentence—ends by standing triumphantly at the top of his greatest creation, a New York skyscraper. The second scenario ends with the heroine rushing to the rescue of the hero, whom the villains have left strapped to a torture machine. When AR had a good plot idea, she did not forget it.

[*AR begins with notes on a book of short stories about railroad workers* (Held for Orders *by Frank H. Spearman*). *Apparently, she considered it as a possible source of ideas for scenarios.*]

(1) *The Switchman's Story:* Shockley

His past. His regeneration through work. His strength and success with the work. His sacrifice to save a friend.

(2) *The Wiper's Story:* How McGrath Got an Engine

An obscure man proves his worth by doing a very dangerous and difficult thing that no one else could do, and gets his reward—what he wanted.

(3) *The Roadmaster's Story:* The Spider Water

The tragedy of a good, strong, wonderful worker—dismissed for lack of education.

(4) *The Striker's Story:* McTerza

Personal courage—in a big fight.

(5) *The Dispatcher's Story:* The Last Order

The tragedy of a fatal mistake committed [by the dispatcher].

(6) *The Nightman's Story:* Bullhead

A man's regeneration through work; a big danger, brought about by his fault, that is [overcome by] a heroic effort.

(7) *The Master Mechanic's Story:* Delaroo

Friendship in work—and professional sacrifice for a friend.

(8) *The Operator's Story:* DeMolay Four

A man's hard, heroic work. Another man's lazy negligence—and the crime or catastrophe from it.

(9) *The Trainmaster's Story:* Of the Old Guard

A fight between his conscience and his work.

(10) *The Yellow Mail Story:* Jimmy the Wind

A big enterprise—saved by one man.

———— ◦ ————

[*AR notes the following idea for a scenario entitled* The Country Doctor.]
A story about a country doctor.

What interesting *situation* can he be in?

He saves the life of his enemy (or his enemy's son).

What kind of an enemy can he have? Who could hurt him and how? *What* can hurt him? To lose his job. His enemy has taken his job away from him.

How could he? The job was in the hands of his enemy. How? Through competition. The enemy opens a hospital and [hires] a new doctor.

Why is the enemy angry? The doctor has done something against his wishes. It must be something good. He helped his son to elope with a girl. How to connect the hospital with the beginning? The job was promised to the doctor and it was his ambition. What can make his position more tragic? His marriage depended on his new job.

He builds his hopes on getting a job in a hospital.

He does not get the job because of his enemy.

He saves the life of his enemy's son and gets his job.

———◇———

[*The following notes pertain to a story about a builder.*]

The strength, energy, heroism of a superintendent.

What can be the energy of the superintendent? What can express it? How can it be shown?

What is the difference between a good and a bad superintendent?

What mistakes can be made? How? How will they be discovered? Can there be a big, fatal mistake? What and how?

What mistakes can be made on the building intentionally, and how? What will be the result of it? How could the superintendent be prevented from noticing it? How does he finally discover it?

Who can be against the construction of a building and why? What can they do? What can threaten a building? What are the difficulties a superintendent meets in his work?

If somebody is against the superintendent, what can they do to hurt him professionally? Who is likely to be against him? Who are the professional enemies he can have? What are the professional tragedies?

Can there be a very dangerous and difficult thing that no one can do— and that one man does? Is there a possibility and an occasion for one-man heroism? Or a professional sacrifice?

What can be the dangerous, tragic consequences of a person's laziness and negligence?

Is it possible for a man to be in a position in which the good of his work interferes with his own good? How?

We want the story of how a building is constructed and everything that gets in its way—the energy of breaking through obstacles. What can prevent the building? Are there any obstacles possible? Can the building of a certain skyscraper hurt somebody? How and why?

The tremendous energy of that work. What expresses it in the best and strongest way?

## The Skyscraper

[*DeMille bought a story entitled* The Skyscraper, *written by Dudley Murphy, and assigned AR to work on the scenario. Many years later, AR recalled:*

*It was the story that gave me the most trouble. The original involved two tough construction workers who were in love with the same girl. The events consisted of them throwing rivets at each other, or almost falling off the girders; they fight but they are really the best of friends—it was that kind of story. DeMille said that I didn't have to follow the original, just do a scenario that projected the drama and heroism of constructing a skyscraper.*

*AR's first attempt is recognizably based on the original story.*]

Strength—energy—work. Steel and sweat.
A story about the building of a skyscraper.
A story about a steel-worker.
The worker saves the building from a fire, risking his own life.
What are the results of it? He rehabilitates himself.
What was his crime? What was he accused of?
He has lost his job. How?
A bum becomes a man, under the influence of the *work* on a skyscraper.
[Characters:] Bill MacCann, Dick Saunders, Hetty Brown, Buddy [O'Brien].
Bill MacCann comes to New York, a down-and-out bum.
Hetty Brown, his former sweetheart, is now engaged to Dick Saunders, a young construction superintendent.
Their meeting, her disappointment, his desire to revenge himself on Dick.
He goes to work on the skyscraper.
He reforms, becomes a man (his success at work, his friends, his promotion).
Dick's friendship with Bill. Hetty in the building. Her gradual love for Bill.
Dick introduces Bill to Hetty.
The bonus money—for the marriage of Dick and Hetty.

The night of the finish. Bill's energy. (Dick in Bill's power. Accident on top of building?)
Hetty breaks her engagement to Dick. Bill-Hetty.
Bill is fired.
Bill saves the building from the fire.

A bum works on a skyscraper to take his revenge. He becomes a man under the influence of his enemy, the superintendent. He loves the superintendent's fiancée.

Think from: Bill getting ready to kill Dick and what follows. Dick's good deed to him—their friendship. Hetty-Bill and Hetty-Bill-Dick.

*Expectation.* Have something *hang over the head* of the audience, something to expect; they know the situation is strange and they know something is going to happen, *has to happen,* so they *wait.* (Examples: "The Angel of Broadway," "Senorita.")

———◇———

[*AR interrupts her work on* The Skyscraper *to write down another idea. This note was titled "F. a. t. D.," probably meaning "Friends and the Duel."*]

A story of two friends in love with the same woman.

What would be the strongest result of it, the most tragic? They fight a duel over her. Why? Because she is the wife of one of them. Then why does the first love her? He loved her before the marriage. Why did the second marry her? He didn't know of the first love. Why didn't the first marry her himself? He could not. Why? He has killed her [former] husband in a duel. How did the second meet her? The first had to go away and left her in his care. What was the first's reaction to the marriage? He loved his friend and he loved her. What was her reaction? She tried to tempt him back.

———◇———

The story of the building of a skyscraper. The energy of the work makes a man out of a bum. Why has he decided to revenge himself? Because the superintendent was engaged to his girl. What does he do when reformed? He gives up his vengeance against the superintendent. What was the bum, or his guilt? He planned to kill the superintendent. Instead, he defends him. Against what? What can be his danger?

The *effort* of the building, the construction—all the details of that effort. The types, what they do, what happens to them and so on.

An epic must have a big idea behind it, an idea related to human lives.

*Achievement is the aim of life.* Life is achievement.

The sense of achievement—breaking through obstacles. Obstacles to the building or to [the man].

Achievement—give yourself an aim, something you *want* to do, then go after it, breaking through everything, with nothing in mind but your aim, all will, all concentration—*and get it.*

———

Bill MacCann, a down-and-out young bum, comes to New York from a far-away small town. He wants to see his former sweetheart, Hetty Brown, whom he had not seen for some years.

Hetty Brown is working in a department store on Broadway. She had not heard from Bill for many years and now she is engaged to another man, Dick Saunders. He is the superintendent of a skyscraper that is being built across the street from the store where she works.

But Hetty has not forgotten her first love. She is very excited when she gets the letter announcing Bill's coming to New York. She waits for him anxiously.

Bill comes. It is a great shock for Hetty, when she sees the ragged, half-drunken, lazy bum he has become. All her dreams about him are shattered and she tells him that there can be nothing between them and that she is engaged to Dick Saunders.

Bill is furious and leaves her. He does not want to show how unhappy he is. He walks through the streets of the big city, lonely, hungry and homeless, hating everybody and everything around him. He swears to revenge himself on Dick Saunders.

Bill goes to the skyscraper and gets a job as a steelworker, for long ago he had been one in his native town. But he is unaccustomed to work and at the end of the first day is bawled out by the superintendent, Dick Saunders. Buddy O'Brien, another worker, tries to help Bill out.

Tom Webbs, the steel-foreman, notices Bill's rage and hatred at Dick Saunders. After the work Webbs takes Bill to a shabby little restaurant, a bootlegger's joint, where he makes him drunk. While drinking, Bill boasts desperately that he is going to kill Dick Saunders at the first chance he gets. Webbs is very pleased. He is Dick's enemy and he encourages Bill in his decision. Bill explains that he will do it when he is alone with Dick somewhere on top of the building, where he can kill him and throw his body down, so that everybody will believe it was an accident.

Bill starts work lazily the next day. But in spite of himself, the strength and energy of the work [inspires] him. When the work stops at lunch time, Dick Saunders praises Bill. It is something quite new to the bum and for the first time in his life he feels proud and satisfied with himself.

Just then, Hetty Brown appears from her store across the street, coming to see Dick, as usual. She sees Bill. She is startled, for she did not expect him to be working here. He looks at her mockingly and turns away when she wants to talk to him. Hetty goes to Dick, who has not noticed the little scene.

Bill comes back to work after lunch, with a tell-tale bottle in his pocket. He is half-drunk with jealousy and the drinks he had. From his carelessness, an accident occurs that almost costs the life of Buddy O'Brien, his new friend. Buddy is saved only by Dick Saunders, who dashes up in time to rescue him. In spite of himself, Bill admires his enemy.

That night, going home, Bill gives his word to Buddy that he will never drink again.

In two weeks' time, the workers can hardly recognize the young bum. Bill's whole appearance has changed and his energy makes him one of the best workers. He is enthusiastic about his work. He cannot resist the influence of the skyscraper. Slowly, it makes a man out of him.

From her store window, Hetty watches Bill's tall, strong figure across the street and wonders whether her love for him is really dead.

When Bill gets his first pay-check, Tom Webbs invites him to the joint. Bill refuses. He is proud of his earned money and he makes a confession to Webbs: on his way to New York he committed his only real crime—he stole a wallet from a passenger on the train. He has not spent all the money. Now he asks Webbs to take it to the police station, for he does not dare to do it himself. Webbs agrees to do it. However, he keeps the wallet to himself.

———◆———

[*The scenario stops here. In the following notes, AR begins another scenario with the same title. I have identified a few paragraphs that were written in Russian; the rest was written in English.*]

[*In Russian:*] The main thing—the building of the skyscraper, no matter what. Plot-line: victory over obstacles. They try to prevent him from building. He sacrifices everything for the sake of the building. How can he sacrifice or lose the woman for the sake of his work? His private life is in conflict with his work.

The story of a *Man*. "The Man and the Building."

Francis Gonda. Something in the past of the man. His passion for the building. "The basement" calls for him—down.

The victory of a man over the town, rising above it, to the sky. The spirit of *Calumet "K."* [Calumet "K," *by Samuel Merwin and Henry Webster, was AR's favorite popular novel. It is the story of a hero's triumph over all obstacles in the construction of a grain elevator.*]

The building rises in the night as a white column, with drops of water rolling like tears on the joyously glistening walls, in the rays of spotlights. On top of the building, a man is standing, his head thrown far back—just a man looking at the sky.

[*In Russian:*] The basic plot—the building of a skyscraper. The line is man's strength. How can strength be expressed? The ability to bear calmly an enormous disaster.

[*In Russian:*] Question of interest: will Francis triumph over the city or not?

"It's a challenge we have thrown to the city! It's a war declared! We are going to build the greatest of buildings. We are going to rise higher [than anyone before]!"

Francis Gonda—"The Man Victorious," the Master Builder.

[*A fantasy poster sketch with the words:*]

Cecil B. DeMille presents

*THE SKYSCRAPER*

by Ayn Rand

from a story by Dudley Murphy

with William Boyd and Lena Malena

*Francis Gonda.* "The Skyscraper." An epic of construction.

*The active power*—Francis' ambition, his passion for building (and his passion for the woman).

[*Characters:*] Francis Gonda, a steel foreman, a typical worker, the roof dancer, a bank owner, and John [Scott].

———◦———

[*In the scenario that follows, the name of the hero is changed from Francis Gonda to Howard Kane.*]

Howard Kane is the hero of New York. He is a young architect, who has won a big competition arranged by a newspaper, and is now building a skyscraper that is expected to be one of the highest and most unusual in the city. He is architect and superintendent of the construction. John Scott, a famous established architect, had hoped to win the competition. Now he is madly jealous of Howard Kane, who had formerly been employed on his buildings, starting as a simple worker at the very bottom.

Howard is not popular among the workers. They resent his restless energy and the severe discipline he has established on the building. Howard's only friend is Jimmy, a little newsboy who is selling evening papers near the structure and is very proud of "our architect."

John Scott has one of his faithful men employed on Howard's building: Tom Riggins, the foreman of a steel-workers gang. Together they have a scheme to ruin Howard's success. Riggins is working on it. Scott's construction company is interested in preventing Howard, their brilliant new competitor, from finishing the building.

One summer morning Howard goes to the steel mills outside the city to look over certain steel beams that are to be shipped to his building. As he is riding back on one of the steel-laden trucks, an elegant little roadster driven by a young girl crashes into the truck. Howard helps the girl out of the wreck of her car. She is not hurt and he proposes to drive her home to the city. She arrives at the door of a very fashionable hotel, riding gaily on the steel beams of a heavy truck. She gives Howard her name—Danny Day.

When he returns to his building, Howard sees posters on the roof-cabaret next to his structure, announcing the first appearance of the famous dancer Danny Day, returned from her European tour.

The next evening, working a night shift, he watches from his building as Danny dances on the next roof. She sees him and waves gaily to him.

Among the brilliant crowd that fills the roof-cabaret are John Scott, who is an old admirer of Danny, and Mr. Clark, owner of the newspaper that is building the skyscraper. After the performance, Danny asks Mr. Clark permission to visit his building. A group of guests goes to the structure. Howard is busy on top of it. Danny jumps into the cable loop of a hoist and goes up to him. As they are on a narrow girder, Danny misses a step. Howard has the time to catch her, but her wrap falls down. She remains almost naked in her follies costume. They are alone, a terrific height above the city. He kisses her.

Danny Day is renowned for never having been in love. She does not want to admit that she is now. She goes down, trying to look cold and angry.

Howard leaves his work for the first time the next day, when he goes to see Danny and ask her forgiveness. They go for a ride together. The public cheers when they recognize Howard Kane, the hero of the hour.

Before leaving him, Danny admits that she loves him. He promises to come and see her again that evening.

Meanwhile, in Howard's absence, John Scott has sneaked into the building. He watches Tom Riggins' men carrying out his scheme: on a part of the building, they are riveting the steel girders in such a way that they will not be able to stand the pressure of the upper stories and the steel frame can collapse at any moment.

Late that evening Howard is ready to leave the building, when little Jimmy, the newsboy, comes up to see him. A girder gives way under the child's weight, and he falls a story. He is not seriously hurt. Howard rushes to examine the girder, and he discovers the mistake that has been done on purpose. He sees that a whole part of the skeleton is barely holding together and at any moment the steel giant can crash down on the crowded street below.

The workers are panic-stricken and want to run. Howard orders them to remain and save the building by carefully removing the girders and riveting them again. The workers refuse, for it is very dangerous work. Howard seizes his revolver and orders them to work, threatening to shoot the first man who leaves the building.

They work through the night, Howard's will alone ruling the terrified, trembling mob of workers.

Danny is waiting for Howard. Time passes; he does not come. She is desperate at the thought of being neglected by a man to whom she has admitted her love. Then John Scott comes to see her. Her pride is so much hurt by Howard that when Scott starts making love to her, she says "yes" to his proposal.

With the first light of the morning, the work on the building finishes. The skyscraper is saved. But several workers are seriously hurt.

Howard Kane is arrested on a charge of criminal negligence and violence. At the trial, Tom Riggins claims that he worked according to Howard's instructions. Howard is sentenced to ten years in jail.

On a Broadway corner, with tears in his eyes, Jimmy is selling extras with big headlines announcing this news.

Using all his power and influence, Mr. Clark, the building's owner, succeeds in releasing Howard on bond—just to finish the skyscraper, for no one else can do it.

Howard comes out of jail. New York is indignant at his being allowed to work again. The public hates and despises its former hero. As he walks to his building, the boys on the streets throw stones and mud at him. Everybody laughs at the "convict-builder."

He comes to the skyscraper. The structure is in a state of perfect dejection. No work has been done without him. He gives orders. The old energy returns to the construction. He tells [the workers] that the steel frame must be finished that night.

While working, Howard sees a party on the next roof. He sees Danny among the guests. He is happy. When he has a moment to spare, he goes to the cabaret. He stands in a corner before approaching Danny. He hears the announcement of Danny Day's engagement to John Scott—this is their engagement party. Howard approaches the table. Danny did not know that he had been released already. She jumps to her feet, wants to run to him and stops, realizing her position. John Scott and the guests laugh at Howard, the "convict-builder." Howard does not say a word and returns to his work.

That evening when Howard leaves the building to take a short sleep, for he has to work at night, the workers gather to talk over their indignation. They don't want to work under a convict. They decide to strike. But Tom Riggins whispers to some of his friends that he will get rid of Howard once and for all.

When Howard is returning to the building, Tom Riggins waits for him on a dark corner and shoots him. Then Riggins returns to work, so that there would be no suspicion of him.

Howard is lying on the sidewalk unconscious. An automobile passes by and stops. Danny is returning home alone and sees Howard. She takes him to her house. She bandages his wound. When he opens his eyes, she tells him that she loves him, that she will break her engagement to John Scott.

But Howard remembers that he has to spend ten years in jail. He does not want to ruin Danny's life. He struggles with himself. He forces himself to look cold and indifferent, and saying that he does not love her, he leaves Danny and returns to his building.

He appears strong and steady, hiding his suffering from the wound, calmly taking command of the work again. Tom Riggins is terrified. Howard does not pay any attention to him. They work late into the night. The workers are exhausted—Howard is not. At last, their patience ends, they refuse to work for the "damned convict." They declare they are going to strike and ask for another superintendent. The big mob of workers gathers on the lower floor of the building. They order Howard to give up his job.

Then, alone before the threatening mob, Howard tears open his shirt, tears off the bandage and shows the wound on his breast. He tells them that he is not going to denounce the criminal, that he only asks them to work, to finish the building, for he has sacrificed his whole life for his skyscraper.

The workers are stricken with a respectful awe, when they realize that

Howard has been working wounded. They hesitate. Jimmy, who is present, throws himself to the defense of his friend, shouting to the mob that they are a "bunch of yellow guys." Some workers take Howard's side. The others refuse.

Then some policemen, attracted by the tumult, appear at the building. They ask Howard what happened. Tom Riggins trembles. The workers are silent. Howard answers calmly that nothing happened.

When the policemen leave, a roar of enthusiasm greets Howard. The workers push away Riggins and his little group. Cheering, they surround Howard Kane, their leader. And the work starts again, with an enthusiasm such as never before.

Under Howard's direction the building seems to grow, to rise toward the sky. Danny Day is dancing on the cabaret roof. He tries not to look down. He thinks only of his skyscraper now.

---

Howard Kane's building is finished. Only the wooden scaffolding that surrounds it still remains to be removed. The proud skyscraper towers over Broadway, before the admiring eyes of the [people below].

Howard must return to jail that evening, for his bond has expired with the completion of his work. Alone in the building, he is taking a last look at it.

Danny Day is going to her wedding, for this is her wedding day. She is riding in an automobile through New York's streets. She cannot tear her eyes from the automobile's window. Above the roofs of the small houses, she sees in the distance Howard Kane's skyscraper. It appears behind every corner, in every opening between the houses. It seems to follow her. She cannot stand it. She gets out of the car and runs. But the skyscraper is still there, before her. She loves the buildings of Broadway. She feels so small and helpless at their feet. She feels for the first time all the majesty of the world's greatest structures. And she is drawn irresistibly toward Howard's skyscraper.

She comes to the building and meets Howard. Both cannot hide their love any longer. But they have to part. Howard goes to Mr. Clark to say farewell.

Mr. Clark, however, has another plan. He tells Howard that he is so grateful for his work that he is willing to lose the bond money and he asks him to run away. Howard agrees.

Meanwhile, John Scott calls Tom Riggins. He is furious that the building has been finished on time. He bribes Riggins to set fire to the wooden scaffolding. And Riggins does it.

Howard and Danny are riding away in an automobile. They hear the newsboy shout about the police searching for the escaped Howard Kane. Then suddenly they see a red glow that sets the sky aflame and they see the burning skyscraper. Howard wants to save it. Danny implores him not to give himself up and to run away. But he rushes to his building.

The skyscraper is a blazing tower of flames. The firemen are unable to stop the fire. The water hoses are helpless before the 700-foot-high flaming monster. An immense crowd is gathered before the tremendous spectacle.

Policemen rush to Howard when they see him. But he runs to the building and starts climbing up, through the flames, to the water tower on top. He rises through the fire, climbing, falling, climbing again. It seems that all of New York is watching him breathlessly.

Meanwhile, Tom Riggins is arrested, for he is suspected. He is terrified and announces that John Scott is guilty of the fire, as well as the first catastrophe at the building.

Howard reaches the water tower at the top. He releases the water. The building is saved.

Far below, the crowd is cheering wildly for Howard Kane, the hero. The skyscraper rises in the night like a victorious white column. His clothes, hanging in rags, his body burned and bleeding, Howard Kane is standing on top of his building, his head thrown back—just a man looking at the sky.

[*DeMille did produce* The Skyscraper *in 1928, starring William Boyd and Alan Hale. The movie followed the original story, not AR's scenario; according to AR, "it was a lousy picture."*]

---

[*The following notes were written in Russian.*]
An epic:

1. Spans an entire epoch.
2. Has a large theme, a grand theme—and an enormous conflict (external or internal).
3. Exhausts and integrates everything related to the theme; it represents the essence, in the best possible form.
4. A concrete story expresses the universal essence; it is not an exceptional occurrence.
5. The story applies to everyone, not just to an individual soul.

How it is expressed:

**1.** Expresses various main ideals, ideas, and events of a given epoch.

**2.** A large theme, closely related to the epoch's character.

**3.** The most interesting, universal traits and facts are expressed in the most [*illegible*], interesting, and characteristic story.

**4.** A concrete story is built in such a way as to express the idea, the universal traits, in the most colorful way.

**5.** Do not push the hero into the foreground too much, do not express everything *only* from the hero's point of view and as being for the hero; implicitly let it be felt that the hero is a means, not the end.

**6.** The plot [should] express and unite everything, all the concretes. The plot flows from the essence of the theme; one constructs the plot after analyzing the theme, the epoch.

---

[*The following is the second complete scenario. In order not to give away the story, I have omitted one page of plot notes.*]

### The Siege

Ellen Darrow, her millionaire father Mr. Darrow, and her fiancé Dick Saunders are paying their last visit to Peking. The American Consul, their friend, advises them to leave China as soon as possible, for it is dangerous for foreigners to stay there with all the disorders and insurrections.

Ellen has been noticed by a Chinaman of bad reputation, Jung-Tzan, who had seen her in a restaurant. She has been saved from him by the two Americans, who were present there. Mr. Darrow is very nervous and promises the Consul that they will leave tomorrow.

They return to their hotel to spend the last night there. This hotel is a strong building, reminiscent of a Chinese castle. It is situated in a picturesque but lonely spot among rivers and woods, miles from Peking. The manager is a European and the residents are all Americans and Europeans, a very exclusive crowd of society people. The only Chinaman in the place is the janitor.

That night, when the lights of the hotel go out, a young American, Kenneth Hartley, slips into the building through an open window. He isn't a resident of the place. He's just a crook and his aim is the safe in Mr. Darrow's room.

He is opening the safe when Ellen, in her room upstairs, hears the noise. She rushes downstairs, revolver in hand, and stops Kenneth just as he had opened the safe. Mr. Darrow and Dick Saunders arrive at her call. Kenneth is disarmed. Dick is about to put handcuffs on him, when they hear shots outside and a loud knocking at the door.

The hotel is surrounded by a mob of Chinese bandits led by Jung-Tzan, Ellen's enemy. The terrified hotel guests are in a mad panic. They don't know what to do and are too frightened to act. The only man that realizes the position is Kenneth.

In a few moments he organizes the defense of the hotel. All of the doors are strong iron and most of the windows have iron bars and shutters. The residents have quite a big supply of firearms. Kenneth assigns a post to every man in the place.

The Chinese mob attacks the hotel and the attack is forced back by the hotel guests, under Kenneth's orders. Knowing that they can't hold for a long time, Jung-Tzan orders his bandits to remain around the building in a regular siege. He had previously cut off all the hotel's telephone wires. There isn't a living soul for miles around. He knows that the place is in his power, with all the money, jewels, and women in it.

A few days pass. Kenneth is the supreme chief and dictator of the besieged hotel. He leads the defense and the helpless society people know that their lives are in his hands. There is not much food nor many weapons in the place for a long siege and Kenneth manages it, spending as little as possible.

Dick Saunders is very drunk and jealous, for he notices a growing friendship between Ellen and Kenneth. After one of the Chinese attacks, Kenneth is slightly wounded and Ellen bandages his wound. During that battle Ellen has seen and recognized the Chinese chief, and it adds to the anxiety of Mr. Darrow, her father.

That night, Kenneth is watching over the hotel and surveying the Chinese camp. All seems quiet, when he suddenly sees two Chinamen climbing up the old stone wall towards Ellen's window. He rushes to Ellen's room and enters it noiselessly. Ellen is asleep. For a moment he looks at her, forgetting the enemies and everything. Then, mastering himself, he goes to the window and shoots at the Chinamen, just as they are approaching. One is killed; the other—Jung-Tzan—runs away.

Ellen wakes up and runs to Kenneth in terror. Then she realizes that she is in his arms and steps away from him, just as her father and Dick rush in.

The next morning, Kenneth finds a strange letter in his room. It is from Jung-Tzan. The Chinese chief tells Kenneth that he is the only one they fear and offers him a big sum of money for surrendering the place. Kenneth throws the letter away disdainfully, wondering how it got there.

That day, while putting iron bars on the window in Ellen's room, Kenneth sees Ellen and, forgetting himself, tries to take her in his arms. She tears herself from him. She does not speak to him that day, and tries to be especially tender to her fiancé, Dick Saunders, as though to convince herself that she still loves him. Kenneth is dark and silent, tortured by jealousy.

The hotel guests notice it all. It worries them, and their worry changes to terror when one of them finds Jung-Tzan's letter in Kenneth's room. They are afraid that Kenneth will betray them. They call Ellen. They ask her to pretend to love Kenneth, to prevent him from surrendering the hotel. Ellen is indignant. But they all plead with her, asking her sacrifice to save them from a terrible fate. Even Dick Saunders does not object to it.

Ellen agrees at last. She tries to convince herself that her task is more disagreeable to her than she really feels it is.

Meanwhile, as a last hope, Mr. Darrow decides to send the Chinese janitor to Peking, hoping that he might be able to slip through the Chinese lines and inform the American Consul. The janitor is let out through a little side door.

In a short time, Ellen has conquered Kenneth. And when she is in his arms, when she loves him, she is afraid that she is not playing a part. But she does not want to admit it to herself.

Kenneth asks her to marry him right away, for he wants her and they cannot be sure of the future, with the terrible danger hanging over them. Ellen struggles with herself, then agrees.

Mr. Darrow has to agree, too. Kenneth is radiant with happiness and tells them that he is going straight forever.

There is a priest among the hotel residents. Everything is ready for the wedding. The ceremony is about to start when there is a knock at the little door. The janitor returns. He announces that he has informed the Consul and American soldiers are on their way to the hotel: they will be there in a couple of hours.

A roar of enthusiasm greets the news. Dick Saunders stops the wedding, says that Ellen does not have to play the part anymore. Ellen wants to protest, but cannot, for Kenneth is stricken with the discovery of her deception.

And the guests' attitude toward Kenneth changes. They don't need him anymore. They are mocking and disdainful. To them, he is the crook again. They even put handcuffs on him, but Ellen takes them off. Kenneth is too stricken to protest or say anything.

Some of the guests run to the roof of the building and fire their last bullets into the air, as a signal to the coming soldiers.

Kenneth is alone in a dark corner when the janitor approaches him. The janitor is laughing triumphantly. He tells Kenneth that he is in Jung-Tzan's service and the news is a fake, nobody is coming to the rescue, but that Jung-Tzan's offer to Kenneth is still good and maybe he will accept it, now that he sees how his people have treated him.

Kenneth runs to the cellar; there is no food left and hardly any bullets. He returns to the janitor and tells him to bring Jung-Tzan in secretly through the little side door to discuss his offer.

Jung-Tzan comes. Kenneth says that he will agree to open the doors to him, under two conditions: first, Kenneth will be the master and the Chinese will obey his orders; second, the woman, Ellen Darrow, will belong to him. Jung-Tzan hesitates, but finally agrees.

In the evening, the hotel guests are all dressed in their best evening clothes, waiting for the soldiers, when Kenneth opens the doors and lets the Chinese mob in. It is a terrible scene. At Kenneth's orders the guests are all made prisoners in a few moments. They are horrified at Kenneth's betrayal, which seems so hideous. Kenneth orders them all to be locked in the hotel's cellar and the key brought to him.

Ellen is the only one that is not locked. He takes her to his room. She struggles desperately, but he drags her roughly up the stairs, while the China-men laugh.

When they are alone in his room, Kenneth tells her that he brought her here only because he could not trust Jung-Tzan. He explains that this was the only way to save them all. He is going to let them all escape, in two of the Chinese trucks, while he will remain here and keep the Chinese from following them.

Ellen is horrified. She does not want him to remain. She tells him how much she loves him and they have a sincere love scene this time. But Kenneth has to remain to save the others. While the wild Chinese mob is robbing the house, breaking the safes and drinking the remaining wine, Kenneth leads all the prisoners to two trucks, parked in a lonely, dark spot, and they speed away. He remains.

He does all he can to keep the Chinamen from going into the cellar. He drinks with them and tries to amuse them. Then Jung-Tzan suggests that they must prepare tortures for the prisoners. Kenneth tries to keep them at it as long as possible, inventing more and more tortures, but knowing that he is the only one on whom they will be used.

Finally, they grow impatient. He tells them that he has lost the cellar key. They go downstairs, they break the door. The cellar is empty.

They rush to Kenneth. He faces them with a calm [expression].

The hotel guests reach Peking. Mr. Darrow asks for American soldiers to be sent to the hotel immediately. He and Ellen go back to the hotel with them.

Taken by surprise, the Chinese mob in the hotel surrenders immediately. Ellen runs madly through the rooms, searching for Kenneth. She finds him at last, tied to a torture machine, but still alive.

### circa February 1928

*In 1928, at the age of twenty-three, AR made her first attempt in English to plan a novel. The working title was* The Little Street.

*Its theme is that humanity—warped by a corrupt philosophy—is destroying the best in man for the sake of enshrining mediocrity. By far AR's most malevolent story, it provides a sharp contrast to the "benevolent universe" of the earlier scenarios, in which the hero is victorious. Here she is bitterly denouncing a world that seems to have no place for heroism.*

*Later, AR emphatically rejected the "malevolent universe" premise that evil is powerful and the good helpless. But the premise does dominate* The Little Street. *What kind of factors may have led her temporarily to accept it?*

*She grew up in Russia, a man-made model of a malevolent universe (see* We the Living*). Then, in America, she was astonished to discover that the same anti-life ideas that had destroyed Russia were on the rise here. The result seems to have been periods of profound indignation, when AR felt that the whole world was dominated by evil and that she was a metaphysical outcast. It is from this perspective that the story was conceived.*

*In her mature writings, AR stressed that she advocated rational selfishness, not the whim-worshipping subjectivism of the man who says: "The good is whatever I want." She regarded the whim-worshipper with particular contempt, arguing that such a man entirely lacks the virtue of selfishness (see "Selfishness Without a Self" in* Philosophy: Who Needs It*). But in the following notes, AR is focused on a single question: whether a man is motivated to act for himself or for others—and not on the epistemological issue of whether he acts by reason or whim. Consequently, she praises any expression of egoism, even when it seems to be the pseudo-egoism she would soon begin to denounce.*

*Furthermore, AR has not yet distinguished clearly between the independent man and the man who seeks power over others (e.g., between a man like Howard Roark and one like Gail Wynand). She writes admiringly of the strong individual who wants to "command," rather than "obey." Later she recognized that such a choice is a false alternative: "The choice is not self-sacrifice or domination. The choice is independence or dependence." The notes for* The Little Street *were written nearly eight years before she began work on* The Fountainhead.

*Occasionally, AR describes certain fundamental attitudes or character traits as "innate" (e.g., her hero's innate egoism). These passages contradict her advocacy of free-will; it might appear that AR believed in some form of biological determinism. In fact, even in these early notes, her dominant premise is that men are responsible for the ideas they choose to accept and the actions they choose to take. For example, she cites the ideas that have led to the moral corruption in the world, and her implication throughout is that men can choose to accept these ideas or not. She is inconsistent in this story, because she does not yet see the contradiction between free-will and innate virtues.*

*All of the above confusions reflect the influence on the early AR of Friedrich Nietzsche, whom she had read and admired, especially for his eloquent expression of a heroic sense of life. There are several references to him in these notes. In due course, however, she discarded all these Nietzschean elements, and defined "heroism" in rational terms, by reference to her own distinctive philosophy of Objectivism. For her final view of Nietzsche, see the introduction to the twenty-fifth anniversary edition of* The Fountainhead *and the title essay in* For the New Intellectual.

*Despite the flawed statements, it is easy to recognize AR as the author of the following notes. Her trademark—the reverence with which she regards man's life, her intense passion for values—comes through clearly. In its combination of value-passion and moral indignation,* The Little Street *is similar to AR's early screenplay* Ideal *(see* The Early Ayn Rand*).*

*The notes also include AR's earliest formulations on several key topics: her sense of life; the unity of thought and feeling which is experienced by a "clear mind"; the effect of the morality of sacrifice on self-esteem and moral ambition; moral compromise as an unmitigated evil; the motivation of a soul who insists that the meaning of one's life is to be found outside oneself.*

*At the age of twenty-three, AR knew that she was not ready to portray her ideal man. Her goal here is less ambitious; she wants only to project her ideal man's sense of life. The protagonist, Danny Renahan, is an independent, uncompromising, nineteen-year-old boy with a passionate hunger for life. Some of Danny's characteristics are based on an actual nineteen-year-old boy, William Edward Hickman, who was the defendant in a highly publicized murder trial that had just taken place in Los Angeles. Hickman was accused of kidnapping and murdering a young girl. He was*

*found guilty and sentenced to death in February of 1928; he was hanged on
October 20, 1928.*

*Judging from the newspaper accounts of the time, Hickman was articu-
late and arrogant, and seems to have enjoyed shocking people by rejecting
conventional views. The public furor against him was unprecedented. For
reasons given in the following notes, AR concluded that the intensity of the
public's hatred was primarily "because of the man who committed the crime
and not because of the crime he committed." The mob hated Hickman for his*
independence; *she chose him as a model for the same reason.*

*Hickman served as a model for Danny only in strictly limited respects,
which AR names in her notes. Danny does commit a crime in the story, but it
is nothing like Hickman's. To guard against any misinterpretation, I quote
her own statement regarding the relationship between her hero and
Hickman:*

[My hero is] very far from him, of course. The outside of Hickman, but not
the inside. Much deeper and much more. A Hickman with a purpose. And
without the degeneracy. It is more exact to say that the model is not
Hickman, but what Hickman suggested to me.

The Little Street *is not the only early work of AR's in which she chose a
criminal to symbolize an independent man. In her first play,* The Night of
January 16th, *the hero commits financial fraud on a grand scale and then
attempts to escape by faking his own death. She explains her use of the
heroic criminal in the introduction to the play, written in 1968. Her comments are applicable here.*

*Night of January 16th* is not a philosophical, but a sense of life play. . . .
    This means that its events are not to be taken *literally*; they dramatize
certain fundamental psychological characteristics, deliberately isolated and
emphasized in order to convey a single abstraction: the characters' attitude
toward life. The events serve to feature the *motives* of the characters'
actions, regardless of the particular forms of the actions—i.e., the motives,
not their specific concretization. The events feature the confrontation of
two extremes, two opposite ways of facing existence: passionate self-
assertiveness, self-confidence, ambition, audacity, independence—versus
conventionality, servility, envy, hatred, power-lust.
    I do not think, nor did I think when I wrote this play, that a swindler is
a heroic character or that a respectable banker is a villain. But for the purpose of dramatizing the conflict of independence versus conformity, a

criminal—a social outcast—can be an eloquent symbol. This, incidentally, is the reason of the profound appeal of the "noble crook" in fiction. He is the symbol of the rebel as such, regardless of the kind of society he rebels against, the symbol—for most people—of their vague, undefined, unrealized groping toward a concept, or a shadowy image, of man's self-esteem.

That a career of crime is not, in fact, the way to implement one's self-esteem, is irrelevant in sense-of-life terms. A sense of life is concerned mainly with consciousness, not with existence—or rather: with the way a man's consciousness faces existence. It is concerned with a basic frame of mind, not with rules of conduct.

If this play's sense of life were to be verbalized, it would say, in effect: 'Your life, your achievement, your happiness, *your person* are of paramount importance. Live up to your highest vision of yourself no matter what circumstances you might encounter. An exalted view of self-esteem is a man's most admirable quality.' How one is to live up to this vision—how this frame of mind is to be implemented in action and in reality—is a question that a sense of life cannot answer: that is the task of philosophy.

*AR did not get far in planning* The Little Street. *The project was too alien to her deepest premises. The notes are undated, but it seems likely that they were made over a short period when she was feeling particularly bitter toward the world. This was not a novel that she could have written; to her, the purpose of fiction writing is not to denounce that which one despises, but to exalt that which one admires.*

## The Little Street

*The world as it is.*
Show it all, calmly and indifferently, like an outsider who does not share humanity's feelings or prejudices and can see it all "from the side."

Show all the filth, stupidity, and horror of the world, along with that which is supposed to atone for it. Show how insignificant, petty, and miserable the "good" in the world is, compared to the real horror it masks. Do not paint one side of the world, the polite side, and be silent about the rest; paint a real picture of the whole, good and bad at once, the "good" looking more horrid than the bad when seen together with the things it tolerates. Men see only one part of life at a time, the part they have before their eyes at the moment. *Show them the whole.*

Show that *humanity is petty.* That it's small. That it's dumb, with the

heavy, hopeless stupidity of a man born feeble-minded, who does not understand, because he *cannot* understand, because he hasn't the capacity to
understand; like a man born blind, who cannot see, because he has no organ
for seeing.

Show that the world is monstrously hypocritical. That *humanity has no
convictions of any kind*. That it does not know how to believe anything. That
it has never believed consistently and does not know how to be true to any
idea or ideal. That *all the "high" words of the world are a monstrous lie*.
That nobody believes in anything "high" and nobody wants to believe. That
one cannot believe one thing and do another, for such a belief isn't worth a
nickel. And that's what humanity is doing.

Show *that humanity is utterly illogical*, like an animal that cannot connect together the things it observes. Man realizes and connects much more
than an animal, but who can declare that his ability to connect things is perfect? The future, higher type of man will have to perfect just this ability [to
achieve] the clear vision. A clear mind sees things *and* the connections
between them. Humanity is stumbling helplessly in a chaos of inconsistent
ideas, actions, and feelings that can't be put together, without even realizing
the contradictions between them or their ultimate logical results.

A perfect, clear understanding also means a *feeling*. It isn't enough to
realize a thing is true. The realization must be so clear that one *feels* this
truth. For men act on feelings, not on thoughts. Every thought should be part
of yourself, your body, your nature, and every part of your nature should be
a thought. Every feeling—a thought, every thought—a feeling. [*This is AR's
earliest statement regarding the harmony of reason and emotion that follows
from a proper integration of mind and body.*]

Show the silent terror that is life at present, the silent terror that hangs
over us, chokes us, that everybody feels and nobody can define, the nameless thing that is the atmosphere of humanity.

Show that the mob determines life at present and *show exactly who and
what that mob is*. Show the things it breaks, the precious enemies that it
ruins. Show that all humanity and each little citizen is an octopus that consciously or unconsciously sucks the blood of the best on earth and strangles
life with its cold, sticky tentacles.

Show that *the world is nothing but a little street*. That this little street is
its king and master, its essence and spirit. Show the little street and how it
works.

*Religion:* show what it means when thought out consistently; what it
does to man; who needs it; who defends it with all the ferocious despotism
of a small, ambitious nature. The great poison of mankind.

*Morals* (as connected with religion): the real reason for all hypocrisy. The wrecking of man by teaching him ideals that are contrary to his nature; ideals he has to accept as his highest ambition, even though they are organically hateful and repulsive to him. And when he can't doubt them, he doubts himself. He becomes low, sinful, imperfect in his own eyes; he does not aspire to anything high, when he knows that the high is inaccessible and alien to him. Humanity's morals and ideals, its ideology, are the greatest of its crimes. ("Unselfishness" first of all.)

*Communism, democracy, socialism* are the logical results of present-day humanity. The nameless horror of [these systems], both in their logical end and in the unconscious way that they already rule mankind.

*Family-life:* the glorification of mediocrity. Elevating the "everyday" little man's existence into the highest ideal for mankind.

Show that humanity has and wants to have: existence instead of life, satisfaction instead of joy, contentment instead of happiness, security instead of power, vanity instead of pride, attachment instead of love, wish instead of will, yearning instead of passion, a glow-worm instead of a fire.

All the "realistic" books have shown the bad side of life and, as good, have shown the good of today. They have denounced that which is accepted as bad and set up as a relief or example that which is accepted as good. I want to show that there is *no* good at present, that the "good" as it is now understood is worse than the bad, that it is only the result, the skin over a rotten inside that rules and determines it. I want to show that all the conceptions of the "good," all the high ideals, have to be changed, for now they are nothing but puppets, slaves and accomplices to the horrible [stifling] of life. There are too many things that people just tolerate and don't talk about. Show them that *it can't be tolerated, for all their life is a rotten swamp, a sewer, a dumping place for more filth than they can ever realize.*

Show that the real God behind all their high words and sentiments, the real omnipotent power behind their culture and civilization, is *the little street*, just a small, filthy, shabby, common *little* street, such as exist around the center of every town in the world.

Show them the real, one and only horror—*the horror of mediocrity.*

## The Characters

*Danny Renahan.* The boy.

He is born with the spirit of Argon and the nature of a medieval feudal lord. Imperious. Impatient. Uncompromising. Untamable. Intolerant. Unadaptable. Passionate. Intensely proud. Superior to the mob and intensely, almost painfully conscious of it. Restless. High-strung. An extreme "extremist." A clear, strong, brilliant mind. An egoist, in the best sense of the word.

He is born in a small town, into a poor, *very* average family. He grows up lonely, hating everybody and being hated by everybody. (?) Very unpopular in school—for his imperious, masterful character. No love-affairs or drinks. Too straightforward and too absolute for the rest of the boys. Dangerous, too. People don't trust him, instinctively, feeling him to be an "outsider."

Show his battle with the world. He is too impatient to toil slowly through the years for the things he wants. Too uncompromising to succeed in the way of the popular young men who know how to get along with those in power. Too intolerant to "get along" with anybody. Too passionate not to burn with disgust for life as he sees it and with humiliation at not being above the mob, crushing it under his feet, giving it orders instead of trying to satisfy it, of crawling before it for its good graces. He is unable to understand how he can act and live as an equal with those he knows to be inferior to him, those he despises and has a right to despise. More passionate than strong. Daring and courageous; but without the patient courage that can fight through, slowly, against disgust. A man that can slash with an [ax], but can't saw patiently. Too brilliant and fiery a nature to be able to handle any "job" and make money. Crushed by a stupid, ignoble poverty. Too restless and innately, unconsciously romantic to "make good" in the way of the model, average, hard-working young man.

As a result, he is perfectly cynical. Stone-hard. Monstrously cruel. Brazenly daring. No respect for anything or anyone.

He is medium height and slender. Has strong, rather irregular features, as though cut by quick, sharp blows. Not a beautiful face at all but fascinating because of its strength. Deep, dark eyes, dark more through their expression than through the color, burning with the intense fire of a strong, restless soul. His gaze is piercing and threatening under two straight, severe eye-brows. Rather frightful eyes, that make people feel uneasy. He has a large mouth, like a wound slashed in his face. The lower lip is thicker than the upper. He has a habit of an ugly grin that twists his mouth so that one corner only is raised and the upper lip curled, as in a snarl, which gives him an expression of disgusted cruelty.

He has a brilliant sense of humor. Rather a cruel, sardonic kind of humor. Being conscious of his superiority to the rest of mankind, he cannot help seeing their absurd, ridiculous, idiotic smallness. He has no respect for anything; therefore he can laugh at everything and approach all things lightly, with an attitude of superior disdain. His mind is brilliant enough to see the ridiculous side of everything. He gets immense enjoyment from shocking people, amusing them with his cynicism, [ridiculing] before their eyes the most sacred, venerated, established ideas. He takes a real delight in opposing people, in fighting and terrifying them. He has no ambition to be a benefactor or a popular hero for mankind. [. . .] Subconsciously, this is the result of a noble feeling of superiority, which knows that to be loved by the mob is an insult and that to be hated is the highest compliment it can pay you.

He is born with a wonderful, free, light consciousness—[resulting from] the absolute lack of social instinct or herd feeling. He does not understand, *because he has no organ for understanding,* the necessity, meaning or importance of other people. (One instance when it is blessed not to have an organ of understanding.) Other people do not exist for him and he does not understand why they should. He knows himself—and that is enough. Other people have no right, no hold, no interest or influence on him. And this is not affected or chosen—it's *inborn*, absolute, it can't be changed, he has "no organ" to be otherwise. In this respect, he has the true, innate psychology of a Superman. He can never realize and *feel* "other people." (That's what I meant by thoughts as feelings, as part of your nature.) (It is wisdom to be dumb about certain things.)

[William Edward] Hickman said: "I am like the state: what is good for me is right." That is this boy's psychology. (The best and strongest expression of a real man's psychology I ever heard.) The model for the boy is Hickman. Very far from him, of course. The outside of Hickman, but not the inside. Much deeper and much more. A Hickman with a purpose. And without the degeneracy. It is more exact to say that the model is not Hickman, but what Hickman suggested to me.

The boy is a perfectly straight being, unbending and uncompromising. He cannot be a hypocrite. He shows how impossible it is for a genuinely beautiful soul to succeed at present; for in all [aspects of] modern life, one has to be a hypocrite, to bend and tolerate. This boy wanted to command and smash away things and people he didn't approve of. He could not compromise with that which he despised and knew he had a right to despise. All life is compromising, at present. *A man that could not compromise.*

At the end, when his last appeal has been refused and the execution awaits him, he throws away all protective hypocrisy and shouts to his jailers and the newspaper reporters what he thinks of the world. It must be the essence, the very heart of the book: his wild, ferocious cry. It must be the strongest speech ever uttered in condemnation of the world. It must strike people like a whip slapping them in the face. It must be scalding in its bloody suffering, like the yell of an animal with an open, torn wound.

He has a wonderful "sense of living." He realizes that he is living, he appreciates every minute of it, he wants to *live* every second, he is unable to *exist* as other men do. He doesn't take life for granted and live as he happens to be living—just calm, satisfied, normal. For him, life [must be] strong, high emotion; he has to live "on top," "breathing" life, tense, exalted, *active*. He cannot spend eight hours each day on work he despises and does not need. He cannot understand men spending their lives on some work and not liking that work, not doing with it what they please. He knows that he wants to live and that the whole damn world hasn't the right to deprive him of it!

He doesn't have people's attitude toward life, that is, the general way of existing calmly day to day and [experiencing] something strong and exalting only once in a while, as an exception. *"Everyday life" does not exist for him.* His normal state is to be exalted, all the time; he wants *all* of his life to be high, supreme, full of meaning.

All this is unconscious in him. He cannot reason it out and explain it. It's unconscious, because it's innate, it's his natural state of mind, it's organic in him, and he cannot realize it, because he cannot quite understand the common attitude toward life, which is too monstrous for his Superman's consciousness [to grasp].

He half-consciously realizes that he possesses something sublime, and that he is going to be condemned for possessing it. From this—his tense, wild, ferocious attitude.

Most people lack [the capacity for] *reverence* and *"taking things seriously."* They do not hold anything to be very serious or profound. There is nothing that is sacred or immensely important to them. There is nothing—no idea, object, work, or person—that can inspire them with a profound, intense, and all-absorbing passion that reaches to the roots of their souls. They do not know how to value or desire. They cannot give themselves entirely to anything. There is nothing *absolute* about them. They take all things lightly, easily, pleasantly—almost indifferently, in that they can have it or not, they do not claim it as their absolute necessity. Anything strong and intense, passionate and absolute, anything that can't be taken with a snickering little "sense of humor"—is too big, too hard, too uncomfortable for them. They are too small and weak to feel with all their soul—and they disapprove of such feelings. They are too small and low for a loyal, profound reverence—and they disapprove of all such reverence. They are too small and profane themselves to know what sacredness is—and they disapprove of anything being too sacred.

The boy is just their opposite. He is all passion, will, and uncompromised absolutes. He takes everything seriously. Life is very serious and sacred to him. And, as Nietzsche said: "The noble soul has reverence for itself." He has a profound reverence for himself, a determination to keep himself and his life clean, untouched, and beautiful, because they are the most sacred of all sacred things. And when he wants something—he *wants* it.

The tragedy of a man with the consciousness of a god, among a bunch of snickering, giggling, dirty-story-telling, good-timing, jolly, regular fellows.

All this is quite unconscious in the boy. He does not and cannot recognize it. He is too much of an "outsider" to understand the "inside." He understands only enough to hate and despise it, as only he can hate and despise.

The boy has a marvelous, fascinating laugh. I must describe it in the beginning of the story, as Danny's introduction: a clear, ringing laugh, the laugh of an unhesitating, unquestionable joy, the laugh of a sunny soul, the laugh of the real life itself. That laugh must show more than anything else what that boy is and what they are destroying.

The probable story: he is unjustly hurt and deeply insulted by a popular, "respectable" pastor, who is a condensed representative of the "little street." [The injustice is such] that it damages, if not ruins, his life and career. He murders the pastor, as a revenge. The public is horrified, for the pastor was a very popular, "beloved" figure. The crime takes the aspect of a blow against the church, religion, civilization, humanity, etc. "The greatest crime ever . . ."

The boy is alone against all of society. He is everybody's personal, hated enemy. He is caught, tried, and condemned to death. He escapes from jail. He is recognized on the outskirts of the town by a sneaky little man with a shiny old coat, protruding chin, tobacco-stained yellow lips and bad teeth. He is surrounded by a mob and lynched. Torn to pieces, beaten to death on the pavement with the water of the gutter running red.

The story ends with Hetty, the girl who loved him, going to a grocery store on a rainy November evening, sent by her mother to buy some hamburger and ten cents worth of chopped pickles.

And the last cry of the story, as the girl looks at the little street:
"I'm afraid, Mother, I'm afraid!"

*Hetty, the girl.*

A clear, *straight* soul. Like the "Prince-Flower." [AR may be referring to a Grimms' fairy tale, *The Carnation,* in which a beautiful girl is turned temporarily into a flower by a prince.] Very sensitive. Lonely. Not a strong, ambitious career woman, but—a woman. Bewildered by life. Unable to adapt herself to things as they are. In the end, left aimless, with nothing to live for and a terror of living—showing how empty a place this world is for one who does not and cannot share its vices and vicious virtues.

She is the only daughter of a stupid, indifferent father and a petty, [pushy], house-wife mother. The household is rather poor—it has too much to be shabby and not enough to have any education or refinement.

She loves the boy with a wilder passion than she can realize. She is usually too calm, restrained and frail to think herself capable of such a primitive, raw feeling, almost beast-like in its overwhelming [intensity]. She is the only one who feels the Super-Being in the boy, feels it, without completely understanding it. She is frightened by him sometimes, but she is always ready to take his side against everybody. She might sometimes *think* he is wrong, but she always *feels* he is right. Her antagonism to common life, her infinite longing for something above it, centers on him, as the only relief from it she has ever met. She is not a strong, active, fighting enemy of that life. She does not even fully realize [the nature of] that life, because she is straight, honest, and "outside of it." But she feels, blindly and instinctively, the horror of that life and she feels the boy is the only one who is so far and *so high* above it. Without her realizing it, her love for him is her love for life—her religion, hope, ambition, pride, and future—all these things having no particular meaning to her, the intensity of her feeling centered on one thing: him.

The whole of her tragedy is brought out in the last scene. He escapes from jail after being sentenced to death, and comes to her because she is the only person he can trust. But he is [forced to leave] her house; her mother is threatening to call the police and her father is expected to return home any moment and would be sure to denounce the criminal who is loathed by all mankind. In these moments, when she sees herself alone against the world, when she sees herself so little and helpless in facing the monster of humanity, when she sees the octopus that has caught in its sucking [tentacles] the one who is sacred beyond all sacredness to her—then she understands life for the first time. (And so must my readers.)

(The model for the girl: the "Prince-Flower," qua modern; and myself, qua weak—the idealistic, longing side of me.)

She is medium height, very slim, rather frail. Not beautiful, but exquisite in her own way. Thin features. Brown hair. Gray eyes with long eyelashes. A fascinating smile that makes her look beautiful: a very feminine, delicate, and tempting smile.

The boy is not in love with her. He has never been in love. But he knows that she loves him. And he feels something like love, although it is more physical desire in the last scene when he kisses her wildly; he is feeling the call of life, when he is so near to losing it.

Just as the boy [embodies] the perfect egoism and will to live—the girl [embodies] the perfect love, the kind of overwhelming, intense, absolute passion that is so alien, so out-of-place on the "little street." To her the so-called love problems have always been utterly impossible to understand. She doesn't understand any tragedies of marriage, parents' opposition, social obstacles and such. The love that she knows is something so immense, so dominant, so unquestionable, that she cannot see anything being considered beside it or opposed to it.

As a relief for the whole book, the few moments that she spends with him when he is hiding in her house, when they kiss each other for the first and last time, must be trembling with the intensity, joy, and ecstasy of life. This scene must show what is possible and what is being destroyed by the little street. The stronger the contrast, the better. The reader must feel an actual pain, and the wild desire to yell for something that can't be explained in words—the life that no one knows.

*The Pastor*

[*An early version of Ellsworth Toohey in* The Fountainhead.]

He has everything that "the little street" has and nothing that it should have. A small soul choked with a poisonous ambition to dominate and crush everybody and everything. Not the kind of passion for power that says: "I want to rule because I know that I am superior to others and I must dominate them"; but the kind that says: "I know that I am inferior and therefore I don't want to let anything superior exist." This is subconscious, of course, because one of those muddy souls would never admit it to itself. Consciously, it believes that "we are all equal" and defends that equality with all the jealous, greedy zeal of a bulldog that has his teeth sunk into a piece of meat; the dull, despotic zeal of mediocrity that is [concerned with] the equality of those above, which it wants to pull down, and not with those below, which it [allegedly] wants to pull up.

The pastor has no idea out of the ordinary, the common, the established and he does not want any such ideas to exist. He is not a clever hypocrite that despises the mob and only plays up to it to attain his own aim. He is the lowest, most poisonous, most dangerous type—the ambitious mediocrity. He wants to believe that the mob he serves really *is* the ruler and the lord of the world. He has no aim outside of that mob. He wants to believe that the mob's ideas are the standards of the universe; that he is absolutely right in his petty, narrow little convictions; that everybody must not only obey these ideas, but actually *believe* them.

He knows how much of a blood brother he is to the mob. He also knows that there are those who stand far above it, and he wants to drag them down to the level of the mob, where *he* is the master [because he is] the best, "condensed" representative of that mob. He's a devastating picture of a dull, diseased ambition that has filled [an otherwise] empty soul. The ambition of a skunk that knows the bad smell is his only strength and therefore makes it the highest principle of life on earth.

His ideas are the means for "equality," for bringing higher men down to his level. His thinking is muddy enough to [demand] an absolute obedience to these ideas from others, but not from himself. He isn't above having filthy little love affairs, accepting money when doing so is quite safe although not quite clean, and forgiving in his "friends" the sins for which he would destroy an "enemy" (i.e., an "outsider").

He is tall and rather flabby, although he gives the impression of being thin. Has a narrow, lined, yellowish face with the proud, austere expression of a saint. He has little, damp, lusty eyes and the thin, dry lips of a cold hypocrite. He has white hands with short, fat fingers and shapeless fingernails that are more wide than long. Likes to wear rings. Has thin, straight hair which is beginning to gray, with a bald spot showing rosy and soft like the flesh of a baby. He has a deep, slow, dignified voice and a hee-hee-ing, indecent, insincere laugh.

He is a very prominent figure. Especially popular among the semi-literate lower classes, the ones that are always ready to fall for religious preaching. To some, he is a beloved and respected "father"; others are rather indifferent themselves, but will not tolerate any disrespect or disbelief of him and are always ready to defend him furiously against anyone doubting his authority. The business magnates and such despise him and feel an instinctive disgust toward him, but they have to tolerate and stay on good terms with him for fear of his dark, "backstage" power.

He hates all successful people. A successful man, in any line, is his personal enemy. He rejoices at every failure and at the fall of every idol.

(The model for the pastor: the pastor of the Ku Klux Klan that I read about. The movie censors. All "reformers." An endless list of "little street'ers" that I will note down as they come.)

[*Other Characters*]

A fat woman that has made her immense fortune by having bad houses [*houses of prostitution*]. An influential, respectable citizen. Very proudly conscious of her power. Ambitious to get or buy everything she wants. Convinced that there is nothing so high that she cannot get it. She marries a brilliant, aristocratic, divinely handsome young man, Eric "Goldenlocks." Marries him because she "can afford to have a pretty boy in her bed" if she wants one.

Eric is poor, ambitious, conceited and not very strong. He just sells himself, marrying her for her money, knowing all about her and the source of her fortune. He is tall, with blue eyes, golden hair and all the Siegfried-like, fresh, sparkling beauty of a snow-covered Scandinavian mountain peak on a sunny morning. He marries the woman. We see him later, with a heavy, flabby, ghastly white face, red eyelids, shiny nose, sagging double-chin, unkempt hair, muddled, expressionless eyes and the reputation of a chronic drunkard.

He had been in love, before his marriage, with a charming, brilliant girl from an old family, now poor and barely keeping up a decent appearance to support the dignity of their name. His marriage to the woman is a terrible blow to the girl. A middle-aged nouveau riche, a heavy, common brute, had been courting her in his ambition to possess something he felt to be so above him, a woman of the real aristocracy. She marries him now—in despair. We see her later, overdressed in an expensive and tasteless way, having for a lover a cheap, notorious "heartbreaker." A little detail: before all this, a young college girl—romantic, sensitive, but not very attractive—has committed suicide over her hopeless love for the handsome Eric "Goldenlocks."

A genius gone wrong. A handsome, brilliant young actor with a fine mind and a beautiful soul. Famous and successful, but gone wrong in that he is genuinely unhappy; his life is empty of desires or interests; he is cynical, tired, disgusted with everything—inside. Outside—he leads a wild life full of vice. He is not clear to himself, there is a continual chaos in his mind, regarding himself and the world. He does not know what he lives for or why he lives. *He does not care*—in an immense sense. An example of a fine frame that the little street has filled with its rotten content. Instinctively, he does not accept [the little street's view of life], he revolts against it—but he has no other. And it is too late for another. He shows how empty the little street's ideals are and what a wreck they make of an exceptional being. For they can't fill such a soul and they do not permit the [ideals] that could fill it. He is utterly cynical and does not believe in anything. He could not accept the little street's beliefs; they only killed in him all belief in believing.

The boy of the story shows how the little street wrecks an existing exceptional being. The actor shows how it wrecks such a being before he develops. The boy *is* an exceptional nature, and he is wrecked physically. The actor isn't, but could have been, and he is wrecked spiritually. The boy *is* a wonderful character, in spite of everything. The actor is *not*, but shows signs of what he might have been. The boy has his ego, his pride, his strength. The actor hasn't anything. He does not even respect himself. He is despicable sometimes, and does not care. He is as empty of any high interest or feelings as a human being can be.

A "philosophical" prostitute. A creature that lives for one thing only and does not want to see anything else. Perfectly satisfied and proud of herself. She looks at things straight, realizes her power and is proud. The female representative of the little street—to match with the pastor. Except that she is more honest than the pastor. She sees the world as it is and laughs at all the high words and ideals. She knows their worth. She has no "high ideals." She is openly rotten and satisfied with it, for the world is rotten and she has a right to say it. She is the voice of the little street when she says: that she is the real queen of life; that "decent" women have to share their men with her and be satisfied with what she leaves; that men's respect for their "respectable" women isn't worth a penny; that there is no man too high for her bed; that nothing is higher for men than what she gives them; and so on. She is a filthy creature who spits on all the high ideals of humanity and *has a right to do it*. For she does not lie. She only looks at things as they are and states the facts that the "decent people" are hypocritical enough to overlook and tolerate.

<hr />

*Things that will have to be shown and have characters to represent them*

*Sex filth.* The real horror (and here I must gather all my strength to show it as strongly as possible) of respectable men having love affairs with the lowest kind of female filth. Show that a great man can't be great if he associates (and associates in such a way!) with women he himself despises, that he is despicable himself if he does it. Show great men and young, promising boys with the disgraceful slime they make "love" to. All the things which they tolerate, which they allow themselves, thinking that they still have a right to keep their self-respect.

The hypocrisy of what men call love. A dull, lukewarm feeling of domestic-animal attachment and "respect" for their wives, not affected by affairs with "unrespectable" women.

The wives who tolerate their husbands' unfaithfulness and are unfaithful themselves. Perfectly satisfied with such a marriage.

Mothers who approve of their sons' vices and even help them in [such a course].

Influential, powerful men and the prostitutes who are their mistresses and who through these men get power over respectable people.

White-slavers.

*Associations.* The human herds. All the gatherings of average humanity which have but one aim: to ruin all individuals and individuality, to put "we" instead of "I" everywhere, to have a herd of submissive insiders against everyone outside who "does not belong," everyone who has the courage and conscience to walk alone. The tyranny of number, of the multitude, of the average. Communism already established—unofficially.

*Women's clubs.* The poisonous hypocrisy of a secret revenge given power and influence. The revenge of failed mediocrities that glorify "virtue" because they have no chance to [engage in vice]. Sour old maids—not only physically, but spiritually as well. Women who failed in their private lives given the power to dictate an opinion and exercise an influence over the lives of others. Inferiors, speaking as superiors to society. Wrecks themselves— trying to wreck other lives.

*Prominent, "respectable" citizens.* The intimate details of how they [rose]. Unpunished crooks who commit crimes against "society" and then furiously defend the rights of society against others. "Successful" men and what makes their success. The art of boot-licking. Patriots and their ferocious intolerance. Men killed and crippled for "their country." And *who* and *what* is that country? Show the "great" men—in business, politics, art—and how small they are when one looks closely.

*Home life.* The stupid idealization of it, that tries to make it the highest ideal and aim for everybody. The dull, petty, purposeless existence that it is. The ridiculous smallness of it. Show young, promising people, full of life, and what they become with their "families." The domestic-animal, eat-drink-

and-sleep existence. The chewing-cow-in-the-sun contentment. The heavy, dumb, jail-like monotony of that life, day by day. [*Note AR's rejection of both the "family values" of conservatives and (earlier) the "feminism" advocated by many liberals.*]

*Narcotic-fiends.* Those who buy it—and those who sell it, making fortunes [while remaining] uncaught and unpunished.

I leave these pages empty to be filled with [more descriptions of] those who constitute "humanity" and make up our great civilization, those for whom we are expected to live.

They are the ones who judge the boy when he commits his crime against society.

*Facts that I observe and want to remember:*
*good examples of the "little street"*

I must remember that I do not want to invent or exaggerate anything in this story. Everything must be taken from life. I do not want it to be my furious protest against humanity—made up in my imagination. It has to be true, just life as it is, which is far worse than I could ever invent. The only thing I can do in the story is to put it all together, to show the whole, to bring things a little closer to each other, allowing people to see the close relation between the "good" and the horror of their lives.

*The Hickman Case*

The first thing that impresses me about the case is the ferocious rage of the *whole* society against *one* man. No matter what the man did, there is always something loathsome in the "virtuous" indignation and mass-hatred of the "majority." One always feels the stuffy, bloodthirsty emotion of a mob in any great public feeling of a large number of humans. It is repulsive to see all those beings with worse sins and crimes in their own lives, virtuously condemning a criminal, proud and secure in their number, yelling furiously in defense of society.

This is not just the case of a terrible crime. It is not the crime alone that has raised that fury of public hatred. It is the case of a daring challenge to society. It is the fact that a crime has been committed by one man, alone; that this man knew it was against all laws of humanity and intended it that way; that he does not want to recognize it as a crime and that he feels superior to all. It is the amazing picture of a man with no regard whatever for all that society holds sacred, and with a consciousness all his own. A man who really stands alone, in action and in soul.

A mob's feeling of omnipotence is its most jealously guarded possession and therefore a dangerous thing to wound. The mob can forgive any insult or crime except one: [the act of] challenging its ultimate power. It can forgive a criminal who erred, but who is just one of itself, i.e., has the same soul and ideas and bends to the same gods. But to see a man who has freed himself from it entirely, who has nothing in common with it, a man who does not need it and who openly disdains it—this is the one crime a mob can never forgive.

It seems to me that the mob is more jealous to possess a man's soul than his body. It is the spiritual despotism that is so dear to it. It does not care whether it [physically] possesses a man, as long as the man acknowledges to *himself* that he belongs to it. It cannot stand to see a man who does not belong and knows it. That tyrannical monster, the mob, feels the helpless fury of impotence in the presence of the one thing beyond its power, that it cannot conquer, the only thing that counts—a man's own soul and consciousness. And when the mob sees one of these rare, free, clear spirits, over which it has no control—then we have the [spectacle] of a roaring, passionate public hatred.

Worse crimes than this have been committed. Not one has ever raised such furious indignation. Why? Because of the man who committed the crime and not because of the crime he has committed. Because of Hickman's brazenly challenging attitude.

[It can be seen in] his strange letters, which are a little theatrically melodramatic, but so boastful and self-confident, e.g.: "If you want help against me, ask God, not men," signed "The Fox." [It can be seen in] his utter remorselessness; his pride in his criminal career and in things that are considered a "disgrace"; his boasting of more and more crimes and his open joy at shocking people, instead of trying to implore their sympathy; his utter lack of anything that is considered a "virtue"; his strength, as shown in his unprecedented conduct during his trial and sentencing; his calm, superior, indifferent, disdainful countenance, which is like an open challenge to society—shouting to it that it cannot break him; his immense, explicit egoism—a thing the mob never forgives; and his *cleverness*, which makes the mob feel that a superior mind can exist entirely outside of its established morals.

No: [the reaction to] this case is not moral indignation at a terrible crime. It is the mob's murderous desire to revenge its hurt vanity against a man who dared to be alone. It is a case of "we" against "him."

And when we look at the other side of it—there is a brilliant, unusual, exceptional boy turned into a purposeless monster. By whom? By what? Is it not by that very society that is now yelling so virtuously in its role of innocent victim? He had a brilliant mind, a romantic, adventurous, impatient soul and a straight, uncompromising, proud character. What had society to offer him? A wretched, insane family as the ideal home, a Y.M.C.A. club as social honor, and a bank-page job as ambition and career. And it is not the petty financial misery of these that I have in mind. They are representative of all that society has to offer: a high social standing and a million-dollar business position is essentially the same Y.M.C.A. club and bank-page job, merely more of the same.

If he had any desires and ambitions—what was the way before him? A long, slow, soul-eating, heart-wrecking toil and struggle; a degrading, ignoble road of silent pain and loud compromises. Succeed? How could he succeed? How *do* men succeed? By begging successfully for the good graces of the society they must serve. And if he could not serve? If he didn't know how to beg? It's a long and tortuous road that an exceptional man must travel in this society. It requires a steel-strength that can overcome disgust, which is a worse enemy than fear, and also a steel-hypocrisy, the patient art of hiding oneself when it is wise not to be seen.

A strong man can eventually trample society under his feet. That boy was not strong enough. But is that his crime? Is it his crime that he was too impatient, fiery and proud to go that slow way? That he was not able to serve, when he felt worthy to rule; to obey, when he wanted to command? That boy could not get along with the men that society forgives and tolerates. He could not get along with the majority. He could not lick boots—and one can't succeed without licking boots. He was superior and he wanted to live as such—and this is the one thing society does not permit.

He was given [nothing with which] to fill his life. What was he offered to fill his soul? The petty, narrow, inconsistent, hypocritical ideology of present-day humanity. All the criminal, ludicrous, tragic nonsense of Christianity and its morals, virtues, and consequences. Is it any wonder that he didn't accept it? That it left his soul emptier than it had been before? That boy does not believe in anything. But, oh! men, *have* you anything to believe in? Can you offer anything to be believed? He is a monster in his cruelty and disrespect of all things. But is there anything to be respected? He does not know what love means. But what is it that is worthy of being loved?

Yes, he is a monster—now. But the worse he is, the worst must be the cause that drove him to this. Isn't it significant that society was not able to fill the life of an exceptional, intelligent boy, to give him anything to outbalance crime in his eyes? If society is horrified at his crime, it should be horrified at the crime's ultimate cause: itself. The worse the crime—the greater its guilt. What could society answer, if that boy were to say: "Yes, I'm a monstrous criminal, but what are you?"

This is what I think of the case. I am afraid that I idealize Hickman and that he might not be this at all. In fact, he probably isn't. But it does not make any difference. If he isn't, he *could* be, and that's enough. The reaction of society would be the same, if not worse, toward the Hickman I have in mind. This case showed me how society can wreck an exceptional being, and then murder him for being the wreck that it itself has created. This will be the story of the boy in my book.

### Facts and details that will be useful to me

The insistent efforts of the newspapers to represent Hickman as a coward, to break down the impression of his strength and daring. Immediately after his arrest the papers were full of articles about his being "yellow," his "breaking down," his "hysterical fear," his "white face," his appearance of being "a rat instead of a Fox," and so on, all insisting that even if he seems calm, he really isn't, he must be in a deadly terror. This might or might not have been true. Probably not, judging from his later behavior. Perhaps he was pretending to be insane. But the insistent way in which the papers shouted about his being "yellow" seemed to be a mad, furious attempt to degrade him, to take away any heroic appearance he might have had, to make the public think that they had succeeded in breaking him, while they really had not. It was as though it infuriated them to see strength, pride, and courage in this criminal and to see that they could not break him; it seemed to be the mob's subconscious fury at the sight of such virtues in its enemy. To humiliate, to throw down—that is the mob's greatest delight. (It's going to be so in the story, after the boy's arrest.)

*The jury.* Average, everyday, rather stupid looking citizens. Shabbily dressed, dried, worn looking little men. Fat, overdressed, very average, "dignified" housewives. How can they decide the fate of that boy? Or anyone's fate? If a man has to be judged, why can't he be judged by his superiors, who alone would have a right to do it? Why does he have to be judged by "equals" (and what "equals"!)? (In the story, I must select my jurors very carefully. One or two will have to be prominent characters whom the readers know very well, including all sides of their natures and their own unpunished crimes against society. Several will have to be incidental "background" characters—with enough of them shown to see what "good citizens" they are. The rest will be described by their looks—which is plenty. The whole must make a nice picture of society's representatives, who sit in judgment over the boy even though they are not worthy to lace his shoes.)

*Asa Keyes, the prosecutor.* His [lack of] honesty and conviction was clearly demonstrated in the shady, disgraceful case of Amy MacPherson. Shameful charges were directed at him immediately before the Hickman case. A fat, overindulgent-looking man, with an owl-like nose, narrow little eyes, a big, heavy face and double-chin, a grayish-yellow complexion, a balding head with greasy hair, and the booming voice of a bully, giving an impression of a fat seal or a bull-dog. He made an unintelligent speech, full of common platitudes, showing a complete lack of any imagination or originality. *He* had the nerve to speak in defense of the people, the country, the world and so on! And *he* had the right to yell about Hickman: "He is rotten, rotten!"

All of this is a good example of my "little street" idea. I kept the clipping of his speech, as a wonderful example of how the little street talks, almost exaggeratedly good, couldn't be better if I had written it for him.

(In the story, the prosecutor will have to be a rather prominent character, with a shady case on his hands, right before the boy's case, with all the characteristics of this one—and more!)

*The public who attended the trial. Average* citizenry in all its full bloom. Women and girls—silly, homely, uninteresting and insignificant, over-rouged, just utterly blank in every way. Old-fashioned little women—shabbily dressed, wrinkled and shriveled. God knows from where and why here. "Fellows" with "their girls." Men of all ages and of every profession, high and low, mostly low. Newspaper women with the conceited vanity and superior dignity of mediocrity feeling its importance, of workers smaller than their jobs. The common woman with ugly clothes, a fat, soft white face, and religious pins, a "kitchen-sink" type, who looked on everyday and declared that she had been to all the murder trials. The barefooted, robed "hermit" with a white beard, "Prophet Jonas" written in white oil-paint on a band around his head, and a red banner of prayers in his hand, who claimed that he was a messenger from Jesus Christ, sent to attend the trial. The fat, tall woman in brown with a mustache and a suspiciously kind voice and manner. The young man with the horse's teeth, who was "just curious." And so on. These are the ones I saw. The list can be prolonged indefinitely. The circus show that the mob enjoys when it has a plaything that is going to be murdered.

Harry Carr and his superb indignation at Hickman. (More about him later. I must have a journalist like that in the story, a composite of Harry Carr, Arthur Brisbane, Adela Rogers St.-Johns and several others with newspaper columns.)

Harry Carr's friend, the perfect gentleman who suggested that the proper punishment for Hickman is that he be cut to pieces.

Patsy Ruth Miller, the "big star" who "openly expressed her disapproval of the effort to save Hickman," and who has such a right to express it!

Charlie Chaplin, who came to the door and went away claiming that "one look was enough" and "he didn't want to be seen here." Such a clean, decent, virtuous man! [*The sarcasm here was in part provoked by Chaplin's support of communisn.*]

The prince of Sweden, the "royal presence," a chap with protruding jaws and the blank expression of a half-wit.

Richard Barthelmess who sat for hours in a place where he "could watch every expression on Hickman's face."

Adela Rogers St.-Johns cleverly noted that Hickman is an extremist, a type that can either be very good or very bad. This is true and the idea of the "extremist" is splendid. We should have more extremists—then life wouldn't be what it is. But she says that "an extremist is always dangerous" and we all should be just in between, the "golden mean," the balanced average. This is a wonderful expression of the view exactly opposite from mine. What I want to show in my book is just the horror of that middle: the illogical, inconsistent, weak, tolerant, mediocre, loathsome middle. For if men were extremists they would follow each idea and feeling to its end, they would be faithful to their purposes and to themselves, they would be clear, straight, and absolute in everything. And they wouldn't tolerate a lot of what is tolerated now. This is just what we need.

She says that Hickman could be either a very great man or a very great criminal. Well, it only shows that he is always great and the one thing impossible to him is pettiness and mediocrity. For this reason I admire Hickman and every extremist. [*Later, AR identifies "extremism" as an "anti-concept"; see "Extremism, or the Art of Smearing" in* Capitalism: The Unknown Ideal.]

She says that Hickman was always conscious of himself, always thinking of the effect he produces, always centered on himself. This is one of those things that isn't worth arguing about; the opinion on egoism is organic in every person and can't be changed or argued.

So she is afraid of men being too good or too bad? I think of the man who said: "Oh, that their best is so very small! Oh, that their worst is so very small! And oh, how horrid it is to be small!" [*This is an approximate quote from* Thus Spoke Zarathustra *by Friedrich Nietzsche.*] This is what my book is going to say. Extremist beyond all extreme is what we need!

Agnes Christine Johnston said that Hickman is "surprisingly uncivilized." I congratulate her, although not quite in the way she would expect. Her idea is that civilization is *sympathy*, i.e., a great sympathetic understanding and co-feeling with others. She is perfectly right; that is just what civilization is. But is that *progress*, which is the meaning usually associated with the word "civilization"? Isn't just that "sympathy" in civilization the greatest regress, the greatest danger, downfall and degeneracy of mankind? I know what Nietzsche and I think on this subject.

Johnston says that Hickman has "an ugly soul," that his mind is developed, but his soul is neglected. Well, "ugly" is a relative expression. She concludes with the responsibility of parents to develop their children's souls and mentions her "own three little ones."

(Incidentally, this same Agnes Christine Johnston is the author of a silly play about office-girls' love, about a homely working girl who becomes beautiful, and so on. The play has the deep, significant title of "Funny Little Thing." I mention this as an example of the ideology of those who speak so loudly about "civilization.")

V. M. declared, as though she were dictating a paragraph into my story, that Hickman's greatest crime is the fact that he willingly [detached] himself from "humanity," from the one and only thing that counts in the world— humanity and its progress. She claims that for this he should be killed and destroyed without pity. (She said this last part about *destroying* quite savagely, in a dark, threatening way that sounded so much like that typical, blind mob cruelty.) She says that the main thing in life is to feel that you are contributing to the progress of humanity, or life, or things in general—to feel yourself a part of some vague immense universal progress. She says that she is perfectly satisfied to feel herself a good average human being, and to believe that the other human beings are just as good—or bad—as she is; that the exceptional beings have to use their talent and intelligence to pull the average ones up, because kindness is the greatest thing, the only thing in life; that you are so closely related to other people that you can't tell where you end and they begin; that those who dare to stand alone always become insane.

I put all this down as a good, clear outline of the little street's high ideals.

Her claim that Hickman's greatest crime is his anti-socialness confirmed my idea of the public's attitude in this case—and explains my involuntary, irresistible sympathy for him, which I cannot help feeling just because of this and in spite of everything else.

Hickman said: "I am like the state: what is good for me is right." Even if he wasn't big enough to live by that attitude, he deserves credit for saying it so brilliantly. There is a lot that is purposelessly, senselessly horrible about him. But that does not interest me. I want to remember his actions and characteristics that will be useful for the boy in my story. His limitless daring and his frightful sense of humor, e.g., when he was playing the Victrola while policemen searched his apartment and he offered to help, asking if he could do anything for them. His calm, defiant attitude at the trial. His almost inhuman strength in being able to joke about his death sentence: "The die is cast and the state wins by a neck." His deliberate smiling when posing for photographs after the sentence. His hard, cynical attitude toward everything, as shown in the little detail that he expressed his feelings after the sentence by saying one obscene word. The fact that he looks like "a bad boy with a very winning grin," that he makes you like him the whole time you are in his presence, that he has a personality that would have carried him far if he had gone another way. His decision to die like a man and his promise to walk calmly up the death-steps. His playing jazz records and asking for flowers even in the death cell.

[The depravity of] the pastors who try to convert convicted murderers to their religion. Hickman has been baptized into the Catholic faith. So has Ruth Snyder. The horrible idea of "saving" a murderer's "soul," adding to the "glory" of their religion by demonstrating its power over fear-crazed convicts. The hypocrisy of "saving a soul," of turning a man to a religion of charity and forgiveness like Christianity—and then executing him. The mob tyranny I mentioned, shown in the desire to make a new slave, add a new follower to the herd, break an independent man into submission.

The fact that right after his sentence Hickman was given a Bible by the jailer. I don't know of anything more loathsome, hypocritical, low, and diabolical than giving Bibles to men sentenced to death. It's one of those things that's comical in its stupidity and horrid because of this lugubrious, gruesome comedy.

The newsboy I saw on a crowded downtown corner, a heavy, unshaven young fellow, with a [sickly] complexion, fat lips, narrow forehead and spectacles, who was yelling: "They're gonna hang him!" when the first extras with the sentence appeared. Other adult newsboys, yelling with a bloodthirsty delight: "Hickman to hang! Hickman to hang by the neck!"

The drunken man who murdered his wife for no particular reason, and then regretted it, was Hickman's cell-mate in jail—and beat Hickman up, thinking himself superior.

The twelve-year-old little girl, who wrote a letter to Hickman, asking him "to get religion so that little girls everywhere would stop being afraid of him."

Dale Budlong and other prisoners who "don't want to be mixed" with Hickman, considering themselves so much better.

The woman who wrote a letter to the authorities asking for permission to be present at Hickman's hanging. A great number of other letters making the same request. (!) (The bloodthirsty, blind, carnivorous beast that is hidden beneath the polished surface of our "civilized," religious, *respectable* citizens!)

All the dirty stories about Hickman. In this case they are probably true, but how easily they could have been manufactured to throw dirt at the object of the public's hatred (which will be the case in my book).

### Other examples of the "little street"

Gertrude Stein, when she stupidly said "It's the little things that count!" This is the perfect expression of that despicable attitude of some people— the glorification of mediocrity, the mediocrity that not only doesn't make any effort to rise toward something high, but idealizes its own smallness, glorifies it, makes it the highest thing in life, the only thing "that counts." The purposeful denial of high [ideals], the shameless, insolent sneering of the plebian who says: "I'm small, sure, but that's the main thing—to be small. You big ones, you don't mean anything, you don't count!"

That most repulsive of all things—the pride and vanity of the mediocre.

V. M., when she said: "Original thoughts are dangerous. . . . If an original thinker is anti-social, the more brilliant he is—the more dangerous he is, and therefore original thinkers are to be condemned!" Doesn't need any comment.

She speaks also of being useful to posterity, to the whole human race and so on. This gives me the thought that fear of death may govern those who think too much of the "future" and of "humanity." It is as if they know that their own life will not be enough and they want to have something eternal to believe in outside of it.

Where can I find a man who knows that his own life will be so great and he will fill it with so much, that he doesn't need any "high ideal" outside of it? Eternity itself doesn't matter—to exist is glorious enough!

Arthur Brisbane, who does not sympathize with Voronoff's desire to produce a Superman through heredity. He declares that this is just what humanity *doesn't* need; we don't want Supermen, we want average, equal creatures, for Nature always strives towards equality and balance. He proves [this latter claim] by deep, significant examples such as tall men liking short girls and fat women liking thin men. (And all the results of this poisonous, rotten, sewer-philosophy!)

The thing I heard about Gilbert Roland (too horrid to write down).

The parties at the studios with naked Negro girls dancing.

The way stars make their careers. (The middle-aged woman with pull who can make the careers of young men, or refuse to, telling them sincerely: "I'm sorry, you're not my type!")

The different kinds of mind: the abstract and the "social" mind, the latter being considered the most important for success. And what is it but the art of "getting along" with human beings? (Men like Danny Renahan don't get along.)

I. L. [Ivan Lebedeff, a Russian-born actor whom AR knew in Hollywood], who says that he does things he despises just to lower himself, to feel he is doing something nasty, to get to the level of the mob, and mix into that mob. He is afraid to be above [the mob]; he cannot stand the tragedy of being alone on top, and the horror of what he sees under him and has to live with and tolerate.

I don't know if it's quite so in his case, but the idea is very profound— that those who *could* be above willingly lower themselves, because "the little street" makes it super-humanly hard for a man to remain alone and keep his ideals. Another instance of how the little street works.

The rotten swamp that sucks everything into it. And so it goes: a man has the possibility to be high; he cannot stand it—other men and "society" are too much for him to fight against; he sinks down, to the mob's level; and thus he becomes one of those who stops some other man who could be high. [. . .]

*Incidents in the story*

College-life, the mob-reign par excellence. Danny—the most unpopular figure in college. He doesn't belong to any clubs, societies, or fraternities. He doesn't allow any crazy tricks to be played on him when entering college. He doesn't take part in any sports, that is, any *teamwork*.

Hetty is expelled from college for her attitude in the "Renahan case."

Hetty is one of the defense's star witnesses at the trial; she tries to save Danny.

Hetty implores the Governor to [pardon] Danny. She climbs into his house through a window when he refuses to see her. She pleads with real, human words against the stiff, official, blind answers of the Governor. She falls on her knees: "You can save him! Don't destroy something you can never create again!" He orders her thrown out and advises her to be careful of the reputation she has already soiled, or he may have to send her to a penitentiary to reform her "unnatural, degenerate tendencies!" [*This scene is a precursor of one in* We the Living, *when Leo is dying of tuberculosis and Kira pleads to Soviet officials to save him.*]

———◦———

Danny's death. The little man who recognizes him and attracts the mob to him. The mob appears from everywhere, from every dark corner and alley, like swarming cockroaches crawling out of their holes. The big drunken brute who strikes his heavy, nail-soled foot into Danny's breast, cracking the ribs. The quarter that rolls out of Danny's pocket into the pool of blood and is picked up by one of the men, who wipes it and takes it. The police find Danny's body near the sidewalk, a horribly torn mass. Only his beautiful face is left untouched, now immobile, pale, with eyes closed and long shadows of the eyelashes on the white cheeks; a head of marble, with one thin red stream, like a crack in the marble, on his temple; and only his hair moving slightly around the immobile face, moved by the water in the gutter that streams red.

———◦———

Danny in jail. His perfect indifference to everything—visitors, family, everybody—except Hetty. He does not love her, but he sees, understands, and respects her feeling for him.

The only moment when Danny is afraid of death and wants to live. One night, when he looks out of his cell window and sees nothing but a dark, clear sky and stars, and one luminous spire from a tall building far away; when he does not see the city and it seems to him that he is in some other world, on another planet, where life is clear, pure and luminous like the sky he looks into. And he wants that life, he loves it with all the passion of his life-hungry soul. That is the only moment when he weakens, when he is horrified at the thought: "They are going to kill me! They have no right to *kill* me!"

This episode will probably end with a guard passing by and seeing Danny's emotion instead of his usual calm, and snickering something about his being broken and yellow. Danny turns to him and answers with a horrible swear-word, something as obscene and contrasting with his former mood as the reality he faces is filthy and contrasting with the world he saw for a moment. With that one word, all his regrets are gone, he is back again in the life that makes him indifferent to death, he is again the hard, sneering, cynical convict, indifferent and disdainful of everything.

———◆———

When Danny kills the pastor, he shoots him straight in the face, mad with loathing and the desire to destroy him. He then shoots the rest of the bullets into the body, in his hatred and fury to kill. After that—no regrets, no remorse whatsoever. A clever and calm scheme to escape. He is found and arrested only through the betrayal of a friend.

———◆———

Danny becomes a criminal while he is scheming his vengeance. In one scene, another criminal dies in his arms while hiding from the police. The young man is unable to get help, preferring to die than to be discovered; he dies from bullet wounds, choking with blood. His beautiful last moments and words. The impression it makes on Danny.

———◆———

Danny's "fan mail" in jail. The disgusting letters of hatred and the even more disgusting letters of sympathy. Among the latter: declarations of love from half-witted, hysterical old maids; religious preaching and propaganda; the consolations and sympathy of "good Christians" for a "poor, erring sinner," and so on. Danny orders the jailers to stop bringing him the mail and to instead "use it in the toilet."

———◆———

[The Little Street *ends here. The booklet closes with the following personal notes.*]

From now on—no thought whatever about yourself, only about your work. You don't exist. You are only a writing engine. Don't stop, until you really and *honestly* know that you *cannot* go on.

*Concentration!*

Learn to enjoy action, and effort.

Learn that your work is a certain kind of work and that the state of your mind should be different from that which you have when doing nothing. You can't write and do something else.

*Do you live for action or for rest?*

*Stop admiring yourself—you are nothing yet.*

You must know how to control your moods and your mind. Be absolute master of yourself and your mind. How can you rule anybody or anything, if you can't rule your own mind?

The secret of life: You must be *nothing but will*. Know what you want and *do* it. Know what you are doing and why you are doing it, every minute of the day. All will and all control. *Send everything else to hell!*

Be a tyrant—no compromises with yourself. Do everything *absolutely*.

Try to forget yourself—to forget all high ideas, ambitions, supermen and so on. Try to put yourself into the psychology of ordinary people, when you think of stories. Try to be *calm*, balanced, indifferent, normal, and not enthusiastic, passionate, excited, ecstatic, flaming, tense.

Learn to be calm, for goodness sake!

Look at everything through the eyes of a very skeptical, very prosaic businessman.

Think more of the psychology of your heroes, according to their characters.

Not so straight and crude. The same things can be more complicated and different, as they usually are in life.

## 2

# WE THE LIVING

AR's working title for We the Living was Airtight. In 1930, at the age of twenty-five, she began making notes for the novel in a bound composition notebook. The notebook, presented below in its entirety, contains descriptions of the characters and the unbearable conditions of life in a totalitarian state.

The remaining notes on the novel are unbound, undated, mostly unnumbered, handwritten pages; some are paper-clipped together, and all are collected in a folder. About one-third of this material is offered here. I have omitted her chapter-by-chapter outline because it does not depart in any significant way from the novel. I have also omitted several pages listing known facts of Russian history in the 1920s. The only other material omitted was too cryptic to be of general interest.

It may be surprising that AR made so few notes for her first novel. There are two main reasons. First, no research was required for We the Living, since she already knew the background. Second, AR chose this novel as her first partly because of its relative simplicity. She was not ready to attempt a complex theme or to present her ideal man, but she was ready to write about young people being crushed by a dictatorship.

Since she had little difficulty with the plot, characters, or theme, she did not need to make extensive notes.

## Airtight

### *The Characters*

*Kira Argounova*

Dominant trait: an intense, passionate hunger for life. Beautifully sensitive to the real meaning and value of life—and crushed under the senseless, morbid, suffocating conditions of a miserable existence. Proud and definite. Unbreakable. One of the very few—and the only one in the book—who, as a person, is not in the least affected by the new conditions; who denies them and does not quite understand their right or reason for existence. She fights them—externally; and the fight is the more tragic because, internally, she is left absolutely untouched and unaffected. A sane, healthy individual thrown into the very depths of abnormal, inhuman conditions.

Independent. Self-assured. Educated in a wealthy family by a mother who let her grow up as she pleased, without any restraints or influences, and with plenty of everything she needed. As a result, she has a calm poise and the full, free strength of her own unusual personality that has not accumulated any useless, alien inhibitions from any outside source. No religion whatsoever. Brilliant mind. Lots of courage and daring. Only her calm exterior poise hides her tempestuous emotional nature. A sort of graceful restraint under which one can feel the storming fire.

Rather cold and indifferent to everything that does not interest her deeply. Absolutely proof against all influences. Always alone and, to most people, aloof. Disliked by women. No girlfriends. No "beaux." Indifferent to men. Dimly conscious of her tremendous sexual power—if she wanted to use it. Men are attracted to her and afraid. Nothing flirting or "come hither" in her. The more powerful, then, is her attraction for men with whom she condescended to be a woman, and who saw the woman in her: Andrei and Leo.

Honest and straightforward—the honesty of pride and of superiority. Misunderstood. Hurt by it, sometimes, yet used to her loneliness, intelligent enough to realize that it is unavoidable. A strong determination and disdainful pride—and sometimes, beneath it, an indefinable, charming, feminine weakness and helplessness—something of the frightened child, which she is to a great extent. Always feminine in the best sense of that word, that is, graceful, aloof, charming. Never the masculine, "intellectual," "rough and ready" type of woman [common] in politics, or the alleged "woman of brains." Capable of being cruel. Sometimes conceited—at the feeling of her power.

Her love for Leo—the concentrated strength of all her will to live. He is, to her, the symbol of everything she wants and the meaning of life as she sees it. Therefore, her indifference to others, the clarity of her mind that leaves her cool to many useless emotions and affections, her straightforwardness—these lead her to an all-absorbing passion, almost unbearable for a human being.

### Andrei Taganov

Dominant trait: a born individualist and leader who never discovered it. A great mind and a profound honesty. An iron will and unconquerable strength. A great calm and deliberation—the calm of a man who knows he is master of himself and has learned long ago to have complete self-control. Occasional, very rare flashes of temper that show the real fire in him—a fire, however, that never gets the best of the man.

His father: a factory worker, mixed in politics and sent to Siberia during the Revolution of 1905; died in exile. His mother: died shortly afterwards of poverty and overwork. He, the only son, made his way through the hardest work [with an] iron determination, and a long toil that did not break him, but only taught him patience and hardened him. No school education; self-educated and self-made. Always lonely and aloof, aloof without realizing it. Never a good mixer. Never a popular fellow. In his political career, he advanced through his brilliant ability and unquestionable honesty more than through popularity in the Party, where he is far from being popular. His comrades in the Party are always his political friends, never his personal chums; this is not the result of any deliberate attitude taken by him, but the natural behavior of a man who has devoted his entire life to his political ideals and sees only that.

As to those ideals: they are the result of his early hatred of the existing system of society—not so much hatred, but rather a calm and cool determination of long ago: to do away, someday, somehow, with the inhuman conditions that he went through and in which he started his life. The people whose champion he is stand before his eyes as individuals, as men like himself, whose *life* is crushed by the senseless power of a society that has no right to a man's life. In that, and more unconsciously than hers, his tragedy is the same as Kira's. Both are superior individuals. Both have in their souls the sensitivity, the understanding, the hunger for the real life, as few men see it. Both rise to fight for their rights to that life; and both face the same enemy: society, the state, the mass. She is stronger, in that she realizes the fight and the enemy. He is more tragic, because his fight is unconscious: the fight against society of a man who stands as a champion of the most sociable ideals.

He is a man that would have been a Napoleon—had he been born with less conscience and idealism. He has an iron devotion to his ideals, the devotion of a medieval martyr. Capable of anything, any cruelty, if convinced that his aim needs it. Cruelty for the cause is, to him, a victory over himself; it gives him the feeling of doing his duty against his sentiment.

Yet a profound egoism lies under that devotion to his work, for it is *his* work and *his* aim that he is serving. His ideals have not been inspired by sympathy and compassion for the suffering of the masses. It is his suffering and *his pride* that made him take arms against society. This is subconscious, for it's not his personal interests that he has in mind, it's the victory of *his* idea—and his idea is the uprising of fighters, individuals, strong men of the people crushed under a senseless, ignoble system.

The taste, manners, and tact of an aristocrat—but not conventional manners, just the poise and dignity of a man with inborn good judgment. Instinctive, unconscious understanding of beauty and art; an untrained, but wise esthetic feeling, [which is] dormant, never given much attention or opportunity. Delicate and sensitive to other people's feelings—no violent hatred or prejudices against anyone. No religion.

No conceit. One of the few people who is absolutely untouched by flattery, admiration, or any form of other people's opinion. Not because of a proud disdain, but because of a natural indifference to it. Subconsciously, he knows his superiority and does not need any one's endorsement. Consciously, he is interested only in doing what he thinks is right; [he wants to be] satisfied in his own eyes. A self-discipline learned long ago.

A man who knows how to take serious things seriously. But with hidden beauty, sympathy, even tenderness, and an intelligent sense of humor.

Sexual matters never interested him. Didn't have the time. Accustomed to hard work and making the most of his time, all concentrated in one line and aim. Never had an affair. Not because of a moral effort, asceticism, or self-imposed renunciation, but because of a lack of interest and a slight disgust for sex as he saw it around him. Yet a very strong sense of sensuality, unawakened.

Kira is the first woman who ever attracted his attention. His instinctive sense of values and beauty sees in her what very few men see. Therefore, his passion—unexpected, fierce, primitive, letting loose an energy long restrained—overwhelms him with its intensity. He has sense enough not to attempt any struggle, nor to consider it as interfering with his aim and duty. He just surrenders completely to what is for him a newly discovered beauty in life, the life for which he has a profound instinct. It is characteristic that Kira is an aristocrat, a woman of the upper classes, and that, knowing her hatred of his Party, he never resents it.

*Leo Kovalensky*

[*This section was crossed out. While much of the following obviously applies to the Leo in the novel, the character described here is more flawed.*]

Dominant trait: a man who should be more than he is. A brilliant, but not profound, mind, and a very poor emotional nature. A mind witty, quick, sharp and clear, but not deepened by any great feeling. *Very* good-looking— more than that: beautiful. A face with the proud, haughty, aloof expression of a god, a face promising a superior, profound, fascinating man; and the man not keeping the promise. The greatest lack in him is the lack of any strong desire or ambition; therefore, also, the lack of will. Never had any profound love or hatred, never very happy or despondent, no real interest or enthusiasm for anything. No emotional extremes.

He is brilliantly witty. A light, distinguished sense of humor; too much of it leads to his not taking anything very seriously. A love for paradoxes, for witty ridiculing of any high, serious, revered, or established ideas. Elegant, distinguished, aristocratic—mostly in manner and attitude, not in clothes or [conventional] psychology. His aristocratic [style] is personal, not the class-bound [charade] of formal manners and high ancestry. Sophisticated, bored, slightly cynical. No moral feeling. Would not do anything low or ugly, but more from an esthetic than from an ethical feeling. Has a love for beauty, but mostly beauty of form, beauty of the surface, not deeper.

Likes everything new, exotic, extreme, effective, modernistic, eccentric, original, smart. Affects a modern European or American attitude. Has an aristocratic dislike for work and effort. Nothing can rouse him to any serious effort or struggle. Anything hard is distasteful to him. Lack of perseverance; takes everything easy, nonchalantly. No great ambition of any kind—not definite or positive enough for that.

He is very popular. Always the soul of the party, but not as a "good fellow," rather as a perfectly charming, fascinating man of the world. Always knows how to say and do the right thing at the right time, and is at ease with everyone, everywhere.

His convictions: none. Not even positive about that. Constant only in his indifferent sophistication and skepticism toward everything. Alert and takes great mental interest—in everything new and startling. But no emotional interest.

Religion: hasn't any. Yet is not a decided atheist. Never made up his mind definitely one way or the other. Can be both, according to the mood or effect of the moment.

His political convictions are not definite. While not being in sympathy with the government, he is not as indignantly opposed to it as most people in his circle. While ridiculing and resenting the conditions of life around him, he is not theoretically opposed to communism; he is not [opposed] to anything modern—part of his sophisticated tolerance.

Temperamentally, he does not like to display any emotions. Although he is not of a very intense nature, yet he does get depressed, occasionally, and cannot always hide it. Also, he does show happiness occasionally, but more seldom. Very brave, disdainful of danger—sometimes; and sometimes loses his nerve.

He had a profound affection for his parents and sister, who died.

In regard to sexual matters, he is not highly virtuous; yet he is not oversexed. Has had affairs. Not vulgar or promiscuous about it, however. He is not too interested in sex, and the occasional interest he has is more physical than emotional. Is tremendously attractive to women. Women spoiled him. He is conceited and self-assured with them. Flirts with every woman he meets—rather, just has a flirting manner, highly flattering to women. Of course, he never means it. It is a habit and light diversion for him.

Conceited, but not concerned about it. Not susceptible to flattery—used to it. Has few real friends and none very close—he is not interested. But a vast number of acquaintances. Cruel, in that he is perfectly indifferent to other people's feelings.

He is capable of high emotions and beautiful actions, but seldom roused to them. Has the mind to understand high beauty—and could have been more than he is. Has everything to be a great man. Ambition is all he lacks. Conditions around him subconsciously killed all ambition in him, all real appetite for life. In other circumstances, he would have developed into an outstanding and fascinating man. He is too much the aristocrat and not enough the male to stand up under any conditions and fight his way through. Besides, he did not even have anything to fight for; life around him did not offer any stimulant to his ambitions at the time they could have been formed. He is not the type that would bring his own desires and ideas to life; he has to get them from life—and it did not give him any. While he does not oppose the conditions of life around him very much, they break him internally, without his even knowing it, break him by killing his interest in life.

Kira saw in him "what he could have been." Her romance with him is also her desperate fight to "keep them from getting him." As to Leo, his love for her was the best thing in his life. It was all of his higher sentiments and better self. The "man that could have been" understood Kira, saw the superior woman in her, and loved her more than he had ever loved anyone. He did not love her better [because] he was not capable of a better love. And as his better self slowly dies in him, so does his love for the only real woman in his life. It never dies completely. Something indefinable, nameless, unconscious, remains. He is not happy when he goes [south] to his new life, leaving Kira behind. In his indifferent hopelessness a dull, secret pain always remains, as the scar of a feeling which he could never entirely forget—and which he had not been big enough to keep. [*End of deleted section.*]

### Antonina Pavlovna

Dominant trait: the condensed low female of all times. Selfish like a dumb, brutal monster. Vain. Conceited. Eager for everything that flatters her ego. But mainly: a loose creature out to satisfy herself. Cheaply fashionable, "feminine," "modern," with some pretenses at being "cultured" and "intellectual." "Misunderstood." From a middle-class family, but always aspires to more "aristocracy" and "culture" than is her right.

She is oversexed and promiscuous. Vulgar in her sex affairs. She has many of them—some for profit, some for animal desire. The kept mistress of white officers and Bolshevik commissars. Proud of her position and influence. She is always trying to show her power and make that influence felt. Nothing is too small or too filthy for her.

Her "love" for Leo: the vain female desire to "win" him. Also: the animal desire of an oversexed creature for the gorgeous male that he is.

### Rita

A plain debauchee. She has no feelings or thoughts left. Nothing but loose, uncontrolled, sordid sexuality. She is from a good family, and was given a good education. Divorced from a red commander. Only the thinnest outside cover of some culture left. A menacing specter, a symbol of what lies in the future for the youth of the coming generation.

More obvious, open and younger than Antonina Pavlovna. Not many "intellectual" pretenses.

### Lydia

An average girl, nearing her thirties. Not too attractive nor intelligent. She has wasted her best years, becoming bitter and poisoned.

(Representative of the older half of the younger generation.)

### Vava

A common, sheep-like nature. She is rather attractive, and from a wealthy family. Spoiled. Conceited. Marries, has a child soon, and does her best to live in the favor of the government. Becomes a typical, [lifeless] "soviet citizen."

(The alternative—Rita or Vava.)

### The Picture

A terrific machinery crushing the whole country and smothering every bit of life, action, and air.

A picture of the state, and those who are the state, strangling the individual. A picture of the masses showing who and what those masses are, their ideas, and their rise against the unusual and higher man.

How is it done? By conditions of living unbearable to the higher individual. And the theme of the book—*what these conditions are and how they work*.

The higher and stronger is broken, but not conquered; she falls on the battlefield, still the same individual, untouched: *Kira*. The one with less resistance is broken and conquered; he disintegrates under an unbearable strain: *Leo*. And the best of those who believed in the ideal is broken by the realization of what the ideal really means: *Andrei*.

### How It Is Done

1. *Economic conditions*

*Terrific poverty.* A general misery. People driven to the point where [obtaining] the most common necessities presents a big problem. The horrible, deadening dullness of the hopeless drudgery, when all higher instincts and aspirations slowly die out, stifled by the dumb, animal struggle for a pitiful existence. And the mental atmosphere furnished by the government: a glorifying of the drudgery. A growing habit of considering all luxury—everything unnecessary and charming—to be absolutely and hopelessly out of reach.

*Unemployment.* The frightful lack of work. The humiliations, pull, and struggle one must endure to get employment. The unions. The idiotically cruel refusal of even the right to make a living for people with an aristocratic past. The new merchants and the senseless persecution that follows them. The successful new rich and the grotesque irony of their gains, influence, and position in the "red" society—the class of men uglier even than the ideology of the ruling class that allows them to exist. All the pathetic, tragic, and ridiculous efforts to make a living. Divorces to keep a job. The "cutting off" of employees. The eternal fear and uncertainty. Queer new professions and occupations.

*Physical discomforts.* Hunger. Cold. No living space. Terrible transportation. Disease. Lice. Dirt.

## 2. *Mental conditions*

Everything centered around one idea—one propaganda—and that idea fed to the people until they mentally suffocate. Everything that does not belong to this propaganda, all the natural instincts and ideas, everything that makes up the individual life and the beauty of life—is thrown out and trampled. An unbearable propaganda of an unbearable idea that makes the atmosphere choking, *airtight*, until people get to a state of mental scurvy. The idea itself and the method of propaganda are the very essence of commonplace ideology—intended for and created by the "middle class of the spirit." (When showing the ideas, always show those who create them and make them possible.) The great "average humanity"; show its spirit and what it does to the ones above the average.

*Propaganda:*

*In Education* (schools and universities): students' meetings, the political life, the arrests and exiles, the spies, the "cleaning" of the students, the exile of the old professors, teaching only propaganda, and in high school—the coming youth and its mental mutilation.

*In Art:* theaters, books, paintings, movies: censorship and the propaganda idea—the "proletarian art."

## 3. *Moral conditions*

An existence where men turn into cornered animals. The perpetual fear, struggle, poverty, depression, and hopelessness. A general degradation—men turning smaller than they usually appear, life turning into a shabby, petty, cheap routine.

And the youth of the country starting out on their lives.

The youth of the [former] classes faces a hopeless struggle: a long, tiresome, joyless path. Alternatively, they may sink down into real debauchery, all morals let loose by the strain of the unusual times.

The new youth [is characterized by a] loose morality and a superficial, "patriotic" arrogance.

The older generation faces a hopeless old age.

And the real human being—Kira—caught in the swamp and voicing the theme of the story: "But there is a life, a life that I saw, that I was waiting for—and I have a right to it. Who is taking it away from me and why are they doing it?"

[*The material in the composition notebook ends here. The remaining notes were made on unbound pages and collected in a folder.*]

*Collectivism:* its spirit, influence, ramifications.

*Desperate living conditions:* the people's attitude toward them, and the government's attitude—*glorification.*

*The new red culture:* its hypocrisy, show-offishness, fear, boot-licking, nonsense (museums, schools, etc.).

*Propaganda:* ever-present, at every step and moment. (Artificial enthusiasm.)

*Inefficiency:* the stupid bureaucracy, red tape, bad quality in everything (Soviet matches, Soviet soap, etc.).

### To Show

#### Economical

*Food:* How it's impossible to get: the cards, rations, speculators, standing in line, cooperatives. The monotonous, unhealthy diet: millet, dried fish, linseed oil. Everyday necessities considered as luxuries: butter, eggs, milk, white bread. Excesses of hunger: fallen horse, acorns, coffee grounds.

*Clothes:* The impossibility of getting new materials. Every new article of clothing an event (particularly shoes). Endless altering of old clothes. Pathetic "styles": patent-leather, celluloid jewelry, "batik" handkerchiefs. Worship of imported "foreign" clothes and *silk stockings*. Pathetic awe at the sight of "dressed" foreigners. Smuggling of stockings and cosmetics. The "Soviet" cosmetics (poisonous lipstick). No formal evening clothes. "Soviet" materials—everybody alike. The terrible inefficiency of everything "Soviet."

*Houses:* Crowded to the limit. Encounters with enforced tenants. Frozen water pipes. Lack of wood. Six degrees [Celsius] in the house. "Bourgeoisie" stoves. Linseed oil lamps. Primuses. The house "parliament" and the Upravdom. Dirt. Lice.

*Employment:* The pathetic horror of "cuts" of employees. The vile, low, humiliating playing up to the "red" authorities. The time wasted on stupid, hypocritical "social activities." The "enforced patriotism." Constant propaganda in connection with any work. Persecution of private traders and the unemployed. Impossibility of finding work. Odd forms of earning a living: street peddlers and their pathetic merchandise.

#### Political and Cultural

*The All-Pervading Propaganda:* Its ridiculous, far-fetched connections. Its intentionally vulgar, "popular" style and artificial bravado. Glorifying of the drudgery and the "everyday." Its main methods: *employment*—enforced meetings, "social activities," demonstrations, enforced deductions of pay for "patriotic" enterprises; and *schools*—enforced study of unscientific "social sciences," a "red" angle on all activities.

Talk, talk, and talk. *Endless, enforced talk without the right to say anything.*

The ever-present threat of the G.P.U.: secret arrests, executions, exiles.

*Art:* Old theater—and next to it the awkward new "proletarian" dramas. Movies: the foreign ones cut, the red ones—(!). Literature (books and magazines): all propaganda, and intentionally vulgar. Art: all "red." "Ballet of the Toilers."

The pathetic intelligentsia: the operas, philharmonic concerts, futuristic book covers and china, "modern poets," theatrical settings, foreign translations, and worship of foreign magazines. The pathetic "parties."

## Morality

Hypocrisy at an unbelievable height. Nepmen and "red fighters" like Victor. [*NEP was Lenin's New Economic Policy, which allowed some "private" trading. "Nepmen" was the name for those who grew rich through this policy; they are represented in the novel by the character of Morozov.*]

### Characters

The individual against society at a time when society is at its worst and makes itself felt most strongly. Therefore, show *all* the *mass* manifestations of humanity in general and of the Russian revolution in particular.

Types who represent it:

*Kira*—cannot be broken.
*Andrei*—broken physically, broken life.
*Leo*—broken spiritually.
*Pavel*—"the best of the worst"; representative of those successful with the mob.
*Victor*—same [as Pavel].
*Comrade Sonia*—the "new woman," mob womanhood at its most dangerous.
*Dunaev*—the best in the old world and its tragedy.
*Antonina Pavlovna*—the worst.
*Nepman*—the triumph of the new order.
*Stepan*—the sailor, the fighting idealist.

*Lydia*—the dying old world.
*Galina Petrovna*—the accommodating "intelligent" [woman].
*Alexander Dimitrievitch*—the dying old world.
*Marisha*—the new "loose, red youth."
*Sasha*—the old fighting student.
*Irina*—an average girl, caught by events.
*Acia*—the "new child."
*Maria Petrovna*—a frightened "nothing."
*Vava*—a "flapper" of the old world.

[*AR made the following notes on revising Part 1.*]

## Chapter I

More of Kira's reaction—make Kira's presence felt.
Song of the "Apple"—twice.
Incident of "official business"—? Out.

## Chapter II

Their arrival and the station—shorter.
Shorter description of Nevsky.
Read again carefully the talk with relatives. Insert some touch of propaganda—very little.

## Chapter III

Revise: Place and date of birth, family position, union membership, occupation. Quicker, short examples and sentences. More of Kira, her spirit of adventure, and not in love only—*her hunger for practical beauty, for dreams and reality united.* More distinct propaganda on the official's part. Cut out unnecessary "cruelty" of Kira. Kira's attitude toward sex and love.

## Chapter IV

More of Kira—of her idea of life and of her reaction. A little about the University. More propaganda. Kira—the Viking—the "Song of the Broken Glass" against Soviet reality.
Correct reference to Admiral Kovalensky.
Shorter and sharper—Victor's visit. His conversation—also in the cab—more pointed and typical—the "artist," the "advanced, cultured, hard-working young man," the terrific egotism felt under it.

Synopsize scene in Summer Garden.

Conversation with Leo—more of Leo's bitterness, masterful arrogance and unhappiness.

## Chapter V

Not enough of Kira's reaction to Leo.

Cut out the "no" sequences—except house meeting. [*The "no" sequences have been published in* The Early Ayn Rand.] More of propaganda and living conditions. More of Kira's reaction, her impatience, her thoughts of Leo. The University—a possible beginning; Syerov and talk of "Red Culture." New meeting with Comrade Sonia. Rewrite scene at home.

This chapter should be the opportunity for "everyday" flashes; propaganda also—the Dunaevs.

## Chapter VI

Better beginning. Better description of streets. "Re-touch" meeting with Leo. Out—scene at Dunaevs; move it—modified—to Chapter V. Scene of Dunaev and Kira at market: a little more—and sharper. (Better—about Professor Lesbov—also about his crying over Beauty.) "Re-touch" conversation with Andrei—watch out for naturalness and Andrei's character, his strength. Emphasize: Leo's weariness, Andrei's enthusiasm.

## Chapter VII

A little more of Kira's reaction in scene with soap. Revise theater scene. And the sleigh. More of Andrei's reaction—stern. Meeting with Sonia and Pavel—?

## Chapter VIII

"Re-touch" scene in Communist cell.

## Chapter IX

More conversation with Andrei. Show their friendship, their basic understanding, the things on which they differ and in which they're alike. "Re-touch" ride through streets and walk through snow.

## Chapter X

Last—Leo's warming.

### Chapter XI

Kira-Andrei conversation. More about relationship of Kira-Leo, and their love.

### Chapter XII

Reconstruct party. More of Victor—"soul of the party." Better description of Vava's father. More *fear*.

### Chapter XIII

Cut out "Vorovsky." [*Vorovsky, mentioned in her history notes, was a Soviet envoy in Switzerland who was killed in 1923.*] Check on flashes of Leo's employment-seeking; give them something besides dialogue—a few touches.

### Chapter XIV

Better beginning. A little better about the movie. A few more detailed touches to the quick episodes.

[In general:] *Better dialogue with Andrei.* A more real, personal friendship—not too theoretical. And the theories—clearer.

General misunderstanding and disapproval of Kira—home and Institute.

[*The remaining notes are on particular scenes, beginning with the first meeting of Kira and Leo.*]

*Leo:* Insulting and perfectly indifferent about it.

Their understanding—which leads to questions about her experience, then to her final confession.

*Kira:* Stunned by him, reverent, yet hiding it under a matter-of-fact calm. More reverence than love. A girl full of life, full of vague hopes of which he is the realization.

*Leo:* Mystery as to his identity and position. Bitterness—a general, philosophic kind of bitterness, with just a hint of bitterness against the Soviets under it. *A cynical worldliness and weariness.* Cruelty—and completely indifferent to it. Superior conceit—indifference to women's compliments, a "spoiled by women" attitude.

At first—he is amused, he plays with her. Then—he is interested, impressed—more than he wants to admit—by her straightforward, brave, calm outlook on things.

———◊———

[*The following is for the description of Petrograd in Chapter I, Part 2. In a 1961 interview, AR commented on this description:* "It is the one passage that shows (Victor) Hugo's influence. The style is not mine—it is not the method natural to me."]

The whole: give a picture and feeling of Petrograd as a city—not *any* city, but *Petrograd*.

Its creation: by a will of man where no city should have been—not born, *made*.

Nevsky. Kamenostrovsky. The islands. Neva. Palace and fortress. Side streets. Canals. Little parks. Factories. Unrelieved drabness and plainness.

(The feeling of the city without crossing its doors, without entering its houses.)

Petrograd is complete, it does not grow. It is definite.

Its facets are extreme: man-made, deliberate, perfect for what they are. No nature—*man*.

No folklore or history like that of Moscow or Paris. No legends.

It is not the city of the people, but of the aristocracy and the intellect.

[*The following two sentences were crossed out:*] Its symbol would not be a church or a fortress, but a palace and a night club. It is the city of a high hat and a narrow liqueur glass.

It is "he," not "she" like Moscow.

What the revolution did. (Monuments.)

Spring.

———◊———

[*For the climactic scene between Kira and Andrei in Chapter XIII, Part 2.*]

She is proud of what she has done.

Nothing he can do to Leo will compare to what she has done to him.

His love was only money for Leo. She laughed at his love. . . . Highest woman? Only a prostitute—and he is the one who bought her. She thought of Leo [while she was] in his arms. Every kiss she gave him was given for Leo.

She is not ashamed—she is what they have made her. They who have forbidden life to the living.

In him and to him—she has paid.

Has he learned what his own life is? Will the State be a consolation? Does he know what they are doing? "Airtight."

I could stand all but my highest reverence . . .

———◦———

[*For Kira's death scene.*]

Earth—snow, going up and down, snow lighting the sky, a haze ahead—and she isn't sure whether it's close at her face or miles away. Frightened when she sees a tree—crouches like an animal. Bands of snow rising in the wind as if reaching the low sky in the distance.

Sky—black and gray and patches of blue that could not exist in daytime. Strips of stars that make her uncomfortable. Patches of light from nowhere.

Silence—shadows of sounds. Afraid to stop to listen beyond the sounds of her feet. Long journey—as if there had never been anything else in the world beyond that snow.

*Weariness.* Pain in her knees as if climbing a stairway. Her cheeks frozen. Pain in her finger-joints, in her back, in her shoulder blades. Legs moving as if not her own. Suddenly she feels well, too well. Sudden break of pain. Cannot stop at any price. Bending—to be less to carry.

*Thoughts; She has to get out.* Has she any questions to be answered? To be answered *there*. It won't get her. She can't give up. Looking at stars—head thrown back, arms outstretched—isn't there a place for her in the world? Checking on money in jacket often. Thinks dimly of "Cafe Diggy-Daggy"—repeating it senselessly, nickel plated letters insolent in their simplicity in dull white glass. Doesn't know what awaits her. Knows only that she has to get out. An instinct chasing her, like that of an animal. Nothing behind her—only that ahead. "You're a good soldier."

Growing insane determination: to go on, to get out.

Worries over bills. "Good soldier."

Finds herself in the snow suddenly. "I must have fainted again."

Rolls down side of the hill. Gets up slowly—seems like hours.

Crawls up the side of the hill, on her hands and knees. Rises again.

Pink froth at her lips. Throws away the scarf. Throws away the jacket.

Staggering in the snow, her hair in the wind, bloodstains spreading on her gown.

Calling Leo—the Leo that would have been there, where she is going.

What life had been. The Viking. Murmuring the "Song of Broken Glass."

That which had been promised cannot be denied to her.

Dawn—Beauty in nature, which is more than the beauty of nature, but the beauty of an idea.

A last ecstasy of life. "Life that is a reason unto itself." That which was possible.

**February 2, 1936**

*[An excerpt from an autobiographical note that AR sent to her publisher.]*

I have been asked why I wrote this novel. I think the answer is obvious. I have seen Soviet life as few writers outside Russia have seen it. And while the world at large is deluged to the saturation point with minute accounts of Soviet Russia, including all the latest statistics up to every single tractor produced by the "great experiment," very little has been said about actual life under communism, about living beings, not slogans and theories. Theories against practice—that's something too often overlooked in every important question today. With due apologies to good manners, I don't give a damn about theories. I do give a good deal about human beings. No, not all of them. Only those worthy of the name.

Also, if one takes even the swiftest look at the world today, one cannot help but see the greatest, most urgent conflict of our times: the individual against the collective. That problem interests me above all others in my writing. No country on earth offers such a startling and revealing view of that conflict as Soviet Russia. Hence—*We the Living.* The plot of my novel is entirely fictitious. The background and circumstances which make the plot possible—are entirely true.

# 3

# FIRST PHILOSOPHIC JOURNAL

*AR was twenty-nine when she wrote the following notes in a philosophic journal.*

These are the vague beginnings of an amateur philosopher. To be checked with what I learn when I master philosophy—then see how much of it has already been said, and whether I have anything new to say, or anything old to say better than it has already been said.

**April 9, 1934**

The human race has only two unlimited capacities: for suffering and for lying.

I want to fight religion as the root of all human lying and the only excuse for suffering.

I believe—and I want to gather all the facts to illustrate this—that the worst curse on mankind is the ability to consider ideals as something quite abstract and detached from one's everyday life. The ability to *live* and *think* quite differently, thus eliminating thinking from your actual life. This applied not to deliberate and conscious hypocrites, but to those more dangerous and hopeless ones who, alone with themselves and to themselves, tolerate a complete break between their convictions and their lives, and still believe that they have convictions. To them, either their ideals or their lives are worthless—and usually both.

I hold religion mainly responsible for this. I want to prove that religion breaks a character before it's formed, in childhood, by teaching a child lies before he knows what a lie is, by breaking him of the habit of thinking before he has begun to think, by making him a hypocrite before he knows any other possible attitude toward life. If a child is taught ideals that he knows are

These are the vague stirrings of an unborn (2)
philosopher. To be checked with that I learn when I
master philosophy — then see how much of it has already
4-9-34 { been said, and whether I have anything new
to say, or anything old to say like anything it
hasn't said.

The human race has only two unlimited
capacities : for suffering and for lying.

I want to fight religion as the root of all
human lying and the only excuse for suffering. —

I believe — and I want to gather all the facts
to illustrate this — that the worse curse on
mankind is the ability to consider ideals as something quite abstract and detached from one's everyday life. The ability of living and thinking quite
differently, in other words eliminating thinking
from your actual life. This applies not to deliberate
and conscious hypocrites, but to those more dangerous
and hopeless ones who, alone with themselves and
to themselves, tolerate a complete break between their
convictions and their lives, and still believe that

contrary to his own deepest instincts, [ideals] such as unselfishness, meekness, and self-sacrifice, if he is told he is a miserable sinner for not living up to ideals he can never reach and *doesn't want* to reach, then his natural reaction is to consider all ideals as out of his reach forever, as something theoretical and quite apart from his own actual life. Thus the beginning of self-hypocrisy, the killing of all desire for a living ideal.

Religion is also the first enemy of the ability to think. That ability is not used by men to one tenth of its possibility, yet before they learn to think they are discouraged by being ordered to take things on faith. *Faith is the worst curse of mankind;* it is the exact antithesis and enemy of *thought.* I want to learn *why* men do not use logical reasoning to govern their lives and [solve] their problems. Is it impossible to them or has it been taught to them as impossible?

I believe this last. And the teacher is the church. *Thought* and *reason* are the only weapons of mankind, the only possible bond of understanding among men. Anyone who demands that anything be taken *on faith*—or relies on any super-mental, super-logical instinct—denies all reason.

Why are men so afraid of pure, logical reasoning? Why do they have a profound, ferocious hatred of it?

Are instincts and emotions necessarily beyond the control of plain thinking? Or were they trained to be? Why is a complete harmony between mind and emotions impossible? Isn't it merely a matter of strict mental honesty? And who stands at the very bottom of denying such honesty? Isn't it the church?

I want to be known as the greatest champion of reason and the greatest enemy of religion.

**May 9, 1934**

In regard to free will: Why is it used as an argument against freedom of the will that it is motivated by a circumstance of the outside world? Is there any such thing as will without the content to which it is applied? Isn't will a pure abstraction, not an object? Isn't it a *verb* rather than a noun, and as such meaningless without that upon which it acts? The will does not have to be *without reason*, or motivation, in order to be free. One's act may be motivated by an outside reason, but the *choice* of that reason is our *free will*. An example of the determinists: if a man drinks a glass of water, he does it because he is thirsty, therefore his will isn't free, it's motivated by his physical condition. But he drinks the glass of water *because* he needs it *and decides* that he wants to drink it. If his sweetheart's life had depended on his *not* drinking that water, he probably would not have touched it, no matter what his thirst. Or if it were a question of his life or hers, he would have to *select* and *make the decision*. In other words, he drinks because he's thirsty, but it is not the thirst that determines his action, the thirst only motivates it. *A motivation* is not *a reason*. (Has that anything to do with the question of free will?)

Doesn't the "free will" question come under the general question of human reason—and *its* freedom? If an action is logical—does that mean it is not free? Or is logic considered a restriction? If so—upon *what*? Is there anything conceivable beyond logic? Does a *free* action necessarily mean an *unreasonable* one? And if *mind* (or reason) depends on the outside world for its contents—is it *reason* any the less?

Has anyone properly described logic and human reason?

All philosophy is a set of thoughts. Thoughts are [governed] by certain implacable rules. If we deny these rules—which are an integral part of thoughts—we deny the thoughts. If we deny the thoughts—we deny the philosophy. So why bother at all? (In answer to all those who build transcendental, super-reasonable, super-logical philosophic systems.)

Is there—or should there be—such a thing as emotion opposed to reason? Isn't it merely a form of undeveloped reason, a form of stupidity?

How and why can will be considered apart from the mind? If thinking is free from subconscious influences—why not the will?

And if, as according to [H. L.] Mencken, the question of "freedom of the will" has to be studied on the basis of psychology with all its dark complexes—then what are we actually studying? Will as it is expressed in subnormal cases? Or in normal, average cases? Or in the highest instances of the human [mind]?

Are we studying will as *it is* actually in the majority of cases—or as *it can be essentially*, as a human attribute?

Do we judge all human terms as applied to existing humanity or to humanity's highest possibility?

If we are trying to form a general conception of a "stomach," do we study a hundred diseased stomachs and form our general conception from them, so that "stomach" as such is something with a number of diseases attached to it—or do we find the healthy stomach first, in order to learn what it is, and *then* judge the others by comparison?

Is ethics necessarily and basically a social conception? Have there been systems of ethics written primarily on the basis of an *individual*? Can that be done?

Are ethics at all a matter of history? Does it matter how and where they developed? Is a history of ethics necessary? I believe only a *system of ethics* is necessary, and it has to stand or fall on its own merits—*not* on any history or far away beginning. For instance, when discussing the social instinct—does it matter whether it had existed in the early savages? We do not judge the value of an automobile by the first chariot ever used in the history of men. Supposing men were born social (and even that is a question)—does it mean that they have to remain so?

"Social life," said Kropotkin, "that is, *we*, not *I*, is the normal form of life (in man). *It is life itself.*" Good God Almighty!!!! [*Petr Alekseevich Kropotkin (1842–1941) was a Russian socialist who advocated the revolt of the "working class."*]

This is *exactly* what I'm going to fight. For *the exact opposite is true*.

If man started as a social animal—isn't all progress and civilization directed toward making him *an individual*? Isn't that the only possible progress? If men are the highest of animals, isn't *man* the next step?

**May 15, 1934**

In regard to *The Revolt of the Masses* [*by José Ortega y Gasset*]: Isn't it a terrible generalization—that can be interpreted in too many different ways—to say that a "noble" man strives to serve and obey, and the "mass" man to do as he pleases?

If what is meant is the noble man's servitude to his own standards and ideas—is that to be called servitude? If the standards are his, isn't he precisely obeying himself and doing what he pleases? No truly noble man is going to obey standards set for him by someone else. *That* is the action of the *mass* man. It is the mass man who *cannot* do as he wishes, because he has no wishes; he has to have his standards—or the nearest to that word that he can come—dictated to him.

This leads me again to a question that is part of the general "free will" question. What exactly is freedom? Surely, freedom does not mean an empty blank. If a man obeys his own ideals—how can that be called servitude? If a man has no ideals at all—why is that called freedom? How can any human quality, such as freedom, be disconnected from its content? Isn't there a terrible mistake of abstraction here? Isn't it as Nietzsche said: "Not freedom *from* what, but freedom *for* what?"

This leads to another question—my question of the "supreme egoism." There exists that body of ideas which represents all the so-called intellectual and spiritual values: ethics, philosophy, etc. (This requires a better definition and analysis—which has to be done later.) My "supreme egoism" consists of the right to apply these values to oneself and to *live them*. For example: if a man is convinced that religion is wrong, he has to *be* and *profess* to be an atheist.

The vile, dangerous habit of today is to admit, for instance, that religion is valuable to the majority and, therefore, go to church, profess to be religious, etc., in order to gain something by playing down to the masses. As a consequence, the horrible paradox of our time is that intellectual values are left only to the masses, that they become a special, exclusive privilege of the masses, who not only have no right to them, but lack completely even the elementary *organ* for anything approaching intellectual ideas. It is as if one left sight only as a privilege of the blind. The so-called "selfish" man of today uses "ideas" only as means to attain *his own* end. But what is that end? What is accomplished if the man attains power and prominence at the cost of playing down to the masses? It is not *he* that triumphs, it is not his ideas and standards. It is only his physical frame. Essentially, he is only a slave to those masses. [*This idea was later to find dramatic expression in the character of Gail Wynand in* The Fountainhead.] This explains my meaning when I consider the "selfish," ambitious man of today as essentially *unselfish*, or rather *selfless*. The true selfishness is that which demands the right to *its own* higher ideas and values. The "supreme egoism" is that which claims things for their *essential*, not their secondary values.

An example from my own experience, which, at the present time, affects me most, is the fact that few men have the ability *or the desire* to judge literary work by its *essential* worth. To most men, that work becomes valuable only after it has been recognized as such by someone else. They themselves do not have any standards of their own (and they do not feel the lack). The same is true of any other field of mental activity: scientific, philosophical, etc. This is the great unselfishness of today. As a matter of fact, unselfishness is merely *selflessness*. The true, highest selfishness, the exalted egoism, is the right to have *one's own* theoretical values and then to apply them to practical reality. Without that *self* there are no values. Here again—*ethics based on self*, not on *society*, the mass, the collective, or any other form of selflessness.

From this—to another question. There have been too many philosophical abstractions, too much intellectual *"algebra"*—as is illustrated best by that statement from *The Revolt of the Masses* about the noble man's servitude. It is an algebraic formula into which [are inserted] too many different arithmetical contents. What we need is an *"arithmetic"* of the spirit. Algebra—spiritually—is too much of the mob, of the masses, the collective, being too general. The individual is the *arithmetical* quantity of the spirit. And in things spiritual—or intellectual (which is essentially the same)—it is only the individual and the particular, concrete problem that counts. Algebraic constructions are only a convenience. In practice, they have no use, unless the proper arithmetical content is inserted into the formula. But in the field of philosophy today there is this tendency of considering the algebraic formula as *final*, and therefore philosophy has no practical significance or application. Returning to what I said at the beginning of these notes, there is no need for theory which cannot be applied in practice. More than that, such theory is not only useless, but dangerous and fatal, for it lies at the bottom of that frightful phenomenon of believing one thing and living another. If by practical reality I mean the *actual living* of an individual, then there is no need for anything which is not this practical reality, which is not actual living. This is a point which can and will be strongly debated, but it has to be the cornerstone of my philosophy—proving the supremacy of *actual living* over all other considerations, in fact proving that *there are no other* considerations. As a result, my "arithmetic" of philosophy has to be philosophy brought *up* to the realm of actual living. (I say intentionally brought *up* to it, not *down*.) This—I expect—will be its vital strength. [*We can see the first seeds of AR's later theory of concepts in her identification of the relation between abstractions and concretes as similar to that between algebra and arithmetic. Her primary concern here is to reject the Platonic rationalism that detaches abstractions from concretes, and affirm the Aristotelian premise that only concretes exist. However, her characterization of abstractions as "collective" and "only a convenience" conflicts with her mature views. For a full presentation of AR's theory, see* Introduction to Objectivist Epistemology.]

That philosophical "algebra" is, to my mind, the greatest crime of metaphysics, if I understand that word correctly. It is the result of that underlying error of human thinking—which forgets the distinction between abstraction and reality, thus denying reality. For abstractions are only a convenience, not a fact, a means, not an end. This—for the basis of *philosophy as a science*. For science essentially deals with facts. The next step will be to define just what are *facts*. Which will bring me to *human reason* as the basis of all facts, scientific or philosophical. More about that later.

(All these things are *only* for my own use. They are pretty disjointed and not in any logical sequence. But what will [ultimately] come out of this is an arrangement of the whole in a logical system, proceeding from a few axioms in a succession of logical theorems. The axioms will be necessary— even mathematics has them—[because] you can't build something on nothing. The end result will be my "Mathematics of Philosophy.")

I have to study: philosophy, higher mathematics, physics, psychology.

As to physics—learn *why* mind and reason are so decried as impotent when coping with the universe. Isn't there some huge mistake there?

It may be considered strange, and denying my own supremacy of reason, that I start with a set of ideas, then want to study in order to support them, and not vice versa, i.e., not study and derive my ideas from that. But these ideas, to a great extent, are the result of a subconscious instinct, which is a form of unrealized reason. All instincts are reason, essentially, or reason is instincts made conscious. The "unreasonable" instincts are diseased ones. This—for the study of psychology. For the base of the reconciliation of reason and emotions.

As to psychology—learn whether the base of all psychology is really *logic*, and psychology as a science is really *pathology*, the science of how these psychological processes depart from reason. This departure is the disease. What caused it? Isn't it faulty thinking, thinking not based on logic, [but on] faith, religion?

All consciousness is reason. All reason is logic. Everything that comes between consciousness and logic is a disease. Religion—the greatest disease of mankind.

Some day I'll find out whether I'm an unusual specimen of humanity in that my instincts and reason are so inseparably one, with the reason ruling the instincts. Am I unusual or merely normal and healthy? Am I trying to impose my own peculiarities as a philosophical system? Am I unusually intelligent or merely unusually honest? I think this last. Unless—honesty is also a form of superior intelligence.

**May 16, 1934**

A quotation about Russia, which may be useful, from *While Rome Burns* by Alexander Woollcott [*American journalist and writer*]:

Then at noon the next day, the neat, bustling, inexcusably cheerful station at Stolyce, Poland. The first cup of good coffee in weeks. Flagrantly trivial newspapers to read. And a great buoyancy of one's spirit. All returning travelers mention this curious lifting of the sense of oppression—sometimes unnoticed until it does lift, just as you realize how foul the air of a room has been only when you get a whiff from out-of-doors—this exhilarating relief which even one who has hugely enjoyed his stay in the Soviet Union does experience on quitting its territory. . . . There is nothing mysterious about it. Every man who was ever demobilized remembers this sensation of a recovered freedom. Freedom to sit on a park bench and starve, perhaps. But freedom, brothers, freedom.

The new conception of the State that I want to defend is the State as a means, not an end; a means for the convenience of the higher type of man. The State as the only *organization*. Within it—all have to remain individuals. The State, not as a slave of the great numbers, but precisely the contrary, as the individual's defense against great numbers. To free man from the tyranny of numbers.

The fault of liberal democracies: giving full rights to quantity (majorities), they forget the rights of quality, which are much higher rights. Prove that differences of quality not only do exist inexorably, but also *should exist*. The next step—democracy of superiors only. This is not possible without a very high and powerful sense of honor. This, in turn, is not possible without a set of values from which this honor is to be derived. The new set of values: [my] supreme egoism.

---

From *The Revolt of the Masses* by José Ortega y Gasset:

[T]he apparent enthusiasm for the manual worker, for the afflicted and for social justice, serves as a mask to facilitate the refusal of all obligations, such as courtesy, truthfulness and, above all, respect or esteem for superior individuals. I know of quite a few who have entered the ranks of some labor organization or other merely in order to win for themselves the right to despise intelligence and to avoid paying it any tribute. [In regard to] Dictatorship, we have seen only too well how they flatter the mass-man, by trampling on everything that appeared to be above the common level.

**May 21, 1934**

"Mankind? It is an abstraction. There are, have been, and always will be, men and only men." (Johann Wolfgang von Goethe)

I would change that to go one step further: *man, only man.*

Has there ever been a history written from the viewpoint not of a nation's development through its outstanding individuals, but of these individuals' desperate fight against their nations, for the sake of the development and advancement for which the nation so noisily and arrogantly takes credit after it has made a martyr of the "developer" and "advancer"? History as a deadly battle of the mass and the individual. A scientific task for me: to trace just how many of mankind's "geniuses" were recognized and honored in their own time. And since they were not—as most of them weren't—is there any ground for the conception of any national cultures, histories and civilizations? If there is any such thing as culture and its growth—isn't it the culture of great individuals, of geniuses, *not* of nations or any other conglomerations of human creatures? And isn't history the fight of mankind *against* advancement, not *for* it?

# THE FOUNTAINHEAD

# THEME AND CHARACTERS

*AR's working title for* The Fountainhead *was* Second-Hand Lives. *She kept most of her notes for the novel in three ring-bound notebooks. The present chapter offers the complete contents of her first notebook, which begins with a discussion of the theme and then gives character descriptions of Howard Roark, Peter Keating, and Ellsworth Toohey.*

*To avoid confusion, I have used the names of the characters as they appear in the novel. In these early notes, Ellsworth Monkton Toohey was Everett Monkton Flent, Peter Keating was Peter Wilson, and John Eric Snyte was Worthington Snyte. AR changed the names about two years after her first notes.*

**December 4, 1935**

### Second-Hand Lives

It is not the works, but the belief which is here decisive and determines the order of rank—to employ once more an old religious formula with a new and deeper meaning—it is some fundamental certainty which a noble soul has about itself, something which is not to be sought, is not to be found, and perhaps, also, is not to be lost. *The noble soul has reverence for itself.*

FRIEDRICH NIETZSCHE, *Beyond Good and Evil*

**I.** The first purpose of the book is *a defense of egoism in its real meaning*, egoism as a new faith. Therefore—a new definition of egoism and its living example. If egoism is the quality which makes one put oneself above all—well, in *what manner*? And—*above what*? If one goes ruthlessly after one's aim—*what is the aim?* It is not what one does or how one does it, but *why one does it*. It is the ultimate result, the last consequence, the essence and sum of sums which determines the quality of egoism.

One puts oneself above all and crushes everything in one's way to get the best for oneself. Fine! But *what is that best*? Which leads to the question: are morals, or ethics, or all higher values, a thing outside [oneself], i.e., God's law or society's prescription, something related not to a man, but to others around him, an ultimatum forced upon man and essentially selfless and *un*selfish? *Or* [are these values] a man's very own, his sacred, highest right, his best inspiration, his real life and real self?

And further: what is the *self*? Just the fact that one is born and conscious, just the "I" devoid of all definite content? *Or*—the "I" that values, selects and knows precisely the qualities which distinguish it from all other "I's," which has reverence for itself for certain definite reasons, not merely because "I-am-what-I-am-and-don't-know-just-what-I-am." If one's physical body is a certain definite body with a certain definite shape and features, not just *a* body—so one's spirit is a certain definite spirit with definite features and qualities. A spirit without content is an abstraction that does not exist. If one is proud of one's body for its beauty, created by certain lines and forms, so one is proud of one's spirit for its beauty, or *that which one considers its beauty*. Without that—there can be no pride of spirit. Nor *any* spirit.

If the higher values of life (such as all ethics, philosophy, esthetics, everything that results from a *sense of valuation* in the mental life of man) come from within, from man's own spirit, then they are a right, a privilege and a necessity—*not a duty*. They are that which constitutes a man's life, and if he is an egoist in the best sense of the word he will choose these higher values *for himself* and for himself alone, i.e., for his own sake and satisfaction, not because of a duty to God, fellow-men, the State or any other fool abstraction outside of himself. A man has a code of ethics primarily for his own sake, not for anyone else's. Consequently, *an ethical man is essentially an egoist. A selfless man cannot be ethical.*

To explain what may sound like a paradox: if by ethics we understand all sets of values, all standards of conduct and thought (without specifying at present just what standards are to be considered ethical; i.e., taking merely the quality of valuing, without defining how one should value), then a man who does not consider his values as *his*, but merely as prescribed to him, or who acts virtuously because he *has to*, not because he *wants to*—that man can hardly be considered virtuous or ethical. The man to whom virtue, or that which he considers virtue, is a necessity, not a painful duty, is the truly ethical man. As example: if a man dies for his cause, because he hates to do it, but feels that some higher power—God or State—compels him to, he is a poor hero; if a man dies because it is *his* cause and he wishes no choice but to defend it at any cost—he *is* a hero.

The question as to what constitutes a standard of values will come later. The primary question is only to establish such a thing as a standard of values and its necessity as part of a man's own self—without which there is no such thing as *self*.

Now, then, if a man is a ruthless egoist, just what form does his egoism take? Does he fight, struggle and claim for himself those higher values and his right to follow them? *Or*—? ?—what? The generally accepted example of pure egoism is a ruthless financier who crushes everything in order to obtain money and power—but can he truly be considered an egoist? What does he do with the money? To what purpose does he use the power? Doesn't he merely—and this is always the case with the conventional type of egoist—give up all standards of value, those prescribed to him as well as his own, in order to get the money? Doesn't he play down to the mob in every sense and manner, encouraging its vices, sacrificing his own opinions, serving others, *always others,* as a slave—to gain his own ends? Well then— what ends?

*Who is the true egoist:* The man who crushes his own "I" to succeed with others, to fool them, betray them, kill them—but still live as they want him to live and conquer to the extent of a home, a yacht and a full stomach? *Or*—the man who puts his own "I," his standard of values, above all things, and conquers to live as he pleases, as he chooses and *as he* believes? If a dictator, such as Hitler, for instance, has to play down to the mob in order to hold his influence and rule—*does he rule?* Or does he merely give orders as long as he gives the kind of orders the mob wants to obey? In which case— *who rules whom?* If [William Randolph] Hearst has a great influence because he always sits on the fence and says only that which is "box-office"—where is the influence? When and where can he say what he wants and succeed in getting it? Isn't he the greatest of slaves instead of the greatest of powers?

Is power the possibility to force others into doing what you want—or merely in sitting on a high throne, in the full glare of the public light, executing what others want you to do? If a man who is not a Nazi pretends to be one and goes on pretending to the end of his days in order to have a soft job, money and food—is he to be called an egoist? Or isn't the true egoist the one who starves in exile for the right to believe what *he* believes?

A true egoist, therefore, places his ego and the claims of his ego in the realm of higher values. He demands these values because he wants them, and is utterly *selfish* in his demand. If higher values are the meaning of life, if they *are life*—well then, *an egoist demands the highest.* The man who sacrifices these values for physical comforts does not demand very much. He is not an egoist—*because the ego is absent.*

*An egoist is a man who lives for himself.* In this, I can agree with the worst of Christian moralists. The questions are only: 1) what constitutes living for oneself? and 2) if the first is answered my way, i.e., living for one's highest values, then isn't living for oneself the highest type of living, the only real living and the *only ethical living possible*?

Consequently, my "egoism as a new faith" is a higher meaning and a higher exaltation of the word "I," of that feeling which makes man say and feel "*I.*" Which brings me to the second point of the book.

**II.** The thing which is most "wrong with the world" today is its absolute lack of positive values. [There is a lack] of moral standards (not merely the old-fashioned "Victorian morals," but of *anything* approaching morals, anything that values, differentiates and says "yes" or "no"), a lack of honor, a lack of faith (in a philosophical, not a religious meaning, faith as a set of certain principles, as a goal, aim or inspiration, as a life-system). Here again, it is not the absence of a certain type of values that I mean, but the very act and habit of valuing and selecting in one's mental life. Nothing is considered bad and nothing is considered good. There is no enthusiasm for living, since there is no enthusiasm for any part, mode or form of living.

(Incidentally, this explains the tremendous popularity of communism among people who are not communists at all, particularly the young people. Communism, at least, offers a definite goal, inspiration and *ideal, a positive faith*. Nothing else in modern life does. The old capitalism has nothing better to offer than the dreary, shop-worn, mildewed ideology of Christianity, outgrown by everyone, and long since past any practical usefulness it might have had, even for the capitalistic system. Furthermore, that same Christianity, with its denial of self and glorification of all men's brotherhood, is the best possible kindergarten of communism. Communism is at least consistent in its ideology. Capitalism is not; it preaches what communism actually wants to live. Consequently, if there are things in capitalism and democracy worth saving, a new faith is needed, a definite, positive set of new values and a new interpretation of life, which is more opposed, more irreconcilable, more fatal to communism than its bastard weak-sister—Christianity.)

Returning to the immediate purpose of the book: A new set of values is needed to combat this modern dreariness, whether it be communism (which I may not include in the book) or the sterile, hopeless cynicism of the modern age. That new faith is *Individualism* in all its deepest meaning and implications, such as has never been preached before: individualism of the spirit, of ethics, of philosophy, not merely the good old "rugged individualism" of small shopkeepers. Individualism as a religion and a code, not merely as an economic practice. (What in hell is the kind of "individualism" that allows a man merely to run his own grocery [store] instead of a government cooperative, but sends this same shopkeeper to church on Sunday to pray for "loving his neighbor as himself"?) A revival (or perhaps the first birth) of the word "*I*" as the holiest of holies and the reason of reasons.

Am I wrong? Well—let's consider it. What we actually have today is an individualistic (or at least so-called) form of economics with the most perfect communistic ideology that any Soviet could hope to achieve. In our economic life there still is a chance for the private initiative that made all modern technical progress possible—but it is absolutely absent from our spiritual life. Consequently, we have the appalling spectacle, decried by all, of a highly developed technological civilization along with complete spiritual stagnation. We have developed technically—oh yes!—but spiritually we are far below Renaissance Italy. In fact, we *have no* spiritual life in the grand manner, in the sense it used to be understood.

Is it the fault of machines? Is the twentieth century incapable and unfit for my spiritual exultation? *Or*—is it only that little word "I," which, after twenty centuries of Christianity's efforts, has been erased from human consciousness, and along with it took everything that *was* human consciousness?

It is not the purpose of the book to prove theoretically, point by point, *why* the morality of individualism is superior to that of collectivism, why it is, in fact, the only morality worthy of the name. The purpose is only to show how both of them work in real life: to show the ultimate consequences and results of both—brought to their logical conclusions. Perhaps, in doing so, the question will be answered of itself and the proof will be given. It is not a question of individualism versus collectivism; it is a question of egoism [versus] selflessness. The latter [alternative] is the psychological basis of the former, in concrete human forms. The purpose is to prove that the so-called "selfish" man of today is the true collectivist in spirit, the man who has [renounced] his own "I" for the dictates of others, who has accepted society as his absolute ruler in the realm of spiritual values—and paid the price. As a contrast, as the moral, the theme of the book—[I show] a man who is a true egoist, the man who really "lives for himself."

**III.** What do I mean by "second-hand lives"?

1) All men who have lost the ability to choose, value and pronounce judgment on all questions of spiritual standards. For there is no true judge outside of one's "I." Everything accepted on faith or on someone else's authority is only a warmed-over spiritual hash.

2) All men who have reversed the process of "end" and "means" and to whom the means have become the end. For instance, if an egoist struggles for power to achieve his ambitions and ideals—well and good. But if, in the struggle, he sacrifices his ideals merely to achieve the power, he is accepting a second-hand substitute, a thing that has no meaning, that brings him no value whatever, but takes his values away instead.

3) All men who, by betraying their egos, actually live for others, not for themselves, live only through others (this is the main point). For instance: if a man struggles for power and achieves it by accepting and championing the ideology of the masses, he himself knows that *he has no real power*, but he has it only in the eyes of the mob. If a man is a crook and cheats to achieve his ends—he himself knows that *he is* dishonest, but will struggle and scramble to preserve a respectable appearance and reputation in the eyes of others. If a man wants to be a writer and hires a ghost to do his great epic, then bows and happily accepts popular acclaim—he himself knows that he is a nonentity, but rejoices in being a genius in the eyes of others. All deceits prompted by vanity, all reaping of faked successes, are a second-hand acceptance of something existing only in the minds of our neighbors, not in us, not in our own reality. (Vanity as the most selfless of qualities.) If a man is praised for writing a trashy movie scenario, and glories in the praise, knowing it was trash, he accepts a second-hand achievement in which he himself does not believe. If a man does not create what he likes, but creates that which he *knows* others will admire—it is second-hand creation.

In other words, when a man shifts the center of his life from his own ego to the opinions of others, when those others become the determining factor in all his higher values, when his ideals are one and his actual existence another, when he cheats himself of all reality to create it in others, when higher values become merely a [possession of others to be used] by him for money or physical gain, while he is cheating himself of those higher values and of all life's meaning—he is leading a second-hand life.

Consequently—coming back to where I started—the "great selfishness" of the conventional opportunist is merely an immense betrayal of his self.

(19)

December 22, 1935

To add to what I have written: the great tragedy and problem of the modern age is the absence of all values. The good preachers and moralists yell that capitalistic selfishness is responsible for it, and all those idealistically inclined embrace Communism as the cure for this guilt of selfishness. Exactly the opposite is true: the absence of values is caused by the absence of egos. As explained before, no ethics of any sort are possible without a feeling of egoism. Unless a man wants to be honorable because he wants to be honorable and takes pride in being honorable — he is not going to be honorable. If humanity, for twenty dreary centuries, has been buttered into believing selflessness a virtue and into considering as ideals things which are inherently impossible of attainment (all of Christianity's ethics) — all idealism is gone. All ambition toward an ideal, the something which makes men wish to attain the highest possible is gone, since that highest, as preached by Christianity, is unattainable.

To add to what I have written: The great tragedy and problem of the modern age is the absence of all values. The preachers and moralists yell that capitalistic selfishness is responsible for it, and all those idealistically inclined embrace communism as the cure for this guilt of selfishness. Exactly the opposite is true: *the absence of values is caused by the absence of ego.* As explained before, no ethics of any sort are possible without a feeling of egoism. Unless a man *wants* to be honorable and takes pride in being honorable—he is not going to be honorable. If humanity, for twenty dreary centuries, has been battered by Christianity into believing selflessness is a virtue and into considering as ideals things which are inherently impossible to it—all idealism is gone. All ambition toward an ideal, that which makes men wish to attain the highest possible, is gone, since that highest, as preached by Christianity, is unattainable.

If all of life has been brought down to flattering the mob, if those who can please the mob are the only ones to succeed—why should anyone feel any high aspirations and cherish any ideals? The capitalistic world is low, unprincipled and corrupt. But how can it have any incentive toward principles when its ideology has killed the *only* source of principles—man's "I"? Christianity has succeeded in eliminating "self" from the world of ethics, by declaring "ethics" and "self" as incompatible. But that self cannot be killed. It has only degenerated into the ugly modern struggle for material success at the cost of all higher values, since these values have been outlawed by the church. Hence—the hopelessness, the colorless drabness, the dreariness and empty brutality of our present day.

The same would happen to humanity under communism—if it could ever succeed and take the place now held by the church. As long as men live, their "self" cannot be killed. But it can be distorted into a monstrosity, as any living organism can if reared in improper conditions and under an unbearable strain.

The consequence? *Until man's "self" regains its proper position, life will be what it is now: flat, gray, empty, lacking all beauty, all fire, all enthusiasm, all meaning, all creative urge.* That is the ultimate theme of the book—Howard Roark as the remedy for all modern ills.

The theme, then, goes like this: Howard Roark is what men should be. I show: how and why others are different from him; what forms that difference takes; what reasons create it; what it does to its victims—their successes and their ultimate tragedies. And I show what life [is] to Howard Roark, how he succeeds and what his success means. An illustrated message to the twentieth century—without benefit of Marxism.

Instead of preaching more collectivism, men must realize that it is precisely collectivism, in its logical consequences—a subtle, unnamed, unofficial, but still all-powerful collectivism—that is the cause of mankind's tragedy. It may not be the economic collectivism for which the communists clamor, but it is a perfect form of ethical collectivism, not theoretical, but actual, living, working. And since collective ethics are claimed to be necessary for collective economy—take a look, gentlemen, we have those ethics already. We have them and we don't like them; it is not a pretty picture.

Either "man" is the unit and the final sovereign—or else "men" are. And "men" means the mob, the State, the nation, the Soviet—anything one wishes to call it, anything that implies a *number* of humans, a herd. Man must live for the State, claim the communists. Well, man *is* living for other men, for the *mob*, completely and hopelessly, only we don't say so. I will show what it means to live for others—just exactly what it actually means and how it works. If it's not pretty—well, then, where's the mistake? The old Christian–communist denial of "self." Proper life is possible only when man *is* allowed (and encouraged, and taught, and practically forced) to live for himself.

(Sideline: "But a communist State will do precisely that!" yell the communists. "It will give each individual a chance!" *How?* By inoculating them with a "collective ideology"? There it is, your collective ideology, perfect and logical and working.)

If—and no communist has yet gone this far—they claim that man's higher values will come from his sense of honor before the mob (or his "brothers"), that he will be taught to value popular approval and esteem as reward for his efforts on the State's behalf, that in this way his egoism will become spiritual instead of materialistic—how are you going to teach a contradiction? If he is to value his pride, his feeling of achievement, his personal glory, *as his*, how can he put them into the hands of the mob? How can he want to live for himself if all his actual life, his work, his ambition, his relations with others have to be guided and motivated by the "good of the State," by collective interests and collective gain? How—if he is asked to live for others—is he going to have an incentive for self-respect and for his own higher values? A collective form of life with individualistic ethics and spirituality? That is as impossible as the "rugged individualism" of modern capitalistic society with a collectivist form of ethics and ideals—which is what we have today. The communist utopia of a collectivist state with individual morality would come to the same dreary mess—only it will never come.

To repeat: living for others, i.e., "second-hand living," is exactly what we have today—in actual reality. And if that's wrong, if it doesn't work, if it creates a repulsive, hopeless chaos, then the solution is "living for oneself." Capitalistic democracy has no ideology. That is what the book has to give it.

———o———

Nothing has ever been created except by the will of *a* creator. Civilization is *not* a collective process, the work of many men working together. It is the work of many men working *alone*. Each did what he could and *wanted* to do. No common cause ever tied them to one another.

All civilization, all progress—ethical, esthetical, philosophical, scientific—has been accomplished not by a cooperation between an originator and his followers, between man and the mob, but by a *struggle* between man and the mob. The mob has always been against novelty, originality, everything new and forward moving. It was individual men who made the forward step in each case, only to pay for it, often with their lives, because the mob resented it. But the world did move forward, because life belongs to the leaders and the exceptions. The others follow. They don't want to. They have to. They contribute nothing to progress, except the impediments.

If the best part of life, the mental life, everything above mere material existence, is creation, it presupposes a sense of valuation. How can one create if one does not first estimate—*value*—one's materials? (That applies to science, arts, ethics, and all mental endeavor.) How can there be valuing without those who value? A verb does not exist in a vacuum. A verb presupposes a noun. There is no such thing as an action without the one who acts. And who can do the valuing except *a* man?

A collective valuing would amount to this: one believes what others believe, *because* others believe it. If we have ten people and each one of them chooses to believe only what the nine others believe—just exactly who establishes the belief, and how? Multiply it by millions, on a world scale, and it's still the same. The laws of mathematics work the same for dozens, and for hundreds, and for billions. There has to be a cause of causes, a determining factor, a basic initiative. If it is not taken by a man—by whom, then, is it taken? If a man is not the one to weigh, value and decide—who decides?

A "collective" mind does not exist. It is merely the sum of endless numbers of individual minds. If we have an endless number of individual minds who are weak, meek, submissive and impotent—who renounce their creative supremacy for the sake of the "whole" and accept humbly that "whole's" verdict—we don't get a collective super-brain. We get only a weak, meek, submissive and impotent collective mind.

If a man is the ultimate creator, the one who values, then the worst of all crimes is the acceptance of the opinions of others. [The worst men are those who say:] "A thing is good because others say it's good"; they are the men who lack the ability or the courage to value on their own.

As a ridiculous and petty but clear example of this type: the movie producers and the Hollywood type of mentality. The movies have produced no great work of art, no immortal masterpiece to compare with the masterpieces of other arts. Why? Because the movies are not an art? Rubbish! Because those in charge do not create what they think is good, but what they think others will think is good. Because those in charge have no values of their own (and refuse to have) but accept blindly anything and everything approved by someone else—anyone else.

The movies are the perfect example of collective ideology and of "living for others." Why did all the other arts reach heights the movies never attained? Why did they prosper and survive in spite of the fact that they did not consider the "box-office," the mob's approval? Precisely because they did not consider the mob's approval. They created—and *forced* the mob to accept their creations. But the movies "live for others." And—they do not live at all. Not as an achievement and an end in themselves. Those working in the movies work to make money, *not* to work in the movies. Fine, if that's all they want. But what do they get out of the money? What do they get in exchange for giving up the reality of their work and of their lives? They spend their lives at a *second-hand task*, a task secondary to their real purpose, a task which is only a means to an end. What is the end? Shouldn't the end be precisely that at which they spend their lives? But—they're only second-hand people with second-hand lives!

This is an example which is clearer and plainer than any other form of activity. It applies to other professions as well. The principle is the same. The result is the same.

### December 26, 1935

An important thing to remember and bring out in the book: while Howard Roark, at first glance, is monstrously selfish and inconsiderate of others—one sees, in the end, his great consideration for the rights of others (when they warrant it) and his ruthlessness only in major issues; while Peter Keating, at first glance, is unusually kind, thoughtful, considerate of others and unselfish—in the end, it is clear that he will sacrifice anyone and everyone to his own small ends, whether he has to or not. In other words, those who show too much concern for others and not for themselves, have no true respect for either. Only the one who respects himself can also respect others (and only as a secondary matter, *after* himself). No other neighbor-feeling is possible.

While, at first glance, Howard Roark is a stern, austere, gloomy man, who does not laugh readily, who does not crack jokes and enjoy "comedy-relief," he is [actually] the truly joyous man, full of a profound, exuberant joy of living, an earnest, reverent joy, a living power, a healthy, unquench-able vitality. While, at first glance, Peter Keating is cheerful, optimistic, the "life of the party," the true "good fellow"—he is [actually] a sad, desolate man, empty, desperate in his emptiness, without life, without joy, hope or aim, a bitter cynic hiding his cynical despair under a superficial, forced gaiety.

The truly joyous man does not laugh too much, because there is little to laugh at in life as it is today. The truly joyous man takes himself *very seri-ously*, because there is no joy without self and pride in self. Those who preach and practice "not taking anything seriously" are not the gay, light-hearted ones. They are merely the empty-hearted. "Taking seriously" is the very essence of life. If one does not "take oneself seriously," one can take nothing seriously. And—"the noble soul has reverence for itself." One does not revere with a giggle.

Above all, bring out the noble, all-pervading, joyous energy that perme-ates the being of Howard Roark and his whole life and every action, even in his tragedy. And—the dreary hopelessness of Peter Keating.

### Cast of Characters

*Howard Roark:* The noble soul par excellence. The self-sufficient, self-confident man—the end of ends, the reason unto himself, the joy of living personified. Above all—the man who lives for himself, as living for oneself should be understood. And who triumphs com-pletely. A man who *is* what he should be.

*Peter Keating:* The exact opposite of Howard Roark, and everything a man should not be. A perfect example of a selfless man who is a ruthless, unprincipled egotist—in the accepted meaning of the word. A tremendous vanity and greed, which lead him to sacrifice all for the sake of a "brilliant career." A mob man at heart, of the mob and for the mob. His triumph is his disaster. He is left an empty, bitter wreck—his "second-hand life" takes the form of sacrificing all for the sake of a victory that has no meaning and gives him no satisfac-tion because his means become his end. He shows that a selfless man cannot be ethical. He has no self and, therefore, cannot have any ethics. A man who never could be [man as he should be]. And doesn't know it.

*A great publisher* (Gail Wynand): A man who rules the mob only as long as he says what the mob wants him to say. What happens when he tries to say what *he* wants. A man who could have been.

*A preacher* (?): A man who tries to save the world with an outworn ideology. Show that his ideals are actually in working existence and that they precisely are what the world has to be saved from.

*A movie producer:* A man who has no opinions and no values, save those of others.

*An actress* (Vesta Dunning): A woman who accepts greatness in other people's eyes, rather than in her own. A woman who could have been. [*Vesta Dunning was cut from the novel after the first draft of Part 1 was written. The main scenes with Vesta have been published in* The Early Ayn Rand.]

*Dominique Wynand:* The woman for a man like Howard Roark. The perfect priestess.

*John Eric Snyte:* The real ghost-writer-hirer. A man who glories in appropriating the achievements of others.

*Ellsworth Monkton Toohey:* Noted economist, critic and liberal. "Noted" anything and everything Great "humanitarian" and "man of integrity." He glorifies all forms of collectivism because he knows that only under such forms will he, as the best representative of the mass, attain prominence and distinction, which is impossible to him on his own (non-existent) merits. The idol-crusher par excellence. Born, organic enemy of all things heroic. He has a positive genius for the commonplace. The worst of all possible rats. A man who never could be—and knows it.

**January 15, 1936**

One more variation of "second-hand lives": those who put any secondary considerations before true values. Example: a man who gives a job to a friend, because he is a friend, rather than to the most deserving applicant, even though the latter is what the business requires. A critic who praises the work according to his relations with the author, rather than according to the value of the work. A secondary substitute. A "second-hand" way of living.

This may sound naive. But—is our life ever to have any reality? Are we ever going to live on the level? Or is life always to be something else, something different from what it should be? A real life, simple and sincere, and even naive, is the only life where all the potential grandeur and beauty of human existence can really be found. Are there real reasons for accepting the substitute, that which we have today? No one has shown [today's] life, *as it really is,* with its real meaning and its reasons. I'm going to show it. If it's not a pretty picture—well, what is the [alternative]?

**July 14, 1937**

[*AR often rewrote sections of her journals, essentializing and condensing the material. As a rule, I have omitted these repetitions. However, I include the following summary of the preceding journals, as an example of her method of rewriting. This summary is presented out of chronological order; it was written a year and a half after the original notes.*]

*Main points of plan*

1. *Defense of egoism in its real meaning.*

Demand the best for oneself. What is the best? Why? An ethical man is essentially an egoist. The selflessness of sacrificing one's best for secondary ends, such as money or power, which cannot be used as he wishes. Conventional selfishness—an immense betrayal of one's very self.

2. *The thing most wrong with the world—lack of all values.*

Reason for the appeal of communism. Individualism as a complete new faith. The actual spiritual collectivism of our modern life—and the root of all its evils. Egoism and selflessness presented in all their consequences. Howard Roark as the salvation of mankind. (Our achievements in technique—where individualism reigns. Our degeneration in cultural matters—which have always been collective in America.)

The lack of principle in capitalism drives men to communism as the cure. Precisely the opposite is true. The evil is not too much selfishness, but not enough of it; not lack of collectivism, but too much of it. The cure—not the destruction of individualism, but the creation of it. Christianity as the hatred of all ideals. *Show clearly what real collectivism would actually mean.* (On the basis of what it means already today.)

3. *The meaning of "second-hand lives."*

All those who shift the center of their lives from their own egos to the opinions of others. When those others become the determining factor. When a man cheats himself of all reality in order to create it in others. Types of "second-handedness": 1) Those who have lost the ability to value for themselves and accept on faith or on someone's authority the opinions of others. 2) Those who reverse the process of "end" and "means," and to whom the means become the end. (Like money and power for their own sake.) 3) *Those who actually exist only in the eyes of others, not in their own.* (A crook who tries to be considered respectable. A writer who hires a ghost. An artist pandering to the box-office. The deceits of vanity—the most selfless, second-hand of all qualities.) 4) Those who put secondary considerations before actual ones (like giving a job to a friend, in preference to a man of real ability).

"Second-handedness" destroys the *reality* of living. Our life is always not what it appears to be. Our higher values have no existence in reality. Let us be *real*.

### 4. *The theme condensed.*

Howard Roark is what men should be. I show: what he is, how and why others are different from him, what forms that difference takes, what reasons create it, what it does to its victims—their successes and their ultimate tragedies. And I show what life [is] to Howard Roark, what hell he has to go through and why, how he succeeds and what his success means.

### 5. *All progress as the work of individuals.*

Not a cooperation between man and mob, but a struggle of man against mob. Life belongs to the leader. The others follow. They don't want to. They have to. They contribute nothing to progress, except the impediments.

### 6. *The difference in the attitudes of Roark and Keating* (sub-issue).

Those who show too much concern for others and not for themselves, have no true respect for either. Only the man who respects himself can also respect others (and only as a secondary matter, *after* himself). No other neighbor-feeling is possible.

The truly joyous man takes himself *very seriously*, because there is no joy without self and pride in self. Those who preach and practice "not taking anything seriously" are not the gay, light-hearted ones. They are merely empty-hearted. One does not reverence with a giggle. *Above all, bring out the all-pervading feeling of joy in the being of Howard Roark, and the dreary hopelessness of Peter Keating.*

*Cast*

*Howard Roark:* The man who can be and is.

Gail Wynand: The man who could have been.

Peter Keating: The man who never could be and doesn't know it.

Ellsworth M. Toohey: The man who never could be—and knows it.

Dominique Wynand: The woman for a man like Roark. The perfect priestess. A woman who must give herself—and finds nothing to give herself to (until Roark).

The preacher: The man who tries to save the world with what the world should be saved from.

Guy Francon: The real ghost-writer-hirer. [*Earlier, this was AR's description of John Eric Snyte, who instead became the eclectic.*]


**February 9, 1936**

*Howard Roark*

Tall, slender. Somewhat angular—straight lines, straight angles, hard muscles. Walks swiftly, easily, too easily, slouching a little, a loose kind of ease in motion, as if movement requires no effort whatever, a body to which movement is as natural as immobility, without a definite line to divide them, a light, flowing, lazy ease of motion, an energy so complete that it assumes the ease of laziness. Large, long hands—prominent joints and knuckles and wrist-bones, with hard, prominent veins on the backs of the hands; hands that look neither young or old, but exceedingly strong. His clothes always disheveled, disarranged, loose and suggesting an unknown. No awkwardness, but a certain savage unfitness for clothes. Definitely red, loose, straight hair, always disheveled.

A hard, forbidding face, not in the least attractive according to conventional standards. More liable to be considered homely than handsome. Very prominent cheekbones. A sharp, straight nose. A large mouth—long and narrow, with a thin upper lip and a rather prominent lower one, which gives him the appearance of an eternal, frozen half-smile, an ironic, hard, uncomfortable smile, mocking and contemptuous. Wrinkles or dimples or slightly prominent muscles, all of that and none definitely, around the corners of his mouth. A rather pale face, without color on the cheeks and with freckles over the bridge of the nose and the cheekbones. Dark red eyebrows, straight and thin. Dark gray, steady, expressionless eyes—eyes that refuse to show expression, to be exact. Very long, straight, dark red eyelashes—the only soft, gentle touch of the whole face—a surprising touch in his grim expression. And when he laughs—which happens seldom—his mouth opens wide, with a complete, loose kind of abandon. A low, hard, throaty voice—not rasping, but rather blurred in its tone, though distinct in its sound, with the same soft, lazy fluency as his movements, neither one being soft or lazy.

*Attitude toward life.* He has learned long ago, with his first consciousness, two things which dominate his entire attitude toward life: his own superiority and the utter worthlessness of the world. He knows what he wants and what he thinks. He needs no other reasons, standards or considerations. His complete selfishness is as natural to him as breathing. He did not acquire it. He did not come to it through any logical deductions. He was born with it. He never questions it because even the possibility of questioning it never occurs to him. It is an axiom to him as much as the fact of his being alive is an axiom. He is a man born with the perfect consciousness of a man. [*This passage conflicts with AR's rejection of innate ideas—see John Galt's speech in* Atlas Shrugged.]

He is not even militant or defiant about his utter selfishness. No more than he could be defiant about the right to breathe and eat. He has the quiet, complete, irrevocable calm of an iron conviction. No dramatics, no hysteria, no sensitiveness about it—because there are no doubts. A quiet, almost indifferent acceptance of an irrevocable fact.

A quick, sharp mind, courageous and not afraid to be hurt, has long since grasped and understood completely that the world is not what he is. Consequently, he can no longer be hurt. The world has no painful surprise for him, since he has accepted long ago just what he can expect from it. Indifference and an infinite, calm contempt is all he feels for the world and for other men who are not like him. He understands men thoroughly. And, understanding them, he dismisses the whole subject. He knows what he wants and he knows the work he wants. That is all he expects of life. Being thoroughly a "reason unto himself," he does not long for others of his kind, for companionship and understanding.

He also knows that the world will not give him the right to his work easily. He does not expect it to be given. He enters life prepared to find it a struggle. And although he is a warrior above all, he does not consider himself such. The state of strife and battle is natural to him as a synonym of life. He does not think of himself as "Howard Roark, a soldier." He thinks: "A soldier, because he is Howard Roark."

Consequently, there is no danger of suffering. He does not suffer, because he does not believe in suffering. Defeat or disappointment are merely a part of the battle. Nothing can really touch him. He is concerned only with what he does. Not how he feels. How he feels is entirely a matter of his own, which cannot be influenced by anything and anyone on the outside. His feeling is a steady, unruffled flame, deep and hidden, a profound joy of living and of knowing his power, a joy that is not even conscious of being joy, because it is so steady, natural and unchangeable. If outside life brings him disappointment—well, it is merely a detail of the battle. He will have to struggle harder—that's all. The world becomes merely a place to act in. But not to feel in. The feeling—the whole [realm] of emotions—is in his [power] alone. He is a reason unto himself. He cannot feel differently. He was born that way.

His whole attitude toward himself, life and other men is completely clear to him. He does not even have to ponder about it—it is his very nature to be clear, consistent and logical about everything. His main policy in life is to refuse, completely and uncompromisingly, any surrender to the thoughts and desires of others. He wants to be an architect. He knows what he thinks of his work and what and how he will create. He expects others to accept his creation. Not because *he* needs their acceptance, but merely because they will be the ones to live in and use his buildings. He does not consider his work as concerned with the benefit and convenience of others. They are merely a convenience for his work. He does not build for people. People live for his buildings. He does not expect or wish admiration: he merely expects a humble bow to his superior spirit and its creation—because such is the nature of things and mere justice.

If he cannot get the right to do the work as he wants it done—well, then, he'll take a fifteen-dollar job as a common worker, and wait and work for his chance. Because the rewards of success as such—money, ease and fame—mean nothing whatever to him; his life has to be real, his life is his work, he will do his work as he wants it done, the only way he can enjoy it—or not at all, and perish in the battle. Because the second-hand consolations most people get out of life have no meaning for him, he will not compromise by building inferior buildings, nor by pretending adherence to the prejudices of those in power to gain their favors and their jobs. He will be himself at any cost—the only thing he really wants of life. And, deep inside of him, he knows that he has the ability to win the right to be himself. Consequently, his life is clear, simple, satisfying and joyous—even if very hard outwardly.

He is in conflict with the world in every possible way—and at complete peace with himself. And his chief difference from the rest of the world is that he was born without the ability to consider others. As a matter of form and necessity on the way, as one meets fellow travelers—yes. As a matter of basic, primary consideration—no. And the whole tone of his life is set by that one idea, one feeling—he is "a reason unto himself."

If he chooses the harder way, it is not through stupidity, stubbornness or a desire to be a martyr; it is merely because he knows he can make his way in the manner he pleases and will make it, and because he prefers his manner of making it. He has a tremendous, unshatterable conviction that he can and will *force* men to accept him, not beg and cheat them into it. He will *take* the place he wants, not receive it from others. Consequently, the profound serenity, joy, grandeur of his entire life and whole being.

His emotions are entirely controlled by his logic. Or rather—they are one and inseparable, with the emotions following the logic. (Show how this is possible.)

His whole *philosophy*: pride in oneself, confidence in oneself, placing one's life and fate above all, but only the *kind* of life one wishes.

*Religion*—none. Not a speck of it. Born without any "religious brain center." Does not understand or even conceive of the instinct for bowing and submission. His whole capacity for reverence is centered on himself. Needs no mystical "consolation," no other life. Thinks too much of this world to expect or desire any other.

*Politics*—interested only in not being interested in politics. Society as such does not exist for him. Other people do not interest him. He recognizes only the right of the exceptional [man] (and by that he means and knows only himself) to create, and order, and command. The others are to bow. [*Here we see a remnant of the Nietzscheanism prominent in* The Little Street. *For AR's mature view, see "Man's Rights" in the* Virtue of Selfishness.]

*Ethics*—only a code of his own, and only because he wants it. Doesn't know what the word "duty" means. Plays straight—because he would feel contempt for himself if he were to sneak and lie. Says what he means—whether others like it or not. He is not concerned with their liking it. They will have to accept it. His life and work come above all—nothing and no one can interfere, or even be considered beside it.

*Sex*—sensuous in the manner of a healthy animal. But not greatly interested in the subject. Can never lose himself in love. Even his great and only love—Dominique Wynand—is not an all-absorbing, selfless passion. It is merely the pride of a possessor. If he could not have her, it would not break

him or affect him very deeply. He might suffer—in his own indifferent way,
a suffering that can never reach deep enough to obscure life.

His attitude toward Dominique is not: "I love you and I am yours." It's:
"I love you and you are mine." It is primarily a feeling of wanting her and
getting her, without great concern for the question of whether she wants it.
Were it necessary, he could rape her and feel perfectly justified. Needless to
say, it is she who worships him, and loves him much more than he loves her.
He is the god. He can never become a priest. She has to be the priestess.
Until his meeting with Dominique, he has had affairs with women, perfectly
cold, emotionless affairs, without the slightest pretense at love. Merely satisfying a physical need and recognized by his mistresses as such.

*Ambition*—see life. His whole being. Not even recognized by him as ambition. Merely his natural behavior, the only way he could be and act.

His *manner* is one of profound, inexorable calm. A strong kind of calm.
Nothing can really arouse him—at least not outwardly. A slow, deliberate
manner of speaking. Precise, unhurried movements. Laughs seldom. Does
not joke. When he does—it is merely a quiet, indifferent kind of sarcasm. A
man so far above men that nothing can really reach him. Never an emotional
outbreak. Never loses control of himself.

And yet—a flaming intensity of feeling for his work and creation. And
for life in general. A flame reserved only for himself. No one is ever to see,
guess or witness it. And yet—its radiance is ever-present, in his indifferent
calm itself, a radiance felt by all. Suffering makes him merely tenser and
harder. A great deal of cruelty toward himself. And consequently toward
others. Does not recognize suffering as such, or grant it any privileges and
considerations. By the same token, he will never inflict unnecessary suffering or cruelty upon others. But when necessary, he will do it without even
noticing it, without a shudder or a hint of hesitation.

The book is the story of Howard Roark's triumph. It has to show what
the man is, what he wants and how he gets it. It has to be a triumphant epic
of man's spirit, a hymn glorifying a man's "I." It has to show every conceivable hardship and obstacle on his way—and how he triumphs over them,
why he *has to* triumph.

These obstacles, of course, can come from only one source: other men.
It is *society*, with its boggled chaos of selflessness, compromise, servility
and lies, that stands in the way of Howard Roark. It is every conceivable
form of "second-hand living" that fights him, that tries to crush him as only a

mob can crush—and fails in the attempt. To every second-hand creature he stands as a contrast, a reproach and a lesson.

We follow him from graduation as an architect to his ultimate, highest, complete victory. On the way, there are three main obstacles to face him: professional, economical, emotional. Professionally, it is the natural opposition of the mob to genius: total lack of understanding of his ideas, petty jealousies, resentment of the strange and the new, the stubborn stupidity of conservatism, the "social" angle of refusing opportunity to one who so totally lacks the social [ability of] boot-licking. As a consequence, [he endures] economical hardships, years of struggle with obscure jobs, poverty, silent, grim, relentless work. Every economical humiliation that society knows how to inflict. Emotionally, his first love is thwarted and denied— because of his unconventional, uncompromising attitude (Vesta).

**February 11, 1936**

### Peter Keating

Medium height, slender, graceful. Too graceful, with the studied, perfect, too soft and fluent grace of a ballet dancer. Carries himself erect, a deliberate erectness that seems a living illustration of the good, conventional "chin up" motto. Very pretty hands, always perfectly groomed. *Always* well dressed, well groomed and suggesting the manner of a fashion-plate, even in cheap clothes. A long, rather small, oval-shaped head, with a certain classical perfection in the shape of the skull. Long, narrow, pale face and attractive, almost feminine smooth skin, with a delicate, wax-like, transparent and milky texture. Long, thin nose and a very small mouth, delicate, flower-like and pretty, inclined to pout in a "bee-stung" manner, a mouth that would be small and pretty even on a girl. Dark, well-shaped eyes, alive, alert and softly lustrous. Obviously *smart* eyes, not deep or intelligent, but smart. Well-shaped eyebrows. Rather small, but well-shaped and pale forehead. Very black hair, set in a perfect, natural wave with soft, small ringlets in front. A rather high-pitched voice, softened by a studied, deliberate touch of kindly, velvet smoothness. An unnatural smile, soft, kindly, gentle and too friendly, considered fascinating and charming by all but the most discriminating ones. An unpleasant, insincere laughter, pitched on a high, oily, blurred hiccough sound, inclined to run into giggling.

*Attitude toward life. Vanity* grown out of all proportions. A vanity expressed in only one manner: to convince others of his superiority. Never a thought given to how he himself feels about things or values them; always—*what others will think of him;* and an overwhelming, burning anxiety to have them feel envy. All this never thought out or realized; just a blind, compelling instinct. This instinct has trained him to perfection in the ability to seize upon every thought and circumstance as helpful or detrimental to his main end. A lightning-like, instinctive, unreasoning ability to seize upon every possible advantage to his goal, long before his mind points out to him just where and what that advantage may be.

No philosophy of life ever thought out. No feeling of need for one. Never given to much abstract thinking. No such thing as peace with himself, since even the idea of any "self" to consider has never occurred to him. No internal strife to consider for a long time, and when it does come it is too late, since the strife and the realization of its possibility both come at the same time.

Consequently, no convictions of any kind on any subject whatever. A blind, stubborn idea that convictions are useless and unnecessary. Fooled himself long ago, before he could realize that he was fooling himself, into the belief that his superiority lay precisely in his freedom from the bounds of convictions. Only an instinctive, subconscious resentment and impatient annoyance with those he considers to be "idealists," left in him as a reminder of his unrealized, but subconsciously felt inferiority. This drives him, in self-protection, into a bitter, vicious resentment of men "with ideas."

His main principle: "don't take anything seriously." A cheap cynicism and iconoclastic fury against everything high, noble and exceptional parade under the cloak of a "sense of humor," "practical common sense," and "keeping your feet on the ground." Defending as "reality" all that he wishes reality to be.

## February 12, 1936

[Peter Keating has] an invisible habit of belittling, mocking and dragging down everything high. He greatly enjoys "debunking" biographies of famous men and everything that tends to prove that great men were "only human." Loves to insist that "we're all brothers under the skin." Has accepted as a faith, without thought or conviction behind it, the glorification of the so-called "human element": the equality of men, the average good fellow, kindness, patience, tolerance, good neighborly feelings, love of children, home, family, etc. (Such convictions are not dangerous to his vanity, since they belong to the inferior man.) Doesn't really mean or believe it, but is convinced that he believes it. Abstractly, of course. His "convictions" and his actions are things quite apart and the incongruity never occurs to him or bothers him.

He is as dishonest with himself as he is with others. His great motto: "If anyone has a car, I want two cars. If anyone has two cars, I want three cars. And I want to be sure they know it." Has selected architecture merely because he thinks it will give him a great chance at his kind of "success." No real love or talent for the work. Would have selected street-cleaning or shoe-mending with an equal pleasure, if it promised more advancement.

*Attitude toward men.* A mob man at heart. Completely gregarious. Has no satisfaction or interest in himself, consequently cannot stand to be alone. Prefers and selects inferior people among whom he can shine. Talks a great deal about the "communal spirit," but sees to it that he is always the leader of any "commune." Always plays up to others and revels in his great popularity. Never expresses a definite opinion on any subject, even the weather. Always sits on the fence. Calls it diplomacy. Acts as if each new man he meets is his greatest friend and the most interesting person in the world. Listens with immense interest to everyone else's troubles. Never remembers a word of it. Always ready and delighted to help others—and says so. Never forgets to mention past favors he has rendered. Loves to take credit for the achievements of those he has helped. Fools himself with believing that he is sincere in his altruism. Doesn't realize that it is caused by the subconscious instinct that tells him this altruism will help him a great deal in his cause, his vanity, in the opinions of others. But he will never lift a finger if helping another would really cost him anything or if there is no glory in such helping. And he would not hesitate to cut [others'] throats, even unnecessarily, if he thinks it will help him.

Loves movies and popular plays and vaudeville and, occasionally, magazines of the "Liberty" kind. Loves best-selling novels, particularly the "human interest" ones. Feels genuine respect for anything that has proved popular or has made money, no matter what he himself may have thought about it. Prefers stories about mothers, children, and dogs. Loves animals and declares them superior to men. Donates to orphan asylums and societies for the prevention of cruelty to animals. Shrugs at old classics, particularly those of the heroic type, as being old-fashioned hokum—as opposed to wholesome, "modern" humanness. Loves and enjoys everything that gives him a patronizing feeling of superiority: the weak, the helpless, the meek and sentimental. Dismisses everything high with a contemptuous accusation of "high hat." Announces for all to hear that he would love nothing better than a home and children, particularly children, but does nothing to satisfy his desire.

His manner is soft, friendly, graceful. Extremely popular. The "soul of the party," the "regular fellow," the "dream lover" of many a female. Judiciously mixes seriousness and jokes. Talks in nothing but platitudes. Always has to have friends and "best pals."

*Philosophy*—none.

*Religion*—none to speak of as far as sincerity is concerned. But a great deal of talk about the high principles of Christianity, the simple faith and the inevitable necessity of religion. Makes a show of going to church when advisable. Talks of the "Spirit" and of a "Superior Power" or "Universal Principle." At heart—a dumb, superstitious fear and a vague admittance of something "Above." Refuses to believe that there is "nothing after death" and dreads the whole subject.

*Politics*—interested only as much as it can help him. Joins whatever party is advisable at the moment. Member of every fraternity, club, lodge and order it is possible for him to join.

*Ethics*—none. No conception of the idea. But a great deal of talk about it in the good, accepted, middle-class manner.

*Sex*—highly sexed and completely "dual-personality" on the subject. On the one hand—preaches home, love, marriage, purity and respectability. Considers physical sex low and dirty. Proclaims pure, spiritual love as the perfect ideal. Cries over love stories. On the other hand—loves his physical sex and his women. Dissipates wildly but judiciously. Patronizes whorehouses. But is always discreet—*very* discreet.

*Ambition*—overwhelming, but in one line only, on the line of his vanity. Always belittles his ambition and all ambitions, but never misses a chance to mention his achievements.

He acts servile with superiors and overbearing with inferiors. Goes out of his way to humiliate those under him, with nothing to gain for himself, except a feeling of superiority.

**April 21, 1936**

| *Howard Roark* | *Peter Keating* | *Vesta Dunning* |
|---|---|---|
| His beginning—dreams, plans, ridicule and opposition. | His beginning—out to "sell himself" and gain popularity. | Her beginning—poverty, ambition, heroic dreams. |
| First clashes with others. | His approach to his work. | |
| Work for Snyte. | Work for Snyte. | |
| Beginning of love for Vesta. | Love for Vesta. [*Entry crossed out.*] | Her attitude toward both men—beginning of love for Roark. |
| Hardship and setbacks. | From success to success. | |
| Break with Vesta. | Affair with Vesta. [*Entry crossed out.*] | Surrender to Keating—for her career. [*Entry crossed out.*] |
| Opens own office—failures and hardships. | Goes into partnership with John Eric Snyte. [*Snyte's name was crossed out and replaced by Guy Francon.*] | Gets break on stage and signs Hollywood contract. |
| A few jobs—fame as "freak"—achievements and hardships. Slow rise. | Easy triumphs. Fame. Wealth. Marriage that cinches his career. Slow downfall. | Fame, sensation. Break with Keating. Series of lovers. Dissipation. Bitterness. |
| Meeting with Gail Wynand. | Dope. Drink. Dissipation. | Encounter with Roark—her undefeated, unuttered love for him. |
| Dominique. | Desperate bids for Wynand Building. | "Joan of Arc." |
| Scandal. | Failure. | Last meeting with Roark. |
| Wynand Building. | | Suicide. |

**February 22, 1937**

*Ellsworth Monkton Toohey*

The non-creative "second-hand" man par excellence. The critic, expressing and molding the voice of public opinion; the average man condensed, representing the average man's qualities plus the peculiar qualities which make him the natural leader of average men.

Theme-song: a vicious, ingrown vanity coupled with an *insane will to power*, a lust for superiority that can be expressed *only through others*, whom, therefore, he has to dominate; a natural inferiority complex that subconsciously leads to [the desire to] bring everything down into inferiority. A tremendous ego—without content. No reasons for his egotism—"I am I," that's all, without concern for what this "I" really is.

Important trait to emphasize as a social implication: this type is the one who, once in a position of power, subconsciously, but with an unerring instinct, surrounds himself with his moral and intellectual equals, works to fill other positions of power with his own kind, closing all doors he can to genuine talent and superiority, since this last would be too great a threat for him. None of it is conscious—just an innate instinct of self-preservation.

Here is the place to emphasize that genuinely superior beings are *too* individualistic [in social matters], in the sense that they achieve their own positions and are not concerned with the propagation and advancement of their own kind. It is only the inferior men that have collective instincts—because they need them. But since the superior men live in society, they have to organize for their own protection—a kind of class brotherhood of talent—if they are to survive at all. The only kind of "unselfishness" permissible to the great man is unselfishness to the cause of that superior form of living which he represents, and which has to be protected in the persons of other individuals like him. (Social instinct as the weapon and protection of the inferior.)

Toohey's physical appearance: medium height, rather on the shortish side, skinny, anemic, concave-chested, spindly, slightly bow-legged, ridiculous and offensive in a bathing suit. A glaring lack of vitality—compensated, so he thinks, by his intellectual achievements. Long, narrow face, slightly receding chin, protruding upper teeth, in a sharp, circular, rodent fashion— not too good a set of teeth, nor too clean. Narrow, sharp black eyes, set close together, bright and "intellectual" between slightly puffed, heavy lids. A Hitler-like small black mustache—carefully trimmed. Luxurious hair—black, lustrous and faintly suggesting a wave—thoroughly well groomed, leaving just the faintest doubt between natural carelessness or very deliberate, retouched, marcelled picturesqueness. Not a mane, but somehow suggesting a mane—seeming too large for his light frame, making him vaguely top-heavy—more in impression than in fact. Thin, expressive hands and small feet, with a mincing, uncertain, unsteady, nervous walk.

He has a magnificent voice—a true achievement. Deep, low, well-modulated, clear, precise and expressive. Perhaps a little offensive to some people, because of its smug perfection—but to a very few people. He has made a thorough study of voice-culture, but does not like to mention it—prefers to let people think it is natural. Shrugs deprecatingly when complimented on his voice, but never misses or forgets the compliments.

Went into "intellectualism" in a big way. Two reasons: first, a subconscious revenge for his obvious physical inferiority, a means to a power his body could never give him; second (and primary), a cunning perception that only mental control over others is true control, that if he can rule them mentally he is indeed their total ruler. His vanity is not passive like that of Peter, who is concerned with other people only as mirrors for his vanity; Toohey is very much concerned with other people in the sense of an overwhelming desire to dominate them. This is the lust for power, but it is a "second-hand" power. It is motivated not by some deep conviction of his own to be imposed upon others, who would thus be secondary to him and his conviction, but by subconsciously adopting the convictions of others in order to rule them and thus acquire his own grandeur through the number of people he dominates, deriving his self-satisfaction from them. They are actually the prime factor and he a "second-hand" creature devoid of all personal significance but that given to him by others.

In contrast to Peter, Toohey does believe strongly and earnestly in ideals and convictions, but they must be the ideals he has accepted. He is intolerant, impatient and sarcastic to all intellectual opposition. He believes in "principles," realizing subconsciously that a strict adherence to a set of principles delivers men into his hands when he is the chief proponent of these principles. He is the loud defender of the "intellect," of "brain over brawn" or "mind over matter." Such words as "culture," "civilization," "progress," "the spiritual heritage of centuries," "ethics," "esthetics," and "philosophy" are his favorites, to the point where he has become convinced that he is their living embodiment.

Now as to his convictions. [As a consequence of] his basic lust for power—a "second-hand" power not expressed in any concrete ideal of his own—his convictions are all those which are expedient to his attainment of such power. He has realized ahead of many others the tremendous power of the masses, which, for the first time, are acquiring real significance in all (even the intellectual) aspects of life. In this sense, he is the man of the century, the genius of modern democracy in its worst meaning.

The first cornerstone of his convictions is *equality*—his greatest passion. This includes the idea that, as two-legged human creatures, all possess certain intrinsic value by the mere fact of having been born in the shape of men, not apes. Any concrete, mental content inside the human shape does not matter. A great brain or a great talent or a magnificent character are of no importance as compared to that intrinsic value all possess as *men*—whatever that may be. He is never clear on what that may be and rather annoyed when the question is raised. He avoids it by running to meet it and by silencing the issue with a great deal of talk. He talks of the "human spirit," the "spark of God in all of us," the "man created in God's own image," the "best in the worst of us," etc.

His talk is on a grand scale, staggering, magnificent, its bromides well-hidden under the latest scientific terms, the whole worked out brilliantly on the formula of saying things that sound profound until one stops to think of what exactly they mean and finds that they mean nothing. Inasmuch as beliefs are important to him only as a means to an end, and that is the extent of his belief in beliefs, he is not bothered by his inconsistencies, by the vagueness and illogic of his convictions. They are efficient and effective to secure the ends he is seeking. They work—and that is all they're for.

Once the equality of men is established, the advantages to his type are obvious. It discredits the superior type of man whom he hates, dreads and envies. It minimizes, through a metaphysical, "humanitarian" hocus-pocus, the qualities and virtues which the superior type possesses and which he lacks. It denies superiority and subordinates it to that vague "humanness" which he can claim along with everyone else. But, mainly, it assures him of superiority—his brand of it. Deeply and subconsciously he *knows* that he is a second-rater and a representative of the average. That [knowledge], aided by a certain amount of brains, puts him in the category of "upper-class average"; but he is devoid of all individuality and creative power, which dooms him hopelessly to the average (in other words, he is a plain average man spiritually, but slightly above the mob mentally, in the facile sense of cunning, not wisdom). [Hence] he becomes the true representative, leader and condensation of the average. Once the [men at the top] are removed or discredited, *he* is the top. As the best representative of the masses, he can attain the prominence, distinction and power [which would be] impossible to him on his own personal merits. In an individualistic society, where men have to stand or fall by what they really are in themselves, where they are valued as single men and by no other standard—he is nothing. In a collective mass society, where quantity stands above quality (another unreal, "second-hand" substitution)—he is everything. Hence his profound urge toward equality and collectivism, or his "social conscience," as he calls it.

This "social conscience" is an outstanding, dominant trait in him. He has an instinctive interest in everything concerning others. He is the born spiritual meddler, reformer, and "social worker." Societies, clubs, lodges, organizations of any kind attract him irresistibly. His is not the cruder interest of Peter, who joins for what he can get out of it for himself. Toohey joins to take an active part, for what *he* can do to others. In everything he joins he soon becomes the leading voice and *the* influence. He is no rank-and-file member, ever; he is always *on* the committee or the board of directors. He is not after advancing his own career; he is after molding the lives of others, which *is* his career. (The monstrosity of "selfless" egotism.) One will always find him on the stationery of "Slum Clearance Leagues," "Mass Education Leagues," "Modern Education Leagues," "Recreation for the Poor Leagues," "Social Foundation Leagues," and prize-giving "Art Leagues."

Toohey is a "humanitarian" and a "radical." He is a humanitarian because his great love for and eternal preoccupation with humanity gives him the standing and prestige he does not possess as a man; it fills the void [caused by a lack] of all individual creativity, the void in a man who has nothing to offer in himself, only in, through and for others. (A "second-hand" man par excellence. Only those who have nothing in themselves are too concerned with others.) He is a radical because the theory of the triumphant, totalitarian mass is still a new one in the world, particularly in its spiritual implications and sources, which he realizes full-well, but never mentions explicitly. Up to the twentieth century and Soviet Russia, the world [had offered some degree] of recognition for individual achievement, recognition of leaders and exceptions as opposed to the masses; the trend of "liberalism" and the idea of "freedom" was freedom for "a man" and the fight for the individual rights of "a man." When humanity achieved that freedom after the Industrial Revolution, or came as near to freedom and general equality before the law as it had ever come, one thing became apparent to the deluded idealists who, in fighting for the "rights of man," included *all men*, presumed all men to be equal, or at least potentially equal given equal opportunities. Whether under modern capitalism the best men always won (and undoubtedly they often did not) was not as important as the fact that capitalistic democracy showed plainly that there is a *best*. And that the best [among men] are opposed to the rest of humanity.

The liberals and humanitarians are now faced with a choice: either

admit that there are differences among men more profound and irrefut-
able than those of money or aristocratic birth, and therefore fight for the
rights and the freedom of the *best* among men, rights and freedom which
the average men do not want, do not understand and cannot use or protect,
and stop the damnable preoccupation with the "poor" as such, the poor who
have no distinction beyond their poverty; or—deny these ideals and, keeping
only the philosophical zeal for all humanity, bring mankind down to the
level of the masses, deny to the few the rights which endanger the masses,
benefit the masses by destroying their eternal enemy—the exceptional man,
and instead of fighting *for* the individual rights which have hitherto been
known as "human" rights, reverse the process, fight *against* these rights, for
these rights are the enemy, not the liberation of the masses. [*By "masses"
AR refers here to second-handers who wish to live by exploiting better men.
For evidence of her respect for honest men of average ability, see the characters of Mike Donnigan in* The Fountainhead *and Eddie Willers in* Atlas
Shrugged.]

Communism, the Soviet variety particularly, is *not* merely an economic
theory. It does not demand economic equality and security in order to set
each individual free to rise as he chooses. Communism is, above all, a spiritual theory which denies the individual, *not merely as an economic power,*
but in every respect. It demands spiritual subordination to the mass in every
way conceivable—economic, intellectual, artistic; it allows individuals to
rise only *as servants of the masses,* only as mouthpieces for the great
average. It places Ellsworth Monkton Toohey at the top of the human
pyramid.

Hence, Toohey's natural "radicalism." In it, he is subtler, deeper and
more consistent than many a modern communist. If some communists come
to a spiritual collectivism somewhat reluctantly, as a necessity for achieving
economic collectivism, Toohey reverses the process, much more logically.
He embraces spiritual collectivism first; economic collectivism is only a
means to that ultimate end.

When and if the mob is enthroned as the supreme arbiter of all life,
Ellsworth Monkton Toohey will rule the earth. As a voice of the mob, to be
sure; but to a "second-hand" man this does not matter. What if he is only the
servant spiritually—when there is nothing in his spirit that may wish to rule,
no ideals, no convictions, no creative power strictly his own? Spiritual servility is not abhorrent to a man devoid of spirituality, in the only sense in
which spirituality exists—in the powerful, self-contained, self-reverent ego.
In *actual,* material life—devoid of all spiritual content, as a collective life
must be when the only source of spirt, the ego, is removed—he will be the

ruler. He will have no fear of competition from his spiritual superiors, since they will be destroyed, or if any are still born they will have no chance against him, [because they] lack his power of mob appeal when the mob is supreme. And the only danger to his power—the spiritual or mental life of humanity—will be taken care of by an all-pervading propaganda for the ideals that made his rise possible, the ideals of mob supremacy, a smoke-screen to fill the emptiness of the human spirit, a spirit castrated, denied and offered its own denial to satisfy its hunger.

Such is Toohey's secret dream and Utopia. He knows all the possible approaches to it and his convictions derive from that, have that dream as a motivation. Everything that proceeds from the individual and the exception is bad; everything that proceeds from the masses and the average is good. He takes a great interest in folklore, in anonymous legends and songs, as opposed to individual creations of artists. He proclaims the supremacy of "folk art" over any other art. He adopted the Marxist theory easily and natu-rally, primarily because it discredits the significance of individuals in history in favor of the economic significance of the masses; also, in subordinating the spiritual to the economic, in proclaiming the dependence of the spirit upon the material, it gives men like Toohey a great weapon against their enemy, the spirit: just take control of humanity's economics—[which is] concrete and accessible—and you can (hope to) control humanity's spirit.

In opposing the existing order of society, it is not the big capitalists and their money that Toohey opposes; he opposes the faint conceptions of indi-vidualism still existing in that society, and the privileged few as its material symbols. He says that he is fighting Rockefeller and Morgan; he is fighting Beethoven and Shakespeare. He says he is fighting for a comfortable home with a bathroom for every financially disinherited factory hand; he is fighting for a comfortable throne and a halo for every spiritually disinherited Toohey. Hence his great preoccupation with the poor and the lower classes. He is known as a great, unselfish crusader in unselfish causes; his crusade is thoroughly selfish in the [sense of the] perverted selfless selfishness of the "second-hander."

It is not surprising, therefore, to find him with a reputation of "daring," "progressiveness" and "originality." He is all of that, in the sense that the total supremacy of the masses is a new idea in the world and he, as its apostle, may be considered daring or original. In that sense, he is the cham-pion of everything "new," particularly if it helps in the fight against the indi-vidualism of the old. He is a great champion of the Art Moderne. He is the defender and publicizer for Gertrude Stein in literature, the "surrealists" in painting, the cacophony of "new" music, and the factory-made standardized modern house in architecture. He knows, half-subconsciously, that all these phony fakes are easy for anyone and deny the true originality, genius and rarity of great artists.

In his chosen profession as an Art and Architecture Critic, he defends, above all, *a standard.* He is all for the old academic eclecticism, where it imposes rules, restraints and precedents on individual creation; he started as a rabid defender of eclecticism ("We cannot improve upon the masters of the past, accepted and recognized by whole nations and whole *centuries of nations*") until he discovered a new standardization in the factory-made "moderne," this last move in keeping with his social theories and his general reputation for radicalism. Before the spread of the "moderne," he was opposed to modern architecture. And he has been opposed and is forever opposed to Howard Roark. Peter Keating is his true disciple and protégé, and Peter switches with Toohey from conservative eclecticism to extreme, mechanical, unoriginal modernism. (When convenient. But still continues with his "classic orders"—when convenient.) In the early stages of modern architecture, Toohey decried it and defended the old—on a typical ground: "Why force individual eccentricity and idiosyncrasy on the *will* and taste of the people expressed in their preference for conventional homes?" With the growth of the philosophy of mob supremacy and the emergence of modernism in set mass-forms, a modernism as stiff and frozen and unoriginal as the old traditions—he switched to it easily and naturally.

He realized, on that example, that to be the true "voice of the people" he had to become a radical opposed to the majority sentiment at present—for the sake of an ultimate, complete triumph for real majority sentiment. The mob had not yet been taught to openly and consistently worship itself as a mob; it still had vestiges of respect for individualism ground into it by centuries of aristocracy; it is the duty of Toohey to teach the mob exactly what to believe in order to inherit the earth; it is his job to awaken the mob to its own power. He can be—and it is only [an apparent] paradox—an exception and a rebel against present society, which, after all, is not yet collectivized spiritually—in order to establish conditions which will make him the true and complete "voice of society."

Toohey studies voraciously. He has a magnificent memory for facts and statistics; he is known as a "walking encyclopedia." This is natural—since he has no creative mind, only a repeating, aping, absorbing "second-handed" one. He has nothing new to create, but can acquire importance by absorbing the works and achievements of others. He is a sponge, not a fresh spring. His passively retentive memory has always made him a good scholar; he was a brilliant pupil in school—the kind who always knew his lessons, had the neatest copy-books, preferred his homework to athletic games (in which he would have no chance), wore glasses, often had head-colds, and his mother had to watch his diet. An intellectual child with a delicate stomach.

Since his scholastic achievements took a great deal of painstaking, meticulous work, he has always resented his quick, brilliant classmates to whom study was no effort. Hence, his great defense of hard work as the key to everything ("perspiration is inspiration"), the conviction that hard work can accomplish anything, that talent does not count for so much, because a hard worker can equal and even beat any of "your geniuses." He was not so good at mathematics in school, but great at history, literature, psychology, and penmanship. He went to Sunday School, because of a religious lower-middle-class mother ("Christian Science").

His great asset is the fact that he is by no means dull. He has nothing new to offer, but he is perfect at the old and he can do the conventional better than anyone else—the secret and key to his success. He sells pills of bromides, but he can devise brand new coatings for them—the sure way to popular acclaim. He is genuinely witty—[usually] in a sharp, insidiously sarcastic way. His sarcasm, for which he is famous, is an art: it is subtle, elaborately polite, personal, "deadly" according to those in his frame of mind. Elaborate politeness is another of his specialties. His manners are impeccable. He speaks with a faint touch of the broad "a"—just faint enough to be considered charming and distinguished. "Distinguished" is his favorite adjective to apply to himself.

Sarcasm is his pet weapon—as natural to him as smell to the skunk—as a method of offense and defense. He is magnificently, maliciously catty. He does not fight his opponents by straight argument or logical refutation—he disqualifies them from the game, dismisses them by mockery. Perhaps he has no refutation to offer, but that does not matter for his purpose. He communicates to his audience the feeling of his superiority over his opponents, the impression that he does not answer them because they are not even worth answering. With an intelligent audience this does not work so well, but then he is not after an intelligent audience. With the rest—the vast majority, the pseudo-intellectuals particularly—the trick works like magic. He convinces them and wins them to his point of view by a snappy crack and a superior shrug at the right time.

Individualism, of course, and everything connected with it, is the great butt of his cracks. Everything heroic is dismissed with a: "My dear fellow, this is utter, childish rot. Very pretty, but one must grow up, you know." He goes in a big way for the "scientific spirit" and uses all the latest scientific terms, all the phony, complicated "isms," coining a few of his own, when necessary. His pet convenience is vague generalizations, the terms devoid of all concrete reality, the kind that take volumes to interpret and that can be used nicely to muddle up an issue, while giving the appearance of great scientific precision. The inferiority complex thus created in the audience, which is not so glibly familiar with the terms, is also a great help in making converts and winning his point.

"Above all, let us be modern" is his pet slogan—with "modernity" given his own interpretation. With the help of his erudition, it is easy to point out that the whole process of history has been leading in his direction, has been but a prelude to the "modern" ideas which he represents and which are, as he can prove, the goal, culmination and apotheosis of all human progress. There is also the little trick of astounding and confusing his opponents with his stunts of memory: he can quote, without a second's hesitation, the date of any battle in ancient Greece, of the birth and death of any pharaoh of Egypt or any parliamentary leader of England, along with the date, number of workers and financial damage in dollars *and* cents of any strike. If his opponent doesn't know as much—who, ladies and gentlemen of the audience, is obviously the more educated man and obviously in the right?

Naturally, his sympathies are always to the Left. But he does not assume the pose or appearance of a soap-box proletarian. He is friendly to them, but faintly superior. After all, as he likes to refer to himself, he is "a gentleman and a scholar." He may defend the lower classes, but his consuming vanity will never let him appear as one of them in a society where they are still recognized as the *lower* classes. As long as things are as they are, he will preserve all the outward symbols of superiority as it is commonly understood around him, and, above all, he will be accepted as a superior in his social intercourse. Hence, his immaculate appearance, his exquisite grooming, not too foppish, only slightly so, not too startling, only quietly, conservatively elegant. He likes to think of his "conservative good taste," where personal appearance is concerned. The same applies to his voice and to his style of writing—smooth, elegant, well-rounded, just spiced with his exquisite sarcasm.

His manner with people is quiet, *so* polite, very faintly effeminate—and "brilliant." He is a "brilliant" conversationalist and storyteller. He is an addition to any party and a favorite with hostesses, particularly intellectual ones. He is never offensive; if he wishes to insult someone with his sarcasm—it is done so exquisitely that the insulted one seems offensive. His manner is friendly in a cool, impersonal, slightly patronizing way. He is never emotional and has never lost his perfect poise. If, sometimes, he chooses to make his voice tremble with intense feeling, it is done artistically, like a gentleman, and one gets the impression of great emotion hidden under a perfect self-control, which creates in his listeners admiration and a conviction of his utter sincerity. His pose is eternal and immutable; it is the same in a drawing room, on a lecture platform, in a bathroom or during sexual intercourse: cool, self-possessed, faintly patronizing.

He loves to address an audience—the larger, the better—and never misses a chance to do so. Is perfectly at home on the speaker's platform. He loves and devours publicity—the "dignified" kind, but does not talk about this. ("My dear, I never read my clippings—haven't the faintest idea what they say about me." He knows every word of every clipping by heart.)

He has an attractive, colorful style, with a great deal of merit in form, if not in content, which makes him easy to read or to hear. Wins great popular success through this. He is adept at coining phrases, epigrams and "mots justes"; he loves to know that he is quoted.

When talking beautifully of the proletariat, he never visualizes himself as one of them. He is the superior benefactor, the teacher and leader, the benevolent father of his flock. [He views himself as] "a shepherd," along with the conception of others as sheep. Spiritually, he is very much the condensation of the worst features of a pedagogue. He started life as a teacher; he is now a college professor of esthetics, with art and architecture as specialty. The experience of molding the lives and destinies of young pupils gave the impetus to his absorbing desire to mold the lives and destinies of all men. On the side, as a pet hobby, he is a vocational advisor. He thinks of himself and demands to be considered as the final authority on every subject. He is pettily impatient and intolerant of opposition, of any refusal to take his word as the final proof.

Extremely fastidious in his clothes and his living room, although his bedroom and study are inclined to be somewhat dusty and sloppy. His daily routine is timed to the second and unbroken. He cannot be interrupted during his writing, even if it be a long distance phone call from his dying mother. His meals are eaten on time and his calories scientifically counted, his food rations being weighed on apothecaries' scales. His daily cold shower is timed with a stop watch. The room where he receives visitors is exquisitely simple and modern, its few ornaments consisting of rare and precious art objects and old editions. He is a connoisseur of wines and never orders less than the best, which he cannot afford often. ("What's not good enough for Morgan is not good enough for me.") He proclaims the supremacy and "rhythm" of toil, but his hardest physical exertion is to brush his teeth. ("After all, mental labor is the hardest labor.")

The "friend of humanity" has no friends. A great many admirers and

fans, particularly women-fans who write him passionate letters after every
lecture or radio-broadcast. But no real "pals." His cold pose forbids it. He
does not feel any lack from it. Loving all humanity as he does, he has never
loved a single human being. When approached for help or money, he
refuses, but makes the person who asked feel guilty and cruel at having
imposed on his better feelings. "My dear, I am refusing for your own good.
Believe me, it is harder for me than it is for you. But it is against my principles. It will destroy your feeling of self-reliance." Intent on saving
mankind, he has never helped a man. He does not do favors. When he stuffs
choice positions with his protégés, it is done for his own sake and for the
sake of his principles, never for the protégé. He prides himself on the epi-
thets: "impartial," "fair," "objective" and "incorruptible."

The question of sex is a touchy one to him. Here, as in everything else,
he craves superiority. He is no great power as a male and he is very conscious that his sexual organs are rather inadequate. He makes up for it by the
most exquisite and varied perversions. ("My dear, we must be modern.")
Has a great collection of the most unusual aphrodisiacs (all the "happy
boxes" and then some). Loves to think of himself as a great lover and as irresistible to women. ("For the life of me, I don't see what attracts women to
my unprepossessing self, God knows I'm no Apollo, and you'd never think
that intellectual appeal counts in sex, *would* you?") He has had mistresses—
more than one at a time—but never a *love* affair. Visits whorehouses when
necessary. Is very fastidious about his mistresses—they must be, above all,
beautiful and feminine. Doesn't go for intellectual women. His mistresses
are seldom the pick of the chorus, but a good second best. He will *not* be
seen with an unattractive woman. Makes a point of this. (He will have
nothing but the best.)

Is naturally liberal in his sexual views, contending that the family is a
bourgeois institution, but does not go for the subject of sex much. Too
physical and consequently unimportant. After all, he is concerned with the
purely intellectual aspects of life.

Although raised with religion and having undergone a mild attack of
religious hysteria in his adolescence, he is now an agnostic, rather prone to
frown on religion. After all, religion is a sort of individual refuge and as such
it is dangerous. His insatiable lust for spiritual power would rather focus all
emotion on the earthly collective, because the earthly collective—"c'est
moi."

He is not a member of the Communist Party, because that Party is
still considered lower class. ("Besides, I am a man of science, not a politician.") He is not an open supporter of Soviet Russia. ("After all, I am an

impartial observer.") But his sympathies are with both—fervently, but always "objectively."

He is a man so completely poisoned spiritually, that his puny physical appearance seems to be a walking testimonial to the spiritual pus filling his blood vessels.

**1937**

[*After writing her character description of Toohey, AR attended two lectures by a prominent British socialist, Harold Laski (1893–1950). During an interview in 1961, she recalled:*

*Laski was the soul of Ellsworth Toohey in the flesh. After seeing Laski, I just had to remember how he lectured—his mannerisms, the pseudo-intellectual snideness, the whole manner of speaking on important subjects with inappropriate sarcasm as his only weapon, acting as if he were a charming scholar in a drawing room, but you could sense the bared teeth behind the smile, you could feel something evil—and I would know how Toohey would act in any circumstance; it gave me the complete sense of life of that type. Toohey is larger scale than Laski, who was a cheap little snide socialist, but Laski projected Toohey's essential characteristics. Even his appearance was ideal. I drew a sketch during the lecture, with the narrow cadaverous face and glasses and big ears, and I gave it all to Toohey.*

*The following notes are from the second of the Laski lectures.*]
Extremely well-dressed women (not too young, typically around forty and over) with a vapid and aggressive look—hatred of [the intellect] and insistently trying to acquire it. Only one I saw to be fairly attractive. A good type: a woman nearing fifty, medium height, slender, *very* well groomed; long, narrow face, *mainly nose,* pleasantly smiling, upturned lips (smiling too easily, with such a set, rehearsed, partly patronizing pleasantness), no eyes—all you see is the yellow-white lids and you have the uncomfortable feeling that the face has no focus and no opening, a face with no person behind it; a beige coat of smooth brown fur, a Russian-looking, fancy hat of the same cloth and fur; *and*—most prominent, the first thing you notice— glasses with a heavy black ribbon hanging *ostentatiously* from the corner of her eye.

Also a great many shabby, old-maid-librarian types of middle-aged women, most unbecomingly dressed; the first thing jumping off from them, hitting you in the face, is the fact that you simply cannot imagine a man [making love to] them.

Also—aggressive house-wife types, with old-fashioned hats and dirty-looking complexions.

Also—a great many homely young girls, poorly dressed, of all degrees of homeliness, amazing variations of it, *all* of them with flat shoes and very unkempt, uncombed hair. A sad look of defensive aggressiveness, unconvincing assurance, and that awful feeling of "we're miscarriages physically, but we're making up for it intellectually."

Most of the audience are women. Few men comparatively and these better looking than the women, more prosperous, less freaky. Most of the men seem a little sheepish, quite a few seeming like good Babbitts dragged here by their wives—just as they are dragged to the play of their wives' choice.

Single most unpleasant characterization of this audience—the mouths. There is more meekness and insincerity in the mouth than in any other part of the face. Is that the most expressive and most betraying organ?

Above all impressions—the horrible [spectacle] of intellectual vulgarity. A crowd of this same mental caliber going to a dance hall or saloon is much more attractive, honest and bearable than this phony search for intellectuality. A pretense of brains should not be allowed to anyone except those who have brains. What horrible, horrible things can be done with the mind, *through,* with and for half-brains! How much better no brain is than half a brain!

A woman with horrible piano legs sitting right in the front row on the stage, facing the audience, with a short skirt, her legs crossed and *lisle* stockings! Well-dressed and *flaunting* the stockings; also diamonds on her fingers quite [prominently] displayed.

It's the aggressive, imperious expressions that are awful—on these people who are supposed to stand for equality, freedom, kindness, justice, etc. Isn't that significant? Think of the implications, beyond the obvious ones.

*Here comes Toohey [i.e., Laski]:*

He starts with explanations and *"advice."* The audience laughs before any point is made.

"The *great* world"—"The *grim* reality"—always using important words sarcastically.

"A sovereign state is an anachronism"—"When the pound sterling falls, the heart of the secretary of the U.S. Treasury beats faster."

*Wears glasses.* Long neck, sloping shoulders, too narrow chin, wide temples, large ears.

"The white man's burden has been borne by the black."

"It would be possible to show—if it weren't *impolite* to show . . ."

The audience laughs every time he says "simple-minded."

He looks terribly at ease, a little weary, a little bored—not offensively so, just gracefully so. (He leans limply sidewise against the stand.)

Simplicity and clarity of sentences—yet a few "exquisite" words.

"A stick to beat Mr. Chambers with—and let me say the bigger the stick the more honorable the purpose—" (Note the "witty" asides.)

"The limits of euphemism are infinite."

"The poor, the lame, the halt . . ."

"The government—whose discomfort at public discussion I can wholly understand—"

(The gals on the stage are yawning—the one with the lisle stockings, too.)

"It's pure accident, it just happened that way"—[in regard to] something he quite definitely means was not an accident.

"I made up my mind twenty-five years ago to be a rank-and-file [member] of the Labour Party."


**March 15, 1937**

An agency for writers has on its office wall a huge photograph of a mob (with mob faces) and the big letters: "Don't forget whom you're writing for."(!)


**March 27, 1937**

A typical instance of the rising power of the masses—the open arrogance of inferiors who no longer try to imitate their superiors, but boldly flaunt their inferiority, their [mediocrity], their "popular appeal." A state of affairs where quality is no longer of any importance, and where it is coming to be shunned, avoided, even despised. The paradox of the dregs of humanity actually feeling *contempt* for their betters, *because* they are better. Quantity alone considered important—quality no longer even considered. The masses triumphant.

Example of this: the head of a "charm school," a contemptible racket, having been attacked by a "high brow" magazine, states haughtily: "Why should I worry? In all the years they've been in existence, they have only a hundred thousand circulation. I have a million customers in a year!"

**March 28, 1937**

More about Toohey.

He is vociferously rational while doing his best to deny reason. Basically, he is all for the heart above the mind, emotion above thought. [Superficially], he is strictly scientific, rational, materialistic, with only a few lapses into talk about the "soul." His trick is the same as that of Christian Science. He realizes subconsciously that reason is the enemy of all "heart hokum" and of all spiritual rackets. Consequently, he destroys it by appearing to support it. He defends reason loudly, but [substitutes] for reason his own preposterous brand of pseudo-science. He betrays himself occasionally by his talk about the "pure in heart," the "universal spirit" and other such mystic-Christian-communistic catch-words.

# 5

# ARCHITECTURAL RESEARCH

Before Ayn Rand could work out the plot of The Fountainhead and begin writing, she needed to know more about the profession of architecture. She asked the New York Public Library to recommend a list of books for her research. She read most of them in 1937, making extensive notes in her journal.

More than half of her notes are presented in this chapter. I have included nearly all of the notes in which she comments on her reading, or relates the material to The Fountainhead.

I have omitted many quotes that she copied with little or no comment. I have also omitted passages in which she simply paraphrased factual material, without evaluation. For instance, AR made lengthy notes on Skyscrapers and the Men Who Build Them by W. A. Starrett, concerning such topics as: the methods and problems of constructing large buildings; the division of responsibility among architects, engineers, and contractors; the time required to design, contract, and build skyscrapers; the financing of large buildings and the types of building contracts; the typical problems that arise with contractors and labor unions. Also omitted here are some notes on the training of architects, taken from The ABC of Architecture by Matlock Price, and notes on building codes and zoning laws in New York.

AR found aspects of The Fountainhead's theme and characters everywhere in the actual profession of architecture. Ellsworth Toohey's manner of combining architectural criticism with collectivist propaganda was taken in part from the writings of Lewis Mumford and Bruno Taut. She identified the second-handedness of Peter Keating in the work and writings of architect Thomas Hastings. As to deeper issues, she even recognized the central importance of the concept "unit" while considering the planned design of cities versus individual buildings. These notes are a record of AR's unique philosophic perspective on architecture.

**March 13, 1936**

[*AR made the following notes on two great innovators in modern architecture: Louis Sullivan and Frank Lloyd Wright. Louis Sullivan (1856–1924) is widely regarded as the father of modern architecture and particularly of the skyscraper. He seems to have served as the concrete inspiration for the character of Henry Cameron. Frank Lloyd Wright (1869–1959) is famous for his strikingly original designs, done in a style he referred to as "organic architecture." In his basic architectural principles and in his fight for modern architecture against tradition, Wright served as a model for Howard Roark.*]

### Louis Sullivan

Fight against eclecticism and classicism for an original, creative style.
Ousted by inability to conform to the prevailing mode, the majority.
Started as draftsman. Then—partner. Then—independent.
Incident of church "corrected" by cheap architect. Neglect of civilities. Lack of commissions. Smaller firms appreciated him more than large ones.
Lack of social ability to get jobs. Arrogance with customers. Refusal to comply with their tastes.

### Frank Lloyd Wright

[*AR made the following notes on Wright's autobiography.*]
Apprenticeship in architects' offices. Originality and insubordination.
Resented by his fellow-beginners. Resentment against his originality, independence, lack of "social" qualities, and boss' favor, as well as obvious talent. Slander, ridicule, interference with work. Attempts to get him out.
Incident with [Daniel H.] Burnham. Attempt to bribe [Wright] into submission to prevailing styles and commercial success—on the very basis of the originality of his talent.
Opening his own office—big wish.
"American Institute of Architects," The A.I.A. (Check up on this and on all architectural associations and publications.)
Compromise on a house for money's sake. Subsequent shame at hearing the house praised.
First building praised, admired—and ridiculed. Requests for more houses like the "compromise" and his attempts to talk clients out of it.
Office taken with another architect—but not as partners.
Incident with Cecil [Corwin]—who quit because of envy for Wright's superior talent.

Speeches at clubs. Editorial comments. Antagonism of professionals. Ridicule—and yet notice and inept copying, distorting of his ideas. Gradual growth and development of his own individual style.

His principles in house building: simplicity, elimination of unnecessary details and trimmings; real fireplaces, flat roofs, abundance of windows, light, spaciousness. Elimination of different materials in favor of one. Flat, parallel planes. Straight, geometrical lines. "Organic" architecture. Antagonism to and ridicule of these houses. Calling them "heresy." Misunderstanding and confusion of his work with established eclectic styles.

Interior—spaciousness. Eliminating unnecessary walls and doors— "boxes within boxes."

"Plasticity"—building as a harmonious whole.

Engineers could not help with this structural continuity. Emphasis on the nature and individual qualities of building materials. New materials: steel, glass, concrete.

*Reactions of public to these new buildings:* Bankers refused to finance them. Mill men refused to work for them. Contractors misunderstood the plans. Some of them went broke. The worst type of contractor appeared on the scene. Interior decorators refused to work for owners—because architect had to okay everything.

Refused steadily to enter a competition. [He held that] the world has gained no building worth having by a competition because:

**1)** The jury is necessarily a hand-picked average. Some "constituency" must agree upon the "jury."
**2)** Therefore the first thing this average jury does is go through all the designs and throw out the best ones and the worst ones. This is necessary in order that the average may average upon something average.
**3)** Therefore any architectural competition will be an average upon an average in behalf of the average.
**4)** The net result is a building that is well behind the times before it is built.

Every architect entering a competition does so to win a prize. So he aims at what he conceives to be the common prejudices and predilections of the "jury." Invariably, the man who does this most accurately wins the competition.

Committee decisions, too, are seldom above mediocre unless the committee is "run" by some strong individual.

One such individual gave the commission for the Unity Temple to Wright.

[Wright:] "Why not, then, build a temple, not to God in that way—more sentimental than sense—but build a temple to man, appropriate to his uses as a meeting place, in which to study man himself for his God's sake?"

All artistic creation has a philosophy. The first condition of creation.

Hard work on coordinating minor features with the whole. (This coordination of details to the whole—isn't that the same as plot construction in accordance with your theme?)

Interiors expressed in exteriors—"the living motif of the architecture."

Hardest of an architect's trials: to show his work, first time, to anyone not entirely competent, perhaps unsympathetic. . . .

At this moment the creative architect is distinctly at a disadvantage as compared with his obsequious brother of the "styles." His brother can show his pattern-book of "styles," speak glibly of St. Marks at Venice and of Capella Palatine, impress the no less craven clients by a brave show of erudite authorities—abash them.

But the architect with the ideal of an organic architecture at stake can talk only principle and sense. His only appeal must be made to the independent thought and judgment of his client. The client, too, must know how to think from generals to particulars. How rare it is to go into court where that quality of mind is on the bench! This architect has learned to dread personal idiosyncrasy—offered him three times out of five as substitute for such intelligence.

Fight to persuade the committee. One dumbbell with stupid criticisms, objections, and doubts is always present and dissenting.

Contractors bid after the plans are approved. Most of them refuse—because it is too new, too much of a risk. Those that do bid charge twice too much. No one really wants it. A contractor is needed to "rescue ideas, to participate in creation."

Congratulations after the Temple opened.

[Wright] does not believe in ancient traditional church building—because traditional religion itself is dead. (This is important for architecture as a reflection of the architect's philosophy.)

He gets a commission because the clients saw in his houses "the countenances of principle."

Lack of general response to his work after a period of intensive labor, day and night.

Architect calls in sculptors and artists. Architect—the master of them all.

He sometimes slept "on a pile of shavings" right at the construction works.

A female model posing for sculptors right in a shanty on the building site.

Unions interfering and stopping construction on frequent occasions, on silly pretexts.

Cheap additions, such as a glowing electric sign, that ruin the architect's idea. [. . .]

[Wright:] "Equivocal conduct hurts ten times more those who practice it than those it is practiced upon."

The "eternal triangle"—architect, owner, contractor. Owner often takes contractor's side against the architect.

Owner decides to build and make changes without consulting architect.

Usually it is necessary to defeat the contractor's advice to the client.

He had no real organization. "My office is me."

"I don't know why houses have so much grief concealed in them, if they try to *be* anything at all and try to live as themselves. But they do. Like people in this I suppose."

"The greater the idea, the greater the banker animosity."

Owner choosing contractor and insisting on him.

The architect has to defend the construction of his building continually.

"Where creative effort is involved there are no trivial circumstances. The most trivial of them may ruin the whole issue. Eternal vigilance is the only condition of creation in architecture."

Sullivan—ruined by provincial prejudice against his personal habits. "A genius? That term damned him as it was intended to."

The rarest and most fortunate occurrence in any architect's life: opportunity, ideal site, and a man who understands.

Dangers of construction: building settling because of too great a weight.

Foreign exhibit of photographs, drawings, models. Lectures. Dinners given in architect's honor.

Remark about the worthlessness of courthouse in Milwaukee. Storm in the press. Furious enmity. Even attempts at arrest on trumped-up charge. But big lecture and enthusiastic audience nevertheless.

Speaks at Architect's dinner in New York. Alone and against the majority of speakers. Obvious resentment of others.

[Wright] gets his houses accepted by convincing the client that he (the architect) is right, by explaining the truth clearly.

Other architects try to make Wright out as "difficult," because he does not "stay in line with them," even though he has had no troubles with his clients. Work came to him, instead of his going out after work. He "stayed in line" with his principles, not with salesmanship.

"Eclectics haven't much artist-conscience and what little they have is guilty."

His ideals: The importance of interior space expressed in the exterior, "inside" and "outside" as one. The use of glass to this end. Open buildings as contrast to the "caves" of ancient architecture. "Freedom" substituted for "fear." Steel construction and "plasticity" unknown to ancient architecture. A variety of new materials—each to determine the style of the building it is used on. "Organic" ornament to express the meaning of the whole, not merely for looks and trimming effects.

No more buildings of one material to imitate another (such as: steel made to look like masonry, etc.).

Buildings, just as airplanes, steamships and automobiles, should look like what they are, be what they are.

**February 23, 1937**

Lewis Mumford, *Sticks and Stones*.

Rather strained attempts to connect architecture with sociology, particularly in explaining the prevalence of certain styles at certain times by economic conditions, à la Marx. (The classic style in America because of its "imperial" atmosphere is in keeping with the "imperial" mood of the rising capitalists.) Good for Toohey.

**February 27, 1937**

Arthur Woltersdorf, *Living Architecture*.

The smugness, stodginess, dull commonplaceness of officially recognized architectural authorities, as exemplified in most essays of this book. The only exception—the only architect with something definite and fresh to say—is a pupil of Frank Lloyd Wright and *not* a member of the American Institute of Architects, as are most of the others. Characteristic of officialdom when it tries to "go modern": staleness, a reluctant repetition of the truths proclaimed by the real modern [architects], which are too obvious to be disclaimed and are therefore embraced half-heartedly, mechanically, without conviction, consistency or fire, evidencing an amazing ability to make even a new truth sound like a bromide; at the same time, obviously no desire to accept this modernism as a whole, a struggling and pulling to compromise, to incorporate the old traditions with the new or to explain the old lamely with new formulas borrowed from modernism. A magnificent display of reluctance to say anything positive, important, fundamental or vigorous. A great deal of talk about meaningless details, a re-chewing of trivialities, with all great fundamental principles ignored, with no real faith to proclaim, only a great show of cheap erudition and pseudo-importance in detailed knowledge of many nothings.

A great emphasis on "public spirit," on duty to the community, on being only "servants and expressors of national spirit, general spirit, mood of the people, trend of the times," etc.

Typical quotation: "The problem is to know the past and still be free to speak in a language that will hold the man in the street, so that he will think and talk about architecture as his wife does about her favorite movie star."

Incidental question: a librarian writing about library building insists that libraries must be made to look as accessible to the public as possible—to "bring the library nearer to the people." "Spacious and inviting entrances are placed at grade level, close to the public thoroughfare, with as few steps as possible between the pedestrian and the building." This may be quite sound in relation to library architecture, but the question it raises, in a more general sense, is this: is it advisable to spread out all the conveniences of culture before people to whom a few steps up a stair to a library is a sufficient deterrent from reading? Hasn't that something to do with the attitude behind general education for those better left illiterate?

The advocates of "housing projects" rave about a hideous example of a huge block of buildings all alike, with a series of windows like those in a jail, where your feeling of an individually owned house ("my home is my castle") is reduced to owning three dots of windows out of a myriad of identical bee-hive cells. (This is to be advocated by Toohey—just right for him.)

Another typical quotation—regarding the expression of "true American" architecture:

In experience and expression each individual will contribute some factor common to all. The sum total of these common experiences and modes of expression is the common denominator, the factor which dominates the race or the community; which distinguishes it and individualizes it. The development and enrichment of this factor is not imitation but worthy progression. [. . .]

Climate, Geography, Race, Nationalism must impress and inspire the architect in this desired, if not at once forthcoming, expression. The architect cannot stand alone by himself ignoring the workings of these four great influencing factors, stand alone and endeavor merely to express himself, and achieve an art which shall be so generally and widely expressive of fundamentals as to last and become a permanent influence, as permanent and as lasting in effect as the social organism of which he is part. If he is apart from, rather than a part of, the social order neither the artist nor his words will persist.

(Great for Toohey!)

Isn't the exact opposite true of Frank Lloyd Wright? Doesn't the genius and the new always come as opposite to the "spirit of the community" and have to fight like hell against it? I grant that the genius will not be known and will not influence the general culture unless he is fairly widely recognized. Isn't it then a question of *forcing* that recognition on the community (through the recognition of a few leaders), rather than a question of the genius "expressing" his community—whatever that is? If a genius passes unnoticed, the loss is humanity's, more than his. There must have been many great innovators that never influenced culture because they were not recognized in time. So much the worse for culture. Culture is not the supreme arbiter, always right by the mere fact that it took a certain turn and not another. It is largely chance, the result of the eternal fight between man and masses. And if we judge men in their own time and reality, which is all that counts to men, let them be judged by their intrinsic value, not by their relation to a vague accident called "culture." A work of art is great by what it is, not by how many cheap imitations it has created in its assimilation into a "cultural" movement. ("The vermin of the cultured that feasts on the sweat of every hero"—Friedrich Nietzsche.)

Probably sensing something of the above, [Woltersdorf] says a little later:

Now the artist, especially the architect, not only should reflect the tendencies and right movements of the age (who's to determine the "right movements?" AR)—he should direct them. He should even inaugurate them. He sometimes does; but his work is ineffectual until the society which he is trying to interpret to itself rises to a plane of right consciousness and recognizes itself and its desires in the ideal which the artist is seeking to advance.

(More for Toohey.)

When will this sort of pap stop? What precisely does society recognize and what are its desires—in the sentence above? This kind of vague metaphysical hooey is at the bottom of all "social-consciousness" theorizing. Why assign profundity and ideals where there are none? Why not say honestly that an architect must lead and make the society "rise to a plane of right consciousness," without flattering the mob monster by making it, in some vapid, non-descript way, the inspiration and master of its leader?

This book is a good example of what happens to the ideas of geniuses when "adopted" by lesser [men], of how dead, devitalized, dull, common and flat a great idea can become in average, official, "communal" hands.

---

Darcy Braddell, *How to Look at Buildings*.

Somewhat similar psychological type to the preceding book, in the sense of a desperate struggling for the old along with reluctant concessions to the new. But a type of mentality and attitude that is less vicious and pompous than the preceding. A mild, esthetic mind trying, at least, to be fair. Not fighting vigorously against modernism and giving it its due, when unavoidable. The [concessions to modernism are] done with obvious reluctance and in terms of the old, applying old standards and appearing to justify it on the basis of the old, while actually trying to justify the old by the principles of the new. Frequent recurrence of such statements as: "Even the modernists can't escape well-established fundamentals of architecture, which they have to share with the classics," etc. No viewpoint at all. A thoroughly polite and Milquetoastish sitting on the fence. Plus a yes-man complex, prone to admire indiscriminately every established authority. (Such as the author's silly admiration for [Christopher] Wren's towers, and his weak excuses for their ugliness, his even going so far as to call them "original architecture.")

Not the type to violently oppose a new movement, but certainly not one to encourage or approve it, and certainly not until it is well established; then, perhaps, a little approval, grudgingly, without enthusiasm, in a dull, devitalized manner, strictly formalistic and superficial, not recognizing all the fundamental principles, but carping on details, just as one does about the old eclectic architecture, making a new sort of super-eclecticism, a mixture of eclecticism and modernity.

This is not Toohey's type, but a good source for Toohey, a good type for the minor, work-a-day "art critic," a mass of which makes a good background for Toohey and leaves the field open to him.

Typical quotation:

One thing is quite certain, nobody is ever going to make a simpler (in the true meaning of the word) column cap and base than are already provided by the Classic Orders! Yet it is equally certain that their use is being discarded more and more every day because they are not modern. What, then, is going to take their place? The "flight from the orders" argues a flight from a culture we have all been brought up to revere. For the orders are not a worn-out decorative motif, but part of the language of architecture. They represent ordered expressions of thought.

Also typical is his assertion that modern architecture is merely "dressmaking," only dressing a structural skeleton, but having nothing to do with real structure. This is how much he understands about modern architecture—which, above all, *is* structural, as compared to the "dress-making" of Renaissance and subsequent architecture. [. . .]

Characteristic of this type is a total lack of basic principle or conviction. Vagueness. A great many contradictions. Details and petty measurements for criticism, instead of a complete, unified system of thought.

**March 2, 1937**

C. H. Whitaker, *Rameses to Rockefeller.*

In reference to Louis Sullivan: when the *Journal of the American Institute of Architects* published Sullivan's *Autobiography of an Idea*, many people demanded that the Board of Directors stop its publication. The members of the Board refused "even though some of them were a little fearful." (This was in 1924.)

About Sullivan:

Your country has passed you by. That was what had happened, and I knew, as you read, what the passing by had meant and how you had been hurt. It was plain then that you had been crucified and lacerated, because you challenged the humbug of the art you loved. In every word that you read, I could feel the weight of the tragedy. But, like the voice of the captain rising above the wreckage, I could also feel the exaltation within you that no tragedy could crush. You had seen! You had beheld! You had known the rightness that has forever belonged to craftsmen. You had heard and accepted the everlasting challenge! Ah, that was a wonderful evening, Louis, and I never told you how I felt about it. I guessed that you guessed that I knew. You must have known.

**March 12, 1937**

Same book.

Real pearls of wisdom for Toohey:

It is so easy to give credit for the Parthenon to the men whose names have come down to us by the historical method—Pericles, Callicrates, Ictinus, and Phidias, whom Plato called "a wise stone-cutter"—and so easy to forget, by the same very defective historical method, the long procession of building craftsmen who, year by year, played with their changing ideas of form and proportion as succeeding variations passed the ultimate test by which like and dislike were determined.

Had it not been for this great unsung host of stone-carvers and stone hewers, there could have been no Parthenon. It did not spring from any single mind. It was not born of any single concept. Rather was it the fruit of a slowly ripening experience over a century of trial and error. Year after year the builders studied the result of their labor, looked at it, lived with it, and noted what pleased them and what did not. . . .

Thus the historical method of giving credit for a building to some particular person seems ungenerous. No building ever had a single author. One cannot point to a single feature of building, anywhere, and say that it first appeared in this building, or that. The whole historical method, in so far as it applies to credit and authorship, rests only on the concept of society as a struggle for individual glory and reward. It completely denies . . . the endless procession of workers and thinkers, each making his humble contribution.

Could anything be sweeter and clearer?

**March 28, 1937**

Same book.

As a slogan for Toohey's idea of architecture:

As a beginning—for the builders who shall at last set to work for a society that is resolved to build a civilization—what could be a better mark to aim at than for everyone a fine and spacious room, sun-lighted or sun-shaded, as one might choose!

Fine degree of selective freedom!

This is the best book for all the lying, evasions, and sophistries of

Marxism as applied to architecture. Toohey's exact psychology at work. Always the attempt to give credit to the masses. In Greek architecture—by pulling facts in by the ears, as in the quotation above [i.e., the March 12 entry]. In Gothic—great praise, because it is the anonymous architecture of collective workers. Blaming all the faults of the post-Renaissance architecture on the rise of the individual architect. Phony examples of exploitation as expressed in buildings, such as this explanation of the Parthenon columns: "[T]he temple was meant to advertise certain ideas that would inspire respect and make people pray and go to war without too much murmuring. . . ."

A dishonest, disgraceful, stinking book.

———◦———

Claude Bragdon, *Architecture and Democracy*.

An idiotic, unimportant book. The only thing of interest is the author's combination of communistic leanings and great talk about the "Long Denied" with a silly mysticism that denies reason completely and puts the "heart" above the "brain." Typical process of subconscious adjustment to purpose.

Use this. Show the process, particularly obvious in the Catholic Church and in Communism, through which all convictions, even on points [that appear to be] far from the main issue, are subconsciously, in individuals, and deliberately, in ideologies, constructed in such a way as to support the main issue somewhere, in its consequences or in its hidden roots. The "style" of ideologies.

A good example of sheer drivel, of putting one's point across where it does not belong, is Bragdon's interpretation of Sullivan's Prudential building:

> One feels that here democracy has at last found utterance in beauty; the American spirit speaks, the spirit of the Long Denied. This huge, rectangular bulk is uncompromisingly practical and utilitarian; these rows on rows of windows, regularly spaced and all of the same size, suggest the equality and monotony of obscure, laborious lives; the upspringing shafts of the vertical piers stand for their hopes and aspirations, and the unobtrusive delicate ornament which covers the whole with a garment of fresh beauty is like the very texture of their dreams.

This is the way Toohey criticizes buildings.

A sample of collectivist-mystic balderdash: "Now materialism is the very negation of democracy, which is a government by *demos*, the over-soul. . . ."

Glorification of the masses as against genius:

But in every field of aesthetic endeavor appears here and there a man or a woman with unclouded vision, who is able to see in the flounderings of untrained amateurs the stirrings of *demos* from its age-long sleep. These, often forsaking paths more profitable, lend their skilled assistance, not seeking to impose the ancient outworn forms upon the Newness, but by a transfusion of consciousness permitting it to create forms of its own. . . .

His (the architect's) problem, in other words, is not to interpret democracy in terms of existing idioms, be they classic or romantic, but to experience democracy in his heart and let it create and determine its new forms through him. It is not for him to *impose*, it is for him to be *imposed upon*.

If he is at a loss to know where to go and what to do in order to be played upon by these great forces let him direct his attention to the army and the army camps. Here the spirit of democracy is already incarnate. (!!!)

A great truth, not at all in the way the author intended!

**June 4, 1937**

Alfred C. Bossom, *Building to the Skies*.

The author praises the pseudo-classic architects of the Chicago World's Fair of 1893. He shows his eclecticism, praising the "modern" skyscraper, [while he is] devoid of true architectural convictions, of all inner fire or integrity—"anything goes with the fashion of the moment." In the list of great American architects of the early skyscrapers—not a word about Sullivan. (Nor about Frank Lloyd Wright.) Yet the author exhibits a plate of a junky building that got first prize in 1921. Typical instance of accommodating mediocrity.

He praises women's interest in the architecture of the home. (That's the reason for the monstrosities we have!) Some architects will not work for a woman client, regardless of the fee. (Good for them!)

Relatively simple regulations for American architects as compared to England. *(Check on this.)*

According to the author, an American architect has to be a walking bureau of business information. He has to advise the client as to what type of building to erect on a certain site or even choose the site; what the prospects of the neighborhood are, how large a building it can sustain and make it pay, etc. (He has to consult the American Telephone Company that always knows all prospects.) Every skyscraper-building office has one or two employees, technical advisers on this point. Author refused to build a bigger building than the location warranted; he felt his reputation would be hurt if he were associated with a beautiful building which turned out to be a commercial failure. (??) (*Check up on this by all means. Is this the general attitude? Where does the creative instinct come in on this?*)

Investors sometimes ask an architect to select a site and tell them what to build on it.

Working practice of the author: after the site and the type of building is approved, he "settles all the fundamental problems of the new building himself," then turns the problem over to his designers who *compete* for the actual design of the building. (!) (*Check up on this! Is it the usual practice? Is the businessman really the boss who hogs the credit, while the creative designer is only a minor employee? Is it usual or is it just a typical instance of second-hand practice? Good for John Eric Snyte.*)

Even the smallest firm building skyscrapers employs 20 to 25 draftsmen. A larger firm would have 60 on its permanent staff and double this number during a rush. The head architect travels a great deal on inspections. (Spends ten nights a month in a sleeping car.) A regular [payroll] of about $15,000 a week. Permanent overhead—$250,000 a year.

Preliminary drawings for a small (million-dollar) building take about two months. Every tiny detail is included. Separate sets made for the main sections of the job. In all, there are hundreds of them.

From the moment he starts on his drawings, the architect is in constant touch with structural engineers, contractors, manufacturers and suppliers of materials, and the heads of thirty-two trades that will work under him. Free exchange of opinions and information. Cooperative spirit. Open publicity about everything on job. Drawings and specifications posted in building, so that every worker can read them. Contractors bid for the job. The winner, in turn, opens the bidding for sub-contractors.

A "cost-plus" contract allows the contractor the cost of the building plus a fixed fee for himself (this is apart from the architect's commission); anything the contractor saves is split between himself and the owner. This helps to save in buying materials, as the contractor is most experienced and acquainted with the market.

*Typical and valuable instance of mob-spirit:*

[Raymond Hood is] an architect of the modern type who preaches and practices cooperation. He has no use for the architect who "shuts himself up in his office to make a design and then sends it out to a contractor to build or to an engineer to fit up with the plumbing, heating and steel as best he can." Nor has he any use for the architect who "goes up to a Communion on Mount Sinai and hands the results to the owner, the engineers and the public." In his view, as in my own, the best designs, at any rate for the building of skyscrapers, come from "a group of minds in which the architect is one link in the chain."

So speaks the mob. The results—the "Daily News Building" [designed by Hood] and [Bossom's] buildings—speak for themselves: they are the ugliest, flattest, most conventional, meaningless, unimaginative and uninspiring buildings in the book.

This type of architect works "by conference," in which all parties concerned take part, discuss his drawings, make suggestions, etc. (A Hollywood story conference.) The result is a collective creation—"an average on an average." (This method and these convictions, absolving the architect of all creative responsibility, are good for *Peter Keating*. Check up on just how much conferring and cooperation is done by an architect such as Frank Lloyd Wright.)

Good touch: workers who steal rides on trains and get tools out of a pawnshop in some town where the architect is working—in order to work again under him. [. . .]

———◦———

The author talks a great deal about daring, courage and leaving the way free for new inventions. Yet—he is an eclectic artistically. His "newness" applies only to the technical, scientific side of new methods and materials, *not* to new esthetic ideas. No daring, courage or novelty in his architectural designs. No talk at all in the book of the artistic problem of skyscrapers. No esthetic convictions.

But a great deal of talk about cooperation. Let's get together. The skyscraper cannot be the product of one man. It is all collective. A great many attacks on "separatism." [He is] a second-rater and second-hander, following popular trends, praising engineering and Greek orders in skyscrapers with equal ease, naturally anxious for everyone to share ideas, in order to pick up what he can pick up. (Beware of those too eager for sharing—in wealth or in ideas; they're the ones who know that they'll get more than they'll give in such a pool. Those with much to give do not talk of sharing—they do not need it.)

*This author is just right for Peter Keating.*

————◦————

An important side-idea to bring out [regarding] the building of a skyscraper: If led by a strong personality, superior in knowledge and talent to the others, representing the complete authority and final judgment in all matters, with a pyramid of ranks under him, widening toward the bottom—the perfect organization with the proper spirit of cooperation and discipline results, and the created building is a magnificent monument. If cooperation means equality, with everyone's voice as good as the next fellow's and all the fingers in the pie—an eclectic mess results. (Check up on how, through what exact steps and means, these two methods work in practice.)

**June 10, 1937**

Matlock Price, *The ABC of Architecture.*

The best architectural training is to be had in the Architectural Department of one of the large Universities, or in a Technical School.

"In the University it is possible to begin architectural training in the first year and carry it on, with other and more general studies, through the four years of college." After this, it is very desirable to take from two to four years post-graduate work, specializing entirely in architecture. (Check up on all this.)

The author also states that many architects consider a year or two of European travel as the best preparation. (Rubbish!)

University program:

First year: history of architecture, drawing, "thorough training in the Classic Orders," simple problems of architectural design, freehand drawing, a general fine arts course.

Second year: making "measured drawings," courses in perspective, shades and shadows, simple building construction, more advanced design problems.

The next two years—the same subjects carried still further in more advanced problems.

At the same time courses in higher mathematics.

Post-graduate work—design problems as advanced as the actual profession of architecture itself.

He may, at this stage, compete for a Traveling Scholarship which will pay his expenses for a year or two of special study in Europe, usually at the American Academy in Rome.

If the student intends to become the designer of important public buildings, he should spend a few years at the Ecole des Beaux Arts in Paris. (More rubbish!)

Because of their belief in the value of the Beaux Arts training, a group of New York architects who originally studied there, founded the "Society of Beaux Arts Architects" with a working studio, or atelier, where any ambitious architectural student may come and work on problems similar to those of the French Beaux Arts School, under the direction of the Beaux Arts architects themselves, who generously give their time to this work. And every year a "Paris Prize" is awarded, which sends its winner, with all expenses paid, to spend a year in the Ecole des Beaux Arts in Paris.

(Look into this. Sounds perfectly anti-Roark. Try to meet one of them. What prompts such a business?)

The step from draftsman to architect is seldom an easy one. In a small firm a draftsman may be taken into partnership, if his work is valuable; more likely if he can bring with him a "job"—"if through social connections he can develop a client." With money, he can buy himself into a partnership.

In large offices, where it is more difficult, he may do work in his spare time, working at night or on holidays, if through some personal means he can get a building to design.

Sometimes, if two fellow draftsmen can get work of their own to do, they give up their jobs and set themselves up as architects. If they have no money they must be very economical. [They may set up] a small office, two drafting tables, bought second-hand, and do all their own work. While working on their first "job," they must do all they can to find another to follow up with.

"*Sometimes one plucky fellow alone* makes the jump from draftsman to architect in just this way."

———◦———

About this particular book: a commonplace, plodding little author, well-meaning, but completely conventional. To wit: the advice about the Beaux Arts School. Equal notice for classical revivals and Frank Lloyd Wright. "Anything goes." Scholarly and without convictions about it all.

Naively funny descriptions of all the jumbled eclectic adaptations of architectural styles in America. Such sentences as "the best French chateau in America," etc. After listing the English, French, Dutch, Spanish and Italian buildings in this country, he adds quite seriously: "The Floridians have been even more adventuresome in architecture, achieving surprisingly successful adaptations of North African architecture, in stucco houses that are extraordinarily suggestive, in their essentials, of the houses of Tunis or Algiers." (!)

Note: The peculiar preoccupation of architects such as this author and the previous one with "proportions," "moldings," "scholarly faithfulness to Classic examples," etc. Worrying about every little thing, except the main one—the composition and its meaning as a whole. Isn't it like the people who worry greatly about fine points of "style" and grammar in literature, without caring what the writing is about? Again, the "how" against the "what." (Yet, the "what" determines everything else, just as the end determines the means, not vice versa. I do not intend that the end should justify lousy means, either. The "how" should always be worthy of the "what," but determined by it.)

**July 12, 1937**

Le Corbusier, *Towards a New Architecture*.

He claims that the most beautiful forms are the simplest geometrical forms, the easiest to see. (Danger of over-simplification of modern architecture here.) Thus he considers Classic, Egyptian, Roman and some Renaissance architecture good, but Gothic bad, or at least not pure architecture. (Lack of the true principle of Frank Lloyd Wright here.)

Architecture is the first manifestation of man creating his own universe. [...]

There is one profession and one only, namely architecture, in which progress is not considered necessary, where laziness is enthroned, and in which the reference is always to yesterday....

He claims that the terrible houses of today destroy the family, by being unlivable. Advises modern houses to save family life.

He claims that we must establish definite standards for architecture, in order to elaborate these into perfection. (Danger of a new standardization and new set of rules for all architects to follow—just as in the following of old styles.)

Elementary satisfactions—decoration. Higher satisfactions—mathematics. The Parthenon and the automobile—both products of selection.

We must not assert with too much conviction that the masses give rise to their man. A *man* is an exceptional phenomenon occurring at long intervals, perhaps by chance, perhaps in accordance with the pulsation of a cosmography not yet understood. [. . .]

Art is this pure creation of the spirit which shows us, at certain heights, the summit of the *creation* to which man is capable of attaining. And man is conscious of great happiness when he *feels that he is creating*.

Advocates planned towns. (What will Roark say about that? Give it some thought.)

Interesting book, but too much emphasis on mass-production houses. Beautiful theories—but in practice, in the illustrations of the man's work, too much standardization, too much reliance on the principle of "the beauty of modern tools," not enough of that superior architectural beauty which the author himself advocates.

---

David Gray, *Thomas Hastings, Architect.*

The **most** disgusting book that I have read to date. The perfect picture of everything that stands against Roark. To be used plenty, for Peter Keating and all the others, particularly for John Eric Snyte. The perfect set-up of what has made modern architecture impossible. The perfect crystallization of the conventional architect, at the head of the profession, the kind responsible for Architectural Societies and all that prevents real creative genius and fights not to give it a chance. Smug, arrogant in a vulgar way, vain, self-contented, bitter and nasty toward all who are not like them, attacking genius with a phony, angry contempt, but without reasons or explanations, attacking only with ugly adjectives and curses, but never mentioning any valid grounds. [They] theorize in empty talk, seeming to accept all the best teachings of modern architecture and then distorting them by their own petty, silly, preposterous sophistries.

Only actual quotations can do justice to the picture of such an architect as Hastings:

The man and the artist seemed inexplicably detached one from the other. So to speak, one never met them both at the same time; and meeting the one gave little clue to the nature of the other.

As artist he was single-purposed, concentrated, intense, withdrawn into himself, obeying the mystic guidance of his genius with an almost ruthless energy and devotion. As a man in his human relations his qualities were those of a lovable child, generous, affectionate, sunny-natured. It was his good fortune never to have grown up in a worldly sense. He believed in everybody, was disposed to like everybody, was troubled by no spiritual questionings. He found the world the best of all possible worlds, and that, though he had worked his way through it from bottom to top by his own talent and industry. In this he was truly an amazing example of the preserving grace of simplicity and love.

### Sic!!!
Such damning twaddle is presented in the book in the spirit of the greatest compliment. It speaks for itself—for the man and also for those who admired him.

Hastings had a "salon" that gathered for a "business man's lunch." "Charming" informality, "humor" and "quaintness." Just a nice, big show to yell to the world: "See what lovely, regular fellows we are!" A description of Hastings' entrance into one of these gatherings:

She stopped him with the observation that he never had had an idea except to build his clients a fire house if they ordered a dog kennel. It was their habitual play together and Hastings went on with his part, sputtering protestingly, calling on someone to protect him. As he peered, blinking through his pince-nez and recognized first one friend then another, he gave exclamations of delight and went the rounds with his greetings, pouring out affectionate extravagances, wringing hands, holding Miss Marbury's and begging her to elope with him.

Lovely? Just a good back-slapper that knew damn well how to get along with his fellow men. It must also be noted that the struggle "from bottom to top" mentioned in the previous quotation was in reality from the security of an established family to his first jobs through the pull and protection of his family's friends.

Some more about the lunches:

Hastings in this milieu was like a boy out of school: gay, irresponsible, affectionate, charming. His old friends all called him "Tommy" and chaffed him incessantly. It was characteristic of the relation between him and those who were fond of him, and he enjoyed it. At each new and affectionate insult he would rock with laughter and mock indignation.

It is characteristic all right.
Hastings entertaining a guest at lunch:

It was characteristic of him to make much of the stranger and put him at his ease. First he produced a wire puzzle—he was habitually buying such things from street vendors—and challenged her to take off a ring which was apparently irremovable. When she had given it up, he held the thing below the table with an air of mystery and triumphantly produced it in two pieces. Then he told her his story of the father who asked his advice as to whether his son should embrace architecture or dentistry. At this Dunne observed that if Hastings' father had consulted a good architect, Tommy might now have been a good dentist.

Shaking with laughter, Hastings went on to explain to [his female guest] that no dentist could have the anxieties of an architect; that when he was a beginner he was always afraid that his houses were going to fall down but now when he saw them again he was afraid that they weren't.

Such wit!
Contrast this—if the mere rapprochement of the two in one thought is not too much of a sacrilege—with the chastity of a Howard Roark. [. . .]
No early signs of his [aptitude for] architecture, except a "talent for drawing." At seventeen, he gave up his preparation for college and entered the offices of a firm of furniture makers and interior decorators, as student and draftsman. His first solo assignments were rooms to redecorate. He attended a "Sketch Club," heard talk of the Paris Ecole des Beaux Arts and decided to go there. Went to Paris at age twenty. He was "affectionate, social, fun-loving, and boyishly exuberant. . . . Though very young he appeared to escape those sentimental and passionate predilections which blind the mind to work of equal merit but of a different kind." He liked everything. No ideas of his own, no positive taste, no artistic, creative convictions. The above quotation is also given in the book as a compliment.

He studied at the Ecole for four years. Returning to America, at age 24, he entered the office of McKim, Meade and White as a draftsman. Here he met John M. Carrere, another Ecole man, and their friendship led to the forming of a partnership a year later. Hastings did the designing and Carrere handled the business side. His first big commission, which warranted his going into business for himself, was for a hotel in Florida, given to him by a friend and parishioner of his father. He built the hotel in the Spanish Renaissance style.

Hastings' opinions:

At any given point in this historic evolution he saw the architect building in the manner which his own period had devised rather than selecting styles from the past. Architecture, therefore, had ever been modern and of its own time.

Fine, but here is the conclusion:

He maintained that as far as modern architecture could have a name and recognized style, it must be Renaissance; for our life and civilization were still motivated by the forces which brought about the Renaissance. Therefore, the modern architect must be logically a Renaissance architect and such he conceived himself to be.

Best example of sophistry I've ever heard. [*Ralston Holcombe expresses this view in the novel.*]

In 1897 (at the age of 37) he won the competition for the construction of the New York Public Library. He wanted to make it more monumental than the original utilitarian plan.

The measure of this determination and tenacity is the fact that he wrung upwards of nine million [dollars] from a not overwilling city government, instead of two and one half million. . . . Its Renaissance elevation was to him equally logical and essentially modern. As he saw it, the aesthetic treatment lay inevitably in those principles of design and ornament developed since the revival of learning and the arts. . . . How the self-styled modernist who condemns this work as academic, who denies the heritage of the past and exalts originality above beauty, would have conceived an appropriate monumental repository for the printed record of man's intellectual achievement is an interesting though perhaps not important speculation.

Here speaks arrogant mediocrity. Note the constant attacks on originality both from Hastings and from his enthusiastic admirer, the author of this book. Such little phrases as "exalting originality above beauty." Nothing is ever said about originality that *is* beauty. [. . .]

During the years of work on the Library, Hastings had more than two hundred other commissions. He specialized in "monumental" works. Built a great deal for Fairs and Expositions. The most important of his works in this period was the New Theater in New York. He also won this in a competition. (Remember what Frank Lloyd Wright said about competitions! This is the best supporting evidence.)

"As he matured and gained authority, the teacher and evangelist in him became more evident." He went to great lengths in preaching his architectural ideas. He also went heavily for "public service." In 1910 President Taft appointed him one of the original members of the National Commission of Fine Arts. "This body was to exercise a general supervision of the National Government's activities in the field of aesthetics and in particular of the architectural development of the National Capital." (A fine example of what happens when National Governments go in for art.) In this capacity, Hastings had a great deal to do with the building of Washington, D.C. [. . .]

"He regarded architects who ignored tradition as uneducated, which was usually true, or as actuated by a frivolous and vain desire to be original at any cost." (Mediocrity going snobbish and on the defensive.) Speaking of a Renaissance architect, he said: "It would have been impossible for him actually to define the style of his own period. That is for us, his successors, to do." (Fine consciousness in creation!) An architect, he goes on to explain, [should] study the best that he can find in the past and use it to solve his modern problems. (Very creative!)

Hastings at fifty:

In 1922 he was awarded the King's Medal by the Royal Institute of British Architects, bestowed hitherto upon but two Americans, Richard Hunt and Charles McKim. He was a fellow of the American Institute of Architects, President of the Society of Beaux Arts Architects, member of the Architectural League of New York and of the American Academy of Arts and Letters. He had served seven years as a member of the National Fine Arts Commission. France had awarded him the Legion of Honor. He was continually consulted by the municipal authorities of New York in regard to its architectural projects and executed various public commissions.

*Here* is the complete picture of society and collectivism at work. Who gave medals and titles to Louis Sullivan or Frank Lloyd Wright? All this was going on in the same years when Sullivan was dying of a broken heart because his country would not recognize him, not even give work to him. If this doesn't damn society, what can? [. . .]

Hastings' views:

How near can we come to determining what is modern architecture, or what is the proper style of architecture for our time? Surely it should not be the deplorable creation of the would-be style-inventor, or that of the illogical architect, living in one age and choosing a style from another.

The important and indisputable fact is not generally realized that from prehistoric times until now each age has built in only one style of architecture. In each successive style there has always been the distinctive spirit of the contemporaneous life from which its roots drew nourishment. But in our time, contrary to all historic precedent there is a confusing variety of styles. Why should we not have one characteristic style, expressing the spirit of our own life? Has the world of art always been in the wrong until today? Does our actual work warrant the conceit of the assumption that we know more about it than has ever been known at any time or by all artists for the last three thousand years? History and the law of development alike demand that we build as we live.

(Note the awful borrowing of modern ideas, only to lead up to such conclusions as he makes.)

He further claims that architecture always follows the political, religious, economic and other cultural developments of history, i.e., it follows the "spirit of the age." And then:

Therefore, before we can in any way indicate what style properly belongs to our time, we must first realize our historic position and the distinctive characteristics of our civilization. What determining change have we had in the spirit and methods of life since the revival of learning and the Reformation to justify us in abandoning the Renaissance, or in reviving medieval art, Romanesque, Gothic, Byzantine, or any other style?

(What indeed? This passage beats them all!)

Out of these necessities of the times the Renaissance style was evolved, and around no other style have been accumulated such vast stores of knowledge and experience, under the lead of the great masters of Europe. Therefore, whatever we now build, whether church or dwelling, the law of historic development requires that it be Renaissance.

All branches of art have contributed to the embellishment of this style; no other is so thoroughly expressive of the artistic feeling of the age in which we live. . . .

We should study and develop the Renaissance and adapt it in our modern conditions and wants, so that future generations can see that it has truly interpreted our life. We can interest those who come after us only as we thus accept our true historic position and develop what has come to us. Without this we shall be only copyists or be making poor adaptations of what never was really ours.

(What a mental hodge-podge!)

And here comes the best of all: since the most practical solution is always the most beautiful, the gentleman claims that we should not concern ourselves with the practical. Just make it beautiful and it will hold. No need of mathematical calculations: if a pier is beautiful it will automatically be strong enough. Calculations are needed only for verification. (What are you going to do with a mind like that?)

> I believe in such calculations for purposes of verification, but in general the piers will be about as safe to build upon when studied by an educated architect as when calculated by engineers. . . . It is really architecture and well-proportioned masonry *versus* engineering and iron girders. Each has its use, but they are not interchangeable. Buildings have stood for centuries without a knowledge of modern engineering, solely because their plans were so well studied, so thoroughly artistic and beautiful, that constructive difficulties were avoided. . . .

He is at his most vicious when attacking the skyscraper on every point possible: esthetic, moral, interference with the value of the neighbor's property, depriving neighbors of light and air, traffic congestion, etc. Everything but the boll weevil. "There is no hope for any continuity of lines and simple regularity in domestic or privately owned buildings, which in any great city ordinarily form a beautiful background of a much needed monotony for its outstanding monuments, all of which together form the physical make-up of a great municipality." (It must be remembered here that he specialized in monuments.) With all the viciousness of the little man aroused, he runs to Mamma and demands laws against skyscrapers. He was a member of a two-man committee sent to Albany for that purpose. He demands taxation of skyscraper property, if he cannot get direct laws against them. He yelps that he is fighting not for esthetics, but for "justice." Justice to the little fellow, the small property owner, etc. Here is the anger of a mass-man, who has had his way too long and is furious when a new development, truly original and modern, triumphs in spite of him, and he cannot stop it no matter what he does. When the phony prestige built on cheap imitation and fraudulent loud talk about high art does not work any longer, he reverts to the one recourse of his type—the mass, i.e., the State. "There should be a law against it"—the cry of all cornered collectivists. Incidentally, he holds the cities of Europe as the ideal and would like to see New York resemble them, with all their old-fashioned restrictions on free building. [. . .]

With badly hidden resentment, he writes of originality in a contemptuous, skeptical way, evading the real question [by turning to] side-issues:

> Originality is only a natural and spontaneous effort to solve the practical conditions imposed upon an architect, and it is generally a good test of the merit of his design when it looks as though it has been done before, however different it may be from everything else. . . . When we consider originality, how often do we give credit where it really belongs? This is a fair question, not only in architecture, but in everything else, and yet, after all, what difference does it make?

He goes on to say that it is often impossible to determine who originated a certain thing or idea. Is this the point? Isn't it a guilty conscience speaking and rationalizing itself?

He attacks the critics. Demands that only professional architects be allowed to criticize architecture in writing. (And of course he and his pals will see to it that no architect can practice unless he is one of their kind.)

He attacks the engineers. "One danger in bridge-building is the engineer. In two cases out of three an engineer is employed. He sees the quantitative side rather than the qualitative point of view; he is apt to disregard the beauty of design." (Top of presumption.) Incidentally, if the practical is always beautiful, as he claims, why is it that the engineers do not achieve beauty? Or does this work only one way, his way, and not the other?

To sum it all up, I must not forget the words of the book's author in his preface: "The circumstance that, alone of the notable practicing architects of his generation, Hastings formulated in writing his philosophy of art, his ideals, convictions, and critical comment would seem to warrant the assumption of this responsibility (to publish the book)." *This* was written after Sullivan had published his *Autobiography of an Idea* and Frank Lloyd Wright had published his *Autobiography*. !!!

If I take this book and Wright's autobiography, there is practically the entire story of "Second-Hand Lives."

**November 22, 1937**

[*AR obtained a job with Ely Jacques Kahn, a prominent New York architect, for the purpose of learning about the daily activities of the profession. She worked in his office for six months as a filing clerk, typist, and general assistant. Later, she remarked about Kahn: "As a type, he was Guy Francon. He was so much the socially acceptable architect. He was abler than Francon, and he was modern—within careful limits. But his career was strictly dominated by Francon methods. And he had that manner—very elegant and charming."*]

*Notes taken in office.*

Frank Lloyd Wright used to advise his lady clients to wear gowns cut in lines and made of materials to harmonize with the houses he had created for them. (Interesting, even if slightly silly.)

Hugh Ferris: "The nature of the architectural forms and spaces which people habitually experience are potent factors in determining the nature of their actions, their emotions and their thoughts." (I think he's a phony, but this may be an interesting thought, if not carried too far into preposterousness.)

Swell touch of advance propaganda where it doesn't belong: Lewis Mumford in *The New Republic*, July 6, 1927, criticizes the defects of a building by blaming them on the expensiveness of the site.

It is as if even the great powers of industry and finance were not capable of controlling the forces by which they have sprung into being, as if they, too, must submit to the system which they nominally dominate.

Also—the building is "cold and hard"—a perfect symbol of modern business to Mr. Mumford. (!?!) (For Toohey.)

I find it (the building) more interesting because of its finely humanized interior than because of its stupendous bulk against the skyline of the city.

People, as well as cultures, have definite leitmotifs. Toohey's can be seen very readily here. Follow up its manifestations as it consistently, even if subconsciously, asserts itself. Roark's theme will be quite different. An important part of the book and the whole idea is *this subconscious themesong in the psychology of men. This base and all the practical results. There are only two fundamental bases: Roark's and Toohey's. Show them at work.*

———o———

Some unknown architect writing a "review" on the Squibb building declares flatly that "the building would have been better with color." Then, praising the white brick, he wishes for a law to make all New York buildings of white brick—"with colored trimmings." (Just pass a law to have all buildings done as he likes them! A sample of the "there-oughta-be-a-law" psychology.)

———o———

There has been an influx of socialites into the architectural profession. Careers are made solely on family connections. Important work is not given to architects of established fame and great achievement (generally recognized, practical achievement, not even an "arty" fame) because they "do not belong to the 400." It would be only natural for these people to be eclectics and to defend eclecticism as "culture"—because they have nothing else to offer.

———o———

The "society-playboy-architect" [Kenneth Murchison] who has never built anything, but is quite famous. Writes articles and makes great caustic fun of known architects. Specializes in staging the "Beaux-Arts" ball for the Beaux-Arts Society of Architects. (The dirtier and sexier the ball—the more funds for the educational work of the society. Great society!) [*Murchison was the model for Athelstan Beasely in the novel.*]

**November 28, 1937**

The following is from *Modern Concepts Concerning an Organic Architecture from the Work of Frank Lloyd Wright* (a proclamation sent by Wright to Kahn and autographed):

Individuality realized is the supreme attainment of the human soul, the master-master's work of art. Individuality is sacred. Let us dedicate this republic to multiply and elevate that quality in all art and architecture in all men in all life.

From the first issue of Frank Lloyd Wright's magazine *Taliesin* (which perished after the first issue from a lack of subscribers):

> We are all possessive and we are all egoistic. Ingloriously so, the present impasse can show. But neither "possessive" nor "egoistic" need be inglorious.
>     There is probably no suitable economic system not founded upon human egoism.
>     There is probably no great society where individual possession is not something to be respected and encouraged.
>     Nor is there a society worth considering where individuality is not the desirable cultural product of human life. . . .

[Wright's description] of organic architecture: "I got the sense of architecture as a reality no longer consisting in walls but inherent in the space within the walls to be lived in."

His amendment of Sullivan's formula: "Form follows function by way of the nature of materials."

He objects to making "good architecture" a matter of "good taste." (Interesting point. Not a matter of taste, but of incontrovertible principle—or do I understand it right? It should be so, and for all art, but what really is to be the principle, concretely and definitely and in a "legally" clear definition?)

From the article "Matter" by [Wright] in same issue: his enthusiasm for natural materials as potential weapons to use for his own creation. "And then I wish both mill and gravel heaps endlessly subject to my will." (*There* is a Roark emotion.)

> Gold and silver, lead and copper, tawny iron ore—all lying in drift to yield themselves up to roaring furnaces and to flow obedient to the hand of the master mind: all to become pawns to human will in the part human imagination plays in the human game we call civilization. . . . Wood, stone, pottery, glass, pigments, and aggregates, metals, gems cast into the industrious maw of mills, kilns or machines all to be worked to the architect's desire by human skill in labor. All this to his hand as the pencil in that hand makes marks that dispose of all as he dreams and as he wills.

**December 3, 1937**

From "Selling Architectural Services Today" by Rion Bercovici, in *Architecture*, April, 1933:

> In order to sell his services today, the architect must be able to talk to business men in their language. He must present his case from the angle of his ability to do work that will sell—merchandise, services, floor space, and anything that is housed. The architect cannot just be a merchant of even the most expert *architectural and building counsel*: he must be a merchant of *auxiliaries to salesmanship* in one form or another. To do this successfully he must adjust himself to the rhythm of the times.

(What horrors and crimes aren't always being excused by this great buck-passing to the "rhythm" or "spirit" of the times?)

Kahn's insistence on the "crafts"—too much. It is *not* part of architecture. He believes that: "There is a potential and currently neglected field for architects in industrial designing of fabrics, metals, and so forth." I'm not sure, but it seems to me that such a "field" would, to Frank Lloyd Wright, be what writing for Hollywood is to a writer.

Such advice to architects as telling a store how they can sell more groceries by changing their lighting. (Practical, perhaps, but is it architecture or window-dressing?)

———o———

A 1932 conference between four big architectural organizations discusses plans for training architects and admitting them to practice. A suggestion is made that the organizations themselves make the rules about admission of a young architect to practice. (Sic!—this is the organization to which Frank Lloyd Wright does *not* belong!)

One of the guys there expresses the hope that they should make "A.I.A. membership synonymous with qualifications for practice." (!!!)

Kahn explains that this was done to unify the license requirements in various states. Most states have examinations for licenses. When an architect has been in practice for 15 years, he can take an examination for a National License, which allows him to practice all over the U.S.A. Kahn's experience with this examination: the examining board was composed of "eminent" professors of architecture who had never put up a building.

The meeting of architectural organizations planned to pattern the licensing of architects on that of the Medical profession. (But medicine is not a creative art. Architecture is. Even at that, the American Medical Association has done much harm along with the good, such as the accusation often heard, possibly true, of keeping important discoveries off the market in order not to lose valuable practice. Wouldn't the same happen to architecture? And how safe is the distinction between purely educational tests and esthetic tests for the admittance to practice? What if this becomes an artistic dictatorship? (Check up.)

**December 5, 1937**

Let us decide once and for all what is a unit and what is to be only a part of the unit, subordinated to it. A building is a unit—all else in it, such as sculpture, murals, ornaments, are parts of the unit and to be subordinated to the will of the architect, as creator of the unit. No talk here of "the freedom of craftsmen" for sculptors and the like.

Also—*man* is a unit, not *society*. So that man cannot be considered as only a subordinate part to be ruled by and to fit into the ensemble of society.

(I really believe that a building is a unit, not a city, so that city planning should not control all buildings. Because a house can be the product of one man, but a city cannot. And nothing collective can have the unity and integrity of a "unit.")

Much of the confusion in "collectivism" and "individualism" could be cleared up if men [knew] what constitutes a unit, what is to be regarded as such.

As to the rules about this—my job of the future.

[*AR completed this "job of the future" in* Introduction to Objectivist Epistemology.]

———⚙———

From: *The Life-Work of Frank Lloyd Wright.*

Wright's principles of architecture (from his "In the Cause of Architecture," 1908): "Simplicity and Repose are qualities that measure the true value of any work of art." A building should have as few rooms as possible, taking account of its needs. Openings should be integral features of the structure, and if possible its ornamentation. Eliminate unnecessary details and ornaments. Avoid appliances or fixtures. Avoid too many pictures on walls. Most or all the furniture should be built in as a part of the whole scheme. "There should be as many kinds (styles) of houses as there are kinds (styles) of people and as many differentiations as there are different individuals." "A building should appear to grow easily from its site. . . ." Follow the color schemes of nature. "Bring out the nature of materials, always let their nature intimately into your scheme." "Buildings like people should be quiet, sincere, true and then withal as gracious and lovable as may be. Above all, integrity."

At the beginning of his career, Wright found exceptions to the prevalent eclecticism "chiefly among American men of business with unspoiled instincts and untainted ideals. A man of this type usually has the faculty of judging for himself."

At the beginning he had great trouble with everyone: workers, mills, financiers and all. Millmen in Chicago refused to work on a drawing bearing Wright's signature; contractors even cut [the name] out, but millmen recognized the work and refused to "hunt for trouble." (Incidentally, how about this for standardization? How can one get the "right" standardization? What protection is there within it for new ideas?)

He fought against the cheap imitators of his work, who copied his forms without understanding his principle, who made a new "style" and formula out of his forms.

---

Lewis Mumford [claims that] architects in America either pursue empty eclectic styles, or turn into engineers, consider utility only, devoid of art.

Wright differs from other modernists in that he wants to humanize the machine, make it serve artistic and human purposes, while the others want to make the machine and machine-principles dominant, eliminating all ornament entirely, all beauty and art, beyond the barest utility.

Mumford, with what seems to be the typical near-sightedness of a "pinkish" critic, has the presumption to ascribe Wright's lack of recognition in America to his being "regional"; Wright's buildings, according to Mumford, are suited only to prairie country, but not to all of the U.S. This is as much as Mr. Mumford can see. He goes so far as to say that Wright's buildings are "not completely successful." The problem of a new architecture will require, he claims, "the work of a hundred Wrights."

Typical: one critic in the book praises Wright highly, but claims that he is "personal," not "universal." Another one praises him particularly for being "universal." (Doesn't it all seem like a lot of rot? What is universal? Is there such a thing? Isn't it merely something individual copied by a great many people? As such, does it acquire any added value? Should there be any such conception as "universal" at all?)

Note how the "pinks" in art circles stuck to Wright like leeches, how they tried to use his fame and influence to their own ends, misinterpreting him entirely, ascribing to him their own pet sociological implications which he never intended or meant in a quite different way.

For instance, from Pieter Oud [a prominent Dutch architect]:

That which Wright desired, viz., an architecture based on the needs and the possibilities of our own time, satisfying its requirements of general economic feasibility, universal social attainableness, in general of social-aesthetic necessity, and resulting in compactness, austerity and exactness of form, in simplicity and regularity; that which he desired, but from which he continually escaped on the wings of his great visionary faculty, was tried in more actual consistency in cubism.

(Near enough, but how far! If I understand him, this is not at all what Wright preached and wanted and meant.)

H. H. Sullivan says that two great ideas confront each other in the world: the idea of tyranny, appealing to man's fear, and the idea of freedom, appealing to man's courage. [He says] we now have mental slavery, even though physical slavery is gone. But the idea of freedom is awakening, freedom of each individual's own expression. (All this is fine, but what is this freedom and who threatens it? I wouldn't call it democracy, as Sullivan always called it. Didn't he really mean individualism?)

Sullivan is opposed to all abstract philosophy (Platonism, Neo-Platonism, German Transcendentalism) as sterilizing life. (Wonder if he means what I would mean by this?)

**December 6, 1937**

Raymond Hood states that "architecture is the business of manufacturing adequate shelter for human activities" and asserts that this conception imposes only one restriction: "That the product must be adequately practical as a shelter for human activities."

Hood is a second-hander trying to be strictly "modern" in his terminology—which he stole from Le Corbusier, incidentally. Did he come to this "principle" himself? Did he fight for it? Or didn't he just appropriate it when the battle had been won by others, by the suffering of others, and then parade it as his own great wisdom and gain prestige as a "foremost architect" thereby?

———◦———

John Cushman Fistere, "Poets in Steel," *Vanity Fair*, December, 1931.

Here's Toohey in full colors. Listing America's ten greatest architects, he starts off by being sarcastic about people naming Frank Lloyd Wright as first.

Nevertheless there are many who believe that Mr. Wright is more genius than architect, and who justify their opinion by pointing to his characteristic idiosyncrasies, and to the still more significant fact that he has designed comparatively few buildings to support his manifold theories. Even his most zealous disciples have difficulty in listing his actual achievements: the Larkin factory, "that hotel in Japan," and the glass and steel apartment house for New York that has never been built. As an architectural *theorist*, Mr. Wright has no superior; but as an architect he has little to contribute for comparison.

May I be forgiven for copying this! This is Toohey par excellence— god damn him!

Further from same:

Number two on nearly everyone's list of the ten great skyscraper architects would be Raymond Hood, seemingly less of a genius than Mr. Wright, but perhaps more of an architect. Unfortunately for the purposes of promoting him, Hood has no theories to advocate, is anathema to the intellectuals because he opposed the appointment of Wright to the World's Fair Architectural Commission, and is happier sticking to [architecture] than he is in making speeches and giving interviews. Hood already has three buildings to his credit to support the claims of his friends that he, and not Wright, is the first architect of the country.

(Nice friends, ain't they?)

Hood's most promising trait is his inconsistency. . . . "I would never build the same building twice"—that is the explanation of Hood.

("I would also build anything, because I have nothing to say" can be his explanation as well.)

This Hood interests me. I may be wrong, but there's something sinister about the man. He was broke and ready to give up architecture, when he won the Chicago *Tribune* competition by going in "partnership" on the design with a prominent architect who had been "invited" to participate in the contest. Hood did the design, and shared the glory with the other man, who got $40,000 out of the $50,000 award. The building was eclectic, Gothic, and none too good. This was after Sullivan, after Wright, when Mr. Hood could have discovered modernism if he had wished to listen, let alone "invent" it. But he goes Gothic "because embroidery was in vogue."

He prospers on the reputation gained by this contest. He gets big buildings to do. Modern architecture is gaining. The shrewd gentleman realizes it—I imagine he was a very good businessman. He switches to modernism with a bang—the Daily News Building. He is successful and sensational. He likes it. It is now safe to be sensational. He speedily appropriates the language of the modernists—Le Corbusier, Sullivan and all. He is admired for it. He is "the foremost *modern* architect of America." He is a prophet—neatly and nicely, with someone else's prophecy and genius, and with someone else's struggles and suffering having paved the way for his victory.

It is now embarrassing to know that the words are stolen. He would like to believe himself that he is what he has managed to make himself appear. So he hates the men he has robbed. He fights them. *He* keeps Wright from the Chicago Fair. He hates Wright for being actually what he, Hood, only appears to be. And—an interesting parallel: Wright refused to participate in the Fair, unless he could have complete say over it; Wright did it because he had an idea of what he wanted done with the Fair and he wished no interference with the idea; he had a truly beautiful and important thing to create. ("Terrible and megalomaniacal," comments Kahn.) Hood, on the other hand, made no such demand; but, according to Kahn, Hood *was* the ruler of the exposition. And an ugly mess resulted; Mr. Hood compromised or was incapable of anything better; he had no idea and nothing to create; he merely wanted the honor of bossing other people and being the "ruler" in their eyes, even if he had nothing for which to rule. And, of course, he had to keep Wright out of it; Wright was the only danger to this kind of phony, secondhand supremacy and the one who could steal the thunder from and the spotlight off Mr. Hood. Isn't that typical and significant? Isn't that "secondhandedness"? (I think I've analyzed it correctly. Check up.)

---

*From the "Symposium on Architecture" at the Decorators' Club:*

Kahn mentions that the plans for the Rockefeller Center were originally to be Gothic, because of Mr. Rockefeller's love for the Gothic [style]. Plans had even been drawn in Gothic. But practical necessity, such as windows and lighting, led to the adoption of a modern design. When I asked him about this personally, Kahn hastily denied that Gothic plans had been drawn. (?) *Hood* was the guiding hand among the eight or ten architects of Rockefeller Center. (Any wonder he got in? Would Wright draw up Gothic plans and then "talk" Rockefeller out of it? Where is the great integrity and "modern" convictions of Mr. Hood? And Rockefeller Center is a mess, compared to what it could have been. As to its sculpture—I wonder if Hood had a hand in the giving out of *that* commission?)

As to the whole meeting: a lot of insufferable drivel. A bunch of wealthy idlers in evening clothes listening smugly to a re-hash of things they could read in any book in ten minutes. Two dotards pattering smugly about Classic and Gothic architecture. Kahn—the only one to say a little of something and to say it with conviction. The others—drooling about a "house in Pompeii," which we are invited to inspect "from a magic carpet," and about the long nave of a Gothic cathedral symbolizing "the long way of a sinner to redemption" (sic!). The well-fed morons listening contentedly, certain that they are acquiring "culture." Tickets at $2.20 a head. And Wright could not raise the money to publish his magazine!

**December 7, 1937**

Samples of phony architectural language (from Kurt Jonas, in the *South African Architectural Record* ):

Here we find, indeed, a four-dimensional composition of space enclosed by solids. Especially the north and north-west aspect of the house shows a dynamic balance of forms, such as it would be hard to surpass. At the same time, it is not lacking in that interpenetration of spaces which brings out the hollow character, full of fluctuating life, which is the expression of architecture as compared with sculpture. . . .

The sphere of architecture is space. We must define space. But we cannot. For space is defined by movement. And movement presupposes time. Therefore we should speak more correctly of spacetime. . . . Architecture is a four-dimensional art. . . .

[T]his is a contradiction not due to the [average] man's poor logic, but to the higher logic, the dialectics of all life and art. To emphasize this I started that essay, *Towards a Philosophy of Architecture*, with the statement: "Modern Architecture is the realization of a contradiction in itself."

That not all things are so simple as some people believe, that there are inherent contradictions in life and in art, is no fault of mine. It is the task of the writer to show and to express this dialectic state, not to cover it with a torn fig leaf of simplifying logical construction, all for the sake of a mentally lazy layman.

Here is a typical one of Toohey: muddle the issue, appear deep by being unclear, down with logic in the name of a "higher logic"; this is the spirit of Gertrude Stein and others, again denying superiority by denying reason—the sole danger to mediocrity. Remove reason—and what ground is there for greatness or smallness? Aren't all equal when the scales have been destroyed? [*AR made use of the above "phony language"—see Gordon Prescott's testimony at the Stoddard trial.*]

"Modernist" architects build their own homes in the most conventional, old-fashioned way. The exception—Frank Lloyd Wright.

A silly *New York Times* article (1931) gloats over this, emphasizing that even so-called "modernists" (such as Hood) do not live in "modernistic boxes," that their homes are as old and eclectic as the homes of the conservative architects; [the article] stresses the fact that the [modernists'] homes are ancient, reconditioned, part old barns, etc., and goes mushy over ancient cherry-trees, lawns, flowers and birdies and the like. One of the "modernists," when asked about his home, got sheepish, then admitted that he didn't build it for himself, but for a client: his wife, who "didn't like modernism." Could Wright have done this—wife or no wife? Could he stand living in a house he hated? Could any man with sincere and profound convictions about his art, the art that is his life, live in a house that denies all his ideals? Could I, for the sake of a husband or for Jesus Christ, read nothing but Kathleen Norris? [*Kathleen Norris, a novelist, wrote* Mother *(1911),* Saturday's Child *(1914),* Sisters *(1919),* The Sea Gull *(1927), etc.*]

**December 9, 1937**

Lewis Mumford: "A critic who deals with the whole field of American culture." A swell description of Toohey.

———⊶———

[*The following note pertains to an item clipped from a newspaper.*]

The Beaux-Arts Ball (January 23, 1931) where famous architects wore costumes representing one of their buildings. "Human Skyline for Beaux-Arts Ball."

(Note the little guy with the glasses peering through a hole in his head-piece—the Waldorf-Astoria.)

**December 11, 1937**

Note the difference of approach to their profession between all these successful New York architects and Frank Lloyd Wright. He wouldn't go on a stag trip to the "Alma Mater" in Paris. He wouldn't go to a ball dressed as his building. This is the difference between the "common touch" and the ideal, between art as a business and art as a religion. The difference in the men is also in their buildings. It is this feeling I want for Roark—the burning reverence as against the "meal-ticket" architecture.

Note also, for Toohey, the measly trick in the *Vanity Fair* article quoted previously, of not coming out with a direct statement of the writer's own opinion, but hiding behind such phrases as: "There are many who believe" and "his friends claim."

**December 22, 1937**

A. T. North, "The Passing Show," *Current Architecture*, September, 1930.

This gentleman criticizes someone for saying that an architect must have convictions about his style—"as though the architect must have a style conviction just like one has a religious conviction." (**Precisely!** That's what he *must* have.)

We expect our tailors and modistes to produce equally well any selected pattern or style of garment, our physician to correctly diagnose and prescribe for all ailments, and our attorneys to conduct any manner of litigation—but the exceptioned architect cannot render any and every style equally well because he would be "so lacking in convictions." Unfortunately, too many architects make a cult of style. Style "conviction" in architecture?—it is amusing.

What logic! Here's mediocrity speaking.

Ugliness can be produced only by abnormal persons, the normal persons always desire beauty.

Now what is beauty? Who is to decide? By what rules?

**December 24, 1937**

Pictures of the A.I.A. convention: terribly stodgy, pompous, either "Babbitt" or "Social Register" faces of prominent architects. What a figure Howard Roark will be among them!

**December 30, 1937**

In December, 1935, Mayor La Guardia announced a list of fifty architects who would get all the big municipal work [in New York City].

The jurors who selected the fifty architects were Phelps Stokes, Ralph Walker, and Kenneth Murchinson. These last two are architects (I don't know about the first). Murchinson is the life-of-the-party of the architectural profession; he hasn't built anything to mention—but what power! He is always in the thick of things, particularly in "social activities."

The men who selected the jury were all presidents of various architectural organizations. Two of these electors were named among the list of fifty. One of the two—Upjohn—spoke utter drivel about Gothic architecture at the meeting I attended. ("The long nave is a symbol of the long road of the sinner to redemption.") And he was president of the A.I.A.! Such is the power and the glory of organized mediocrity.

**January 1, 1938**

Notes on a conversation with Kahn:

Plagiarism in architecture: plenty of it. Buildings which are copies of Kahn's buildings. Copies of his ornament. Case of client who asked him to build a replica of a certain building, and upon going to see the model, Kahn discovered it to be a copy of one of his own buildings, which he showed to the client, much to the latter's amazement. Case of bank which planned a building; Kahn was asked to submit a sketch, which he did; no further action was taken upon it and Kahn was informed that the plans had been abandoned; upon returning from Europe some months later, he found his building done and erected, very badly done and unskillfully interpreted from his rough sketch, but still his very building. The bank had taken his sketch and given it to some friend of theirs to build. Nothing done about this. Kahn did not sue or receive any payment for the sketch. Later, some "arty" book on architecture mentioned this particular building as the best building of that year, giving credit to the plagiarist-architect.

———

A draftsman in an architect's office is usually called "a designer" and typically does the actual designing of his bosses' buildings. If a draftsman refused to work in the style ordered, he would be fired immediately.

———

Frank Lloyd Wright, *Modern Architecture*.
The preface to this book mentions instances of Wright's lack of consistency and logic, and quotes the following: "When asked to write *The Logic of Modern Architecture*, Wright replied: 'Is the rising sun logical? It is natural and that is better.' " (This is sheer drivel. I am afraid that Wright has some of it once in a while. When is logic going to be fully explained and vindicated?) From the same preface: "Whose likes and dislikes are logical? We are now finding that logic, as a convention of human thinking, will not confine within its premises art and life as creative activities." (Rubbish!)
[Wright] calls the A.I.A. the "Arbitrary Institute of Appearances."

———

Arthur T. North [editor]: *Contemporary American Architects*, by E. J. Kahn.
The abysmal idiot who wrote the preface [A. T. North] displays quite a different spirit and approach to architecture than that in the writings of Frank Lloyd Wright. Thus, in praising Kahn's work, he has nothing of greater significance to say than the following, which he considers to be important architectural criticism:

Appraisals of buildings to determine their real contribution to architecture must include inquiries as to whether they "work"—fulfill their intended purpose—and are sound financial projects. In both these respects the buildings designed by Mr. Kahn are successful and at the same time he has complied with all legal and economic requirements.

Such inspired writing!

[North writes] of Kahn: "His democratic manner, interested consideration of matters brought to his attention, tolerance for the views and opinions of others, and amiable disposition, cause him to be held in friendly regard and respect." What a tribute to pay to an architect! This, then, constitutes Mr. North's idea of a great architect. Certainly, Kahn's work deserves more serious consideration and more valuable comment. Yet, here is Mr. North as editor of works on modern architects and as publicist of ideas on architecture. What chance would Frank Lloyd Wright or Howard Roark have here, [since they] are *not* "tolerant of the views and opinions of others"?!


**January 9, 1938**

Bruno Taut, *Modern Architecture.*


In building, no personal isolation of the individual actually exists. The process of building, by reason of the participation of innumerable artisans and workmen and the considerable expenditure involved, which again represents labor, is in itself of a collective nature. [. . .]

The test with regard to the collective attitude of mind of the architect is of particular value in this case, in that he is bound to hold sternly aloof from any favorite constructive ideas, particularly dear to his own personal taste. [. . .]

The small individual house, built in accordance with the wishes of an individual man or woman, is possibly still more indicative of the general standard of the delirium of individualism. . . . The construction of a dwelling-house not only shows that a feeling of ownership is a menace to this quality, but even, so it would appear, is in a degree opposed to it. For where the owner-builder is the more disposed to waive his possessive rights in favor of something really good and useful, there will not only disappear the sentimental, romantic delirium, but the houses will come to bear a certain resemblance and suitability, the one to the other.

(What logic!)

Should it not be impossible still to speak of taste, after the Stuttgart exhibition of 1927, for instance, proved that sixteen architects (all of whom differed greatly one from the other, even apart from the fact that they came from five different countries), without concerning themselves about any of the houses not actually of their own design, were yet able to evolve a suburb of a highly uniform character? A suburb in which each of them experimented in the most varied directions, proving that it was their common mental attitude which produced the unity of effect, thus excluding the question of taste. And yet, in view of the illustrations in this volume, many will assuredly contend: "That may be all very well thought out, but it does not happen to be my taste." To which one can only reply: "Questions of taste are social questions."

(Note: the Stuttgart exhibition is nothing but a collection of trashy, shoe-box houses, none of which means anything, consequently all of which can be considered to produce an effect of unity, the unity of nothingness.)

The coming world is most clearly expressed in its architecture, no matter from what angle it is regarded. Painting and the plastic arts keep within the calm of the studio, entangled in their problems regarding artistic form. The heroic attempts of a Picasso to set up a general consistent formula on constructive foundations are greatly to be appreciated so far as the standard of painting is concerned; yet his vacillations from Cubism to Classicism, and again from Cubism to Abstractism, must surely be indicative of a certain want of clarity as to how painting was to be linked on to the social whole. [. . .]

*This,* then, is Toohey in the flesh speaking. Little can be added to the gentleman's own words, except to note that he has quite a bit of praise for the awful monstrosities of cast-iron columns used when iron first came into use in architecture. He praises Renaissance architecture, when necessary. He has no conception of what Wright's fight for modern architecture means, nor its spirit, nor its purpose. All he has grasped is the "down with ornament" idea. Which is, of course, nothing but glorifying mediocrity, making architectural creation of such nature that it is open to anyone; anyone can build this senseless, awkward, common junk; genius or intelligence or taste are no longer necessary; taste particularly is deliberately denied and mocked. Note the remarks about Picasso—an attempt to connect idiotic modern painting to "the social whole," to set up standards that deny ability, and open art to anyone and everyone. There's Toohey's little system.

**January 10, 1938**

A. T. North, *Raymond Hood*.

[Hood has little] to say about general principles of architecture. The book [focuses mainly on] explanations of details of his buildings, plus some second-hand statements on form following function, old re-hash of what has been said a million times before, without adding a single new thought. The illustrations of his buildings show a magnificent absence of individuality. There is no such thing as a spirit or style of his own. Anything goes. The buildings could have been done by twelve different men. Appalling lack of imagination. Plenty of Renaissance and Gothic. Modernism à la Germany. When he tries to depart from precedent in decoration and to create patterns of his own, they are horribly Renaissance, awkward and meaningless. A great deal of stealing from Wright and from E. J. Kahn. This is the man claimed by many to be the great American architect.

A glance at his list of "societies" explains it all. Note also that he has worked always with someone else, hardly ever on his own, and if he did work on his own, he produced nothing of importance in those times. He has changed a great many partners. Evidently he didn't care with whom he worked, or so it appears from the numerous list of collaborators. Whether he was in each case the original designer or not does not matter. I do not trust people with instincts for collaboration.

**January 12, 1938**

A. T. North, *Ralph Adams Cram*.
A lovely compliment to Cram & Co. from Mr. North:

In this (their use of Gothic) they have exerted a steadying influence on American ecclesiastical architecture by retaining always its essential Christian character and spirit. At the same time, they have drawn on other sources with equal success. In their design of collegiate buildings they have drawn on many architectural sources [. . .] with the same facility and discrimination. In all of their work they have applied a serious and scholarly effort that produces an architecture which is appropriate to its purpose and in harmony with the best human attributes.

Observe the art of sounding profound and meaning nothing whatever, such as in the last sentence.

**January 17, 1938**

*Architectural League of New York, 1930:*

All the eclecticism in the world. Modern structures, such as the Empire State Building, and some of the oldest junk. The firm of Voorhees, Gmelin and Walker has, in the same issue, a modernistic building (Roerich Museum) and a bank building in New Jersey with Greek pilasters at the entrance. Anything goes with these architects. There is a home by Delano & Aldrich (society boys) which is rather simplified à la modernistic, but with a dome in the center and a Greek portico for an entrance. There is a Sewage Disposal Plant with Greek moldings.

It is almost pathetic to see the way in which the architects feel forced to simplify their facades, yet hang on to the Greek trimmings, porticoes, orders and such—in a slightly simplified form. (As if these were the only forms of which they felt sure and they cling to them desperately, seeing nothing beyond them.)

The above applies only to commercial buildings. In the field of domestic architecture it is still the dark ages. *Not one* modern building. Not even a touch of modernity on the old monstrosities. The only modern [design] shown is a model home built or projected by *House & Garden*.

**February 15, 1938**

N. C. Curtis, *Architectural Composition*.

A silly book, musty, naive and old-fashioned, smelling of the XIX century, even though it is published in 1935. Written by a professor of architecture. Gives a marvelously clear picture of what the academic mind thinks of architecture and of what it teaches to students. [. . .]

A lot of drivel on the idea of making a plan attractive in itself, not in what it represents, but in itself, as a picture. This seems hard to believe, even for the old days. (Check up on this.)

Advice to students in learning to make beautiful plans: "Progress will only come through practice; by the study of beautiful plans, chiefly through tracing them."

Throughout the book, a continuous emphasis on the "monumental," which seems to be the one type of architecture the author is most interested in—and the one most useless.

Traditional architecture, the great body of the master works of past epochs of architecture, is the store house from which we ought to draw and in most cases to draw all the inspiration that goes to make for the greatness of our contemporary designs. The greatest commentators are no uncertain advocates of this doctrine. Let us hear what M. Gaudet has to say:

"I know that to speak of tradition now passes far behind the times; the present tendency is to scorn tradition. That means to despise long efforts continued through centuries by the industrious generations preceding us; to seek generally to conceal ignorance by affecting to scorn the unknown in order to avoid the effort necessary to know it. Preserve yourselves from this error! Progress is slow and must be sure. Whoever proceeds slowly is sane, and whoever is sane goes far. Do you know what is very strong and original? It is to do very well what others have merely done well. The finest epochs are those in which tradition was most respected, when progress was continually perfecting, when there was evolution and not revolution. Never has there been spontaneous generation in art. Between the Parthenon and the temples preceding it are only shades of difference. Furthermore and especially for studies is tradition precious. To dare to become free from it one must judge it, and to do this it must be known. Tradition is a paternal patrimony; to dissipate it independently, one risks finding himself wandering at random and must at least know how to find himself another shelter."

This sounds like the despair of a bunch of quacks or witch doctors, who have held power for a long time by reason of their specialized knowledge in a field made mysterious, cluttered with minute details and requiring years of study, such dull and useless study of so much that is inessential, that few would enter it and the witch-doctors, consequently, held sway and ruled all architecture. When the people are leaving them, at last, they rack their brains for some excuse to hold on to their phony position of prestige: we gotta have tradition, and if not, we gotta study it anyway, at least in order to discard it, etc. But *please* study it, because this is our field, our second-hand claim to prestige and distinction! [. . .]

This is a magnificent sample of what every thinking person in any line is up against.

Simple and regular type forms of buildings, often of colossal dimensions, have been employed in all ages to embody purely idealistic concepts, or other ideals removed from the merely useful or material. Such are the temples, mausoleums and monuments of antiquity and the great cathedrals and churches of Christian epochs.

Here is an important point of difference. Howard Roark will make *all* buildings "idealistic," for every phase of life. Real life on earth, not in heaven, can and must be made beautiful.

Research and careful study of the masterworks of architectural art are most essential factors in training. By strengthening taste, discrimination is thereby made more sure and the novice will have the right to feel that he has climbed many steps when he is able to select the good from the inferior. It is well to remember that in the study of design it is far better to copy something that is really good than to try to create out of a limited imagination. After all imagination is rather largely a matter of memory, if it is not all that. In architecture, it has been said, the sort of originality that consists in the use of old materials is quite satisfactory for all purposes. It was good enough for the Greeks, why not for us?

(Sic!)
In conclusion:

I am only paraphrasing the words of Sir Joshua Reynolds, when he said: "The habit of contemplating and brooding over the ideas of great geniuses, until you find yourself warmed by the contact, is the sure method of an artist-like mind."

Isn't there something here to explain why geniuses are so often recognized only after they're dead? When they are alive, they're a menace to the second-handers. But when they are dead, their glory can be appropriated safely by these second-handers who then accept the prestige of specialists in that which their own kind would never have acknowledged while the author was there to claim his own glory. (Also: how many of these recognized geniuses are such and how many the creation of the second-handers?)

———◦———

Frank Lloyd Wright, *The Disappearing City*.
No notes. More of Wright's ideas. Some beautiful, a great many not clear. More about sociology than about architecture. [He speaks of] architecture as a force shaping society. (Which it isn't.)

**August 15, 1938**

From a speech by Charles D. Maginnis, president of the A.I.A., at the Institute's convention in New Orleans, April, 1938 [published in the May issue of *The Architect's World*]:

It is to be remarked that the world of our youth, to the understanding of which our minds were so very painfully adjusted, is in the act of tumbling about our heads and we are largely engaged in testing the validity of the fragments in the expectation of constructing a better one. Inevitably the process is attended by violent conflict of opinion. In the political order, for instance, we had been deeply grounded in the faith that, with all its familiar inefficiencies, the democratic type of society offered the highest exercise and the most lasting satisfaction for the human spirit. We now confront a mounting philosophy based upon its complete denial. More profoundly still we had believed in the cogency of the Divine principle in civilization. A strange new world rejects it as an anemic and disturbing anachronism. . . .

This is terribly important. Here is a man who fights modern architecture and individuality, as later quotes show, an eclectic and a second-hander par excellence. And he is precisely the type that would state and accept as a fact that "the world is tumbling about our heads." Who told him it was tumbling? What grounds has he to believe so? Only the Red propaganda, which he has accepted promptly and readily because he thinks that that is the way the wind is blowing. He has never had any standards and is, therefore, willing to abandon what he thought to be standards, willing to abandon anything. He is willing to gather the fragments and "build a better world." Better—with the denial of democratic rights included? This is to be stressed. It is men like Peter Keating who make men like Toohey possible; by denying standards, they are ready to accept any standards handed to them by anyone, or forced upon them. Keating will submit to Toohey as he submitted to everyone and everything else. Toohey is the type who knows how to reap the harvest of the second-handers.

After grudging, half-hearted, bromidic, meaningless compliments to modern architecture, the speaker shows what is really in his heart:

And so, in this attitude of reserve, we may welcome the stimulation of the new movement with all the challenge of its bitter rationality. That there is refreshment in it we have already noted in the clarity, vitality and independence it has brought to all design, even as we remark that, unlike Europe, we have not as yet yielded to its complete implication. Whether it hold the gift of completely alienating the past still remains to be proven. We have not yet seen the convincing evidence and it is always to be remembered that an artistic philosophy must propitiate the eye no less than the reason. This may take a little time. The human spirit has a way of finding its own satisfactions, and logic does not figure too largely in the matter.

(Note the second-hander's invariable disparagement of logic in favor of "spirit" or "sentiment.")

It may well be that the modern thesis is over-bold. It comes to one, for instance, that of the new materials with which its philosophy is identified, it is perhaps the single weakness of steel that, with all its thrilling capacities, it cannot make for interesting ruins. It is a point not to be overlooked, for even ruins have their eloquent and venerable importance. Always it has been architecture which has given us testimony of the ages. Someone has said: "show me the buildings of a people, and I will tell you its history." If we are content to render our own civilization in an architecture dependent upon steel, a reasonably remote posterity can have no visual knowledge of us, which might be a pity. In this there may be hint that the historic principle of structure is not quite discredited and that walls will still be built against which our posterity may bark its shins. For it is worthy of remark that it is the walls and not the space which have so intelligently survived. Perhaps it may not be too hazardous a prediction that the great and significant buildings of the generations will be built in the future, as they have been always built, in terms of articulated and enduring masonry.

(**This speaks for itself!** The most priceless bit I have yet found.)

# PLOT

*After two years of working on* The Fountainhead, *AR was clear on the theme and characters, and had learned a great deal about architecture. But she had not yet worked out certain key elements of the plot. In particular, she did not yet have the idea for the climax of the story, i.e., Roark's dynamiting of Cortlandt Homes and the subsequent trial. Long after the publication of* The Fountainhead, *she recalled her difficulties:*

I had the most impossibly difficult time, and nothing in the story could be set firmly, only tentatively, until I had the climax. And that was a real mind-breaker. I needed an event which was connected with architecture, but which would put Roark in the position of real danger and of antagonizing the whole of society. And, incidentally, I found that dramatizing events of an architect's career is enormously difficult, because the art itself is physical, it doesn't deal with people. All the conflicts have to be ideologically tied to the building, but they are not about the building as such. A lawyer or a doctor would be much easier to dramatize. And I remember cursing the profession for that reason. . . .

*It was while working in the office of E. J. Kahn that Ayn Rand thought of her dramatic climax. Kahn mentioned to her one morning that the biggest technical problem in architecture was the design of low-rent housing projects. That day, while eating lunch in a nearby cafe, she arrived at the idea of Roark designing and dynamiting Cortlandt Homes. She had solved the most difficult problem in planning the book—she finally had the essential element of the plot. The following notes begin in March of 1938, shortly after this breakthrough, at about the time that she quit her job with Kahn.*

*Approximately two-thirds of her notes from this last pre-writing period are pre-*

*sented here. I have omitted outlines that are repetitive or that merely describe events as they happen in the published novel.*

**March 8, 1938**

### Tentative Plan

Introduction: Roark's ambition, setting him against society. Graduation, with flashback to school days; work as draftsman, one definite break with boss. 1923
*First commission and own office:* society reacts—*his first tragic failure.* 1926
*Poverty—work as quarryman.*
(Attempt at bribe to Ecole des Beaux Arts.) 1928 [*This seems to refer to an attempt to bribe Roark into submission to conventional architectural standards, by offering him some prestigious honor from the Ecole des Beaux Arts.*]
Personal—*meeting with Dominique.*
*Back in New York Commission.* First critical fury. Beginning of a grudging recognition.
*Personal—secret affair with Dominique.*
Setbacks: The competition which Peter wins. Personal: Dominique marries Peter. The unfinished building? 1929–32
Dominique-Wynand. Their marriage. 1933
Peter's zenith and beginning of downfall.
*Roark's rise.* 1934
Wynand commissions Roark to build country home.
Roark-Wynand. Roark-Dominique. 1935
Roark-Peter: The housing project. 1936
"Ford" Building.
*The crisis. Trial.* Dominique-Wynand. 1937
The Wynand Building. 1938

---

Roark meets Dominique: 1928 (summer). He is 28, she is 25.
Their affair: 1929–30.
Dominique marries Peter: early 1931.
Dominique marries Wynand: 1933.

Wynand engages Roark to build home: 1935.
Crisis: 1937.
Roark-Dominique united: 1938 (he 38, she 35).

*Outline of Roark's architectural career.* (Highlights of his important buildings and his worst tragedies.)
Outline of Peter's career. (Highlights of his buildings and rise. Highlights of his downfall.)
*The affair of Roark-Dominique. Their break.*
Personal life: Peter-Dominique.
Personal life: Wynand-Dominique.
*The change which forces Dominique back to Roark.*
The relationship: Roark-Wynand.
The career and life of Toohey.
*The climax—Roark's crime and trial.*

### The climaxes and points to build to:

Part I: That Roark fails and Peter wins.
Part II: That Roark loses to Toohey. The burden of Peter's glory.
Part III: That Roark overcomes Toohey. Beginning of Peter's downfall.
Part IV: That Roark overcomes everyone. Peter's downfall.

### Next points:

Roark's first women and his personal life up to Dominique—*all of first part.*
Roark's women after Dominique's marriage to Peter.
*Toohey's trick against Roark.* (Involve Dominique, Wynand's editor, the young millionaire, Toohey's whole technique and his definite advancement with the Wynand papers.)
Roark's friends.
Roark's temptation? Is there or is there not a situation for him? *Not.*
Roark-Dominique: what finally brings them together?

### For Roark-Dominique lawsuit:

What would make Roark sue?
What can Toohey do to bring it about and to make Dominique say it?

What advantage results for Toohey, other than Dominique being
fired?
What damage to Roark?
Precisely what makes Toohey want Dominique to be fired?
Toohey's technique and illustration of his whole character?

**1938**

*To think over.*

Trouble for Dominique (early)—?
Wynand's sadism (luxury for people out of the gutter)—?
Wynand's one big attempt against Roark. (Roark's heroic reaction,
Wynand's turning point toward Roark and all things.)
Roark's activity about securing jobs.
*Roark's activity about his kind of joy in life.* (?) (Greatest part of
book to last part and climax.)
*Influence of Roark on all who come in contact with him.* Roark
brings out either the worst or the best in people. (The worst—
Toohey. The best—Wynand.) Think this over in connection with
every point in the outline of Roark's career.
In construction: *first*—philosophy, second—architecture.

———◦———

Roark-Wynand, Roark-Dominique, Roark-Toohey, Roark-Peter: In these
[relations], the things which happen to these people affect Roark or vice versa.
But he motivates them and all the major events of their lives.
On what occasions can Roark demonstrate his utter anti-socialness?
Opportunities for second-handedness:

*professional*—obedience to opinions of others, the end becomes the
means, existence only in the eyes of others, nepotism;
*personal*—fear of public opinion, conventions and prejudices, sacrifice of one's real self to others.

(Try to think out a type and a dramatic occasion for each.)
Roark's situations come from his peculiar attitude and his disregard of
all that would constitute tragedy to average people. As far as the plot and

physical body of the novel is concerned, all the main events are motivated by the second-hand psychology (or Roark as its opposite).

The last part of the book is mainly Roark-Wynand. Consequently, the rest is preparation for it which is resolved in the main climax. This is: Dominique, Peter, Toohey. Concentrate on this for first part—building toward last.

(What if Roark is brought to Wynand, not through a house to build, but by the editor, as a rescue, as [Wynand's] greatest prey?) [*This sentence was crossed out.*]

**March 31, 1938**

*Roark and Wynand*

*What is Wynand's stage when he meets Roark?*

Wynand is at the height of his success—and sick of it. He has married Dominique. His love for her is getting to a stage of mania—the despair of holding on to one thing in which he sees salvation and self-respect. One thing which he really wants—and now he wants her with all the passion of every other "wish he might have had." His bitterness about his kind of life is growing steadily, but vaguely, obscurely, hidden. He denies it to himself, evades it, hides from it behind Dominique. He has not missed and betrayed everything, he tells himself, he *has* Dominique. But precisely for that very reason, one serious devotion in his life leads him to feel more strongly that which he has missed; it makes him realize—subconsciously, against his will—everything that he has betrayed.

Consequently, his attitude to Dominique is a feverish mixture of exaggerated joy and involuntary, exaggerated despair. This last is rarer. But there are sudden moments, like explosions, like subterranean grumblings of the earthquake to come, when he is madly bitter, unhappy at her—without reason. These are the first signs of the man breaking up. No one notices it except the editor [Alvah Scarret], who does not like it.

His attitude toward men around him is the same strange mixture, somewhat reversed; his spurts of sadism intensified, sometimes out of all proportion, to the limits of the permissible. He has never been as bitter toward men. He is getting worse, people say. The fact is that he is getting better—and does not know it, and does not *want* to know it. He now has strange moments of relaxation in his taunting of men, moments of dead calm, a hopeless, weary calm that [suggests] his greatest danger—indifference.

Even this pastime no longer interests him. He is beginning to realize—
subconsciously, for he would not yet admit it to himself—that even this
means nothing, that it proves nothing and *redeems nothing*. This subconscious conclusion terrifies him, drives him to excesses. But it will take Roark
to make him admit the conclusion in so many words. The editor, wise in his
own way and in his unerring second-hander's instinct, sees and recognizes the danger signs. He knows the coming loss to the second-handers'
camp of a great ally who has never really belonged to it. Consequently,
Wynand's excesses worry him less than his occasional terrifying indifference. Once, when Wynand refuses to act true to form, the editor goads him
to it desperately.

This is the groundwork for Roark's entrance into Wynand's life.

*What is Roark at the time?*

This is the definite beginning of Roark's final [triumph]. Not much
money as yet, but much fame. Notoriety, rather, of the resentful kind. Complete self-assurance. He knows he has won. His indifference to people
can afford now to be tinged with the slightest pity. There is a glow about
him—of a great battle won. His calm is a challenge to others. His honesty—
arrogance.

*How does Roark take Wynand?*

He sees through him at once. He sees more than the editor, more than
Wynand himself. He is amused, at first; then soon begins to pity him, with a
kind pity that respects, not insults. Ends by liking him. *(One occasion of
Roark's gesture of faith in Wynand—either before or after Wynand's
attempt against him.)*

*How does Wynand take Roark?*

Wynand is fascinated, at first. Completely and in spite of himself. Or
rather, he does not fight against it, does not even analyze it. It is a complete,
spontaneous emotion, so rare in him. He surrenders to it simply, naturally,
and happily. He knows only that here is a man whom he really likes—which
has never happened to Wynand before—a man to whom he likes to talk,
simply, directly, sincerely. This after the first few taunts—and quite involuntary, unpremeditated. Then he realizes—with a little frightened start—that
he actually respects the man. It is an entirely new feeling for Wynand; he
enjoys it with an interested curiosity. So much for the beginning.

**April 4, 1938**

Then Wynand realizes the trap into which he has fallen—too late. He
has one spurt of ferocious hatred against Roark, a last gesture of self-

defense. Roark wins—which only makes Wynand like him more. (This may be the point where Wynand suddenly cancels the construction of his country home—for no apparent reason at all, only to take it up again shortly afterwards, knowing that nothing will make him cancel his house or lose Roark.) Perfunctorily, almost as a matter of conscientiousness, Wynand goes through a few "temptations" of Roark—such as offering him huge real estate projects if he surrenders his ideals. It does not work. Not at all. Roark does not even hesitate for a moment, makes no great show of heroism and sacrifice in refusing. He refuses simply and immediately, as a man who does not ever see two, but only one course open to him. He does not even give Wynand the satisfaction of being indignant. If anything, he is slightly amused. He sees through Wynand's game—the first victim to do so. To the editor's terror, Wynand—instead of being furious at his defeat—is openly delighted. Openly even to himself. Not to Roark, of course, but openly enough for the editor to see it and for Wynand himself to realize it fully, to admit it to himself. In any future, lesser attempts, Wynand is now anxious for Roark to defeat him. Roark does.

And the great Gail Wynand comes to a point where Roark becomes the most precious thing in his life. Above Dominique, though Wynand does not admit it. Roark becomes his revenge against society, against that mob whom Roark is defying and to whom Wynand has surrendered. Wynand, at this stage, does not yet admit this surrender to himself, but he knows it already subconsciously, hence all his vague anguish, his peculiar spiritual hysteria. The full, conscious knowledge of it will come later, when he is forced to betray Roark.

At the moment, Roark becomes an obsession to him. In the most spiritual sense only, without the slightest possibility of the merest hint of sexual perversion, Wynand is actually in love with Roark. There are no definite events, no concrete speeches in which this is displayed. It is there, nevertheless. It is an instance of Wynand's masochism, of which he has quite a taint. The torture of loving a man whom in many other ways he hates appeals to him. He hates him for everything that Roark is and he, Wynand, isn't. He hates him as a challenge to his whole life, as the embodiment of his conscience. He loves him for these very reasons. Unrealized, there is in Wynand's mind a twisted feeling of atonement in his love for Roark—his worst enemy. He is punishing himself for what he has done—by bowing before what he should have done. The bowing hurts him. He enjoys it for that. By being hurt—at this late date—he thinks he is atoning for the many hurts he has avoided: he is suffering for an ideal—for the first and last time in his life. As a gesture to all the ideals he should have, but did not, suffer for.

He now has two centers in his existence—Dominique as a joy he wished and obtained, Roark as a suffering he chose and accepted. He loses both at the same blow.

How he takes Roark's love for Dominique is another great point to be considered at length separately.

———

*Another important second-hander:* The kind that does not form opinions because others hold them, but because they know instinctively this is what others *will* hold (e.g., Toohey, the editor). Toohey approves of a book, not because it is already popular, but because he *knows* unerringly that it will be popular. The barometers of the mob. The deadliest kind of second-handers.

### Plan of the Last Part

Roark blows up the housing project.

His arrest. Wynand offers help immediately. ("I know. I understand. I admire. My entire resources at your service in your coming fight. G. W.") Old lawyer comes out of retirement to take the case. Wynand supplies Roark's bail.

Fury of indignation in the press all over the country. Roark maintains complete silence—no explanations given. Wynand papers come out alone to defend Roark. (Incident of woman who wants house by Roark.)

Toohey urges his union to strike against the "Ford" building. He does not hope or intend to win. Just a gesture to "finish" Roark. Wynand's greatest crusade. His insane determination. The editor's fight with him. Dominique's threat-promise. ("I will love you if you stand by him. You don't know what you'll lose—if you don't.")

Utter failure of the Wynand papers. Boycott against them on a grand, general scale. His board of directors and the editor deliver an ultimatum. Wynand surrenders. His papers come out against Roark.

Wynand's own, silent tragedy. He sees his second-hand power for what it is, fully, clearly and completely. He knows now the failure of his whole life. (Incident with housewife buying newspaper.)

Wynand-Roark. Wynand begs him to escape and jump bail. Roark refuses.

April 4, 1938

(1)

<u>Summary of last part</u>

Roark blows up housing project.

His arrest. Fury of public indignation. Strike against Ford building.

Wynand's crusade + failure. He turns against Roark. Wynand's tragedy.

Dominique—Roark. Her confession of love. He agrees to escape. ~~~~~~
Their night together at her country house.

First day of trial, Roark absent. That night — drive to airport.

Fire on Ford building. Roark's arrest.

Wynand's return from Washington. He learns the truth.

Wynand—Dominique. Her confession. Wynand gives "carte blanche" to editor.

Next morning. "Wynand"'s statement in the papers. His scene with Dominique.

The trial. Rise of Wynand papers during trial.

The verdict — "not guilty". Roark at Ford building, plan to re-build housing project.

Dominique leaves for Europe. Wynand's divorce.

Wynand's decision about his building. Roark—Wynand.

Dominique's return from Europe. Dominique at the Wynand building.
Her ride in the elevator.

Dominique's decision to escape with Roark the day before the trial. She tells him that she loves him. Begs him to escape and to continue his work abroad. She will pay Wynand his bail. She is "buying him from the State of New York." Roark agrees.

Their escape [the night before the trial] to her country home (which he built). Old servants who see them there. Their first night together after many years.

Day of trial. Wynand is in Washington trying to use "pull" to save Roark. Roark does not appear. Alarm sent out for him.

That night. Dominique has arranged for private plane. Drives with Roark to the airfield. Mails letters to Wynand on the way. Fire in the "Ford" building—set by the strikers. Roark sees it on the way [to the airfield], rushes to building in spite of her protests. The situation of the unconnected water tank. Roark rushes up through the flames to save the building. Dominique tries to stop him. She falls down after trying to hold the elevator. Looks up into a battery of cameras.

Roark's fight against the fire on his way up. He connects the tank and saves the building. Does not even care or notice when he is arrested. [*Note the similarity here to her earlier story,* The Skyscraper.]

Next morning. Wynand flies back to Washington in private plane. He knows nothing of the events of the night before. Drives to office from landing field. Sees extras in street, pays no attention. Peculiar reception of his office staff. He bawls them out for "missing a scoop." They run away from him. The editor rushes into his office. "I told you so!" If he means Roark's escape, Wynand laughs, why, he is delighted. The editor hands him a copy of a rival paper with the picture of Dominique in the mud, on the front page. The whole story of the fire is there, plus the information already gathered by the police about Roark and Dominique spending the night together at her country home. The editor is frantic as to their policy in this crisis. Wynand doesn't even hear him. Wynand is quiet, gentle, the gentleness of a man who is not alive any more. He asks only where Dominique is, and hearing that she is at home, leaves the office, ignoring the editor's hysterical questions.

Wynand-Dominique. When he comes home, he learns that she has just returned from the jail hospital (where Roark is) and that she is waiting to see him, Wynand. Their scene. He tries desperately to prevent her from saying one thing which he dreads. He starts by telling her that if she says the story isn't true, it *won't be true*; his great power will make it untrue. He begs her, in other words, to deny it. It's true, she tells him. She laughs: his great power, what did it do for *Roark*? Wynand then talks hysterically, as if putting words into her mouth, telling himself what he has not heard from her, but wants to hear: that it is only an affair, he doesn't mind, he was expecting it sooner or later, they will go abroad and forget it all. There are not reproaches from him, no anger, no thought of giving her up. Only a desperate plea for her not to leave him.

She tells him that she loves Roark. When she says it, she realizes that that is what he had been dreading. She expects an explosion. She defies him. She tells him everything and how much Roark really is to her. There is no explosion from him. No reaction. No words, after his recent outburst of them. He only mutters dully that if she wants a divorce, he'll let her divorce him. He leaves the room. Her letter and check of the day before arrive. . . . The editor phones, begging frantically for instructions on their policy. Wynand tells him to do anything he pleases. The editor holds him to that, makes him repeat it. Wynand does not care.

Next morning. After a sleepless night, the full force of the blow has come to Wynand. It is his last outburst of emotion. He goes to Dominique's room, begs her, threatens her, offers her anything to remain with him; she can have all the lovers she wants, but not *that one*! She can even leave him, Wynand, if she insists, and go with any other man, but *not Roark*. Anything, but not Roark! She is kind to Wynand this time; she understands, she is sorry for him. She lets him see that it is hopeless; that she will live or die for Roark. She knows that she and Wynand have both found the same thing in Roark; only it is too late for Wynand. . . .

She is now leaving to go to the trial. (She can't do that! he objects. *He* can't, she answers, but she can. She is not the Wynand papers.) And before leaving she tells him that there is not much that he can do now, anyway, about their marriage: she hands him a copy of his own paper, where, on the front page, is a statement signed "Gail Wynand," denouncing Dominique, insulting her, putting all blame on her, announcing to the world that he is going to divorce her. Wynand is unable to speak. Dominique can now feel pity for him. "Don't, Gail. I understand. I know who wrote it. Don't blame him too much. He had to. You had to." She leaves for the trial.

The trial. Roark enters, his head bandaged, his left arm in a sling. He is greeted by cheers, applause and hisses. The public sentiment is now divided about him. The judge threatens to clear the court, "if they don't remember that it is a courtroom, not a news-reel theater." The photographers have a swell time photographing Dominique as she enters. She pays no attention. She sees no one but Roark.

The progress of the trial. The prosecution has an army of witnesses. (Perhaps even Dominique—to supply the motive as Roark's hatred for

Peter.) The defense tactics—"no questions." No cross-examination whatever, not even of Peter, who has some terrible moments on the stand and behaves like a piece of pulp. Peter, however, does not confess the truth and is not asked to.

Wynand does appear in the courtroom—once. Thereafter, the editor prevents it. When the defense's turn comes, the old lawyer has but one witness to call—Howard Roark. After the first formalities of name, profession, etc., the lawyer asks: "Mr. Roark, what connection did you have with the project known as [Cortlandt Homes]?" Roark answers, very quietly: "I designed it." [Then comes] the whole story of the contract with Peter. The contract is introduced in evidence. Before Peter can be warned by the prosecution or collect his wits, he has admitted his signature and the truth of the story. The defense rests.

The old lawyer's closing speech—summation of what Roark is, of his standards, of his value to mankind. No plea for pity. No apology. A quiet defiance. A "This-is-what-he-is-now-dare-to-convict-him,-if-you-can" feeling. The jury retires to deliberate.

Jury out all evening and night. Possible scene of Roark, Dominique, old lawyer, some others waiting together for verdict. Roark talks—of everything but the jury and trial. The only time he can be poetic, almost tender(?).

Next morning. The verdict: *"Not guilty."* The judge furious. It comes out that the first ballot was eleven . . . guilty to one . . . not guilty. The one swung the eleven. (Plant this one man earlier, his reasons, his psychology.) Dominique leaves courtroom as soon as verdict is rendered. She does not approach Roark. "Home and to bed!" the old lawyer orders him. "To the Ford building!" orders Roark.

Ovation of workers at the Ford building. (They have been listening on the radio to the verdict.) Then at Roark's office: The one "capitalist" on the housing project has announced that he is buying it from the state and will have Roark do it as it was intended. Other commissions—from sensation seekers. . . .

Then Roark comes home. Dominique is waiting for him there. Their one real, complete love scene. She will go away, not to disturb him now when his work needs him; also to "find herself"—adjust herself to her new life. Then she will come back. They will be together forever.

———◦———

The Wynand papers have been doing beautifully during the trial. Circulation is boosted by a "succes de scandale." Everyone reads the Wynand papers to see how they "take it." The editor takes advantage of it. He prints hints, double-meanings, "between-the-lines" allusions, things that will be quoted and discussed and gloated over; he builds up Wynand as a moral, outraged man. He is delighted with and boasts to Wynand (without noticing Wynand's horror) about the tons of fan mail arriving for Wynand, letters of sympathy and advice from good housewives, proposals of marriage from spinsters who promise not to "treat him that way" and to "make him forget." And Dominique, whom Wynand had tried so desperately to keep from the mob, whose pictures were never allowed in the press, is now splashed across every front page in the country, including the Wynand papers. (Incident with paper in the gutter.) When a political event occurs that is in line with the Wynand papers' policy and throws a great deal of sympathy to them, when a noted gossip columnist decides to join the Wynand papers, the editor's victory is complete. The Wynand papers are back. The editor even goes so far as to say before Wynand that the whole affair was a swell stunt for them, after all.

Wynand takes it all as in a daze, with the greatest indifference possible. He lets it be done. He does not even wince often. Dominique leaves for Europe. Wynand divorces her—in a short, horrible scene in which he repudiates her publicly. It is Wynand's greatest agony. He goes through it like an automaton. He is led by the editor completely. He has not gathered the pieces of his spirit enough to act for himself.

Peter's complete downfall. Short scene of his accepting an inferior commission, a home in the "Greek" style ("like his library").

Toohey's defeat and new plans, grander than ever.

---

Very shortly after the divorce, the question of the Wynand Building comes up. The time is considered "just right" in view of "the triumph." The board of directors is in session to decide on the architectural competition for "the greatest building in the world." This is Wynand's last gesture. All that he has gathered of his spirit now goes into this—as a challenge to that new triumph which he hates. He rises. "Gentlemen, there will be no contest. I have chosen the architect who will do the Wynand Building. His name is Howard Roark." Dead silence. The sole reaction is one choked hiccough from some unimportant little guy. Wynand looks at the stunned faces, pouncing on them ferociously: "Well? Has no one here anything to say? I take it that you approve of my choice, gentlemen?" In the silence, the editor gasps: "You're mad, Gail!" Wynand whirls on him: "Why? Because he's sleeping with my wife? Because I hate him more than any man living? And because he alone can give us the greatest building in the world? . . . The matter is settled, gentlemen. I wish you a good day." He leaves the conference room.

Nothing can sway Wynand in this, his last, his only real decision. To the frantic pleas of the editor, he answers only that he does not give a damn any more about "his public" and "his papers." He has enough to live on. He doesn't care whether the papers go on or fail. He has no heirs to leave them to. The public will accept it—he doesn't care; the public won't accept it—he cares less. But he will have this one thing out of his life, when he has lost all the rest; one thing that *he wants*.

Roark is informed. He is called to Wynand's office. He comes. Wynand meets him alone in his office, coldly, formally. There is no allusion to anything but the building. Wynand informs him briefly, generally of the requirements, the kind of building he wants from the angle of utility, its purpose. The rest is up to Roark. He will have an unlimited budget. There will be no orders given by anyone but him. He is to design and build it as he pleases. It is to be the greatest building in the world. He does not even have to submit his design for approval; it is approved in advance. If Roark accepts the job, he will find the contracts ready in the outer office; Wynand has signed them; all Roark has to do is to sign. Roark accepts. He is as calm, as cold, as unsurprised as is Wynand.

Then Wynand says, with a little different note in his voice: "I do not wish ever to see you again. I do not wish to speak to you. You will find my manager ready at any time for any orders you may want to give. I do not have to see you." His hatred, almost his insult, is apparent. Roark agrees calmly. Then, without looking at him, Wynand says softly what that building had been intended to be and mean, how he had planned for it through the years, the crowning glory, the symbol of his life. He looks at Roark suddenly. He adds: "I have nothing to crown now, nothing to celebrate. I have nothing to go into that building—except what you'll put into it." He rises. His greatest moment. The sum and the summit of his life. Everything he has is in the words: "Build it as a monument to that spirit which is yours . . . and . . . could have been mine."

---

About eight months later (less, if possible). Dominique returns from Europe. She has not written to Roark of her return. She goes to his office— he is at the Wynand Building. She goes to building. The steel skeleton is up.

She stands looking at it. Then she notices a thing which makes her tremble suddenly and lean against a wall. She looks at the street, at the people around her. She feels suddenly the greatest of all events, the greatest of all triumphs, the victory of all the "great unsung" over all the filth of the pavements and those upon them; she sees all of society in a flash—and what it means; she sees all those whom it has crushed and passed by—and their vindication. She has seen a small, dirty tin plate nailed to the scaffolding of the Wynand Building:

"Howard Roark, Architect"

She goes into the building. She is told that Roark is above, on top of the building. She takes an open freight elevator to go up. As it begins to rise slowly, we rise with her above the pavements, above the shops, the theaters, the houses, the church spires, above all that men do and are. (The writing accelerates here with the growing speed of the elevator as it rises.) She is above everything, with nothing but the sky and the distant ocean rising on the horizon. Then she sees, alone, tall, erect against the sky, Howard Roark on the top of the building, his red hair flying in the wind.

**April 25, 1938**

*I. 1922–1928: Peter Keating* (6 years)

From graduation to Roark's failure. The competition which Peter wins and his definite establishment. This is Peter's story.

*II. 1928–1931: Ellsworth M. Toohey* (3 years)

From quarry to start of summer resort project. The affair of Roark-Dominique. Dominique marries Peter. Roark-Toohey. This is Toohey's story.

*III. 1931–1935: Gail Wynand* (4 years)

No relations between Roark-Dominique. Roark's slow rise. The summer resort project's "J'accuse" [*in reference to the discovery of the fraudulent investment scheme*]. Dominique marries Wynand. Peter's problems and beginning of downfall (the Exposition). Wynand's story.

*IV. 1935–1938: Howard Roark* (3 years)

Roark's commission for the Wynand Country House. Dominique's regeneration. The housing project. The Ford Building. The trial. The Wynand Building. Roark's story.

**May 15, 1938**

Roark and Toohey as the two poles of good and evil.

Everything that happens to the others in the book is according to the principles either of Roark or of Toohey. These principles are illustrated by the actions of the two men. In their relations to these two, and in the influence of these two, the [other] characters play out the drama which illustrates the two life-principles.

The others are: Dominique, Peter, Wynand.

*Dominique:* The Toohey principles have forced her into a bitter cynicism about all life. She is born above these principles, and not ready as yet for those of Roark, because nothing in life has ever taught her the Roark philosophy. Her story is the struggle against the Toohey principle to win through to Roark.

*Wynand:* He has lived according to Toohey all his life and has never believed in it. He is only too ready for Roark and knows it the moment he meets him. His story is the conscious struggle against the Roark principle, only to surrender to it in the end.

*Peter:* Unfit for any principle. The clay with which Toohey builds. He could have, perhaps, achieved a shadow of self-vindication with Roark. He reaches the bottom of waste and tragedy with Toohey.

———◦———

*Roark:* integrity, loyalty to yourself.

*Toohey:* exist for, by and through others.

Roark brings out and encourages every form of truth to self. Toohey destroys every vestige of it, leaving about him a sterile desert.

**June 15, 1938**

*First Draft of Chapter Plan*
*Part I: Peter Keating*

I

Spring, 1922. Howard Roark alone in the mountains. His return to the city. The interview with the principal about his being expelled.

## II

Same day. Peter Keating at the commencement celebration.

## III

Same evening. Peter comes home. Vesta Dunning. Roark's plan for their life together in New York.

## IV

In New York: the new household. Peter's introduction into Francon's office. Roark–old master [Henry Cameron]: first meeting, hired.

## V

One week later. Roark's first work for old master. Scene where Roark is fired—and their first real understanding. At home: Vesta-Roark. Peter.

## VI

Fall, 1922. Peter's first accomplishments in the Francon office—professional and personal. The affair: Roark-Vesta.

## VII

Winter, 1922–23. Roark's struggle with old master. Peter's loves. The beginning of Vesta's conflict with Roark.

## VIII

Winter, 1923–24. Peter has moved out. Peter's rise with Francon. Old master gives up.

## IX

Peter brings Roark to Francon's office. The clashes. Mike.

## X

Winter, 1925. Roark fired. Break with Vesta.

## XI

Beaux Arts bribe. Roark in new job.

## XII

Peter sees Dominique in Francon's office.

## XIII

Spring, 1926. Roark gets his first commission from the critic [*Austen Heller, whom she refers to as "Mencken" in one cryptic note from this period*]. Peters meets Dominique.

## XIV

Summer, 1926. Peter's attempts at romance with Dominique. Critic's home finished. Public reaction—or lack of it.

## XV

Winter, 1926–27. Other commissions for Roark. His struggle. His second mistress [*Heddy Adler, who was later cut from the novel*]. The competition for the library.

## XVI

Summer, 1927. Roark's struggle.

## XVII

Winter, 1928. Roark's downfall. Staking all on one commission. He refuses his mistress' proposal. Peter-Dominique, their kiss, her indifference. Peter beginning to dislike her definitely.

## XVIII

Spring, 1928. Peter wins the competition. Roark refuses to take commission he was counting on. Roark leaves for Connecticut. The party celebrating Peter's partnership in Francon's firm.

———◦———

[*AR made similar outlines for the rest of the book. I have included here only those descriptions in which AR makes a comment of special interest or mentions an event that did* not *occur in the novel.*]

[*Part II: Ellsworth Toohey*]

## V

Toohey—past, present, future. Toohey and the Wynand paper. Dominique-Toohey, Peter-Toohey. [*Note added later:*] Incident about Roark's building—"Independent as an insult, isn't it?" [. . .]

## IX

Summer, 1929. Escape of contractor for Unfinished Symphony. Toohey-Dominique. She prints the libel.

## X

Lawsuit and love affair. Roark-Dominique.

## XI

Fall, 1929. Roark wins the suit. That night. Next day—Symphony stopped. A few days later—Dominique marries Peter. Her wedding night with Roark. Next morning—she tells him. Their break. [. . .]

## XVI

Fall, 1930. Roark loses [the Stoddard Temple] lawsuit and everything. Sculptor's [Steven Mallory's] suicide—"for Roark's sake." Roark goes to live in Unfinished Symphony. Toohey and the Wynand Settlement project. Plans for Peter, and for Dominique to meet Wynand. Temple altered by Peter. Scene of Roark on steps of Temple, at night, in the snow, his hat off, his hands patting the steps. Scene: Roark-Toohey.

### Part III: Gail Wynand

## III ·

Roark's [commission for] the nightclub. Roark living in Symphony. Meeting with young writer. [. . .]

## VIII

Spring, 1931. Young writer's death. Roark leaves for summer [resort] project. Peter and the Wynand Settlement. Peter-Toohey. [. . .]

## XII

Dominique's reactions to Roark's mistresses. Dominique-Wynand.

## XIII

Spring, 1933. Opening of summer resort. Great success. Panic of promoters. Roark and mistress at opening. Dominique there alone.

## XIV

The flood. Night. Next morning. [*AR's original idea was that Monadnock Valley was subject to periodic flooding, and the promoters had counted on the summer resort being destroyed by a flood. Their plan fails because Roark designs the resort such that it can withstand the floods.*] [. . .]

### *Part IV: Howard Roark*

## VI

Peter marries blonde. Scene: Toohey-niece.

## VII

Summer. On the construction site. Roark-Dominique. Roark-Wynand encounter. One furious spurt of Wynand's hatred for Roark. Wynand cancels the construction. [. . .]

[*The events after Roark dynamites Cortlandt Homes are the same as those described in her "Plan for the Last Part" written on April 4.*]

**June 21, 1938**

### *Chapter III*

Francon's office. Keating arrives for work—a little before 9 a.m. The entrance lobby of the office. The reception clerk. The employment manager.

The drafting rooms. The head draftsman. Keating shown his locker, told a few brief instructions, put to work.

Keating tracing blue-prints. First nervousness. Then looking about, loses all fear of the men, knows he is better.

The great activity. Looks at the city. "It comes from here."

Keating and the drawing. "Francon? No, so-and-so did it."

The afternoon. Keating sent to Francon. Francon with a slight hang-over. His brief talk with Keating about his, Francon's, duties. Leaving, Keating sees woman client in reception room.

---

Cameron's past.

Roark comes to Cameron's office. The office (overlooking one of Cameron's buildings).

The interview. Roark ordered to come to work tomorrow.

Cameron's reaction.

Roark looking at the streets.

Roark comes home. Vesta doing Joan D'Arc. Roark-Vesta. His interest. Her reverent enthusiasm. Peter comes home. She changes, does a fool imitation. The dinner she has prepared.

---

Cameron—the austerity, the devotion, the tragedy.

Francon—big business (show, pompousness, kowtowing to clients, utter indifference to the *reality* of the work).

**June 25, 1938**

### Chapter 1

Roark in the mountains—his body, the earth around him, the complete ecstasy of the complete man, his thoughts on architecture and the material around him (nature as his clay to mold as he pleases). The swim. The fact that he has been expelled.

Roark on his way home: the interreaction of Roark and others around him.

Roark home. Mrs. Keating. First reference to Peter. Mrs. Keating's quite obvious joy at Roark's expulsion and her pride in Peter, her "sweetness" and her ferocious ambition, her hatred for Roark (and for every other student at the Institute). She tells Roark of Dean's call.

Roark on his way up. Incident with Vesta's closed door and her rebuff to him.

Roark in his room—his drawings. He forgets call. Mrs. Keating reminds him. He goes.

Interview between Roark-Dean. Establish why he's been expelled. Lay a brief and clear foundation for the two basic opinions on architecture—Roark's and the eclectics'. The Dean's mention of Cameron; Roark's reaction. Roark's background—where he came from, that he has worked as building constructor during his way through Institute. No friends, no fraternities. Roark's utter, shattering indifference. "Your opinion, Mr. Roark, is not the most important thing that counts." "It is the only thing."

As Roark leaves, he is distracted by the stone in the Institute building—his thought as to what he would do with it.

———◦———

[*AR elaborates the above in the following notes.*]

Rocks like a fortress wall, enclosing everything, a circle, a planet or world of its own. Rocks like a frozen explosion—a struggle, the harmony of conflict, the hard unity not of peaceful balance, but of opposite forces holding one another in check. Sharp angles, like clenched muscles, deep gashes like wounds worn as decorations, a million sparks in the granite, the rock flaming, a hard luster, the polish of heat, as if the air were a liquid, so dry that the stones seem wet with sunrays.

A few tufts of green—a luminous green tumbling in the wind, like green bonfires burning on the fuel of granite. One tree—as a banner, victorious over the rock, rising to proclaim its place in this world of stone. [*This last sentence was crossed out.*]

The lake—an enclosed canyon, quiet, guarded, mysterious. Cold, obviously cold even in its fire; in spite of it or because of it. Subterranean spring. No bottom. [*The preceding three sentences were crossed out.*]

A thin silver film cutting, midway, the walls of granite. A luminous bowl—lighting the sky. The sky—clear, blue with nothing, not a single cloud to give it limit or reality—as a mirror for the lake. The rocks continue into the depth and then there is the sky. So that the whole place seems suspended in space, with the sky below and above it, an island floating on nothing, a circle, a coral reef of the sky, anchored only by the two feet of the man on the rock.

The place is wild, untouched, no trace of the existence of men.

His laughter as the meaning of the earth around him, as its song, as the release of its tension. Triumphant, the complete ecstasy. (See Nietzsche about laughter.) [*Elsewhere in her notes, AR copied the following from* Thus Spoke Zarathustra*: "O my brethren, I heard a laughter which was no human laughter—and now gnaweth a thirst at me, a longing that is never allayed. My longing for that laughter gnaweth at me: oh, how can I still endure to live! And how could I endure to die at present!"*]

It's the lines of his body that give meaning to the struggle around him, it's the struggle known and possible to his muscles, to his veins, to the thin lines beating under his skin.

———❧———

The township of Stanton began with a dump. Billboards advertising soap and gasoline. A church—carpenter Gothic with spire à la Wren. Streets—all alike and all awful. Consumptive, public, tight little houses, "fancy" architecture with the paint peeling. Garbage can. Diapers on a line. A pampered dog on a cushion. A man's behind—planting nasturtiums. A woman sprawled, legs spread apart, on a porch. A woman pushing a perambulator and wiping the sweat off with the back of her hand.

Roark amidst it. Everyone looks at his hair. Most people turn away too quickly. Some stare with a blind, nameless, instinctive hatred. All uncomfortable. The alien. What had been joy in him is now arrogance, what had been strength is now a challenge, what had been freedom is a nameless threat. As to him—he sees no one. He walks, as he swam, straight to a given point. For him the street is empty. He could have walked there naked without concern.

Main square—shops about a lawn, a movie theater in competition with the stock theater. Signs in shop windows welcoming the "Class of '22," which is graduating today. He turns off into a side street at the end of which, on a knoll, stands the house of Mrs. Keating over a green ravine.

———❧———

Roark versus the eclectics. ("Have you thought of clients?" "Yes, I have thought of clients. I do not presume to consider myself the only man of good taste in the world.") Mention of Cameron.

Lead up to his utter selfishness. Dean mentions that he has no friends, has refused to join fraternities. "Won't you reconsider? You have worked hard for your education." (Sketch his past.) "No, I won't reconsider." Whom to notify? No one. No parents. No guardians. Who was his father? He has no one now.

"We have decided. I believe, as was stated at this morning's meeting, that the profession is not for you. You're giving it up, aren't you?"

"Oh, no. I'm just beginning."

"Who'll give you work?"

"I believe I know someone who will."

Dean's anger. "You are dangerous." End of interview.

("I haven't the time to waste on exercises in calligraphy, copying. I'm here to learn. When I'm given a project, its only value to me is to learn to solve it as I would solve a real one. I did them the way I'll build them.")

### The Eclectics

#### Artistically

Everything beautiful in architecture has been done already. We cannot improve, we can only try to repeat.

There is something good in every style. We can only choose from the great masters. Who are we to improve upon them? Of course, we must make proper adaptations to meet modern conditions.

That is *tradition*. We cannot break with tradition. It is our sacred heritage. Nothing worthwhile is invented by one man in architecture. The proper creative process is a long, slow, gradual, collective one, in which each man adds his little bit to what has gone on before. This is the splendid march of civilization. And will always be so. The modernists? A passing mode, a freak fury of exhibitionists trying to attract attention. Look at Cameron.

#### Sociologically

An architect is not an end in himself. He is only a small part of a social unit. He does not build to please himself. Cooperation is the key word to the modern world and to architecture particularly. Furthermore, the designing and artistic inspiration is only a small part of an architect's equipment. He must also be a business man and a diplomat. Above all, he must consider the client. *The Client*, above all. It's his cash that pays for the luxury of your artistic inspirations, isn't it? He's the one to live in the house. Who are you to tell him what he must live in? You're only an employee, like his secretary, his chauffeur and his cook. You are only to execute his desire, in the best manner you are able and give it the proper artistic form.

*Roark*

*Artistically*

Why do you think the Greek style beautiful? Just because your grand-father did and told you so, and his grandfather, and millions before him?

I am a man. I choose a work to do. I must do the very best possible to me. I am the sole judge of that best. If I give up that right of valuing, I might as well give up the right to all thought. If I think, I value. I alone. How do I know who is right among the others? I can only judge of what is right to me, for me.

Times have changed. New means, new materials. We put up awful imi-tations, we're uncomfortable, wasteful, dirty. Why?

Architecture—the most important of the arts. Changing the face of nature, man's background, that against which his whole life is played. In no other art are there set standards. The artist works as he alone pleases. Why not, then, in architecture? [*AR's formulations here are open to a subjectivist interpretation; see* The Romantic Manifesto *for her defense of the objec-tivity of esthetic standards.*]

Form follows function. Consider the reality of what you're doing.

*Sociologically*

The people do not know what they want. There is no such thing as the spirit of a people. [Someone must] *tell* the people what they want. There are men born to tell and men born to accept. *That* is cooperation. I do not build for a client. He only [offers] a problem for me to solve. I am glad to have a client so that I may build. Not vice versa. The client is my means, not my end. The building is the end.

# 7

# NOTES WHILE WRITING

AR began writing The Fountainhead on June 26, 1938. She finished four and a half years later, on December 31, 1942. The writing went slowly at first, in part because of the difficulty of the task, and in part because financial troubles caused her to interrupt the work. In 1939, she wrote two plays: an adaptation of We the Living (entitled The Unconquered) and a philosophical murder mystery, Think Twice (published in The Early Ayn Rand). In 1941, she took a job as a reader for Paramount Pictures. Her (unpaid) campaign work for Wendell Willkie in the 1940 presidential election was another major interruption. As a result, nearly two-thirds of the novel was still unwritten when she signed a contract with a publisher (Bobbs-Merrill) in December 1941. She had to write at a furious pace to complete the novel by the agreed-upon deadline of January 1, 1943.

The above history is reflected in the present chapter. Whereas Part I involved detailed analyses in her journal, there are comparatively few notes that pertain to specific scenes in the last two-thirds of the novel. By the time these scenes were written, of course, her ideas were clear and she had little need to make notes.

The vast majority of her notes while writing are included here. Some of the material is undated; I have specified the year when it is known. I have omitted a revised outline of Part IV because it describes events as they happen in the published novel; the only other notes omitted were repetitive or cryptic.

**July 18, 1938**

*Chapter II*

Francon's speech (his distinctions).

The audience. Peter in it. Peter's thoughts about everyone noticing him, he and others. Peter's qualifications: star student, president of student body (he has always been elected), star of track team, fraternities.

Peter receiving his degree, Paris scholarship, gold medal. Congratulations of the boys and of professors, Petechin among them (referring to his one building), mention of Peter's graduation project. Francon's mention of a job.

Peter at the banquet. His talk on architecture. Peter's thoughts about Roark. Roark's help. Party of boys planned for later that night.

Peter goes home. Wonders if people notice him or know who he is, determines that he'll *make* them know who he is. His and Mrs. Keating's past.

Peter comes home. Roark and Tony on the porch—Tony's protestations to Roark—slight encounter between Peter and Tony. Tony doesn't like Peter, Tony leaves.

Peter-Roark. Peter "wants to speak to him." Peter's condolences. The friendly scene. Mrs. Keating rushes down, hearing his voice. She's been waiting for him; he's annoyed. Peter is gloating about Francon's offer and hesitating about the Paris trip. Mrs. Keating settles that. Peter asks what Roark will do. His horror at the mention of Cameron. Peter raises the question of living together—with Mrs. Keating keeping house for them. Roark refuses.

Vesta comes down. Vesta—appearance and status. Her brusqueness and forced nonchalance. Roark insists on knowing what's the matter with her. She confesses. Roark's plan for the three of them to move to New York. Peter and Vesta agree. Mrs. Keating's horrified protests overruled.

Roark goes to pack, Vesta to dream, Peter to his party.

Peter on way to party. Complete intoxication of success. The great things he will do.

What did he graduate in? Oh yes, architecture.

**October 16, 1938**

Roark: feature one building in each important line, show how he knows the important activities of life—and what he thinks of them.

*Friendship*: Roark is the only one capable of real friendship—because he is able to look at people in themselves, *un*selfishly—because he is *too* selfish, because they are not a part of him in any way. He does not need them basically, does not need their opinion of him, and [therefore he] can value them for their own sake, a relationship of two equals. Roark does not want to impress himself upon others, because he does not need it.

Other people cannot be friends, because in their petty selfishness—in their concern with themselves *through* others—they can be interested in friends *only* as those friends concern them. They become tyrants, because they need the slavery of others to inflate them.

[Show] not only what second-handedness (as an abnormal, *basic* preoccupation with others) does to the person himself, but also to those others, to his relation with them. (Hatred of all who *don't belong*. If one isn't too concerned with others—why want them to "belong"?) You can have real freedom (in every sense, freedom from one another) only when you stop being too concerned with others.

**November 8, 1938**

For the whole—*every stage of the lives motivated by certain principles*. Every detail of how a certain conception of existence works, what it does—*and what are the results*.

**November 10, 1938**

It's terribly bad to be conscious of yourself as others see you, [whether they see you as] good or bad. Take yourself for granted. The consciousness that feels alone—without the weight of other eyes watching—is the only healthy consciousness.

Another aspect of second-handedness: The horror of being nothing; every person one faces is not a person, not a rational, cognizant being, but a blind, deaf agglomeration of bits from everyone else, unthinking and impotent, without the will of decision, so that nothing in that person can be reached, nothing can act or respond. It is the hopelessness of attempting to speak to an animal—there is no language, there is no possibility of a language, there is a barrier that can't be broken. The silent, universal, omnipresent beast of "other people"—unreachable, irresponsible; vague and intangible, yet more real than the concrete beings who represent it, who are only its fragments.

[*The following note was added on February 21, 1940:*]

Toohey is the one to capitalize on this. The soil is ready, begging for some seeds, because it is empty. Toohey gives them the seeds. Toohey molds public opinion. And Toohey is the one to do it, not someone better, not the Roark type, because what Toohey preaches is in accord with and in support of the one certainty of the mob: its rightness in being second-hand, its fear of the single, the strong and the definite. Toohey makes this second-handedness, this cowardice and universal "equality," into a virtue. And he is thus armed to fight the Roark type.

**December 12, 1938**

*For Roark-Dominique:* She likes to think of the granite broken by his hands, [when] under his hands.

*For Toohey:* His great enthusiasm for and preoccupation with books on children and animals, such books as *Ferdinand* or *Tapiola*, such movies as *Snow White* and all of Walt Disney. It would be Toohey who'd find philosophical significance in Donald Duck. Why? It's not Donald Duck that he's boosting. It's philosophy that he's destroying.

*For Roark:* Watch and trace the development, the growth of his ideas on architecture and what he does with them, the changes in his work.

[*The life of William Randolph Hearst, the newspaper publisher, suggested to AR several concretes for the life of Gail Wynand.*]

John K. Winkler, *W. R. Hearst, An American Phenomenon.*

The principles of "circulation getters":

Be first with the news. Go out and get it. In case of need, make it. Display it strikingly, distribute it swiftly and sell it cheaply. Avoid brain-racking comment upon it. Follow it up until the evening of the day before the public wearies of it. Then get something fresh. . . .

What is news, and to whom? To the circulation-getters, pure and simple, it is what will cause most excitement among the widest public. It is a common denominator of ordinary minds. It is what will capture the crowd. . . .

The most glaring of his faults, it has been said, is that Hearst and the men he placed in charge of his growing enterprises have too often denounced the successful merely because they were successful, and painted rainbows of hope for the unsuccessful merely because they were poor—and numerous. . . .

Hearst loves to astonish. Yet there is something in his enigmatic temperament that keeps him from warm, intimate friendship. The man is Oriental-minded. . . . The Orient whispers to Hearst in many ways—in his lordly opulent living, his unceasing quest for the beautiful, his curious instinct for watching others squirm, his habit of falling away from a wolfish world and embarking upon long pilgrimages attended by one faithful and obedient courier. [. . .]

Within two years the twenty-six year old editor, owner and sole pro-prietor, had converted the Examiner into the greatest feature newspaper in the West—and within five or six years the paper had become by far the greatest money-maker on the Coast. No man ever mastered the root ele-ments of journalism so speedily as the youth fresh from Harvard. From the first, as Roosevelt said, he manifested uncanny ability at cutting across lots and anticipating public opinion. He knew what would please the mass even before the mass began to move toward his bargain counter with its gaudy headlines, juicy morsels and (later) colored supplements, cartoons and comics. [. . .]

Hearst was very interested in machinery; he always introduced the latest in his newspaper shops, and even did inventing and improving himself.

Camaraderie with his subordinates, fun and excitement in the office, in his early days in San Francisco.

Hearst got the best newspaper talent he could get—and did not spare money to buy it. He paid very high salaries.

Sample of his methods:

Word filtered into San Francisco that the famous Hotel Del Monte at Mon-terey, some 200 miles down the coast, was in flames. While the other papers waited for the news to reach them in the leisurely, traditional way, Hearst chartered a special train, filled it with staff writers and sketch artists and rushed south. The following morning the Examiner came out with a fourteen-page extra containing one of the most vivid stories of a disaster that had ever been published in the West. . . . Most of the headlines and legends had been written by Hearst himself. Three editions were run off to appease the popular demand.

Hearst enters civic problems in his paper:

A new city charter was proposed. The paper fought the charter on the ground that it would entrench the bosses in power. The charter was defeated. Then the Examiner proposed a new charter that would give the people a greater measure of home rule, and carried it. It opened a crusade to force a privately owned water company to lower its rates. It won that, as well as a campaign to force the electric companies to place their wires underground in the suburban district.

Hearst went after local bosses of the Democratic Party and caused their indictments by a grand jury.

One of his woman reporters pretended to faint on the street, was taken to the city receiving hospital and then wrote an exposé of it, which caused reforms.

A baby was born in the City Prison Hospital to a drunken prostitute. The child would have become a charity charge had not Hearst stepped in. The birth occurred a few weeks before Christmas. The Examiner started a fund for the baby and called it "The Little Jim Fund."

The baby died, and Hearst applied the money to build a hospital for crippled children. He personally guaranteed the entire sum, while trying to raise it by appeals in his paper.

One of his reporters jumped off a ferry boat in order to see how much time would be taken to rescue him (he was an expert swimmer). This caused reform of ferry apparatus and drills for life-saving.

Hearst's bitterest early battle was against the Southern Pacific Railroad, which controlled the state. Hearst got hold of letters written by the Railroad's attorney and published them, creating a sensational scandal.

Hearst bought the New York *Morning Journal* in 1895. He was thirty-two years old. He lost a great deal of money before he made this paper pay, but he spent the money heedlessly. He started a battle with Pulitzer's *World*. He cut the price of his paper under that of the *World*. He raided his rivals. He took their best men away from them; he doubled the men's salaries. At one time he lured the entire staff of the *Sunday World*: editors, artists, writers. He signed all the best writers and famous names he could get. "Invariably he

would go into the composing-room at midnight to help make up the paper,
and his gift for striking display and news arrangement was the marvel of his
associates." His greatest concern was to build circulation at any cost. [. . .]

> One night he came into the composing-room and looked over the make-up
> of the first page. He said the story they were playing as second in impor-
> tance was really more interesting than the first and suggested that they
> should remake. "I agree with you," said the make-up man, "but I am afraid
> there is no time to reset." Hearst smiled, pushed the whole form off the
> table, making a beautiful pile of pied type, then asked: "Now, is there time
> to reset? . . . There is always time to make a thing better."

Hearst started on what he called the "new journalism." His slogan was
"While others talk the *Journal* acts" and "What is everybody's business is
the *Journal*'s business." He decided to be the champion of the people not
only in words but in action. His paper started bringing legal actions and
injunctions against corporations and public abuses, e.g., an injunction preventing the Board of Aldermen from granting a gas-franchise, which the
*Journal* found illegal, and others like that. [. . .]

"A mobile 'murder squad' was formed to solve criminal mysteries
independently of the police (by the paper). Liberal rewards were offered."
One murder was actually solved by the *Journal*, when it published reproduc-
tions of the oil-cloth in which the body was found, and one of the reporters
traced the purchaser of the cloth and exposed the murderer.

Hearst liked features with "women appeal":

> On one occasion the entire third page was given over to "Stories of Love
> and Romance Gathered From the News of the Day." Each of the seven
> columns were headed by heart-shaped illustrations. Soon "Letters From
> the Lovelorn" blossomed out. [. . .]

The incident when two editors of Hearst's escaped to Europe, from
overwork, and Hearst sent a reporter after them, found them, took them back
and never reproached them for it. "He greeted the deserters politely, without
a word of reproof or admonition, just as though he had seen them every day
for the past month."

Hearst helped many people, but always concealed his personal charities.

Hearst started agitating for the Spanish-American War in order to
create "live" news. There was a story, unproved, but considered possible:
Hearst sent special correspondents to Cuba, one of whom was

Frederic Remington, the eminent artist, who drew notable sketches of Spanish cruelty. After a short time Remington sent this telegram from Havana: "W. R. Hearst, New York Journal, NY: Everything is quiet. There is no trouble here. There will be no war. I wish to return. Remington." This is the answer Hearst is said to have written: "Remington, Havana: Please remain. You furnish the pictures and I'll furnish the war. W. R. Hearst." [. . .]

When Hearst opened a paper in Chicago, he had to fight a war with other papers. They all hired thugs to interfere with the distribution and selling of one another's papers. But this did not discourage Hearst and his paper remained. [. . .]

Hearst obtained and published letters written by the vice-president of Standard Oil. (He bought the letters from minor employees who stole them and let Hearst take photostats of them.) The letters showed corruption of senators and others. They created a great scandal. It was even rumored that the President asked Hearst whether he had any letters referring to him. "Nothing that I intend to publish at this time," replied Hearst blandly.

Hearst started publishing magazines in 1903. One of his greatest successes was *Good Housekeeping* which appealed to women and to advertisers, with its innovation of tests for the products advertised. [. . .]

One artist who was invited to work for a Hearst magazine answered: "The only enterprise in which I shall ever voluntarily join William Randolph Hearst will be one of self-destruction."

Hearst went into motion picture production, but had to give up, losing a great deal of money. (His political career, after terrific ballyhoo, was also a failure. He lost the election for governor of New York and the nomination for president.) [. . .]

He has a special system to check up on all his publications. He keeps a man to read them and to see that they carry out Hearst's instructions. If they don't, they get a note of warning from Hearst. This gives the impression that he personally reads all of them.

Hearst's executives have a vast respect for and a very appreciable terror of their chief. Hearst derives Machiavellian delight in sitting in the wings and relishing quarrels between the figures on his stage. When he has had his fun, and is convinced the scrap has gone far enough, he takes a hand. Generally, he "suggests" a holiday to one or the other disputant. [. . .]

Hearst's belief about journalism:

The important thing for a newspaper to do in making circulation is to get excited when the public gets excited. People will buy any paper which seems to express their feelings in addition to printing the facts. . . .

Why, then [asks Winkler], is he not the uncrowned King of America, a truly great leader? Because the average American citizen distrusts his motives. The average citizen is willing to be amused or entertained by him but has no confidence in Hearst's intellectual sincerity. That is why he is one of the most melancholy figures of our time. Hearst has a thousand readers to one follower. The readers enjoy his comics, his high-pressure editorials, his provocative pictures, but they have deep distrust of his motives. They no longer follow the shifting winds of his fancy. [. . .]

Hearst does not allow his papers to have his biography in their "morgue."

"Newspaper work is the best line of work that I know of," says Hearst. "If I had my life to live over again, I would be a newspaper man, and merely try to be a better one."
If he had his life to live over, one wonders if Hearst would tread the same path. Would his motto again be: "Capture the crowd at any cost"? Or would he elect to employ his astonishing talent to ennoble, to spiritualize the crowd? No one can tell.

This book lists (1928): Twenty-seven Hearst newspapers, nine magazines in America and three in England, one book publishing corporation, eight film and news services.

**Undated**

Watch out for Roark being too heroic and always right too easily. (In particular, in scene with building he saves, Chapter V.)
*For Roark-Holcombe.* Roark asks him why one must copy the Parthenon. Holcombe answers: "Not the Parthenon. You're quite right, Saint Peter's Cathedral."

### For Dominique

Disillusionment—sees through people and everything—and doesn't like it.

Fierce independence—nothing in such a world will hold her.

Enjoys destruction and deliberate nastiness—her answer to life and the only way to make it interesting.

Has denied herself all desire or enthusiasm—because life can hold her through that and she will not give it such an opportunity.

She has contempt for all ideals—because of the ideals that she has been taught (Christian brotherhood).

### For Roark-Dwight

When Roark is broke, before going to Connecticut, he does not hide the fact from Dwight at all; he has no inkling of the idea that he should keep up his prestige for the sake of Dwight, who looks up to him. [*Larry Dwight, a minor character that AR cut from the novel, was a draftsman whom Roark met while working for John Eric Snyte.*]

**Undated**

[*The following fragment is from an early draft of Part I. It describes Heddy Adler, a mistress of Roark's who was later cut from the novel. Heddy is reminiscent of Jinx in the short story* Good Copy (*see* The Early Ayn Rand). *She represents a type that AR liked, but never found a place for in her novels.*]

She was utterly incapable of two things: of lying and of denying herself a desire; she did not quite grasp the possibility of either process. It was just as plausible to her to push her way through a crowd [to see] a steam shovel as it would have been [to see] a royal coronation; she would have enjoyed either. She had been spoiled and sheltered, accustomed to seeing her every wish granted; she had emerged from it completely sure of herself, neither arrogant nor offensive, but irresistible in the bright, innocent self-assurance of a person who had been spared all contact with pain. She acted as one would act if this were a dream world and life contained nothing to make lightness feel guilty and men were free to give beauty and significance to the insignificant gestures of their every moment. She was completely real in being unreal. [. . .]

She was not afraid of Roark and she did not question the things she could not understand in him. She had not expected that she would love him, but she never needed reasons or explanations for the unexpected. He was not exactly like other people; she neither approved of it nor condemned it; she took it for granted; she never thought of resenting it, she was too avidly curious; and one universal trait had passed her by entirely; it never occurred to her, upon meeting anything strange and different, that that strangeness and difference were to be taken as some deep personal insult to her. She did not doubt herself; she had no compulsion to doubt others. [. . .]

**Undated**

### To do:

When Part I is finished—go over it and make separate schedules for the development of Roark, Cameron, Keating, Toohey, Wynand, Dominique, Katie. (Minor: check on Vesta, Heller, Francon, Mrs. Keating.)

Where and how much is given of Roark's architectural philosophy? How much is necessary?

More important—and watch this for schedule: Roark's philosophy of life.

How about the mind versus the emotions? How much of that can or should be included? Where? In what form?

Roark's egotism versus Keating's egotism? Where to stress and explain this?

---

Remember: "Form follows function"—in the writing and planning.

(Enough of the glorification of the people as "natural" and "true." Show what the *people* are.)

**Undated**

[*Here are the "character development schedules" referred to above. AR names what is shown about the character in each scene.*]

### Roark

CHAPTER I: *In the mountains. Exaltation at thoughts of architecture. Expulsion. Talk with Dean.*

Appearance, great love for architecture, modernism, some of

his convictions on architecture, independence, self-assurance, cold indifference to people, mention of his past.

CHAPTER II: *Scene with Keating.*

A touch of gentleness and understanding. The courage of his decision to work for Cameron.

CHAPTER III: *First meeting with Cameron.*

Quiet assurance. Gets what he wants without saying much. Respect for Cameron.

CHAPTER IV: *Scene of Cameron firing him.*

The calm that nothing can shake. A glimpse of what awaits him—he accepts it.

CHAPTER V: *Meeting with Vesta. Incident at building with Cameron drunk.* [*These scenes were cut and later published in* The Early Ayn Rand.]

A touch of the unconventional with Vesta. Indifferent interest in her. His attitude on the site of a building under construction. His ability and quick decision. Knocking out the contractor. Talks with Cameron—his understanding and devotion to work.

CHAPTER VI: *Affair with Vesta. Scene of Cameron having expected commission. Help to Keating on his first project.*

His indifference to Vesta, his absorption in his work and ideas, her reaction to him—fear of him, his taking her as an act of cruelty. His terrific work on the commission—and calm in the face of defeat. His ability in helping Keating—and calm contempt.

CHAPTER VII: *Cameron gives up.*

His calm in the face of a disaster.

CHAPTER VIII: *Peter's offer. Clash with Vesta. In Francon's office. Mike.*

His closed attitude on people and Vesta's fear of it. His cold indifference to her and snub to Keating. His silent torture in Francon's office. His love for actual sites of construction. His ability with building work—Mike's admiration, his response to a person like Mike.

CHAPTER IX: *Fired. Looking for job.*

First real test of his integrity—he loses job. His calm about looking for work, reactions of people to him, his inability to worry too much, his immovable faith in the future.

CHAPTER X: *Job with Snyte. Break with Vesta.*

The difference between Vesta's feeling for life and his. His cold ruthlessness in breaking with her.

CHAPTER XI: *The Heller house.*

His attitude on work with Snyte—ability to forget. His wonder about the world around him. His direct ruthlessness in taking commission for Heller house.

CHAPTER XII: *The building of the Heller house.*

His passionate happiness in his first work. Cameron's prediction. Some of his ideas on architecture.

CHAPTER XIV: *Gowan's Station. Talk with Heller on commissions. Three refused clients. Fargo Store. Sanborn House. Heddy.*

His unsocialness—as expressed by Heller. His quiet stubbornness with clients. More of his thoughts on architecture. A touch of the unconventional in meeting with Heddy. His "caste-system" with people. [*This last reference is to the following passage, later cut: "He seldom looked at women; there were few whom he could want, as there were few people to whom he could speak. He had an instinctive caste-system of his own; he looked for a mark upon each forehead; a mark clear to him in the lines of a face, unseen by everyone else; without that mark men did not seem to exist for him, nor women; they lost all reality to him and he lost all response. When he found that mark, the stamp of a peculiar freedom that was more than freedom, he looked upon his finds with interest and eagerness. . . ."*]

CHAPTER XV: *Idleness. Heddy. Holcombe's bribe. Help Keating with competition project.*

Calm in the face of idleness. Lighter touch with Heddy. Takes no advantage of his connections. Refuses Holcombe—wonders about Holcombe's reasons. Won't enter competition.

CHAPTER XVI: *Scene with Keating. Refuses bank commission. Leaves for Connecticut.*

Contempt for Keating—won't take money he needs. Torture and almost breakdown from waiting. The great bank commission. Refuses. Ruthlessness toward himself in his decision to work as common laborer.

*Keating*

CHAPTER I: *Reference to him by Mrs. Keating.*

His brilliance as a student.

CHAPTER II: *Graduation. Talk with Roark. Decision about job.*

Brilliance and popularity. His second-hand absorption with his relation to other people and with his superiority to them. Insincerity with people. Touch of sincerity with Roark—his helplessness and lack of assurance. Lets mother influence him, even though he neither loves nor respects her. Mother pushed him into career.

CHAPTER III: *First day in Francon's office.*

Lack of assurance—gains it only from comparing himself to others. Clever playing up to Francon—dig at Stengel.

CHAPTER IV: *Relations with Francon, takes over Davis' work, scene with Katie.*

Taking Francon into his hands, insincerity and shrewdness in dealing with Davis, sincerity and vagueness with Katie, his own better side which he cannot sustain, confesses to her his real opinion of Francon and his career, exhibits good touch in refusing to meet Toohey.

CHAPTER V: *Establishes himself in office, betrays Davis.*

Servility and appeal to clients, unprincipled ruthlessness in advancing himself, weakness in avoiding Katie, cheap love affairs, touch of hypocrisy with mother.

CHAPTER VI: *Gets rid of Stengel. His first designing job.*

Subtle diplomacy, treachery to Francon in his manner of eliminating Stengel, orgies with Francon. Attitude on his work—only fear, no real ideas or creative impulse. Runs to Roark—accepts his help and resents him.

CHAPTER VII: *Steady advance. Proposal to Katie.*

Beginning of fourflushing with money and position. Hints about Francon's daughter. He is greatly satisfied with himself—has lost the sincerity of admitting anything to Katie, doesn't see it any more, loves Francon and his position, wouldn't mind meeting Toohey, indifference to work, concentrates on the social side of it. But proposes to Katie—somewhat unexpectedly, as a last flash of his better self.

CHAPTER VIII: *Gets Roark into Francon's office.*

Fourflushing before Roark. Needs Roark, uses him, yet in a way feels superior, enjoys subtly insulting Roark and ordering him about.

CHAPTER IX: *Does nothing for Roark after Roark is fired.*

Drops Roark when he feels he needs him no longer.

CHAPTER X: *Strike. Protest meeting. Sees Dominique.*

His restlessness and doubts when left alone and idle. Needs Katie. His fear at her absorption in Toohey. Sees Dominique—and decides to follow it up, even though he fears and dislikes her.

CHAPTER XI: *Holcombe's party. Meets Dominique. Francon's hints.*

Pursues Dominique, plans to take advantage of Francon—even though he doesn't really like Dominique.

CHAPTER XII: *Scene in Roark's new office.*

Resents Roark's success and advancement over him. Instinctively, not understanding it and bewildered by it. Later—nasty, patronizing remarks about Roark.

CHAPTER XIII: *Luncheon with Dominique. Scene when Katie asks him to marry her—and the consequences.*

Goes after Dominique without warning her. Realizes he's planned two futures; decides to let future decide and drifts. His love for Katie asserts itself when he is ready to marry her, has feeling of his own danger, but lets his mother and the considerations of other people—career, Francon, society, church, etc.—stop him. Would have gone through if Katie insisted, but she doesn't and he lets it go. His uncertainty and reliance upon others.

CHAPTER XV: *Campaign against Heyer. The Cosmo-Slotnick competition. Love scene with Dominique.*

Ruthlessness in his hounding of Heyer. Weakness on the Cosmo-Slotnick competition, dread of another winner, hysterical vanity, runs to Roark again. Is physically infatuated with Dominique, is terribly disappointed, but still proposes to her.

CHAPTER XVI: *Heyer's death. Wins competition. Scene with Roark. Celebration of partnership.*

Horrible cruelty to Heyer. Triumph of vanity and "second-handedness" in his attitude on winning competition. Slight hint of conscience in thought of Roark. Attempts to talk Roark into conventional attitude—doesn't know what prompts him. Attempts to bribe Roark—and screams his hatred of him, realizing Roark's contempt. Celebration of partnership—"second-hand" satisfaction.

*Toohey*

CHAPTER IV: Article in *New Frontiers*—first hint of his philosophy.
CHAPTER VI: Katie's talk about him—hints on his manner and methods. Small mention—Keating's fear of him.
CHAPTER VII: "Sermons in Stones"—radicalism, criticism of present economic system, down with individuals, glorifying the masses, glorifying the united and the obedient, attack on modern architecture. Brilliance of style and erudition.

Katie about him: the beginning of her absorption, his indif-

ference to the clippings, and yet . . . his making speech at
Union.
CHAPTER X: His column on the Banner. The situation on the strike,
the noble gesture of a public martyr. The speech—stress on organiza-
tion and the lack of freedom in individual choice. The magnetism of
his voice. Katie's absorption in him frightens Keating.
CHAPTER XI: Dominique on Toohey—the perfect skunk, the mono-
lith, his threat to the world, the testing stone.
CHAPTER XV: Said nothing about the Heller house.
CHAPTER XII: Katie's fit of terror of him.
CHAPTER XV: On Cosmo-Slotnick competition jury.

*Wynand*

CHAPTER V: First mention of papers—"gas-station murder."
CHAPTER VI: Cameron's mention: "legs, crusade against wealth,
rights of the downtrodden, unwed mothers, recipes, utility companies, horoscopes." Circulation growing.
CHAPTER IX: Francon's reference to Lili Lansing. The castle, the
party (Caesar Borgia) and the photos with children.
CHAPTER X: Wynand on the strike. Reverses principles when it hits
him. His real estate operations. His unpredictable inconsistency. The
appeals to trashy patriotism. People's dread of him and his
vengeance. Heller's reference to him. The startling gesture toward
Toohey.
CHAPTER XI: Dominique on Wynand—great art lover and perfect
sideshow baiter. Decadent.
CHAPTER XII: The slums campaign. Wynand on a world cruise.
Alvah Scarret.

**February 18, 1940**

[*AR critiques her first draft of Part I.*]
[The Chapter I scene in] Roark's room: Is it necessary at all? If so—do
better, put in more character.

CHAPTER I: Roark planted too soon—too much of him given—too
obviously heroic—the author's sympathy too clear. (?) Don't like
Roark's outbreak with Dean—can be treated differently. *Don't* dialogue thoughts—narrate them (such as the Dean's and Mrs.

Keating's). Roark changing his drawing—too much detail. (?) In this first chapter—plant Roark: ornament—that his buildings are not modernistic boxes?

CHAPTER II: Change Mrs. Keating's approach to a subtler and meaner one—like the one she uses later about Katie. Give one speech on Keating's attitude about architectural convictions. (?)

CHAPTER III: Miss Bisbee—unnecessary? Too long about Francon's office—can be cut. Cameron's biography should be gone over—some awkward passages. Cameron's criticism of Roark's drawings—don't like it.

CHAPTER IV: Details about Tim Davis—unnecessary. Make it shorter. Roark's life and his tenement room—can be done better, simpler, there's a little too obvious an effect there. Cameron giving Roark a raise—too much niceness. (?) Don't have Cameron dropping his head on his arms.

CHAPTER V: Roark looking for the "stamp" on faces—should be planted earlier and separately and more importantly. Omit incident with faked plans—too much and too detailed. Change it to narrative of Davis simply becoming useless, being crowded out—and never knowing how it was done and Keating remaining his best friend and even giving him a job and boasting of this "good deed." Don't like all of incident with Roark fixing building—too long—technically dishonest—and Roark too able. Cameron's struggle against contractor unnecessary—reserve that for Roark's future. [*AR cut this last scene—it has been reprinted in* The Early Ayn Rand.]

CHAPTER VI: First reference to the Wynand papers should be separate and more important. On Vesta's first resentment [of Roark]—here is the place to put the other side of her character—the "social" one.

The Dunlop incident—couldn't it be cut? Important psychologically and as example of Keating's methods—but perhaps too detailed for a mere incident. Keating's first job of designing—shorter and clearer. Roark's corrections—all the details or none. Narrative would be better than dialogue. The Cameron sequence from Austen Heller to flashback and back again is bad. Put flashback and [summary] of past year first, then on to Heller and the Wynand papers. *This* is the place for the first mention of the Wynand papers.

CHAPTER VII: Better last paragraph of office closing sequence—more emphasis for drawing on the wall. In resume of Keating's rise— stress more (and *most*) the second-handedness: his worrying about people's admiration for him and people's envy, his comparing his

achievements with others, his "good deeds"—and boasting of them.
Mrs. Keating's arrival not very well worded. Also—the transition to
Katie.
CHAPTER VIII: Cut some of Keating's cruder insults to Roark.
Keating must be much subtler in this. More about Mike—show why
Roark likes him and why Roark would like him immediately.
CHAPTER IX: Shorter on Roark's looking for a job. No need for
single incidents; they can all be blended into one narrative—all
except Prescott.
CHAPTER X: Lead up into the strike—simpler and more authentic.
CHAPTER XI: Better and clearer summary of Roark's six months with
Snyte.
CHAPTER XII: Cut out Heller's thoughts on men's interdependence.
*Much* too early. Leave just the friendship angle—the unselfish devotion. Don't like Roark's talk on architecture—give it better build-up,
lead into it better, and also better wording and more original thoughts
and expressions. Heller's biography—very last. More pointed and
fresher.
CHAPTER XIV: Cut out Heddy entirely. I don't think that Roark needs
another love. Cut out Sanborns—too detailed for this part of the
book—not detailed enough in itself. Perhaps cut Fargo Store—
another way of covering this period has to be found.
CHAPTER XV: Cut out Heddy. Cut out Holcombe incident—or put in
another one like it instead.
CHAPTER XVI: In conversation with Mike—plant that Roark does not
want a white-collar job. Control the obvious, pointless exaggerations
in the description of the movie furor.

---

*About first part in general:*
Do not dialogue thoughts. Control adjectives—cut the weakening ones.
Do not use adjectives unless they are different and illuminating. Don't
go into over-detailed analyses of psychology—unless it's something new
and illuminating to say. Don't give any details whatever—in sentences or
thoughts—unless you have something new to say.
Stress the second-handedness whenever possible, particularly in
Keating, but a different facet of it each time. Cut out episodes that do not
bear on that theme. The book is not about architecture, it's about Roark
against the world and about the workings of that thing in the world which

opposes him. Give only enough pure architecture to make the background real. But only *as a background*. Eliminate bromides or convenient colloquial expressions ready-made, even in places that are mere transitions, such as "and it made film history," "round of nightclubs," etc.

**Undated**

[*For the scene by the granite quarry, when Roark and Dominique speak for the first time.*]

Estrangement—antagonism.

Her putting him in his place as a worker.

Her directness and defiant wit.

His mockery in his quiet acceptance of the position she is imposing upon him—and when she attempts (faintly) to bring in the personal, it is he who refuses, sticking to the "Yes, Miss Francon" attitude of a respectful worker.

[Roark:] "You want me and I know it and I'll make it vile, to show you the enormity of your desire, because you'll want me still. I'm obedient to you now, I'm nothing before you—and it won't change things. I'll crush you in spite of it, *because* of it, when the time comes."

[Dominique:] "I have you in my power. I'll torture you. I enjoy it. I want you to know that. I enjoy debasing you, because I'm debasing myself through it, because you'll conquer me some day—I want it—I hate you and I'll punish you for it."

All this on what appears as a discussion of his living conditions and her interest in the workers.

"You're boasting." "No, but . . . it changes so little." "In what?" "In your interest in workers. In the future. There are so many unchangeable things."

**February 21, 1940**

Toohey [promotes] Keating—because he *knows* that Keating did not design the Cosmo-Slotnick building.

Toohey writes a *profound* article on Keating's work, and tests Keating by asking him if he did mean all those things, knowing quite well that he, Toohey, has made them up. Keating agrees that he did—and Toohey is happy. Keating isn't quite sure whether he did mean all that or not and is not sure whether Toohey knows it or not, but is very sure that Toohey is pleased. (These touches in Toohey must be very subtle, vague and rare—only as a hint, particularly at first. Most of Toohey must seem to be very authentic, noble and "humanitarian.")

Toohey builds Keating up in print. Gives him commissions. Organizes the "Youth Club" of the A.G.A. with Keating as head. He controls the architectural profession through Keating. Disgrace to young sculptor on one of the buildings. (When Toohey switches to modernism, "Youth Club" switches with him.) The "youth"—and Keating—want to be "deep," learn nothing, are glad to have it given to them by Toohey. He drives Keating into complete spiritual dependence upon him. He inflates Keating with false, empty values—knowing they are empty, knowing that Keating will feel the emptiness without understanding it—and will, therefore, be ruined for any values. The emptier he is, the more Keating will need Toohey.

Toohey alone among his associates guesses at Wynand's real nature—at least to the extent of knowing that Wynand is not a mob-man at heart. Toohey, contrary to the dictates of his usual clever diplomacy, tries very hard to appear as a hero and a "man of integrity" before Wynand. Wynand ignores him completely, never considers him worth breaking. This makes Toohey furious—relegating him to the kind of man he knows himself to be.

### February 22, 1940

Part II must show Keating at his height, enjoying himself immensely (his idea of enjoyment, and the essential meaninglessness of it)—and plant the first seeds for his later downfall (mainly through Toohey getting hold of his spirit, because of the emptiness of that spirit).

### February 24, 1940

Toohey's [purpose is] to ruin the strong, the single, the original, the healthy, the joyous—with the weapon of "other people," of humanitarianism. To excuse all sins in kindness—and thereby to destroy all virtue. To kill happiness—in order to have slaves. No man is dangerous to him—except the happy man. He exists like a maggot—on wounds and sores.

### Undated

Toohey's greatest enemy—independence of spirit.
The first result of [independence] is great creation.
Toohey destroys all independence in people and all great achievement.
*For the first:* independence causes happiness. Toohey is out to destroy

and discredit—philosophically and practically—all happiness. Unhappy people look for a yoke—and they come to him.

*For the second:* To discredit great achievement, he sets up standards which are easy for the phonies. Hence—Toohey and Gertrude Stein, Walt Disney, and *Ferdinand the Bull.* [*Gertrude Stein seems to have been the model for the character Lois Cook, whose first name was originally Gertrude.*]

*For the first:* Catherine, Peter, Dominique, Dick Sanborn, attempt (later) at Wynand. (Also Vesta.) [*This is the last mention of Vesta Dunning in AR's notes.*]

*For the second: Roark,* sculptor, young writer, *Heller,* Peter as architect, death notice on Cameron.

The author of *Ferdinand the Bull* made into a "philosopher" by Toohey, as against the young writer.

**February 28, 1940**

For Gertrude [Lois Cook]: deliberate sloppiness—as careful as grooming—and for the same purpose.

Toohey's behavior after the assassination attempt—"theatrical only in too complete an absence of anything theatrical." Toohey is on his way to some "humanitarian lecture."

### *Advance questions for Part II*

Change which Roark would not make and which ruined contractor? (?)

What libel could really be dangerous to an architect's career? (Unsafety of construction.)

**March 4, 1940**

### *Part II: Revised Schedule of Chapters*

Chapters I and II: written (Roark-Dominique in quarry)

### III

October, 1928. Peter—his high standing. (Peter enters office. The newspaper. Story of Toohey's inheritance. Peter—on not meeting Toohey and no write-up.) The Cosmo-Slotnick building and incident of sculptor—

past—and sculptor has just been fired. Peter looking for another one. Review of Cosmo-Slotnick building and note from Toohey. News of attempt at Toohey's life. The story of the attempt. Peter's meeting with Toohey. (Toohey knows Peter did not design all of Cosmo-Slotnick building—and is pleased by it.) Peter accepting Toohey's ideas on his building. Toohey hints about his "committee of architects"—in the future. Toohey and Gertrude's commission. Toohey about Peter's romance with Catherine.

### IV

Sketches in papers and accounts of Roark's building for Enright. Peter-Catherine, her first "social worker" job. Peter meets Gertrude—her house. Gertrude's literary career. Their romance. Toohey's reference to Roark's building—"if it were important, I would have remembered it." Toohey questions Peter most significantly about Roark. Peter is surprised that all the questions are personal about Roark, not architectural at all. The meeting of the "committee of architects." Peter is president.

### V

Dominique's return to New York. Dominique-Toohey. Meeting of youth group. Peter—her looking for him.

### VI

Roark, the Enright Building, Austen Heller. The prospective client. The party. Roark-Dominique. Roark-Toohey. Toohey-Dominique.

### VII

Dominique's article against Roark—Toohey objects. Toohey-Dominique about past relationship of Roark-Peter. Dominique getting important commission for Peter. Interview: Roark-owner. Roark-Dominique—their night together.

### VIII

Early winter, 1929. Commission for "Unfinished Symphony." Reactions to that. Toohey and writer. Dominique-Roark. Dominique helping Peter. Toohey throwing Dominique and Peter together.

## IX

Campaign against "Symphony." Dominique-stockholder. Toohey makes Dominique lose her column. Dominique votes against Symphony. Work stopped (Fall, 1929). [*Note that the chapter on Toohey's background is missing here.*]

## X

Peter-Catherine. Dominique at "Symphony." Next day—Dominique marries Peter. Her night with Roark. Next morning—their break. [*The main events that AR planned in connection with the "Unfinished Symphony" were later transferred to the Stoddard Temple sequence.*]

## XI

Winter, 1929–1930. Toohey and old millionaire [Hopton Stoddard]. Roark gets commission for Temple. Roark and sculptor. Life of Peter-Dominique. Roark calls on her. Dominique posing for statue.

## XII

Fall, 1930. Temple finished. The scandal. The lawsuit. Cameron's death. [*In the novel, Cameron dies much earlier (towards the end of Part I).*]

## XIII

Early winter, 1931. Roark loses suit and everything. Goes to live in "Unfinished Symphony." Temple altered by Peter. The Wynand real estate project. Toohey's plans for Peter. Dominique is to meet Wynand. Scene of Roark on steps of Temple.

**March 1940**

### Main Questions

(1) Unfinished Symphony—example of the triumph of second-handedness.
(2) Toohey-Dominique.
(3) How Dominique loses her column (possible connection with Wynand).

**(4)** Toohey and the Wynand papers.
**(5)** Dominique-Roark: why she leaves him.

### Subordinate Questions

**(a)** Wynand. (Prepare him as a complete scoundrel. The oddness of his villainies. His passion for art.)
**(b)** Toohey-Heller. (The beginnings of the break. The parting of the ways. The two kinds of liberals.)

———————

Heller's foundation for relationships—Toohey objects. In connection with (b) above.

Dominique at Unfinished Symphony, sees man and his dirty action, sees all of society that will hurt her as this act has hurt her—decides to marry Peter. (Before this—lying at Roark's feet—in silence, in complete sincerity.) [In connection with] (5).

Toohey, knowing Wynand's tricks, deliberately builds up a writer of integrity, creates the occasion for a great display of integrity, in order to tempt Wynand to [crush] it—which Wynand does. (In connection with Unfinished Symphony? Heller?) [In connection with] (4) and (a).

Toohey, knowing what Wynand has prohibited, deliberately tells Dominique that it's prohibited—and she changes her mind to the opposite of what she intended to write and is fired. (Unfinished Symphony and Heller?) [In connection with] (2) and (3).

Toohey has to eliminate the top off the papers—Dominique and the writer whom Wynand ruins. [In connection with] (4).

**April 22, 1940**

[*For Kiki Holcombe's party, where Dominique discovers that Roark is the architect who designed the Enright House.*]

What do I wish to show by the party (besides the meeting of Roark and Dominique)? *Second-handedness.* What kind? *The social kind.* Which is?

A desperate desire to make an impression on others. They are not there to see but to be seen. Each wants to dominate the other and will crawl, lick feet, and make a fool of himself for that domination. They cannot talk shop. They cannot raise controversial subjects. Don't antagonize—above all. You've got to please them all. Don't mention what you're really interested in; it makes you too important. You gain importance here by being unimportant—in inverse ratio. Others are not interested in you as your own self; you offend them by presuming that they are. Become only a mirror for them, while they're trying to be a mirror for you. The vicious circle. Toohey as the one to start the circle rolling, because he [provides] a direction compatible with all those people's hidden aims. They all want importance—they can find it only in others. They want to be invited in order to get work in order to be invited here. (Use people to make money to use to impress people with.) There are no values—that is why they cling so desperately to people.

*I show this by (?):*

Attitude toward Howard Roark. ("The Enright House is almost as good as the Cosmo-Slotnick Building." "He will be another Peter Keating.") They know nothing about his work and are nothing. They are interested in: the cost of the Enright House, how did he get the commission from Enright, is he related to the Roarks of Schetwick? Don't give a person reality by inquiring into his ideas, i.e., into what *he is*. Detract from his importance by confining your interest to other people around him: tie him to family, acquaintances, bosses.

The conversations are about facts, not thoughts or opinions. Thoughts and opinions give personality to the one expressing them and *require personality* to be expressed. Facts are impersonal. They want it kept impersonal, because personality is dangerous. Or—they express opinions that are so bromidic as to be public property and safe. Resentment if anyone takes it out of that class. (On the one hand, things must be impersonal. On the other—utterly personal, that is, they want everybody to agree with them, because what is personal to them is tied irrevocably to others. They have no personality apart from others—so others must not have it either.)

Toohey's social technique: he insults the person, but includes himself in being insulted, points out a real weakness, but excuses it.

**1940**

[*With one third of the manuscript completed, AR began to submit* The Fountainhead *to prospective publishers. She wrote a synopsis, apparently intended to be sent with the manuscript, which contains a surprising idea for the climax. There is no evidence that this synopsis was ever sent to a publisher, and no other mention of the idea in AR's notes. Many years later, she remembered hesitating over her original idea for the climax (the dynamiting of Cortlandt Homes). She was concerned that it might be difficult to make it "plausible objectively" why Roark would be justified in such dynamiting. It may have been this doubt that prompted her to consider—perhaps only for a single day—an alternative climax.*]

Toohey has risen to a position of great power in society. He is the undeclared dictator of the intellectual and cultural life of the country. He has "collectivized" all the arts with his various "organizations," and he allows no prominence to anyone save to mediocrities of his choice, such as Keating, Lois Cook, and others of the same quality. He has to stop Roark. And when events come to a point where he can destroy Roark's career once more, it is Dominique who comes to Roark's assistance. She has learned a great deal from her strange marriage to Wynand. Dominique kills Toohey. It is more than a murder—it is the destruction of everything Toohey stood for. Roark takes the murder upon himself—the circumstances are such that either one of them can be accused and Roark forces her to remain silent; she agrees, but only until the outcome of the trial—she will speak if he is convicted.

This, then, is the sensational trial—Roark against society. There is a great deal of public indignation at the murder of a "humanitarian" and a "saint" such as Toohey. Wynand alone tries to stand by Roark—but public clamor forces him to betray Roark, to reverse the policy of his papers and demand Roark's conviction (see character outline). During the trial, the affair between Roark and Dominique is made public (though not her part in the murder).

Roark is acquitted—through the efforts of Austen Heller and his other loyal followers. Wynand is forced to divorce Dominique—his prestige with his respectable "Ladies' Club-home-church-family" audience demands it. He betrays and loses the only two human beings who had ever meant anything to him.

All his life, Wynand has dreamed of erecting a "Wynand Building" to house his newspapers, a monument to his achievement. Now, left alone and broken in spirit, his journalistic empire tottering, knowing that this empire will not survive him, Wynand makes one last gesture. He decides to erect the Wynand Building as his swan song. And he gives the commission to Roark. He barely speaks to Roark now, he wants no personal contact, no feeling between them; he gives the assignment to Roark in a short, blunt, businesslike interview, in cold, impersonal words. And only when Roark accepts and turns to leave the office, does Wynand add: "Build it as a monument to that spirit which is yours—and could have been mine."

When Dominique is freed of all ties to Wynand and comes back to Roark, never to leave him again, she finds him at the construction site of the Wynand Building, where the skeleton of Roark's greatest achievement is beginning to rise into the sky.

[*One can guess the reasons why AR quickly rejected the idea of Dominique murdering Toohey. First, the climactic action is taken by a secondary character rather than the hero. Second, such a climax would undercut the novel's theme by implying that Roark must be saved by a lesser character acting on the "malevolent universe" premise. Since Roark is the ideal, both morally and* practically, *his victory must result from his premises and his actions.*]

**December 11, 1941**

*For Toohey-Dominique:* "Don't fool yourself. You're not a bitch—you're a saint, which is much worse." A saint can't help but turn into a destructive, vicious monster like Dominique in the world as it is—consequently down with the saints, they make the world much too uncomfortable by seeing it too clearly.

---

*For Roark-Dominique:* His love for her declared for the first time when she leaves him—after she tells him that she's married. "I won't tell you that it's unselfish love—it's much greater because it's selfish, because it's my need." Power over another person is clean only when you can be proud of the person that you have in your power—perhaps love is the only place to know and exercise power. "You have much to learn—yourself—I can't help you." "Not until you come back, of your own will, completely, forever, and on your knees."

**December 17, 1941**

[*On this date, AR made her final chapter outline for the second half of Part II (she seems to have written up to Chapter VIII). She had recently contracted with Bobbs-Merrill to complete the novel by January 1, 1943.*]

**December 31, 1941**

For Roark: "The first man entering a fresh, clean world for the first time."

**1942**

*[The following notes pertain to the description of Gail Wynand's background in Chapter I, Part III.]*

### Gail Wynand

Gun—indifference.

His day. (Incident with Toohey and housing development.) Incident to show Wynand's powers, luxury, arbitrariness and his particular methods of pleasure.

Back to gun—thinks of his life.

First scene—tight figure against wall—fight—show his will to rule— his parents—relationship with father. Left alone at twelve.

**1)** Incidents to show: will to dominate, impatience with stupidity and being forced to obey stupidity, knowing that he knows best—and showing that he does. Ferocious independence.

**2)** Incidents to show: disappointment in human integrity and desire "not to be a sucker." Idealism turned to utter cynicism.

**3)** Forces his way into a newspaper. His rise. Unscrupulous incident of getting money to buy the newspaper.

**4)** Development of newspaper empire, stock market speculations, real estate speculations.

**5)** Wynand at the top—his public reputation, his private life. Incidents to show the constant use of his power. (The secret art gallery.) Back to gun—drops it. Finds [Toohey's gift]—scene with Toohey.

———◦———

Incidents:

**1)** *Childhood will to power and fight against stupidity.*
    **1.** First fight.
    **2.** Beating by longshoreman and later revenge.
**2)** *Disappointment in human integrity.*
    **1.** Columnist (?)
**3)** *Brilliant and unscrupulous methods of rise.*
    **1.** Starving while working free in newspaper office.
**4)** *Same—later*
**5)** *Typical Wynand attitude now*

1. The contest.
2. The reversal of destinies (the suicide).
3. Murder over a woman he didn't want.
4. Attitude on women.

———————

Gun—indifference.

The bedroom and the apartment and his appearance. (Cynicism.)

His day: breakfast, arrival at office, scene with his type operator, crossed-out copy, talk to coast editor, phone call to Senator, board meeting, housing project, Alvah Scarret about Toohey, lunch at Women's Club, editorial on prohibition, talk with Toohey—about [gift]. Dinner with mistress.

Back to gun—decides to think of his past.

Fist fight—over looting and gang leadership.

His father and mother.

Delivers newspapers—incident of advice to employer—"You don't run things around here."

Bootblack on ferry boat—dreams of future New York—"You don't run this place."

Incident in school—"You're not the only one here."

Walks through fallen parts of city—stolen book—looting of bookstore.

Scene with beating by longshoreman. (Only time he asks for help.)

Goes to work for *Banner*—incident of dime.

The woman. (He never needs a lesson twice.)

The idealistic editor (only time he thanks anyone).

Put in charge of paper by political gang—owns paper and destroys gang.

Success through sensationalism. ("It is not my function to help people preserve a self-respect they haven't got.")

Newspaper war—incident of ruthlessness.

Rise: real estate, chain of papers, magazines.

(People who want to use him.)

At his height—power. Private art gallery.

After forty-five—fight against integrity. (Power for power's sake.)

Back to gun, drops it, goes for drink, sees statue, calls Toohey, agrees to meet Dominique.

**July 2, 1942**

[*AR wrote her final chapter outline for Part IV on this date.*]


**Undated**

[*It seems that AR once considered prefacing each part of* The Fountainhead *with a quotation from Friedrich Nietzsche. The first two quotations below were copied into her journal and may have been intended for Parts I and II; the last was placed after the title page to Part IV.*]

Vanity is one of the things which are perhaps most difficult for the noble man to understand: he will be tempted to deny it, where another kind of man thinks he sees it self-evidently. The problem for him is to represent to his mind beings who seek to arouse a good opinion of themselves which they do not possess—and consequently also do not "deserve"—and who yet *believe* in this good opinion afterwards.

Ye preachers of equality, the tyrant-frenzy of impotence crieth thus in you for "equality": your most secret tyrant-longings disguise themselves thus in virtue words!

But from time to time do ye grant me—one glimpse, grant me but one glimpse only, of something perfect, fully realized, happy, mighty, triumphant, of something that still gives cause for fear! A glimpse of man that justifies the existence of man, a glimpse of an incarnate human happiness that realizes and redeems, for the sake of which one may hold fast to the *belief in man*!


**Undated**

[Regarding Roark:]
A whole life lived on a certain principle. The highlights of that life. The quality of that life, proceeding from that principle—with the result of grandeur, heroism, beauty, pride, honor, truth, *joy*. Not *for* anyone, but in itself, in the man—and secondarily in those he touches and in his benefit to society—*only secondarily* and precisely because of the first, because of his disregard for society. (Steel-will, hardness, cruelty—the cruelty turning into his own brand of almost unbearable beauty.)

**1942**

*Possible additions:*

In last scene with Katie—on how hard it is to do what one wants—Keating says: "Why did I choose a profession I hated?"

The deliberate destruction of the prime movers by the second-handers—Mallory's "the genius recognized too well."

The second-handers [offer] substitutes for competence, such as love, charm, kindness—*easy* substitutes—and there is no substitute for creation.

We must be *ashamed* to admit second-hander's motives—acts of altruism.

*On second-handers:* [they are] always concerned with people—not facts, ideas, work or production. What would happen to the world without those who think, work and produce? [*For the answer, see* Atlas Shrugged.]

**1942**

[*For the scene in which Wynand wanders the streets after he has betrayed Roark.*]

Bottle caps. Pawn shop. Subway grating.

Flashback.

Housewives, pushcart, grocery markets—"my masters."

Power—slavery to those you rule—or—the Toohey kind. The self as thought; they escape from thought; [this escape is turned] into a system and a virtue. I never had any power. The destructive mass.

Shakespeare movie—Tchaikovsky juke box.

Austen Heller and the *Globe*, whom he despised.

Roark was my own self—the kind of victory I could have had.

He buys paper and reads editorial (to anyone who wished, for the sum of three cents, I have sold Howard Roark).

Hell's Kitchen—"I never got out—I surrendered to the grocery man and the ferry boat sailors."

What I had wanted—"The defense rests."

Skyscrapers. (I've betrayed you—I have no right to love the city.)

I deserved it, I unleashed the monster.

A great many *Banners*—the one with Roark and the heel print.

That I built it—I was the prime mover—I made it possible for the beast—the unforgivable—hatred of own life—no gallantry. (Forgivable for the "little people"—not for him.)

Will go back to Dominique—only pity—the kind of marriage she wanted.

The unforgivable sin.

**1942**

The worst crime of all on earth—to repeat a borrowed opinion. (We can't all be geniuses, but independence of judgment is involved in any act or comment.)

The irresponsibility of the second-hander. *This* is the drooling beast [referred to by the character Steven Mallory]: that the man acts, but his reasons are so scattered that they're nowhere and he cannot be reasoned with.

Play up to the opinions of people? But most of them have no opinions. The vacuum—until someone (like Toohey) chooses to fill it.

Second-handedness (even its true altruistic form) is so much easier than self-respect. Oneself is the person one can never fool.

Wynand is a great tragedy—the reverse of the famous geniuses—they were creators in their work, second-handers in their personal life. Wynand is reversed—but the same tragic contradiction and inner battle. (Wynand says he'll achieve his purpose when he wishes.)

When people believe that others are their prime virtue, they have only two alternatives: do what others believe (slavishness) or force their own belief for the good of others.

**1942**

[*The following seems to be for Roark's speech.*]

What is life? Consciousness, thought, valuing, creation—all egotistical conceptions. That is the ego.

What are second-handers? Those who place their basic reality in other people's eyes. (Keating, Toohey, Wynand, dictators, "devoted" mothers, vain society women, etc.; the destructive envy—Eleanor Roosevelt.) Reflected reality.

Why altruism had to become second-handedness and can be nothing else.

Selfishness—not crush others, but *independent* of others.

Not "egotism" and "altruism" but "selfishness" and "second-handedness."

Toohey's words about antonyms—the basic test—that which is of life and that which is of death.

The great reversal—the joke on mankind.

The virtues and the vices—vices are collective.

One cannot eat for others.

Christ and Nietzsche.

What we permit—what the test of virtue should be.

The second-handers against men who rule nature.

**1942**

### Roark's Speech

"Thousands of years ago, the first man discovered fire . . ."

The persecution and exploitation of the Action Man—martyrs of history.

Action Men live for themselves.

Everything we have comes from them—all they ask is to give.

Before one can give, one must create.

Usefulness—but it cannot be reversed.

What do they ask in return?—their freedom, their right to exist for themselves.

Cooperation, but not collectivism. Each for himself. Use the product of others and add that which is new and yours. The first man finding a new world for the first time—the only form of giving.

I refuse to exist for anyone or anything else.

The world is perishing from an orgy of "sacrificing."

I had to state my terms—here they are. I gave you that building.

You have worshipped slaves and rulers, but fear the independent man above all. "Each man classifies himself."

In the name of Henry Cameron, Steve Mallory and all the others. "For a man who doesn't want to be named, but who's sitting in this courtroom and knows that I'm speaking of him."

What you do to me does not matter to me.

(I'm an architect and I can read blueprints—I understand yours.)

"The lights are going out all over the world."

**Undated**

[*The following lengthy paper was written for prospective publishers, probably in 1940.*]

Theme of *Second-Hand Lives*

The theme of this novel is individualism versus collectivism, not in politics, but within a man's soul. It is the conflict of these two principles in their fundamental aspect.

As a consequence, it is also a definition of what constitutes selfishness and a defense of selfishness in its true spiritual sense.

The four men, after whom the four parts of the novel are named, present four different attitudes toward these two basic, irreconcilable principles.

*Howard Roark*, the hero of the novel, is a man utterly devoid of the collective sense. He is not an enemy of mankind, but much more than that: he is spiritually unconscious of the existence of other men. Basically, life is consciousness; to live means to think; the fundamental process which constitutes life itself is the process of thought; thought is the creator of all values; the practical application of thought is man's work, his labor, his creative activity—and all labor is a creative activity to some degree. In these two realms—his thought and his labor—Roark is utterly independent of all other men. He faces life as if he were the first man born. Nothing stands between the evidence of his senses and the conclusions his mind draws from them. He does not even reject the conception of: "I must believe this because others believe it"—he goes much beyond rejection: he simply is unable to understand the possibility of such a conception. An entity such as "others" does not exist in the roots of his consciousness. Thus, the aim of his life—and his desires in life—lie within him alone.

He is an architect. He builds as he wishes to build, as he considers right to build. He is true to his own truth—he knows no other. Tradition and custom—what others have done before him or what others wish him to do now—have absolutely no meaning for him. He is a first motive, a prime mover, a creator of values, a creator in the only possible sense of the word. He is the life-giving principle itself, personified in a man. His work is his only reality and his only great passion. His happiness depends on nothing but his own achievement. And he finds, in that achievement, a sensation beyond happiness, a sensation for which the word ecstasy is inadequate, a sensation which is a reason in itself, which justifies all existence: Man at the highest possible to him.

His valuation of himself depends on nothing but the concrete reality of his achievement. He is good if he is convinced that his work is good. What others think of it or of him does not matter. His happiness, his pride, the motive power of his will to live concern no one but himself and depend on no one else. Of course, he needs other men; but that need is secondary, not primary. As an architect, he needs clients; he needs people to live in the buildings he designs; but the difference is this: he needs clients in order to build; he does not build in order to have clients; while creating, he is essentially alone; the creation is the end, people are the means, a secondary means; he does not achieve *through* other men nor *for* other men; he achieves through and for himself alone, then offers it to others.

Thus, spiritually he is a paragon of selfishness. And his life presents a strange paradox: outwardly, his life follows the course conventionally considered as that of an unselfish man; he sacrifices everything to his convictions, to the integrity of his work; he is not concerned with wealth, fame, admiration or physical comfort; he lives in poverty; he is a martyr to an ideal. Thus the devotion to an ideal, the noblest feeling possible to man, is also the most selfish.

The second paradox is in Roark's relations to other men. Basically, he needs nothing from them; so he demands nothing of them. And thus, when he is a friend, he is the only true friend those around him possess. He does not love all men abstractly and indiscriminately. His love, as everything else he experiences, has to have a basis in his own reason. Men have to earn his love. And what he respects and appreciates in men is the same kind of spiritual independence as his own. But when he likes a man, he likes him for that man's own sake; not for what he, Roark, can get from that man, not for what that man can give him. His love is respect for the other man's own value—apart from himself, apart from any relation to himself. Thus his attitude towards other men is completely selfless—in the only noble and benevolent meaning of that word. He will not sacrifice himself for others; neither will he sacrifice them for himself. He will not let others enslave him; neither will he enslave them. He does not exist for the sake of others; neither does he expect them to exist for his sake. Having no fundamental need for other men, he can have no motive for bearing ill will towards them; and more than that: he bears towards them the only good will of any real meaning—the recognition of their own independent value. Such is Howard Roark.

The second man of the novel, *Peter Keating*, is—basically—the utterly selfless man. His spirit is an empty space which other men have to fill. In himself alone, he has nothing to offer—to himself or to the world. He cannot exist, save through others. His consuming ambition is to be great—in other people's eyes. Thus, at the root of his spirit, others take precedence over his own self. Others establish all his values. Others become the motive power of his will to live. He is an architect. He builds as his clients wish him to build. His work is not an end in itself; it is the means to satisfy other men and to obtain from them in return the one gift he needs so desperately—the gift of their approval and their admiration. He has no convictions of any kind about his work; it is good if others like it; he has never stated to himself a code of right or wrong in relation to his creative activity; to him, right is that which other people consider right, wrong is that which they consider wrong. In his own mind, he does not even ask for the reasons upon which others have based these valuations; to him, the judgment of others is sufficient reason as such. He finds no happiness in his own work; his happiness comes *second-hand*, through the reaction of others to his work.

He achieves the first great triumph of his career when he wins an important competition with a building which he claims to have designed, but which was actually designed by Roark, though no one knows this save Keating and Roark; Keating is happy in the general admiration, even though he knows that he doesn't deserve it; he is happy in the fact that millions of men consider him a great architect, even though he himself knows that the achievement they admire is not his. If Roark were given the choice of being great in all eyes save his own or of being great in his own knowledge, with all other men ignorant of his greatness—he would choose the last. Peter Keating chooses the first. Thus, to Keating, all reality is second-hand— through others, by others, for others. Fame, above all else, is his greatest desire; the admiration of others for his person is his greatest need. His life is an eternal concern with what others will think, what others will say, how others will react to him.

Outwardly his life follows a course conventionally considered as that of a selfish man. He is not one to sacrifice for an ideal—he has no ideal. He struggles for fame, admiration, prominence, money. He has no scruples in the struggle and he does not hesitate to sacrifice other men who stand in his way. But, fundamentally, he does all this for the spiritual sake of others—or, rather, for the satisfaction of his own spirit which depends on others so completely. He needs the fame and the admiration in order to have the judgment of others grant him his own value; he needs the money in order to impress others with a tangible evidence of his value; he needs the prominence in order to establish his superiority over others. The quest for superiority is his obsession; it is touched with hysteria; it is the most sensitive spot in his soul. Since he has no objective, independent standard by which to establish his own dignity, his pride and his self-respect, he can establish them only by comparison. He is a success to the extent to which others have failed; he is great to the extent of his ability to surpass others. His selfless greatness consists essentially of the degradation of his brother men.

And this is the paradox in Keating's relations to men: basically, he is completely dependent upon them; thus he is forced to demand a great deal from them; selfless in spirit, he makes other men his victims, he sacrifices them to his own emptiness, to fill his own void. His success does not depend upon the intrinsic value of his own work; his success is to be obtained *through* and *from other men*; thus he has to fight men, to cheat them, to force one man after another from a position he desires; he has nothing to fight with, save his ability to outwit and outmaneuver other men; each man is his natural enemy. The spiritual independence of another man is the greatest threat to him; being only a mirror that reflects others, he expects others to be only a mirror for him. A man unconcerned with the person of Peter Keating is an enemy; for within that man, Peter Keating is dead; and Peter Keating has no life save within other people's minds. To exist he must force the consciousness of his existence upon them. He spends his life cultivating friendships—and he is no friend to anyone. Spiritually enslaved, he carries the principle of slavery to all those around him. He is a man without a soul, who has never felt the need of a soul. When he begins to understand the truth about himself—it is too late.

*Gail Wynand*, the third man of the novel, is a man who sold his soul. Independent in spirit, with a potentiality for greatness such as Roark's, he chooses deliberately to betray his own self. Fundamentally, he does not need other men in that deep, primary, personal sense in which Keating needs them. But instead of keeping himself apart spiritually, Wynand chooses to seek power over men. His conception of greatness is not in following other men, not in being admired by them, like Keating, but in ruling them.

A man of brilliant intellect, of great daring and imagination, starting life from the abject poverty of a slum childhood, he rises to become a great publisher, head of a journalistic empire. He achieves his success by giving people what they want; nothing is too low or too sensational for his newspapers to exploit; he plays upon men's worst instincts; he develops an unerring sense of public opinion, and the policy of his newspapers is to follow it faithfully. He does not allow himself the luxury ever to express an editorial judgment of his own; his editorials say what he knows his readers want him to say. The difference between him and Keating on this point is that Keating would have accepted, in his own mind, this judgment of his readers as final and valid; Wynand does not accept it; Wynand despises his readers and all humanity; but Wynand thinks that power over men is his best defense against them. His only relief from men is his love for great art, which he understands and appreciates.

In his innermost consciousness, Wynand is free; but he does not possess Roark's single-minded consistency; he does not carry his spiritual reality into action; Roark is too selfish to feel the need of imposing himself upon others in any way; Wynand is selfless enough to need power. In acquiring power over others, he loses his own freedom; he has no outlet for his own convictions, no way to translate them into reality. Potentially a prime-mover like Roark, i.e., a man who thinks and feels through his own mind, he denies himself the possibility of an idea to follow. But the need of such an ideal is deep within him. And this need, frustrated, turns into an active hatred of all ideals. Keating does not understand the conception of idealism; Wynand understands it too well. The more successful he becomes in his career, the greater his impulse to destroy in others that which he himself has missed, that which he has sacrificed to them. The only personal pleasure he finds in life is a sadistic delight in breaking the integrity of other men. He will pay any price to force a writer of radical sympathies into becoming a champion of conservatism, or vice versa. The commercial careerist holds no interest for him. It is only men in whom he senses a sincere, profound devotion to their convictions that he chooses for his victims. He wrecks lives on his way, he drives some to suicide. He believes that he is merely proving to himself the triviality of all human idealism. He believes that he is prompted by contempt for human integrity. He cannot allow himself to realize that he is prompted by a great love of integrity, that he tries to destroy it in order to prove to himself that it does not exist, that he has not missed much—knowing only too well that it does exist and that he has missed more than he dares admit to himself.

He has never allowed himself a complete, profound, personal desire of his own. But, at the climax of his life, an overwhelming personal issue forces him to put his power over men to an actual test. He attempts, for once, to sway the public opinion which he thought he controlled. He attempts to use his newspapers to champion an unpopular cause crucially important to him. He finds himself helpless. Public opinion will not follow him. Men are deaf to his commands and to his pleas—men who have never been given cause to respect him. He sees, for the first time, that he has no power over men, but has surrendered himself into their power instead, that he does not rule, but is ruled, that he has been a figure-head sitting on a throne which they had created and which he could occupy only so long as he pleased them, that he is the creation of his own slaves, that he is the puppet and they hold the strings, that his life and his power have been second-hand. And the monster he helped to feed is now unleashed against him: the voice of other men, the pressure of public opinion force him to betray his own cause, to reverse the policy of his papers in obedience to the general desire and against his first and only ideal.

*Ellsworth M. Toohey,* the fourth man, is a creature of perfection in his own kind, just as Roark is a creature of perfection in his—and the complete antithesis of Roark. Toohey is successful at the evil of which Keating and Wynand are victims. Toohey is the paragon of spiritual "second-handedness."

Basically, Toohey is non-creative. He has nothing of his own to offer—to himself or to others. His evil lies in [the fact] that he knows it, accepts it and glories in it. He begins where Keating and Wynand ended. Keating sought superiority after his own fashion; he wished for good, even though his conception of good was false; when he discovered the basic lie of his life, when he saw that he had been neither superior nor good—the discovery brought him spiritual ruin. Wynand sought power as a means of independence; when he discovered the true nature of his power—he was ended spiritually. Toohey began by seeing and accepting what these two could not accept; he knew himself to be incapable of intrinsic superiority or independence; he made of this his virtue; he dedicated himself to the destruction of all superiority and all independence. He accepted consciously the negation of all values, of all ideals, of all that is high and noble in man—with a full realization of the meaning of such values. Not in frustrated longing for an ideal, but in cold and deliberate hatred of all integrity. He chose to be consciously evil. He is the great Nihilist of the spirit.

Toohey understands human greatness and the motive-power of human greatness better than any other man in the story. Roark *is* great, but too unselfconscious to analyze or understand it—for a long time. Keating and Wynand seek greatness blindly. Toohey knows its roots. He understands fully the basic antithesis, the two principles fighting within human consciousness—the individual and the collective, the one and the many, the "I" and the "They." He knows that the source of all greatness, of all that is free, creative, forward-moving, and—ultimately—benevolent to all men is a man's basic independence of spirit, his integrity of thought untouched, fundamentally, by any concern for others. He knows that the source of all evil and all sorrow, of all frustration and all lies is the collective sense, the intrusion of others into the basic motives of a man. And since he is dedicated to the destruction of greatness, he becomes the enemy of the individual and the great champion of collectivism.

Toohey knows that each man must be judged by what he has achieved through the creative labor of his own mind, not by what he has or has not done for others; that his creation is the greatest gift he can bring to others, such as the creations of all great thinkers, artists, and scientists, creations made possible not because of their brothers, but in spite of the opposition of their brothers, made possible only by the profoundly selfish integrity of the spirit of the great creators. Toohey knows that a man's achievement is the only measure of his value and of his superiority. And Toohey knows that in such a competition he has no chance at superiority; he is basically sterile; he has no great passion for anything and no great interest in anything save other men. Thus he decides not to attempt to seek superiority, but to do better: to destroy its very conception. He cannot rise. He can pull others down. He cannot reach the heights. He can raze them. Equality becomes his greatest passion.

His life program is simple: to destroy men by tying them to one another; to preach self-sacrifice, self-denial, self-abasement; to preach the spiritual slavery of each man to all other men; to fight the great creator and liberator—Man's Ego. Toohey is famous as "The Humanitarian."

Any form of personal happiness is a form of freedom. To destroy men he must destroy their joy in living; to destroy their joy in living he must destroy all that is personally dear and important to them. Such is his first instinct in relation to any human being he meets. He wrecks the life of his niece, Catherine, by destroying the only important thing of her existence— her love for Peter Keating. He destroys Keating by killing such self-respect as Keating did possess. He attempts to destroy Dominique Francon, the heroine of the story (more about her later), by encouraging her perverse desire to resist all desires. He has no personal concern for Keating, Catherine, or Dominique; it is only their inner selves which he wishes to annihilate. Men who are happy live for themselves; Toohey cannot allow men to live for themselves; unhappy men turn to others for consolation, attempt to fill the emptiness of their failure by existing for the sake of others; and this is the state to which Toohey wishes them reduced. "Let all live for all. Let all sacrifice and none profit. Let all suffer and none enjoy. Let progress stop. Let all stagnate. There is equality in stagnation." Such is Toohey's secret motto. And it is the more frightening since he truly seeks nothing for himself. He does not wish to subjugate men to his own will. He wishes to subjugate all to the will of all. Which means—to the will of none. Universal slavery—without even the dignity of a master. Slavery to slavery. A great circle and an utter equality. Such is Ellsworth M. Toohey.

His chief weapon is mockery. A great, all-embracing nihilistic ridicule. Allow nothing to remain sacred in a man's soul. Earnestness towards any conception whatever, the mere conception of earnestness itself, is the base of reverence. Allow nothing to be important to a man's spirit. Laugh it out of existence. Laughter, not as joy, but as destruction. Fight ideals, not by denial, but by internal corruption. Toohey is wiser than Wynand; Wynand tried to destroy integrity by crude force from without, which merely tore that integrity, intact, out of a man's soul. Toohey is subtler and deadlier: he makes integrity rot slowly within that soul. He uses a man's integrity against itself; he makes it become loyalty to principles basically destructive of all integrity. He destroys idealism in men, not by denying it, not by preaching the vanity of all ideals, but in precisely the opposite manner: by professing the great value and glory of idealism in men and then directing their idealism toward objects basically destructive of all ideals. Thus, he holds out unselfishness as the supreme goal of the spirit; thus he holds out brother-love as the sublime virtue. He does not deny the conception of superiority among men, but destroys it by glorifying the worthless as superior. Thus, fully recognizing the genius of Roark, he holds him up to ridicule; fully recognizing the mediocrity of Keating, he hails him as a great architect. An art critic by profession, Toohey manages to reach into every field of creative endeavor; and in every field he enshrines mediocrity—in order to destroy all shrines. Keating in architecture; Lois Cook in literature—a phony "modernist" who writes "words on words," "words above meaning" and thus destroys both words and meaning; in painting—a creator of the pork-chop-fur-lined-tea-cup school; and so on. Do not fight human achievement in the open. Destroy it from within. Destroy by internal corruption. Destroy the rare, the difficult, the exceptional, the original by substituting standards of achievement open to the abilities of any and all. That, also, is Ellsworth M. Toohey. That he is a Communist in his political convictions is only incidental; he proclaims that he fights Rockefeller and Morgan; he really fights Shakespeare and Beethoven.

Thus the four men of the story are: Howard Roark, who is great and knows it; Peter Keating, who could not be great and does not know it; Gail Wynand, who could have been; and Ellsworth M. Toohey, who could never be and knows it.

A few words about Dominique Francon and about the general course of the story.

Dominique's basic passion is a fierce love of independence. But it is an independence that turns upon itself—in protest against the world she sees around her. Capable of great desire, she makes it her aim to desire nothing. Actually a saint, in that her subconscious demand is perfection—from herself and from all others—she finds a vicious delight in lowering herself to whatever action she considers most contemptible; since she cannot find perfection, she prefers its opposite extreme to compromise. But such conscious self-degradation is only her manner of a quest for the sublime. Her redemption is in that she never accepts spiritually the vile depths to which she descends; she defies the depths by descending.

It is quite obviously inevitable that she should love Roark and that her love for him should be final, complete and immediate. It is a love too great to be endured in acceptance; she can bear it only by denying, by resisting it, by degrading it, by trying to destroy it. Like most women, and to a greater degree than most, she is a masochist and she wishes for the happiness of suffering at Roark's hands. Sexually, Roark has a great deal of the sadist, and he finds pleasure in breaking her will and her defiance. Yet he loves her, and this love is the only passion for another human being in his whole life. And her love for him is essentially worship, it becomes her religion, it becomes her reconciliation with life, with humanity and with herself—but not until many years later.

Roark's life is the simple, single-tracked pursuit of his only goal—architecture. It is the continuous struggle of his own truth against men. He experiences every hardship, every defeat, every agony that men can place in his way. But it leaves him untouched—within. His conflict is with the outside world, not with himself. He never achieves universal recognition—which he never sought. But he wins the freedom to work as he believes, he fights through to the chance of creating great buildings. His buildings—not his love nor his compliance—are his gift to the world. And by ignoring men, he gives them creations of great value. At the end of the story, we leave him at the height of his work and of his power. And in that work, he has found a height of happiness unknown to most men, he has made the world a better place by the fact of making such happiness possible, by the fact of making it exist within his own soul—and the realization of man's capacity for ecstasy is the only reason for this world's existence. Or so the author believes.

Keating achieves the kind of success he seeks, early and easily. He wins great popular acclaim. But the emptiness and the uncertainty within him allow him no happiness. He has never known peace with himself. Such joy as he finds in life is only a guilty, unhealthy, unsafe satisfaction. He has not the courage of his own desires—and he passes up the only chance at happiness he had, his sincere love for Catherine. His success goes as it came—through the whim of others. His popularity fades as that of all current fashions; undeserved from the first, his fame dwindles and dies; he is replaced by other popular heroes of the same type. And it is only when people begin to desert him that he begins to question his own soul, to realize dimly what it was that he missed, what it was that he had always envied, feared and resented in Roark. When he understands it, it is too late. We leave him, a man without hope, without future, without past, a man who had lived through others, had brought them nothing but sorrow and left them nothing but bad imitations of every bad building created before him.

Toohey proceeds successfully on his chosen course of destroying all those whose lives touch his. He fails only with three human beings: Roark, Dominique, and Wynand. Roark is the great, consuming hatred of his life, the symbol of all that he must destroy. He is helpless before Roark; he cannot touch Roark spiritually—and he knows it. So he marshals every social weapon he controls—to break Roark's career. And Toohey holds a great power over society, carefully built up through the years. But he fails. He cannot prevent Roark's ultimate triumph. In regard to Dominique, Toohey is one of the few who understand her real nature. He goads her on to self-destruction. He helps to bring about her marriage to Wynand—a marriage he hoped would destroy them both. He has a special interest in Wynand: he works slowly, through many years, to obtain editorial control of the Wynand papers, on which he is employed as a special columnist-commentator. He understands Wynand. He knows that Wynand's bitter cynicism is only a mask for the kind of spirit Toohey dreads; he knows that Wynand is not basically corrupt. He hopes to achieve that corruption through Dominique, whom he considers to be the worst possible influence that Wynand could encounter. He fails in his calculations. At the end of the story, he loses that particular battle by losing his position with the Wynand papers. But another great newspaper signs him up at once. Toohey, like time, marches on.

Wynand's retribution comes first in the person of Dominique, in that he falls desperately in love with her; desperately—because it is his first complete, sincere and personal emotion. When he marries her, he knows that she does not love him, but he does not know that she loves Roark, that the marriage is only her way of defying and degrading her love for Roark, the bitterest way she could find. She chooses Wynand as the most completely vicious man she knows. She is disappointed in this; she herself brings the first awakening of Wynand's essential self. His love for her becomes the symbol of everything he has missed in life: an experience completely his own, to be guarded savagely against all other men, those other men whose public property he is.

But it is Roark who is life's final revenge upon Wynand. When [they] meet, Wynand is 54, Roark is 37. Wynand does not suspect that Dominique had been Roark's mistress, and his attitude toward Roark has no relation to Dominique. Instead of the usual hatred which men of Roark's integrity had always aroused in him, Wynand's reaction is a great, irresistible, unformulated wave of recognition and admiration. He does not understand or analyze it for a long time. He knows only that he needs Roark in some odd, unaccountable manner. Slowly, through their strange relationship of unspoken understanding, Wynand begins to realize that Roark is the symbol of everything he has betrayed; Roark achieved what he had lacked the courage to achieve; Roark is his own self, as he might have been; Roark is his revenge against society, against that mob whom Roark defies and to whom Wynand has surrendered. And although Roark is an external reproach to him, although the mere fact of Roark's existence brings him the first spiritual suffering he has ever allowed himself to experience—Roark becomes Wynand's obsession. Wynand is actually in love with Roark. It is love in every sense but the physical; its base is *not* in homosexuality; Wynand has never had any tendency in that direction. It is more hero-worship than love, and more religion than hero-worship. Actually, it is Wynand's tribute to his own unrealized greatness. This love has no relation to his love for Dominique; it is not faithlessness to Dominique; and yet, were he ever asked to choose between the two, Wynand would have chosen Roark. Wynand welcomes the torture of loving a man whom he should hate. He finds a dim, twisted sense of atonement in his love for his worst spiritual enemy. He is punishing himself for what he has done—by bowing before what he should have done. It is his first acceptance of an ideal—and his first suffering for its sake. Roark becomes the most precious thing in his life.

Roark's attitude toward Wynand is a deep understanding; in a way—respect; and the only pity he has ever felt for any human being. As to Dominique, she sees the situation, resents it and is frightened by it. To her, there is no other reality and no other concern but Roark. She is jealous of Wynand, of any feeling Roark might have in response to Wynand's adoration of him. It is a triangle—in which the husband and wife are both in love with the same man.

It is when—through Toohey's efforts—Roark becomes the center of a sensational scandal and faces a trial involving a possible sentence of life-imprisonment, that Wynand attempts to defend Roark through the influence of his newspapers. Roark is the object of great public indignation. Wynand wants to defend him, more passionately than he would want to defend his own life. But he cannot fight the monster of public opinion. He is forced to make his papers clamor for Roark's conviction. He is forced to betray his first and only god.

It is Wynand's final tragedy. He faces the full understanding of his own spiritual degradation and of that illusory power over men for the sake of which he had allowed his degradation. Roark is acquitted. In the circumstances surrounding the trial, Wynand learns the truth about the past of Roark and Dominique, and that they still love each other. He loses them both. He is forced to divorce Dominique. He has nothing left but his newspaper empire, which he now hates—with all its energy, spirit and prestige gone.

Dominique comes back to Roark—completely, finally and voluntarily, understanding through him the meaning of life as he has lived it, as she is prepared to live it for the first time.

This, very generally and very roughly, is the story.

**December 13, 1943**

[*Shortly after* The Fountainhead's *publication, Warner Brothers bought the movie rights. The following notes were made as AR began work on the screenplay.*]

*General Theme:* Man's integrity.

*Plot Theme:* Howard Roark, an architect, a man of genius, originality and complete spiritual independence, holds the truth of his convictions above all things in life. He fights against society for his creative freedom, he refuses to compromise in any way, he builds only as he believes, he will not submit to conventions, traditions, popular taste, money or fame. Dominique Francon, the woman he loves, thinks that his fight is hopeless. Afraid that society will hurt and corrupt him, she tries to block his career in order to save him from certain disaster. When the disaster comes and he faces public disgrace, she decides to take her revenge on the man responsible for it, Gail Wynand, a powerful, corrupt newspaper publisher. She marries Wynand, determined to break him. But Roark rises slowly, in spite of every obstacle. When he finally meets Wynand in person, Dominique is terrified to see that the two men love and understand each other. Roark's integrity reaches Wynand's better self, Roark is the ideal which Wynand has betrayed in his ambition for power. Without intending it, Roark achieves his own revenge—by becoming Wynand's best friend. Dominique finds herself suffering in a strange triangle—jealous of her husband's devotion to the man she loves. When Roark's life and career are threatened in a final test, when he becomes the victim of public fury and has to stand trial, alone, hated, opposed and denounced by all—Wynand makes a supreme effort toward his own redemption. He stands by Roark and defends him. Wynand loses, defeated and broken by the corrupt machine he himself had created. But Roark wins without his help—wins by the power of his own truth. Roark is acquitted—and Dominique comes to him, free to find happiness with him, realizing that the battle is never hopeless, that nothing can defeat man's integrity. [*Note that the movie's plot is to focus on Roark, Wynand, and Dominique; Keating and Toohey are not even mentioned.*]

---

*Specific theme, as presented in screenplay:*

Independence—as against obeying the wishes of others, as against the "social" spirit, which is: Keating, who tried to live by public polls; Wynand, who tried to use the mob; Toohey, who consciously used collectivism for the purpose of gaining power and enslaving mankind.

Therefore, Roark's speech must summarize the above, give it a statement—the *good* is not the *social*, but the *individual*, not the herd-instinct, but independence; to live for yourself or for others is an issue of the spirit, the choice between one's own judgment and the surrender of one's judgment, between integrity and mental prostitution. The form of a society will be the result of this basic issue.

**May 3, 1948**

[*Almost five years later, Warner Brothers began to make the movie. Shortly before the start of principal photography, the director (King Vidor) asked AR to write instructions for the scene in which, after Kiki Holcombe's party, Dominique comes to Roark's apartment. Patricia Neal, Vidor said, needed a better understanding of Dominique's psychology. The instructions helped; AR commented later that this was "the best acted scene in the movie."*]

*Notes on Scene in Roark's Apartment*

*Dominique's Psychology*

This scene contains the entire progression of Roark's and Dominique's love affair in the book. Dominique's part in the scene gives her a chance to show every aspect of her character.

Dominique's basic attitude is the violent conflict between her passion for Roark and her despair. The more she admires him, the more certain she is that he will be destroyed. She is so hurt herself that she is driven to hurt him, but her cruelty to him is only an extreme expression of her love. We must be certain that there is never a touch of feminine cattiness, vanity or malice in Dominique's performance. She defies Roark because she worships him. She defies him for the pleasure of seeing him master her. Her real desire is always to see him win.

The different aspects of Dominique's character and mood in the scene go in this order: Defiance—bitterness—sex—feminine helplessness.

**1.** At the beginning of the scene, Dominique is coldly, arrogantly defiant. This is her way of paying Roark for the rape. Her attitude, in effect, is: Well, if you want to break me down, I will break down with a vengeance, I will go all the way—and it won't do you any good. She is challenging him by overdoing her surrender. To achieve this effect, she must read her lines coldly, arrogantly, with an undertone of bitter mockery. When she speaks of how much she loves him and how much she missed him, her voice must sound as if she were throwing insults in his face, throwing them coldly, contemptuously and deliberately. Then the lines will sound as if they are torn out of her against her will—and this will convey a feeling of passion for him much greater than any sentimental reading could achieve.

**2.** These are the speeches where Dominique shows all her bitterness against the world—and, in doing it, she shows her own uncompromising idealism and her admiration for Roark. In this bitter form, she pays him the greatest compliments. This is her real declaration of love for him—because here she states the reasons for her love: she loves all the things which the world hates him for. While she speaks about his business and clients, her voice has more emotion than she showed in the preceding moments when she spoke of love. This is where she begins to show despair, but not openly; it is merely in the bitterness and tension of the way she speaks; she must speak as if every word hurt her.

**3.** Here we see Dominique's sexual violence. This is the first time when she gives in to Roark physically and voluntarily. Her response, when he seizes her in his arms, is a contradiction of everything she has said. She has spoken coldly about wanting to leave him, but the moment he touches her, her response is one of desperate, irresistible hunger for him. While she is in Roark's arms, she is her real self, free for a few moments. She is, frankly and openly, a primitive sexy female—in the highest sense of the words. When Roark says, "I had to let you learn to accept it," her silent answer shows that she has more than accepted it: the way she kisses him has the same quality of open desire as his, it is she who seizes him as he had done it to her before. The purpose of this part of the scene is to explain why Dominique decides to marry Wynand: Her physical hunger for Roark is so great that she knows she will not be able to resist it. She knows she will not escape, but will keep coming back to him in spite of all her convictions—so she has to tie herself in some irrevocable manner to keep herself away from Roark. That is the motivation and purpose of her marriage to Wynand.

**4.** This is the last and startling transition of Dominique's attitude in the scene. It is the only time we will see her break down completely—and it *must be* the breakdown of a strong woman, not of a weepy little girl. Her despair has been growing throughout the scene and now it breaks into the open. Here she is completely feminine, helpless, pleading—but never weak. She has a desperate urgency and sincerity—she does not realize the preposterousness of what she is asking—so that when she speaks about cooking and scrubbing floors, it does not sound homey, but tragic. When she says, "Don't laugh, I can," Roark has not given the slightest indication of any desire to laugh. In fact, this is where he listens to her most earnestly, because he knows that this is real despair.

When Roark refuses her and she gets up to reach for her wrap, her manner becomes that of the cold, detached, Madonna-like woman which she is through most of the picture. But the rest of the time, she gives the impression of a person who feels nothing; here, she is a person who has felt too much—she is drained of all emotion, life or hope.

At the very end of the scene, when she is in Roark's arms again, her desire for him returns, but now it is not enjoyment, it is a tortured, involuntary surrender. She really wants to escape from him—her manner must be the direct transition to the next scene where she goes to Wynand.

*Roark's Psychology*

Roark's attitude throughout the scene is much simpler. There is no conflict in him. He knows what he wants—but he learns in this scene that he cannot have Dominique, at least not for a long time.

At first, his manner is a direct continuation of his attitude in the quarry sequence. It is self-confident, mocking, with an undertone of triumph—because she has surrendered by coming to him, which is what he was waiting for. He listens to her first speeches with the faintest hint of a mocking smile. He is enjoying it. He likes her defiance, because he likes a victory over a strong adversary.

The first change in his attitude comes when she says: "I love you, Roark." This is more than he expected. He knows that coming from her it is a danger signal.

When she tells him why she is certain that he will be destroyed by the world, he listens calmly. He knows that he won't be destroyed. He is so sure of himself that he will not argue with her about it. He knows she is wrong and, therefore, he feels confident that he can win her.

His only answer is to sweep all her objections away simply by showing her the greatness of their love for each other. To him, the world can never be a threat and can never stand in the way of his own happiness.

It is only when Dominique falls down on her knees and starts pleading with him that he realizes completely the extent of her despair. Then he understands that he cannot force her into his own attitude toward life, that she will have to learn it herself. He acts toward her on the same principle as he acts in his professional career. He wants a voluntary acceptance, he will not force his ideas on anyone. He raped her only because he knew that she wanted it; but she is not ready for happiness and he cannot force her to be. His action here is quietly heroic. He could have demanded anything he wished of her, and she would have obeyed. Instead, he lets her go. His last speech must be delivered very quietly and with great self-confidence, so great that it needs no obvious emphasis, no raised voice. It is a man speaking with absolute certainty, even when he suffers, and he does suffer here.

Their last embrace is in the nature of a farewell—though not an *immediate* farewell. This will be their last night together, and Roark knows it, but he does intend to have that last night.

———◆———

*Notes About the Set*

It is *extremely important* that Roark's room be kept completely in character with him. He is quite poor at this time. He knows that whatever money he got for the Enright House will have to last him for a long time, and he is not the type of man who would waste money on personal luxuries. Also, he is too great an artist ever to want any second-rate junk around him. Therefore, his room must be extremely, startlingly simple. It is not the simplicity of squalid poverty, but the simplicity of deliberate intention. The room must be large, with a feeling of space and with an absolute minimum of furniture. He would want his home to be as functional as his buildings. He would have only the things he needs and nothing else. He would never make attempts at homey comfort or prettifying. *Above all*, there must not be any pictures on the walls. The walls must be bare. There must be one large window, a couch, a drafting table, a few chairs, a dresser, a wooden filing cabinet for his drawings—and that is all. No curtains, no rugs, no boudoir pillows, no *books*, no fancy lamps or ash trays and, for the love of God, no vases or knick-knacks. The furniture must be modern and very simple—the kind of good, but inexpensive modern that one finds sometimes in New York. An impression of beauty can be achieved by the proportions and the relations of the objects in the room. The effect of the room must be the same as the effect of Roark's character: direct, stark, purposeful, austere. Since the love scene is to be played in evening clothes, its effect—against the simplicity of a room that looks ascetic like a monk's cell—will be most startling.

———◆———

*Suggestions*

In the love scene, Roark sits down, not in a chair, but on a couch. The way I would suggest doing it is as follows: They stand near the couch when Roark seizes her in his arms. After his line: "You'd rather not hear it now? But I want you to hear it. I love you," he kisses her and they lean back and go down together, without breaking the kiss, his mouth not leaving hers.

For the last embrace my suggestion is this: Dominique is wearing a strapless evening gown; when she is about to leave, she reaches for her wrap and puts it on. She has it on when Roark takes her in his arms. Show the embrace in a close-up that includes their heads and shoulders. As he holds her, while she moans that she wants to leave him, the wrap slips off. We do not see her gown, but only her naked arms, back and shoulders; we see Roark's hand moving slowly from her shoulder down her back.

# TRANSITION BETWEEN NOVELS

PART 3

TRANSITION BETWEEN
NOVELS

# 8

# THE MORAL BASIS OF INDIVIDUALISM

Shortly after completing The Fountainhead, AR contracted with her publisher, Bobbs-Merrill, to write a short nonfiction book giving a systematic presentation of the novel's ethics and politics. Her working title was The Moral Basis of Individualism.

AR's notes for this book provide a fascinating record of her philosophic development during the period between The Fountainhead and Atlas Shrugged. In the course of these notes, she is discovering and clarifying many of the ideas that became essential in John Galt's speech. Her formulations here should not be interpreted as Objectivism; rather, they are her notes to herself while she is working out how to present Objectivism as a systematic philosophy.

Her journal for The Moral Basis of Individualism can be viewed as a progression with three stages. She begins in September of 1943 by writing a "tentative outline," a foreword and an unworked draft of the first three chapters. She then stops work on the draft and instead begins asking herself questions and thinking aloud on paper. Finally, in the summer of 1945, she critiques her original draft and rewrites part of it before deciding to drop the project.

There seem to be two reasons why she lost interest in writing this book. Years later, she recalled that in the early stages of planning she had concluded that "it was useless to present a morality without a metaphysics and epistemology." Second, her primary interest was fiction writing. In her journal from May 4, 1946 (see Chapter 11), she explains that

> the idea of writing a philosophical non-fiction book bored me; in such a book, the purpose would actually be to teach others, to present my ideas to *them*. In a book of fiction the purpose is to create, for myself, the kind of world I want and to live in it while I am creating it; then, as a secondary consequence, to let others enjoy this world, if, and to the extent that, they can.

**August 18, 1943**

*Tentative Outline*

### I. The Life Principle

The "nature" of man—the primary matters of his existence—the rational process—the particular qualities of man as creator (the Roark qualities)—the law of his survival (the Active Man). Show how the "action spark" has the same application today as in the primitive jungle. How to define and recognize it.

### II. The Death Principle

The only other possible way of survival—through the brains of others. The second-hander, his particular qualities (the Passive Man). (Altruism and Collectivism.)

### III. The Moral Law

*The exposition of the new moral law*—examples to range over the whole field, in history, politics, economics, personal relations. Not serve *or* hurt others—the basic position and the basic realm is neutral, *independent.* Express the idea of the "sin of omission."

### IV. Individualism and Collectivism

The mind cannot be added. Brute force is the only form of expression possible to a collective—but even force cannot be exercised without reason.

### V. Man and Men

The proper relationship of man to men, deduced from the moral law. Traders, *not* servants. But trade only that which *can* be traded—hold on to the untradable. Altruism is an absolute evil. (The evil escape which it permits and becomes.)

### VI. The Moral Society

The proper society deduced from the proper relationship. (The advantages of society to man—but *only* on the above basis. What is the use of advantages that take his life in exchange, by crossing the basic limit of his rights?)

### VII. How It Works

The Capitalist System. Selfishness—and the benefits to others as a *secondary* consequence. Government as protection of the individual against the collective. (The police protect single men against mobs—*not* a collective against single evil-doers.)

### VIII. The Immoral Society

Duplicate the same process in brief, starting from the altruistic principle and leading to an outline of a consistent collectivist society. (Collectivism as the principle of race prejudice and of every form of injustice.) First—theory, then show examples from practice.

---

*Notes*

To start with: Man exists and must survive as man. This is not for those who do not believe in reason and logic. (?) [*This last sentence was crossed out.*]

The reversal of all moral values when taken from the individual realm into the collective.

Altruism is spiritual cannibalism. If it is so wrong to eat another man's body—why is it right to feed upon his soul for one's own survival?

The man who wishes to live for others is merely confirming his inferiority. The infallible test of a man's value is the degree of his indignation against the idea of compulsion and against the idea of being like others, of being unoriginal. (Look at the others—is *that* what you are proud of being like? If not, do something about it, don't hold it as a virtue.)

Man is *not* his brother's keeper. (All responsibility *must* carry with it the authority to enforce it.)

The altruist's inevitable concern with the inferior—its reasons and results.

The "good of a collective" that demands the sacrifice of an inventor in order to avoid unemployment.

Man cannot give life to himself. But it is up to him to maintain it.

(For "free will": you cannot change the basic materials—nature, natural law, your own nature—but you are free in the use you make of it; you exercise choice among given materials. Be careful here of the definition of "your own nature"—how much is given to you, how much you can alter. You do not make an automobile nor can you make it perform what it can't perform, such as flying, but you can drive where you wish.)

It has to begin with pride in self, with that which constitutes *man*—the reasoning mind. The rights or application of the mind is unlimited, except for the right to deny itself—if a mind denies itself, it cannot enjoy the rights which belong only to it. To deny itself means to deny the mind's essential [nature as] an *individual* entity. The mind can conclude anything it wishes— except that [it may] impose its will by force upon other minds.

The root of the desire to abase man—as in the idea of smallness before nature.

Altruism as a weapon of exploitation. The creators are disarmed. They have the genius, the life gift. But the second-handers have virtue.

If it is good to suffer for others, a true altruist has to make others suffer for still others—thus he is doing them good by making them virtuous. If anyone thinks that this sounds fantastic in theory, look at the way it works out just like that in practice and ask yourself why. There is and can be no other explanation. (If it is good to sacrifice oneself for others, then one makes these others vicious by making them accept one's sacrifice—since the giver is virtuous and the receiver evil. Thus the altruist achieves virtue at the expense of the virtue of others—is this altruism? But it can mean nothing else. Logically, one would have to land in some such silly situation as the Japanese exchange of gifts.)

No relation of man to man is possible without a moral principle. If there is no such principle, brute force is the only recourse and the only form of relationship. But in any relation between men the unstated and accepted principle [of altruism] is that each must sacrifice himself to the other. Each must attempt to achieve not his own advantage but that of the other man. Both know this to be impossible. No definition [of a moral principle] can be made this way—and no deal. So both drop all moral considerations whatever ("business is business, morality has nothing to do with it") and both attempt to squeeze all they can out of the other, to sacrifice him to oneself— as the only alternative to an impossible self-sacrifice. *No decent or fair relation among men is possible on the basis of altruism.* Only when one begins with the principle that the other man does not exist for one's sake, that the other has a legitimate and *moral* right to his own advantage, only then is a fair relation possible. *Never demand of another man that which would constitute his sacrifice to you. Never grant him that which would constitute your sacrifice to him.*

Never initiate the use of force against another man. Never let his use of force against you remain unanswered by force.

Love as exception-making. The vicious implications of the idea of "loving everybody." Not love—but a benevolent neutrality as your basic attitude to your fellow men. The rest must be earned by them. Justice, *not* mercy.

Remove the idea of altruism from your mind—then look at the collectivists. See these shabby, sordid men of horror for what [they are], without the aura of virtue that idea gave them. What, but that idea, could make men tolerate and accept that horror?

What kind of a person are you? What do you see when you think of "man"—a hero or an Okie? This question is the decisive one—it holds everything. The style of a soul. (If you're confused, try this. It will tell you everything. Then try to untangle it.) (The worm who wrote to Pat about the Wright brothers—the deliberate belittling of greatness.) *We do not attempt to acquire the virtues of heroes—we attempt to give heroes our vices.* [*"Pat" refers to Isabel Paterson, author of* The God of the Machine *and a friend of AR's in the 1940s.*]

[In regard to] the Passive Man—stress obedience and following. The first desire of the Active Man—to do things alone and in his own way. The first desire of the Passive Man—to obey and not to be responsible. [The Active Man wants] neither to impose himself upon others nor to be imposed upon. Best results and most moral method of action—alone, *not* together. Tests of school children. Hollywood scenarios. Mob actions— lynchings. Cooperation, not collectivism. Government's only duty—protect individual rights for individuals, *not* create encroachments for pressure groups. There can be no individual action without productive or economic freedom. There can be no such freedom without property rights. The "body" and "soul" of human rights. Who can rule best—the one or the many? Nei- ther. As little ruling as possible. Then—go to the Capitalist System.

**September 4, 1943**

### The Moral Basis of Individualism

*I do not recognize anyone's right to one minute of my life. Nor to any part of my energy. Nor to any achievement of mine. No matter who makes the claim, how large their number or how great their need.*

*I wished to come here and say that I am a man who does not exist for others.*

*It had to be said. The world is perishing from an orgy of self-sacrificing.*

*—*HOWARD ROARK, *The Fountainhead*

### Foreword

Mankind is committing suicide.

The peculiarity of the present world disaster is that every group of men in every country is the originator of its own destruction. Men are not fighting one another for self-preservation. They are each fighting all for the right to annihilate oneself as fast as possible.

Intellectuals, such as Trotsky, worked to bring about the dictatorship of the proletariat in Russia; they have been murdered by that dictatorship. Industrialists, such as [Fritz] Thyssen, and church leaders, such as [Martin] Niemoller, worked to bring about the Nazi regime in Germany; they have been exterminated. [*The preceding two sentences were crossed out.*] American labor union leaders caused the creation of Labor Boards; these are now the instruments through which labor union leaders are being sent to jail. Republicans who decry the New Deal usurpation of power are now advocating the passage of a labor conscription act which would give the New Deal its last, winning step toward total power over this country. Conservatives, anxious to preserve capitalism, are supporting this measure which would turn citizens into serfs—which would be the end of capitalism, for it cannot function through serfs. Leaders of racial minorities are advocating the destruction of the American system of government—which is the only system that ever has or can protect a racial minority. Intellectuals have embraced, en masse and in toto, the doctrine of collectivism—under which the intellectual professions are the least possible and the first to go. Name a group of men and you are naming that group's murderers.

There must be a reason for a suicidal mania that has infected a whole world, particularly when the suicide is not conscious or willing, when the victims are thrashing about in wild despair, wondering who is destroying them, swatting at everyone in sight, dragging their brothers along as they race down into the abyss and scream that someone is pushing them.

It is generally recognized that mankind has achieved, since its rise from savagery, a miraculous progress in the realm of its material culture—and none whatever in the realm of its ethics. Our homes are superior to the cave of the Neanderthal man, but our morals are no better than his—worse, if anything, for we do not have his excuse of ignorance. There is no act of inhumanity which he perpetrated and which we do not perpetrate, except that he did not possess our exquisite means of perpetrating it and he could never equal our present scale. In a recently published book (*The Spirit of Enterprise* by Edgar M. Queeny), the author—intent upon a hymn to human progress—spends five pages describing man's material triumphs. Then he adds: "Our morals have come a long way, too. The mere thought of a feast on a loose piece of human flesh, which to the Bushmen brings mouth-watering longing, is to us horrid and nauseating." This is all he can offer, without equivocation, for ten thousand years of man's spiritual growth. And even this claim is open to question, because cannibalism occurred in Soviet Russia in the famines of 1921 and 1933, and God only knows or can bear the sight of what is occurring in Europe now.

Why has man displayed such magnificent capacity for progress in the material realm and yet remained stagnant on the level of savagery in his spiritual stature? This discrepancy has been recognized, decried, deplored, denounced by everyone. It has never been explained. Countless explanations of evil and remedies for it have been offered through the centuries. None of them worked. None of them cured or explained anything.

Yet that which mankind holds as its moral ideal has been known and accepted for centuries. The basic principle of men's morality has not changed since the beginning of recorded history. Under their superficial differences of symbolism, ritual and metaphysical justification, all great ethical systems from the Orient up, all religions, all human schools of thought have held a single moral axiom: the ideal of selflessness. That which proceeds from love of self is evil, that which proceeds from love of others is good. Self-sacrifice, self-denial and self-renunciation have ever been considered the essence of virtue. In no other matter has mankind held to such total unity, so completely and for so long. Altruism is the doctrine which holds that man must live for others and place others above self. Humanity has proclaimed its moral ideal unanimously. It has never been questioned. It has always been the ideal of altruism. [*Later in this chapter, AR notes that the cultures of ancient Greece and capitalist America were at least partial exceptions to this rule.*]

This ideal has never been reached. In spite of its statement and re-statement, in every land, in every age, in every language, in spite of its professed acceptance by all, mankind's history has not been a growing record of benevolence, justice and brother-love, but an accelerating progression of horror, cruelty, and shame. Baffled, men have accepted the explanation that man is essentially evil; man is weak and imperfect; *he doesn't want to do good*. The noble ideal of altruism is never quite to be achieved, only approximated; man is immoral by nature.

But look back at mankind's record. Every major horror of history was perpetrated—not by reason of and in the name of that which men held as evil, that is, selfishness—but through, by, for and in the name of an altruistic purpose. The Inquisition. Religious wars. Civil wars. The French Revolution. The German Revolution. The Russian Revolution. No act of selfishness has ever equaled the carnages perpetrated by disciples of altruism. Nor has any egotist ever roused masses of fanatical followers by enjoining them to go out to fight for his personal gain. Every leader gathered men through the slogans of a selfless purpose, through the plea for their self-sacrifice to a high altruistic goal: the salvation of others' souls, the spread of enlightenment, the common good of their state.

It is said that self-seeking hypocrites used these virtuous sentiments to delude their followers and achieve personal ends. Doubtless, there have been such and a great many of them. But they never caused the bloody terrors caused by the purest "idealists." The worst butchers were the most sincere. Robespierre asked and wished nothing for himself. Lenin asked and wished nothing for himself. But the record of Attila is that of an amateur compared to theirs. At the apex of every great tragedy of mankind there stands the figure of an incorruptible altruist. Yet, after every disaster men have said: "The ideal was right, but Robespierre was the wrong man to put it into practice," (or Torquemada, or Cromwell, or Lenin, or Hitler, or Stalin) and have gone on to try it again.

But what is one to think of creatures who are willing, century after century, to bear every form of agony, every kind of martyrdom, for the sake of that which they consider as their moral ideal? Are they creatures devoid of moral instinct? Is not the determination to act according to one's conception of right, no matter what the price, precisely the attribute of a high moral sense? Men have been robbed, enslaved, tortured, slaughtered in the name of altruism. They have accepted, forgiven, and borne it, because their ideal demanded it of them. The price they have paid in unspeakable suffering should have granted them, at least, a badge of virtue.

But the nature of their ideal has robbed them even of this earned honor.

A true premise, once accepted, leads to a greater truth and a clearer knowledge with each subsequent step deduced from it. A false premise leads to a greater falsehood and a blacker evil, until, followed to its ultimate conclusion, it brings total destruction, as it must. The spiritual tragedy of mankind has now reached this last step. The spectacle of horror which the world presents at this moment has never been equaled and cannot be surpassed. This is the end of the blind alley of men's thinking. And there is no way out—save all the way back, to the beginning, to the first principle which permitted men to be led into this.

The ideal of altruism has now taken its ultimate toll. We are the witnesses of its climax. We see mankind destroying itself before our eyes. We see the price it is paying. We glance back at its history and we see the price it has paid. But we look on and say: "This noble ideal is beyond human nature, because men are imperfect and evil."

Isn't it time to stop and to question that noble ideal instead?

**September 6, 1943**

*Axiom*

Moral law is a code of right and wrong. The moral law of man must be based on his nature as man. This is implicit by definition. That which is right and proper to man must be right and proper to man. A moral code not based on man's nature would have to be stated like this: that which is right and proper to man is that which is improper and impossible to him. Whatever such a statement might be, it is not a statement of morality, but of total evil, by its own terms. It leaves man no choice but to acknowledge himself as evil by nature, in which case no morality is possible to him, or to destroy himself. ([*Note added later:*] "In order to exist I must be evil. If I do not wish to be evil, I must not exist. Existence is evil." This is where I'll discuss the morality of altruism.)

What is man's nature? The definitive factor must be that which is peculiar to man, that which distinguishes him from all other entities, objects or creatures. The attribute peculiar to man is the rational faculty. It is that which, in all known nature, is possessed only by man. ([*Note added later:*] Define the rational faculty here. Truth to the facts of the outside world.)

Man exists. He is alive. He is distinguished from all other existing objects and living creatures by the faculty of reason. He is a rational being.

Every species of living creature survives through the exercise of that attribute which is its particular, distinguishing faculty. All its other attributes are adapted to the mode of existence set by the one which is its means of survival. If it were otherwise, if two fundamental attributes of a creature, both essential to its nature and to its survival, were in irreconcilable conflict ([*note added later:*] nail *this* down)—the creature would have to perish. The attributes and nature of a bird are set by the determining factor of flight as its means of survival. The attributes and nature of a tiger are set by the determining factor of predatory hunting as its means of survival. That which in art is style, that which in music is leitmotif—the central theme, the basic principle, the determining conception which sets and rules every detail of the whole—is, in living nature, the creature's means of survival.

Man survives through the exercise of his rational faculty.

That is his sole means of survival.

Man comes on earth unarmed. His brain is his only weapon. Animals obtain food by force guided by instinct. Man has no claws, no fangs, no horns, no great strength of muscle, and no instinct to guide him. He cannot obtain sustenance for his body except through the exercise of his rational faculty. He must plant his food or hunt it. Planting requires a long, consistent process of thought—of observation and logical deduction. Hunting requires weapons; man cannot hunt with his hands, his quarries are his superiors in speed or force, and making weapons requires a process of thought. Man could not survive even as an herbivorous creature by picking fruit and berries at random. He has no instinct to tell him which plants are beneficial to him and which are a deadly poison. He can learn it only by conscious experimentation or by the observation of other living creatures who do not touch poisonous plants—a procedure which, in either case, is a process of thought.

([*Note added later:*] Here the transition from the material to the spiritual.)

From these simplest primary necessities on through his every other need, his clothes, his shelter, his philosophy, on to his greatest achievements, from the flint and arrowhead to a modern skyscraper, everything man is and everything he has comes from a single attribute—the function of his reasoning mind. The Empire State Building was not erected by instinct.

But it is the nature of the rational faculty that it implies choice and the possibility of error. Instinct is infallible within the limits of its sphere. Nature gives an animal both the means and the method of survival; he cannot do wrong in his method; he does what he must; if he is confronted by a fact outside the provisions of his instinct, he can do nothing and he perishes. (This can be observed in any country road: wild creatures that run from the approach of man or horse do not run from a speeding automobile; instinct has not armed them against an automobile, as it has not armed cows off railroad tracks. The formulation of an abstraction—such as the rule that two bodies cannot occupy the same space at the same time—is not done by instinct.)

([*Note added later:*] He is given the tool; the nature of the tool sets the method of its use, but man must discover that method. Reason applies to nature—and to himself.)

It is man's distinction that he is given the means, but not the method of survival. He must discover the method himself. The process of discovery is a long series of steps—of observation, deduction, conclusion. The possibility of error hangs over every step. Nothing guarantees in advance the correctness of his deductions. It is up to him. One error in the process grows with each succeeding step—until, if pursued far enough, it leads to the final proof of error, to destruction. Man's life ultimately depends upon every conclusion within his brain.

The process of deduction is a succession of answers to questions, on a single basic pattern: "Yes" or "No." The possibility of differentiating between a "yes" or a "no" is the capacity of choice. Choice is the ultimatum of man's existence. The process of differentiating is an act of choice. The rational process is a succession of such acts. The first commandment of an animal's survival is only: "Act or perish." The act is prescribed. The first commandment of man's survival carries a fateful responsibility: "Choose right before acting or perish."

But the responsibility goes deeper than that. It is not only that man survives through the rational faculty which functions through constant choice. It is that he also has the choice of exercising his rational faculty or not. He can make an error in judgment. He can act against his own judgment. He can suspend all judgment. ([*Note added later:*] Explain what it means to act without judgment.) An animal cannot act against his instinct nor suspend it. He enjoys a safety man can never have—the invariable operation of his means of survival. He cannot act against his own nature. Man can. Man can stop his source of existence. Man can choose not to act as a rational being. Man can choose not to function as a man. His destruction will be the ultimate price—but it will not be the immediate consequence. The rational faculty operates through time. It does not grant man the safety of an immediate retribution for error. The greater man's knowledge, the more complex the factors involved in any given act—the longer the interval before the consequences of that act become evident to him. At any moment of his existence, man lives with the possibility of acting as an agent of his own destruction.

Just as man must discover the methods that permit him to obtain sustenance from the physical world, so he must discover the methods that permit his means of survival—his rational faculty—to function. Nothing is granted to him automatically, neither the results of the operation of his reason nor even the operation itself. He must discover the rules which that operation requires. He must direct his actions by these rules. He must learn to act in accordance with his nature as a rational being.

Man cannot give life to himself. But its preservation and continuation are up to him. Life is given to him—survival is not.

Man cannot change his nature. But its realization and fulfillment are up to him. Being a man is given to him—remaining a man is not. He is the only creature who can slip beneath his own stature. He is man only so long as he functions in accordance with the nature of a rational being. When he chooses to function otherwise, he is no longer man. There is no proper name for the thing which he then becomes. It is not an animal—it does not possess the animal's equipment of survival. It cannot survive, but it has that interval of time at its disposal before the consequences of its choice catch up with it, an interval as a prelude to destruction, a process of disintegration like a slow-rotting disease. Thus it exists for a while—a thing of corruption and death.

A flea does not have the responsibility of remaining a flea. It can be nothing else. A tiger does not have the responsibility of remaining a tiger. Man must remain man through his own choice. Nature guarantees him nothing, not even his own nature. Such is the penalty and the honor of being a rational creature. ([*Note added later:*] Careful here. It may be [asked]: well, if his nature is something relative, arbitrary—how can you base morality on his nature? His nature must be achieved by him. The process here, in effect, is this: man is raw material when he is born; nature tells him: "Go ahead, create yourself. You can become the lord of existence—if you wish—by understanding your own nature and by acting upon it. Or you can destroy yourself. The choice is yours.")

Such is the origin of man's moral faculty.

The moral faculty—the ability to distinguish between right and wrong—is implicit in the rational faculty. The act of choice is the act of establishing values: the accepted and the rejected. Yes or no, right or wrong, good or evil. ([*Note added later:*] Unwarranted jump. A transition is needed.)

A moral code is man's statement of the principles that permit him to function as man. It is his protection against becoming his own destroyer. It is his code of rules for the preservation of that entity of consciousness which we call his soul or his spirit.

The first, most earnest, most crucial question man asks of himself is: Am I right? An animal cannot conceive of such a question. Man cannot escape it. In one form or another, it rings through his whole life. It sets the leitmotif of his existence—the style of his soul. No matter what he has accepted as his conception of the "good" and no matter how often he betrays it, his desire to remain good has the fierce intensity of a primary instinct. His quest for moral justification has a quality of desperate urgency. Men have died willingly for an ideal. It is said, of such cases, that their moral instinct was stronger than their instinct of self-preservation. ([*Note added later:*] *This is* their instinct of self-preservation.) This is not true. The fact is that men—whether they have consciously stated it or not—know that their moral instinct is the first condition of their self-preservation.

All moral systems speak of spiritual death as penalty for immorality. This statement contains all the dangers and possibilities of deception inherent in any half-truth. Man is urged to save his soul at the price of his physical destruction—an unwarranted contraposition. It is true that man destroys his spirit in breaking the principles of morality. But the whole truth is much wider than that. The whole truth is that man cannot preserve his body unless he preserves his soul. His spiritual survival precedes his physical survival—the last is not possible without the first. And if man is placed in a situation where he must choose between spiritual evil or physical death, he chooses the last, because the choice is death in either case; only, in the first case, it is a dreadful form of slow disintegration which no man can choose once he has understood it. The moral man is the one who understands.

([*Note added later:*] This is where altruism cut man's soul off from his physical reality.)

But if a moral code is a necessity of man's survival, what happens when his code is in opposition to his survival? Then man finds himself in a state of perpetual internal war—a civil war against himself. This is the state in which he has lived for centuries. Let us now clear away the wreckage—and the rubbish.

The establishment of values requires a standard. What is the standard by which moral values are to be set? Good and evil? Good—for what? Evil—to whom?

The nature of man sets the standard of his moral code. Man's survival sets the purpose. A moral code in opposition to man's nature or survival would mean immediate destruction, if actually adopted.

The axiom of the only morality proper to man is:

*Man exists and must survive as man.*

All that which furthers his survival is good. All that which obstructs it is evil. The conditions and qualities required by the function of his rational faculty constitute the Life Principle and are, therefore, good. The conditions and qualities that proceed from or result in the obstruction of his rational faculty constitute the Death Principle and are, therefore, evil. [*AR later rejected the idea that ethics begins with an axiom. For her proof of man's life as the standard of moral value, see John Galt's speech in* Atlas Shrugged *and* "The Objectivist Ethics" *in* The Virtue of Selfishness.]

Any morality not based on this axiom would have to claim either that a) man does not exist, or b) he exists, but his survival is not desirable, or c) he can survive as a sub-human creature. The viewpoint of those who might wish to propound any such morality can have no pertinence in any human discussion. ([*Marginal note:*] *Good!*)

If one accepts man for what he is—a rational being—any hypothesis one may hold upon his origin or the origin of his rational faculty will not contradict man's proper moral code. If it is held that man is created by God, endowed with an immortal soul and with reason as an attribute of his soul, it still holds true that man must act in accordance with his nature, the nature God gave him, and that in doing so he will be doing God's will. If it is held that man is a wholly material creature of unknown origin and that his rational faculty is an attribute of his physical body, a superior manifestation of material energy—it still holds true that man must act in accordance with his nature, of which that rational energy is the free, dominant and determining part. [*Later, AR recognizes that an objective ethics is incompatible with an irrational metaphysics. When she rewrites these notes in 1945, this passage is eliminated.*]

The only metaphysical viewpoint that cannot accept or be accepted in this discussion is the old doctrine which has a long, disreputable history, as many variations as a skin disease, and can best be identified in its present version by its current title of "dialectic materialism." It is the doctrine which denies the existence of the rational faculty in man. It holds choice as an illusion and reason as a by-product of physical environment, nutrition and "conditioning," operating without volition, automatically and unalterably. There is a catch in that doctrine, however. Its proponents claim to have reached it by rational deduction. They urge us to take action upon it, to improve our physical environment in order to improve the by-product, our brain, and they beg us to take such action through a conscious decision of—our rational faculty. It is an embarrassing contradiction which no dialectic materialist has ever explained away. Until it is explained, the doctrine is not worth considering or discussing.

There is an axiom implicit in the act of reading or writing any book— the axiom that a book can be read or written. There is an axiom implicit in any book on morality—the axiom that morality is possible. ([*Note added later:*] Not necessarily.) There can be no morality without the rational faculty. There can be no rational faculty without the act of free choice. If this is not accepted as self-evident, no conception of morality nor of a book is possible. Animals and imbeciles are neither rational nor moral. This book is for men.

**September 18, 1943**

*Theorem I: The Basic Alternative*

[*AR here presents independence as the primary virtue in her morality (the "basic alternative" is the choice between independence and dependence). Later, she identifies independence as a derivative, an aspect of the*

*primary virtue of rationality. See John Galt's speech, where she writes:*
*"Thinking is man's only basic virtue, from which all the others proceed."*]

. . . There is nothing in nature to hinder the function of man's rational faculty. That function follows a simple pattern: to observe through his own senses, to make the proper deductions through his own reasoning power. Nothing must stand between the material and man's mind. No intermediary is possible. What can assume the role of such an intermediary? Only other men. The conclusions, the thoughts, the opinions, the wishes or the orders of other men. Man can, if he chooses, accept the ideas of others without examination, repeat what he is told, follow instead of inquiring, shift to others the responsibility of choice, judgment and decision. But whatever he does in such case, it is not an act of reason. The only threat to man's rational faculty lies in the person of others. ([*Note added later:*] This point must be illustrated concretely. Tremendously important step—not well stated. Not clear.)

In this thinking, each man must be as the first man facing a new world for the first time.

Nothing can guarantee that he has made the right deductions, and nothing can prove that he has made the wrong ones—except the consequences, observed and examined by his own mind. His own mind remains the ultimate criterion, the court of final appeal. Other men can find a better solution for any given problem and show to him the error he has made. But this error must be demonstrated in rational terms—and the demonstration is not conclusive or valid to him until he has become convinced of its truth by the operation of his own reason. He must examine a theory presented to him by other men exactly as he examines any fact of physical nature, by the same method, through the same act of independent rational judgment. He is as alone in the presence of an idea as in the presence of a jungle. He can make an error; so can any other man; so can any number of other men. The fact that others hold an idea to be true is no proof of its truth. The idea must be examined on its own merits by his own mind. Nothing else is relevant, nothing and nobody. The responsibility of final judgment is still his. The immutable question remains: "Is this true?"—not "Do others believe this to be true?" ([*Note added later:*] But truth is not "subjective." Only the responsibility is.)

In the delicate, exacting, infinitely strenuous process of reason, there is one deadly consideration man must escape, a trap which, once closed upon him, stops the process dead: the conception of other men as authority. If, at any point in the process, man makes a step because others tell him to, if he accepts a conclusion based on nothing but the unexamined pronouncement of others, if that alien judgment assumes the role of an unquestioned ruler in his mind—his rational process is ended (in this specific instance).

It does not matter whether the idea he accepted is true or false. The act of substituting the word of others for one's own judgment is an act of suspending one's rational faculty—the primary act of man's self-destruction.

And thus the first condition required for the operation of man's rational faculty, the demand inherent in its nature, is *independence*. Man's independence from all other men. The reasoning mind can accept no outside authority. It cannot work under any form of compulsion. It cannot be curbed, sacrificed or subordinated to any consideration whatsoever. Nor to any other man. Nor to any number of other men. The rational faculty demands total independence—in function, in action, in motive.

The man who surrenders this independence destroys his means of survival. He surrenders the responsibility of thought. Then others must carry it and he will live as a parasite on the products of their thinking. But who are the "others"? If every man waits for others to do the thinking he will borrow—no thinking will be done. Then no man can survive.

The man who surrenders this primary independence commits the act of slipping below his nature, into the sub-human. He will survive for a while—as a parasite survives, not as a man. He will be able to satisfy his physical needs—by the grace of those who had the strength to remain men. But nothing will stop the disintegration of his spirit—because he is acting against the nature of man, he is acting on the principle that represents man's destruction.

If *"Man exists and must survive as man"* is the axiom of man's morality, then the first moral principle deduced from it, the first commandment to guide man in his relations with other men, is the principle of independence. Independence of man from men is the Life Principle. Dependence of man upon men is the Death Principle. All that which proceeds from man's independence is good. All that which proceeds from man's dependence upon men is evil.

To preserve the independence of his mind is man's first and highest moral duty. It stands above any other precept. It takes precedence in any conflict.

Man's first moral duty is to himself. No other man can have a claim upon him [that supersedes this right]. This right is primary. All relations of man to other men are secondary.

Left alone, man has a single alternative: think or perish. When man lives in the society of other men, the working intelligence and productive energy of others give him the possibility of another alternative: think or be supported by the thinking of others. Without effort, ability or responsibility, he has a margin of time at his disposal, a margin which he might believe to include his whole lifespan, when he can survive as a parasite. Most societies man has known have made this form of survival seem easier and more practical [than independence]. ([*Note added later:*] Be more specific. Illustrate.)

The choice man makes here is the crucial choice; primary in its nature, based on the manner of his survival, on the issue of life or death, this choice will determine all his subsequent behavior, his actions, his motives, his character, the style of his soul. ([*Note added later:*] Because it is the basic principle.) This choice is the root of good and evil.

We are far removed from the immediate realities of the process through which man obtains his sustenance; a complicated society and the heritage of centuries behind us disguise the primary forms of that process, and have disguised it for man since the beginning of recorded history. So the basic choice assumes a different form in the minds of men. The essence of the choice remains: producer or parasite. The form becomes: independence or dependence.

This is the only real division among men. These are the two irreconcilable antagonists within the human species. Every other distinction—of birth, race, class, position—is artificial and superficial. This one is fundamental—and it is made by voluntary choice. Each man classifies himself.

What makes man choose to be a parasite? A great many motives, of which the common denominator is fear. Independence is a terrifying responsibility. Man has gone to any length and any depravity in trying to circumvent the fact that his survival is in his own hands and that no outside power can offer it to him as a gift. [The motives are] fear of responsibility, fear of effort, fear of his own incompetence, envy of the abler and the better endowed, greed for unearned and undeserved rewards. ([*Note added later:*] And he has been taught to regard independence as evil.)

The modes of survival of the producer and the parasite are diametrically opposed; so the conditions they require in order to function are opposite; their needs are opposite; their codes of behavior are opposite. [. . .]

Such are the Active Man and the Passive Man.

The Active Man is the producer, the creator, the individualist, the egotist, the life giver.

The Passive Man is the parasite, the imitator, the borrower, the collectivist, the altruist, the death-carrier.

As we shall demonstrate fully when we examine them both in action and in detail.

**September 29, 1943**

*Theorem II: The Life Giver—the Active Man*

Since man's physical survival depends upon his rational faculty, the realm of his mind precedes and determines every other sphere of his activity. That which is not proper in this realm cannot be proper in any of his actions.

A man's mind is an attribute of his self, of that entity within him which is his consciousness. That entity can be called spirit. It can be called soul. It remains—no matter what its origin—a man's self. His "I." His ego.

If to preserve the independence of his mind is man's first moral duty, what choice is he to make when his thinking clashes with the thoughts and convictions of others? Such a clash occurs at every step of a man's life, most particularly when his thinking results in a new, original discovery—as every new discovery must originate in one brain, that is, with one man, and therefore must be apart from or in opposition to whatever convictions men previously held on that subject. What is man's choice in such a conflict? It is a choice of authority. "I think" or "They tell me." Whose authority is he to accept? Upon whose authority is he to act? Who must be placed first: his ego or other men?

The independence of man's mind means precisely the placing of his ego above any and all other men on earth. It means acting upon the authority of his ego above any other authority. It means keeping his ego untouched, uninfluenced, uncorrupted, *unsacrificed*.

In the realm of man's mind, the principle of altruism—the placing of others about self—is the one act of evil, the original sin. [*Marginal note on the last two paragraphs:*] *Good!*

Man's virtues are the qualities required for the preservation of his independence. They are personal qualities, unsocial by their nature and antisocial in any conflict of man against man. They are unsocial, because man cannot derive them from other men, cannot receive them as a gift from an outside source, but must generate them from within his own ego. They are profoundly *selfish* virtues, for they proceed from his ego, pertain to his ego and cannot be sacrificed to any consideration whatsoever. Without these virtues man cannot survive nor remain man.

Integrity—the first, greatest and noblest of all virtues—is a synonym of independence. Integrity is that quality in man which gives him the courage to hold his own convictions against all influences, against the opinions and desires of other men; the courage to remain whole, unbroken, untouched, to remain true to himself. It is generally recognized that a man who is true to himself is a man to be admired. But the sloppy confusion of human thinking has prevented men from understanding their own words or hearing what they are actually saying. "True to himself"—what does that mean? True to his own ego. True to the duty of holding his ego apart from all other men—above them and against them when necessary. A man of integrity cannot place others above self. Here again, the principle of altruism is an act of evil.

The virtue of courage is the strength to face any threat and to fight back. Fight what? Nature, as well as other men when necessary. If, however, one must place others above self—then it is evil to resist them; then one must surrender if a conflict arises. But the man of courage is the one who does not surrender. In an issue of courage, altruism becomes cowardice—an act of evil.

The virtue of honesty is implicit in the function of the rational faculty. Man requires the greatest, the most ruthless honesty of observation and reasoning in order to reach as correct a conclusion as his rational capacity will permit. A man willing to fool himself will collapse—and does—in his first attempt at thought. The incentive to dishonesty comes when man deals with other men. What is the exact procedure of a dishonest action? A man says a thing which he knows to be untrue or commits an act which he knows to be wrong—in order to obtain something from other men or achieve some end that depends upon others. Whether he does it for personal gain or for any other reason, does not alter the procedure. The motive is irrelevant to the nature of the action. The nature of the action is that man acts upon what he believes to be agreeable or desirable to others, not upon his conception of the truth, that he acts to deceive others, they are his first concern, they determine his conduct. This is the placing of others above self. The procedure of dishonesty is the procedure of altruism—and an act of evil.

A sense of honor is a selfish virtue by definition, because it implies the honor of one's own self. Of one's ego. A man with a sense of honor will not submit to certain things nor permit them to be done to him—the things which he considers dishonorable. Dishonorable to whom? To him. Will not permit them to be done—by whom? By other men. What, then, does a sense of honor require? The placing of self above others. The principle of altruism applied here would become abjectness and depravity—an act of evil.

The virtue of self-confidence is made clear by the very term. It is not confidence in others, nor reliance upon others, but confidence in one's own ability, in one's strength, one's courage, one's judgment, one's vision. Confidence in one's own ego. When is this virtue called upon? In a conflict with others. Here altruism would mean trust in anyone and everyone above self—the behavior of a Milquetoast of the spirit—an act of evil.

The virtue of strength implies all the same considerations. Strength of character, strength of will, strength of spirit—all attributes of the ego, needed in conflict with others, all making an application of the principle of altruism an act of evil.

The love of freedom is a synonym of independence. Freedom from what? Nothing can take a man's freedom away from him—except other men. *Freedom means freedom from others.* A man who places others above self should have no objection to being a slave. In fact, that is the condition he should desire. Here altruism means enslavement—an act of evil.

A sense of justice is an intellectual quality—totally selfish, because it cannot be exercised except through one's own judgment, one's own rational faculty. Here man cannot accept the pronouncement of others, as he cannot accept it in any process of reason. A just man acts upon that which he has concluded to be just. If he places others above self in a matter of justice, he is committing the equivalent of joining a lynch mob. Here altruism assumes one of its blackest forms of evil.

The virtue of wisdom implies all the same considerations as above. One cannot be wise except through one's own brain and acting upon one's own thoughts. It is not necessary to repeat what altruism would mean here.

All these virtues are contained in, enhanced by, based upon one fundamental virtue—that of *self-respect.* Self-respect is implied in each of them. A man who does not respect himself can have no integrity, no courage, no honesty, no honor, no strength, no wisdom, no virtue of any kind. Self-respect implies that a man considers himself an entity of value—a purely egotistical consideration.

These virtues are primary. They pertain to the realm of man's mind and spirit. And in that realm, altruism is either impossible or evil, or both. [. . .]


**September 30, 1944**

*The relation of the immediate and the long-range in morality.* (The impression that "evil pays.")

After we have defined the good and the evil—what are the proper methods of fighting the evil?

A Peter Keating [type might make the] argument: "Since I have a second-hander's social talent, why should I not exercise it to the limit and get more than I could by my own ability?" Here comes the question of the proper relation between the primary and the secondary matters, between basic individualism and functioning in a society of exchange.

(Note on a good argument about the position of an unemployed man in a capitalist society: the primitive condition of fighting nature directly is always open to him (Pat's argument), but the advantages left to him by others, by civilization, more than balance the hazard of having to seek employment through other men. He is asking for a chance created for him by others.)

*Think very thoroughly* on the relation of theory to practice, covering every possible instance where it looks as if theory does not have any meaning in practice. Is it in any sense true that in a free society a basic right can become meaningless and without application? Analyze cases such as: cameramen blacklisted by Hollywood ([Albert Mannheimer's] question); the closed shop disaster to the New York stage (you are not forced to deal with established producers, but in practice it means that you cannot have a producer); the hypothetical case of a monopoly (say, telephone) free to refuse services to an individual or a group of men or a branch of business.

In this last case, it is obvious that the inventor's monopoly has such an absolute right. Does it mean, however, that individualism then degenerates into its opposite in practice, into collectivism? Has the size of an enterprise (made possible by the scope covered by modern inventions) anything to do with it? In other words, does an invention such as the telephone give the individual who controls it a *collectivist's* power by the sheer size of his business? (*No*, I think.)

Granted that such monopolies would be destroyed by counter-inventions, if man's ingenuity is left free—what happens to individual victims in the meantime? (Here again, the relation of the immediate and the long-range.) Also, a single individual denied service by one of these gigantic enterprises has no recourse unless there is a *collective* of men in his position—or else no competitor will start to compete against the monopoly. Is there a principle involved in such a possibility? Is there a possibly legitimate argument that if huge private companies control everything—individualism becomes meaningless in practice? (*No*, I think.)

Still, the point here seems to be *size*. Before modern inventions, enterprises were within the personal scope of one man's control and ability. Modern inventions *seem to* make enterprises "collective" in scope and nature. (I may be terribly wrong here, but I must analyze this "seeming.") A man can compete against a hand forge—can he compete against the Radio Corporation of America? The main point is: does he *have to* compete? Is there or is there not room left for individualism *in practice*—under the most extreme consequences of "laissez-faire" that can be imagined and legitimately supposed to happen?

This is probably the point at which people now go in for collectivism

and statism. Since collectivism is not the solution, but only the complete surrender into the very evil one is opposing—is there a solution? Or is it that
civilization *must* periodically collapse because it always becomes collectivism and stops? And that the moment any economic activity grows beyond
the "controllable capacity" of one man—the limit has been reached and we
go into the dark ages again? All of these questions are probably nonsense—
but an awfully clear statement and definition is needed.

Here is the seeming contradiction: mass production gives inestimable
advantages to the individual through the cheapness of products made possible by a "collective" of customers—but then the individual is tied to that
collective task. Or is he? It's individual inventors and producers that make
mass production possible. It's individuals and minorities that support new
inventors and teach the masses to appreciate them. Obviously, it starts with
prime-movers and followers. But what about the results? Here again, a *most*
careful statement of the relation between individualism and a society of
exchange is needed.

Does all this mean that an individual acquires "*collective*" power
through a great invention that becomes a mass industry, and that to compete
with him, or to be independent of him, another man needs "*collective*"
power?

And if we say that voluntary collectives (such as unions, closed shops,
employers' agreements) are *evil*, but cannot be stopped by law—and we rely
only on men's wisdom and proper choice—will it work in practice? Since
the majority are second-handers by nature, will they necessarily and always
destroy a free system by starting with voluntary collectivism? If the prime
movers are clear on the idea that there must be no state interference, but the
second-handers are the majority with the political power, then is every civilization only to have a very brief period (such as Greece's 150 years and
America's 150 years) before the second-handers unavoidably destroy it?
Just a brief period of magnificence once in many, many centuries—and then
destruction? Is that the inevitable fate of mankind? Is it basic and eternal—a
small group of prime-movers feeding the rest and being destroyed by those
they feed? (For *The Strike*.) [The Strike *was the working title for* Atlas
Shrugged*; this is the first reference to the novel in her notes.*]

*Or are second-handers in the majority?* That, perhaps, is the heart of
the question. Maybe not. Maybe Pat is right—the fault is in men's thinking,
not in man's nature. (Think, think, think on *this* point.)

Granted that collectivism and statism are brought about by minorities—
as [Ludwig] von Mises proves. What can the minority of prime-movers do
about it? Are the collectivists' methods open and proper to prime-movers?

Won't the majority always follow the collectivists if given a clear choice? (*No*, I think.) Isn't it actually true that even among collectivists and statists it is always a prime-mover off the track who does the real damage?—so that the world is destroyed by the Wynands, not the Tooheys? (I think so.) [*Here AR is grasping an idea essential to* Atlas Shrugged: *that evil is impotent—it has no power except that which the good grants it.*] But if so—can it ever be stopped? What can stop prime-movers from going off the track for one reason or another? I suppose the answer is: Nothing. There is no automatic fool-proof and error-proof [way]. If there were, there would be no free will. Nothing can ever replace man's necessity to make a free, conscious choice—the necessity of an effort of reason. All we can do is indicate the right way, the proper principles—and then *fight, fight, and fight* for them.

That a man knows the right idea is not enough. He must still act upon it. There are, then, two acts of the free will: the will to know the truth and then the will to act upon it. The first does not lead automatically to the second.

**October 25, 1944**

In answer to the question "If a morality is not based on the common good, what is it then based on?": on a definition of the moral individual and on that which is good for *him*. The moral individual is the best and highest possible to man. By what standard? By the essence of man's nature. The man living in accordance with his nature is the moral man and the "surviving" man—he carries the life force, the life principle, he is the self-renewing "energy" and the fountainhead. What is man's nature? Man is a *reasoning* being.

And since morality is a matter of free will, open to all but the insane—the good of the moral man is good for all, i.e., for all those who wish to be moral.

What is good? That which is in accordance with the life principle of man. The independent, the self-reverent, the self-sufficient.

Do I set myself up as an arbitrary elite and formulate a morality for my own kind of elite, at the expense of others? No, because it is not to be enforced upon "others" or anyone. "Others" are free not to accept it and not to subscribe to it; they may have their own kind of collectivism, altruism or whatever they wish. *But* they are not free to enforce it upon me and my "elite"—they are not free to arrange their collectivism at *our* expense. The objective dividing line is: *no man exists for the sake of another man.* There can be no moral justification for a collectivism [forcibly imposed] on one man for the sake of the others. But, the collectivists would say, our survival depends upon enslaving this exceptional individual; haven't we a right to do it? *No.* First, it does not and cannot depend upon such enslavement; second, if it did, it would not work just the same, the enslaved creator would not save them; third, if it did, it would still be evil and no such universe is worthy of existence, so that it would be moral to let the collective, the creator, and the world go to hell altogether.

*This point*—no man exists for the sake of another man—must be established very early in my system. It is one of the main cornerstones—and perhaps even the basic axiom. [*For AR's final view of this issue, see the introduction to* The Virtue of Selfishness.]

———◇———

In relation to my earlier notes on individual competition against big near-monopolies: take notice of Mr. Hazen's complaint about the impossibility of an independent producer competing with big movie companies because "the big companies won't loan their stars to independents." [*Joseph Hazen was president of Hal Wallis Productions.*] Mr. Hazen wants to compete with ready-made tools to be handed over to him by the competition. He doesn't want to start at the beginning—he wants to expropriate that which the competition has created (and use it against the competition), he wants to be boosted to an equal level to start competing, he wants to be handed an unearned advantage. Is the way open to him to compete from a clean beginning? Obviously, *yes*, in this case. He *can* and *should* create his own stars, and all his other tools.

Isn't the situation the same in every other line of business where men yelp about the impossibility of competing with bigness? Monroe Shakespeare [*a businessman in Kalamazoo, Michigan*] says that he can't compete with automobile manufacturers and he wants to expropriate the patents that they created—which is exactly like Mr. Hazen's stars. What's to prevent Shakespeare from inventing his own patents? What if he can't—why should he demand the property or discoveries of others? And if there are no new patents to be invented in connection with the automobile—why should he go into that business and expect an unfair advantage? Even from the angle of "the common good," why should society help [establish] him in a branch of business which society doesn't need, since the existing companies cover it perfectly?

If he has, not a basic patent to offer, but an improvement on the existing ones, which he cannot use without the consent of the original patent's owners—then he has to sell his idea to these owners. They won't see it?

That's too bad—but that is the basic condition of an exchange society—the voluntary consent of those involved in a transaction. (*Yes*, even if a lot of men are blind, stupid and unable to see their own advantage. *That* is the basic law of an exchange society. It includes the right of fools to make mistakes. Any kind of *sin of omission* has to be permitted—there's no way out of that. *But no sins of commission.*)

But, Shakespeare might say, in such a case the owners of the original patent would dictate terms and take unfair advantage of the new inventor. Not necessarily. Not if he holds out and if what he has is good enough and they want it badly enough. Again—the rule of a free exchange society. (And, as a matter of fact and history, the fools cannot hold a valuable invention down, nor close the road to it by being unable to see it and thus not giving it a chance. They cannot stop the inventor or the invention. It is the history of every great innovation that it [overcame] fools. And it's the fools who suffered—not the inventor, nor society. *Provided* the social system is *free*, and the inventor has a chance to fight. He *does not* need ready-made encouragements. All he needs is—no barriers. Hands off and out of my way! Don't help me—but *don't stop me.*)

———◆———

In answer to the argument that "man doesn't know what is best for him—in this day of specialization a man cannot know what is best for him as well as a doctor can." First, the primary choice is still with the man—does he wish to call in a doctor and what doctor? If he doesn't want any, no moral right can force him, even though he might die. He has the right to choose to die. *Freedom includes the right to make mistakes.* There's no definition of what's good for a man—except that which a man chooses as good for himself. He is the final and total judge of that—*provided* his choice does not include the use of *force* upon other men. (Incidentally, doctors can be wrong, and so can engineers, and any specialists. There is no [automatically] defined *good* for everybody. Only the right to choose one's own good. To suffer through the consequences of one's own error is a proper part of the existence of a being endowed with free will. But to suffer through the mistake of another which is forced on one for one's own good is an inexcusable, unnatural evil.) [*For AR's view of the good as objective, see "What is Capitalism?" in* Capitalism: The Unknown Ideal.]

But *second*, and most important: if the choice here is between a genius subjected to the will of a moron or a moron deprived of the help of a genius—the first is the evil, the second not. Here is a *good case* of the sins of commission and omission. The first is a positive sin of commission. The second is only a sin of omission—*which is not a sin.* (This distinction must be covered very thoroughly, completely and unanswerably. It is a cardinal point; it is the root and source of altruism.)

---

Minor point: if the majority of men cannot know what is good for them, each for himself, how can they know what is good for others by proxy? If they are to be controlled by "specialists," because they cannot know everything themselves, how and by what standards will they choose the specialists? This is where communism runs into fascism—the rule of a collective by an elite for the sake of the collective.

How many men are incapable of living by independent effort in a system of free enterprise, based on merit? Only a small, subnormal minority are incapable. Thus collectivism is not even the sacrifice of a brilliant minority for the sake of the average majority—but the sacrifice of everybody, of the *majority*, to the worst and lowest minority: the incompetent and subnormal. Collectivism is not even "the greatest good for the greatest number," silly and vile as such a formula is. Collectivism is the sacrifice of the greatest number for the greatest good of the vilest and smallest number. And besides, it won't work—even for the benefit of the morons.

### October 26, 1944

A possible definition of a *right*: a "right" is that which it is morally permissible to defend by force. Here I have to be *very* careful. This might be totally wrong. If carelessly handled, it could be used as justification for the right of a communist to murder an employer who does not give him a job. Again, "sins of omission" come in. This is only a hint, a possible clue to be thought out very carefully, from every possible angle and in every possible application. It is no good—*unless* a total *proof* of it can be given. As a clue to it: it would have to be clearly stated that only that which does not depend *primarily* upon other men can be considered "a right"—such as life, liberty, and the pursuit of happiness. But again—the definition of the principle and its application in reality has to be given—"the long-range and the immediate." Such as: "My happiness depends on my work—what about the man who refuses to give me the job I want?" Here again—the definition of basic individualism in an exchange society. (Clue: Nobody is forced to provide you with the means of exercising a right. But nobody must *stop* you from exercising it.) [*See "Man's Rights" in* The Virtue of Selfishness *for AR's final definition.*]

Could it be that *virtues* (toward other men, *socially only*) are virtues of *omission*, while sins are only of *commission*? There's something important here. Of course, the real and primary virtues are individual and positive, virtues of commission, such as: integrity, courage, wisdom, honesty, independence. But in the social realm—in relation to others—the virtues are all of omission, that is, *hands off.* While the sins are of commission—positive violence.

The whole relation of man to society has to be defined, its proper order stated: Man, the entity, first—*then* his relation to society. Society is only the sum of individuals, therefore the order is natural, logical and proper: individual entity, rights, and morality *first*, then the secondary matters pertaining to society, to the established entity's relation with others. If relations are placed first—*who is it* that's having relations, *whom* are we talking about?

In any clash between the *individual* and the *social*, the *individual* must win, the individual has the right and the priority. (But be sure that the individual is *strictly* individual and clearly defined as such.)

**October 28, 1944**

The force which a proper government exercises against criminals is *not* in defense of *society*, but of an *individual*. A murderer did not hurt "society"—he killed an individual man. He violated, not a "social" right, but an individual right. Secondarily, the punishment of a murderer benefits society [because] society cannot exist unless individual rights are protected. Here again, the social is secondary, a natural consequence of the individual—and beneficial *only* in that secondary manner.

This point is extremely important. It is the sloppy fallacy that a policeman protects "society"—that he is there to combat crimes against society—that creates the acceptance of the idea that we can exercise force for the "*social*" good. There *is* no "social good" and it can never be defined. Only in serving *individual good* can we accomplish any *social* good at all. And the clear, objective standards defining the individual good are inalienable individual rights. Force can be exercised *only* in the protection of these rights. [*Here we see AR's respect for the rights of every man, genius or not; her individualism has led her* away *from Nietszche.*]

The policeman is not protecting a community (a collective) against single individual malefactors. He is protecting individuals against the possibility of collective violence. The only protection the individual needs is against the collective, and the only action which a collective can take (as a collective) is violence—physical force. A society based on the prohibition of the exercise of physical force between its members is an anti-collectivist society. (Force is the only specifically "collective" method.)

(Breach of contract comes under the same category. If a man is up against a single man and a contract is broken, the man can deal with the breaker by force. But he cannot [protect himself] if the breaker has a collective of followers under his command. Then the intervention of government—of law to protect contracts—is needed, because this keeps the issue between two men and their rights, allowing no recourse to violence in which the man with the most followers would win. Again, a contract society is an anti-collectivist society.)

### November 6, 1944

The art of writing is the art of doing what you think you're doing.

This is not as simple as it sounds. It implies a very difficult undertaking: the necessity to think. And it implies the requirement to think out three separate, very hard problems: What is it you want to say? How are you going to say it? Have you really said it?

It's a coldly intellectual process. If your emotions do not proceed from your intellect, you will not be able to apply it, even if you know all the rules. The mental ability of a writer determines the literary level of his output. If you grasp only home problems well, you'll be only a writer of good homey stories. (But what about Tolstoy?)

### February 13, 1945

*Note on altruism:* in private and voluntary instances of help to another person (and this is only *kindness,* not *altruism*) it works well *only* when the recipient of help is a worthwhile person (essentially an "action" person) who is temporarily in need, purely through accident, not through his own nature. Such a person eventually gets back on his own feet and feels benevolence (or gratitude) toward the one who helped him. But when the recipient is essentially a "passive" person, chronically in need through his own nature, the help of another gets him deeper into parasitism and has vicious results: he hates the benefactor. Therefore, here's the paradox about "helping another": *one can help only those who don't actually need it.* With the others, help leads only to disaster. Help is proper only in a catastrophe or emergency—such as rescuing a drowning man. It seems right by the very nature of things: a catastrophe is the opposite of the normal; therefore, that which is proper in a catastrophe is the opposite of that proper to a normal, healthy human existence.

Besides, all instances of legitimate help seem to be of a physical nature—rescues in illness or physical disaster. The possibility of spiritual help seems doubtful. Incidental assistance—yes. Real, crucial help—no. But material wealth is the result and consequence of a spiritual effort—work and thought. Why should it be distributed according to a rule (altruism) inapplicable to the primary sphere, to its source, the spiritual life of man?

*Proper relation of men*—justice. A fair exchange to mutual advantage—not charity. No, not in any way. A man owes his fairest judgment to another man—nothing else. This is a moral law—up to each man, not to be imposed by force or by the state.

### March 25, 1945

"Only a man fit for solitude is fit for human association." He must bring an entity to his relationship with others; otherwise his own vacuum creates a suction, he *must* feed on the *substance* of others, he becomes "a second-hander who cannot exist except as a leech on the soul of others."

### June 29, 1945

*[AR now critiques her original draft. The foreword is referred to here as the "Introduction"; "Axiom" is Chapter 1; "Theorem 1: The Basic Alternative" is Chapter 2; "Theorem 2: The Life Giver—the Active Man" is Chapter 3.]*

Notes on the written part of *The Moral Basis of
Individualism Introduction*

Excellent in content and general effect. Bad in language—too journalistic and uncertain. Shaky. No unity of style, because no unity of method and approach. Reorganize and rewrite, keeping the same beginning and end. Go easy on and be careful of "journalistic" references—keep them specific and general at once—general primarily, and specific only to the extent needed to drive the idea home, only in the nature of a concrete illustration. (But remember that it must be clear to the contemporary reader, and clear to any reader at any time. When in doubt, aim for the latter.)

In speaking of [altruism in history], cover the point that your statement holds true *even* if most of the followers of an altruistic leader acted for "selfish" material gain. (Such as—"the real purpose of the Crusades was Oriental trade.") If [the motives were selfish], why didn't the leaders recruit men for the purpose of "selfish" looting? *And*—if an ideal is such a handy cover-up for the lowest "selfish" purposes—isn't there something wrong with the ideal? Isn't it because the ideal cannot be defined and is impossible to practice?

## Chapter I

To cover more thoroughly the [point that] "reason" is the determining faculty of man: it is obvious that man's physical survival and progress have been achieved *only* through his reason. If that is the prime law of the survival of his body—can his soul (or spirit, or consciousness) have a contradictory, opposite prime law of survival? Reason is a faculty of the spirit. Applied to the physical realm it has performed miracles. It has never been applied consistently to the spiritual realm—to ethics, which is the code of spiritual laws—and look at the state of our morality!

*If we cannot survive without our rational faculty, our prime laws of conduct must be those required by the rational faculty.*

Chapter I should *begin* by stating the axiom. Then define man's nature. Then ask [*AR interrupts her thought, crossing out the preceding two words*]. *Or*—begin by asking whether a moral code is necessary? Prove that it is— for a rational being. What is the rational? That which is true to *facts*. To exist one must be true to facts. If one goes contrary to the facts of existence—one perishes, simply by being or making oneself *unfit* for existence. [*Here we see AR grasping the crucial point that ethics begins by asking not "What are the right values?" but rather "Why are values necessary?"*]

What is the rational? To be *right*. What is the moral? To be (or do) *right*. (Why is the same term used?) A code of ethics must be totally, profoundly, completely *practical*—or else it is a means of self-destruction (as altruism is). It is altruism that has caused the idea that morality is "impractical," something for which one must suffer, that "virtue is its *own* reward," meaning its *only* reward, and that "idealism" or "theory" are the opposite of reality and practice.

[Regarding the point that man must choose to be man:] This might be the place for the statement that: "Man screams in terror at his own greatness,

(4)

Chapter I should begin by setting the axiom. Then define man's nature. ~~~~~~ Or — begin by asking whether a moral code is necessary? Prove that it is — for a rational being. What is the rational? — That which is true to facts. To exist one must be true to facts. If one goes contrary — one perishes, simply by being or making oneself unfit for existence — going contrary to the facts of existence.

What is the rational? To be right.
What is the moral? To be (or do) right. (Why is the same term used?) A code of ethics must be totally, profoundly, completely practical — or else it is a means of self-destruction (as Altruism is.) It is altruism that has caused the idea that morality is

begging by every possible means to be delivered from it. The greatness is being a *free agent*."

Chapter I is not well-organized; it leaps into side-lines, does not follow a straight progression. *Reorganize* the material and the order of presentation.

When you speak of "reason" and "the rational faculty," illustrate the concrete application of what you mean once in a while.

## Chapter II

An additional point here: if someone says "But so many crucial mental conclusions in a man's life are made under the *influence* of other men (or proceed from other men)"—the answer is: "Quite so. For *some* men. But some other man had to think of it in the first place. Even if it's only a small improvement on the material left by others—if it is an improvement and a new step, some *one* man had to think of it." And as general historical illustration and proof—the greatest achievements and advances were made in individualist societies, when men worked alone—*not* in collectivist ones, where men were encouraged and *forced* to work together. Also, the great epoch-making discoveries (such as the Wright brothers' airplane) were made by single, individual men. Only the minor improvements and variations are made by collectivists (such as the boasted discoveries of Nazi Germany or Soviet Russia). There is almost a law here: if a man gets his major impetus from the material (or influence) of others, he is of lesser stature than the man who strikes out the farthest by himself. And the achievement of the first will be less than that of the second.

Point to cover: Edison, born in the jungle, would not have invented the electric light. But he would have invented the torch—or some other equivalent of his achievement—equivalent in the sense of a tremendous step forward in comparison to what was known before. The savage who died in the swamp at that time, having achieved nothing, still exists today—he is every man who has never held a thought of his own. It is not society that made Edison's achievement possible (nor the social heritage)—it is Edison.

The important point: the thoughts of others (the heritage of civilization) can be of tremendous help to man—but *only* if weighed, examined and accepted by his own reason. They become a death trap and a menace when accepted merely on *the authority* of other men.

[*Regarding the disintegration of spirit in the parasite:*] Clarify this thought. I mean here: if he persists in this action *or* to the extent to which he persists. He may still act as a rational being in other spheres—but the poison is planted and will continue to grow. *And*—the more he indulges in the non-rational (the second-hand), the more he acts on the death principle and the faster he comes to one form or another of actual destruction.

[*Regarding social relations:*] Before you come to "any principle as a guide in his relations to other men," cover the point of how the morality of reason applies to man alone—even to a man on a desert island. The first commandment is to exercise his reason. *Morality is not social* (and don't forget the evils that come from thinking that it is). Only after you have established this, can you come to morality in relation to other men. [*Here we see AR's transition, in regard to the primary virtue, from independence to rationality.*]

[*Regarding the choice to be a parasite:*] This needs the added statement that the *degree* of a man's intelligence is not the essential, determining factor here—the *exercise* of his intelligence *is*. (And a necessary addition to this is: if you cannot venture independently into difficult intellectual spheres—*don't venture* into them. There is no moral obligation to know and solve everything, to have an independent judgment upon everything. There *is* a moral obligation that such judgments as you *do* hold *must* be your own. Let your sphere of concern be as large or as small as you feel capable of handling (and you're the sole judge here)—*but it must be* the sphere of your independent rational judgment. There is *never* an obligation upon man to handle more than his intellect will permit him. If he finds himself in a position where it seems that he has to—he has brought it upon himself, through second-handedness. If a writer steals, because he cannot invent, he had no business being a writer. The test for a person in any field is the question: What do I know about this by myself, without having heard it from others?)

Chapter II is extremely confused. The material is out of sequence and covers too many fields too soon.

## Chapter III

Excellent in thought, but not definite in statement and much too soon in sequence. I take virtues for granted, instead of proving that they are virtues. Since it draws parallels between egoism and altruism, it must come later, after both have been stated, defined, and analyzed.

## For Chapter I

Man's sole means of survival is the rational faculty. It is a spiritual faculty through which he controls matter. Yet he has excluded it from his spiritual field—and does his damnedest to find himself excuses to be set free of it. (Man screaming against his own greatness.) He doesn't want to realize that he himself must be controlled by the same faculty—and by himself. He dreads the responsibility. He wants the license of chaos within himself. What for? ("It's such a big responsibility really to desire something.")

**June 30, 1945**

### General Notes

Be very careful to keep in mind that the axiom of your morality is *not* "Man must survive," *but*: "Man must survive *as man*." This is the crucial point; otherwise it becomes an issue of any kind of survival, and any criminal moron can claim that he is moral when he murders, because that is his only means of survival. This point, clarified, must cover such cases as when a man chooses to die, rather than compromise with evil. Since man's status as man is within his own keeping (and he is the only such creature, *that* is his crucial distinction), the basis of his morality is the preservation of himself *as man*, not just the preservation of a physical hulk (which, incidentally, cannot be preserved without the preservation of his human spirit).

A possibly helpful point toward a clear definition of what constitutes one's own judgment and what is merely taken on second-hand authority: an independent rational judgment is one which we know how to apply to the concrete. Every statement or judgment is an abstraction; when we repeat an abstract statement with no clear idea of its concrete application, we are [being] intellectually second-handed; we destroy our connection with reality and our sole means of handling it—the very fact of our consciousness.

It is useless to accept generalities second-hand, i.e., on the authority of others, because generalities are of no value except when and as applied to the concrete, and each man must do that for himself, applying principles to the concrete events of his life. He cannot do it with a principle he has not understood.

Man has a right (and a moral duty) to state the terms of his existence (again, since his nature is in his own keeping). At a certain point, he must tell his brothers: "*This* is the kind of existence *I* do not accept." At that point, he [may] face a firing squad rather than submit to others. *Think this point over carefully:* it leads to an extremely important fact—that morality is *not* social, but in certain respects *anti-social*. Morality is unsocial in essence: it applies to and proceeds from *man*, not society. But when it involves man's relation to other men, it becomes anti-social; it is man's protection *against* society. ("Rights were not given to man *by* society nor *for* society, but *against* society. They are man's protection against all other men.") And, incidentally, only when each man is thus protected can one have a *good* society. Let society always remain what it is—a consequence, not a determinant, an effect, not a cause, *the secondary, not the primary.*

**July 3, 1945**

Nail down—thoroughly, completely, once and for all—the fool idea that good is merely a matter of good will or good intentions. Here's another abstraction without relation to the concrete—a "floating abstraction." [*AR's first written use of this expression.*] Before you can have "good will," i.e., before you can want to do good, you must know what is the *good*. In effect, fools say that all the problems, personal and political, can be solved by finding "men of good will." But the "good" is never defined. And actually, most of the evil in this world is done by and through "good" intentions. The cause of evil is *stupidity*, not malice. "Good" is an intellectual concept.

———◈———

Regarding the golden rule: "Do unto others as you'd want them to do unto you." This is used in support of altruism. In that way, it would imply that you must give out to charity because you want to be an object of charity yourself. Or—you must sacrifice yourself to others because you want them to sacrifice themselves to you. Actually, the golden rule can work *only* in application to *my* morality: you do not sacrifice yourself to others and you do not wish them to sacrifice themselves to you. You may want to be helped in an emergency or a catastrophe—but *only* in such cases. You consider such cases a calamity—not your normal and proper state of existence. You *do not wish* to live as an object of charity—and you do not hand charity out to others.

**July 5, 1945**

*General Plan*
*Part I: Morality*

**1.** The nature, necessity, and axiom of morality. (Morality *must* be practical.)
**2.** Define the morality of egoism.
**3.** Define the morality of altruism.
**4.** Virtues—under both moralities.
**5.** Human relations (personal, economic, political)—under both moralities.
**6.** Conclusion—the spiritual wreckage and corruption caused by altruism. The spiritual status of an egoist.

*Part II: Politics*

The reference of political forms and ideas to morality—and to both systems of morals.

———————◆———————

**Blast**—once and for all—the horrible notion that love is in the nature of a handout, that it's alms, charity, something undeserved but handed down out of generosity or pity. This idea leads to the impossible precept of loving everybody. If love is undeserved, one can love everybody; then, the less the object deserves it, the nobler is the love, since it makes the one who loves more generous. Therefore, the noblest emotion would be, not to love a Roark, but to love the lowest, vilest, most contemptible moron one could find. This has been actually preached. Yet, in common sense, people do not love that way.

Love is exception-making and *it must be deserved*. This means [it must be] an exchange—the one who loves gets a personal, selfish happiness out of the virtues or qualities he admires in the object of his love, and love is his payment for them.

It is the idea of love as alms that leads to the idea of parents' love for their children as a generous sacrifice. But if the parents get no happiness out of their love for their children—their sacrifice is of no use and they're vicious parents (other things being normal). If they do get personal happiness and their love is authentic, they'd better stop prattling about self-sacrifice.

———————

When society makes claims on the individual—the individual also starts making claims on society (such as "my right to a beautiful street"). Then no untangling [of "rights"] and no justice is possible. The ultimate recourse is brute force. Without individual rights, no peace among men is possible. By herding men into "unity," one creates total disunity and chaos. Instead of peace, one gets war of all against all, and general hatred.

**July 6, 1945**

The contradiction in the collectivists' view of mankind: They hate mankind and believe that men cannot rule themselves for their own good, [because of] malice or stupidity or both. Yet they advocate giving total power to this vicious, incompetent majority. This is where the idea of a Nazi elite comes in—fuhrers ruling others for the others' own good.

Every collectivist hates mankind because he hates himself.

The collectivists have such a tender concern for the dregs of humanity. What is their attitude toward humanity's heroes?

**July 8, 1945**

For morality as non-social: it is most important (and hardest) to be *honest* with oneself. The person who lies to himself is much more revolting and corrupt than one who lies to others.

———————

Why is the word "virtue" used as a synonym for "strength" or "effi-cacy"? There is here the same connection as between "right" used for "true to facts" and for "morally correct." Obviously, the conceptions of morals and virtues were [meant] to be *practical*—not the complete opposite of prac-tice. Altruism made them this last.

There is also the question: practical for whom? If ethics had always been considered as a social matter and based on collectivism—obviously the "good" and the "virtues" were set to profit collectivism, to work for the collective (for society). But collectivism doesn't work. Therefore, the ethics of collectivism didn't and couldn't work. Men *had* to live as individuals—at least partially—in order to survive at all. Thus ethics and "ideals" became the impractical, the impossible. Thus all beauty, dignity, and inspiration were taken out of men's actual lives. Men functioned on the conviction that their actual existence and their deepest reality were vicious, depraved, contrary to all ideals. And every attempt to reach the ideal resulted in suffering, horror, and evil.

No, ethics are *not* set arbitrarily, with some utilitarian purpose in view (as the dialectic materialists may claim at this point); that is, ethics are *not* *relative*, set "pragmatically." No, we cannot have: "bourgeois ethics," "capitalist ethics," "collectivist ethics"—for the sake of a class, a state or any other "sake." Ethics *are* absolute and objective. They must be based—not on an arbitrarily chosen purpose—but on the very nature of man. And the nature of man is individualistic. And the only ethics that will work are the ethics of individualism.

———◆———

In ethics, when we ask the question: Practical for whom? Good for whom? we must give a reason for the answer. Good for the collective? *Why?* No reason can be given. Good for the individual? *Why?* Here there is a reason and an unanswerable one: because such is man's nature.

———◆———

Account for the fact that man is not "a social animal." Explain the facts [regarding] human affection and loneliness.

———◆———

Men have always thought—for some reason (think this out)—that morality must be difficult. The morality of egoism is much—oh, much!—more difficult than that of altruism (if difficulty is any relevant criterion at all). *But it works.*

———◆———

Altruism works like every cheap [fraud]—by blaming the victim. As a spiritualistic medium tells you that your "vibrations are wrong" if you see nothing in his demonstrations, altruism tells you that it's you who're evil if you end up in a sea of blood by following consistently the dogma of altruism.

**July 9, 1945**

Even though men have been commanded to love their neighbors—they feel no love when facing a neighbor; they feel only an immediate sense of guilt: "I should love this man, but I don't. I'm no good." An emotion cannot be achieved by command—only by *rational conviction*. The acceptance of arbitrary authority is so counter-rational and, therefore, so counter to human nature that men cannot force themselves to make it a conviction. Even though Christ commanded men to love their neighbors and men have accepted the idea that Christ is God-like and, therefore, right—they still cannot experience an emotion on the basis of: "I don't know any reason for it, but Christ told me so, therefore it must be right."

Emotion can come only from actual rational conviction.

If men say that their emotions are a chaotic, contradictory mess—well, look at their convictions. They have none—or, to be exact, they have a grab-bag of undigested, unapplied, contradictory generalities, acquired at random, without volition, choice or examination. The state of their emotions is the result. A mess can produce only a mess. If you treat your mind like a garbage can, a recipient for any chance refuse, then your emotions will be garbage—useless, disconnected hunks of a little bit of everything, leading to nothing but decomposition, rot, suffering. Mental activity is the production and emotions are the consumption of your spirit; you have nothing but garbage to consume when you have produced nothing but garbage.

**July 13, 1945**

The moral man is not necessarily the most intelligent, but the one who independently exercises such intelligence as he has. He is not the man who has, potentially, the greatest brain power (if this can even be measured or determined), but the one who exercises his own brain power independently. Thus, a college professor who makes the intellectual error of collectivism or second-handedness somewhere in his thinking turns out in his theory and practice to be a vicious man (same with criminals, dictators, social reformers). But a plain man concerned only with his own life and his own job, not venturing beyond the limits of his own intellectual capacity, is usually a moral man in every sense. Therefore, the moral faculty is *not* something independent of the rational faculty, but directly connected with it *and proceeding from it. The moral faculty, however, is not dependent upon the amount of intelligence, but upon the proper exercise of intelligence*—its exercise according to the rules its nature demands, *independently*. In other words, the intelligent man is the moral man if he acts as an intelligent man, i.e., in accordance with the nature of his rational faculty. (He has the choice not to act in accordance with his rational faculty. That is why ethical laws are necessary. The laws of any function are implicit in the function. But man must discover and formulate them.)

———◦———

My greatest personal mistake is ever to allow a word or a moment that "doesn't count," i.e., that I do not refer to my own basic principles. *Every word, every action, every moment counts.*

(This is also the pattern on which everybody makes mistakes [or] becomes irrational—not relating their one action or one conviction to another.)

———◦———

*Why must man's morality be that of individualism and egoism?* Because otherwise the best is sacrificed to the worst. If we establish the virtues which a rational man needs in order to survive, and then say that the goal of his virtuous action must be service to those who do not have such virtues—we place virtues in the service of vice, we penalize virtue and give a reward to vice (or weakness). [In regard] to survival, the altruist formula would read: *the man capable of survival must not make his own survival his goal, but the survival of the man incapable of survival.* ([*Note added later:*] If he works for his own survival, he is vicious. He can justify it only by helping the unfit. If he doesn't do so, he had no right to survive.)

If we refer to happiness or the enjoyment of life, the altruist formula would be: the man capable of achieving enjoyment or the means of enjoyment must not make his own enjoyment the goal—but the enjoyment of the man incapable of achieving it.

If we formulate a moral code, the man who lives up to its every provision is the perfect, ideal moral man. If then we formulate our ideal man and make him a servant of others—it comes to sacrificing or subordinating the perfect to the imperfect, the ideal to the corrupt.

If the ideal moral man is the mark at which we must aim—how can we wish to reach the ideal if, when we reach it, our life shall be sacrificed to our moral inferiors?

(Here the question of natural endowments enters—to be defined and covered.)

A moral code must be the code of man at his best—at his best in every way, including natural endowments, since these are desirable. A moral code is the code of establishing *values*. Desire (or purpose) establishes *values*.

Suppose we imagine a man with all the perfect natural attributes: intelligence, strength, talent, health, beauty—every conceivable natural qualification. He is then a perfect entity, an entity perfectly fitted for life. But how will he live? Life is action. He must decide on his own action, set his own purpose. His choice must be guided by the moral law—he must also be morally perfect. (Here again I need a definition of *why* man needs a moral law. Moral law is a code of good and evil. Whose good and evil? Man's. What man? The most perfect man conceivable.)

Now if it is asked: but what about the imperfect man, since most of us are imperfect? We can act only on the basis of our *degree* of perfection, trying to approach perfection; we cannot live on the basis of our flaws. For instance, if we are sick, we must try to get well—we cannot base our life on being sick. If a man is incurable, e.g., blind, he cannot expect the healthy to live by the rules set for his blindness.

[Man's] actions and his observance of the moral law are up to him. The purpose of life is happiness—and if we adopt the morality of altruism, then the man most fitted for life has the least right to it (or to its enjoyment, to happiness). The more endowed he is, the less right he has to his own enjoyment. And the less endowed the moron is, the more right he has to enjoy himself and to demand the sacrifice of everyone else. This is the irrational paradox of altruism—and it is vicious, since it is irrational and unnatural. This is the process by which qualities (virtues) desirable in fact become undesirable in morality (and also desirable natural attributes are made undesirable). This is why virtue becomes impractical. Altruism is the morality of death and destruction (and it leads to death and destruction in practice) because it holds as desirable the opposite of the qualities needed for man's survival, the qualities of *life*.

The ideal is composed of all the attributes which we consider desirable. Why, then, should the final goal and purpose of the desirable be the undesirable? Why should a genius serve the happiness of the moron? Why—as an example—should a beautiful woman give up her evening gown to an ugly one?

Here enters the differentiation between *ideal* and moral ideal. The moral code must be the code that is needed by and is fair to the best possible type of man born naturally: the most intelligent, the ablest, the healthiest, the most beautiful. The average, lesser man cannot be sacrificed to this code; the better man doesn't need his sacrifice. But more than that, the lesser man also can live only by such a code—to the degree of his abilities—and his rewards will be commensurate with this. But if it is said: "What about the man who cannot live by such a code at all?" The answer is: "Then he cannot live at all—because this is the only code by which man can survive." No man must survive at the expense of another man.

(One of the roots of altruism is [a man's] fear of his inferior natural ability.)

### July 14, 1945

Man is afraid to consider himself and his happiness the final end—because to achieve happiness is a great effort, a great responsibility, and most men are incapable of it. Or, achieving what they think is their happiness (some form of second-handedness) they *feel* it's low and shoddy—and long for something "higher." In effect, what they feel is: "Is that all? That's not worth living for. Something must be worth living for—and it's not in me, since my best happiness is so low and unsatisfying." This is the pattern of their "instinct" for "something high and noble."

### July 17, 1945

*The short-range must not contradict the long-range.* The distinction between immediate pleasure and happiness is that a pleasure which is part of your general happiness, a step towards it, is proper—but one which has to be paid for with suffering later is improper. Example: if your long-range happiness depends upon your marriage (by your own choice and definition, i.e., you have accepted it as happiness), then an affair with some chance woman may give you pleasure for the moment, but will destroy the thing you prize more. (In most marriages, the trouble is that the marriage is only a compromise, not happiness, and so is the affair—neither chosen nor accepted fully and consciously.) If you overeat it may give you pleasure for the moment, but destroys your stomach and health the next day. The long-range is your guide and standard for the immediate. What if you have nothing of long-range value to you? Well, you won't be happy. What if two "compromises" clash—as in the conventional marriage? Choose by your own definition which you prefer. But you can't expect to have your cake and eat it, too.

### July 18, 1945

Since man must establish his own values, accepting a value above himself makes him low and worthless. Allow nothing to stand between you and the world. The worship of something above you (like God) is an escape, a switch of responsibility—to permit you anything.

A code of ethics is man's statement of his instinct of self-preservation, and it must be based on his conviction of his value.

The first law of ethics: demand the best. (If you demand the worst, you betray the good—and yet ethics are supposed to be a code of good and evil.)

Establish your values—then go after the best.

———※———

Nature never gave to a creature instincts contrary to its own survival. All instincts are aimed at survival. If we assume that man has instincts that are contrary to his rational faculty, then nature has given him instincts opposed to his survival. That does not seem likely, unless we assume that he is slated for destruction and extinction (like the lemmings). And—as an "instinct" species—man certainly *is* on his way out. (Perhaps we are really in the process of evolving from apes to Supermen—and the rational faculty is the dominant characteristic of the better species, the Superman.)

———※———

Regarding the argument that "we must live for the whim of the moment": nature doesn't function by the whim of the moment. The rational faculty works by observing and discovering immutable laws of nature. And the rational faculty functions through time. If you let one moment contradict your long-range decisions, you're acting immorally.

———※———

Altruism poisons a man's happiness. When he has achieved something and is happy, he is forced to think: "But I am not serving anyone. Therefore I'm vicious."

———※———

Why are there more neuroses nowadays? Because, as men learn to think more and better, the evil of their original false premises catches up with them and makes it impossible for them to go on. (This is assuming that men have really learned to think more—or have tried to. It is possible that man's ethics have been the cause of the fact that men have not achieved any intellectual progress. The ethics of altruism, of course, is the cause of men's failure to achieve happiness or any progress in morality.)

———

An example of the vicious injustice of applied altruism: a man gives a job to a half-wit, on the basis of pity. He tells himself that he's done something noble, he's sacrificed the better service he could have had—for the sake of the inferior creature. Is he the only one whom he's sacrificed? He's sacrificed his customers—in effect, society—to the extent of the poorer service his business offers (and if he continues on this policy he'll have to go out of business). But, above all, he's sacrificed the better man, the able applicant, who expects and deserves justice—i.e., expects to have his ability recognized. The able man has been rejected for being able—for a virtue. The employer has committed an evil and immoral act. (Virtue includes the ability to recognize and appreciate virtue—this is *justice*.)

———

*Two crucial questions to formulate—the two most important steps or key points:* (1) define the *need* of morality, and (2) prove why (proceeding from the rational faculty) man's morality must be that of individualism and egoism (*independence*).

———

To exercise conscious rational control is man's first responsibility, duty and moral commandment. (To assert his will against circumstances—like the man in the snow.)

**July 19, 1945**

*My Outline*

1. Man's morality must be based on his nature.
2. Man's nature is that of a rational being. The rational faculty is his

only means of survival. His physical faculties are of no use to him without the guidance of his mind.

**3.** The function of the rational faculty is to observe the physical world and draw conclusions about it, thus establishing a certain *truth* about it. Man must then act on the basis of this truth. The rational faculty operates through a series of acts of choice.

**4.** The rational faculty is not automatic. Nothing assures man of the correctness of his conclusions in advance. Nothing can prove an error to him—except the consequences, observed by his rational faculty.

**5.** Even the use of his rational faculty is not automatic. Man can choose not to exercise it—or, rather, not to exercise it in certain acts or in certain spheres of activity. He can choose to act as a robot (or second-hander). It is here that he becomes his own destroyer.

**6.** Man needs a moral code as a set of rules on what is right or wrong for him as a rational being. The moral faculty is a necessity of the rational faculty.

**7.** Man observes nature and concludes what is true of it or not. He then has to act upon his knowledge. To act, he has to set himself a purpose. He estimates what is right or wrong for his purpose. The purpose determines the value he places on his acts—as means to an end. (For example: he observes that a seed grows when planted in the ground, but not when thrown on a rock. If his purpose is to grow wheat—it is right to place seeds in the ground; it is wrong to scatter them on rocks.) Now if man has accepted it as his first moral axiom that his survival is good, this becomes the standard of his moral code—"Man must survive as man." His moral code is a standard for his valuation of himself—he cannot consider himself good if he acts as his own destroyer. He must look at himself as a moral entity to be created by himself.

**8.** What is the purpose of man's survival? Happiness. Whose happiness? His own. If man's survival is made the means to some end— and if at any point this end [conflicted with] his survival, he would have to be motivated by self-destruction. Therefore, the placing of any goal as the standard above his survival is evil. If man is not to survive for his own happiness, but for someone else's—then, if the claims of this other interfered with his own happiness, he would have to survive in suffering. Therefore the placing of anyone's happiness above one's own is evil.

**9.** There are, therefore, only two axioms to be accepted as self-evident in my morality: (1) man must survive, and (2) man must be

happy. But both of these axioms imply—"as man." Man's survival
and happiness are not automatically "human." These two axioms
apply only to man as a rational being. When man chooses to act in a
sub-human manner, it is no longer proper for him to survive nor to
be happy. There is no reason in fact by which he can claim these two
rights as natural. He cannot survive at all, if he acts on another basis;
if he cannot survive, he cannot have any happiness.

**10.** The rational faculty is individual. The only threat to its exercise lies
in other men. The first demand of the rational faculty is *independence*.

---

*My three cornerstones:* man is an end in himself; no man exists for the
sake of another man; each man exists for his own happiness (to be achieved
by his own effort).

*My chief virtues:* self-reverence (the sense of the heroic in man); self-
sufficiency (independence, integrity, the capacity of happiness—which is
self-contained and self-justifying); worship of the ideal (define your ideal,
then live by it, work toward it, find your happiness in it—make your happiness be a response to man at his highest, not at his lowest).

---

People suffer because they are not appreciated—not because they get
no alms. Alms, pity, and charity is precisely what they *don't* want. But when
their better qualities get no justice or appreciation, they lose faith in themselves, in men and, above all, in ideals. It is at this point that they turn
cynical and vicious.

But before you can get appreciated—ask yourself: "For what?" You
cannot be appreciated for a potentiality you have not exhibited. Act, before
you demand any appreciation from others; give them objective evidence of
what it is you want them to like and admire in you; be sure you have objective (rational) standards for your achievements. (*This* is an example of the
fact that the rational is the only bond possible between men, and the only
standard in all their relationships.)

**July 20, 1945**

By proclaiming his willingness to sacrifice himself, man acquires the
right to sacrifice others. If it is asked: but is self-sacrifice easy?—it is the

easiest thing in the world for the man who has no self. First, he makes a virtue of his one most dreadful deficiency. Second, his desire to destroy others is his most burning desire—once he has dropped his own self-respect. *The man who does not respect himself can have no love or respect for others.*

In practice, the actual satisfaction of all dictators is to command, humble, humiliate, hurt others (which means precisely to *sacrifice* others). What enjoyment except this one can a dictator have when he lives in debauched animal luxury and in constant fear, hatred, suspicion of even his closest friends? Not love, but *sacrifice* of men becomes his only desire in relation to them.

---

If a man bases his values on brute force—he is saying to himself, in effect: "This method cannot keep me alive, but I can make it work by enslaving those who can keep me alive." Then he must realize that the method he's chosen as proper to him is not the one proper to those who must keep him alive. Then his code of values will destroy them—and when they are destroyed, he will perish; thus he has destroyed himself. So he cannot claim that his method and his code of values are based on man's survival, not even on his own. It is based on man's destruction—because it is not human and cannot work for man.

---

If men claim that the rational faculty is an innate gift (which it is, or rather its power is, just as the degree of any physical talent varies from birth) and, therefore, a man cannot be blamed if he is born with a mental capacity insufficient for his survival, and he cannot make it the standard of his survival—the answer is that he has no choice except to exercise his mind to the full extent of his capacity—and let the overflow of the better minds of others help him (which it does, but *not* at his demand). He cannot impose his need as a standard of value upon his betters, i.e., upon those who have to help him survive. If he has no capacity of survival, then it is precisely his *self-interest*, his desire to survive, that must make him accept the standards and values of those on whom his survival depends.

---

A parasite (in the physical world) destroys that upon which it feeds—like a virus that attaches itself to a living cell and kills it. Man has to destroy himself if he lives as a parasite upon the work and souls of other men. Yet altruism has made him just that. No other species exists as a parasite upon itself. Man does. (There is a difference here, though: an animal destroys his food, in the sense of killing another creature. But he does not try to exist by destroying his fangs, horns, or whatever is his tool of survival. A human parasite does just that: he destroys his tool—the human brain. That is why he can be defined as a creature unfit for existence—an embodied death principle—the actual evil.)

A crucial issue exists between the conception of "self-as-is" and "self" as a rational free agent. For instance, it is considered noble to have an "impersonal" attitude toward knowledge. It is implied that a *personal* attitude would be, not the desire to know the truth, but the desire to gain some advantage. Yet it is only the most *personal*, *independent* element of a man—his rational faculty—that is capable of acquiring knowledge. Truth, therefore, is presumed to be somehow detrimental to a man's interests. By what, then, does he establish his interests?

If men feel: "I've got to live such as I am, on the basis of my flaws," the answer is: "You can't live on the basis of your flaws. Such as you are, you can live only on the basis of your virtues." Here the idea of "getting by" enters.

The "individual," the "subjective," has always been held to be the irrational. Yet it is only objective reality and the tool that masters it—the rational faculty—that permit man any individuality at all. And for man, objective reality demands *individualism*.

The "subjective" school says, in effect: "I yam what I yam and that's all I yam." The answer is: "Fine. But what are you?" They say: "I am born or conditioned or determined this way—and therefore I can't be blamed for it, I'm not bad, therefore I'm good—as is and whatever it is." The answer is: "You are neither good nor bad. You are nothing at all. If you are a 'determined' creature—no conceptions of morality, nor even of values, can apply to you. Nature has not given you any values automatically—nor can you define them to yourself or to others. You may try to exist by whatever it is you claim is your code of values. When you come to dealing with the physical world—in order to satisfy your instincts, hunches, or conditionings—you'll see what will happen to you. You don't know what you want nor why you want it. How do you expect to get it?" (To *want* anything, one must have a standard of values.)

———◈———

Man may be justly proud of his natural endowments (if they are there objectively, i.e., rationally), such as physical beauty, physical strength, a great mind, good health. But all of these are merely his material or his tools; his self-respect must be based, not on these attributes, but on what he does with them. His self-respect must be based on his actions—on that which proceeds from him. His survival depends on the *proper* kind of action. His appreciation of himself must be on the same principle. Every animal (and even plants) exhibits self-respect or a kind of self-pride—an attitude of considering itself valuable, i.e., good. And it exhibits [this attitude] in direct proportion to its fitness for survival. Man's fitness for survival lies in his rational faculty. The survival of the fittest—as applied to man? It is the survival of the best mind; the best mind is the most independent; the most independent man is the most moral man. If we understood this correctly—the survival of *the fittest* does mean *of the best*. But *the best*—for man—is not brute force, nor cunning, nor slyness, nor any quality that depends upon the existence (and sacrifice) of other men in order to be exercised.

If a man says: "But I realize that my natural endowments are mediocre— shall I then suffer, be ashamed, have an inferiority complex?" The answer is: "In the basic, crucial sphere, the sphere of morality and action, it is not your endowments that matter, but what you do with them." It is here that all men are free and equal, regardless of natural gifts. You can be, in your own modest sphere, as good morally as the genius is in his—*if* you live by the same rules. Find your goal within yourself, in whatever work you are honestly capable of performing. Never make others your prime goal. Demand nothing from others as an unearned gift and grant them nothing unearned. Live by your own rational judgments. Be independent in whatever judgments you hold or actions you undertake, and do not venture beyond your own capacity, into spheres where you'll have to become a parasite and a second-hander. You'll be surprised how decent and wonderful a human being you'll become, and how much honest, legitimate human affection and appreciation you'll get from others.

As to material rewards, you'll get what you deserve, what you have produced. The greater rewards received by men of greater ability do not concern you—*because they were not taken from you.* There is no point and no sense in your hating the man of superior ability because he has more material wealth than you have. It is his ability that produced the wealth. If he had no such ability or if you destroyed him—it still would not make *you* able to produce that wealth. All you can do is rob him. His ability does not hamper yours, it merely surpasses it. And so do the material rewards. There is no point in your hating a beautiful woman for being more beautiful than you are; if she lost her beauty or if you killed her, it would not make you more beautiful. You'll say, but men would consider me more beautiful then, without the comparison? Not necessarily. Standards of beauty, like any standards, are set by a certain ideal of perfection, usually personal to each man. You will not be any nearer to perfection by eliminating a rival who was nearer.

No, moral virtue is not its only reward. But it cannot give you rewards you have neither earned nor deserved. Moral virtue will give you just what you deserve—and this is quite a great deal. (Particularly if you choose to make it a great deal and exert the needed effort.) Moral virtue will give you justice. And more than that neither men nor nature can give you.

If men's desperate rebellion against the objective world, reason, and justice is, at [root], a rebellion against the shortcomings of their own natural endowments, if men scream so much against the "injustice" of being born without some special great talent or desirable faculty—*why don't they exercise such faculties as they have, instead?* Most of their unhappiness in this line (with the possible exception of physical beauty) comes from second-handedness. They don't want to write—they want the fame, money, and prestige of a writer. If they had an actual, personal desire to write, i.e., if they had something to say—without any second-handedness involved, no desire to impress, nor any desire to re-hash some plagiarized ideas—*they would have the talent.* Men usually have the talent for that which they want to do— *if they really want to do it,* i.e., if their primary motive is personal, not second-hand.

———◦———

The pattern of spiritual human relationship under my code of ethics has the form of a sale—value for value received; the pattern under the code of altruism is that of graft—of a bribe.

**July 21, 1945**

Advice to people on what to do under my ethics: name your action by its actual name, i.e., be conscious at any moment of what it is you're doing. Above all, be conscious of what you're doing in the long run, of your overall meaning and goal. People think from moment to moment—they don't connect—they have not acquired the idea of a whole life. That is why they whine in middle age: "What was it all about?" (They exist in the manner of consciousness of an animal.)

---

Make a note of the way in which people actually lose all capacity to think when they appoint themselves as thinkers for others, as molders or expressers of "public opinion." They do make sense in their specific, individual and selfish job. But there is a peculiar, special kind of rottenness that [takes hold] in them the moment they begin to think in or for "the public."

This applies both to such cases as a reader who has good independent judgment until he becomes an editor—and to such cases as when a man has to defend his views in public. This last may be due either to the innocent fact of being unprepared and not connecting new ideas fast enough—*or* to the much more vicious fact that a man feels no necessity to have any "wider" convictions (philosophical, social, or political), but feels he must have them as window-dressing, so whatever nonsense he spouts, he spouts only to make a "cultured" impression on the listener. He doesn't want to believe, he only wants to convince you he believes something. Now *this* is real second-handedness in operation; abstract convictions, ethics, ideals, philosophies are [regarded as] only a social convention, only a means to an end. That is the real absence of an ego.

How do those people exist? Not too well. Obviously they're not happy and they're running from themselves. But can anything be taught to them? Can they be shown their own emptiness? This is hard to answer. I suppose, not until they *want* to see it. Not until some form of suffering makes them question themselves. The thing that puzzles me is only: how do those people exist at all, without realizing that central emptiness? Isn't it something they should discover for themselves and at once? The truth is probably that they have some most peculiar, logically twisted substitute or excuse or justification. The thing that bothers me here is: how can people live in inconsistency? The immediate answer would be: because it's so difficult to be consistent and rational (and besides they have been trained not to be). Therefore, they take inconsistency as a law of existence, they're bewildered, they can't untangle things—but they have to go on living, so they let it go at that.

The main difference between me and them is that I try to keep my thinking straight and give my complete, honest, interested attention to any intellectual argument. They either don't want to try, or are indifferent, or actually resent it when brought face to face with the necessity to think and connect. I try to live consciously, from the basic principle on up to every detail. They live, essentially, by chance. The most important questions are the ones they won't or can't face.

**July 22, 1945**

Knowledge grows from basic premises like a plant from a seed. The seed is like a basic premise in which all the details and consequences of the future plant are contained—and only a certain plant can grow from a certain seed. Once you have accepted a basic premise, you will have to follow and accept all the consequences, because they *are* in the seed. You have no power to change the nature of the universe, the nature of matter or its laws; and you have no power to change the nature of a logical sequence. But where is your freedom and the field of your free will? In exercising [your reason] to understand [nature] and use it as material to fulfill your purpose. You set the goal and the meaning; the field of choice and possibilities is immense; the only necessity involved is that you use the material as it is and your tool (reason) as it is—that you understand them for what they are before you choose or achieve a purpose.

Do not call it a "limit." The basic fact of reality is a "limit"—the fact of existence, which presupposes an entity, which means a thing differentiated by certain intrinsic, essential attributes from that which it is not. "To be" implies a "limit"—a distinction from that which is not. If you demanded "freedom" from the natural world—you would demand, in effect, an undifferentiated chaos, the non-existence of entities, actually more than death— the annihilation of the conception of the possibility of living.

———◦———

We apply reason to the material world, but not to the spiritual, not to ourselves. The material world gives us an objective standard, a starting point, a solid fact, the something from which we have to proceed—since we cannot create something out of nothing, or base something on nothing. There is no such standard in the spiritual world. Yet the rational faculty should be that starting point. And a moral code should be that standard.

In dealing with physical nature each man is an independent judge: he will consider a car good if the car runs—and he will make sure that he *sees* the car running. But in the spiritual world men are second-handers: they place the quality of judgment within the consciousness of others, being lost and unsure within their own. So we have the paradox that in physical matters the actual value and performance of the product is the standard (people will buy a car if it is a good car), but in spiritual matters (precisely in the realm of greatest, absolute individualism) the collective counting of noses is the standard (a book is good if people buy it). Physical values are thus ethical (based on value-judgments) and personal—but spiritual values are non-moral and "commercial" in the most vulgar sense of the word. Physical values become an end in themselves, moral values a means to an end. (There is here a strange circle. Our rational faculty *is* the means of obtaining satisfaction from the physical world. But the satisfaction is spiritual, since the physical is only a means to the satisfaction of our desires—and of more than our physical desires.)

———⋄———

The essence of morality is to *desire that which is good*. But we must define what is good—and that is the purpose of a code of ethics.

This point must cover and account for the fact that some people admit virtue without desiring it—such as Mallory's "the genius recognized too well—the people who see it and don't want it"; or "He's a saint—I don't like saints."

Is the cause here the fact that people think of morality as an arbitrarily prescribed code of ethics, the Christian code, and rebel against it? Isn't the greatest error of all morality the fact that the moral systems prescribed concrete rules, arbitrarily, instead of general principles that would allow men precisely the essence of morality—a free choice between good and evil? *Think this over.* The key here is the relation of the abstract to the concrete, of the general to the particular—and the need is that of a clear statement of the line dividing the two and of the relationship between the two.

What actually happens when men get lost in abstractions? What is the nature and cause of a "floating abstraction"?

Think over the relation of "survival" to happiness, the exact point in the process of man choosing a goal. And the relation of the material to the spiritual.

Humanitarians claim to hate suffering, and therefore to make it their goal to eliminate it. They take for granted that happiness is automatic, but suffering is not and therefore we must direct our actions at eliminating suffering. But it is precisely *happiness* (or good or virtue) that is *not* automatic and must be achieved by effort and purposeful action. Suffering comes automatically from the absence of action. (To be exact, the absence of the right action; if you do nothing at all, or if you make a mistake and do nothing to correct it, *that's* when suffering will come automatically as your proper, natural punishment. Everything *good*—desirable—has to be achieved.)

But you want to act to relieve the suffering of others? Can you? To what extent? And why should you? And at what price? And is that the chief goal of life? Is your goal to run around correcting errors—or to act straight?

———————————

Here there enters the question of what it is you love when you love "Man." Again, a reversal of the abstract and the concrete that destroys the concrete. By loving "Man" as an abstraction in the sense of loving any and all men, you end up by loving the worst of men. By loving "Man" as an ideal, you love actual men and the best among them. What is the difference between "abstract" and "general"? Between "archetype" or "ideal" and "average"? There might be an important key here.

### July 23, 1945

The person who believes in determinism (personal or historical) merely confesses the truth about himself: he is not a prime-mover, he does not know what makes him act or how or why—therefore he assumes that others are equally "determined," floating non-entities pushed around by chance. Having no prime-moving ego within himself, such a person assumes one of two things: either that others are equally uncertain—therefore "something" outside moves us all; or that others know and decide, while he can't—so he accepts them as the mover and the standard. Usually it's both, since the essence of a second-hander's thinking is that he does not think, therefore none of his premises are too clear and all of them are contradictory. If this were not so, if he were completely consistent with anything, he wouldn't be a second-hander.

———◆———

Can purpose determine entity? Purpose presupposes the one (a consciousness) who sets the purpose. And man is that one—the standard, the point of beginning. *Think this over.* (Plato said function determines virtue. I mean something much more than that.)

**July 27, 1945**

An animal can have self-respect automatically—"I am good such as I am," because the capacity of self-destruction is not within him. A man's self-respect (and instinct of self-preservation) must be conscious (based on a standard of values) because he *can* be his own destroyer. That is his great innate fear—and one of the causes of his rebellion against reason, against the terrible responsibility which the rational faculty involves.

———◆———

The tendency of all civilization has been toward *division* of labor—not collectivization. Toward splitting jobs into separate activities—not toward doing things more and more "together." All economic progress has come from that. But, it may be said, since each man does only a part of the whole—shouldn't there be a collective direction and shouldn't the whole direct the parts? The whole does direct the parts—by the mechanism of supply and demand, which is actually the verdict of the majority upon what kind of work it wishes done. But it is the whole as a number of individual units acting independently, each exercising his judgment for his own good. It is not the artificial arrangement of a "whole" out of units that cannot be added together, a whole that involves the sacrifice of some parts to others and is not, therefore, a whole. Each man should have a say about economic production and consumption? He does. By producing and by buying. In this way, each man decides for himself, and the "whole" is the sum of such decisions. In the collectivist way, each would have to decide for all—which is impossible in practice and vicious in concept, since it is the diametric opposite of human nature.

The mental and moral corruption of so-called intellectuals is due to the fact that they are the real class of "exploiters." Men cannot be enslaved by sheer force alone—it would take too many people, so no parasitical minority could enslave the productive majority. The enslavement has to be done by spiritual means, by making men feel that their slavery is "right." (This was done by every tyrant in history and by modern dictators.) Therefore it's the "intellectuals" who become the spearhead, the professional tools and source of any human enslavement. They're second-handers, collectivists, altruists—and getting paid for nothing. They believe that one can build that mode of living into a system.

Defeat collectivists and altruists by the single method of contempt. Take away their aura of holiness. Look at them for what they are—parasites.

---

The usual reason [given for] moral corruption is hatred for mankind—a man uses collectivism as an excuse for his own rottenness—"he can't help it, others are vicious, he's got to get along." Thus he switches the responsibility. "Others" are his excuse. But there is no excuse. A man's estimate of mankind is only a reflection of his estimate of himself. You think man as such is rotten? (Not the majority, but man as such.) It's only you who are rotten. If you think you're capable of virtue, but others are not—you're a human being, therefore man as such *can* be virtuous. The majority can't? Why should that concern you? Keep the majority (or anyone) from power, keep society free—and you have nothing to worry about.

[*AR is here rewriting and expanding on her notes from September 6, 1943. The first few pages have been omitted because the content was not significantly different from the 1943 notes.*]

The purpose of a moral code is the preservation of man's nature, i.e., the preservation of man as man.

Every living thing exercises a form of choice—to the extent of assimilating only those elements which are necessary to its survival, not any and all elements indiscriminately. A plant absorbs particular chemicals out of the soil. An animal hunts particular foods. To live, a living thing must have a code of values: that which is good for it and that which is not. Its survival is the standard, the measure of value. But for a plant or an animal, the standard, the values, the method of survival and the exercise of that method are automatic; no other choice is possible; no conscious choice is necessary.

Man's method of survival is not automatic. He must establish it by conscious choice based on a rational observation of nature and of himself; he must discover what he is, what he needs, how he must act in order to exist. He must establish his own code of values. Its standard must still be the same: survival. But the values he establishes must be the ones needed by and appropriate to his one and only means of survival—the human means—the rational faculty.

A moral code is man's statement of the principles that permit him to function as man. It is his protection against becoming his own destroyer. It is a set of values upon which he bases his rules of conduct, the rules of what is right or wrong for him as a rational being. The moral faculty is a part and a necessity of the rational faculty.

The establishment of values requires a standard. The concept of "value" presupposes an entity to whom an object or action is valuable. Moral values constitute a code of good and evil. By what standard are they to be set? Good—for whom? Good—for what?

Man's nature sets the standard of his moral code. Man's survival sets the purpose. His proper morality is based on a single axiom:

*Man exists and must survive as man.*

All that which preserves man's nature as a rational being is good. All that which destroys it is evil. All the actions based on, proceeding from, in accordance with man's nature as a rational being are good. All the actions that contradict it are evil. All the forms and conditions of existence that permit man to function as a rational being are good. All the forms and conditions of existence that prevent it are evil.

The actions, conditions, motivations, and qualities required by and for the function of man's rational faculty are man's virtues—by sanction of the fact that they constitute man's life principle, his means of survival, the forms, expressions and essence of his living energy.

It must be carefully noted, at this point, that the word "man" denotes a concrete, specific, existing entity—not "mankind," which is a collective abstraction. An entity survives by surviving; a "kind" may attempt to survive by slaughtering nine-tenths of the entities composing it.

Before we proceed to analyze in detail the implications contained in the above axiom and the specific code of behavior it demands, we must stop to examine and fully understand the nature of the axiom itself.

It consists of three facts which must be accepted as self-evident: 1) that man exists, 2) that man is a rational being, 3) that man's survival is desirable.

1) Any conception or discussion of man's existence is an axiom implying three parts: that man exists, that an objective world exists around him, and that he has the faculty of rational consciousness which enables him to know the external world. [*This is AR's first discussion of the axioms of existence and consciousness; see John Galt's speech for her definitive formulations.*]

These three facts need not and cannot be proved. Any proof rests on them and implies them as axioms. Proof by physical demonstration implies a physical fact (in the external world) demonstrated to an observer (man) who grasps it through a faculty of consciousness which permits him to grasp it (the rational faculty). Proof by rational demonstration implies an entity (man) who possesses a faculty of consciousness (the rational faculty) which permits him to acquire knowledge about facts (in the external world). Proof cannot begin in a vacuum. Existence begins by existing. Proof begins with something that exists proving something about something that exists.

The *nature* of man and the *nature* of the world in which he lives are *not* self-evident. It is the function of man's mind to give him knowledge of himself and of the world—the knowledge of *what* he is and of *what* it is. But that he *is* and that it *is* are axioms implicit in the mere fact of consciousness, axioms preceding and permitting the perceptions, conceptions and definitions which constitute his knowledge.

A stupendous amount of writing has been done as an alleged demonstration of the fact that no objective world exists outside of man—or that man does not really exist—or that he exists but has no mind—or that nothing really exists at all. But since all the volumes of such demonstrations simply amount to: "My observations of the world lead me to conclude that it doesn't exist, that there's nobody observing it and that there's no faculty to observe it with," we can safely take these theories and their authors at their own word—as non-existent.

2) The assertion that man has no rational faculty is a contradiction in terms. An attempt to lift oneself by one's own bootstraps is the physical counterpart of a man proclaiming as a fact the fact that he has no capacity for grasping facts. ([*Note added later:*] By means of *what* does an irrationalist demonstrate that reason doesn't exist?)

The anti-rationalist doctrine (remember that "anti-rationalist" means "anti-necessity-to-make-sense") is extremely old, has a long, bloody history and as many variations as skin disease. That doctrine has no intelligible content—but a most intelligible purpose, since the rational faculty is the badge of man's freedom. That doctrine has always preceded and accompanied the slaughter and enslavement of men. Its current version is known as "dialectic materialism." It holds that man has no mind. It holds choice as an illusion and reason as a by-product of the physical environment, nutrition, and some sort of a voodoo process named "conditioning," which makes reason operate without volition, automatically. Translated into human language, this doctrine claims that the operations of reason work on the following pattern: if you had oatmeal for breakfast, you will think that two and two make four; if not, you'll think it's six.

A statement such as: "Man's thinking is conditioned by his background" is merely a confession that the speaker has no conception of what constitutes *thinking*, and that those to whom the statement might apply are not men whose thinking is conditioned, but men who do not *think* at all. The appalling collection of miscellaneous garbage which present-day men hold to be their intellectual convictions has no resemblance to or connection with the act of thought. It would be useless to argue that some backgrounds bring some men to a state where they cannot think. The only men who *cannot* think are those who are or belong in insane asylums. That a great many men do not choose to think is another matter. There are reasons for such a choice, which we shall examine later; the chief reason can be mentioned now—*thinking* is not done automatically.

The proponents of the doctrine that denies the existence of man's rational faculty claim to have reached their doctrine by—rational deduction. They urge us to improve our physical environment in order to improve the by-product, our brain, and they urge us to take such action through a conscious decision of—our rational faculty. If a dialectical materialist asks at this point: "But why should I have to make sense?"—the answer is: "You don't have to. Just remember that you don't."

Then there is a school of opinion which describes itself loosely as "naturalistic" or "realistic." The arguments of this school amount to: Man's body has many similarities to an animal's body, therefore man's consciousness is like that of an animal, therefore man is ruled by instincts, therefore reason is a delusion, therefore the way a rat goes about getting to a piece of cheese in a maze is the way man goes about building the Rheims Cathedral.

By this type of argument one could say that an animal's body has so many similarities with a plant's that the animal's consciousness and manner of living ought to be like a plant's, therefore his basic distinction—the power of locomotion—is an illusion, therefore an animal ought to dig his paws into the ground and stay there, because it is unnatural for him to do more.

It is precisely by observing nature that we discover that a living organism endowed with an attribute higher and more complex than the attributes possessed by the organisms below him in nature's scale shares many functions with these lower organisms. But these functions are modified by his higher attribute and adapted to its function—*not* the other way around. Plants possess digestive and reproductive organs; animals possess digestive and reproductive organs plus the power of locomotion. An animal's stomach is not that of a plant; it is not adapted to the needs of an organism attached by roots to the ground, but to the needs of an organism that obtains its food by moving.

Man possesses digestive and reproductive organs, plus the power of locomotion, plus the faculty of reason. The distinction of an animal from a plant is the power of a self-moving body; the distinction of a man from an animal is the power of a self-moving mind. Whatever organs and attributes man may possess, they are modified by and adapted to the needs of a being who survives through the use of his mind. His nature is not to be discovered by what he has in common with lower animals—but by what he has and they haven't.

If it is biased not to notice similarities between a man and an amoeba— what sort of bias prompts those who do not notice the differences? Man is a rational being, according to the plain, hard, material facts of reality. Those who imagine themselves as harsh realists when they say: "Man is just an animal ruled by his stomach," had better remember what puts food into a human stomach and what must be preserved if there is to be any food—or any stomach.

Since no road is ever muddy enough but that someone will rush to plump himself into its middle, there are a great many middle-of-the-roaders on this issue, who claim that man has a mind all right, except that he's not able to use it. Man cannot, they say, be called a rational being because his actions are not motivated by his mind; his mind is like his Sunday clothes, kept in a dark closet and donned reluctantly on rare occasions; and when donned, it makes him stiff, uncomfortable and unhappy, because it never fit him well in the first place. What man does on weekdays, they say, is to gallop about stark-naked, on all fours, because it reminds him of his mother who gave him a complex, and to whirl around catching his own tail which he hasn't got but feels he has; that is what he does because it makes him happy. Reason? Reason, they say, is just something he uses in such negligible, incidental matters as earning a living. ([*Note added later:*] There's no basic contradiction or conflict between the "physical" and the "spiritual." There are no different sets of rules or principles for them. They're based on and proceed from the same principle.)

It is pointless to argue with the instinct—feeling—urge—emotion—compulsion—sub-conscious boys and to debate what percentage of man's nature can be called rational. It is simpler to take them at their word. Even if we suppose that man is not a rational being, but a howling neurosis endowed with one percent of rationality—it still remains true that in order to survive he must take rational actions rationally thought out from rational motives, and that unless he does so, he won't be there to enjoy his sub-conscious. Let it be but one percent of his nature, his rational faculty is all that matters in him and all that counts. It must still be taken as his dominant trait—because it is his sole lease on life. He can survive only to the extent that he is able to exist in accordance with it. When and if he is unable to do so—he has stated and signed his death warrant. There is no point in discussing the way of life proper to a creature who has no means to keep itself alive.

Your inexplicable emotions? Your great big dark mysterious urges? Your irresistible impulses? Your desires for you don't know what you don't know why? Go right ahead and roll in them as in any other gutter. But remember that when you lie on a barren stretch of soil, with a single seed of wheat in your hand, all your emotions, urges, and desires will not make the seed grow. Only your mind will.

3) Every living thing is motivated by the instinct of self-preservation. This is implicit in the mere fact of life. Life is a matter of motion and activity; a living thing not motivated by self-preservation would not and could not preserve itself. But a plant's or an animal's method of survival is automatic, i.e., instinctive; therefore its motive is an instinct. Man's survival is not achieved instinctively; therefore an instinct is inadequate to motivate it. His motive must be conscious.

([*Note added later:*] Most men actually have no desire to survive—in fact, they act as if they had accepted the opposite premise; their actions are consistent with a hatred of life.)

Man needs a rational decision, an axiom understood and consciously accepted: I wish to survive—my survival is desirable. In accepting this, he has accepted the standard and the first axiom of morality.

In morality man's life is taken as the supreme value. It is the gauge by which the value of every part, aspect and action of his existence is to be measured.

If anyone now asks: But why do I have to hold my survival as desirable?—The answer is: You don't have to. It is an axiom, to be accepted as self-evident. If it is not self-evident to you, you have an alternative: admit that your survival is not desirable and get out of the way. There is no middle-ground and no middle choice. The act of evading this issue, making no decision, closing your mind and just floating along, is precisely the act of suspending your rational faculty—of refusing to observe a fact, to identify it and to understand it. It is the primary act of your self-destruction. With that as your first premise, you will not survive—and the span of life you have at your disposal will be a succession of acts leading to your self-annihilation, as the history of mankind and of most private lives has amply demonstrated. You have many choices open to you, but the choice is saying: "I don't have to decide whether life is desirable, I'll just live" is not one of them. That choice is not given to you because the life you refer to is a human life, and a human life is not preserved automatically.

A moral code is not a sentimental luxury, nor a pretty dream, nor an arbitrary decree, nor an impractical abstraction. It is the hardest, most practical of all necessities—because without it no practical action nor any kind of life is possible.

But a moral code—like any other rational conception—cannot be forced upon men. It must be accepted. Those who wish to accept what is to follow, are asked to accept as self-evident a single axiom:

*Man exists and must survive as man.*

**August 3, 1945**

The "common man" doesn't understand the gibberish of the "intellectuals"—because the common man relates abstractions to the concrete. It takes a second-hander, a collectivist intellectual, to run amuck among "floating abstractions."

**August 4, 1945**

It is the doctrine of altruism that stops men from thinking. They have been battered by altruism and have accepted it before they reach the age of reason and begin to think. Then altruism stops them—because the very nature of thinking is not merely unsocial, but anti-social: it is profoundly *selfish*, it implies setting oneself apart from and *above* all others. So men feel (and justly, by their standards of morality) that they are doing something vicious when they attempt to think. (Why is every thinking, independent person called "hard," "conceited," "arrogant," "selfish"?)

**August 11, 1945**

When fools say that technical progress destroys man, that the machine is bad for him, it makes him evil, etc.—the actual fact behind the phenomenon they describe is that man's moral thinking is centuries behind his scientific or "practical" thinking. He has never discovered the morality that would permit him to use and enjoy the machine properly. He has not discovered that reason is his only weapon and standard for dealing with both physical nature and with himself.

---

For self-reverence: we must begin with love for the conception of man as a rational entity, free to create himself—and then we must live up to it.

---

To start his code of ethics, man must recognize himself for what he is: an independent entity. On that basis he can demand his own happiness. (His happiness and all the means to it must be created by himself.)

If, by the altruistic code, a man is evil if he is happy, but good if he makes others happy, then those others are either: 1) evil because they are happy, therefore a man is good by making others evil, or 2) good because they are happy not through their own efforts but through an unearned gift. In this last case they are considered good because they have not acted in accordance with man's nature, which demands that he produce what he consumes.

Nature demands just one thing of man: "Make sense"—"Use your rational faculty"—"Don't expect me to be what I am not."

**August 22, 1945**

*The Rational Faculty*

The rational faculty is an attribute of the individual.

There is no such thing as a collective brain. There is no such thing as a collective thought.

A thought held by many men is not held "in common." It is held by each individual man in his own individual mind. If three men think that "Life is desirable," the idea is not broken up into three separate parts, one held by each man—one man holding the concept of "life," another the concept of "is," the third the concept of "desirable"—and the three parts uniting somewhere in the ether to form a complete idea held collectively.

We may multiply to infinity the number of men involved or the complexity of the idea they hold—and the fact remains the same.

An idea, simple or complex, cannot be held in half by two men, working together as a Siamese-twin unit or collective. A man cannot say in reference to his ideas: "I've only got the nouns and the adverbs—my brother Joe's got the verbs and the adjectives—we think kinda like a team." An idea is not a jig-saw puzzle whose pieces can be scattered among various participants, while a mystical super-entity—the collective—puts the picture together, with none of them seeing or grasping the whole. An idea, an intelligible mental conception, is held in its entirety in the mind of one man. Another man may hold the same idea—in its entirety and in his own mind.

A scientist who has arrived at a complicated scientific theory is not the repository of a collective thought composed of contributions by Aristotle, Roger Bacon and on down; his own mind has grasped, understood and passed judgment upon a great many ideas presented to him by a great many men through the ages, has eliminated some of them, has accepted others, and has reached a conclusion, which constitutes a rational conviction. If his mind has not done that, but merely contains an undigested junk heap of unrelated information, such content is not thought, nor is it related to thought, nor is it related to the process of a human mind, but to the process and content of a dictaphone [*a machine, now obsolete, to record dictated material*].

Different men may hold knowledge of different facts, which, when put together, lead to new ideas and a wider knowledge. But such putting together can be done only by a rational process in the mind of one man who assimilates the new knowledge supplied to him by others, relates it to the fact that he knows, forms conclusions and produces a new, coherent, intelligible whole. Any of the other men involved may perform the same process. But each has to perform it alone, in his own mind, rationally grasping every step in the process if he is to grasp the whole. If none of the men has performed the process and none has grasped the whole—there is no whole. There is no new idea born. There is no collective brain for it to be born in.

An agreement reached by a group of men, in which separate men have contributed separate parts, is not a collective thought. It is the result of thought, the product, the secondary consequence. The primary act—the process of reason, the process of observing, considering, passing judgment— had to be performed by each man alone. If one of the men involved corrected his own conclusion because of the convincing evidence presented by another man, he has done so by an independent act of his own reasoning mind; if he has not performed such an act, but has merely agreed, blindly and without judgment—what he has done is not an act of thinking, nor is the final agreement a thought in his mind, nor has he contributed anything to any agreement or thought, nor will that final agreement reached by others do him any good.

Men may share their *knowledge*, not their thinking. Knowledge is not thinking; it is the *result* of thinking, the product of the process of thought. The process of thought is one activity—among many others—that cannot be performed collectively.

That which man produces can be shared but not that which made him capable of producing it. A man can chop up a pile of wood and divide among other men the logs he has cut—but not the strength of his arm. A man can perform a rational process and offer to others the conclusions he has reached—but not the power of his brain. All the functions of man's body and mind are private, personal, individual. They cannot be shared or transferred.

We can divide a meal among many men. We cannot digest it in a collective stomach. No amount of love and self-sacrifice will enable a man to use his lungs to breathe for another man. No quantity of G.P.U. agents will enable a man to think through the brain of another.

Any consultation among men, any exchange of thoughts, is only an exchange of products. Every man involved must perform an independent process of reason before he can accept or reject an idea. No possible effort by the others can give him anything of value without that basic capacity of his own. The product is secondary—the capacity primary. A thought cannot be imparted to a man incapable of thinking. The rational faculty is like a broadcasting station: its product cannot be transmitted to those who lack a receiving set.

The rational faculty can neither be shared nor added. It does not grow by addition. It has a singular, but no plural. Men can unite their physical force, but not their brain power. Two young boys can join their strength to lift a weight, and their combined strength will equal approximately that of an adult man. Two half-wits do not equal one intelligent man. Nor do two intelligent men united produce an entity of double intelligence. The combined physical power of a group of ten average men is ten times that of each member of the group. The combined mental power of a group of ten average men is exactly that of the most intelligent member of the group—and no higher. The rational faculty has no plural.

Even the addition of men's physical power is possible only in a few instances of its many applications—such as in lifting weights or in destroying and smashing things. If a group of men were lined up and ordered to run a race together, as a collective, maintaining a united front or unbroken line throughout—their combined speed would not equal the sum of their individual speeds, nor even the speed of the fastest man among them, *but that of the slowest.* Their collective effort would not lift them to the level of the best, but reduce them to the level of the worst. The lowest common denominator is always just that—the lowest.

If a group of men were ordered to solve an intellectual problem together, as a collective, acting in unison, taking no step without common assent and understanding—their combined effort would not equal the capacity of the best brain among them, but of the dullest. And, as a matter of fact, the actual result—if any—would be somewhere below the result produced by the dullest one working on his own; because, left alone, he would be unhampered.

Thousands of years ago, one man, somewhere in a forgotten jungle, looked at trees and thought of gathering their branches into the shape of a hut for shelter. Others saw his work and copied it. Their descendants inherited the hut. One among them thought of planting posts upright to support horizontal beams. The hut became a house. The post-and-lintel house became the Parthenon. Men discovered the principle of the arch—and the Parthenon became the Pantheon. Men discovered the principle of the flying buttress—and the Pantheon became the Rheims Cathedral. Men learned to make structural steel—and the Rheims Cathedral became the Empire State Building. But all through the process, what men inherited from other men was only the product of their thinking. The moving force in the process—the determining force—was man's rational faculty that took the product as material, used it and originated the next step.

In each new step, the achievement was not that of the originator's predecessors; *their* achievement had been there before; the part of a newly created object which constituted an achievement was not that which had been known before, but that which had not been known; not what the achievement was based on, but what had been added to that base. It was not the inventor of the hut who made the skyscraper possible—he made the hut possible; nor was it the designer of the Parthenon, nor any of the men who left their achievements to their heirs. The skyscraper was made possible by the thought of the man who designed it—to the exact extent to which the thought was new, i.e., his own.

In any period of mankind's progress, the credit for what is done does not belong to a collective achievement of the past. First, it was not a *collective* achievement, not the group production of a group working as a group—but an aggregate of single, specific achievements by single, individual men.

Second, even if viewed vaguely and inaccurately as a "collective achievement" in the sense of representing a sum, the past achievements in any period are just that: *past*. They are done, finished, completed—inert. What is done from then on, what is added to them, what is discovered, defined, invented, created for the first time in what constitutes the achievement. The credit belongs to the man who made the new step.

No matter how many steps were taken to reach any stage in the development of any particular human product, no matter how many men perfected single details—each step was the work, the creation and the achievement of some one individual man. Someone had to think of it.

If several men thought of it simultaneously, as when inventors make similar discoveries independently of one another, it still remains true that each had to arrive at his conclusion through a rational process of his own. An argument such as "If Columbus hadn't discovered America, somebody else would have," is pointless and meaningless. Yes, somebody else would have—if he had acted as Columbus did, i.e., if he had ventured out on an untried journey guided by an idea of his own, unshared and unsanctioned by the majority of his contemporaries. It is of no importance how many men could have equaled the achievement of Columbus and discovered America. The fact remains that he did and they didn't.

The usual cry of mediocrities about [what] they could have invented if someone else hadn't beaten them to it can be answered simply by pointing to the inexhaustible potentialities still open and unexplored in every field of human endeavor. Let them design a new safety-pin before they start whining about how the Wright brothers beat them to [the discovery of the airplane].

It would be pointless to debate whether one man actually thought of making a hut all by himself, or whether the first hut represented a long series of steps invented by many men in succession. The process of achievement remains the same: a single man making a new step, in some cases a small, imperceptible step—in others, a gigantic leap forward. We do not know the authors of mankind's first achievements because their names have not been recorded. But we do know from recorded history that no achievement, great or small, has ever burst upon mankind spontaneously out of nowhere and nobody—nor, as fools believe, out of everywhere and everybody. It came from some one man.

We can also observe that the development of every particular sphere of man's creative activity has not been an even, microscopic succession of contributions, like a procession of ants each adding a grain of dust to the common line. In every sphere—art, literature, music, science, invention, philosophy—the line of progress has shot from mountain peak to mountain peak, from one single burst of light to another, from a key name marking a turning point to another key name at the threshold of a new direction. The valleys, the candle drops and the modest footsteps between such points were filled by many men, each elaborating some one detail of the giant's heritage. The accomplishments of these modest men are not to be despised; they were authentic contributions and they must be given their value—but no more than their value. It is not out of their collected efforts that the basic, crucial, epoch-making achievements have come. It is these great, single achievements that gave them a field in which to work, each to the extent of his own talent.

If anyone wishes to claim that the greater the achievement the more men were required to reach it, the history of every creative profession will prove the exact opposite: the greater, the more primary, the more cardinal the achievement—the fewer men were responsible for it. Only the sphere of polishing, elaborating, pressing seams and ironing wrinkles involved many small contributions by many different men. The design of an in-built ashtray *is* a contribution to the appearance and comfort of an automobile; it is not the same kind of contribution as that made by the man who designed the internal combustion engine. The automobile is not their collective product on equal terms.

There is no anonymous achievement. There is no collective creation. No step was taken anywhere—no single nail was designed—by a group of men working in unison under the guidance of a majority vote. Every step in the development of a great discovery bears the name of its originator. Behind the most complex of modern inventions we find the names of five or ten men—out of the billions who lived and died during the years when the invention was being perfected. There was no collective achievement involved. There never has been. There never will be. There never can be. There is no collective brain.

### March 22, 1946

[Some men] think that being "instinctive" or "spontaneous" is being oneself—that is, if no rational process is involved. But what lies behind one's "spontaneity"? Isn't it the thinking one has done? And isn't rational thinking the most truly personal and independent activity of all? Has Aristotle's idea—that the rational in us is "God" or "the impersonal"—something to do with this? The rational *is* God-like, i.e., *independent*, but it is *not* impersonal. The truly *independent* is the truly *personal*.

This is for "reason and emotions."

# 9

# TOP SECRET

---

*In 1944, AR was hired as a screenwriter by Hal Wallis, the producer of* Casablanca. *Wallis had just opened his own production studio, and she was the first screenwriter he hired. Her contract called for her to work for him six months a year for the next five years.*

*In late 1945, Wallis suggested that AR write an original screenplay about the development of the atomic bomb. Although she was interested in the project, she recalled years later:*

> I told him I wouldn't because we would probably disagree politically.... I told him that I couldn't undertake such a thing unless I had an agreement with him that nothing would be put into the picture that clashed with my political ideas. If he were willing to do that, then I would do the script.

*AR wrote a paper for Wallis explaining the essential ideas that her script would contain. The paper, entitled* An Analysis of the Proper Approach to a Picture on the Atomic Bomb, *is presented below.*

*Wallis did agree to AR's approach, and she began her research. She interviewed several of the key men who worked on the bomb, including Dr. J. Robert Oppenheimer, the scientific director. AR's notes from these interviews are presented here, followed by her synopsis of the proposed screenplay.*

*Regrettably, the movie was never made. When Wallis began the project, he knew that MGM was already working on a movie about the bomb. After AR had completed about one-third of the script, Wallis sold the rights to her work to MGM. But MGM had no interest in her script; apparently, it simply wanted to terminate a rival project. So AR stopped work on* Top Secret *in March 1946 and began full-time work on* Atlas Shrugged.

**January 2, 1946**

*An Analysis of the Proper Approach*
*to a Picture on the Atomic Bomb*
(Confidential)

An attempt to make a picture on the atomic bomb can be the greatest moral crime in the history of civilization—unless one approaches the subject with the most earnest, most solemn realization of the responsibility involved, to the utmost limit of one's intelligence and honesty, as one would approach Judgment Day—because *that* is actually what the subject represents.

The responsibility of making such a picture is greater than that of knowing the secret of the atomic bomb. The atomic bomb is, after all, only a piece of inanimate matter that cannot set itself in use. Whether it's used and how it's used will depend on the *thinking* of men. The motion picture is a most powerful medium of influencing men's thinking. To use such a medium on such a subject lightly or carelessly is inconceivable.

If there is any reason why this picture cannot be made honestly—it is better not to make it at all. There is no possible reward that can be worth tampering with such a subject and its consequences. Money? All of us are quite rich—and even if we were broke and starving, we could not permit ourselves to make money that way; it would be more honorable to become hold-up men. Prestige? What prestige? One does not achieve prestige through a dishonest thing. We all have names which are respected—and we will dishonor ourselves by earning the contempt of the thinking people and of the plain, honest public. We cannot fool anyone; the tone of a picture that fudges, evades, and compromises is recognized immediately by everyone.

But if greatness, nobility, patriotism, and the salvation of mankind are not mere sentences to spout in public, if we mean any small part of it—this picture could be an opportunity seldom offered to any man. It could be truly an immortal achievement, an event of historic importance and a great act of patriotism.

To do this, we must take our task seriously.

To take it seriously, we must think.

To think, we must begin by realizing fully what this subject involves.

It involves the life or death of mankind.

Unless we understand *what this means and how and why*, unless we keep this in mind constantly—we will be committing the crime of children who light a fuse, then run and say: "I didn't explode the thing—I only struck a match—it blew up by itself." We will have on our conscience millions of charred bodies—those of our children.

This is not a subject for petty politics, cheap generalities, evasions or the "well, it's a matter of different opinions" attitude. Every man who speaks about this has to be as certain of his opinions as he is of his own life; which means that he has no right to an "opinion," but must have a *conviction*. A conviction is a profound certainty reached on rational grounds, after considering every aspect of the question to the best of one's intelligence. The responsibility is so great and so terrifying that unless we have the courage for it, we'd better leave the subject alone.

The courage needed is the courage of honest and serious thought. In order to be certain that we do not, unwittingly, preach death and horror—we must be very clear in our own minds on what we want to say. If we're not clear, the picture will run away with us and become one more instrument of world destruction. This will happen without our conscious intention, because the ramifications and implications of this subject are tremendous, because they are of an intellectual and sociological nature, because we cannot escape them and, therefore, this is not a subject to be treated *unconsciously*.

The analysis that follows is broken into two parts:

   **I.** General considerations.
   **II.** The specific problems of the picture.

Do not be afraid of Part I. It is not intended to be included in the picture. It is merely a preliminary discussion, in the nature of ground-breaking. It is a statement of the issues involved which we must consider before we approach the picture. They are not issues which *I* want to attach to the subject. They *are* attached to it. We cannot ignore them—therefore we must give them attention and thought. We cannot say: "But we're not interested in politics." We *have to* be interested, because the subject *is* political—though not in a narrow sense of the word. A picture on this subject will have political implications, whether we want it or not. Therefore we must face the issues, examine them carefully and make sure that our implications will be of the kind we want.

None of our Part I discussion will get into the picture. It is intended only for ourselves. It is an exposition of the nature of our responsibility. After we have understood and accepted it, we will be ready to discuss the picture itself.

## I. General Considerations

Let us begin at the beginning. The first question we have to ask ourselves is: what is the *specific* danger of the atomic bomb to mankind?

The specific danger is that the bomb constitutes a weapon of total destruction and if it exists at a time when men and nations are bent on a course of destruction, it will wipe out mankind.

Therefore, we cannot permit ourselves to preach anything that will push men further along that course.

What is that course?

Are men at present involved in a world catastrophe and in unprecedented destruction? They are. Have they been going in that direction with steps of progressive violence in the last hundred years? They have.

Everyone—of any political shade of opinion—agrees that the world is in a mess. And the mess is getting worse day by day, not better. Why?

If we want to know the reason, we must observe the growing disintegration of the world in the last hundred years and ask ourselves: What is the idea that has been growing in the world at the same time? What is the social philosophy that has been spreading and gaining ground in the same proportion, in the same era?

It is the idea of Statism.

This is no time and subject for evasion and dishonesty. To be honest, we must be specific. *Statism* does not mean just Gestapo agents running around shooting women and children. That is the final result of Statism, not the cause; one of its manifestations, not its essence. The essence of Statism is the idea that government must be all-powerful and must control the existence of men.

There are all kinds and forms and variations of this idea, but all the differences are merely trimmings. We hear piles of superficial nonsense about "good" Statism and "bad" Statism, about differences between "Aryan" and "Proletarian," "for a selfish goal" or "for an unselfish goal," control "by the rich" or "by the poor"—and all of it is just so much childish tripe. The basic idea—an all-powerful government—is the same in all these theories. *And in practice we see that the results are exactly the same under all of them.* And not only under the modern versions of Statism, but under all the variations of it that have existed in history.

*Now,* in our day, the basic issue of the world—the crucial conflict—is between Statism and freedom. Specifically: between an all-powerful government and free enterprise.

During the eighteenth century the trend of men's thinking was toward free enterprise, and as a result we got the nineteenth century—a period of achievement, progress and prosperity unequaled in history; a period during which there were fewer government controls than at any other time, before or since; *and*—most important to our subject—*the longest period of peace* ever recorded (between the times of Napoleon and Bismarck).

But while free enterprise was accomplishing these miracles, the thinking of men, who did not understand the issue, was turning in the opposite direction. The turning point occurred approximately in the middle of the nineteenth century. Stunned by the rush of an unprecedented progress which they'd had no time to digest and analyze, men began to think that they could improve shortcomings by the short-cut of government action. They began advocating and establishing government controls.

For the last hundred years, the world has been going toward Statism, gradually, in one form or another. If Statism were the right principle, this would have made the general condition of mankind progressively better, in corresponding degree. Instead, it has made conditions progressively worse—under every form of Statism and no matter who held the power. We have not seen more general wealth and a rising standard of living throughout the world—but a growing poverty and now literal starvation. Not more freedom—but concentration camps and torture chambers. Not peace—but more wars, each more horrible than the last.

*Statism leads men to war* because that is its nature. It is based on the principle of force, violence and compulsion. This means, on the principle of destruction. Statism cannot maintain itself because it kills the productive activities of its own subjects; therefore it cannot exist for long without looting some freer, more productive country. This is a fact demonstrated by world history. It is the Statist nations—the *controlled* nations, the nations of dictatorial government—that have always resorted to violence and caused wars. Statist Sparta against Athens. Statist Carthage against Rome. Statist Spain against England. Statist Napoleon against the whole of Europe. Statists Bismarck of Germany and Napoleon III of France, against each other. Statist Wilhelm II of Germany and Nicholas II of Russia who, between them, plunged the world into the First War.

And now what about this last war? Who started it? The alliance of two dictators—Hitler and Stalin. Now observe a most significant point: the American-British strategy throughout the war was to destroy the production centers of the enemy and knock him out—because America and England were not after loot, they had nothing to gain by war, they were the productive nations and were merely defending themselves. Was that the strategy of Germany and Russia? No. While Germany was overrunning Europe, she was very careful to spare industrial centers, to seize them intact, and promptly loot machinery and entire factories for shipment into Germany. And Russia did precisely the same while occupying Germany—and is still doing it. If we want to know who and what leads the world to war, destruction, bloodshed and horror—isn't the answer blatantly obvious in practical demonstration? Or are we still going to prattle like high-school boys about "capitalist greed" and "rich munitions-makers"?

So long as Statism had only guns and dynamite with which to enslave men, mankind had a chance against it. After every havoc wrought in history by one dictatorship or another, mankind could still recover, rebuild and start over again. The destruction was partial and limited. But notice that with the improvements in the technology of weapons, each war left behind it more ruin than the one before. *Now,* with a weapon such as the atomic bomb and with a trend such as Statism in the world, there is no more chance left and our days are literally numbered—*unless the trend is reversed.*

An atomic bomb is safe only in a free society—because a free society does not function through violence and does not cause wars. Such a weapon would be dangerous in the world at any time. At a time when most of mankind has embraced the faith of Statism—a world suicide is most surely ahead of us, unless men learn a different faith.

The best sociological minds of this country say: "Mankind has just one more generation to exist. This is a final ultimatum to us. Now men must be free—or perish."

The horror and the responsibility in that statement is the fact that our generation will probably have a chance to muddle through irresponsibly to our normal graves—that we know it instinctively and so refuse to think about it too deeply. But our children will not survive. Nobody who is under twenty now will escape it. And it is *we, now,* who are going to blast them into bloody vapor—we, who will decide the issue by what we do and think—we, who'll pass the sentence on them and throw them into a screaming horror—while we ourselves escape. *This* is what I, for one, will not have on my conscience. And I don't see how anyone else can wish to have it [on his conscience].

This is not a subject for quibbling or evasions. When we say "men must be free or perish," let us be specific and honest about what *"free"* means. It means free from compulsion; it means free from rule by force; it means free from government control of enterprise.

Since the issue of free enterprise versus Statism is so fundamental, since everything we do or say affects it, since every bit of propaganda relates to it—we cannot touch a subject such as the atomic bomb without knowing clearly where we stand. There is no fence to straddle here, no compromises, no neutrality, no appeasement policy possible. [. . .]

The atomic bomb is now the focus of everybody's sociological thinking. All people agree that mankind must reconsider its whole direction in a world that contains the atomic bomb. The question is: What direction?

The Statists are already making propaganda capital out of the atomic bomb by yelling that now we must have a bigger and better Statism, a world slave state with a world totalitarian government—for the sake of harmony and peace. Well, this last is true: we must have peace or it will be the end for all of us. But harmony is not achieved by force. Brotherhood is not achieved by compulsion. Peace is not achieved by appeasement.

Harmony, brotherhood and peace can be reached only voluntarily—or not at all. Only free men are peaceful men. When we need peace as desperately as now, we must have freedom.

It is true that mankind must reverse its direction. But its direction has not been toward free enterprise. Its direction has been toward Statism. *That* is the trend which must be reversed.

The world is still stunned by the atomic bomb and is groping desperately for some understanding of its significance. Therefore anything we say or hint or imply or suggest in a picture on this subject will have tremendous consequences in influencing the thinking of a muddled, confused, bewildered public.

Let us realize and remember that the atomic bomb as an argument can be more powerful and destructive spiritually than it is as a weapon physically.

To sum up, the crux of our responsibility in making the picture is this: (1) It is precisely *because* of the atomic bomb that the world *must* return to free enterprise; (2) The atomic bomb is a tremendously potent argument. If we use it as an argument for Statism—we will have blood on our hands. If we use it as an argument for free enterprise—we will make an inestimable contribution toward saving mankind; perhaps, a historic and immortal contribution.

*The whole history of the atomic bomb is an eloquent example of, argument for and tribute to free enterprise.* It would be monstrous to disregard the lesson, to ignore it or to twist it into the exact opposite. We don't have to attach artificial propaganda to the picture. We must let the facts speak for themselves. We must only present the truth. But we must present the truth, the *whole* truth and *nothing but the truth*.

## II. The Specific Problems of the Picture

If our picture is to be a tribute to free enterprise, does it mean that we have to enter into a controversy and antagonize a lot of people? Not at all. Since we will treat the subject in a broad, philosophical manner, we will find everybody in agreement with us. We will present the issue in such a way that we will leave no room for argument and nobody will dare disagree with us, except the out-and-out Fascists and Communists.

How do we do that? Very simply. By presenting the issue not in superficial, political terms—but in its deeper, essential terms. We state our theme like this: "Man's greatest achievements are accomplished through free, voluntary action—and cannot be accomplished under force, compulsion and violence."

If we stick to this theme intelligently and consistently, who will want to disagree? In order to object, a person would have to admit that he is against freedom and in favor of violence.

Do we touch on any political issue in the narrow sense of contemporary American politics? No. None of that is pertinent. We are not for or against Labor or Capital or Republicans or Democrats. We are presenting only a fundamental issue. If, after seeing our picture, the audience walks out with the conviction that personal freedom is desirable and that the use of force is neither good nor practical, that is all we want to accomplish, and it will be a great accomplishment.

However, we cannot do this by merely tacking on a few cheap speeches about freedom, worded in such a general way that it can mean anything or nothing. Our theme must be explicit, clear-cut and expressed not in speeches, but in action. It must be integrated into the structure of our story.

Do we have to attack our own government and criticize the New Deal? No. (So long as we don't start glorifying the New Deal, either!) As far as I know without further research, our government seems to have behaved properly in regard to the atomic bomb. All we have to do is show the government's actions factually, stressing that in this case it acted as a free country's government should act: it did not use compulsion.

But where we must express our theme full blast is in our treatment of the governments of the countries from which the scientists escaped. This is the heart of the real issue historically—and this is the crux of our theme. We must show how Statism destroys, exiles and paralyzes men of genius—why these men could not work under compulsion—why they could produce what they produced *only* in a free country. Will anyone object to our showing that dictatorships do things at the point of a gun, by force, by decree, by orders in the name of the State? A person who objects to *that*, deserves to have every returned soldier spit in his face.

So much for our general approach to the subject. Now let us examine the particular key points.

## 1. What made the creation of the atomic bomb possible?

This is the most important question our picture has to answer.

In presenting the strictly factual history of the bomb, we will not be able to avoid a slant of unintentional propaganda, one way or the other. The history of the bomb is long and complex. We cannot literally present *all* the facts. We have to exercise choice in what we select to present, how we present it, what significance we attach to it, what meaning we convey. In order to present the truth, we must be able to distinguish the essential from the inessential. Any record can be falsified by omission of the essential and overstressing of the inessential. This is where we have to be careful.

For instance: it is a fact that Roosevelt gave to the scientists the funds necessary for their experiments. How are we going to treat this point? If we show or imply that *that* was the crucial factor in the creation of the bomb, we throw at the world the most powerful piece of propaganda for Statism that could be devised. We tell the audience, in effect: "See what a strong government can do? Many people objected to Roosevelt's arbitrary use of money for secret purposes—yet look what he gave you! The proper way to run the world and achieve the best results is for you common men to shut up, to trust a leader implicitly, to let your government decide for you and plan for you without your knowledge or consent." *This* is what our audience will walk out of the theater with.

Do we want to say *that*?

Do we want to feature the superficial aspects of the case and release on the world a thousand converted Statists with each showing of the picture? Do we want—in presenting the greatest achievement of free enterprise—to make "a picture whose hero will be Roosevelt," as I have heard suggested?

If not, does it mean that we should falsify Roosevelt's contribution? Certainly not. We must give him full and exact credit for the part he played. Not less than that—*and not more.*

Here is the first point where clear and honest thinking is required: if it were true that the atomic bomb was an achievement of strong government—why didn't Germany achieve it? Hitler's government was much stronger than ours—if by "strong" we mean strong-arm, total control, dictatorial power, arbitrary use of money and resources. Hitler certainly wanted to find the secret of the atomic bomb—and he tried. He started preparing for war long before we did. He could and did throw the entire resources of his country into his war machine. What good did it do him? He *did not* get the atomic bomb.

That is a *fact*. How do we treat it? If we ascribe it to sheer luck, just an accident of fate in our favor—if we say that Hitler *could have* got the bomb, that he was just on the verge of it, only we beat him to it—we miss the whole significance of the story of the atomic bomb. We are then committing a moral crime by falsifying a historical lesson of tremendous importance.

There is no factual evidence to support the idea that Hitler was about to discover the bomb. There is plenty of evidence to the contrary. But here is what will happen if we accept that idea: we'll be saying to the audience, in effect: "A totalitarian system is just as good and efficient as ours. Even more so. They can do anything we can. It was quite a feat for us to beat them."

Is that true?

The fact is that Germany did not, could not and never would have created the atomic bomb; nor Italy; nor Russia.

Is it an accident that since the beginning of the machine age, all the great, basic, epoch-making inventions and discoveries have come from America and England? Mostly from America, secondly from England—and with very few contributions from all the other countries. Why? Anglo-Saxon superiority? No. The inventors were of all races and nationalities. But they all had to work either in America or in England. The other countries then elaborated on the discoveries, worked out some details and variations, made minor improvements; but never produced anything crucially new, never made a discovery that was a turning point in science; nothing to compare with the steam engine, the electric light, the automobile, the airplane, the telephone, the telegraph, the motion picture, the radio. For God's sake, can we ignore *that*? Are we going to say "sheer accident?" How many accidents of this nature do we need to be convinced? And if, through our own fault, an atomic bomb drops on us in a few years—are we going to say that was an accident, too?

The simple fact is that invention, discovery, science and progress are possible *only* under a system of free enterprise. If you want to know why and how, in detail, please read *Science and the Planned State* by John R. Baker, a British scientist. It is a short book, recently published. It presents the whole case, with facts, names, dates, records, reasons and unanswerable proof.

*This* is the crucial point of our approach to the picture. If we take the greatest invention of man and do not draw from it the lesson it contains— that only free men could have achieved it—we deserve to have an atomic bomb dropped on our heads.

Now let us look at the history of the bomb in detail. If there is a God, it is almost as if He had staged it that way on purpose—to give us an object lesson.

Some of the key figures in the development of the bomb were [Albert] Einstein, [Niels] Bohr and [Enrico] Fermi. They had to flee from Germany, Denmark and Italy. The Statist dictators had these men and had the knowledge of their original discoveries. And it did not do the dictators any good. These scientists laid the foundations of their future achievements in their own countries. But they could not continue to work there. They had to escape to a free country.

Then there is Dr. Lise Meitner who made her first important experiments right in Nazi Germany—and had to escape. Her colleagues who remained behind, Hahn and Strassman, continued the work and got no results. She continued the work in a free country—and got results. There are many, many other refugees from dictatorships among the scientists who contributed to the atomic bomb. The object lesson is eloquent.

How are we going to treat it? Are we going to say that these refugees were victims of racial prejudice? That is not an explanation. Racial prejudice was a symptom, not a cause; a manifestation of Statism, not its basic essence. Racial prejudice as such does not cause exiles and concentration camps; it can't; it does not rule society; it remains the province of bums and the lunatic fringe. It is only when racial prejudice acquires *political* power, only when it establishes a system of Statism where man's individual dignity and individual rights are destroyed, only then can it actually start to shed blood. Without individual rights, there are no minority rights; without minority rights there are no majority rights either. And an individual is the smallest minority on earth.

To say that Einstein and Lise Meitner were thrown out of Germany on account of racial prejudice is the truth—but not the whole truth. It was racial prejudice *armed with State power*. And what about Fermi and the others? There was no racial prejudice involved in their cases.

The whole truth is that no achievements can be made under a Statist system because: (1) Statists always throttle and destroy the ablest men among their subjects because Statist systems are based on blind obedience; men of ability are dangerous, independent and not easily ruled; (2) Even when a few men of ability survive in a Statist system and are begged or ordered to produce—they cannot produce because they cannot work under orders, controls and compulsion. Nothing new and great can be or *ever has been* done that way. (See *Science and the Planned State*. See the whole of history. Try to name one exception.)

*That* is the point our picture must make. *That* is the lesson of the atomic bomb. *That* is the greatest glory of America, its noblest distinction and its highest pride. And if anyone objects to our saying that, he does not deserve the name of a human being.

## 2. *The actual history of the atomic bomb*

To tell the whole truth about the atomic bomb means to show the entire process of its creation, at least in highlights and key-points.

This is essential to our theme and to historical accuracy. Furthermore, it has the value of great public interest. The public is eager to know just what the atomic bomb really is and how men made such a discovery. Therefore we must tell our story from the beginning.

The first step was Einstein's equation on the conversion of matter into energy, which he formulated before the First War. After that, there was a long, progressive series of steps, achieved by single scientists working independently of one another all over the world. Quoting now merely from a newspaper account (this has to be checked by fuller research), the key steps seem to have been: the discovery of the neutron by Sir James Chadwick, in England, in 1932; the splitting of a uranium atom by Lise Meitner, Hahn and Strassman, in Germany, in 1939; the elaboration upon this experiment by Niels Bohr in Denmark and Enrico Fermi in Italy; the meeting of Bohr and Fermi in America in 1939, when the first discussion of the possibility of an atomic bomb was held; Fermi's proposal to representatives of the Navy; the creation of the atomic bomb project; the two years of work there; the test in New Mexico; the bomb dropped on Hiroshima.

That, in a very general outline, is the story we have to tell. What is its significance? To whom does the credit for the atomic bomb belong?

By the time Fermi approached the Navy with his proposal, the basic scientific work was done; scientists had discovered that the atom could be split and knew how to do it; what remained was the practical application, specifically to the purpose of a bomb. Who had given to the world the crucial basic knowledge? The single, voluntary, unplanned, unregulated efforts of individual scientists, each following his own line of research. Was it a "collective" achievement? No. They did not work together under a common plan, nor under directives, nor by majority vote. It was not the achievement of *one* individual—nor the achievement of an organized group. It was—as all civilization—the sum of free, individual efforts.

I quote from *Science and the Planned State*: "We may turn to any part of science and we are likely to find the same thing: the fundamental discoveries are commonly made by single workers."

I quote from Einstein: "I am a horse for single harness, not cut out for tandem or teamwork."

Now we come to the last stage—the work on the atomic bomb project. That was an organized effort. Organized by whom? By one man or five men—we don't know the number—but we know that work was done under the absolute guidance of a few top scientists. Was that a collectivist method of working? Well, the members of that "collective" didn't even know what they were working on. There was no "democracy" about it, no majority vote, no "collective bargaining." Shall we then consider it an example of Nazi methods—a small, ruling elite and a blindly obedient mass? No. *Because none of those men was forced into that project.*

What was it then? Why, simply and exactly the same method as that of any large enterprise carried on by a free industrial concern. Any enterprise has to work under a single guidance—so long as it is *one specific task*. The employee in a private industry has to take orders from the boss, and cannot and must not vote upon the boss's policy—or you get chaos; but beyond and outside the specific work which the employee has voluntarily undertaken to perform, the boss has no power over him; and within his particular task, an employee must be left free and must exercise his own effort to achieve results. Isn't that the pattern of free industry? And isn't that the way the work on the bomb project was done?

A splendid example of cooperation and discipline? Of course. So is any Ford plant. The biggest and most successful examples of large-scale organization have always been American. Because *this kind of cooperation is possible only among free men by voluntary agreement.*

Is that collectivism? No. Collectivism is compulsion. Compulsion and cooperation are not synonyms. They are opposites. Collectivism is group action by decree—and in matters where no group action is possible. Cooperation is a highly complex *division* of individual labor. Collectivism is not division, but *herd* action, in theory—and a gun stuck in your back in practice. You don't cooperate at the point of a gun. Only free men can cooperate.

*This* is the crucial difference between the method of free enterprise and the method of Statism. *This* is why one succeeds and the other fails. *This* is why the scientists could not work under dictatorships, but could work in America. *This* is why an organization such as the bomb project could not exist in Germany.

We must keep this clearly in mind in order to show the real historical significance of these events. We must not get into a childish interpretation of secondary matters. We must not give the impression that the secrecy, the military discipline, the walled-in cities were responsible for the achievement. These things were required to protect a secret—not to solve it. They were necessities of wartime and of the fact that the work involved a military weapon. They were not necessities of scientific research. We must keep these two aspects clearly defined and apart.

Now we come to the part played by the government. What was the most significant thing about it? *The fact that the government did not attempt to run the bomb project.* The government and the Army took orders from the scientists—not vice versa. The government provided the means—and let the scientists do the work as they wished. We must show this clearly.

Otherwise, there is a great danger of the usual superficial interpretation.

The audience will make a conclusion such as: "It was a government project, wasn't it? And it turned out well, didn't it? So government control is good." It is by such crude, blanket conclusions and unanalyzed, unwarranted generalizations that all the errors in sociological thinking are made.

The part played by the government in the bomb project is not the part people advocate when they speak of government control. A government project is *run* by the government. A private industry controlled by government *takes orders* from the government. This is the exact opposite of what happened on the bomb project. For once, the government literally acted as *the servant* of the people involved, *not the master*. The government put itself at the disposal of the scientists and carried out their wishes without questions. This is illustrated nicely in the little incident of General Marshall giving a $250,000 check to one of the scientists, without knowing or asking what it was for.

This behavior of the government is highly commendable and if we present it exactly as it was, it will be the best compliment we can pay to the government in this case, and it should please every official involved. Do you think officials will be offended if we show that they acted as free men toward free men—and not as Gestapo agents or Commissars?

This is a point that must be shown and stressed. It displays the contrast between a free country and a Statist dictatorship. Under a dictatorship, men would be forced into the project, assigned to it by command, frozen in their jobs, prohibited from leaving under penalty of death, and ordered to work. (And therefore no work would be done.) Materials would be confiscated. (And therefore there would be no materials.) The government would decide who does the work, where and how; there would be the usual unholy mess of directives, regulations, red tape, commands—and bloody purges to punish lack of progress, men executed in order to make the survivors work better through terror. (But achievements and creation are not done through terror.) There would be the usual inquisition on who belongs to what race and whose political beliefs are or are not in strict accordance with the official party line. Now are we still going to wonder why no achievements ever come out of dictatorships? Sheer accident?

The atomic bomb was *not* a creation of government—but of *the free cooperation of free men*. And it is essential to show its whole history—from the single steps by single scientists—to their exiles and escapes—to their coming together for their last effort under the guidance of the best among them. We must not start the picture with the final stage, something like Roosevelt calling the scientists together and saying: "Boys, make me an atomic bomb." That's not the way it was done. If that were the way, Hitler would have done it.

We must not fall into a naive Statism by featuring a government project and saying: "Government did it." That would be equal in intelligence to a man who comes out of a movie theater, saying: "The theater owner is the one who created that wonderful movie. He provided the theater, didn't he?"

And while we show the part played by the government, with proper and exact credit—we must also show, with proper and exact credit, the part played by private industry. The tremendous material and technological resources that were required to make the atomic bomb came from and were created by private American industry, by free enterprise—and were not and could not be created anywhere else by any other method. Statist nations could not have manufactured the bomb, even if they had invented it. The atomic bomb was the end product of a huge, complex industrial structure made up of private achievements and ingenuity—a structure which Statism can neither accomplish nor copy. This must be said and shown.

The plants built for the bomb project in Tennessee and in the state of Washington were built by the DuPont Company—"without profit and with a repudiation of all patent rights" (*N.Y. Times*). This must be shown. Patent rights mean that the DuPont Company had contributed some original inventions. This must be shown.

In our handling of the public names and figures involved, we must maintain the strictest fairness, accuracy and impartiality. If we present Roosevelt in a favorable light, we must also present the DuPonts in a favorable light. Nobody will or can object, so long as what we present is factually true.

---

In the manner and terms I have here described, the general tone of our picture will be that of a great tribute to America—an epic of the American spirit. We will not do it in any phony flag-waving way (we must never even say it nor make speeches about it); we will merely show the American method and its results. We will dramatize that which is the essence of America.

An abstract, general theme of this nature will give deeper significance to the specific events we present, will lift the picture above the class of a documentary film of the moment into that of a great historical work, and will give it the importance and the dignity which the subject demands.

Our picture will say: "This is what America has done—she is the only one who could have done it—this is how and why she was able to do it."

If the above exposition does not represent your approach to the picture, I cannot permit myself to take upon my conscience the contribution of a single line to it.

If you agree with this exposition and wish to make the picture on this basis—I shall consider it an honor and a privilege to work on the screenplay.

**January, 1946**

### Theme

*The mind against brute force;*
therefore—
The mind is that which cannot be forced and will always win against force;
therefore—
Freedom from compulsion;
therefore—
*The methods of free enterprise against the methods of the totalitarian state.*

---

Show throughout that what applies to men applies in exactly the same way to states and nations. (Men are the atoms of society. Matter is organized according to the nature of atoms—not atoms according to what one would like to do with matter.)

First part: scientists fight a lonely, losing battle as the world moves toward totalitarianism, the rule of force, the climax of which is Hitler.

Second part: the world, lost in a chaos of brutality, has no recourse but to appeal to scientists (the mind) to save it from unleashed brutality.

**January, 1946**

*[AR prepared the following list of questions for the first of two interviews she conducted with Dr. J. Robert Oppenheimer, the physicist who served as scientific director of the atomic bomb project at Los Alamos.]*

### Questions for J. Robert Oppenheimer

When did he start in Chicago? Summer, 1942.
When in New Mexico? March, 1943.
Who selected the scientists for New Mexico? How were they invited? What was their attitude? Incidents?
How was the work done? To what extent [was it] controlled? To what extent [was it] free? If controlled—by whom? How many free,

unexpected discoveries were there? How many men were responsible for crucial, basic points?

*Incidents to show **progress** of the work?*

Were there crucial turning points, i.e., milestones of the progress?
What points or events stand out in *your* mind?

*Was there any one specific day or event when they knew they had it?*

Was there a specific event when they started manufacturing the
actual bombs used?

(Our picture is to be a *tribute to the scientist*—as a representative of
free inquiry and the independent mind.)

Contributions of industries?

Incidents of German work on the atomic [bomb]? What happened to
Otto Hahn? [*Otto Hahn was a German chemist and physicist who
received the Nobel prize in 1944 for splitting the uranium atom
(1939). He collaborated with the Nazis in their effort to develop the
atomic bomb.*]

*Did scientists really fear German success and consider it a race—or
were they contemptuous of the German efforts?*

What does he consider the *best* in people as demonstrated in connection with this project?

What does he consider the *worst*?

Any trouble or interference which he cares to mention?

Incidents typical of the men as scientists?

What does he consider his most important contribution to atomic
physics—before the project?

How was he picked to be head of Los Alamos—was he chosen or did
he volunteer? When and how did he first hear about the project?

**January 8, 1946**

*Notes from interview with J. R. Oppenheimer*

No theoretical problem. "Approved for destruction." Some parts
ready two years before.

Scientists—[almost] no one turned him down. (One refused. Two
quit the project.)

Project had a bad name at the beginning.

[Obstacles to hiring scientists:]

1. Scientists already employed.
2. Project's bad name.
3. Remote location.
4. Hated to work for Army.

Town run by Army—commanding officer in charge.

[Oppenheimer was] called by Dr. Arthur Compton in spring of 1942. Group came to Berkeley in summer of 1942.

Staff of laboratory at maximum of 3,500—scientific staff about 900. In the last three years—scientific work at Los Alamos, production at the other two labs [located in Oak Ridge, Tennessee, and Hanford, Washington].

Early part—working out scientific schemes for the other two plants. Group at first meeting being told about work in single teams.

All 900 knew the scientific principles—and others after six months residence were told what they were making.

*They kept it secret without rules—merely by making it a principle to keep it secret.*

Bohr was not closely associated—brought some slight information— not essential to work.

Fermi contributed enormously.

Scientific high points (prior to project):

      Rutherford—discovery of nucleus.

      Quantum theory.

      [James] Chadwick—discovery of neutron.

Dr. Bush important, "had President's ear." [*Dr. Vannevar Bush was director of the government's Office of Scientific Research and Development.*]

Refugee scientists responsible.

Summer of 1942—decision to manufacture bomb was made. Theoretical work was done.

Conant and Bush presented evidence to Roosevelt. [*Dr. James B. Conant was chairman of the National Defense Research Council during World War II.*]

**January 15, 1946**

*Questions* [for Dr. J. R. Oppenheimer]

Describe typical day.

How was work done? On assignment—or free investigation of assigned problems?

When did he move to live in Los Alamos?

Bodyguard?

*Theoretical scientist:* Give one incident about himself prior to project.

Incidents typical of the men as scientists?

Control of Army?

Hiroshima.

*Notes from* [*Second*] *Interview with Dr. Oppenheimer*

Seminars—free discussions ("give and take").

Tormented by something he can't solve.

*Memories:*

>Moral doubts.
>
>Bohr arrives at his house—evening, it is snowing. Went for walk. Talk about German work.
>
>About a year ago—terrible jam on equipment—working 24 hours a day—shop burned down—"evening of extreme [weather conditions]"—snow, inadequate water pressure.
>
>Three or four people at first (March, 1943)—cold—conferences in half-built rooms.
>
>Waiting for news of Nagasaki.
>
>Surprises—came out in conferences—about eight people talking. Trouble about freedom and getting their own personnel and supplies. Trouble with engineers who wanted to start building. First model of bomb had nothing in common with actual bomb.
>
>Scientists ran it—they decided what they needed.
>
>Formal parties—like Englishmen in the Congo.
>
>Hiroshima—Sunday at Los Alamos—brother called and they went for ride—took children to go swimming. Next morning he got phone call at lab—everything all right. On Tuesday night—a colloquium—800 scientists—worried that the next one might not work.

Assembly of first bomb (Trinity). [*This was the bomb used for the test in New Mexico.*]

Compton left—got scared—in early days.

*Bodyguard:*

Sentry at house—standing all night. One of two guys had to go out with him.

Driver assigned to Compton.

June 1943—guard assigned—couldn't [leave] often.

*His achievements:*

Theory of cosmic ray particles—that neutron particles were cosmic rays—1936.

*Typical day:*

Talking with individuals about their problems; trying to give them a feeling of confidence; correcting them while making them think they did it themselves.

Conferences: two on technical subjects, one on administration. One meeting a week to describe progress.

———————

General Groves was the only boss over Oppenheimer.

Scientists given choice of problems. *Reasons* instead of *authority.*

*Free* to solve problems.

Scientists like music. Long walks, skiing, horses.

*No one ever gave an order at Los Alamos.* [*AR recalled this part of the interview years later: "I asked him whether the scientists worked under orders. He looked at me in the way that my best characters would have, and said in a morally indignant tone: 'No one ever gave an order at Los Alamos.'* "]

They did things they didn't want to do—only because they understood the necessity. A great scientist ran the machine shop. People who ran calculating machines and other dull jobs.

After a hundred experiments—"we're getting something."

[*AR's meetings with Oppenheimer proved useful later: he became the model for Robert Stadler in* Atlas Shrugged. *In a 1961 interview, she recalled: "Oppenheimer set the character of Stadler in my mind, which is the reason for the first name of Robert. It's the type that Oppenheimer projected—that enormous intelligence, somewhat bitter, but very much the*

*gentleman and scholar, and slightly other-worldly. Even his office was what
I described for Stadler—that almost ostentatious simplicity."*]

**January 16, 1946**

*Notes on interview with General [Leslie R.] Groves*

Groves—top in his profession (Army engineering)—took chance on
disgrace if project failed.

He was told of his appointment first in hall of Congress building—
came out of Military committee where he testified—met General
Somervell—asked his opinion on taking assignment with General
overseas—Somervell told him the Secretary of War had another
assignment for him "which might win the war." Groves [complained
about being] given a research job; [at first] he thought it was fantastic
and doomed to failure.

Groves didn't know project would succeed. "I thought we had a 60%
chance—and had to take it before anyone else did."

Groves had to make crucial decisions—often against the advice
of his scientific advisors. (In the case of starting Oak Ridge from
[Dr. E. O.] Lawrence's "speck of light.") Groves had no organization
set up—there was no time—he ran things himself—appointed the
right men and almost never changed them.

Groves was "salesman" to get big industries to take the contracts.
They could have refused—but not one of them did. The story of
DuPont—the board of directors—the meeting and the papers face
down—Chairman speaks—not one paper is turned over (among
those who didn't turn the paper over was Lamont DuPont, who owns
60 million [dollars worth] of DuPont stock). [The papers contained
classified information on the Manhattan Project, which the Department of Defense was willing to divulge if necessary.]

Groves says he would like to see stressed "teamwork and American
management"—no other country could have done it.

Groves went to Milwaukee to see a contractor; he solved two technical problems for [the contractor] while in a hotel room conference.
One method of doing a certain scientific process had to be abandoned
after spending a huge sum.

**January 23, 1946**

*Interview with Dr. Kaynes*

[*Dr. Kaynes was apparently a scientist who worked with Richard Feynman in the computing group at Los Alamos.*]

Conflict of scientists who were in Army. But [they were] free in the laboratory. Never worked under compulsion.

What is the critical mass?

One works with cross-section (cyclotron involved).

Neutron reflector—looked for damper—tried to "freeze design."

At request of Fermi, made calculations to see if the world would blow up.

Dr. Hans Bethe gave talk at colloquium before test; they were terrified when they realized how little they knew.

Dr. Kaynes accepted job knowing nothing about it. Arrived in early 1944. Used first names. Dr. Bethe told him they were making a new element. Told everything. Asked: "What do you want to do?"

Worked with a "screwball"—Richard Feynman.

(Scientists dressed sloppy. Only big shots dressed—Bethe and Oppenheimer, but not Fermi.)

Bohr and son came often. Fermi eventually came and stayed there about a year before test. Chadwick was stationed there (for British) almost from beginning. Lawrence visited. Dr. Bethe. Dr. [George B.] Kistiakowsky—White Russian.

(Ideal of most professors—university without undergraduates.)

Feynman was Kaynes' group leader (about age 27). He traveled to Albuquerque to see wife, who was dying of T.B. Beat tom-toms right in laboratory—the more noise, the harder he was thinking. Wife died. No one paid attention to work hours.

One hundred tons of TNT used to test instruments—a few months before atomic test.

Dr. [William George] Penny got word his wife in London was hurt in bombing. Later learned his wife died—intense hatred.

Los Alamos originally planned for 75 scientists, grew gradually.

Polish scientist who could not find his wife in Warsaw.

Columbia—started work with Fermi—men came out all black from carbon. Fermi—scientific. Compton—administration.

(Communists not allowed on project.)

Art Wahl (chemist) discovered plutonium—E. O. Lawrence's laboratory at Berkeley.

**January 25, 1946**

*Interview with Mrs. Oppenheimer*

Test was referred to as "Trinity." Test was on a Monday—the next Saturday Mrs. Oppenheimer gave a party—evening dress. Mood was one of relief.
After Hiroshima they did not feel like celebrating.
The Oppenheimers were the first family to move to Los Alamos.
[The town] had about 30 people then—a big dormitory for scientists in one of the schoolrooms. The Oppenheimers lived in one of the masters' houses of the old school. Community life was much friendlier and more harmonious than in other cities—higher mental level.
Dr. Oppenheimer took job only on condition that his essential workers would know the secret.
A great part of their work was spent in meetings and conferences.
At first, scientists were afraid of possible German atomic research, but later learned there was none. Scientists worked in order to save lives and end the war.
Was it in order to beat the Germans to the discovery? "Good God, no!"

**January 29, 1946**

*Interview with Colonel Nichols*

[*Colonel K. D. Nichols served under General Groves, and had responsibility for the design, construction, and operation of the plants which produced the fissionable material required for the bombs.*]

Spies tried not to be promoted.
Nichols, [General George C.] Marshall, and a civilian wandered for a day, choosing the site.
Plans about center of town—useless planning.
Ore refined at other plant [Oak Ridge, Tennessee].
Scientists impatient with engineers.
Main problem: critical size and detonation.

Detonation—crucial—the gamble.

Lawrence [influential in] selecting Oppenheimer.

FBI security men—separate organization. Foreign spy. Feed back answers to Germany. (Phony answers written by scientist.)

Miss Tracey (Compton's secretary): "I have a husband on Iwo Jima. You don't have to ask me."

Better work when they knew what they were doing. "Never saw such a change in a town" (as took place after they knew).

Mrs. Nichols—story of how she heard news that it was a bomb.

Community troubles with scientists who hated restrictions, such as no choice of schools for their children.

**January, 1946**

### Philosophic Notes

Answer to Oppenheimer's worry:

"Scientists are the representatives of free inquiry. They will protect you—and they will *not* work for or under compulsion. The atom bomb and the sudden ruling position of the scientist shows that *force* is not practical. Force needs *brains* to be applied. Without thought, you cannot even indulge in violence. Brute force is nothing—thought and principles everything.

"The atom bomb is a weapon of *defense*—it is not good for looting—and dictatorships are looters. The atom bomb is the weapon of a free country."

For "overall" guidance:

Wars are caused by the anti-rational, pro-force psychology of men. If we do not deal with one another through reason—nothing is left to us but brute force. *Whenever anyone advocates the achievement of anything whatever through the use of force or compulsion on men—he is planting the seeds of war.*

Have a sequence where somebody wonders what causes war—and scattered, "human" examples of the above psychology.

"What causes wars?" can be a kind of overall theme and unifying line.

"Just as a tiny, invisible atom holds forces that determine the shape of matter—so you, each man, by the ideas you hold, determine the

shape of world events." ("Do not worry about anything except your
own ideas and responsibility. It will work.")

Everything we have comes from someone's thought.

Scene where mother says "nobody wants war"—and we show all the
preaching of violence: worker—"take the property of the rich by
force"; industrialist—"make workers work by force"; teacher—
"educate people by force"; writer—"make people go to my plays by
force"; farmer—"prohibit the sale of milk from other states by
force"; dietitian—"make everybody drink orange juice by force."
"Since society is complex—we need force." (Then show scene at
construction site.)

The antagonists: the Nazi ideal—a horde of armed brutes; the free
ideal—a scientist, alone at a blackboard. (Sequence about the ancestors of both sides.) England in ruins—"our only defense"—Chadwick.
Conclusion from "teamwork" is not "any man is unimportant, only
the team counts," but "every man is important."

"All human activities are like a chain reaction; somebody has to be
the first neutron."

Don't forget line (toward end): "It was not an accident."

Someone (maybe Chadwick) looks at sky and says: "God did give us
a means for right to win over might: the mind which can find the
secrets of the universe and which cannot work for evil, because it
cannot work under compulsion." (Evil [men] steal the ideas and
achievements of free men; it is up to free men to protect themselves
and the world from that—by protecting freedom.)

The men that a dictatorship needs most (if it's real power that it
wants) are the first to turn into its bitterest enemies (Fermi, Einstein)—by the very nature of the idea of dictatorship.


**January 19, 1946**

*[The following is AR's "general outline" of the screenplay.]*

We open with an immense shot of the night sky—the stars and planets—
the vast mystery of the universe. Camera tilts to include the earth below—a
dark spread of hills, wide and desolate under the sky. A single pinpoint of
light shows somewhere in the hills; it looks like a feeble, futile competition to
the flaming spread of the stars. Camera moves forward slowly, and we begin
to distinguish the figure of a man standing in the hills. He seems helpless and
small, totally insignificant in the face of the immensity of the universe.

The man is about thirty years old. He is looking up at the sky. His face is weak and bitter. He turns slowly and walks toward the light we have seen; it is the lighted window of a small, modest house somewhere in the hills of California.

Inside the house, a young woman is lying in bed. The man, her husband, comes in. He speaks bitterly of the fact that man is only a worm in the universe—a helpless, insignificant worm—and what is the use of anything? The young wife reproaches him gently—that is no way to talk on the day when their son was born. And we see the new-born child beside her.

The young mother is full of hopes and dreams for her son. She expects him to have a great life in a great new world; the war has just ended, there will never be another war. She asks her husband what important events took place on the day of her son's birth. The father picks up a newspaper—it is the year 1919. He glances through the pages, briefly naming the big events of the day. Somewhere at the bottom of a page, he finds a small item announcing that Sir Ernest Rutherford, British scientist, has succeeded in smashing an atom of nitrogen. He drops the paper contemptuously; he does not consider this of any importance; scientists, he says, are useless; this is the day of the practical man, the man of action.

There is a photograph of Rutherford in the paper. From it we dissolve to Rutherford himself, in his laboratory in England. He is being interviewed by a couple of reporters—it is not considered a big story—the reporters are not too impressed. Yes, Rutherford says, he can explain his experiments so that the laymen would understand—he is not sure, however, that it would interest many people. He proceeds to explain briefly the nuclear theory of the atom, which he had formulated in 1912, and his present experiment by which he transmuted nitrogen into hydrogen. Of what practical use is that?—asks one of the reporters. A little astonished, Rutherford, the theoretical scientist, answers: "I don't know." "Then why are you interested in that kind of research?" Rutherford answers, very quietly: "Only because it is knowledge of the truth."

We dissolve to the young father saying: "What is the truth? There is no such thing as objective truth." He is saying it to his son, now ten years old. It is the year 1929. The boy is an earnest, intelligent child; his face shows future strength and character. (For the purpose of this outline only we'll call him John X—he can be anyone, he is the young generation of today.) The father is reproaching him for his scholarly inclinations—the boy studies too much, reads too much, asks too many questions. The father wants him to go out more, learn more about the world and become useful when he grows up; people who think are useless; the mind is a superstition, truth is a superstition, everything is relative, we mustn't question anything, we must learn to take orders. The father is a kind of petty-Fascist type, a shiftless failure who wants to run everything and does nothing, who takes out his own incompetence in hatred for the world; he represents the cheap cynicism, the irrationalism, the contempt for moral standards and intellectual principles which characterized his generation all over the world.

Tied into this scene we show, with brief explanations, a scene of Dr. E. O. Lawrence, at the University of California, with his new invention—the cyclotron; and a scene of Dr. Robert J. Van de Graaf, at Princeton, with his new giant electrostatic generator—two important points in the progress of atomic science.

Then, as the father complains about the state of the world—there is nothing to do now, after the stock market crash, no frontiers left to conquer—we go to a plane flying over the desolate wastes of North Canada. Gilbert Labine discovers the black rock on the shore of a lake. We show his expedition through the snow the next year, the discovery that the rock is pitchblende [uranium ore], the establishment of his company.

———⚬———

*1932.* John X is 13 years old. He shows signs of becoming nervous, restless, bitter—as he studies in secret from his father. He has to smuggle the latest scientific magazines into his room and hide them. In connection with his studies, we show scenes of: the Cockroft-Walton experiments, in England, splitting atoms with protons; Sir James Chadwick, in England, discovering the neutron; Prof. Harold Urey, in America, discovering heavy water.

———⚬———

*1934.* Niels Bohr, in Denmark, formulates his theory of the structure of the [atomic nucleus].

Enrico Fermi, in Italy, invents the technique of bombarding an atom with slow neutrons.

Scene of Fermi's clash with Fascist officials who hamper his work. (I would like to have information from Fermi about an authentic incident— also the exact date and manner of his escape from Italy.)

John X is now fifteen. There is a violent scene when he tells his father that he wants to become a scientist. Scientists, the father declares, are no good, because they "live in ivory towers." Man must act, not think. His son must learn to be practical; take, for instance, that fellow who's growing so powerful in Germany; of course, the father says, I don't approve of some of his ideas, but nobody will deny that he's *practical*, a realist, a smart man with an efficient system who'll get what he wants. As an illustration of how one goes about being practical, the father seizes the boy's books and throws them into the fireplace.

As the books burn, we dissolve to a huge pile of books burning in the square of a German city, under swastika flags. And we see the "practical man," Hitler, in his office, bending over a map of Germany. He tells his assistants that he controls all of it—he boasts about his power—to hell with principles and theories—thinking is a weakness—the brain is evil—action and force are all that counts—a powerful State can accomplish anything—the individual doesn't matter—the mind doesn't matter (exact quotations from *Mein Kampf* to be used here). Camera pans to the window of the office: there is a light in a distant window of the dark city outside. Camera moves toward that window and into the room. It is a modest study. A solitary man sits working at a desk. The desk holds nothing but books, papers, abstract formulas. The man is Einstein.

Scene of Einstein leaving Germany. (I would like to have the date and authentic details from Einstein.)

*1936.* John X, seventeen, is entering college. He has given in to his father and given up his ambition of becoming a scientist. As a result, he is a listless, frustrated, embittered youth, cynical, without fire or faith, without much interest in anything—like most of the youth of that time. His father, very pleased, accompanies him when he enrolls at the University of California to study whatever it is his father has selected for him. Actually, the father is not interested in any education, but wants him to become a great college athlete. ("The brawn is mightier than the brain.") As they walk down a hall of the University, they see—through a half-open door—a man at a blackboard in a modest office. The man has his back to us and is writing incomprehensible formulas on the blackboard. From a friend or a minor college official accompanying them, they learn that the man is working on some mysterious studies of the mesotron and cosmic rays. "There!" says the father, "do you want to end up like that?" The boy shakes his head. As they pass the door, we see the sign on it: "J. R. Oppenheimer."

*1939.* John X is struggling through college—miserably. The brilliant boy has become a worthless student. He cannot do well the things he hates. He has flunked many examinations and doesn't care. He is drinking, running around to parties, driving recklessly—without any real joy. When somebody mentions to him the unusual scientific discoveries being made in the world and shows him a scientific magazine—he flings it aside angrily. He is beginning to hate the subject of science, because it is tied to his renunciation of his one real desire.

We go to Germany—to the laboratory of Otto Hahn and Lise Meitner. We see the experiment in which uranium atoms are split for the first time. Hahn and Meitner are puzzled by it—they do not understand the significance of their own experiment—the presence of the element barium. They attribute it to some impurity in the material or some mistake on their part.

Lise Meitner is forced to leave Germany. On the train going to the frontier, she is snubbed and pushed around by arrogant Nazi brown-shirts; the Nazi State has damned her on three counts: the old are useless, women are useless, Jews are useless. She sits alone in a corner of the train, her mind intent on the inexplicable experiment; she makes calculations on a piece of paper. A solution occurs to her suddenly; it is a stunning solution—but she must keep quiet about it. At the frontier, Nazis search her luggage: they take from her an old camera, a typewriter, and other such physical objects; nothing of value to the State, they declare, can be taken out of Germany. We see a close-up of Lise Meitner—the broad forehead, the intelligent eyes. What she is taking out is in her mind.

In Denmark, Lise Meitner explains her solution—that the uranium atom was actually split in half—to Dr. Otto Frisch, another refugee scientist. Together, they communicate the discovery to Niels Bohr. Realizing its tremendous importance, Bohr sails for the United States.

Bohr informs Einstein, Fermi, and other scientists in the United States. The experiment is repeated at Columbia—and [there is] a tremendous release of energy, as predicted by Einstein's formula.

*January, 1939.* Bohr and Fermi attend a conference on theoretical physics in Washington. Their report creates a sensation among the scientists. Fermi suggests to some of his colleagues the possibility of a military application of the new discovery.

*March, 1939.* Fermi and Pegram approach representatives of the Navy Department with the suggestion of an atomic bomb.

*October, 1939.* Fermi and his friends enlist the help of Einstein and Alexander Sachs to approach Roosevelt. Sachs obtains an interview with Roosevelt, reads excerpts from Einstein's letter. Roosevelt forms first "Advisory Committee on Uranium."

*November, 1939.* The committee reports; Roosevelt approves first purchase of materials—for $6,000.

*Summer of 1940* (after the fall of France). Einstein gets first news from the underground that Germany is doing some work on atomic research. Sachs urges more effort—by contacts with Roosevelt. The "National Defense Research Committee" is formed, with Dr. Vannevar Bush in charge. Bush makes contracts for uranium research with many University laboratories. He finds Labine and has him reopen his mines, closed by the war, to get uranium ore.

Parallel scenes in Germany, showing the Nazi method: slave labor operating the uranium mines in Czechoslovakia. A department of the Kaiser Wilhelm Institute in Berlin is ordered to work on atomic research; the top scientists are kicked out and a good Nazi put in charge.

*Spring, 1941.* University laboratories report progress—the possibility of isolating U-235 and of producing plutonium.

*November, 1941* (just before Pearl Harbor). The government approves $300,000 in contracts. Dr. Conant is put in charge, under Dr. Bush. An American mission (Pegram and Harold Urey) is sent to England to confer with British scientists.

*December, 1941* (after Pearl Harbor). Roosevelt tells Dr. Bush to go ahead, he will provide any funds needed. It is decided that British scientists will join in the work in the United States. The project now becomes secret.

---

*1942.* John X goes to war—he is assigned to military intelligence and sent to Europe.

*Summer, 1942.* The Manhattan Project is formed and Gen. Groves is put in charge. (Scenes of Gen. Groves' nomination for the post as he described them to us.)

Prof. Lawrence solves problem of the electromagnetic method of separating U-235. (I believe this is the experiment described by Beatty, with the pinpoint of light and Gen. Groves called to observe it. If chronologically correct, we use this scene here.)

*December, 1942.* Fermi succeeds in producing a [nuclear fission] chain reaction in a basement of the University of Chicago.

*Parallel scenes:* Vain attempts by German scientists to produce a chain reaction. (They made thirteen attempts—without success.)

---

*1943.* Gen Groves, in his role of "salesman," arranges the first industrial contracts to build Oak Ridge. Construction begins on February 2, 1943.

*Parallel scenes:* The Germans in charge of the heavy water plant in

Norway. We show the methods of terror, expropriation and slave labor. Even though this plant was based on the discovery of an American (Urey) and built by Norwegian industrialists, the Nazis believe they can run it successfully through sheer force. Their attitude is, in effect: "You fools do the work, then we'll take it over by force, because force is all that counts."

*February 28, 1943.* The Norwegian plant is blown up—under the leadership of two Norwegian scientists, formerly of this plant.

(If this is technically and historically possible, I would like to have John X connected with this explosion and wounded in subsequent action.)

*Spring of 1943.* John X, who has been wounded in action and sent back to the United States, recovers and is summoned to the office of his chief. Under the impact of his war experiences, the boy is now a wreck spiritually; he is embittered, disillusioned and firmly convinced that his father was right: nothing matters in the world but brute force. His chief informs him that he will be entrusted with an assignment of extraordinary responsibility: he is to serve as bodyguard to one of the most valuable men on earth. "Who?" asks the boy. "A professor of physics," is the answer. The boy feels contempt for his assignment—he thinks he is being thrown into the discard because of his wound. Scientists, he remarks bitterly, live in ivory towers; of what importance are they? "You'll find out," says the chief.

That evening, John X meets the man he is to guard—Dr. Oppenheimer.

Oppenheimer has been placed in charge of the planned Los Alamos laboratory. Together, he and the boy drive to Los Alamos—over the desert and the mud roads—to the future site where there is nothing but an old school-building now. The attitude of the scientist and the bodyguard is one of hidden mutual antagonism. The scientist resents the necessity of being watched. The boy is skeptical about the scientist's work and importance.

It is from this that the drama of their relationship will come: the gradual understanding—the boy's growing admiration for the scientist—the boy's final regeneration and return to spiritual values, as he sees them exemplified in the work at Los Alamos.

The exact sequence of incidents we'll use to illustrate the next two years (1943–1945) cannot be decided upon until all the research material is in. I should like to use as many real incidents as possible—and invent episodes only where no factual information is available, to illustrate the general trend and progress of the work.

Some key spots, which we have and will use, are:

Incidents illustrating the activities of Oppenheimer and Groves: Oppenheimer persuading scientists to come and work at Los Alamos, overcoming their objections to "the project's bad name"; Groves "selling" industrialists on undertaking dangerous and almost impossible contracts.

*Parallel scenes:* In Denmark, the Nazis try to persuade Bohr to work for them. He refuses. Why should they need him? Didn't they say that an individual is of no importance, only the race matters? They threaten him. He asks them contemptuously: "How are you going to force a mind? How are you going to tear out of it an idea not yet born? You have destroyed millions of human brains. Can you make one single brain work? You wish me to produce for you something you can't produce—yet you consider yourselves the masters of the world. Isn't there, perhaps, an error in your theories? One single crucial error?" The Nazis are stopped—they cannot kill him, he is too valuable. [*Note the similarity to the scene in* Atlas Shrugged *when Galt is tortured.*] They threaten to torture his son. The underground arranges the escape of Bohr and his son—first by boat to Sweden, then by plane to England. Here we have the incident of Bohr's head being too large for an oxygen mask—and the great scientist arriving in England barely alive.

Scene of Bohr's arrival at Los Alamos (as described by Dr. Oppenheimer)—dinner in the stone kitchen of the schoolhouse—the walk through the snow, talking of their problems.

*Late in 1943.* Oppenheimer needs 190 of the finest precision-tool makers. We show the recruiting of these workers—and the scene of the old man, with sons in the Army, who abandons a better job for the hardships of living and working at Los Alamos. In connection with this, we show a scene where John X asks angrily why so much fuss is made about getting these workers, why aren't they just drafted and forced to come here, since they're needed so badly for such an important job? Oppenheimer smiles and explains to him that the precision work needed is so fine a human breath can ruin it. Can you make a man do that kind of work by force?

*Parallel scene:* A German laboratory where a worker ruins a delicate, valuable piece of equipment. The Gestapo agents are stumped: was it an accident or sabotage? Neither they nor we will ever know.

Incidents to illustrate the magnificent sentence Dr. Oppenheimer said to us: *"No one ever gave an order at Los Alamos."*

Scientists given a choice of problems and allowed complete freedom to work out the solutions as they wished. Men doing difficult and unpleasant work "only because they understood the necessity" (Oppenheimer). "We used reasons instead of authority" (Oppenheimer).

Scene of Gen. Groves getting the heads of the DuPont Company to accept a difficult undertaking. (I presume this was the construction of Hanford.) The DuPont board of directors meeting, with the thirty papers face down on the table. The Chairman speaks, explaining the great importance and secrecy of the undertaking. "Those who wish to know what it is may turn their papers over." The board accepts [the contract]—and not one paper is turned over.

---

*1944.* Scenes of the construction and the work at Oak Ridge, Hanford, and Los Alamos. Here scientific incidents will have to be integrated, whenever possible, with the human elements of pioneer living conditions and the "melodrama" elements of secrecy, guards, etc. I want to have as many concrete, specific scenes as possible—and reduce the use of an impersonal montage to a minimum, in order to avoid a newsreel effect. Here John X will serve as a legitimate connecting link between the laboratory, the living conditions, and the "secrecy" aspects of the story. He is both a participant and an observer—and the fact that he is a skeptical, slightly hostile observer will help to give conflict, drama and meaning to the incidents.

*A few highlights of December, 1944:*

The Japanese balloon that landed on a Hanford power line.

The Nobel Prize dinner in honor of Dr. Rabi—the prize being given for his work in atomic science, much to the discomfort of those in charge of keeping that subject and Dr. Rabi's connection with it secret.

The telephone call to Dr. Oppenheimer at Los Alamos; he comes back into the room smiling happily. His fellow-scientists think he has received some good news about their work, but the news he received is about the birth of his daughter.

Incident of the scientist whose little son asked him for an atomic bomb for Christmas.

---

*1945.* Some time early in the year, Dr. Oppenheimer decides that they will be ready to start on the actual construction of the bomb by February 28, 1945. It is he who then proceeds to correlate the enormous amount of knowledge and information gathered in two years of experiments. By February 25th, it looks as if they are as far from the solution as ever. But by February 28th, they do have what they wanted—and the actual manufacture of the bomb can begin.

It is early in 1945 that material from Oak Ridge and Hanford (U-235 and Plutonium) begins to arrive at Los Alamos. This material—after the tremendous amount of work at the two giant factories—arrives in small bottles, under heavy guard.

*Spring, 1945.* Truman is told the secret of the atomic project right after his inauguration.

Some time in June (or earlier), the bombs are shipped to San Francisco. Incident of yard master who refuses the bomb car priority and sends torpedoes first.

*Late June, 1945.* Test of tower in New Mexico desert with small ordinary bomb. Lightning strikes tower and explodes the bomb. Better insulation has to be made.

*July 12, 1945.* The atomic bomb, unassembled, is taken to site of test. The next few days—as described in official reports.

*July 16, 1945.* The test explosion—as described in official reports.

Same day—the *Indianapolis* sails from San Francisco for Guam.

Scene where Truman decides that bomb will be used—to save American lives (as described by Truman).

*August 5, 1945.* On Tinian. Word comes that the first bomb mission is on. Capt. William Parsons, designer of the bomb, supervises its assembling. From Los Alamos, Oppenheimer keeps in touch with Tinian, by teletype.

*August 6, 1945.* The take-off of the plane—as described in official reports.

The bombing of Hiroshima.

That day (Sunday) at Los Alamos: Oppenheimer waits for word of results, spends day in normal activities, hiding suspense. Next morning—he gets phone call that everything is all right.

Scene where Mrs. Groves is asked to listen to radio—and discovers she is "married to Flash Gordon."

Tuesday night—colloquium of 800 scientists at Los Alamos. Terrific applause when Oppenheimer enters and makes report.

Night. Oppenheimer and John X walk in the hills around Los Alamos. Oppenheimer tells him that the achievement was not an accident—only free men in voluntary cooperation could have done it—so long as they're free, men do not have to fear those who preach slavery and violence—because the mind is man's only real weapon, and the mind will always win against brute force. The boy is looking at the stars—just as his father did 26 years ago. But his face is shining with pride, courage, self-confidence. Now man does not look like a worm in the face of the immensity of the universe—his figure looks heroic, that of a conqueror. The boy's last line is: *"Man can harness the universe—but nobody can harness man."*

# 10

# COMMUNISM AND HUAC

*This chapter begins with an open letter addressed "To All Innocent Fifth Columnists," which AR wrote in late 1940 or early 1941, when she was encouraging conservative intellectuals to form a national organization advocating individualism. I believe she wanted the letter to be issued by such an organization.*

*The rest of the material dates from 1947 and deals with Communist propaganda in the movies: it includes AR's testimony before the House Un-American Activities Committee (HUAC), as well as her notes to herself on whether HUAC had violated the civil rights of Communists.*

**circa 1940**

### To All Innocent Fifth Columnists

You who read this represent the greatest danger to America.

No matter what the outcome of the war in Europe may be, Totalitarianism has already won a complete victory in many American minds and conquered all of our intellectual life. You have helped it to win.

Perhaps it is your right to destroy civilization and bring dictatorship to America, but not unless you understand fully what you are doing.

If that is what you want to do, say so openly, at least to your own conscience, and we who believe in freedom will fight you openly.

But the tragedy of today is that you—who are responsible for the coming Totalitarian dictatorship of America—you do not know your own responsibility. You would be the first to deny the active part you're playing and proclaim your belief in freedom, in civilization, in the American way of life. You are the most dangerous kind of Fifth Columnist—an innocent, subconscious Fifth Columnist. Of such as you is the Kingdom of Hitler and of Stalin.

You do not believe this? Check up on yourself. Take the test we offer you here.

**1)** Are you the kind who considers ten minutes of his time too valuable to read this and give it some thought?

**2)** Are you the kind who sits at home and moans over the state of the world—but does nothing about it?

**3)** Are you the kind who says that the future is predestined by something or other, something he can't quite name or explain and isn't very clear about, but the world is doomed to dictatorship and there's nothing anyone can do about it?

**4)** Are you the kind who says that he wishes he could do something, he'd be so eager to do something—but what can one man do?

**5)** Are you the kind who are so devoted to your own career, your family, your home or your children that you will let the most unspeakable horrors be brought about to destroy your career, your family, your home and your children—because you are too busy now to prevent them?

Which one of the above *are* you? A little of all?

But are you really too busy to think?

Who "determines" the future? You're very muddled on that, aren't you? What exactly is "mankind"? Is it a mystical entity with a will of its own? Or is it you, and I, and the sum of all of us together? What force is there to make history—except men, other men just like you? If there are enough men who believe in a better future and are willing to work for it, the future will be what they want it to be. You doubt this? Why then, if the world is doomed to dictatorship, do the dictators spend so much money and effort on propaganda? If history is predestined in their favor, why don't Hitler and Stalin just ride the wave into the future without any trouble? Doesn't it seem more probable that history will be what the minds of men want it to be, and the dictators are smart enough to prepare these minds in the way they want them, while we talk of destiny and do nothing?

You say, what can one man do? When the Communists came to power in Russia, they were a handful of *eighteen* men. Just *eighteen*. In a country of [170,000,000] population. They were laughed at and no one took them seriously. According to their own prophet, Karl Marx, Russia was the last country in which Communism could be historically possible, because of

Russia's backwardness in industrial development. Yet they succeeded. Because they knew what they wanted and went after it—historical destiny or no historical destiny. Adolf Hitler started the Nazi Party in Germany with *seven* men. He was laughed at and considered a harmless crank. People said that after the Versailles Treaty Germany could not possibly become a world power again, not for centuries. Yet Hitler succeeded. Because he knew what he wanted and went after it—history or no history. Shall we believe in mystical fates or do something about the future?

If you are one of those who have had a full, busy, successful life and are still hard at work making money—stop for one minute of thought. What are you working for? You have enough to keep you in comfort for the rest of your days. But you are working to insure your children's future. Well, *what* are you leaving to your children? The money, home or education you plan to leave them will be worthless or taken away from them. Instead, your legacy will be a Totalitarian America, a world of slavery, of starvation, of concentration camps and of firing squads. The best part of *your* life is behind you—and it was lived in freedom. But your children will have nothing to face save their existence as slaves. Is *that* what you want for them? If not, it is still up to you. There is time left to abort it—but not very much time. You take out insurance to protect your children, don't you? How much money and working effort does that insurance cost you? If you put *one-tenth* of the money and time into insuring against your children's future slavery—you would save them and save for them everything else which you intend to leave them and which they'll never get otherwise.

Don't delude yourself by minimizing the danger. You see what is going on in Europe and what it's doing to our own country and to your own private life. What other proof do you need? Don't say smugly that "it can't happen here." Stop and look back for a moment.

The first Totalitarian dictatorship happened in Russia. People said: well, Russia was a dark, backward, primitive nation where anything could happen—but it could not happen in any civilized country.

The next Totalitarian dictatorship happened in Italy—one of the oldest civilized countries of Europe and the mother of European culture. People said: well, the Italians hadn't had much experience in democratic self-government, but it couldn't happen anywhere else.

The next Totalitarian dictatorship happened in Germany—the country of philosophers and scientists, with a long record of the highest cultural achievements. People said: well, Germany was accustomed to autocracy, and besides there's the Prussian character, and the last war, etc.—but it could not happen in any country with a strong democratic tradition.

Could it happen in France? People would have laughed at you had you asked such a question a year ago. Well, *it has happened in France*—France, the mother of freedom and of democracy, France, the most independent-minded nation on earth.

**Well?**

What price your smug self-confidence? In the face of the millions of foreign money and foreign agents pouring into our country, in the face of one step after another by which our country is [moving] closer to Totalitarianism—you do nothing except say: "It can't happen here." Do you hear the Totalitarians answering you—"Oh, yeah?"

Don't delude yourself with slogans and meaningless historical generalizations. It *can* happen here. It can happen anywhere. And a country's past history has nothing to do with it. Totalitarianism is not a new product of historical evolution. It is older than history. It is the attempt of the worthless and the criminal to seize control of society. That element is always there, in any country. But a healthy society gives it no chance. It is when the majority in a country becomes weak, indifferent and confused that a criminal minority, beautifully organized like all gangs, seizes the power. And once that power is seized it cannot be taken back for generations. Fantastic as it may seem to think of a dictatorship in the United States, it is much easier to establish such a dictatorship than to overthrow it. With modern technique and modern weapons at its disposal, a ruthless minority can hold millions in slavery indefinitely. What can one thousand unorganized, unarmed men do against one man with a machine gun?

And the tragedy of today is that by remaining unorganized and mentally unarmed we are helping to bring that slavery upon ourselves. By being indifferent and confused, we are serving as innocent Fifth Columnists of our own destruction.

*There is no personal neutrality in the world today.*

Repeat that and scream that to yourself. In all great issues there are only two sides—and no middle. You are alive or you are dead, but you can't be "neither" or "in between." You are honest or you are not—and there is no neutral "half-honest." And so, you are against Totalitarianism—or you are for it. There is no intellectual neutrality.

*The Totalitarians do not want your active support.* They do not need it. They have their small, compact, well-organized minority and it is sufficient to carry out their aims. All they want from you is your *indifference.* The Communists and the Nazis have stated repeatedly that the indifference of the majority is their best ally. Just sit at home, pursue your private affairs, shrug about world problems—and you are the most effective Fifth Columnist that can be devised. You're doing your part as well as if you took orders consciously from Hitler or from Stalin. And so, you're in it, whether you want to be or not, you're helping the world towards destruction, while moaning and wondering what makes the world such as it is today. *You do.*

The Totalitarians have said: "Who is not against us, is for us." *There is no personal neutrality.*

And since you are involved, and have to be, what do you prefer? To do what you're doing and help the Totalitarians? Or to fight them?

But in order to fight, you must understand. You must know exactly what you believe and you must hold to your faith honestly, consistently and *all the time*. A faith assumed occasionally, like Sunday clothes, is of no value. Communism and Nazism are a faith. Yours must be as strong and clear as theirs. They know what they want. We don't. But let us see now, before it is too late, whether we have a faith, what it is and how we can fight for it.

First and above all: what is Totalitarianism? We all hear so much about it, but we don't understand it. What is the most important point, the base, the whole heart of both Communism and Nazism? It is not the "dictatorship of the proletariat," nor the nationalization of private property, nor the supremacy of the "Aryan" race, nor anti-Semitism. These things are secondary symptoms, surface details, the effects and not the cause. What is the primary cause, common to both Soviet Russia and Nazi Germany, and all other dictators, past, present and future? One idea—and one only: *That the State is superior to the individual.* That the Collective holds all rights and the individual has none.

Stop here. This is the crucial point. What you think of this will determine whether you are a mental Fifth Columnist or not. *This* is the point which allows no compromise. You must choose one or the other. There is no middle. Either you believe that each individual man has value, dignity and certain inalienable rights which cannot be sacrificed for any cause, for any purpose, for any collective, for any number of other men whatsoever. Or else you believe that a number of men—it doesn't matter what you call it: a collective, a class, a race or a State—hold all rights, and any individual man can be sacrificed if some collective good—it doesn't matter what you call it: better distribution of wealth, racial purity or the Millennium—demands it. Don't fool yourself. Be honest about this. Names don't matter. Only the basic principle matters, and there is no middle choice. Either each man has individual, inalienable rights—or he hasn't.

Your intentions don't count. If you are willing to believe that men should be deprived of *all* rights for a *good* cause—you are a Totalitarian. Don't forget, Stalin and Hitler sincerely believe that their causes are *good*. Stalin thinks that he is helping the downtrodden, and Hitler thinks that he is serving his country as a patriot. They are good causes, both of them, aren't they? Then what creates the horrors of Russia and of Germany? What is destroying all civilization? Just this one idea—that to a good cause *everything* can be sacrificed; that individual men have no rights which must be respected; that what one person believes to be good can be put over on the others *by force*.

And if you—in the privacy of your own mind—believe so strongly in some particular *good* of yours that you would be willing to deprive men of all rights for the sake of this good, then you are as guilty of all the horrors of today as Hitler and Stalin. These horrors are made possible *only* by men who have lost all respect for single, individual human beings, who accept the idea that classes, races and nations matter, but single persons do not, that a majority is sacred, but a minority is dirt, that herds count, but Man is nothing.

Where do you stand on this? There is no middle ground.

If you accept the Totalitarian idea, if the words "State" or "Collective" are sacred to you, but the word "Individual" is not—stop right here. You don't have to read further. What we have to say is not for you—and you are not for us. Let's part here—but be honest, admit that you are a Totalitarian and go join the Communist Party or the German-American Bund, because *they* are the logical end of the road you have chosen, and you will end up with one or the other, whether you know it now or not.

But if you are a Humanitarian and a Liberal—in the real, not the prostituted sense of these words—you will say with us that Man, each *single, solitary, individual Man*, has a sacred value which you respect, and sacred, inalienable rights which **nothing** must take away from him.

You believe this? You agree with us that *this* is the heart of true Americanism, the basic principle upon which America was founded and which made it great—the Rights of Man and the Freedom of Man? But do you hear many voices saying this today?

Do you read many books saying this? Do you see many prominent men preaching this? Do you know a single publication devoted to this belief or a single organization representing it? You do not. Instead, you find a flood of words, of books, of preachers, publications, and organizations which, under very clever "Fronts," work tirelessly to sell you Totalitarianism. All of them are camouflaged under very appealing slogans: they scream to you that they are defenders of "Democracy," of "Americanism," of "Civil Liberties," etc. Everybody and anybody uses these words—and they have no meaning left. They are empty generalities and boob-catchers. There is only one real test that you can apply to all these organizations: ask yourself *what is the actual result of their work under the glittering bromides*? What are they really selling you, what are they driving at? If you ask this, you will see that they are selling you Collectivism in one form or another.

They preach "Democracy" and then make a little addition—"*Economic* Democracy" or a "*Broader* Democracy" or a "*True* Democracy," and demand that we turn all property over to the Government; "all property" means also "all rights"; let everybody hold all rights together—and nobody have any right of any kind individually. Is *that* Democracy or is it Totalitarianism? You know of a prominent woman commentator who wants us all to die for Democracy—and then defines *"true"* Democracy as State Socialism [*probably a reference to Dorothy Thompson*]. You have heard Secretary [Harold] Ickes define a *"true"* freedom of the press as the freedom to express the views of the majority. You have read in a highly respectable national monthly the claim that the Bill of Rights, as taught in our schools, is "selfish"; that a *"true"* Bill of Rights means not demanding any rights for *yourself*, but your giving these rights to *"others."* God help us, fellow-Americans, are we blind? Do you see what this means? Do you see the implications?

And this is the picture wherever you look. They "oppose" Totalitarianism and they "defend" Democracy—by preaching their own version of Totalitarianism, some form of "collective good," "collective rights," "collective will," etc. And the one thing which is never said, never preached, never upheld in our public life, the one thing all these "defenders of Democracy" hate, denounce and tear down subtly, gradually, systematically—is the principle of *Individual Rights, Individual Freedom, Individual Value. That* is the principle against which the present great world conspiracy is directed. *That* is the heart of the whole world question. *That* is the only opposite of Totalitarianism and our only defense against it. Drop *that*—and what difference will it make what name you give to the resulting society? It will be Totalitarianism—and all Totalitarianisms are alike, all come to the same methods, the same slavery, the same bloodshed, the same horrors, no matter what noble slogan they start under, as witness Soviet Russia and Nazi Germany.

Principles are much more consistent than men. A basic principle, once accepted, has a way of working itself out to its logical conclusion—even against the will and to the great surprise of those who accepted it. Just accept the idea that there are *no* inalienable individual rights—and firing squads, executions without trial, and a Gestapo or a G.P.U. will follow automatically—*no matter who holds the power, no matter how noble and benevolent his intentions. That* is a law of history. You can find any number of examples. Can you name one [counter-example]? Can you name one instance where absolute power—in any hands—did not end in absolute horror? And—for God's sake, fellow-Americans, let's not be utter morons, let's give our intelligence a small chance to function and let's recognize the obvious—*what* is absolute power? It's a power which holds all rights and has to respect none. Does it matter whether such a power is held by a self-appointed dictator or by an elected representative body? The power is the same and its results will be the same. Look through all of history. Look at Europe. Don't forget, they still hold "elections" in Europe. Don't forget, Hitler was *elected*.

Now, if you see how completely intellectual Totalitarianism is already in control of our country, if you see that there is no action and no organization to defend the only true anti-Totalitarian principle, the principle of *individual rights*, you will realize that there is only one thing for us to do: to take such action and to form such an organization. If you are really opposed to Totalitarianism, to all of it, in any shape, form or color—you will join us. We propose to unite all men of good will who believe that Freedom is our most precious possession, that it is greater than any other consideration whatsoever, that no good has ever been accomplished by force, that Freedom must not be sacrificed to any other ideal, and that *Freedom is an individual, not a collective entity*.

We do not know how many of us there are left in the world. But we think there are many more than the Totalitarians suspect. We are the majority, but we are scattered, unorganized, silenced and helpless. The Totalitarians are an efficient, organized and very noisy minority. They have seized key positions in our intellectual life and they make it appear as if they are the voice of America. They can, if left unchecked, highjack America into dictatorship. Are we going to let them get away with it? They are not the voice of America. We are. But let us be heard.

To be heard, however, we must be organized. This is not a paradox. Individualists have always been reluctant to form any sort of organization. The best, the most independent, the hardest working, the most productive members of society have always lived and worked alone. But the incompetent and the unscrupulous have organized. The world today shows how well they have organized. And so, we shall attempt what has never been attempted before—*an organization against organization*. That is—an organization to defend us all from the coming compulsory organization which will swallow all of society; an organization to defend our rights, including the right not to belong to any forced organization; an organization, not to impose our ideology upon anyone, but to prevent anyone from imposing his ideology upon us by physical or social violence.

*Are you with us?*

If you realize that the world is moving toward disaster, but see no effective force to avert it—

If you are eager to join in a great cause and accept a great faith, but find no such cause or faith offered to you anywhere today—

If you are not one of those doomed jellyfish to whom the word "Freedom" means nothing—

If you cannot conceive of yourself living in a society without personal freedom, a society in which you will be told what to do, what to think, what to feel, in which your very life will be only a gift from the Collective, to be revoked at its pleasure at any time—

If you cannot conceive of yourself surrendering your freedom for any collective good whatsoever, and do not believe that any such good can ever be accomplished by such a surrender—

If you believe in your own dignity and your own value, and hold that such a belief is not "selfish," but is instead your greatest virtue, without which you are worthless both to your fellow-men and to yourself—

If you believe that it is vicious to demand that you should exist solely for the sake of your fellow-men and grant them all and any right over you—

If you believe that it is vicious to demand everyone's sacrifice for everyone else's sake, and that such a demand creates nothing but mutual victims, without profiting anyone, neither society nor the individual—

If you believe that men can tell you what you must *not* do to them, but can *never* assume the arrogance of telling you what you *must* do, no matter what their number—

If you believe in majority rule *only* with protection for minority rights, both being limited by *inalienable* individual rights—

If you believe that the mere mention of "the good of the majority" is not sufficient ground to justify any possible kind of horror, and that those yelling loudest of "majority good" are not necessarily the friends of mankind—

If you are sick of professional "liberals," "humanitarians," "uplifters" and "idealists" who would do you good as *they* see it, even if it kills you, whose idea of world benevolence is world slavery—

If you are sick, disgusted, disheartened, without faith, without direction, and have lost everything but your courage—

—**come and join us**.

There is so much at stake—and so little time left.

Let us have an organization as strong, as sure, as enthusiastic as any the Totalitarians could hope to achieve. Let us follow *our* faith as consistently as they follow theirs. Let us offer the world *our* philosophy of life. Let us expose all Totalitarian propaganda in any medium and in any form. Let us answer every argument, every promise, every "Party Line" of the Totalitarians. Let us drop all compromise, all cooperation or collaboration with those preaching any brand of Totalitarianism in letter or in spirit, in name or in fact. Let us have nothing to do with "Front" organizations, "Front" agents or "Front" ideas. We do not have to proscribe them by law. We can put them out of existence by social boycott. But this means—no compromise. There is no compromise between life and death. You do not make deals with the black plague. Let us touch nothing tainted with Totalitarianism. Let us tear down the masks, bring them out into the open and—leave them alone. Very strictly alone. No "pro-Soviet" or "pro-Nazi" members of the board in our organization. No "benevolent" Trojan horses. Let us stick together as they do. They silence us, they force us out of public life, they fill key positions with their own men. Let us stick together—and they will be helpless to continue. They have millions of foreign money on their side. We have the truth.

As a first step and a first declaration of what we stand for, we offer you the following principles:

We believe in the value, the dignity and the freedom of Man.

We believe:

—That each man has inalienable rights which cannot be taken from him for any cause whatsoever. These rights are life, liberty, and the pursuit of happiness.

—That the right of life means that man cannot be deprived of his life for the convenience of any number of other men.

—That the right of liberty means freedom of individual decision, individual choice, individual judgment and individual initiative; it means also the right to disagree with others.

—That the right to the pursuit of happiness means man's freedom to choose what constitutes his own private, personal happiness and to work for its achievement; that such a pursuit is neither evil nor reprehensible, but honorable and good; and that a man's happiness is not to be prescribed to him by any other man nor by any number of other men.

—That these rights have no meaning unless they are the unconditional, personal, private possession of each man, granted to him by the fact of his birth, held by him independently of all other men, and limited only by the exercise of the same rights by other men.

—That the only just, moral and beneficent form of society is a society based upon the recognition of these inalienable individual rights.

—That the State exists for Man, and not Man for the State.

—That the greatest good for all men can be achieved only through the voluntary cooperation of free individuals for mutual benefit, and not through a compulsory sacrifice of all for all.

—That "voluntary" presupposes an alternative and a choice of opportunities; and thus even a universal agreement of all men on one course of action is neither free nor voluntary if no other course of action is open to them.

—That each man's independence of spirit and other men's respect for it have created all civilization, all culture, all human progress and have bene-fited all mankind.

—That the greatest threat to civilization is the spread of Collectivism, which demands the sacrifice of all individual rights to collective rights and the supremacy of the State over the individual.

—That the general good which such Collectivism professes as its objective can never be achieved at the sacrifice of man's freedom, and such sacrifice can lead only to general suffering, stagnation and degeneration.

—That such conception of Collectivism is the greatest possible evil—under any name, in any form, for any professed purpose whatsoever.

Such is our definition of Americanism and the American way of life.

The American way of life has always been based upon the Rights of Man, upon individual freedom and upon respect for each individual human personality. Through all its history, this has been the source of America's greatness. This is the spirit of America which we dedicate ourselves to defend and preserve.

In practical policy we shall be guided by one basic formula: of every law and of every conception we shall demand the maximum freedom for the individual and the minimum power for the government necessary to achieve any given social objective.

If you believe this, join us. If you don't—fight us. Either is your privi-lege, but the only truly immoral act you can commit is to agree with us, to realize that we are right—and then to forget it and do nothing.

There is some excuse, little as it may be, for an open, honest Fifth Columnist. There is none for an innocent, passive, subconscious one. Of all the things we have said here to you, we wish to be wrong on only one—our first sentence. Prove us wrong on that. Join us.

The world is a beautiful place and worth fighting for. But not without Freedom.

**1947**

[*AR wrote the following article for the Motion Picture Alliance for the Preservation of American Ideals. It was published in the November 1947 issue of* Plain Talk, *a conservative political magazine.*]

## Screen Guide for Americans

The influence of Communists in Hollywood is due, not to their own power, but to the unthinking carelessness of those who profess to oppose them. Some dangerous Red propaganda has been put over in films produced by innocent men, often by loyal Americans who deplore the spread of Communism throughout the world and wonder why it is spreading.

If you wish to protect your pictures from being used for Communistic purposes, the first thing to do is to drop the delusion that political propaganda consists of political slogans.

Politics is not a separate field in itself. Political ideas do not come out of thin air. They are the result of the *moral premises* which men have accepted. Whatever people believe to be the good, right and proper human actions—*that* will determine their political opinions. If men believe that every independent action is vicious, they will vote for every measure to control human beings and to suppress human freedom. If men believe that the American system is unjust, they will support those who wish to destroy it.

The purpose of the Communists in Hollywood is *not* the production of political movies openly advocating Communism. Their purpose is *to corrupt non-political movies*—by introducing small, casual bits of propaganda into innocent stories—and to make people absorb the basic premises of Collectivism *by indirection and implication*.

Few people would take Communism straight. But a constant stream of hints, lines, touches, and suggestions battering the public from the screen will act like the drops of water that split a rock if continued long enough. The rock they are trying to split is Americanism.

We present below a list of the more common devices used to turn non-political pictures into carriers of political propaganda. It is a guide for all those who do not wish to help advance the cause of Communism.

It is intended as a guide, and not as a forced restriction upon anyone. We are unalterably opposed to any political "industry code," to any group agreement or any manner of forbidding any political opinion to anyone by any form of collective force or pressure. There can be no "group insurance" in the field of ideas. Each man has to do his own thinking. We merely offer this list to the independent judgment and for the voluntary action of every honest man in the motion picture industry.

## 1. Don't Take Politics Lightly.

*Don't* fool yourself by saying, "I'm not interested in politics," and then pretending that politics do not exist.

We are living in an age when politics is the most burning question in everybody's mind. The whole world is torn by a great political issue—freedom or slavery, which means Americanism or Totalitarianism. Half the world is in ruins after a war fought over political ideas. To pretend at such a time that political ideas are not important and that people pay no attention to them is worse than irresponsible.

It is the avowed purpose of the Communists to insert propaganda into movies. Therefore, there are only two possible courses of action open to you, if you want to keep your pictures clean of subversive propaganda:

**1.** If you have no time or inclination to study political ideas—then do not hire Reds to work on your pictures.
**2.** If you wish to employ Reds, but intend to keep their politics out of your movies—then study political ideas and learn how to recognize propaganda when you see it.

But to hire Communists on the theory that "they won't put over any politics on me" and then remain ignorant and indifferent to the subject of politics, while the Reds are trained propaganda experts—is an attitude for which there can be no excuse.

## 2. **Don't Smear the Free Enterprise System.**

*Don't* pretend that Americanism and the Free Enterprise System are two things. They are inseparable, like body and soul. The basic principle of inalienable individual rights, which is Americanism, can be translated into practical reality *only* in the form of the economic system of Free Enterprise. That was the system established by the American Constitution, the system which made America the best and greatest country on earth. You may preach any other form of economics, if you wish. But if you do so, don't pretend that you are preaching Americanism.

*Don't* pretend that you are upholding the Free Enterprise System in some vague, general, undefined way, while preaching the specific ideas that oppose and destroy it.

*Don't* attack individual rights, individual freedom, private action, private initiative, and private property. These things are essential parts of the Free Enterprise System, without which it cannot exist.

*Don't* preach the superiority of public ownership as such over private ownership. *Don't* preach or imply that all publicly owned projects are noble, humanitarian undertakings by grace of the mere fact that they are publicly owned—while preaching, at the same time, that private property or the defense of private property rights is the expression of some sort of vicious greed, of anti-social selfishness or evil.

### 3. **Don't Smear Industrialists.**

Don't spit into your own face or, worse, pay miserable little rats to do it.

You, as a motion picture producer, are an industrialist. All of us are employees of an industry that gives us a good living. There is an old fable about a pig who filled his belly with acorns, then started digging to undermine the roots of the oak from which the acorns came. Don't let's allow that pig to become our symbol.

Throughout American history, the best of American industrialists were men who embodied the highest virtues: productive genius, energy, initiative, independence, courage. Socially (if "social significance" interests you) they were among the greatest of all benefactors, because it is they who created the opportunities for achieving the unprecedented material wealth of the industrial age.

In our own day, all around us, there are countless examples of self-made men who rose from the ranks and achieved great industrial success through their energy, ability and honest productive effort.

Yet all too often industrialists, bankers, and businessmen are presented on the screen as villains, crooks, chiselers or exploiters. One such picture may be taken as non-political or accidental. A constant stream of such pictures becomes pernicious political propaganda: it creates hatred for all businessmen in the mind of the audience, and makes people receptive to the cause of Communism.

While motion pictures have a strict code that forbids us to offend or insult any group or nation—while we dare not present in an unfavorable light the tiniest Balkan kingdom—we permit ourselves to smear and slander American businessmen in the most irresponsibly dishonest manner.

It is true that there are vicious businessmen—just as there are vicious men in any other class or profession. But we have been practicing an outrageous kind of double standard: we do not attack individual representatives of any other group, class or nation, in order not to imply attack on the whole group; yet when we present individual businessmen as monsters, we claim that no reflection on the whole class of businessmen was intended.

It's got to be one or the other. This sort of double standard can deceive nobody and can serve nobody's purpose except that of the Communists.

It is the *moral*—(no, not just political, but *moral*)—duty of every decent man in the motion picture industry to throw into the ashcan, where it belongs, every story that smears industrialists as such.

## 4. **Don't Smear Wealth.**

In a free society—such as America—wealth is achieved through production, and through the voluntary exchange of one's goods or services. You cannot hold production as evil—nor can you hold as evil a man's right to keep the result of his own effort.

Only savages and Communists get rich by force—that is, by looting the property of others. It is a basic American principle that each man is free to work for his own benefit and to go as far as his ability will carry him; and that his property is his—whether he has made one dollar or one million dollars.

If the villain in your story happens to be rich—*don't* permit lines of dialogue suggesting that he is the typical representative of a whole social class, the symbol of all the rich. Keep it clear in your mind *and in your script* that his villainy is due to his own personal character—not to his wealth or class.

If you do not see the difference between wealth honestly produced and wealth looted—you are preaching the ideas of Communism. You are implying that all property and all human labor should belong to the State. And you are inciting men to crime: if all wealth is evil, no matter how acquired, why should a man bother to earn it? He might as well seize it by robbery or expropriation.

It is the proper wish of every decent American to stand on his own feet, earn his own living, and be as good at it as he can—that is, get as rich as he can by honest exchange.

Stop insulting him and stop defaming his proper ambition. Stop giving him—and yourself—a guilt complex by spreading unthinkingly the slogans of Communism. *Put an end to that pernicious modern hypocrisy: everybody wants to get rich and almost everybody feels that he must apologize for it.*

## 5. **Don't Smear the Profit Motive.**

If you denounce the profit motive, what is it that you wish men to do? Work without reward, like slaves, for the benefit of the State?

An industrialist has to be interested in profit. In a free economy, he can make a profit *only* if he makes a good product which people are willing to buy. What do you want him to do? Should he sell his product at a loss? If so, how long is he to remain in business? And at whose expense?

*Don't* give to your characters—as a sign of villainy, as a damning characteristic—a desire to make money. Nobody wants to, or should, work without payment, and nobody does—except a slave. There is nothing dishonorable about a pursuit of money in a free economy, because money can be earned only by productive effort.

If what you mean, when you denounce it, is a desire to make money dishonestly or immorally—then say so. Make it clear that what you denounce is dishonesty, *not* money-making. Make it clear that you are denouncing evil-doers, *not* capitalists. Don't toss out careless generalities which imply that there is no difference between the two. *That* is what the Communists want you to imply.

### 6. **Don't Smear Success.**

America was made by the idea that personal achievement and personal success are each man's proper and moral goal.

There are many forms of success: spiritual, artistic, industrial, financial. All these forms, in any field of honest endeavor, are good, desirable and admirable. Treat them as such.

*Don't* permit any disparagement or defamation of personal success. It is the Communists' intention to make people think that personal success is somehow achieved at the expense of others and that every successful man has hurt somebody by becoming successful.

It is the Communists' aim to discourage all personal effort and to drive men into a hopeless, dispirited, gray herd of robots who have lost all personal ambition, who are easy to rule, willing to obey and willing to exist in selfless servitude to the State.

America is based on the ideal of man's dignity and self-respect. Dignity and self-respect are impossible without a sense of personal achievement. When you defame success, you defame human dignity.

America is the land of the self-made man. Say so on the screen.

### 7. **Don't Glorify Failure.**

Failure, in itself, is not admirable. And while every man meets with failure somewhere in his life, the admirable thing is his courage in *overcoming it—not* in the fact that he failed.

Failure is no disgrace—but it is certainly no brand of virtue or nobility, either.

It is the Communist's intention to make men accept misery, depravity and degradation as their natural lot in life. This is done by presenting every kind of failure as sympathetic, as a sign of goodness and virtue—while every kind of success is presented as a sign of evil. This implies that only the evil can succeed under our American system—while the good are to be found in the gutter.

*Don't* present all the poor as good and all the rich as evil. In judging a man's character, poverty is no disgrace—but it is no virtue, either; wealth is no virtue—but it is certainly no disgrace.

## 8. **Don't Glorify Depravity.**

*Don't* present sympathetic studies of depravity. Go easy on stories about murders, perverts and all the rest of that sordid stuff. If you use such stories, *don't* place yourself and the audience on the side of the criminal, *don't* create sympathy for him, *don't* give him excuses and justifications, *don't* imply that he "couldn't help it."

If you preach that a depraved person "couldn't help it," you are destroying the basis of all morality. You are implying that men cannot be held responsible for their evil acts, because man has no power to choose between good and evil; if so, then all moral precepts are futile, and men must resign themselves to the idea that they are helpless, irresponsible animals. *Don't* help to spread such an idea.

When you pick these stories for their purely sensational value, you do not realize that you are dealing with one of the most crucial philosophic issues. These stories represent a profoundly insidious attack on all moral principles and all religious precepts. It is a basic tenet of Marxism that man has no freedom of moral or intellectual choice; that he is only a soulless, wit-less collection of meat and glands, open to any sort of "conditioning" by anybody. The Communists intend to become the "conditioners."

There is too much horror and depravity in the world at present. If people see nothing but horror and depravity on the screen, you will merely add to their despair by driving in the impression that nothing better is possible to men or can be expected of life, which is what the Communists want people to think. Communism thrives on despair. Men without hope are easily ruled.

*Don't* excuse depravity. *Don't* drool over weaklings as conditioned "vic-tims of circumstances" (or of "background" or of "society"), who "couldn't help it." You are actually providing an excuse and an alibi for the worst instincts in the weakest members of your audience.

*Don't* tell people that man is a helpless, twisted, drooling, sniveling, neurotic weakling. Show the world an *American* kind of man, for a change.

## 9. **Don't Deify "The Common Man."**

"The common man" is one of the worst slogans of Communism—and too many of us have fallen for it, without thinking.

It is only in Europe—under social caste systems where men are divided into "aristocrats" and "commoners"—that one can talk about defending the "common man." What does the word "common" mean in America?

Under the American system, all men are equal under the law. There-fore, if anyone is classified as "common"—he can be called "common" only in regard to his personal qualities. It then means that he has no outstanding abilities, no outstanding virtues, no outstanding intelligence. Is *that* an object of glorification?

In the Communist doctrine, *it is*. Communism preaches the reign of mediocrity, the destruction of all individuality and all personal distinction, the turning of men into "masses," which means an undivided, undifferentiated, impersonal, average, *common* herd.

In the American doctrine, no man is *common*. Every man's personality is unique—and it is respected as such. He may have qualities which he shares with others; but his virtue is not gauged by how much he resembles others—*that* is the Communist doctrine; his virtue is gauged by his personal distinction, great or small.

In America, no man is scorned or penalized if his ability is small. But neither is he praised, extolled and glorified for the *smallness* of his ability.

America is the land of the *uncommon man*. It is the land where man is free to develop his genius—and to get its just rewards. It is the land where each man tries to develop whatever quality he might possess and to rise to whatever degree he can, great or modest. It is *not* the land where one is taught that one is small and ought to remain small. It is *not* the land where one glories or is taught to glory in one's mediocrity.

No self-respecting man in America is or thinks of himself as "little," no matter how poor he might be. *That,* precisely, is the difference between an American working man and a European serf.

Don't ever use any lines about "the common man" or "the little people." It is not the American idea to be either "common" or "little."

## 10. **Don't Glorify the Collective.**

This point requires your careful and thoughtful attention.

There is a great difference between free cooperation and forced collectivism. It is the difference between the United States and Soviet Russia. But the Communists are very skillful at hiding the difference and selling you the second under the guise of the first. You might miss it. The audience won't.

*Cooperation* is the free association of men who work together by voluntary agreement, each deriving from it his own personal benefit.

*Collectivism* is the forced herding together of men into a group, with the individual having no choice about it, no personal motive, no personal reward, and subordinating himself blindly to the will of others.

Keep this distinction clearly in mind—in order to judge whether what you are asked to glorify is American cooperation or Soviet collectivism.

*Don't* preach that everybody should be and act alike.

*Don't* fall for such drivel as "I don't wanna be dif'rent—I wanna be just like ever'body else." You've heard this one in endless variations. If ever there was an un-American attitude, this is it. America is the country where every man wants to be *different*—and most men succeed at it.

If you preach that it is evil to be different—you teach every particular group of men to hate every other group, every minority, every person, for being different from them; thus you lay the foundation for racial hatred.

Don't preach that all mass action is good, and all individual action is evil. It is true that there are vicious individuals; it is also true that there are vicious groups. Both must be judged by their specific actions—and not treated as an issue of "the one" against "the many," with the many always right and the one always wrong.

Remember that it is the Communists' aim to preach the supremacy, the holy virtue of the group—as opposed to the individual. It is not America's aim. Nor yours.

## 11. **Don't Smear an Independent Man.**

This is part of the same issue as the preceding point.

The Communists' chief purpose is to destroy every form of independence—independent work, independent action, independent property, independent thought, an independent mind, or an independent man.

Conformity, alikeness, servility, submission and obedience are necessary to establish a Communist slave-state. *Don't* help the Communists to teach men to acquire these attitudes.

*Don't* fall for the old Communist trick of thinking that an independent man or an individualist is one who crushes and exploits others—such as a dictator. An independent man is one who stands alone and respects the same right of others, who does not rule or serve, who neither sacrifices himself nor others. A dictator—by definition—is the most complete collectivist of all, because he exists by ruling, crushing and exploiting a huge collective of men.

*Don't* permit the snide little touches that Communists sneak into scripts—all the lines, hints and implications which suggest that something (a person, an attitude, a motive, an emotion) is evil because it is independent (or private, or personal, or single, or individual).

*Don't* preach that everything done for others is good, while everything done for one's own sake is evil. This damns every form of personal joy and happiness.

*Don't* preach that everything "public-spirited" is good, while everything personal and private is evil.

*Don't* make every form of loneliness a sin, and every form of the herd spirit a virtue.

Remember that America is the country of the pioneer, the non-conformist, the inventor, the originator, the innovator. Remember that all the great thinkers, artists, scientists were single, individual, independent men who stood alone, and discovered new directions of achievement—alone.

*Don't* let yourself be fooled when the Reds tell you that what they want to destroy are men like Hitler or Mussolini. What they want to destroy are men like Shakespeare, Chopin and Edison.

If you doubt this, think of a certain movie, in which a great composer was damned for succumbing, temporarily, to a horrible, vicious, selfish, anti-social sin. What was his sin? That he wanted to sit alone in his room and write music! [*The movie AR refers to is* A Song to Remember; *her review of it is presented later in the chapter.*]

## 12. Don't Use Current Events Carelessly.

A favorite trick of the Communists is to insert into pictures casual lines of dialogue about some important, highly controversial political issue, to insert them as accidental small talk, without any connection to the scene, the plot, or the story.

*Don't* permit such lines. *Don't* permit snide little slurs at any political party—in a picture which is to be released just before election time.

*Don't* allow chance remarks of a partisan nature about any current political events.

If you wish to mention politics on the screen, or take sides in a current controversy—then do so fully and openly. Even those who do not agree with you will respect an honest presentation of the side you've chosen. But the seemingly accidental remarks, the casual wisecracks, the cowardly little half-hints are the things that arouse the anger and contempt of all those who uphold the opposite side of the issue. In most of the current issues, that opposite side represents half or more than half of your picture audience.

And it is a sad joke on Hollywood that while we shy away from all controversial subjects on the screen, in order not to antagonize anybody—we arouse more antagonism throughout the country and more resentment against ourselves by one cheap little smear line in the midst of some musical comedy than we ever would by a whole political treatise.

Of all current questions, be most careful about your attitude toward Soviet Russia. You do not have to make pro-Soviet or anti-Soviet pictures, if you do not wish to take a stand. But if you claim that you wish to remain neutral, *don't* stick into pictures casual lines favorable to Soviet Russia. Look out for remarks that praise Russia directly or indirectly; or statements to the effect that anyone who is anti-Soviet is pro-Fascist; or references to fictitious Soviet achievements.

*Don't* suggest to the audience that the Russian people are free, secure and happy, that life in Russia is just about the same as in any other country—while actually the Russian people live in constant terror under a bloody, monstrous dictatorship. Look out for speeches that support whatever is in the Soviet interests of the moment, whatever is part of the current Communist party line. *Don't* permit dialogue such as: "The free, peace-loving nations of the world—America, England, and Russia . . ." or, "Free elections, such as in Poland . . ." or, "American imperialists ought to get out of China . . ."

## 13. Don't Smear American Political Institutions.

The Communist Party line takes many turns and makes many changes to meet shifting conditions. But on one objective it has remained fixed: to undermine faith in and ultimately to destroy our American political institutions.

*Don't* discredit the Congress of the United States by presenting it as an ineffectual body, devoted to mere talk. If you do that—you imply that representative government is no good, and what we ought to have is a dictator.

*Don't* discredit our free elections. If you do that—you imply that elections should be abolished.

*Don't* discredit our courts by presenting them as corrupt. If you do that—you lead people to believe that they have no recourse except to violence, since peaceful justice cannot be obtained.

It is true that there have been vicious Congressmen and judges, and politicians who have stolen elections, just as there are vicious men in any profession. But if you present them in a story, be sure to make it clear that you are criticizing particular men—*not the system*. The American system, as such, is the best ever devised in history. If some men do not live up to it—let us damn these men, *not* the system which they betray.

## Conclusion

These are the things which Communists and their sympathizers try to sneak into pictures intended as non-political—and these are the things you must keep out of your scripts, if your intention is to make non-political movies.

There is, of course, no reason why you should not make pictures on political themes. In fact, it would be most desirable if there were more pictures advocating the political principles of Americanism, seriously, consistently, and dramatically. Serious themes are always good entertainment, if honestly done. But if you attempt such pictures—do not undertake them lightly, carelessly, and with no better equipment than a few trite generalities and safe, benevolent bromides. Be very sure of what you want to say—and say it clearly, specifically, uncompromisingly. Evasions and generalities only help the enemies of Americanism—by giving people the impression that American principles are a collection of weak, inconsistent, meaningless, hypocritical, worn-out old slogans.

There is no obligation on you to make political pictures—if you do not wish to take a strong stand. You are free to confine your work to good, honest, non-political movies. But *there is* a moral obligation on you to present the political ideas of Americanism strongly and honestly—if you undertake pictures with political themes.

And when you make pictures with political themes and implications— *Don't* hire Communists to write, direct or produce them. You cannot expect Communists to remain "neutral" and not to insert their own ideas into their work. Take them at *their* word, not ours. *They* have declared openly and repeatedly that their first obligation is to the Communist Party, that their first duty is to spread Party propaganda, and that their work in pictures is only a means to an end, the end being the Dictatorship of the Proletariat. You had better believe them about their own stated intentions. Remember that Hitler, too, stated openly that his aim was world conquest, but nobody believed him or took him seriously until it was too late.

Now a word of warning about the question of free speech. The principle of free speech requires that we do not use *police force* to forbid the Communists the expression of their ideas—which means that we do not *pass laws* forbidding them to speak. But the principle of free speech *does not* require that we furnish the Communists with the means to preach their ideas, and *does not* imply that we owe them jobs and support to advocate our own destruction at our own expense. The Constitutional guarantee of free speech reads: "Congress shall pass no law . . ." It does not require employers to be suckers.

Let the Communists preach what they wish (so long as it remains mere talking) at the expense of those and in the employ of those who share their ideas. Let them create their own motion picture studios, if they can. But let us put an end to their use of our pictures, our studios and our money for the purpose of preaching our exploitation, enslavement and destruction. Freedom of speech does not imply that it is our duty to provide a knife for the murderer who wants to cut our throat.

[*AR later remarked: "When the Screen Guide was first printed, the major studios generally ignored it. Then I began hearing of one studio after another ordering dozens of copies from the Motion Picture Alliance. And the*

# AYN RAND®
## Information

"Throughout the centuries there were men who took first steps down new roads armed with nothing but their own vision."
— Ayn Rand

If you find the ideas in this book engaging and would like to learn more about Ayn Rand and her philosophy, mail in this card to receive free information about:

- The Ayn Rand Institute: the authoritative source for information about Ayn Rand and her ideas

- Books, recorded lectures and courses, CDs, and DVDs by Ayn Rand and others on her philosophy

- Conferences, seminars and other Ayn Rand-related events.

- University clubs, programs and activities

Information on all these is yours FREE, with no obligation. Just fill out this card and drop it in the mail today or go to www.aynrandinfo.com.

Ayn
Rand
Institute
ARI®

NAME

STREET ADDRESS                          APT.

CITY                          STATE          ZIP

E-MAIL (OPTIONAL)

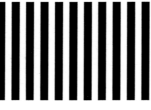

# BUSINESS REPLY MAIL
FIRST-CLASS MAIL    PERMIT NO 14564    IRVINE CA

POSTAGE WILL BE PAID BY ADDRESSEE

AYN RAND INFO
PO BOX 51808
IRVINE CA 92619-9930

*attacks on businessmen as villains disappeared; if you watch the old movies, you can see the difference."*]


**1947**

[*The following was probably also written by AR for the Motion Picture Alliance for the Preservation of American Ideals.*]

The pictures reviewed below are offered as examples of the technique of implications. There are many other pictures which contain scenes, episodes or lines of dialogue favorable, wittingly or unwittingly, to the general cause of collectivism. But there is no point in listing all such pictures, nor in denouncing anyone for past mistakes. Our purpose is not to denounce specific films, but the methods which they represent. With the help of the points given above, anyone who wishes to keep the Red trend off the screen will be able to detect it himself in any particular script or picture.

Most of the people connected with the production of the pictures reviewed below were not Communists nor Communist sympathizers. *That* is what makes the situation both needless and tragic. Any man has the right to produce any picture he wishes and to preach any ideas he believes. But it is shocking to see the talent, the skill, the technical knowledge and the wealth that went into the making of these pictures, turned to the furthering of a cause which does not represent the convictions of the men involved and which they are the first to repudiate when it is named.

It is the methods by which this is done that we wish to expose to its victims; not as a reproach, but as a warning. If anyone still wishes to permit these practices after he understands their nature—that is his right. And it is ours to denounce him.

Nobody has ever been endangered by being offered poison in a bottle bearing a label with a skull-and-crossbones. Poison is usually offered in a glass of the best wine—or, modern version, in a quart of the milk of human kindness.


### The Best Years of Our Lives

Many passages of this picture preach patriotism and sympathy for veterans; this helps the unwary to accept, under the guise of patriotism, the attacks on the free enterprise system which this picture also contains.

**1.** A returning war hero is denied a seat on a plane, to make room for an offensive businessman who is obviously rich. What is the point of this episode—if not the implication that the vicious, unpatriotic rich are grossly indifferent to war heroes? What impression can this leave with the audience—if not resentment against businessmen? The episode is the more offensive when we remember that it implies a distortion of real facts. It was not the businessmen [during World War II], but the bureaucrats who controlled priorities on air travel. If any plane seats were obtained unfairly, it was not money that bought them, but political pull. And the only instance of this kind that attracted nationwide attention involved soldiers who were thrown off a plane, not to make room for a businessman, but for a dog belonging to an amateur politician of pronounced left-wing tendencies. If the picture episode had no such counterpart in real life, it would be bad enough. But to attach to a businessman the specific offense committed by a prominent business-baiter is an act of cynical, sickening dishonesty.

**2.** The returned war hero takes a job in a drugstore owned by a national chain, where he is treated unfairly, offensively and antagonistically. What does this imply—if not the idea that businessmen discriminate against veterans? What impression will this give to nerve-wracked young soldiers—if not the idea that they will get no chance in civilian life so long as jobs depend on private business and private employers? There is another distortion of facts here: most of the drug companies give special preference to veterans applying for jobs; and so do most other business concerns. If anyone claims that this sequence in the picture is not to be taken as a reflection upon business—let him answer whether he would make a picture showing a labor union discriminating against veterans, and then claim that it is not to be taken as a reflection upon labor.

**3.** The picture denounces a banker for being unwilling to give a veteran a loan without collateral, a refusal which is treated as if it were an act of greedy selfishness. *This* is a demagogue's conception of economics. Nobody but a moron could really believe that the money involved in a bank loan belongs to the banker; that he refuses loans out of personal heartlessness, and that he ought to hand out the money not on the basis of his depositors' security but on the basis of the applicant's need. If some banker took the admonition of this picture seriously, who would suffer most and lose their life-savings but the very people that the Leftists love to cry over—the small depositors, the widows and orphans? [*This idea was later dramatized by the character of Eugene Lawson in* Atlas Shrugged.] This incident is, perhaps, the all-time low in irresponsible demagoguery on the screen. To spread such ideas of economics is to take advantage of the most naive and least educated members of the audience. It can have no result except to arouse the worst instincts—the desire to loot—in some helpless illiterates who might get the idea that the banks are holding out on them.

**4.** In the drugstore fight episode, an obnoxious character is presented as being anti-Communist, and he soon turns out to be anti-Semitic and anti-Negro as well. It is implied that these two attitudes go together, that anyone who is anti-Soviet is pro-Nazi. When we consider that the majority of people in this country are now most bitterly anti-Soviet, the consequences of what this episode suggests to them are frightful to contemplate.

Americans are often confused about economics, and they may be uncertain on whether this picture is or is not an attack upon the American economic system. So we shall quote from an expert. An Associated Press dispatch of May 12, 1947, from Moscow, states that the Soviet newspaper *Culture and Life* denounced American movies for spreading propaganda favorable to capitalism and the American way of life. Commentator Yuri Zhukov wrote that American producers were cooperating with the State Department and "monopoly capital" to glut the world market with films "giving a distorted sweetened picture of life in the United States." Zhukov, however, praised one American film—*The Best Years of Our Lives.*

He ought to know.

[The Best Years of Our Lives *won seven Academy Awards in 1946.*]

### A Song to Remember

This is a curious and revealing phenomenon—a *philosophical* picture. It presents, not superficial politics, but the fundamental essence of the philosophy of collectivism. If anyone thinks that collectivists are merely out to destroy some sort of "bloated bankers" or "economic exploiters"—let him see this picture and learn what they are really after.

In order to present a vicious theory, the picture distorted historical events and characters—but this is not astonishing, since a vicious theory cannot be true to facts. The story presents Chopin's struggle between good and evil, as personified by a young Polish girl on the one side and by George Sand on the other. George Sand, according to the picture, is evil because she provides a beautiful, private retreat where Chopin can live in peace and luxury, because she takes care of his every need, attends to his health, and urges him to forget the world and devote himself exclusively to the work of writing music, which he is desperately eager to do. The young Polish girl, according to the picture, is good because she urges Chopin to drop the work that he loves and go out on a concert tour in order to make money. (Yes, *money*—strange as this may sound in a story representing an ideology that damns the capitalist system for inducing artists to be commercial.) The girl, in this case, is collecting money "for the people," for a cause that is identified as national or revolutionary or both, and this is supposed to justify anything and everything; so she demands that Chopin renounce his genius, sacrifice his composing and go out to entertain paying audiences—even though he hates concert playing, is ill with tuberculosis and has been warned by the doctors that the strain of a tour would kill him.

When Chopin locks himself in his room to avoid his nagging friends and to work, the picture treats it as an act of selfishness. When George Sand tells his friends to leave him alone, the picture treats her as a vicious, antisocial creature. The Polish girl and a sniveling old music teacher are held up as samples of self-righteous virtue, the virtue being granted to them by the fact that they demand the sacrifice of another man's life and do not balk at sacrificing the life of a genius to a fund-raising campaign.

After much inner suffering, Chopin escapes from Sand's "selfishness," goes on tour, breaks under the strain—and dies. This monstrous self-immolation is presented as an apotheosis of virtue. There is even a final scene where George Sand asks one of the collectivists what they gained by destroying a great life. The answer is that they gained the inspiration given to thousands of humble people. To translate this into specific and modern terms, one would have to suppose that they meant they gained propaganda value—and the audience is supposed to feel: What's the life of a genius, or of any man for that matter, as compared to "inspiring" the masses?

*There* you can see collectivism in the raw. There you have it stripped of all the humanitarian trimmings and dialectic contradictions. This is the concrete illustration of the collectivist doctrine which holds that man exists to serve others, that he has no right to any personal aim, motive, desire or life, and that his only proper purpose is to sacrifice himself to the needs of the collective; therefore, a creative artist is a selfish monster, not because he hurts or exploits anybody, but because he wants to be left alone to do his own work; and the creative artist's proper place is in a gang of fund-moochers or ditch-diggers, if the collective so demands.

Now, this much is true: creative work *is* a personal, individual, totally independent endeavor; his art means more to the creative artist than any social problem, more than anything or anybody. But who—outside the ideologies of Soviet Russia or Nazi Germany—will dare to hold the creative artist as evil?

**October 20, 1947**

[*The following is AR's testimony before the House Un-American Activities Committee on October 20, 1947, as reported in the Government Printing Office record ("Hearings Regarding Communist Infiltration of the Motion Picture Industry"). The Committee's chairman was J. Parnell Thomas; Robert Stripling was Chief Investigator.*]

**The Chairman:** Raise your right hand, please, Miss Rand. Do you solemnly swear the testimony you are about to give is the truth, the whole truth, and nothing but the truth, so help you God?

**Miss Rand:** I do.

**The Chairman:** Sit down. [. . .]

**Mr. Stripling:** Where were you born, Miss Rand?

**Miss Rand:** In St. Petersburg, Russia.

**Mr. Stripling:** When did you leave Russia?

**Miss Rand:** In 1926.

**Mr. Stripling:** How long have you been employed in Hollywood?

**Miss Rand:** I have been in pictures on and off since late in 1926, but specifically as a writer this time I have been in Hollywood since late 1943 and am now under contract as a writer.

**Mr. Stripling:** Have you written various novels?

**Miss Rand:** I have written two novels. My first one was called *We the Living*, which was a story about Soviet Russia and was published in 1936. The second one was *The Fountainhead*, published in 1943.

**Mr. Stripling:** Was that a best-seller—*The Fountainhead*?

**Miss Rand:** Yes; thanks to the American public.

**Mr. Stripling:** Do you know how many copies were sold?

**Miss Rand:** The last I heard was 360,000 copies. I think there have been some more since.

**Mr. Stripling:** You have been employed as a writer in Hollywood?

**Miss Rand:** Yes; I am under contract at present.

**Mr. Stripling:** Could you name some of the stories or scripts you have written for Hollywood?

**Miss Rand:** I have done the script for *The Fountainhead*, which has not been produced yet, for Warner Brothers, and two adaptations for Hal Wallis Productions, at Paramount, which were not my stories but on which I did the screen plays, which were *Love Letters* and *You Came Along*.

**Mr. Stripling:** Now, Miss Rand, you have heard the testimony of Mr. [Louis B.] Mayer?

**Miss Rand:** Yes.

**Mr. Stripling:** You have read the letter I read from Lowell Mellett?
**Miss Rand:** Yes.
**Mr. Stripling:** Which says that the picture *Song of Russia* has no political implications?
**Miss Rand:** Yes.
**Mr. Stripling:** Did you at the request of Mr. Smith, the investigator for this committee, view the picture *Song of Russia*?
**Miss Rand:** Yes.
**Mr. Stripling:** Within the past two weeks?
**Miss Rand:** Yes; on October 13, to be exact.
**Mr. Stripling:** In Hollywood?
**Miss Rand:** Yes.
**Mr. Stripling:** Would you give the committee a breakdown of your summary of the picture relating to either propaganda or an untruthful account or distorted account of conditions in Russia?
**Miss Rand:** Yes.

First of all I would like to define what we mean by propaganda. We have all been talking about it, but nobody has stated just what they mean. Now, I use the term to mean that Communist propaganda is anything which gives a good impression of communism as a way of life. Anything that sells people the idea that life in Russia is good and that people are free and happy would be Communist propaganda. Am I not correct? I mean, would that be a fair statement to make—that that would be Communist propaganda?

Now, here is what the picture *Song of Russia* contains. It starts with an American conductor, played by Robert Taylor, giving a concert in America for Russian war relief. He starts playing the American national anthem and the national anthem dissolves into a Russian mob, with the sickle and hammer on a red flag very prominent above their heads. I am sorry, but that made me sick. That is something which I do not see how native Americans permit, and I am only a naturalized American. That was a terrible touch of propaganda. As a writer, I can tell you just exactly what it suggests to the people. It suggests literally and technically that it is quite all right for the American national anthem to dissolve into the Soviet. The term here is more than just technical. It really was symbolically intended, and it worked out that way. The anthem continues, played by a Soviet band. That is the beginning of the picture.

Now we go to the pleasant love story. Mr. Taylor is an American who came there apparently voluntarily to conduct concerts for the Soviets. He meets a little Russian girl from a village who comes to him and begs him to go to her village to direct concerts there. There are no G.P.U. agents and nobody stops her. She just comes to Moscow and meets him. He decides he will go [with her], because he is falling in love. He asks her to show him Moscow. She says she has never seen it. He says, "I will show it to you."

They see it together. The picture then goes into a scene of Moscow, supposedly. I don't know where the studio got its shots, but I have never seen anything like it in Russia. First you see Moscow buildings—big, prosperous-looking, clean buildings, with something like swans or sailboats in the foreground. Then you see a Moscow restaurant that just never existed there. When I was in Russia, there was only one such restaurant, which was nowhere as luxurious as that and no one could enter it except commissars and profiteers. Certainly a girl from a village, who in the first place would never have been allowed to come to Moscow without permission, could not afford to enter it, even if she worked for ten years. However, there is a Russian restaurant with a menu such as never existed in Russia even before the revolution. From this restaurant they go on to this tour of Moscow. The streets are clean and prosperous-looking. There are no food lines anywhere. You see shots of the marble subway—the famous Russian subway out of which they make such propaganda capital. There is a marble statue of Stalin thrown in. There is a park where you see happy little children in white blouses running around. I don't know whose children they are, but they are really happy kiddies. They are not homeless children in rags, such as I have seen in Russia. Then you see an excursion boat, on which the Russian people are smiling, sitting around very cheerfully, dressed in some sort of satin blouses such as they only wear in Russian restaurants here.

Then they attend a luxurious dance. I don't know where they got the idea of the clothes and the settings that they used at the ball and—

**Mr. Stripling:** Is that a ballroom scene?

**Miss Rand:** Yes; the ballroom—where they dance. It was an exaggeration even for this country. I never saw anybody wearing such clothes and dancing to such exotic music when I was there. Of course, it didn't say whose ballroom it is or how they got there. But there they are—free and dancing very happily.

Incidentally, I understand from correspondents who have left or escaped from Russia later than I did, that the time I last saw it, which was in 1926, was the best time since the Russian revolution. At that time conditions were a little better than they have become since. In my time we were a bunch of ragged, starved, dirty, miserable people who had only two thoughts in our mind. That was our complete terror—afraid to look at one another, afraid to say anything for fear of who is listening and would report us—and where to get the next meal. You have no idea what it means to live in a country where nobody has any concern except food, where all the conversation is about food because everybody is so hungry that that is all they can think about and that is all they can afford to do. They have no idea of politics. They have no idea of any pleasant romances or love—nothing but food and fear.

That is what I saw up to 1926. That is not what the picture shows.

Now, after this tour of Moscow, the hero—the American conductor—goes to the Soviet village. The Russian villages are so miserable and so filthy. They were [that] even before the revolution. What they have become now I am afraid to think. You have all read about the program for the collectivization of the farms in 1933, at which time the Soviet Government admits that three million peasants died of starvation. Other people claim there were seven and a half million, but three million is the figure admitted by the Soviet Government as the figure of people who died of starvation, planned by the government in order to drive people into collective farms. That is a recorded historical fact.

Now, here is life in the Soviet village as presented in *Song of Russia*. You see the happy peasants. You see they are meeting the hero at the station with bands, with beautiful blouses and shoes, such as they never wore anywhere. You see children with operetta costumes on them and with a brass band which they could never afford. You see the manicured starlets driving tractors and the happy women who come from work singing. You see a peasant at home with a close-up of food for which anyone there would have been murdered. If anybody had such food in Russia in that time he couldn't remain alive, because he would have been torn apart by neighbors trying to get food. But here is a close-up of it and a line where Robert Taylor comments on the food and the peasant answers, "This is just a simple country table and the food we eat ourselves."

Then the peasant proceeds to show Taylor how they live. He shows him his wonderful tractor. It is parked somewhere in his private garage. He shows him the grain in his bin, and Taylor says, "That is wonderful grain." Now, it is never said that the peasant does not own this tractor or this grain because it is a collective farm. He couldn't have it. It is not his. But the impression he gives to Americans, who wouldn't know any different, is that certainly it is this peasant's private property, and that is how he lives, he has his own tractor and his own grain. Then it shows miles and miles of plowed fields.

**The Chairman:** We will have more order, please.

**Miss Rand:** Am I speaking too fast?

**The Chairman:** Go ahead.

**Miss Rand:** Then—

**Mr. Stripling:** Miss Rand, may I bring up one point there?

**Miss Rand:** Surely.

**Mr. Stripling:** I saw the picture. At this peasant's village or home, was there a priest or several priests in evidence?

**Miss Rand:** Oh yes; I am coming to that, too. The priest was in the village scenes, having a position as sort of a constant companion and friend of the peasants, as if religion was a natural and accepted part of that life. Well, now, as a matter of fact, the [policy on] religion in Russia in my time was, and I understand it still is, that for a Communist Party member to have anything to do with religion means expulsion from the Party. He is not allowed to enter a church or take part in any religious ceremony. For a non-Party member it was permitted, but it was so frowned upon that people had to keep it secret if they went to church. If they wanted a church wedding they usually had it privately in their homes, with only a few friends present, in order not to let it be known at their place of employment because, even though it was not forbidden, the chances were that they would be thrown out of a job if it was known that they practiced any kind of religion.

Now, then, to continue with the story, Robert Taylor proposes to the heroine. She accepts him. They have a wedding, which, of course, is a church wedding. It takes place with all the religious pomp. They have a banquet. They have dancers, in something like satin skirts and performing ballets such as you never could possibly see in any village and certainly not in Russia. Later they show a peasants' meeting place, which is a kind of marble palace with crystal chandeliers. Where they got it or who built it for them I would like to be told. Then later you see that the peasants all have radios. When the heroine plays as a soloist with Robert Taylor's orchestra, after she marries him, you see a scene where all the peasants are listening on radios, and one of them says, "There are many millions listening to the concert."

I don't know whether there are a hundred private individuals in Russia who own radios. And I remember reading in the newspaper at the beginning of the war that every radio was seized by the Government and people were not allowed to own them. The idea that every poor peasant has a radio is certainly preposterous. You also see that they have long-distance telephones. Later in the picture, Taylor has to call his wife in the village by long-distance telephone. Where they got this long-distance phone, I don't know.

Now, here comes the crucial point of the picture. In the midst of this concert, when the heroine is playing, you see a scene on the border of the U.S.S.R. You have a very lovely modernistic sign saying "U.S.S.R." I would just like to remind you that that is the border where probably thousands of people have died trying to escape out of this lovely paradise. It shows the U.S.S.R. sign, and there is a border guard standing. He is listening to the concert. Then there is a scene inside a guardhouse where the guards are listening to the same concert, the beautiful Tschaikovsky music, and they are playing chess. Suddenly there is a Nazi attack on them. The poor, sweet Russians were unprepared. Now, realize—and that was a great shock to me—that the border that was being shown was the border of Poland. That was the border of an occupied, enslaved country which Hitler and Stalin destroyed together. That was the border that was being shown to us—just a happy place with people listening to music.

Also realize that when all this sweetness and light was going on in the first part of the picture, with all these happy, free people, there was not a G.P.U. agent among them, with no food lines, no persecution—complete freedom and happiness, with everybody smiling. Incidentally, I have never seen so much smiling in my life, except on the murals of the world's fair pavilion of the Soviets. If any one of you have seen it, you can appreciate it. It is one of the stock propaganda tricks of the Communists, to show these people smiling. That is all they can show. You have all this, plus the fact that an American conductor had accepted an invitation to come there and conduct a concert, and this took place in 1941 when Stalin was the ally of Hitler. That an American would accept an invitation to that country was shocking to me, with everything being shown as proper and good and all those happy people going around dancing, when Stalin was an ally of Hitler.

Now, then, the heroine decides that she wants to stay in Russia. Taylor would like to take her out of the country, but she says no, her place is here, she has to fight the war. Here is the line, as nearly exact as I could mark it while watching the picture: "I have a great responsibility to my family, to my village, and to the way I have lived." What way had she lived? This is just a polite way of saying the Communist way of life. She goes on to say that she wants to stay in the country because otherwise "How can I help to build a better and better life for my country?" What is meant by "better and better"? That means she has already helped to build a good way. That is the Soviet Communist way. But now she wants to make it even better.

Taylor's manager, an American, tells her that she should leave the country, but when she refuses and wants to stay, here is the line he uses: he tells her in an admiring, friendly way that "You are a fool, but a lot of fools like you died on the village green at Lexington."

Now, I submit that this is blasphemy, because the men at Lexington were not fighting just a foreign invader. They were fighting for freedom and what I mean—and I intend to be exact—is they were fighting for political freedom and individual freedom. They were fighting for the rights of man. To compare them to someone fighting for a slave state, I think is dreadful.

Then, later, the girl or one of the other characters says that "the culture we have been building here will never die." What culture? The culture of concentration camps.

At the end of the picture one of the Russians asks Taylor and the girl to go back to America, because they can help them there. How? Here is what he says, "You can go back to your country and tell them what you have seen and you will see the truth both in speech and in music." Now, that is plainly saying that what you have seen is the truth about Russia. That is what is in the picture.

Now, here is what I cannot understand: if the excuse that has been given here is that we had to produce the picture in wartime, just how can it help the war effort? If [the goal] is to deceive the American people, if it is to present to the American people a picture of Russia that is better than it really is, then that sort of an attitude is nothing but the theory of the Nazi elite—that a choice group of intellectual or other leaders will tell the people lies for their own good. I don't think that is the American way of giving people information. We do not have to deceive the people at any time, in war or peace.

If it was to please the Russians, I don't see how you can please the Russians by telling them that we are fools. To what extent we have done it, you can see right now. You can see the results right now. If we present a picture like that as our version of what goes on in Russia, what will they think of it? We don't win anybody's friendship. We will only win their contempt, and as you know the Russians have been [treating us with contempt].

My whole point about the picture is this: I fully believe Mr. Mayer when he says that he did not make a Communist picture. To do him justice, I can tell you I noticed that there was an effort to cut propaganda out. I believe he tried to cut propaganda out of the picture, but the terrible thing is the carelessness with ideas, not realizing that the mere presentation of that kind of happy existence in a country of slavery and horror is terrible propaganda. You are telling people that it is all right to live in a totalitarian state.

Now, I would like to say that nothing on earth will justify slavery. In war or peace or at any time you cannot justify slavery. You cannot tell people that it is all right to live under it and that everybody there is happy.

If you doubt this, I will just ask you one question. Visualize a picture [set] in Nazi Germany. If anybody laid a plot just based on a pleasant little romance in Germany and played Wagner's music and said that people are happy there, would you say that that was propaganda or not, when you know what life in Germany was and what kind of concentration camps they had there. You would not dare to put just a happy love story into Germany, and for every one of the same reasons you should not do it about Russia.

**Mr. Stripling:** That is all I have, Mr. Chairman.

**The Chairman:** Mr. Wood. [*John Stephens Wood was a Democratic congressman from Georgia.*]

**Mr. Wood:** I gather, then, from your analysis of this picture your personal criticism of it is that it overplayed the conditions that existed in Russia at the time the picture was made; is that correct?

**Miss Rand:** Did you say overplayed?

**Mr. Wood:** Yes.

**Miss Rand:** Well, the story portrayed the people—

**Mr. Wood:** It portrayed the people of Russia in a better economic and social position than they occupied?

**Miss Rand:** That is right.

**Mr. Wood:** And it would also leave the impression in the average mind that they were better able to resist the aggression of the German Army than they were in fact able to resist?

**Miss Rand:** Well, that was not in the picture. So far as the Russian war was concerned, not very much was shown about it.

**Mr. Wood:** Well, you recall, I presume—it is a matter of history—going back to the middle of the First World War when Russia was also our ally against the same enemy that we were fighting at this time and they were knocked out of the war. When the remnants of their forces turned against us, it prolonged the First World War a considerable time, didn't it?

**Miss Rand:** I don't believe so.

**Mr. Wood:** You don't?

**Miss Rand:** No.

**Mr. Wood:** Do you think, then, that it was to our advantage or to our disadvantage to keep Russia in this war, at the time this picture was made?

**Miss Rand:** That has absolutely nothing to do with what we are discussing.

**Mr. Wood:** Well—

**Miss Rand:** But if you want me to answer, I can answer, but it will take me a long time to say what I think, as to whether we should or should not have had Russia on our side in the war. I can, but how much time will you give me?

**Mr. Wood:** Well, do you say that it would have prolonged the war, so far as we were concerned, if they had been knocked out of it at that time?

**Miss Rand:** I can't answer that yes or no, unless you give me time for a long speech on it.

**Mr. Wood:** Well, there is a pretty strong probability that we wouldn't have won at all, isn't there?

**Miss Rand:** I don't know, because on the other hand I think we could have used the lend-lease supplies that we sent there to much better advantage ourselves.

**Mr. Wood:** Well, at that time—

**Miss Rand:** I don't know. It is a question.

**Mr. Wood:** We were furnishing Russia with all the lend-lease equipment that our industry would stand, weren't we?

**Miss Rand:** That is right.

**Mr. Wood:** And continued to do it?

**Miss Rand:** I am not sure it was at all wise. Now, if you want to discuss my military views—I am not an authority, but I will try.

**Mr. Wood:** What do you interpret, then, the picture as having been made for?

**Miss Rand:** I ask you: what relation could a lie about Russia have with the war effort? I would like to have somebody explain that to me, because I really don't understand it, why a lie would help anybody or why it would keep Russia in or out of the war. How?

**Mr. Wood:** You don't think it would have been of benefit to the American people to have kept them in?

**Miss Rand:** I don't believe the American people should ever be told any lies, publicly or privately. I don't believe that lies are practical. I think the international situation now rather supports me. I don't think it was necessary to deceive the American people about the nature of Russia.

I could add this: if those who saw it say it was quite all right, and perhaps there are reasons why it was all right to be an ally of Russia, then why weren't the American people told the real reasons and told that Russia is a dictatorship but there are reasons why we should cooperate with them to destroy Hitler and other dictators? All right, there may be some argument to that. Let us hear it. But of what help can it be to the war effort to tell people that we should associate with Russia and that she is not a dictatorship?

**Mr. Wood:** Let me see if I understand your position. I understand, from what you say, that because they were a dictatorship we shouldn't have accepted their help in undertaking to win a war against another dictatorship.

**Miss Rand:** That is not what I said. I was not in a position to make that decision. If I were, I would tell you what I would do. That is not what we are discussing. We are discussing the fact that our country was an ally of Russia, and the question is: what should we tell the American people about it—the truth or a lie? If we had good reason, if that is what you believe, all right, then why not tell the truth? Say it is a dictatorship, but we want to be associated with it. Say it is worthwhile being associated with the devil, as Churchill said, in order to defeat another devil which is Hitler. There might be some good argument made for that. But why pretend that Russia was not what it was?

**Mr. Wood:** Well—

**Miss Rand:** What do you achieve by that?

**Mr. Wood:** Do you think it would have had as good an effect upon the morale of the American people to preach a doctrine to them that Russia was on the verge of collapse?

**Miss Rand:** I don't believe that the morale of anybody can be built up by a lie. If there was nothing good that we could truthfully say about Russia, then it would have been better not to say anything at all.

**Mr. Wood:** Well—

**Miss Rand:** You don't have to come out and denounce Russia during the war; no. You can keep quiet. There is no moral guilt in not saying something if you can't say it, but there is in saying the opposite of what is true.

**Mr. Wood:** Thank you. That is all.

**The Chairman:** Mr. McDowell. [*John McDowell was a Republican congressman from Pennsylvania.*]

**Mr. McDowell:** You paint a very dismal picture of Russia. You made a great point about the number of children who were unhappy. Doesn't anybody smile in Russia any more?

**Miss Rand:** Well, if you ask me literally, pretty much no.

**Mr. McDowell:** They don't smile?

**Miss Rand:** Not quite that way; no. If they do, it is privately and accidentally. Certainly, it is not social. They don't smile in approval of their system.

**Mr. McDowell:** Well, all they do is talk about food.

**Miss Rand:** That is right.

**Mr. McDowell:** That is a great change from the Russians I have always known, and I have known a lot of them. Don't they do things at all like Americans? Don't they walk across town to visit their mother-in-law or somebody?

**Miss Rand:** Look, it is very hard to explain. It is almost impossible to convey to a free people what it is like to live in a totalitarian dictatorship. I can tell you a lot of details. I can never completely convince you, because you are free. It is in a way good that you can't even conceive of what it is like. Certainly they have friends and mothers-in-law. They try to live a human life, but you understand it is totally inhuman. Try to imagine what it is like if you are in constant terror from morning till night and at night you are waiting for the doorbell to ring, where you are afraid of anything and everybody, living in a country where human life is nothing, less than nothing, and you know it. You don't know who is going to do what to you because you may have friends who spy on you, and there is no law or rights, of any kind.

**Mr. McDowell:** You came here in 1926, I believe you said. Did you escape from Russia?

**Miss Rand:** No.

**Mr. McDowell:** Did you have a passport?

**Miss Rand:** No. Strangely enough, they gave me a passport to come out here as a visitor.

**Mr. McDowell:** As a visitor?

**Miss Rand:** It was at a time when they relaxed their orders a little bit. Quite a few people got out. I had some relatives here and I was permitted to come here for a year. I never went back.

**Mr. McDowell:** I see.

**The Chairman:** Mr. Nixon. [*Richard Milhous Nixon was a Republican congressman and future U.S. president from California.*]

**Mr. Nixon:** No questions.

**The Chairman:** All right.

The first witness tomorrow morning will be Adolphe Menjou. (Whereupon, at 4:20 p.m., an adjournment was taken until 10:30 a.m. of the following day.)

[*AR planned to testify further on* The Best Years of Our Lives, *as well as on the wider issues discussed in her Screen Guide. However, she was never given the opportunity. Later, she recalled:* "The Best Years of Our Lives *was the big hit of the period and the movie I particularly wanted to denounce. . . . It was much more important to show the serious propaganda about America—not some musical about Soviet Russia that would not fool anybody, and that had failed at the box-office. . . . But the Congressmen told me that they would not dare come out against a movie about an armless veteran—there would be a public furor against them.*"]

**1947**

[*At some point after her testimony, AR wrote the following notes to herself on whether the Thomas Committee had violated the civil rights of the Hollywood Communists.*]

*Suggestions Regarding the Congressional Investigation of Communism*

The whole conception of civil rights (of free speech, free assembly, free political organization) applies to and belongs in the realm of ideas—that is, a realm which precludes the use of physical violence. These rights are based on and pertain to the peaceful activity of spreading or preaching ideas, of dealing with men by intellectual persuasion. Therefore, one cannot invoke these rights to protect an organization such as the Communist Party, which not merely preaches, but actually engages in acts of violence, murder, sabotage, and spying in the interests of a foreign government. This takes the Communist Party out of the realm of civil law and puts it into the realm of criminal law. And the fact that Communists are directed and financed by a foreign power puts them into the realm of treason and military law.

The Thomas Committee was inquiring, not into a question of opinion, but into a question of fact, the fact being membership in the Communist Party.

The Thomas Committee did not ask anyone whether he believed in Communism, but asked only whether he had joined the Communist Party. Membership in the Communist Party does not consist merely of sharing the ideas of that Party. That Party is a formal, closed, and secret organization. Joining it involves more than a matter of ideas. It involves an agreement to take orders to commit actions—criminal and treasonable actions.

The Communists have been trying to claim that belonging to the Communist Party is the same as belonging to the Republican or Democratic Party. But membership in the Republican or Democratic Party is an open, public matter. It involves no initiation, no acceptance of an applicant by the party, and no card-bearing. It involves nothing but a voluntary and open declaration by a citizen that he wishes to be registered as a Republican or a Democrat for the next primary election. It is a membership which cannot be refused to him and which he is free to abandon any time he chooses. It commits him to nothing but an expression of his ideas at the ballot box, and he is free to change his mind even about that. Thus, it is truly a matter of a citizen's personal ideas and convictions, nothing more.

Membership in the Communist Party is a formal act of joining a formal organization whose aims, by its own admission, include acts of criminal violence. Congress has no right to inquire into ideas or opinions, but has every right to inquire into criminal activities. Belonging to a secret organization that advocates criminal actions comes into the sphere of the criminal, not the ideological.

It is extremely important to differentiate between the American conception of law and the European-totalitarian concept. Under the American law, there is no such thing as a political crime; a man's ideas do not constitute a crime, no matter what they are. And precisely by the same principle, a man's ideas—no matter what they are—cannot serve as a justification for a criminal action and do not give him freedom to commit such actions on the ground that they represent his personal belief.

Under most systems of European law a citizen's beliefs, if contrary to those of the government in power, are considered to be a crime punishable by law. Consequently, an act of violence or a murder committed for a political motive is treated differently from an act of violence or murder committed for a plain criminal motive. Incidentally, prior to World War I, most European governments treated crimes committed for political motives much more leniently and almost honorably in comparison with the same crimes committed for criminal motives. In America, no man can be sent to jail for holding any sort of ideas. And no man is allowed to demand a consideration of his ideas as a mitigating circumstance when and if he has committed an act of violence.

The entire conception of American law is based on the principle of inalienable individual rights. This principle precludes the right of one citizen to do violence to others—no matter what ideas or convictions he may hold. Therefore, any man may preach or advocate anything he wishes, but if he undertakes acts of violence in pursuit of his beliefs, then he is treated as a common criminal. American law is not asked to share *his* conviction—his idea that his rights include the right to use force against other men. (As an example: American citizens have freedom of religion; but if some sect attempted to practice human sacrifices, its members would be prosecuted by law—not for their religious beliefs, but for murder; their beliefs would not be considered or recognized as pertinent to the case.)

Therefore, it is totally irrelevant to Congress whether a man enters a criminal conspiracy for criminal reasons or for reasons he considers political or ideological. This is precisely where his ideas do not concern Congress at all and do not enter the question. When Congress investigates the Communist Party, it is investigating a factual matter, a criminal conspiracy, and not a matter of ideas.

If it is asked why the Communist Party may be objectively classified as a criminal conspiracy—the answer lies in the factual record of the Party, which is a record of proven criminal activities, in its own professed aims, methods, and intentions, and in the fact of its secrecy. Congress was not inquiring who believes in Communism. It was inquiring who belongs to an organization that has defined itself, by its own acts and statements, as criminal.

If the Communist Party were a purely national American organization, the above points would be sufficient to give Congress the right to inquire into its activities. But when we add to it the fact that the Communist Party is an organization which owes allegiance to a foreign power, then it becomes not only a matter of crime, but also of treason. A party which is the agent of a foreign power cannot claim the same rights as an American party—just as a foreign subject cannot claim all the rights and privileges of an American citizen, nor a voice in the conduct of America's internal affairs. An investigation into a man's or an organization's allegiance to a foreign power is not an ideological matter, but a military one.

It is extremely important not to let this whole issue be considered as an issue of the freedom of speech. Nobody has interfered with the right of the Hollywood Ten to their freedom of speech; quite the opposite: they raised a howl because they were asked to speak. No legal penalties of any kind were to be imposed on them for their admission of membership in the Communist Party, if they had chosen to admit it. Yet they are screaming that they were asked to incriminate themselves. To incriminate themselves in what manner?

The Communists claim that the Congressional investigation caused them personal and professional damage, by revealing their political ideas to the public when such ideas are unpopular. Freedom of speech means precisely that a citizen has the right to hold and advocate his own ideas, even when they are unpopular, and that no legal penalty (no restraint by force) will be imposed upon him for it. Freedom of speech is the protection of his right to be an unpopular dissenter, if he wishes, without becoming the subject of any violence by any popular majority. But that same freedom of speech grants other citizens the right to agree or disagree with his ideas.

This is exactly why any man's freedom of speech is no threat or danger to other men: they are free to consider his ideas and not to cooperate with him, if they do not agree. They cannot use force against him, but neither are they forced to assist him in his activities against their own interests, ideas, or convictions.

Now if the Hollywood Ten claim that a public revelation of their Communist ideas damages them because it will cost them their Hollywood jobs—then this means that they are holding these jobs by fraud, that their employers, their co-workers and their public do not know the nature of their ideas and would not want to deal with them if such knowledge were made available. If so, then the Communists, in effect, are asking that the government protect them in the perpetration of a fraud. They are demanding protection for their right to practice deceit upon others. They are saying, in effect: I am cheating those with whom I am dealing and if you reveal this, you will cause me to lose my racket—which is an interference with my freedom of speech and belief.

It is not the duty of Congress to inquire into anyone's ideas—but neither is it the duty of Congress to protect deceit by withholding from the public any information which may involve someone's ideas. If, in the course of an inquiry into criminal and treasonable activities, Congress reveals the nature of the political beliefs of certain men—their freedom of speech or belief has not been infringed in any manner. If, as a consequence, their employers—who had been foolish, ignorant, or negligent before—now decide to fire these men, that is the employers' inalienable right. It is also the inalienable right of the public not to buy the product of these men—in this particular case, not to attend the movies written or directed by the Hollywood Ten. The damage which the Ten claim to have suffered in this case is a private damage, not a legal one, a damage which consists of the refusal of private citizens to deal with a Communist, if they learn that he is a Communist.

And this is another instance where the Communists are attempting to foist a totalitarian conception upon our courts of law, in place of the American conception. They are attempting to claim that there is no difference between private action and government action—that a citizen's refusal to deal with a Communist is equivalent to a government order forbidding him to be a Communist—that a citizen's refusal to employ a Communist is equivalent to a policeman's arresting him—that the disagreement of his fellow-citizens with his views and his consequent unpopularity are equivalent to a concentration camp and a firing squad—that the refusal of his victims to cooperate with their own self-admitted murderer, expropriator, and enslaver is an infringement of his freedom and his rights.

The Constitutional guarantee of free speech reads: "Congress shall pass no law . . ." It does not demand that private citizens lend any form of support to those whose ideas they do not share.

The Communists have perverted the issue of free speech into the following sort of claim: Since a man has the right to hold any ideas he wishes, he must not suffer any kind of loss, discomfort, damage, or penalty, legal or private, as a consequence of his ideas. This is the totalitarian conception which recognizes no difference between public, government action and the private actions of private citizens. This is not the American conception of legality, rights, or free speech.

Under the American system, a man has the right to hold any ideas he wishes, without suffering any government restraint for it, without the danger of physical violence, bodily injury, or police seizure. That is all. Should he have to suffer some form of private penalty for his ideas from private citizens who do not agree with him? He most certainly should. That is the only form of protection the rest of the citizens have against him and against the spread of ideas with which they do not agree.

Should the Hollywood Ten suffer unpopularity or loss of jobs as a result of being Communists? They most certainly should—so long as the rest of us, who give them jobs or box-office support, do not wish to be Communists or accessories to the spread of Communism. If it is claimed that we must not refuse them support—what becomes of our right of free speech and belief?

## PART 4

# ATLAS SHRUGGED

# 11

# THE MIND ON STRIKE

*AR organized her journals for Atlas Shrugged by subject. Her handwritten notes were put in folders marked "Philosophical," "Plot," "Characters," "Outlines," "Research Material," and "Miscellaneous." Here the notes are presented chronologically without regard for subject, so the reader may see the progression of her thought in developing the novel.*

*AR originally envisioned* Atlas Shrugged *as a shorter novel than* The Fountainhead. *In a 1961 interview, she recalled:*

Atlas Shrugged started with the idea of the plot-theme: the mind goes on strike. At first I saw it more as a political and social novel; I remember thinking that it will not present any new philosophical ideas, that the philosophy will be the same as *The Fountainhead*. It will be individualism, only now I'll show it in the political-economic realm. The action will tell the philosophic story with a minimum of comment from me; it will show that capitalism and the proper economics rest on the mind.

Then I started working on the philosophic aspect of it, with the assignment to myself to concretize the theme. Why is the mind important? What specifically does the mind do in relationship to human existence? It's then I began to see that this is going to be a very important and new philosophical novel. There was a great deal more to say than merely what I had said in The Fountainhead.

*Most of the notes in this chapter are from her "philosophical" file. We can see the novel growing in scope as she elaborates and concretizes the theme.*

*Although AR had thought of the plot-theme in late 1943, she did not begin to make notes until January 1, 1945, and only began full-time work on the novel in April*

*1946. The notes in this chapter are largely from this last month –the most prolific month of journal-writing in her life. Nearly all of her notes from this month are included here; I omitted only a few pages in which she was rewriting and condensing earlier material.*

*As with* The Fountainhead *journal, I have used the names of characters as they appear in the novel. In the course of writing, AR changed the first names of several characters. Dagny's name was Marny for a while; Francisco was originally spelled Francesco because AR thought of the character as more typically Italian than Spanish; Rearden's name was Andrew, then William, before she settled on Hank; Danneskjöld's name was Hjalmar, then Ivar, then Kay, before it finally became Ragnar.*

*Atlas Shrugged was a chapter title until 1956 when AR's husband, Frank O'Connor, suggested that it be the title of the novel. Her working title throughout was* The Strike.

**January 1, 1945**

*The Strike*

*Theme:* What happens to the world when the prime movers go on strike.

This means: a picture of the world with its motor cut off. Show: what, how, why. The specific steps and incidents—in terms of persons, their spirits, motives, psychology, and actions—and, secondarily, proceeding from persons, in terms of history, society and the world.

The theme requires showing who are the prime movers and why, how they function; who are their enemies and why, what are the motives behind the hatred for and the enslavement of the prime movers; the nature of the obstacles placed in their way, and the reasons for it.

This last paragraph is contained entirely in *The Fountainhead*. Roark and Toohey are the complete statement of it. Therefore, this is not the direct theme of *The Strike*—but it is part of the theme and must be kept in mind, briefly restated in order to have the theme clear and complete.

The first question to decide is on whom the emphasis must be placed— on the prime movers, the parasites, or the world. The answer is: *the world.* The story must be primarily a picture of the whole.

In this sense, *The Strike* is to be much more a "social" novel than *The Fountainhead*. *The Fountainhead* was about "individualism and collectivism within man's soul"; it showed the nature and function of the creator

January 1, 1945

(1)

# "The Strike"

Theme: What happens to the world when the Prime Movers go on strike.

This means — a picture of the world with its motor cut off. Show: what, how, why. The specific steps and incidents— in terms of persons, their spirits, motives, psychology and actions — and, secondarily, proceeding from persons, in terms of history, society and the world.

The theme requires: to show who are the prime movers and why, how they function. Who are their enemies and why, what are the motives behind the hatred for and the enslavement of the prime movers; the nature of the obstacles placed in their way, and the reasons for it.

This last paragraph is contained entirely in "The Fountainhead." Roark and Toohey are the complete and the second-hander. The primary concern there was with Roark and Toohey—showing *what they are*. The other characters were variations on the theme of the relation of the ego to others—mixtures of the two extremes, the two poles: Roark and Toohey. The story's primary concern was the characters, the people as such, their *natures*. Their relations to each other— which is society, men in relation to men—were secondary, an unavoidable, direct consequence of Roark set against Toohey. But it was not the theme.

Now, it is this *relation* that must be the theme. Therefore, the personal becomes secondary. That is, the personal is necessary only to the extent needed to make the relationships clear. In *The Fountainhead* I showed that Roark moves the world—that the Keatings feed upon him and hate him for it, while the Tooheys are consciously out to destroy him. But the theme was Roark—not Roark's relation to the world. Now it will be the relation.

In other words: I must show in what concrete, specific way the world is moved by the creators. [I must show] exactly *how* the second-handers live on the creators, both in *spiritual* matters *and* (most particularly) in concrete physical events. (Concentrate on the concrete, physical events—but don't forget to keep in mind at all times how the physical proceeds from the spiritual.)

(A new sidelight here: the dreadful desolation of the world, not only in closed factories and ruins, but also in the spiritual emptiness, hopelessness, confusion, dullness, grayness, fear. As keys to that: L. L. and M. K. joining the Catholic Church. *Or:* the relation of people to *me*, what they seem to seek from me—think of Marjorie [Hiss], Faith [Hersey], all my girl friends—and even Pat [Isabel Paterson].)

However, for the purpose of this story, I do not start by showing *how* the second-handers live on the prime movers in actual, everyday reality— nor do I start by showing a normal world. (That comes in only in necessary retrospect, or flashback, or by implication in the events themselves.) I start with *the fantastic premise of the prime movers going on strike*. This is the heart and center of the novel. A distinction carefully to be observed here: I do not set out to glorify the prime mover (that was *The Fountainhead*). I set out to show how desperately the world needs prime movers, and how viciously it treats them. And I show it on a hypothetical case—*what happens to the world without them*.

The difference from *The Fountainhead* here will be as follows: in *The Fountainhead* I did not show how desperately the world needed Roark— except by implication. I did show how viciously the world treated him, and why. I showed *mainly what he is*. It was Roark's story. *This* must be the world's story—in relation to its prime movers. (Almost—the story of a body in relation to its heart—a body dying of anemia.)

I do not show directly what the prime movers *do*—that's shown only by implication. *I show what happens when they don't do it.* Through that, you see the picture of what they do, their place and their role. (This is an important guide for the construction of the story.)

Now to state the theme consecutively: the world lives by the prime movers, hates them for it, exploits them and always feels that it has not exploited them enough. They have to fight a terrible battle and suffer every possible torture that society can impose—in order to create the things from which society benefits immeasurably and by which alone society can exist. In effect, they must suffer and pay for the privilege of giving gifts to society. They must pay for being society's benefactors. That is what happens in [practice] and what society demands and expects in theory, by the nature of its altruist-collectivist philosophy.

The course of each great cultural step forward runs like this: a genius makes a great discovery; he is fought, opposed, persecuted, ridiculed, denounced in every way possible; he is made a martyr—he has to pay for his discovery and for his greatness, pay in suffering, poverty, obscurity, insults, and sometimes in actual arrest, jail, and death. Then the common herd slowly begins to understand and appreciate his discovery—usually when he is too old, worn, embittered, and tired to appreciate that which they could offer him in exchange, i.e., money, fame, recognition, gratitude and, above all, freedom to do more. Or [the appreciation of the genius comes] long after he is dead; then the herd appropriates the discovery—physically, in that they get all the practical benefits from it, *and spiritually,* in that they appropriate even the glory. *This is the most important point of the book.* The public monuments erected to the great men in city squares (for the pigeons to dirty) are only an empty gesture—a hypocritical concession, a bribe. Just like the acknowledgment of the great men's achievements in school books—to bore children with. Nobody takes it seriously. Nobody gives it any thought. Nobody takes it into any spiritual account. Children go on being taught and men go on believing that the "collective" is the source of all virtue, greatness, and creation. The achievements of the great men are embezzled by the collective—by becoming "national" or "social" achievements.

This is the subtlest trick of "collectivization." The very country that opposed and martyred a genius becomes the proud author of his achievement. It starts by using his name as the proof and basis of its glory—and ends up by claiming credit for the achievement. It was not Goethe, Tchaikovsky, or the Wright brothers who were great and achieved things of genius—it was Germany, Russia, and the United States. It was "the spirit of the people," "the rhythm of the country," or whatever. The great man was only the robot—he "expressed the aspiration of the people," he was "the voice of the country," he was "the symbol of his time," etc.

The intent in all this is single and obvious: the expropriation of the great man's credit. After taking his life, his freedom, his happiness, his peace, and his achievement, the collective must also take his glory. The collective wants not only the gift, but the privilege of not having to say "thank you." The collective hates the man of genius—because he is a man of genius. It wants to torture him and expects him to struggle against [the collective]—in order to bring it the gifts, without disturbing its vanity and inferiority. Then it wants to steal the gifts and the giver's glory—so that it would not have to admit to its own filthy, petty, twisted mind that it is an inferior, a charity object, a debtor, a beggar.

(Good examples of this: the Wright brothers against the Smithsonian Institution; any country's boasting of the great artists it martyred, such as France and Victor Hugo; the radio program's slogan—"In a democracy art belongs to all the people"; the Soviet boast about its miserable North Pole expedition being greater than the achievements of individual enterprise, i.e., greater than the man who first discovered the North Pole, and greater than the Wright brothers who created the airplane; the "Zola" movie—where you see France putting Zola through hell for fighting against the collective France of his time, then hear it said at his funeral that Zola represented "the heart of France." *This* is how the genius is made the victim of the collective's crime and the whitewash for that crime.)

Such is the relationship between the prime mover and the collective. It has been such all through history—and it is sanctioned, demanded, expected, held to be virtuous by mankind's moral codes and philosophies. *It is against this that the prime movers go on strike in my story.*

This part has to be kept in mind clearly and covered thoroughly. This is *the basis* of the whole story. I must decide in what way I present it—but it *must be presented.* (I'll have to think over the prologue in this connection.) It is not just that the prime movers go on strike—it's *why* they go on strike and *against what.* The "against what" must be made crystal clear—or the story is pointless.

On the basis of this beginning, the story then proceeds like this: The prime movers say to the world, in effect: "You hate us. You don't want us. You put every obstacle in our way. Very well—we'll stop. We won't fight you or bother you. We'll merely stop functioning. We'll stop doing the things you martyr us for. *And see how you like it.*"

The complete statement of the strike's objective is: "We have had enough of your exploitation, persecution, insults, stealing, and expropriation. Go ahead and try to exist without us. We will not come back until you recognize and acknowledge the truth of the matter. Until you admit what we are, give us full credit for what we do, and give us *full freedom* from your chains, orders, restrictions and encroachments—physical, spiritual, political, and *moral*. Until you accept a philosophy that will leave us alone to function as we please. Until you take your hands off us—*and keep them off.* We ask nothing but the freedom to work and live as we please. You will get gifts and benefits from us such as you can never imagine. But you will not get them until you leave us alone. We are doing this in the name of all the great men whom you martyred in the past—and for the sake of all the great men you intend to martyr in the future. In the name of and for the sake of man's greatness and man's dignity. Once and for all, we will put an end to the torture of the best by [means of] their best—the penalizing of genius for [being] genius."

*This* is the theme of the novel.

The story then shows what happens to the world when its heart stops. *This point* must be thought out carefully, in every detail, in every aspect. In a general way, what happens is total paralysis. Spiritually and physically. The wheels stop—and thought stops. All life, hope, and joy go with them. All energy, fire, color, imagination, enthusiasm. It is a kind of slow, creeping, progressive "rigor mortis." Not horror and violence—but slow disintegration. Slow rot. The gray horror of dullness, stupidity, incompetence, inertia. Most particularly *inertia.*

Show how the world stops entirely. And when it has stopped, when the collective has destroyed itself—the world learns its lesson. The prime movers can come back.

---

To be thought out in detail: (1) every representative aspect of the prime mover who is martyred or stopped by society; (2) every representative aspect of the different way in which prime movers stop and go on strike—the kind of people they are and how they do it; (3) every representative aspect of the way in which the second-hander cannot function by himself and paralyzes the world. Every aspect of how and why and in what way the world has to stop without the prime movers—and does stop.

*Disconnected bits:*

John Galt
Dagny Taggart
Francisco d'Anconia
James Taggart
Eddie Willers

The opening of the story proper with: "Who is John Galt?" The bum in a desolate city street at twilight. The first signs of a city's disintegration. The "afternoon" uneasiness. The calendar on the tower. Eddie Willers thinking of the great oak stricken by lightning, hollow inside—as he comes to the great building of Taggart Transcontinental. The marvelously efficient offices—and the heart of the building, the office of James Taggart. "Don't bother me, don't bother me, don't bother me," said James Taggart.

The introduction of Dagny Taggart as she walks through the offices like a gust of fresh wind.

Dagny and Francisco d'Anconia. "Who is John Galt?"—"Stop using that cheap figure of gutter legend!"

Dagny and the engineer who quits mysteriously.

The girl writer at the book store window: "No, it's not in that window. It will never be in that window." [*The girl writer is the fishwife in the valley; AR initially planned a larger role for the character.*]

The radio talk: "Don't bother trying to choke it off. It can't be done. This is John Galt speaking. . . . How did I do it? You could have had that secret and many, many others."

About John Galt's invention: "In the eighteenth century, it could have been the steam engine. In the nineteenth—the automobile. In the twentieth—the airplane. In *our* day—you'll never learn."

John Galt's answer to the offer of planned power over the world: "Get the hell out of my way."

The last scene: in the mountains of their valley, looking down at a wrecked road—like the roads left of the Roman Empire. A house with a roof caved in—the skeleton of an automobile with its wheels in the air—and in the distance the stubborn fire fighting the wind. John Galt said: "This is our day. The road is cleared. We're going back."

**June 26, 1945**

The key points which will have to be *dramatized* (in concrete events, *not* merely by implication and exposition):

The nature of the *prime movers' martyrdom. That* must be *shown.*

(There must be some equivalent of the prologue—some figure such as the composer—either in action or in flashback, but preferably in direct action.) This is needed not only because it is such an important point, never before covered anywhere—but also because it gives meaning to the strike itself. It is *the spirit of the strike*—and the justification. *It is the very thing that made me want to write this novel.* Without that point, the story would become merely a recital of the physical aspects of the strike, just plot events of a struggle which could not interest us very much because we are not let in on its essential purpose and motive. It would actually feature the second-handers—what happens to *them*, not to the strikers. The predominant emotion left by the book would be contempt, hatred, ridicule, gloating over the second-handers and their plight—but no uplift to the spirit of the strikers. The strikers would become only a kind of plot means to expose the parasites.

I must consider very carefully the statements I made in my [earlier] notes to the effect that *the world* is featured in the story, and *the relation* of society to its prime movers. There is a fine balance of theme and construction which I must achieve here. It is somewhat the same problem as in *The Fountainhead*: the second-handers *must not* be allowed to steal the show, to become the stars of the story. Even though I do not here treat of the *nature* of prime movers, but of *their relation* to society—it is still *the prime movers* who are to be the stars: it is still *their* story. The balance must be: what happens to the world without the strikers—but also, what happens to the strikers.

The general scheme, then, is: society's crime against the prime movers— the prime movers go on strike—society collapses—the prime movers come back.

A question to decide here is: whether there should be a concrete act of *repentance* on the part of society, an act of acknowledgment, the issue understood once and for all—or whether the strikers win merely by default, coming back because their road is cleared. This last is what actually happens historically—but then the implication would be that once the strikers have rebuilt the world, the whole process would begin all over again. The first (the repentance) is difficult to conceive; who is to do the repenting? Are second-handers capable of such an act, of understanding and justice? *This* must be thought out.

[In my notes of January 1], I have the sentence "the world learns its lesson." As a possibility, I might have a specific villain in the story who symbolized the parasites and society, who exploits the prime movers—and who repents at the end. It might be James Taggart. Or it might be several men, each representing a key aspect of society and of the parasite.

The theme stated in its simplest form: it is John Galt saying to an inefficient stenographer: "You presumptuous fool! I have no desire to work for you nor to be martyred for that privilege. You think I should and you think you can force me to. All right—try it."

(A possible lead in thinking out the construction: the story could actually be told in the terms of one life—the personal relationship of one creator to one second-hander. Try to visualize it as that—then translate it into a social picture, by individualizing the separate key aspects of the conflict.)

Keep in mind throughout the story the realistic aspect of the fantastic theme—the *actual* ways in which prime movers *do* go on strike, though it is not a conscious, organized strike. By stressing that, keeping it as the foundation of the characters' psychology, using it consistently for concrete cases, as illustration—I will make the story profoundly *real*, spiritually real. The plot device of the strike will then become only an exaggeration of that which actually happens, an emphasis for purposes of clarity and eloquence—not pure fantasy.

The two realistic ways in which prime movers go on strike are: (1) what happens to talented and exceptional men under dictatorships; and (2) how sensitive, talented people stop functioning when they are disgusted by the society around them, as at the present time here in America.

This last form of striking always happens when gifted men find themselves in a morally corrupt society. (And such a society is always collectivist, or on its way to collectivism, because morality and individualism are inseparable. The degree of individualism in a society determines the degree of its morality.) In effect, the gifted men find themselves dealing with men and conditions that *they do not wish to deal with*. So they do one of three things: (1) they do not function at all and become drifting, aimless bums; (2) they function in some field other than their proper one and produce only enough for their own sustenance, refusing to let the world benefit from their surplus energy; or (3) they function in their proper field but produce less than one tenth of their actual capacity—it is a strained, unhappy, forced effort for them—their natural desire and their energy demanding an outlet, in conflict with their disgust against the conditions under which their energy has to function.

Examples to keep in mind: (1) Gus Vollmer, Linda Lynneberg (?); (2) Frank [O'Connor], Pat's publisher (Earle Balch), Dr. Kramer and all the doctors who wish to retire if socialized medicine is passed; (3) Pat.

**April 6, 1946**

*Questions to think out*

**1.** *The actual plot must contain emotional conflict.* There is the danger of having mere action, without emotional content, if I start with the strikers already on strike. Their decision is then undramatized, behind the scenes—and the story can become passive, like their action of just doing nothing. (Here—show that it is not easy for them to break the ties.)
**2.** The strikers must have something to do more than just strike. Otherwise, the parasites will carry the story by carrying the action. *It still must be the strikers' story—they must carry and motivate the plot.*

*For main line (plot)*

The main activities of mankind.
The three attitudes [*described at the end of the June 26, 1945, notes*].
The steps of growth—reverse [to find] steps of disintegration (and destruction). (Stress "purposelessness" in the progressive steps of TT's [Taggart Transcontinental's] destruction.)
The specific (concrete) form of the final catastrophe. (Specific second-handers, or is it beyond that point? Beyond that point—panic and collapse.)

**April 7, 1946**

John Galt tells one of those who is unconsciously on strike from bitterness and disillusionment: "You think the world is essentially a mixture of good and evil, and one must compromise with the evil, and you're sick of that, so you're giving up the world? Nonsense. Evil, by definition (if we have made the right definition), is the impotent, the impractical, the powerless, that which does not work. So it is no threat to us, it cannot stand in our way—*unless we permit it and help it to do so.* It cannot poison the world for us—unless we carry the poison and spread it. The parasites cannot exploit us or rule us—unless we voluntarily agree to be exploited and hand them the tools with which to rule us. *Let us withdraw the tools.*

"We permit it, and we have suffered this long, for one essential reason: the generosity of the creator. It is our nature that we wish to give, prodigally, recklessly, because we know that the source—our creative energy—is inexhaustible. Being self-sufficient, we cannot conceive of dependence, so we are modest in relation to others, we never think that we are indispensable to them or superior, because we do not consider *them* indispensable or superior to us. We act as equals toward equals—and an exchange between equals is a proper, natural activity. We are glad to give because our creation is a discovery or embodiment of truth, and when others respond to truth we welcome their response, we are happy—not because of the good it does *them*, not because their approval gives us pleasure or is of any importance to us— but because their response is a victory for truth, and what we welcome is their entrance into *our* world, into that world which we know to be good and true.

"We see no danger in giving—we think we're giving to men as rich as we are; we think of it as gifts, not alms. And whenever we come up against an inferior—that he is an inferior is the hardest thing for us to believe; we see the evidence and we think it is a misunderstanding or a temporary misfortune that has affected the man; then we throw ourselves to the rescue, we give, we help, we let him lean on us and bleed us, we carry him—'why not?' we say, we are so strong, we have so much to spare. We are incapable of conceiving of the parasite's mind, so we can never understand him. We are incapable of hatred and malice. We will not accuse him without cause or reason—and we can't find the cause, since we can't understand him.

"So we become helpless and bewildered before him. We never accuse him, no matter what he does to us. He yells that we are selfish, cruel, tyrannical by reason of the very abundance and magnificence of our talents. And we almost come to believe this. "Almost"—because no power on earth can really make us believe this; we are the men of truth, we cannot fall that far into lying; and since our talents, our creative energy, are our sacred possessions, the source of our joy in living, we cannot commit so great a sacrilege against them.

"We allow ourselves to become torn. In a vague, unstated, indefinable way, we begin to feel that we must atone for something, make amends to someone, pay someone for something in some manner. What? We don't know. We can never know. We refuse to admit to ourselves the truth in a clear statement: that we are being damned for the best within us, and that the creature making the accusation is small, inferior, and truly evil. We are generous, and we do not pronounce such a judgment upon a fellow human being. Hatred and anger are unnatural to us; contempt for a human being is totally unnatural to us, perhaps impossible—because we think and act as if we were dealing with men, and it is not proper to despise men, we are worshippers of man, because *we* are men and this is the logical implication of our self-reverence. One's opinion of mankind comes from one's opinion of oneself, which is the only first-hand knowledge of man one can have. The man who respects himself, will carry the respect to his species, to others. The man who despises himself, with good reason, carries the contempt, the malice, the hatred, the suspicion to all humanity. We, the creators, cannot conceive of this. We are bewildered by the parasite's malice—we do not even recognize it as malice, because we don't really know malice.

"But so long as, for any reason, we do not recognize the truth—we are bound to fail and to suffer, in the whole sphere and in all our actions where we have left this truth unrecognized. Our generosity is a good motive? *Nothing* is good if it motivates lying, falsehood, or evasion. There is no morality except an unbending, absolute recognition of the truth, in relation to everything; an absolute will to find, face, and grasp the truth, to the utmost of our capacity, then to act upon it. Nothing is moral but this cold, ruthless, *rational* pursuit.

"But we have not faced or recognized the truth about the parasites—so we fail, we're helpless, we're disarmed, and they've got us. Did they win over us? No, we won the battle for them. *They* rule the world? No, we handed it over to them. The guilt *is* ours, but not in the way they think; in the exactly opposite way. The guilt is that we have refused to see the truth about us and about them.

"What makes a man a parasite? Nothing and no one but himself. We do not classify him as an inferior—he classifies himself. He is the only one who can. What is the specific action of doing this? The recognition by a man, stated or unstated in his mind (and I think it is usually stated), that he is the creature and the product of others, dependent upon them for the content of his soul. The negation by a man of his primary human attribute (his essential attribute, the one and only attribute that makes him human): his independent rational judgment. This is all that's necessary; the rest—all the evils, corruptions, perversions—follow automatically.

"When a man rejects his independent rational judgment he has rejected himself as an entity, as a man, as an end in himself. Whatever happens to him from then on can be nothing but failure and tragedy; he is functioning against his own nature, he is acting against the laws of his own survival. And by the very fact that he *is* a man (or was born to be and can't be anything else), some last conscious remnant of [his betrayal] makes him hate himself.

"He does not know why he has this deep conviction of his own inferiority, of his basic worthlessness, of his being essentially contemptible. He runs, by every means possible, from admitting this conviction to himself, but he knows it's there. He says, in effect, "I *feel* it." He ascribes every possible cause to it—his feeling of helplessness against the universe of which he knows so little, his fear of others, his envy of them, his knowledge that he'll never be able to equal their achievements, that he doesn't possess their talents, or that they'll surely fail to recognize his own. All of it is evasion, beside the point, and a consequence, not a cause. He despises himself because he has willfully negated his nature as a man.

"Were he actually incapable of being an independent rational entity, there would have been no feeling of hatred, evil, misery in him from this negation; he could have no conception of what he had betrayed and no uneasiness about it; a creature cannot hate itself for being what it is. It cannot exist in perpetual pain; pain is a warning of disorder, of the improper, physically or spiritually. A creature born as a physical freak, incapable of survival, would not survive; and such time as it had, would be spent in constant pain, the warning that something is improper, the sign of *the misfit* in the most basic, essential sense. Man survives through his mind, i.e., his spirit. If his spirit were doomed, by its essence and nature, to constant pain, to hatred of himself, he would not survive. If it was proper for a parasite to be a parasite, if he was by nature incapable of independent rational judgment, he would be happy in that state, happy on his own terms. He would go on copying the motions and repeating the ideas of others, as his natural function, like a monkey. A monkey does not hate itself, nor those it imitates. The misery of the parasite is the proof he was not intended to be a parasite; he was not doomed to it by the cruelty of nature—he did it to himself.

"What caused him to do it? That does not matter to us too much. Fear—laziness—the desire to escape the responsibility of rationality—the belief in a malevolent universe and, from that, the conviction that if he learns the truth about the universe he will discover the evil and disasters [surrounding] him, therefore he must avoid knowledge of the truth, therefore he must get rid of his means of knowledge, i.e., his reason—the half-digested teachings of others to which he succumbed in childhood before he had begun to think, the whole vicious mess of irrationalism, altruism, and collectivism—all of that can be and is the cause of his pronouncing the verdict of parasite on himself and rejecting his nature as man. These are his reasons, but what concerns us here are the results as they affect *us*, the results of our relation with the parasite."

**April 10, 1946**

"In what manner do we allow the parasite to rule us, and what happens when he does? He rules us by the break we allow him to make within us. We accept him as an equal, i.e., a rational being. Then we are torn by the awful spectacle of the irrational around us. We find ourselves in a world we cannot understand, we are helpless and lost. *We have allowed him to create around us the kind of world **he** lives in, or imagines, or fears: the senseless, malevolent universe.* We begin to doubt the power of the human mind, the reality or practicality of truth, the possibility of good or justice. We suspect that we might be living in an insane chaos, but *that* is a supposition with which we cannot exist or function. Yet we *must* function, that is the basic law of our nature, and so we are caught in a civil war within ourselves and *we* become objects of perpetual suffering, made so by that very thing which is our life source, our happiness, the moving force of man's survival—our spiritual independence and creative energy. And when we suffer within ourselves in this essential, primary way, we cannot function at our best—and we are disarmed. The parasite has us where he wants us: functioning only enough to support him, but not enough to be happy, to be strong, to shake him off and get forever out of his reach.

"We become like the parasite in every respect save our work. *That* neither he nor any form of suffering nor even our own will can corrupt. *That* remains untouched. In the sphere of our work we remain ourselves, functioning as we should, true to our nature. But in every other sphere—in our private lives, in our relations with men and the world—we adopt the methods and convictions of the parasite, we are just what he is: torn, uncertain, self-contradictory, vicious, lying, evasive—because we're doing the same thing, running from the truth, trying to escape from something we don't want to face. And in such a role, we are, perhaps, more evil than the parasites—if there can be degrees in such a matter. It is then we who poison the world, we who make it evil, we who work for our own destruction. This [applies to] anyone who does not live up to his highest capacity, who betrays his own talent and makes of it his own torture rack. How have we done this? By admitting the parasite into our own soul. By allowing him to be a major concern within us.

"What happens when he rules us? *The kind of vicious world you see, in which the best has been turned into a source of evil, in which competence is the source of failure, life energy is the source of destruction, and the capacity for joy is the source of the most terrible suffering.* In this kind of corrupted world, the parasite can survive comfortably without reproach, he can enjoy it, he can exploit us and he can rule.

*"This is what we have done. Now let us stop it.*

"Withdraw the tools. Put yourself apart. Cut every spiritual connection with the parasite, every emotional tie, and every practical cooperation.

Cooperation with them on their terms (those of collectivism) is not cooperation, but surrender—the voluntary offer to be beaten. Stop it. Face them for
what they are. *And let them learn what you are.*"

———

"Carry to your personal life the same principles on which you function
in your creative life. All of you live on the premise of one kind of universe
when you work—and of quite a different kind in every part of your existence
outside of work."

The above is the actual secret, key and definition of Roark. He was the
embodiment of the perfect man acting consistently on the right moral principle. That moral principle (*the mortality of independence*) is most eloquently obvious in creative work, and actually in every kind of work; this is
proper, since work (creation, production, achievement, purposeful activity)
is man's primary and greatest function. But the same principle applies to all
of a man's life and activities—personal, social, emotional, etc. Roark functioned consistently and consciously on that principle.

The actual case of the genius is often the tragedy of [an internal] civil
war: the principles of the creator in his work, the principles of the second-
hander in every other aspect of his life. Why? All the reasons Galt states
above, plus the fact that no consistent morality of the creator had ever been
formulated. This is what has made geniuses so tortured and so tragic, when
they should have been the ecstatic representatives of humanity. The world is
responsible for torturing them? Yes—but that torture would be easy to bear,
if the genius had not brought upon himself the torture within. It is he who
does the world's dirty work against himself. Otherwise, the pain would go
only down to a certain point—and the genius would triumph, essentially,
even if locked in a jail cell. The world is responsible for the [external] torture of the genius—and as a cause or source of the much greater torture
which he imposes on himself by his wrong conception of the world.

Now it is *this* aspect of genius which I must show—not the pure, consistent genius that Roark is—but the divided victim which most geniuses
have been. John Galt is the Roark in the story, but the others are not, and it is
against the exploitation by the world, particularly this spiritual exploitation,
that Galt teaches them to strike.

———

## Characters needed

*John Galt*—energy. Activity, competence, initiative, ingenuity, and above all *intelligence*. Independent rational judgment. The man who conquers nature, the man who imposes his purpose on nature. Therefore, Galt is an inventor, a practical scientist, a man who faces the material world of science as an adventurer faces an unexplored continent, or as a pioneer faced the wilderness—something to use, to conquer, to turn to his own purposes. In relation to the creators—*he is the avenger*. (He is *"the motor of the world."*)

*A man who is the most tragic victim of collectivist exploitation.* He is the one who finds it so hard to break the ties. Hank Rearden—possibly a great, self-made industrialist, torn by the naiveté of his own generosity.

*The martyred artist.* The composer (Dietrich Gerhardt, who supports his own torturers); the girl-writer. [*AR replaced Gerhardt with the somewhat different character of Richard Halley.*]

*The great man made into a parasite in his private life (or made miserable).* A man who thinks he must pay a price for selfishness.

*The great man who refuses to function and is destroying himself.* Probably a minor character.

*The genius who accepts anything if only he'd be left free to function.* This is Dietrich Gerhardt.

*The young girl who supports a whole family (or the honest kind of tough worker like Mike).* The industrialist's secretary. The worker who fights against Taggart and for Rearden. (She understands the issue.)

*The philosopher.* A kind of Ortega y Gasset—vaguely. A kind of Aristotle if he came back to life today. Or even Thomas Aquinas.

*The farmer.* A man of action [who opposes] the parasites in the most basic, simplest terms.

*Dagny's employee.* The ship owner who sank his ships rather than let them be nationalized (probably an Englishman). (Gerald Hastings)

*The priest.* Father (medieval name), who is the last of the strikers. He withdraws the moral sanction from the world of the parasites. (He represents the last stand for pity.)

*The traitor.* The man in-between who has both potentialities, could go both ways, tries to see both sides, attempting a compromise. He turns out to be the one most destructive to the side of the creators, the one contributing most to the parasites—which he himself cannot

stand, therefore he destroys himself. (He accomplishes James Taggart's triumph over him.) Stan Winslow. (He is also an example of
the two potentialities in the lesser man.)

*The man who goes insane on the idea of charity*—a kind of
"Dostoyevsky."

*The average man.* The actual in-between, who goes to the good in a
society of producers, to the bad in a society of parasites. He can be
an older executive of TT—who, at the end, realizes the horror of his
position.

*The man who makes a virtue of evil*—who claims that his lack of
conviction is a virtue, a sign of some sort of breadth of vision: "To
have convictions is to wear blinders." The damn fool confuses a
view of the opinions of others with a view of reality.

*The mystic of parasitism*—another "Mr. Smith" of Washington.
James Taggart's "best friend," "pull," and guide.

*James Taggart's wife* ("the Cinderella girl"). She may be an example
of the average woman going to pieces without spiritual guidance
(and going through hell with J.T.).

*The man corroded by envy of genius*—because he knows that his
miserable little achievement is swamped out by the magnificent
achievement of the genius. He knows enough to recognize the difference—yet his conclusion is that the genius must be destroyed to protect *him*. That means, by his own definition, that the best must be
destroyed for the sake of the worst. This is the monstrous kind of
second-hander's selfishness—the primary consideration here being
in the others and in measuring one's value by comparison. He considers his own talent worthless, because the talent of the genius is
greater—therefore, to be *best*, he must destroy the genius; his standard of perfection is not absolute, but relative, he wants to do, not the
best possible, but the best others will see. ([*Note added later:*] No.
The man who does this *has no* "little" achievement—whatever he
has is stolen.)

This [latter] man against Galt in the final climax is a good possibility. His
most revealing line: "The genius destroys the individuality of the lesser men."
(?!) (But the god-damn "lesser men" feed on the genius—and that's why they
hate him. This is the fable of the pig and the oak tree.) [*In the fable, the pig
uproots the oak tree to get the acorns, thus destroying his source of food.*]

If the "lesser men" don't want to imitate or follow the genius—then he
can't destroy their "individuality." But if they do want to follow, if it's to

their advantage—then what is it that they resent? Obviously—the impression in the eyes of others. They become "followers," not "great innovators" in the eyes of others. And what "others" does he want to fool? "Lesser men" or "geniuses"? Both, of course, and, above all, himself.

No—not quite. One type simply wants to steal; the other—this type—wants himself and others brought down. (Or are both motives intermixed?) This is the man who has a direct interest in the destruction of genius—steal their achievements, take the credit for your two cents' worth of "improvement," and destroy them, so nobody can challenge you. And then look for another victim.

*The line-up so far:*

*The creators:*

| | |
|---|---|
| *John Galt* | Energy |
| *Francisco d'Anconia* | The entrepreneur (financier) |
| Hank Rearden | The industrialist |
| Dagny Taggart | |
| The girl writer | |
| The young engineer | |
| The girl secretary | "Average" competence |
| Dietrich Gerhardt | The composer |
| *Ragnar Danneskjöld* | The smuggler (the adventurer) |
| The philosopher | Thought |
| Gerald Hastings | The ship owner |

*The parasites:*

James Taggart
The industrialist's wife
The industrialist's mistress and other friends
A "head of the State"—on the order of Truman [*President at the time of these notes*]
Businessmen on the order of Bobbs-Merrill

*The in-between:*

Eddie Willers (to the good)
Stan Winslow (to the bad)
The man of charity (to the *very* bad)

*The strikers (in order of importance):*

> John Galt
> Francisco d'Anconia
> Ragnar Danneskjöld
> The philosopher
> The composer
> Gerald Hastings (the ship owner)

---

*Have characters (or incidents or both) dramatize a world in which:* the best has been turned into a source of evil (Danneskjöld); competence is the source of failure (the young engineer or the girl-writer); life energy is the source of destruction (Francisco d'Anconia); the capacity for joy is the source of the most terrible suffering (the composer, the girl-writer, the industrialist).

"This is what we have done. Now let us stop it."

Here, in effect, the pattern is this: when men refuse to live according to the principles of the good, the principles proper to them, the best among them are forced to turn against them, to become a danger, an enemy, a source of evil to them. (Because the *good* has been declared to be the *evil.*) In a proper society, Danneskjöld would have been a Columbus, the source of infinite benefit to lesser men; in a society of collectivism, he is forced to become a smuggler. Nothing will make him act against his own nature; he will rather act against mankind and all their laws. Danneskjöld doesn't even bother to argue about it; he just acts. (*This is important.*)

**April 11, 1946**

*The worst victim: the industrialist* (probably steel): self-made, extremely active, extremely generous, extremely naive.

*His wife:* a decadent society bitch—neither too beautiful, nor too rich, nor too well-born, but some of all of it. She does not need his prestige or money—her sole aim in life is to keep him down spiritually, to snub and ridicule him, destroy his every personal aspiration, humble him so that she may feel her own personal superiority through the sense of crushing a giant.

*His sister:* a clever, charming, and empty bitch who uses him

unmercifully in every way—socially, professionally, financially—
under guise of her "understanding." Her one concern is always to
make him feel that she gives him more than she receives, to keep
him thinking himself "under obligation"—[she does] this by means
of the "spiritual," as against his gifts which she considers "grossly
material."

*His brother:* a swindling [failure] who is "ashamed of his brother"
and drools that he has no chance because his brother "crushes" him.
A socialist.

*His mother:* an empty old bag who will never let go of the pretense
that her son "owes everything to his mother"—who much prefers her
younger son, a worthless failure—and who makes the industrialist's
life miserable by constant demands that he "make up to his brother"
for his own success.

*Assorted poor relatives and friends*—who "knew him when"—whose
sole theme-song is: "Don't you go high-hat on us," and who feel that
he's betrayed "his people" by rising above them. And they use him
unmercifully. To not "go high-hat on them" means to turn his soul
and pocket-book over to them.

*His secretary:* his exact parallel on a smaller scale. As competent
and honest as he is, and plagued by the same set of parasites with the
same motives, though superficially different.

The scene where the [industrialist and his secretary] realize the similarity of their tragedy. This is either the final or one of the important scenes
leading to both of them joining the strike.

### *Disconnected bits:*

For Eddie Willers and the last train: "Dagny, in the name of the best
within us! . . ."

———◦———

For Dagny's first meeting with Galt: When she opened her eyes, she saw
sunlight, green leaves and a man's face. She thought: I know what this is.
This is the world as I thought it would be when I was sixteen. Now it
is beginning—and the rest of it was just somebody's senseless joke. She
smiled, as to a fellow-conspirator, in relief, in deliverance, in radiant mockery

of all that she would never have to take seriously again. And the man smiled back, in exactly the same way.

("We never had to take any of it seriously, did we?" "No, we never had to.")

Part I—"The End"
Part II—"The Beginning" [*AR planned the novel in two parts. There is no reference in her journal to a Part III until September 1952.*]
Some names of chapters:
    "This is John Galt Speaking"
    "In the Name of the Best Within Us" (Last chapter)
    "The Calendar" (First chapter)

---

John Galt (probably in broadcast): "I am the first man of ability who has refused to feel guilty."

---

The story of the worker who remembers the factory meeting, about twelve years ago, when a slave-labor measure was [passed], and a young man got up to leave the meeting. He was an unknown young engineer. He stood alone against the hundreds, yet he made them afraid. He said: "I'm going to put an end to this, once and for all." As he turned to go, someone asked: "How?" He answered: "I'm going to stop the motor of the world." Then he walked out. No one's heard of him since. The factory is long since closed. But . . . "You see, his name was John Galt."

**April 13, 1946**

*Clues and leads (from "real life")*

*Philip H.*—the insane malice toward me; the dependence on M., yet his desire to crush her and hold her down. (This for James Taggart and the industrialist's wife.)

*Linda L.*—the teachers who refused her a scholarship she had earned and gave it to a less deserving girl "because she needed it more, while Linda could take care of herself." This is the deliberate, specific rewarding of mediocrity and penalizing of competence. (For the policy of James Taggart and others of his kind.)

*The school policy* of grading papers according to [effort] and not according to an objective standard. This is the most essentially vicious and corrupt measure ever devised; it is based on the premise of "to each according to his needs" (at whose expense?) and on the denial of an objective reality, which, in effect, amounts to training children for insanity. It is a denial of the simple fact that a man's need will *not* grow his food, only a man's ability will. It is a denial of the fact that results come from causes, that the achievement (or production) of the able man will be in proportion to and the result of his *ability and effort*, that the equal effort of a man of lesser ability will *not* [result in equal] achievement regardless of how the lesser one feels about it, that this is a fact of nature—and that the lesser one had better act accordingly, rather than attempt to harness the better man to an equality which is contrary to nature, reality and justice. (To carry out such an attempt the inferior man must accept the principle of slavery, with himself as master and the better man as slave. What is rewarded here? Incompetence. This is pure moral corruption.) This method is the total triumph of the irrational.

*Walter* [Abbott]—the sensitive, poetic kind of writer who spends his time writing bloody thrillers; he thinks this is all he has a chance at. That is his form of being on strike.

*Pat*—a person wrecked by a fierce sense of injustice, which she has never analyzed or defined as such. Knowing that she is right and that right *must* be recognized, yet getting no recognition, she has turned to a violent hatred of the world, to an exaggerated pride, to assuring herself too much that she is not hurt by the world—in order not to admit how badly hurt she is. And this is because she will not examine the exact nature of the reasons and motives of those who have hurt her. Also, she has turned to an insane arbitrariness—"I am right because I'm right"—since she has given up the hope of proving rightness in rational terms and having it understood or recognized. (In her particular case, the acceptance of the irrational has a great deal to do with this and with her failure. But that aspect does not concern me here, except to note an interesting question: did she accept the irrational early, because of observing what seemed to be the failure of the rational in the world, and being afraid to face such a universe—or did she accept the irrational first, through some personal fear or feeling of shortcoming, and this destroyed her whole proper life, which should have been that of a great rational thinker? I believe this last.)

The above arbitrariness has turned to hurting those whom she likes, by some peculiar multiple-inversion, like this: the irrational people have hurt her; the rational are the ones whom she needs and likes, the ones who speak her language and with whom she can deal; but she is fiercely determined to avenge herself; she knows that she cannot reach her enemies, the irrational ones, by her proper weapon, the mind; so she turns upon her friends, upon the rational ones, wreaking upon them the very thing she should hate, the thing which has hurt *her—the irrational.*

This is a frightening kind of "collective judgment," of revenge against the world—taking the world as a whole and trying to avenge oneself against its best for what has been done by its worst. It denies the whole conception of individual guilt and individual responsibility. One might say that this is extreme individualism—holding oneself alone against the world as a solid outside unit. But the error here is in considering the world as a "solid unit," in denying individualism as a basic absolute of man's nature, in actually considering the world as a *collective*, with collectivism as the natural law of the universe, and oneself as a noble but doomed outsider, a freak, a kind of Byronic damned, who is damned heroically because he will not accept reality which is evil. (Pat has hinted just that.) This is the same mistake as thinking that an individualist is a man who recognizes only his own rights. *An individualist must recognize man as an individualist.*

I am not sure I want to use this—it belongs in the novel about the mind. [*AR thought of writing a novel showing the primacy of reason over emotions, but it eventually became obvious that this theme was included in* Atlas Shrugged.] I might use only the first part, the terrible bitterness created by injustice; not the second part, not the revenge through the irrational.

*Frank Lloyd Wright*—a man who is a Roark in his professional life, and a Keating in his private life. How does one get to that? Strangely enough, in this case: a lack of self-confidence, personal uncertainty. It seems as if all forms of conceit are sure signs of the exact opposite. Whatever one chooses to express, or achieve, through social means is the denial of that very thing within oneself. If the method is that of the second-hander, this negation is unavoidable. For instance, to make a point of impressing one's superiority upon others is to attach importance to their recognition of one's superiority; if one attaches importance to it, one needs it. Why does one need it? Either as confirmation or as proof of one's own greatness; therefore, one's own conviction of that greatness is either uncertain or totally lacking. If one merely wished to find the understanding and appreciation of friends, one would not exhibit conceit toward them, nor stress one's superiority. One can't wish to have inferiors as friends; nor is the appreciation of inferiors of any sensible value. Therefore, conceit exhibited toward people can only mean a desire to establish superiority by comparison; if so, the primary determinant of superiority is not in oneself, but in others, not in what one can do, but in what they can't do; therefore, one's conviction of superiority has no real basis, no objective standards, no proof, no reality.

Apparently, FLW was hurt and frightened early in life by the hostility and stupidity of people toward his work. Then here was where the principle of collectivism entered: if people stood in the way of his work, it was people that he had to conquer to break his way through. Therefore, people became a crucial objective—and an enemy. On the one hand, he became extremely concerned to win them, to impress them, to get their recognition. On the other, since they are the enemy, he became convinced that he must deal with them on their own terms—through deceit, lying, flattery and rudeness, high-pressure, etc. He concluded that the terms applying to his work—honesty, beauty, intelligence, purposeful clarity, courage, directness—all of that could not apply to his dealings with people, since they were the enemies of his work whom he had to defeat. This is granting a crucial or decisive power to others, actually granting them superiority, at least in what he thinks are the regret-table practical matters, by adopting their terms and methods. (If one must deal with the collective—deal on your own terms, not on theirs. You've accepted the supremacy of the collective and defeated yourself when you accept their terms.)

Here there is a basic misunderstanding of the nature of individualism and of the rational. First, people do *not* hold the decisive power over you, no matter what they do or how you have to deal with them. Second, you can't expect to achieve anything through cheating—you only get what you asked for, a fake something that doesn't actually exist. (This might explain FLW's [*constant*] trouble with clients. Sure, he lies or flatters them into giving him the commission. Then he pays for it by cases such as Aline Barnsdall, or all the abandoned and rushed buildings. Those clients who lasted as a proper source of satisfaction to him were not snared by lies, but by whatever honest argument appealed to the best, the honest or the intelligent within them.)

Most importantly and profoundly, there is again a misunderstanding and fear of the rational. He does not know that his own judgment—exercised to the extreme of his capacity and honesty—is the only criterion of the rational upon which he can act, possible errors included. He does not know that the number of others has nothing to do with the truth of an issue. He sees the majority disagreeing with him about his work. He presumes that they are rational beings, like himself, with rational reasons for their opin-ions. But nothing on earth will make him change his convictions about his work (and rightly so). Then what happens? He can say one of three things: "to hell with my own convictions"—"to hell with the collective"—or "to hell with reason" (because it is reason that tells him the dilemma is unsolvable, contradictory, and he must take a stand). He says: "To hell with reason" (as most of them do). Note how often he makes cracks at reason—the stuff about the sunrise not being logical—yet how everything about his work is based on reason, on function, on purpose.

*In the clash between a man and the collective, the loser is reason* (for most men). A man cannot give up himself—and he dreads to give up the collective, because he doesn't understand it. So he thinks the safe thing is to give up reason; then the dilemma is not irreconcilable—then nothing is irreconcilable, since nothing has to be logical or make any kind of precise sense. (Then the world can dissolve into a kind of haze of overlapping shadows without edges or definitions. *And it does.*) Actually, of all three choices, giving up reason is the most dreadful and the most fatal. It amounts to giving up all three, and everything: all of life, the whole universe (or the ability to recognize the existence of a universe). The first choice is impossible (to give up oneself). This third choice is monstrous and impossible; but it takes a long time to work out its implications, particularly since no man can actually function on such a choice, since he remains rational to the extent that he exists at all, since he only lapses into the irrational occasionally, when he needs escape—and so it is a poison that works slowly, in a prolonged agony. Only the second choice (to give up the collective) is possible—and moral.

(The above is more [relevant] for my novel about the mind.)

Also, FLW is *playing* at living in the kind of world he would like—the effective, dramatic world. But he won't admit to himself that it's only playing. He wants other men to live up to his buildings—to the kind of existence his buildings are intended for (and which, incidentally, he has never defined). He thinks this is up to other people, or depends on them, or he can force them into it. He doesn't realize that none of it is real—since it is forced on people through their acceptance of his superiority (and since there is no conscious rational grasp of it in those people, hence no actual reality as far as they're concerned). Inferiors do not lead a heroic life, nor do they actually contribute anything to the hero. How can they? So his version of the beautiful, dramatic life becomes a show to impress those he despises—the vicious circle of second-handedness. [. . .]

His desire to be "god" or the representation of some sort of universal force is, of course, the desire to be something more than himself. He does not consider it enough to be a great man. This is also, perhaps, the desire to impose himself upon others in a way that the rational terms of man's equality will not permit: to be an authority, not by reason of achievement or rational proof, but just to be an authority: "It's so because I say it's so." Again, the dreadful desire for arbitrary power over others. Isn't the root of that the knowledge or fear that he could not prove or defend all his convictions in rational terms and on rational grounds? (Pat does the same, too.)

All of this leads only to evil, failure, and suffering. While hating people, using and cheating them—he has become completely dependent upon them, constantly begging them for admiration or attention. Trying to make them the means to achieve his world, he ended by living completely in their world, in its worst aspect pretense and deceit. This is an example of the fact that ruling others is still living for and through others, still collectivism. He tried to use the collective—he has become completely dependent upon it.

(The worst part of it is the spectacle of a great man constantly begging others: "Please show me how great a man I am!" It almost amounts to: "Please prove it to me!")

*The girl reader*—a horrible creature—homely, sloppy, physically dirty and unfeminine, unintelligent and inefficient—a person with no single grace to recommend her, but with an insidious bitterness and malice toward the world. She declared smugly that of course she is just a product and creature of her background, of her family, of her race, class, etc.—and of whatever "ideas" she has absorbed from others. She admits her own inferiority, pronounces it a virtue; she sneers at the possibility of anyone being better, regarding anyone's claim to independence as a presumption and a delusion—since she has decided that it is a delusion in her case.

*Nellie Berns*—when she said it's right that she should be compelled to pay for her own social security, by force and law; it's better for her, since she'd never have the character to save or provide for her future voluntarily. This is an admission of weakness and, again, the attaching of one's own sin to the rest of the world. Like this: I deserve to be pushed into line by means of a whip—therefore it's all right for others to be whipped, too, whether they deserve it or not. I need to be led on a leash—therefore, let's put others on a leash, too.

*The publicity boy* who—being a weak, hysterical, touchy kind of failure, the kind who never really made an effort toward anything—criticizes men like Henry Ford and other industrialists of the great school, calls them stupid, considers their success undeserved and in some way expropriated from *him*, and feels that men like Ford should be controlled by men like *him*.

*I. L.* [Ivan Lebedeff]—[a type] that is rather frightening—[he has] the idea that the man of whom he takes advantage must not only help him, but also pretend that no advantage is being taken in order to spare his feelings. This is a case where a man acts like a parasite, but does not want to pay for it even to the extent of admitting that that's what he is, and expects the man he exploits to keep up the pretense for his sake. He denies reality—and expects his victim to deny it, too. He wants to do evil—he knows that it's evil—without paying the price of admitting that it's evil and of having others know it. This is a "compound second-handedness": not merely accepting the judgment of others to estimate his own action, but knowing the nature of his action, expecting others to fake their judgment of it, and then feeling free to accept this faked judgment and to be absolved and vindicated by it. *This is an extremely important point*—it has a place in every variation of second-handedness, in every second-hander's soul. *This is for the priest*—it shows *how* he helps to perpetuate evil, the evil he thinks he's fighting.

### General Direction for Plot

Two main lines to follow for the key events of the plot:

*The progressive paralysis* of the world, the growing disintegration— each time because independent thinking, initiative, originality, fresh judgment were lacking; each time through the cowardly, senseless, automatic repetition of a routine that no longer applies. (This in connection with TT and those businesses that need it or that it needs. TT is acting here as the blood vessels of the world—and we see what happens when the heart is no longer pumping.)

*The progressive disappearance of the prime movers.* As the paralysis grows, they vanish, adding to it. This ties in with the first line—in each specific key case there is a prime-mover involved, who is either disregarded, or hampered, or refuses to make the crucial step and leaves the parasites to their natural fate.

*John Galt* must [embody] that which is lacking in the lives of all the strikers. It is he who specifically (in events essential to and proceeding from his nature) solves their personal stories, fills the lack, gives them the answer.

Here, then, I must decide who are the key strikers of the story and what is their relation to Galt. What they need, what he supplies, in what events this takes shape. ("The man innocent of all sense of guilt.") Most particularly: what does he give to Dagny?

*The climax* must be an event that shows the breakdown of the world. It will be the end of TT—but there must be a specific event that finishes off Taggart and all those connected with TT. This event must be based on and tied to the last major striker—the one who held out the longest, whose tie was hardest to break, but broke at last. (It would be best if this were Dagny.) In connection with this, start by asking yourself: *which, of all their ties and reasons, is the most excusable and the hardest to break?*

(The men who are "mixed" on the problem realize, as the story progresses, that they must take a stand.)

What does Galt do, once he enters the story? Is there no conflict for him? (This should be Dagny.)

**April 14, 1946**

*To think out:*

*Dagny's motive.* (What makes her tick?)
Galt's conflict, if any? (In connection with above.)
Representative strikers.
Representative parasites. In what exact way do parasites perish when left on their own? (Representative aspects of this—and from that, the characters needed and the events.)
The genius-envier as a possible connecting link from Galt's beginning to the climax.
*Representative businesses—the key activities of mankind.* (And how they are connected with TT.)

*For Dagny*

*Three lines of approach:*

Her hunger for her own kind of world. She works so fiercely because she knows she can have her world only by *creating* it—but she makes mistakes about people. (Her consequent bitterness.)
Her attempt (or desire) to be "the spark of initiative and the bearer of responsibility for a whole collective."
Her conflict (it must be concrete, emotional, dramatized, personalized).

**April 17, 1946**

*Note:* The creators work silently, their contribution unknown and their principles unstated, while the parasites climb to the forefront on stolen

achievements (by concentrating on the social, second-hand sphere of activity, and therefore getting the publicity and the credit). [The parasites] preach
their principles to the world, thus making these principles the stated or
public policy of mankind. Example: the real, competent businessman who
[said] that a Peter Keating could not be successful in the business world, that
this is not how business success is made; while every parasite screams that
Keating is the *practical* man, that any kind of success is made only by the
Keating methods, that his technique is *realistic* and *necessary*, and that
*the world* forces us to adopt his method. The question here is: what world?
The world of the parasite, the world which he imagines and according to the
principles of which *he* functions. But *that* world (like the parasite) is a surface sham, an illusion, a mildew on the *real* world, made possible only by
the real world, by its silent, active creators who support the surface mildew
and have no time to protest.

Of course, there are more parasites than creators—so the parasites'
creed is the one heard most often and spread most widely. Plus the fact that
the creators do not talk at all. The terrible thing here is the influence this
creed has on an "in-between," average young man who starts out in life
open-minded, with no particular convictions, and is taught at once that idealism (or any kind of sincerity) is impossible and impractical, that the world
belongs to the Peter Keatings and he had better act accordingly. If he's not
strong and independent enough to rebel against this teaching, he goes the
way of all parasites—and a potentially decent, average man is turned into
another scoundrel, his best potentialities are killed, his worse brought out
and encouraged.

[Further,] the creators themselves are left in a kind of bewildered
muddle. *They* cannot accept the idea that the world is made and moved by
the Peter Keatings—they know better—but they come to believe, with a
kind of helpless, unanalyzed bitterness, that they themselves are freaks or
martyrs, that they must go on functioning in a hostile, vicious world unsuited
to them. Well, the world they see *is* vicious, but it's neither real nor essential
nor necessary—it is permitted only by their own inattention, indifference, or
lack of understanding of it and of themselves. They can shake it off—like a
nightmare—any time they wish, if they understand their own nature, function and place in the world, if they accept their proper morality, declare it to
all men and then act upon it. *Let them awaken.* (This is what John Galt tells
them.)

*The man who thinks that the world demands corruption is the man who
is corrupting the world.* And note that he places his prime motive in others;
*they* demand corruption, he claims, and he has no choice but to accept their

methods and live on their terms. This is an eloquent demonstration of the viciousness, the moral corruption, brought about by second-handers.

Make a point to stress the fact that creators function in silence—both their work and their creed unknown.

Here, tell the creators that they are really functioning on my morality and are afraid to admit it. It's time they admitted it. (It's never been stated for them. But now it's stated.)

(No great man ever says that success is made through fraud; every small man says that. A man's idea of what makes success defines the nature of the man.)

———◦———

The creator's greatest tie to the world is the fact that he will *not* surrender the world to the parasites. He realizes that it is his proper function to shape the world to his wishes. And he struggles to do it no matter what obstacles the parasites put in his way. But by tolerating them or compromising by accepting their terms, he succeeds only in creating *their* world—or in keeping it going.

**April 18, 1946**

General theme in regard to the creators: the creators cannot work or live against their own principles. They only achieve their own destruction and the destruction of everything dearest and most important to them, including their work. This is their error and the cause of their tragedy. This is what they must stop—by defining, understanding, and accepting their proper principles. (They usually try to pay the price in their private lives. They say, in effect: "I am evil in my selfishness—I'll pay for it in my [private] life. I'll accept my suffering—but I'll go on working and being selfish about my work.")

If Dagny is the leading figure and carries the story, then the climax must be the destruction of TT (and almost the destruction of John Galt) by her attempt to deal with the parasites.

(Galt's ultimatum: "Do not function on the collectivist-altruist premise.")

The question here is: *In what specific way and for what excusable reason does she refuse to accept the right philosophy?* (Not stupidity, but a legitimate inner conflict.)

In real life, the creators stop functioning in a collectivist society—but they do it either as victims, forced to stop, or in helpless pessimism, simply believing that collectivism is natural, the law of the universe, and that the universe is evil and they are hopeless, doomed rebels against it. Galt makes them go on strike as a conscious, deliberate protest, with full knowledge of their being in the right; [they] thus demonstrate to themselves and to the parasites their function, their power in the world, and the true nature of the universe.

(As a possibility: flashbacks (e.g., Dagny or Eddie reading about it) of what had been, in effect, the strike of the creators in the past, throughout history.)

*Two aspects of the theme* (to keep integrated):

**1.** What happens to the world without the creators.
**2.** Why the creators go on strike (against what). This shows the manner of their exploitation by the world. Here there are two aspects: (1) material exploitation—by stealing and expropriating their achievements (Dagny); (2) spiritual exploitation—by what is done to the creators inside their souls (the industrialist). This last is made possible by the creators accepting the altruist-collectivist philosophy. They must reject this philosophy—and refuse to *give* to the world. (Then the world sees what happens to it, and whether it can *force* the gifts it needs out of the givers.)

---

The actual form of relationship between men is as follows: in an exchange between two men of equal ability (two creators), the exchange is even; in an exchange between a man of greater ability and a man of lesser ability (a creator and an average man), the lesser one actually receives much more than he gives—and it's all right if he leaves the creator alone; the creator doesn't rob or sacrifice himself, it's only that his ability and his contribution are so great.

As an example: a good, able engineer is needed by a railroad to drive a train engine, and if he works to the best of his ability he makes an honest contribution and he earns the salary which the head of the railroad pays him; it's not charity, it's his, he's earned it, he's produced its equivalent in value. *But he has earned it because the genius* [who runs] *the railroad has created an industry in which the engineer's native ability can earn much more than it could on its own.* The exchange of wages and services between the two men is fair. But the capacity of one has made the capacity of the other greater. If left on his own entirely, the engineer would not produce the equivalent (in comforts or advantages or consumption for himself) of what he produces with the help of the superior capacity of the head genius. (When the head of a company is not a genius, but inferior to his employees, something else happens. In a free society, it will not happen for long. To make it stick, compulsion is necessary. This is the case of James Taggart.)

The relationship works like this: a great, cooperative enterprise of many men is like a pyramid, with the single best brain on top, and then [at lower levels] the ability required is less and the number of men in that category is greater. Even though each man (assuming all work to the best of their ability) earns his living by his own effort and his wages represent his own, legitimate contribution—each has the advantage of all the strata above him, which contribute to the productive capacity of his own energy and raise that capacity (without diminishing their own); each man of lesser ability receives something extra from the men of greater ability above him; while the man at the top (the genius, the originator, the creator) receives nothing extra from all those under him, yet contributes to the whole pyramid (by the nature of his [work]). Now *this* is the creative over-abundance of the genius, this is the pattern of how he carries mankind, properly and without self-sacrifice, when left free to assume his natural course and function.

(What does the genius want for this? Just "Thank you.")

As a parallel example: it's the same process as when a worker makes a hundred pairs of shoes a day with the help of a machine. He gets paid on the basis of having produced a hundred pairs of shoes (the share of the factory owner, inventor, etc., being taken out); but left on his own (without the machine, the management, etc.) he would be able to produce, say, only ten pairs of shoes a day. His productive capacity has been raised by the inventor of the machine. Yet neither of the two men robs the other one; it's a fair exchange; but the worker gives to the inventor less than the inventor has given to him.

A similar relationship and process takes place in the spiritual or intellectual realm among the better and lesser thinkers of the world. All production comes from and is based on first-hand, independent thought. The man who contributes to the world a new thought (whether in invention, philosophy, art, or in any human activity) has made an invaluable contribution, for which no material returns are ever quite an equivalent. And when men deal through free exchange, no matter what fortune a man makes on his new thought, he has still given to other men more than he has received from them.

———◆———

In connection with this: my idea about an exchange between a writer and a composer; the fact that each reader of a book (or listener to a symphony) gets the whole of a tremendous value, for very little in return; each gets the whole, without diminishing it (and this is not just a matter of "mass production"—there can be only one book in existence and it can make the rounds of millions of men, and this still holds true). This has to do with the nature of an intellectual creation.

———◆———

To be exchangeable among men, a creation has to be put into a material shape—and only that material shape is exchangeable (through a material medium of exchange, like money). The spiritual is non-exchangeable. Is it collective? Quite the opposite; it is completely individual, and not subject to exchange. A man who reads my book can get out of it only what he is able to get; I can give him nothing more; and he can give me nothing in exchange; he can give me appreciation and understanding, which are of value to me as a person, but he can give me nothing to help me with *that* book, or with the next one; my contribution has to be made by me alone, and those who want it, take it, for whatever they can get out of it. I do not write it *for them*; they do not read it *for me*. What I can get out of a book spiritually, I get it by writing it. When I give it to others, it's a gift (but without defrauding or sacrificing myself), it's the extra, I can get nothing in return spiritually, it can't be an exchange. (The same pattern applies to me when I listen to a symphony—with me the receiver and the composer the giver.)

I can sell a story when I have put it into a material form, the form of a book. And all I actually *sell* is the material book—say, for three dollars. The actual content of it, the story, cannot be sold or exchanged.

A composer can sell music sheets of his symphony, or records, or performance rights (in this last case, the orchestra, instruments and players are the material form). He cannot sell the content as such—the music.

An inventor sells the physical machine he has devised (or the right to use his idea by putting it into a physical shape or machine). He cannot sell the idea.

A philosopher or theoretical scientist can only sell the book in which he presents the new knowledge he has discovered. He cannot sell the knowledge.

In economics, the realm of material exchange, collectivists demand that a man *give* his idea as well as its physical consequences or manifestations, keeping none of it for himself. He can't get any spiritual payment for his creation—and he is expected to renounce even the physical payment. The physical objects of exchange among men come from someone's ideas, but all men are expected to share in them equally—which [implies] a complete denial of the source of physical wealth and of the rights of its creators. The creators, then, keep the others going for nothing—receiving neither spiritual nor physical reward. And the parasites get the material benefits for nothing, for the mere fact of being parasites—and enslave the creator, besides.

Since the creator needs the material world in order to embody his idea and in order to exist, he is denied the means of creation and of existence by those who could not have these means and could not exist without him.

But in a society of free exchange, the creator gets his fair material reward (by voluntary exchange)—and the rest of mankind gets his idea as a priceless gift.

The spiritual (the realm of consciousness) is the completely individual—indivisible and unsharable. (I do not divide my book among many men, nor do I give it to all men as a collective, to enjoy together, collectively. It is one single book, and it is given individually to single men—those who want it or can get anything out of it.)

The spiritual can be given indefinitely, without diminishing the creator's wealth, because its value depends upon each individual recipient, *his* spirit, and what his spirit can do with the idea. This is individualism again. The recipient has to have the spirit with which to make use of the idea. Still, the idea remains the great gift.

It may be said that a spiritual exchange would be this: I receive all the great inventions, great thinking, great art of the past; in exchange, I create a new philosophy or a new novel. But this is more poetic than exact; there is no direct exchange; there is no way to measure one against the other. [. . .] I do not give anything to the actual source of the gifts I received—to the great creators of the past, each as an individual. I pay the debt to mankind? Why should mankind collect that debt? "Mankind" as a species is only an abstraction. The men living today are not the great individuals of the past, to whom I may say I am indebted; the men of today did not create these great gifts; mankind did not; the gifts were created by specific men, individuals, not by an abstraction; and the pinkish stenographer who may get a copy of my book from the library (and who may hate it) is not a substitute for Aristotle (nor the proper heir to collect his debts).

*Re: Economics.* Since the material proceeds from the spiritual, production from ideas, men must conduct their material existence and their productive activities according to the principles of their source—the principles of the spiritual realm, of man's free, rational thinking. To preserve the effect, one must preserve the cause; to have a river, one must keep free and open the "fountainhead," the source which produces the water. If one attempts to manage the cause by the rules applicable only to the effect (and actually not applicable [even to the effect]), one stops the cause. If one uses the water in the river as the spring gives it, one has both river and spring. If one attempts to regulate the spring by rules derived from considerations of the river without thought of its source, one loses both spring and river. Another example of the collectivist-altruist reversal of cause and effect, of the primary and the secondary.

### James Taggart

He tries to make his *able* employees feel that they are dependent upon him, that he does them a favor by giving them a job. He loses all his good employees that way (among other reasons). He doesn't do that with the incompetent ones, whom he prefers and encourages; in fact, he is "a friend of the workers," he likes to stress his dependence upon them and yelps a lot about "team work." He tries to crush the individual—and fawns over the collective. He tries "to keep in his place" any man on whom he knows himself to be dependent.

### Dagny Taggart

Her error—and the cause of her refusal to join the strike—is over-optimism and over-confidence (particularly this last).

Her over-optimism is in thinking that men are better than they are; she doesn't really understand them and is generous about it.

Her over-confidence is in thinking that she can do more than an individual actually can; she thinks she can run a railroad (or the world) single-handed, she can make people do what she wants or needs, what is right, by the sheer force of her own talent, not by *forcing* them, not by enslaving them and giving orders—but by the sheer over-abundance of her own energy; she will show them how, she can teach them and persuade them, she is so able that they'll catch it from her. (This is still faith in their rationality, in the omnipotence of reason. The mistake? Reason is not automatic. Those who deny it cannot be conquered by it. Do not count on them. Leave them alone.)

On these two points, Dagny is committing an important (but excusable and understandable) error in thinking, the kind of error individualists and creators often make. It is an error proceeding from the best in their nature and from a proper principle, but this principle is misapplied (through lack of understanding of others and of their own relations with others). This is excusable, since it is their nature not to be too concerned with others, therefore not to understand them, particularly when the creators are unsocial by nature, and also could not possibly understand the psychology of a parasite, nor wish to bother wondering about it.

The error is this: it is proper for a creator to be optimistic, in the deepest, most basic sense, since the creator believes in a benevolent universe and functions on that premise. But it is an error to extend that optimism to other *specific* men. First, it's not necessary, the creator's life and the nature of the universe do not require it, his life does not depend on others. Second, man is a being with free will; therefore, each man is potentially good or evil, and it's up to him to decide by his own reasoning mind which he wants to be; the decision will affect only him; it is not (and should not be) the primary concern of any other human being. Therefore, while a creator does and must worship *Man* (which is reverence for his own highest potentiality), he must not make the mistake of thinking that this means the necessity to worship *Mankind* (as a collective); these are two entirely different conceptions with diametrically opposed consequences. Man, at his highest potentiality, is realized and fulfilled with each creator himself, and within such other men as he finds around him who live up to that idea. This is all that's necessary.

Whether the creator is alone, or finds only a handful of others like him, or is among the majority of mankind, is of no importance or consequence whatever; numbers have nothing to do with it; he alone or he and a few others like him *are* mankind, in the proper sense of being the proof of what man actually is, man at his best, the essential man, man at his highest possibility. (The *rational* being who acts according to his nature.)

It should not matter to a creator whether anyone or a million or *all* the men around him fall short of the ideal of Man; let him live up to that ideal himself; this is all the "optimism" about Man that he needs. But this is a hard and subtle thing to realize—and it would be natural for Dagny always to make the mistake of believing others are better than they really are (or will become better, or she will teach them to become better) and to be tied to the world by that hope.

It is proper for a creator to have an unlimited confidence in himself and his ability, to feel certain that he can get anything he wishes out of life, that he can accomplish anything he decides to accomplish, and that it's up to him to do it. (He feels it because he knows that his reason is a [powerful] tool—so long as he remains in the realm of reason, i.e., reality, and thus does not desire or attempt the impossible, the irrational, the unreal.) But he must be careful to define his proper sphere of desires or accomplishments, and not to undertake that which is contrary to the premise of independence and individualism on which he functions. This means not venturing into second-handedness (which will end in certain failure).

Here is what he must keep clearly in mind: it is true that a creator can accomplish anything he wishes—if he functions according to the nature of man, the universe, and his own proper morality, i.e., if he does not place his wish primarily within others and does not attempt or desire anything that is of a collective nature, anything that concerns others primarily or requires *primarily* the exercise of the will of others. (This would be an *immoral* desire or attempt, contrary to his nature as a creator.) If he attempts that, he is out of a creator's province and in that of the collectivist and the second-hander. Therefore, he must never feel confident that he can do anything whatever to, by or through others. He must not think that he can simply carry others or somehow transfer his energy and his intelligence to them and make them fit for his purposes in that way.

He must face other men as they are (recognizing them as essentially independent entities, by nature, and beyond his *primary* influence), deal with them only on his own, independent terms, and deal only with such others as he judges can fit his purpose or live up to his standards (by themselves and of their own will, independently of him). He must not deal with the others—and if he does, he must not fool himself about them, nor about his own power to change them.

Now, in Dagny's case, her desperate desire is to run TT. She sees that there are no men suited to her purpose around her, no men of ability, independence, and competence. She thinks she can run it with incompetents and parasites, either by training them or merely by treating them as robots who will take her orders and function without personal initiative or responsibility, *while she, in effect, is the spark of initiative, the bearer of responsibility for a whole collective.* This can't be done. This is her crucial error. This is where she fails.

But both these errors—of over-optimism and over-confidence—are excusable and understandable, because they proceed from a creator's nature and virtues, because they proceed from strength and courage, not from weakness and fear.

Note (for Dagny or any executive): cooperation is possible only on terms of equality, i.e., between ability and ability (though one man's ability may be greater than another's), *not* between ability and incompetence, nor between intelligence and stupidity. Cooperation must be between equals *in kind*, who might differ in degree—but it can't be between opposite kinds. Cooperation is possible only among independent men, by free, voluntary, rational agreement to mutual advantage, each being concerned primarily with his own personal benefit, and being concerned with the benefit of the other only to the extent of not making himself a parasite, not getting something from the other for which he gives nothing in return.

But you wish to do something involving a great number of men, like running a railroad? *It can't be done,* except on the above terms of cooperation between rational, independent individuals. If you can't find them— *don't wish to do it;* hold your work to the "non-social" scale (that's all your work actually is, anyway); you can't *force* the ability of others; let the scale of your work develop naturally, without your participation or concern; if it doesn't, it means that you're living in a world where it can't—a collectivized world.

**April 19, 1946**

*Dagny* is an example of the material exploitation of the creator, in the sense that her life in the world, with others, is made miserable—*but she is not touched inside.* They use her only in the sense of expropriating the material benefits which are the result of her ability, and robbing her of credit for it. She has to give up (in effect, not quite knowing it) all hope of a real world of her own kind, and live alone in her own world, seeing its expression only in her work.

*The industrialist* is an example of the spiritual exploitation of the creator—exploitation within his soul, by his acceptance of the altruist-collectivist philosophy, therefore his feeling of guilt, therefore his spiritual unhappiness. (This, probably, is also the case of the composer, or some other of the martyred artists.)

The main, concrete dramatization of the methods and forms of how the world exploits the creators must be in the lives of Dagny and the industrialist.

————◇————

Dagny, who is considered so hard, cold, heartless and domineering, is actually the most emotional, passionate, tender and gay-hearted person of all—but only Galt can bring it out. Her other side is what the world forces on her or deserves from her.

————◇————

*The plot line*—the collapse of TT (and of the world).
*The emotional line*—Dagny's quest for John Galt.
*The philosophical line*—Dagny vs. James Taggart (or John Galt vs. James Taggart).

**April 20, 1946**

*The line for Dagny:*

A disappointing attempt at a romance at the age of eighteen.
The railroad worker. (?)
Stan Winslow. (?)
[*Added later:*] Hank Rearden.
John Galt.
She goes on strike as soon as she finds [Galt] in the subway. She quits TT and moves to live with Galt in his garret. (The greatest scientist and the ablest woman in the world are a subway guard and a housewife in a garret.)

James Taggart finds her there. She breaks down once—by coming back to give advice in an emergency, to run the railroad, almost in spite of herself.

James Taggart gets Galt through Dagny (using Galt's love for her in some way—[perhaps] through threat).

Dagny saves Galt (probably with Francisco d'Anconia and Ragnar Danneskjöld).

————◇————

Dagny cries in the subway because she remembers Galt's lines: "We hold, in the world, the jobs which the world wishes us to hold." (The world of the parasites doesn't know or admit that its place for a genius is the job of a subway guard—but that is what the parasite's philosophy implies—so the strikers are living up to it, by way of a demonstration and a lesson.)

### *The gradual desertions:*

John Galt, Francisco d'Anconia, and Ragnar Danneskjöld are the charter members of the strike.

Show them in action, withdrawing the creators from society, "stopping the motor of the world"—particularly Galt doing it.

The strikers who have stopped by the time the story opens are (in addition to the three leaders): the philosopher, the missing millionaire, the ship owner.

The strikers who will stop as the story progresses: the composer, the young engineer, the girl writer, the secretary, the industrialist, Dagny Taggart, and last—the priest.

(Also show the incidents when the help of the missing strikers would have saved the situation—but they're not there; only the James Taggarts are.)

**April 23, 1946**

### *Outline: The Strike*
### *Part I: The End*

[*A restatement of the first scene, already given in her January 1945 notes, then:*]

Introduction of the issue which is threatening TT. ("Who is John Galt?" said again—the connotations made clearer.)

Introduction of Dagny Taggart. The gush of fresh wind in the offices. (?) Or: The girl in a tan coat on the train.

Gerald Hastings (under an undistinguished British name) working as a bookkeeper in the offices of TT. (Somewhere, here or probably later—the story of Hastings' scuttled fleet.)

Introduction of Hank Rearden and Rearden Steel. His wife, his mistress, his son, his secretary. He is Dagny's only real friend—their mutual understanding.

The issue threatening TT ends with a huge loss and discovery that it was brought about deliberately by Francisco d'Anconia. (D'Anconia Copper of Argentina.)

Dagny's meeting with d'Anconia—and whatever revenge or retaliation she attempts. Their "reluctant friendship." ("Oh well, who is John Galt?" "Stop using that cheap figure of gutter legend!")

The composer who quits—this in connection with Dagny's love for his music. (Here we give Dagny's past—the disappointing romance at eighteen.)

Plant the stories of the philosopher who quit, the missing millionaire who vanished, and Ragnar Danneskjöld, the smuggler. Also the "replacers" of the composer and of the philosopher. Here—the influence of philosophy on people like Mrs. Rearden, her son, etc.—and on "the man of pity."

Father Amadeus.

Dagny and the girl-writer.

Dagny and the talented engineer who quits.

Dagny's decision (as a consequence of the d'Anconia disaster) to get supplies from Ragnar Danneskjöld. James Taggart's horrified protests. D'Anconia arranges Dagny's meeting with Danneskjöld—at night, on the coast of Maine. (The friendship of the two men. Danneskjöld's antagonism to Dagny. "It's a rotten joke, Francisco." "We each have our fun in our own way." Then: "I wanted Miss Taggart to learn a lesson." "She won't learn it." "No—not yet.")

Dagny and the disappointing attempt of a weakling at a romance with her. The railroad wreck—her night of work—her first affair, with the railroad worker. The bitter morning after.

Dagny and the discovery that her bookkeeper is Gerald Hastings. His refusal of a better job. She saves him from the police.

Dagny and Stan Winslow. Their romance. Their struggle against James Taggart [and the other parasites].

(Throughout—the John Galt legends.)

The girl-writer and the stranger at the window. She quits.

Dagny sees the talented engineer at an employment agency board. But he refuses her job.

Stan Winslow's romance with a blond dumbbell. Dagny's break with him.

In connection with trouble on TT, Dagny has to appeal again either to d'Anconia or Danneskjöld. The man refuses. She flies after him in an airplane. His plane vanishes in the mountains—with no landing field anywhere in sight. When she attempts to follow—the inexplicable crash.

John Galt. ("We never had to take any of it seriously, did we?" "No, we never had to.") The valley. The new symphony by the composer. The strikers. They refuse her job [offers]. Then she has to leave the valley, promising to keep the secret.

Dagny's search for John Galt—meeting with d'Anconia—return to valley, finding it empty—the anger of the millionaire.

Dagny's resignation—her decision: "I shall live for you—I always have—even if you're to remain only a vision never to be reached."

### Part II: The Beginning

Another step in the disintegration of TT and the world.

In connection with it, the final tragedy of Hank Rearden and of his secretary. Their scene together when they realize the similarity of their tragedies—and the cause. Then—the man who wishes to see Rearden, the name in the sealed envelope—"It must be a gag. . . . What does he look like?" "Like something out of a kind of aluminum-copper alloy."

Hank Rearden quits. The collapse of Rearden Steel. (His secretary quits, too.)

As a consequence, the emergency that threatens TT and the world.

Dagny escapes, in horror, from a banquet where James Taggart and the other parasites discuss the course of action they will take to solve the emergency. She runs into the subway. She sees the subway-guard: John Galt. He looks at her, and walks on without a word. She sits there, sobbing. A bum tries to console her. (The sight of a lady in evening clothes, sobbing in the subway, seems quite natural to him. "Oh well, who is John Galt?") Towards morning, Galt comes back—"All right, come on." Their walk in silence, through the streets in early morning, to his home. At the door, he turns and looks at her for the first time. The same smile as on their first meeting: "We never had to take any of it seriously, did we?" "No, we never had to." They climb the many flights of stairs to his room; she doesn't remember how she climbed the stairs, she knew only that she was rising; she doesn't remember whether it was a long climb—it had taken her thirty years to reach this room. Their night together. He tells her about the strike. Dagny quits—and moves in to live with him. The greatest scientist and the ablest woman in the world are a subway guard and a housewife in a garret.

As a result of (or precipitated by) Dagny's withdrawal—the final emergency which causes the President to announce his world broadcast.

The reason that makes Galt come out in the open.

The chapter called: *"This is John Galt Speaking."* The broadcast: Galt's statement on the cause and purpose of the strike; his demand of complete freedom—the removal of all chains, including the moral ones.

The panic following the broadcast. The government's attempts to say it was a hoax—but nobody believes this. The proclamation of the strikers, signed: "John Galt, Francisco d'Anconia, Ragnar Danneskjöld."

The government attempts to "negotiate" with Galt by secret short-wave broadcasts. His answer—"We do not recognize your right to bargain with us."

The scene of Galt and the priest meeting in a dinky restaurant at night—with the world collapsing around them.

James Taggart (through some connection with Dagny—possibly her one breakdown of giving him advice to save TT) finds John Galt and betrays him to the government.

Galt's arrest and the wreck of his laboratory. ("What was in it? You'll never know.")

The attempts to bargain with him—the banquet—the broadcast—"Ladies and Gentlemen, John Galt to the world!" His speech: "Get the hell out of my way."

The torture of Galt—word of the approaching catastrophe—his one moment of temptation when he almost speaks, out of pity and natural ability, to save them—but looks at the blood running out of the wound on his shoulder and keeps silent.

James Taggart—his hysteria at the realization of his complete evil. His scene with the priest. "I have nothing to say, James. I'm on strike."

Dagny, d'Anconia and Danneskjöld save John Galt. Her ride with him to the valley—the sight of the collapsing world. (The incident with the armed farmer. (?))

The end of Taggart Transcontinental. James Taggart's nervous breakdown. The last train ("The Comet")—and Eddie Willers' effort to save it. ("Dagny, in the name of the best within us . . . !")

The strikers, in the mountains of their valley, look down at a wrecked road: the ruin of a house, the skeleton of an automobile—and, in the distance, the stubborn fire fighting the wind. John Galt says: "This is our day. The road is cleared. We're going back."

---

### The Progressive Collapse of Taggart Transcontinental

The key steps, each worse than the one before and progressively interconnected, are:

## Part I

*First stage:*
    In the first chapter—the trouble.
    This leads to the d'Anconia disaster. (?)
    End on botched achievement.

*Second stage:*
    This leads to Dagny's attempt to deal with Ragnar Danneskjöld.
    The train wreck.
    The events in connection with Gerald Hastings.
    The problems which Dagny fights together with Stan Winslow.
    This leads to her following Danneskjöld to the valley.
    End on first major disaster—the double-cross.

## Part II

*Third stage:*
    In the opening chapter—the serious disaster which will precipitate the collapse. (Here the chain of events must be unbroken and accelerated.) This is the result of Dagny not getting the help she needed from Danneskjöld. (The parasite who gets caught can't supply what she needed—she knew he wouldn't, that's why she went to Danneskjöld.)
    End on parasite's crash.

*Fourth stage:*
    The trouble at Rearden Steel, caused by the above disaster of TT—and, in turn, when Rearden Steel collapses, TT is in its final emergency (and so is the world).
    End on new executive's looting.
    (This leads to President's broadcast.)

*Fifth stage:*
    The panic and the threatened final collapse of TT and everything, which they try to avert through Galt's help. (The psychology of looters and animals—"We only have to last through the next five-year plan.")
    The actual crash—which comes while Galt is being tortured.
    The consequences of the crash—the state of the world after it.

The disaster of *Part II* is actually one single development in progressive steps. (Decide what it is that the steps must lead to.)

In Part I, there are three key points: the original trouble—the problems of Dagny and Winslow—the emergency when Dagny needs Danneskjöld's help.

The pattern of the last emergency must be something like this: if (for a certain expected cause) TT doesn't deliver the ore to a steel factory, there will be no steel; if so, there will be no trucks; if so, there will be no grain transported to farms; if so, there will be no wheat; if so, the country starves.

---

*An important point:* The lesser man thinks he would be president of the company but for the better man. He's wrong. There wouldn't be any company. He thinks better men crowd him out of the better jobs—and all he has to do is destroy the better men, then the jobs will be his. But he destroys the jobs when he destroys the better men. They were not made by these jobs—these jobs were made by them. The lesser man can neither create the jobs of the genius nor keep them. (*There* is an important difference of viewpoint: the creator knows that he makes his own job—the parasite thinks that he can be made by a job prepared for him; the creator knows that wealth is produced by him—the parasite thinks that he is cheated out of his "chance" without the wealth which came out of nowhere. The creator *makes* his job; the parasite *takes over.*)

---

Since the essence of the creator's power is the ability of independent rational judgment, and since this is precisely what the parasite is incapable of, the key to every disaster in the story—to the whole disintegration of the world—is a situation where independent rational judgment is needed and cannot be provided. (Cannot—in the case of the parasites involved; will not—in the case of the strikers.)

### Note on Charity

Charity to an inferior does not include the charity of not considering him an inferior. (This is so by definition.) This is what is demanded by the collectivists now. If the inferior is to be helped on the ground that he is weak and you are strong—let him remember and acknowledge his position (and this is the premise of any voluntary charity).

But charity as a basic, overall principle of morality does lead to this *vicious* circle: if charity (or mercy, as distinguished from justice) is the conception of giving someone something he has not deserved, out of pure kindness or pity, and if this is considered good (a virtue, a moral imperative), then the collectivists are right and consistent in demanding that the principle be applied to the primary sphere, the spiritual, as it is applied to the material sphere, which is only secondary. If, in the material sphere, you give a man a loaf of bread he has not deserved nor earned, so his only claim to it is his misfortune and your pity; then the equivalent in the spiritual sphere would be the kindness of considering him your equal, a status he has not deserved, ignoring his actual worth as a man and handing to him the moral or spiritual benefits, such as love, respect, consideration, which better men have to earn, handing these to him for the same reasons that you hand him a loaf of bread—because it is a desirable possession and he is too weak to earn it.

The collectivists (and all parasites) now demand this kind of charity: give me the bread, because you're strong and I'm weak, and also do me the courtesy of pretending that I'm just as strong as you are, don't hurt my feelings by treating me as if I were weak, hand me an alms of the spirit as you hand me one in physical shape—else you're cruel, selfish and uncharitable.

This is the ultimate logical conclusion and the ultimate viciousness of charity as an absolute principle.

Help to a deserving friend is not charity—by definition. First, you personally want the friend to succeed or overcome his misfortune, you have a reason for it, you consider him good or worthy or valuable, so you have a personal interest in his succeeding. Second, you consider that there is a just reason why the friend should have help—either because his misfortune is accidental, or greater than he deserved.

*Charity* implies that its object does *not* deserve help, but you give it nevertheless, as a bonus; you are not being *just*, but magnanimous or merciful. When you help a genius in distress, you're kind, but not charitable. When you help a bum from the gutter whom you loathe—*that* is charity. You help, not out of compassion for an equal, but out of contempt for an inferior—[you help] *because of your contempt*. And on this premise (which is the exact definition of charity) the collectivists are right when they demand the worship of inferior [men because] of their inferiority; then you do end by rewarding failure, admiring incompetence, loving vices—and penalizing success, achievement, virtue.

This is what happens whenever one attempts to depart from *facts*, i.e., to depart from *justice* (which is to depart from reality). [Regardless of] your motive, the result is still faking reality, evading facts—and the consequences will be those of any lie: corrupt, destructive, and monstrous. There *is no* good motive for lies. Nor for evading reality. There can't be, by definition. What is *the good* in such a conception? *There is no good except truth to facts—which means, the rational method as an absolute.*

There is the same kind of vicious intellectual sloppiness in the idea of "charity" as there is in the idea of brother-love. From the idea that you must love your brother men as a reward or recognition of merit or of lovable qualities (therefore you should love the men who exhibit these qualities, [because that] is only *just*)—it has become the idea that you must *love*, period, without cause or reason, just love everybody and anybody because he is born in human shape—and from that, it has gone "below zero," into "love a man for his vices, love a man *precisely because he shouldn't be loved.*"

From the idea of: "When in doubt about the evidence, be merciful, lean toward giving a man the benefit of the doubt, be a little kinder rather than a little harsher when you are not sure of the exact justice"—it has become: "Be kind, no matter what the evidence, do not even dare to look at the evidence, just be kind"—and then: "Look at the evidence and be kind only to those who deserve the worst punishment; their evil is their claim upon your kindness."

It's like this: first, "Love the hero, hate the knave and be kind to the average man, giving him credit for such good as he does possess, and not hating him altogether for such bad as there is in him." Then: "Love everyone equally and indiscriminately, their personal virtues or vices must have nothing to do with the love you owe them all without questions or reasons." And then: "Love the knaves, because they're the unfortunate ones and misfortune is the only claim to love. Hate the heroes—they cannot claim love, since they cannot claim pity or charity. *Love is a coin used only for alms, never for exchange or reward.*"

*That* is your logical altruism and charity. (And the parasites want it because it's an escape from the responsibility of acquiring virtues to be loved for, an escape from free will.)

From the idea of respecting another man's *rights* because he is a human being, and these rights are his by nature and not subject to your grant or sanction, therefore do not ever rob or cheat another man nor obtain anything from him by force without his voluntary consent, nor expect anything from him without earning it by a free, mutual exchange—it has become: "Give him the shirt off your back, if he wants it—he has a right to it, that is how you must respect other men's rights." From: "Do not take that which is not yours," it has become: "Take nothing and give away anything to anyone who wishes to take it. Misery and misfortune are the only claim checks he must present." (Nothing is yours—everything is everybody else's.)

*God damn it, I must put an end to the idea of misfortune as an all-embracing pass-key and a first mortgage on all life! That's what I must blast.*

The idea behind this damnable worship of misfortune is the denial of free will. Men are not considered responsible for their fortune or misfortune.

Dagny's and Galt's attitude should be *a profound mistrust of suffering.* There is a difference between the way Dagny bears pain inflicted on her by others, bears it defiantly, never allowing it truly inside her, hating the idea of pain, in herself or others—and the way James Taggart, who is a "solid screaming pain" inside, [uses] his suffering to make himself a mortgage on better people.

(This aspect has to do with the final dilemma of the priest.)

———◊———

James Taggart makes use of the idea of charity—on the receiving end.

On the giving end, it is the priest. But the priest cannot go to the depths of depravity which this idea demands. If there is room for it, I might have to have another character to exemplify *that*—a man going insane in the attempt to live by the idea of charity, which he has accepted as a basic premise and axiom, accepted intelligently and consistently, i.e., with all its implications. This would be a kind of Dostoyevsky.

*Line for the "man of charity":* he starts by loving Galt and hating James Taggart; then, to be charitable, he makes himself love Taggart as much as Galt, love them both equally—hating himself in the process and considering his own suffering as a sign of virtue. Then, to be more consistently charitable, he loves Taggart and hates Galt—at which point he commits one of the worst acts (against the strikers) in the whole story, one of the most irrationally twisted, corrupt, monstrous acts—and he ends up insane (and probably dies in some bloody horror which he has brought about).

Starting from hatred of suffering, and from his motive of pity for and desire to relieve suffering, he ends up by becoming a complete sadist.

### The Pattern of the Parasites

The primary attribute of the parasite is his inability or unwillingness to produce.

Since all production rests on original thought and personal effort—

these are the two qualities lacking in a parasite: he cannot produce an original thought and he will not exercise any personal effort.

In respect to thinking, there seem to be two different (though related)
aspects of it: original thinking and assimilating thinking, i.e., the ability to
discover new knowledge and the ability to understand a new thought discovered by someone else (not merely to memorize principles or knowledge, but
to assimilate them through full rational understanding). The necessary
rational process seems to be similar in both instances—the ability to grasp
and connect a rational chain—but it is here, I think, that the degrees of men's
intellectual ability, the degrees of intelligence, become apparent: a great
mind is able to make new rational connections, never made before by
anyone else, from objective evidence; the lesser mind is able to grasp the
connections made by others when these others present their conclusions to
him. (He must be able, when an argument is presented to him, to know
whether it is correct or not, rationally tenable or not, and accept or reject it
accordingly; but he cannot initiate a new chain of reasoning.)

Of course, there are infinite degrees of intellectual ability. A sane but
very stupid man will never understand higher mathematics—simply because
it would take him too long to absorb all the logical steps and knowledge necessary for such understanding. He has the potential capacity to understand
it—if he went step by step and if a better mind guided his understanding all
along the way (this is also supposing that he could retain and assimilate that
much logic and knowledge). But since such a long effort is not necessary for
him, and since no genius is going to help him in that way, it is safe for him
just to leave the subject alone and exercise his mind in a smaller sphere, to
the extent of his capacity. And if it is true that there is a limit to a man's
capacity for intellectual absorption (this is a matter of which I am not certain), [such that] even if he were to start studying higher mathematics slowly
and conscientiously step by step, he would reach a point where he could not
hold it all—then the advisable practical conclusion is the same: he must
leave this field alone, leave it to those who can handle it, and deal only with
such matters as he can handle by the independent rational process of his own
mind. If he ventures beyond that, he is venturing into second-handedness.

Here may be the source of a certain kind of collectivist's resentment
against genius. The collectivist makes the following argument: a world
geared to the genius is impossible for the lesser man to live in; in theory, it
demands of the lesser man a mental effort that he is congenitally incapable
of performing—and in practice, the genius hoards all the material wealth
produced as reward for his genius, since his genius produced it; so the lesser
man has no way to survive, his meager little contribution has no market in

competition with the tremendous production of the genius. Therefore, down with the genius, let us all live on a lesser scale, on a more miserable standard, both spiritually and physically—otherwise, we cannot live at all, we're doomed to destruction, since most of us are only average men and the genius, by the nature of his relation to us, will destroy us. (This is the pattern of what lies behind all the anti-city, anti-machine-civilization, back-to-the-soil, back-to-handicraft movements.)

But this argument is based on a parasite's view of genius, a parasite who does not understand the nature of genius. By the nature of cooperation among men and the nature of intellectual achievement, the genius always gives to others more than he receives from them; no matter what material wealth he gets from men in exchange for his idea, he has given them more than he receives; he has raised their own capacity to produce wealth. He cannot "hoard the material wealth of the world, leaving nothing to the lesser men." Being the source of material wealth, he always leaves to others the greater part of the material consequences of his idea, the greater part of the material wealth he has made possible—by increasing their own capacity to produce it, by augmenting their physical and mental ability through the gift (or lesson) of his discovery.

Besides, it is precisely the differences of intelligence that make cooperation among men possible, fair to all and beneficial to all. For example, a genius who makes an abstract scientific discovery turns it over to the lesser, but still brilliant man—the practical inventor—who discovers a way to make a machine based on it; [the inventor] turns it over to the lesser, but still talented man—the businessman—who starts an industry based on the machine; and so on—down to the man of least ability, the unskilled laborer who only turns a crank, or digs a ditch for the factory, or sweeps the factory floors. The least of these men receives more material benefits through this cooperation than he could get if left on his own (or, in corresponding degree, if any of the better abilities above him had been eliminated).

And, of course, the idea that the intellectually strong crushes or exploits the weak is sheer nonsense. By definition, if he is stronger in ability, he does not need the inferior talent or contribution of the weak and has no cause to exploit him. The weak, of course, has every cause to exploit the strong. In any specific profession, the better man will, of course, crowd out the lesser one, e.g., a good engineer will get a job away from a bad one. But the bad one has no business competing with the man of superior ability—nor expecting his rewards. Let the bad one go into some lesser line of endeavor; let him be foreman, instead of company president; or plain worker, instead of foreman—whatever his ability permits in free competition in a free society.

Never mind the instances of injustice, of ability being passed up and second-handers making a success through pull or palaver—in a free society, such instances defeat and eliminate themselves (though not instantaneously); ability *will* be rewarded, the second-hander *will* fail—if you leave men alone. But the greater the spread of the principles of second-handedness, parasitism, and collectivism in a society—the more injustices occur and the longer they hold. Make collectivism permanent and the injustices are frozen in place, made permanent. But then society collapses. [. . .]

**April 24, 1946**

A man incapable of producing an original thought (or [not in sufficient] degree to affect his practical life or contribute to general knowledge) can still be a moral man and a valuable member of society, if he exercises his own intelligence honestly and to the best of his ability. He can be a good "absorber." He becomes an excellent—and needed—executor of the ideas of others. He does not become a scientist, but a good engineer; or, he does not become an engineer, but a good mechanic.

And he cannot be considered a second-hander, if he does not indulge in any of the second-hander's motives or "social" [methods], if he is honest about himself and his work, does not wish or pretend to be an innovator, but understands his own sphere, his own work, likes it and does it well. In this way, he is being perfectly moral, since he does not place his prime concern within others or into any comparison. He says, in effect: "Others may be men of greater ability, but that is not my primary concern; they offer me an idea in exchange for my work; I give them my best honest effort in return; we're dealing as equals in free exchange to mutual advantage. I like my work in carrying out their ideas—and the work does require a first-hand, independent effort of intelligence on my part. I am happy in my own effort, work, and life. That is all that matters. That somebody is a greater man than I am is none of my concern—except that I appreciate him, I like him for his genius—and, perhaps, I am also a little grateful to him (though not in the primary manner of a dependent)." This is the stand applicable to all good, moral men of average ability.

But the parasite does not take this stand. This is not his attitude nor his method. (The above man is an *active* man; the parasite is not. The above man is a producer; the parasite is not.)

The parasite discards his status as a human being, his attribute of survival—the independent rational mind. Only those who discard it are incapable of producing, since the independent rational mind is the source of all production. The parasite is not insane nor a congenital idiot; he has his rational mind; he could function as the moral average man above (call him "the executor"); but he doesn't want to function as an executor—so he does not exercise even such ability as he has. Now what makes the parasite do it?

*It is the desire to get more than he deserves,* in both the spiritual and the material realm. It may have started only with the material, but now, in this stage of civilization where material abundance is so lavish for all, due to the work of the geniuses of the ages, the desire for more than one deserves has gone mainly into the spiritual realm—and there it is most vicious and deadly (this is not to discount plain grafters and looters, but they are not the real menace today). This is the root of all modern collectivism.

The man who renounces (by statement or by implication) the basic axiom of living by his own independent rational mind has, in effect, announced his desire for more than he deserves and his status as a parasite. (This applies to every philosophy or attitude that is anti-reason.) The axiom [of living by reason] implies most powerfully, without room for escape, that each man stand essentially on his own and get nothing except what he deserves. (Which means: what he earns, what he produces, what qualities he possesses—all of his claims must be based on reality, on objective *fact*.) *The escape from reason is the escape from reality.*

Now if a man declares that he wants to discard reality, it means that he wants to acquire something that reality can't give him; something *more* than he deserves in hard fact. (To admit this is to admit his own inferiority, to say: "I want to be more than I actually am, because I know I'm small, inferior, rotten," but this does not bother a parasite. In fact, it is to escape just such a realization that he discards the validity of reason, logic, or any kind of fact, so that he does not have to face or accept this conclusion. He says: "Oh, it may be so—in reason. But reason is an illusion. Reason doesn't work. Life is not reasonable. Nothing is reasonable. I can say that I am an inferior and consider myself a superior at one and the same time.")

What does the parasite want? Anything that is of value, spiritually or materially.

Materially—he wants more wealth than his own effort is worth; here we have any bureaucrat or politician, any man who wants to gain through restricting competition, any man who seeks economic advantages through political power, i.e., through force, any man who tries to make a success through pull, through the "human" rather than the business angle, through friendship rather than merit, any Peter Keating, or any man who chooses his profession because of the returns he sees others getting from it, not because of his actual ability or desire to do that work (the man who wants to be a writer, *not* to write).

Spiritually—the parasite wants an immense, vague, undefined field of advantages, and it is here that his attitude has that peculiar quality of viciousness, corruption, weakness, touchiness, and hysteria. This is the real sphere of the complexes and the neuroses. A Peter Keating is healthy and even active compared to the primarily spiritual parasites. (P.H. is the best example of such a parasite that I know personally.) This type wants a sense of superiority, which he lacks. (Note that he wants, *not* greatness, but *superiority*.) Therefore, this sense must be given to him by others, second-hand; but this is impossible—so the parasite is never satisfied, never reaches any kind of happiness, his demands grow, the more others give him the more he demands of them, and, in fact, he hates them for giving (actually hating himself for accepting).

He wants, from others, any reward given to human values or virtues—without possessing these values or virtues. Above all, he wants admiration (without an achievement to admire, without even giving to himself any reason why he should be admired). He wants authority, unearned and causeless; he wants to be obeyed, he wants power and the feeling of influencing others. He wants love and affection—[while] never loving anyone himself. He wants prestige—of the comparative kind, being considered *better* than others. He wants fame. He wants fawning, kowtowing and the sense of having inferiors around him. He wants, hysterically and forever, to *beat* somebody at something; *not* to do something *good*, but to do something *better than* somebody else has done it. (This last is indicative of his motive, of the basic cause that made him a parasite.)

He wants, actually, to reverse cause and effect—thinking that the effect will create in him the cause. He doesn't think that admiration proceeds from achievement—he thinks that achievement can be made to proceed from admiration; only he isn't really concerned with achievement.

Where would a parasite get the conception of more than he deserves? From observing others, of course. [. . .] The "material" parasite in modern life is the man who wants to get more than he deserves, by riding on the achievements of others: the hack popular writer who makes a comfortable living by thinly disguised variations on the writings of others; the dress designers who steal from Adrian, etc. (An inferior dress designer isn't satisfied with the income he can make on "Broadway Shoppe" designs; he wants to get some of the income brought in by Adrian dresses—without possessing Adrian's ability; the only way to do that is to steal Adrian's ideas.)

In the spiritual realm, the parasite wants every reward he has seen being given to better men. He would have no conception of admiration, since he never produced anything to admire, if he hadn't seen the genius being admired for his achievements. He wants the reward, without the reason; the effect, without the cause. He wants the admiration—for nothing. His irrationality makes such a conception or desire possible. (Conception?—that belongs to reason. He doesn't even have to consider whatever it is that's going on in his head as a "conception"; nor to state it, nor to define it. Just want it. Just *"feel."*)

What does all this do to the parasite's relation with other men?

The parasite began by being a second-hander. His first premise was accepted on the second-hander's basis—the basis of comparison. He said: "I am inferior, because I see others who are better than I am. I must escape from my inferiority—and from those hated men who made me conscious of it, from those better ones." Then he becomes an irrationalist in order to achieve this [escape]. A man's estimate of and attitude toward himself will, of course, determine his attitude toward everything else: others, life, the universe.

Having started with the idea that value is established by comparison (or else having started by hating himself for some flaw and considering himself inferior without comparison—the result being the same when he confronts others), the parasite will naturally hate the genius, and any man of ability, virtue, or superiority of any kind. In effect, he will have the insane idea that he can become great simply by eliminating those who are better. Values have no absolute existence for him; they are all relative. He doesn't want to grow ten bushels of wheat; he will be happy if he grows two, [as long as] everybody else grows only one. (Marcella B. and her "two cars." [*AR is referring to a young woman she met while working at RKO in the early 1930s. When AR asked the woman about her goals, she said: "I'll tell you what I want. If nobody had an automobile, then I would want to have one automobile. If some people have one, then I want to have two."*]) (Of course, a second-hander can have no absolute values; they have to be relative; his standard and measure is in others, or in his own comparison of himself to others; absolute values require an independent rational judgment.)

The parasite hates competition—because he sees all life as a competition. He knows he can't hold his own, on his own independent terms (he has none), against the genius; hence his desire for "security," "controls," and "collaboration." Yet, as a non-producer (who has discarded the necessary precondition of a producer: the independent rational mind) he sees all life as a race for a static, given amount of benefits. He doesn't think that material wealth is created by the energy and intelligence of men—an inexhaustible source; he thinks that there's just so much material wealth (a static amount) and whoever gets rich takes that much away from him; his "share" is that much smaller. (He doesn't realize that in a free society of producers each wealthy man *adds* to the total wealth, that each creates his own new wealth, and also adds to the wealth of others by his ideas and his energy. But to realize this would be to cease being a parasite.)

He thinks the same in the spiritual realm; he sees spiritual values as a static sum total, so anything gained or possessed by another man is taken away from him. If another man is loved, this reduces his chances of being loved. If another man is admired, it reduces his possible share of admiration. If another man has any personal virtue—intelligence, courage, integrity, beauty—his own virtues are thereby diminished or destroyed (as if virtues were something distributed around out of a common grab-bag—and there's only so much of it to divide). This is the non-producer's, the irrationalist's, the collectivist's, the parasite's view of the world, spiritual and material. (This is the miserable trembling for one's share of the "common pot"—since everything is common, collective, isn't it?)

If it is said that what the parasite dreads is competition for a specific goal—such as one particular job, or the love of one particular woman—and what he fears is that the better man will beat him in that specific instance, then it's still second-handedness. The creator (or any "active" man) attaches no crucial importance to anything that comes from others, from the will of some one other man; he may regret losing a job or losing the woman he loves to someone else, but it is not a crucial tragedy for him, nor the breaking of his life, since it never was his primary concern. He wants a job in his particular line of work, but not necessarily any one specific job. He may love only one woman in his life and he may lose her, and this *is* a tragedy—but *not* the end of him, since he did not exist primarily for that woman, nor for any other human being. His primary goal is within himself.

It is said that this is fine for the genius who's sure of his superiority and chance to win out against others in any competition for a specific object— but what about the lesser men who know they're doomed to be the losers? The answer is: If such are the facts, there's nothing they can do about it; hatred and destruction of the genius will not change anything. They must face the facts and accept the lesser rewards, those they've deserved; they can have nothing more anyway. If there is no genius (or better man) around, it does not mean that the woman whom the lesser man wants will necessarily want him; she may not want anyone at all—the lesser one will never satisfy her. (Personal love is the nearest one can come to a situation where the gain of one consists of the loss of another—and even then it doesn't quite hold; in fact, it doesn't hold at all.)

If the competition is for jobs, the lesser man cannot hold the job which is actually above his capacity—the job which the genius would have taken, if the lesser man had not decided to destroy the genius. *Here, in fact, is one of the key pillars of my story:* if the lesser man is afraid of the competition of the genius for a top job, and thinks that the job would be his, if it weren't for the genius, and so all he has to do, in legitimate self-interest and self-preservation, is to destroy the genius—he will learn that the job, created by genius for genius, *is not for him.* Such a job—created by superior ability and requiring superior ability to be filled, in an advanced civilization which represents the accumulation, the end product, of centuries of thought, effort and genius—cannot be filled by him. (And he ought to know it by his own definition of himself, the genius, and the job.) If he forces his way into it—by compulsion, collectivism, and destruction of the genius—he will not hold the job or get its advantages; he will merely destroy the job—and himself. (*This is important*—James Taggart.)

From such premises, it's logical that the parasite's most frequent and strongest emotion is envy. Envy of ability, of achievement, of virtue, of happiness. This is why the parasite comes to wish ill to everyone, to rejoice in anyone's misfortune and resent anyone's happiness. This is why he will hate any success and relish every failure. This is why he will love the incompetent. This is why he will hate the men of ability, try to crush, stop, or destroy them—and why he will surround himself with mediocrities, with his inferiors, why he will help them, encourage them, push them forward. (And since he is a dreadful mediocrity himself, and has quite a sensitive instinct about recognizing his superiors—boy! how low he has to go in order to find inferiors!) Envy is his constant, corroding, consuming emotion—and his strongest motive (perhaps his only motive). Since emotions come from reason, from the premises one has accepted, this is logical and unavoidable: the premise of second-handedness can produce only the most second-hand of all emotions: envy. If that is his dominant principle, that will be his dominant emotion.

Now what is the exact pattern of the parasite's actions in exploiting the genius?

The simplest and most primitive: if there were only two men in the world and the genius were producing the food needed to exist—the parasite, who produces nothing, would do one of two things: he can descend upon the genius, kill him and seize his food, but then he himself will starve when he's consumed the food and can't produce any more; or, he can try to enslave the genius and make him work, taking as much of the genius' production as he can get away with.

The last is the basic pattern of what has been done to the genius throughout history.

But the genius doesn't work under compulsion; the nature of his genius is the independence of his mind, so the necessary condition for the exercise of his genius is destroyed when he is enslaved. The greater his genius—the greater his sense of independence, of being an end in himself, and not the means to anyone else's ends, not anyone's servant. Whatever altruist-collectivist theory he might have absorbed merely makes him miserable, tortures him and causes a civil war within him. With respect to his work, and to the extent to which he lives in accordance with and by the principles of his genius—he will maintain his independence, fiercely and passionately.

Also, an incompetent ruling a genius, a non-producer trying to control and direct the productive work of a producer, can result only in disaster. The actual performance of men in society is a constant, fierce, undefined struggle between the genius and the parasite. [In order] to function, the genius must have his freedom and his independence—whether by stated, accepted principle, or by unstated default, or by open rebellion against the stated principles of collectivism in society. To the extent of his actual independence, he is able to function. But he is crippled, hobbled, tied, held back constantly by the encroachments and restrictions of the parasites who get their unearned sustenance from him.

How do the parasites do it and what is their long-range policy?

They do it by two means: through actual force—this is political power, the regulated society, *collectivism*; and by spiritual poisoning—this is the philosophical means to disarm and enslave the genius from within, the corruption by the parasite's morality of *altruism*.

(My story must show both methods. Galt leads the revolt against both.)

As parasites, they have no long-range policy. Long-range planning belongs to the producer. The parasite acts on the psychology of the animal or the savage: grab the kill or the bananas of the moment and don't worry about tomorrow; tomorrow you will start looking for another victim.

The parasites will not face the fact that they are destroying their own providers, their own means of survival. If they think anything at all on the subject, it's something like this: there will always be some genius around, we can milk one of them dry, destroy him, and then pick on the next one. The geniuses will always come along to be picked—it's only a question of how much we can get away with. And this has always been true: the geniuses did come along and the parasites got away with as much as the traffic of any particular time would bear. When the parasites went too far, a civilization collapsed into dark ages; then the geniuses were free (by default, by the parasites' impotence amidst ruins) to rebuild the world, and then the parasites climbed on their shoulders—and it started all over again. (This is what Galt wants to stop once and for all.)

How do [the parasites] act toward any man of ability in practical life? In a way which is as contradictory as their philosophic premise. First, they hate him. Second, they want to get all they can out of him. They want to destroy him and to use him at the same time. They put every possible impediment in his way and want as much production as they can get out of him. They refuse to recognize his rights—but they want him to recognize and accept their right to exploit him. They act on the premise of exploiting the better man—yet refuse to admit that he is better. They act on the premise of exploiting his productive genius—yet refuse to admit that production comes from his genius.

Above all, they want him to think (and they want others to think it and would like to fool themselves into thinking it) that what they get out of him is not charity and alms, but is theirs by *right*. The theories and methods to achieve this and the rotten trickery involved are infinite—but it all comes down to collectivism and altruism. (They do not mind so much if their exploitation is thought of as *loot*—this gives them a sense of having bested the genius in some way—but they do not want it to be called charity. This is the touchy vanity of the parasite.)

(This is the attitude of James Taggart toward Dagny, Rearden, the young engineer, and any man of ability he encounters.)

*Now*—what happens in a world where there is nothing but parasites left? What happens in a world run by parasites? What happens to the parasites when they are left on their own, left to their own devices and methods?

**April 25, 1946**

Before answering the last question, one more note on the parasites. Is parasitism basically a desire for undeserved material wealth, which then leads to the spiritual parasitism? Is the basic motive material—and the spiritual evil only the means to an end, the justification, a result of and a disguise for it? *No.* The material proceeds from the spiritual, not vice versa. The material is the expression of the spiritual, the form of the idea, the flesh of the soul. The spiritual intention determines its material expression. Not the other way around.

Therefore, the parasite's basic motive, premise, and evil is spiritual. It is, of course, *self-hatred* [caused by] the discarding of his rational faculty and of the kind of life (the only kind possible to man) which the rational faculty implies and demands. The first crime is against his own *ego*. All the other crimes follow.

What makes a man do that? This is a huge question by itself. It seems that self-reverence (which is the root of self-confidence, which is the root of independence) is a primary axiom for man—the axiom of survival, the life principle. This must be thought out in detail. Here, I trace the course of the parasite from that first crime on. (Nowadays, of course, the reason is the huge pressure of the teachings of altruism. But what is the essential cause here? What was the reason of the primary, original error? Was it fear? If so, what cases that kind of fear?)

If a parasite hates himself, he has to become an irrationalist, in order to survive. Otherwise, he would have to destroy himself, to be consistent.

Once he has [rejected] reason, he has lost or discarded his capacity to produce, his understanding of the source and nature of production, and also his spiritual entity, his *self*, and the entire realm of his spiritual life. No spiritual life is possible without the mind, without *reason*; the spiritual *is* the rational. On the irrationalist premise, there is nothing but a sickening chaos left, since the man is doing constant violence to himself, acting contrary to his nature—and, of course, suffering constant pain, as he would physically if he insisted on acting contrary to the requirements of his body. Also, no spiritual life is possible [to a man who] hates himself; spiritual life has to begin with a strong, proud, happy sense of identity; but that is precisely what the parasite has discarded and is trying to escape. Without the rational faculty, no independence is possible, i.e., no inner existence at all. The parasite is trying to escape from any inner reality; he has discarded the essence of what constitutes life.

But he goes on existing. So he has to find a substitute [for reason]—he thinks that's possible, just as he thinks it's possible to exist without self, without identity. (The process without object? The movement without that which moves?) The obvious substitute of the spiritual is the material. The reversal is similar to what he has already done. As a second-hander, he placed others first, above self. Actually, all relations with others are secondary, and a result of one's entity, one's attitude toward oneself; but he decided that his entity will be determined by and emerge from that relation. ("My virtue is to be determined by the good I do for others," etc.) So now he performs another reversal: instead of realizing that man's material activity and production is the result of his spiritual entity (his thinking, his desires, his purposes) and that the material is meaningless except as the form given to the satisfaction of a primarily spiritual need—he decides that his spiritual happiness will proceed from the material, that the material will give him a spiritual entity. He places the material first.

A simple example of this reversal is the man who wants a big, beautiful, luxurious house—without realizing that the [value] of such a house depends on what he wants to do in it. What if it's big—but he has nothing to do in the rooms and all that space is wasted? What if it's beautiful—if he has no standards, understanding, or appreciation of beauty? What if it's luxurious—when luxury is the lavish satisfaction of desires, and he has no desires? The material is only an answer to a spiritual need, an expression of it, a tool of it. Otherwise—it's meaningless. Without a purpose in his activity, without standards of judgment, without desires—the man might as well live in a rotting shack (or not live at all). He won't acquire these spiritual possessions from the house—the house had to come from them, be an answer to them.

(Sex is a very eloquent and complex example of that, too. Think it over in detail sometime.)

The parasite thinks that the material will give him, not only the happiness he lacks, but also the capacity for happiness which he has discarded. And not understanding (or not admitting to himself) the source of material wealth, he thinks that he can acquire wealth second-hand, through others (as he expects to find virtue, happiness, or importance through others). (He is not a second-hander because he wants to be fed by others; he wants to be fed by others because he is a second-hander; the spiritual reversal, or crime, was first.)

From this [reversal], the parasite acquires two qualities: first, an exaggerated greed for material wealth, with no purpose for which to use it, wealth as an end in itself, and not as the means to an end (which is all that material wealth can be); second, the conviction that the way to get wealth is through others, that his activity must be directed toward the human, not the objective, productive aspect. (This is the source of: "A creator's concern is the conquest of nature. A parasite's concern is the conquest of men." [*This quote is from Roark's speech.*])

This is why the parasite wants, not to make, but to "take over." This is why he is concerned not with merit, but with pull; not with actual performance, but with faking a performance for someone else's eyes. That is why he sees no necessity to produce anything—but only the necessity of convincing someone that he's gone through the motions, so that he gets paid. That is why he doesn't think it necessary to do a good job, but only to please the boss; and it doesn't matter whether he fools the boss into thinking it was a good job—he aims to please the boss through means *not connected* with the job, such as personal flattery or social charm; he even thinks that the safe way to please the boss is one *unrelated* to the job, to the actual performance and result; wealth, he thinks, is acquired through these side-means, through any means, except production.

How—in view of this attitude—he manages to escape facing the implication that somebody else produces the wealth he wants to expropriate, by quite different methods, is an interesting question. Of course, he never quite escapes it. Hence his miserable uneasiness and uncertainty. Hence, also, the disgusting, undefined, untenable theories (they are really shouted slogans, not theories) about wealth being a matter of natural resources (forgetting who and what made resources out of matter that was useless per se), about wealth and success being just a matter of luck, and all the variations of determinism. (Under determinism, nothing has to be explained too clearly: other men produce wealth in some unstated manner, because they're predetermined, or conditioned, that way; he, the parasite, isn't; he's predetermined to *his* method, and it's all a matter of fate, nothing can be changed, it works that way because it has to work that way, so it's quite all right.) Besides, irrationalism helps him to avoid the implications and the contradiction. A "contradiction" is a rational conception; an irrationalist doesn't have to make sense.

Now, then, the parasite concentrates his ambitions and activities on getting material wealth. He may invent all sorts of minor spiritual justifications to cover up his material parasitism, but these are secondary; the parasitical convictions are not accepted in order to permit him to loot; the desire to loot was the result of the original parasitical conviction, the primary spiritual act of second-handedness. And since no "existence through others" is possible, the nearest a parasite can come to it is to exploit others materially, getting physical sustenance or unearned wealth from them, expropriating the results of their work, enslaving them.

[As part of the] proof that the parasite's primary motive is not material: *material wealth never gives him any happiness and he doesn't know what to do with it if he gets it.*

It is not a paradox that the creator, who is not primarily concerned with material wealth, can and does enjoy it when he has it, and the parasite, who places wealth first, goes to pieces with it.

This is why the successful parasites, the Peter Keatings, are completely miserable when they reach success; this is why [so many] celebrities turn to drink, dope, or dissipation at the height of their success; this is [the source of] the vicious talk about success being only a disappointment, and the striving is better than the achievement, and the striving is all there is to do, we must always strive, never succeed, and "a man's reach should exceed his grasp," etc.

Of course, the parasite's kind of success is the deadliest disaster for him. (Since the goal is improper, its achievement can only be disastrous.) He has hunted wealth as a substitute for his inner entity; he has thought that he would get a spiritual life out of his material possessions, that he would get virtue, happiness, inner satisfaction, all the spiritual values which he lacks. He discovers that he doesn't get any of it; that he has not escaped from himself nor found a substitute for himself. He has nowhere else to seek and nothing to do. He is in a blind alley. From this point on, the parasite goes to pieces.

This is why those who preach "selflessness" spiritually are so inordinately concerned with material wealth—why the collectivists think that material "security" is the supreme ideal that will solve everything, while the individualist, who defends a system of private property and so-called greed, attaches little importance to material wealth, can do without it and is not afraid of poverty; he is the man who *makes* wealth and he knows its exact meaning.

Therefore, the "material parasite" and the "spiritual parasite" are interrelated aspects of the same thing, different stages of the same disease (and the two stages are never quite separate—one is merely more pronounced than the other in any particular man at any particular time). The "material parasite" seems somewhat more pleasant, more healthy, than the spiritual one; at least he is active, though in his own disgusting way; he works at being a parasite—like Peter Keating. The spiritual corruption and secondhandedness are there, of course, but total disintegration has not yet set in. When Peter Keating succeeds he reaches the stage of P.H. or M.F., who were born with money, and he discovers what they have already discovered—the impotence of material wealth in regard to their problem. Then he goes to pieces, as they did in the first place. Then he turns to their neuroses, their purposeless existence, and their malice toward the whole universe. They are merely advanced stages of his disease.

So there is no essential difference between the two types of parasite, not in what they do if they succeed, nor in their ultimate goal and fate.

There is one more stage for the parasite, the third and final stage, which they do not always reach (some may die before they reach it or succeed in avoiding it all their lives). This is their real hell and their real retribution. It is the stage when a parasite discovers—or is forced to face—the truth about himself.

His whole, twisted, tortuous, miserable performance has been a search for personal value; he wanted personal virtue—but he tried every possible substitute for virtue; he ran from the realization of his own worthlessness or inferiority, and he has spent his life trying to fool himself about that, in every way possible, including the attempted denial of any value, virtue, or objective reality. In his stage of spiritual parasitism, he was still fighting against any realization of the truth—hence his malice, his mysticism, his collectivism, etc. But if and when some event forces him to see the truth—to see himself as he really is—to see and admit to himself, in full, his own evil—*that* is probably the worst thing a human being can go through. This is Peter Keating after Toohey's speech. This is James Taggart after the priest's refusal. In that stage, there's literally nothing left of the parasite—not even the activity of malice. Then it's total indifference—the passive—the Nirvana.

I suspect that a parasite who reaches this stage either goes insane, commits suicide, or soon dies from a lack of the will to live. (He doesn't know that he actually discarded that will long ago in his first act of second-handedness, when he discarded his rational faculty, man's means of survival; now the ultimate consequences have caught up with him in the only form that was possible, the form he asked for: self-destruction.)

Since success is the worst punishment for a parasite (the success of a man functioning on the principle of destruction *has to be* destruction), the worst thing the creators could possibly do to the parasites is precisely what John Galt does: let the parasites succeed, turn the world over to them—and let them see what happens.

Of course, the parasite's greatest wish (in practice) is to exploit and enslave the creator, but the wish is a contradiction in terms: the creator cannot be enslaved, he cannot function that way; what we see in actual life is only his miserable struggle for the scraps of freedom he tears out of the parasites' hands, and he functions only to the extent of those scraps. So the parasite's wish, in factual terms, is to destroy the creator. To enslave the creator is to destroy him. ("The purpose of the fraud was to destroy the creators. Or to harness them. Which is a synonym.")

Therefore, John Galt grants the parasite his wish: he removes the creators. He doesn't destroy them, of course, but they do not exist as far as the parasite is concerned; they take no part in his world, they contribute nothing, they do not interfere with him or oppose him. He gets what he wanted—a world without creators. Then the horror follows—the destruction of the world—the logical consequences of the parasite's principle of death; and the parasite's inner horror must match, if not surpass, the horror of the world's material collapse. (This is for the last scene with James Taggart and the priest.)

The parasite could exist only so long as he had the creators to lean on, to be fed by, to exploit; in this sense, the creators were responsible for him— by permitting him to do it. This is just like totalitarian economics that can exist only on the energy stolen from the free economies, who thus create their own Frankenstein monsters. This is what John Galt wants the creators to understand and to stop.

This, then, is the meaning of John Galt's strike. *This* must be *shown* clearly, explicitly, and unmistakably (in detail, in more and broader ways than just the disintegration of James Taggart).

### Notes

*Dietrich Gerhardt*—as the composer on the pattern of Shostokovitch (but *not* of that nature), who, by dealing with his enemies, helps to per- petuate their hold on him, to perpetuate his own slavery and precipitate his own destruction (this last, in symbol, through the destruction of a woman he loves, a singer, or of a talented young composer-protégé).

*James Taggart's* hysterical fear of Galt—before he even sees him or hears of him, just fear of *someone like Galt*, from his own knowledge that such a person must exist, his knowledge that *this* is what is missing in the world and *this* is the retribution that will come some day. Taggart's insane, irrational attempts to avoid that day—and the climax is when he comes face to face with Galt. (That is Galt's place in *his* life.) (Taggart hates the expres- sion *"Who is John Galt?"*—instinctively, without reason.)

As a possibility: *the scene where James Taggart finds Dagny in her garret,* scrubbing the floor. (He's had detectives looking for her.) He finds that he cannot beg, bribe, or force her back—that he has nothing to offer her. He wants something from her—he has nothing to give in return. The posi- tion of any parasite—the exploitation made possible only by the generosity of the creator. And Dagny is cured of that. (This scene can show the *exact* nature of charity.) Dagny tells him that the cleanliness of her floor means more to her than the millions of bushels of wheat in the stomachs of the millions of people who need the train to get the wheat. What do those people intend to do to her with the energy they'll get from the wheat she gives them?

———◦———

*For the politicians:* Do not name their exact political positions. Keep it vague and general—as it deserves. They are nonentities and their titles or jobs do not matter—all that matters, the essence of it, is that they are useless, faceless mediocrities, parasites and exploiters—as exemplifying the kind of government they represent. Therefore, avoid the honorable connotations attached to such a title as "President of the United States" by another era and a different principle of government. All you have is "Head of the State" or "Washington Officials." The Head of the State is known and referred to throughout as just "Mr. Parker" (or Mr. Smith, or Mr. Johnson, or the most typically undistinguished name you can find). So are the other officials: always Mr. so-and-so, and *no first name.* The anonymity of mediocrity.

As to Europe—keep it in a gray, ominous, evil fog. Nothing clear about it—only intimations that Europe is finished, there's only a chaos of impotent collectivism left. If you refer to their forms of government, it's always only: "The People's State." (You do all this by hints about the breakdown of communications—there's little left of the radio, the telegraph, the mail, the boats, any kind of press, any kind of reliable source of information. People in the story take this for granted, as normal, matter-of-fact, implying that Europe has been like that for a long time.)

**April 26, 1946**

[*In the following notes, the collapse of a society run by parasites is analyzed into five stages. Later, AR refers to this analysis as the "Pattern of Disintegration."*]

Now to answer [my earlier] question: *What happens in a world run by parasites?*

Since the parasite's basic premise is escape from reason, since he has discarded his capacity for independent rational judgment (and dreads the necessity of such rationality), the most evident and all-embracing manifestation of a parasite's world will be the miserable scrambling to evade personal decisions and personal responsibility.

In every issue—business or personal—the parasites will, primarily, try to stall. They will neither say "yes" nor "no"—on anything. They will evade—in effect, hoping that their inactivity will somehow eliminate the issue. It is not even a conscious decision to wait or temporize—that's still a decision—but just plain evading, which means giving the issue no thought at all and thus avoiding the necessity of examining it or even of admitting its existence.

The pointless stalling everywhere will be appalling; the kind of shifty-eyed, edgy, uneasy stalling that bursts into inexplicable, resentful, disproportionate anger whenever anyone as much as mentions the issue, let alone asks for a decision. This—everywhere, on any matter, big or little, in business offices and in homes, in professional relations and in love-affairs, in public speeches and drawing-room conversations. Nobody will make a definite statement. Nobody will "commit himself," since nobody is sure of anything. Everything is said by indirection, circumlocution, vagueness, a kind of tangled ceremonial empty verbosity, in which the only thing that is clear is the absence of anything definite having been stated.

The one unforgivable sin that makes everyone jumpy, venomous, suspicious, makes them consider you a dreadful boor of bad manners, is to say anything definitely. It is a crime to be sure that the sun is shining and say so. The preferred form is: "It seems that the sun is shining," or "I believe the sun is shining," or "It is generally conceded that two and two make four." (The theories about "nothing is absolute," "nothing is certain," "nothing is real" are enormously popular.) It is not any particular statement they dread, but the mere fact of a definite statement, and of a man being able to make it— because this implies their own need to make [such statements].

Such a world must be first bewildering, then totally unbearable to an intelligent person—like an insane asylum, which it is. Only, the insane cannot deal with reality because of their inherent incapacity to do it; these people refuse to deal with it by intention, which may be even more dreadful. (And, of course, everyone is extremely pleasant to everyone else, smilingly blank, because anger is a definite emotion, a definite stand.)

When things catch up with the parasite and he can stall no longer, he scrambles to pass the buck and shift the responsibility. The parasite will not make a decision; he will look for someone else to make it, then he will subscribe to it—halfway, cautiously, always leaving himself an out, an "escape clause." If the decision turns out well, he will take all the credit and be extremely touchy about minimizing the credit for the man who made the decision. If the decision turns out badly, he will be the first to turn upon the decider and tear him to pieces. This kind of double-crossing, patsy-finding, pushing cat's paws to pull chestnuts out of fires is a general policy, almost expected and taken for granted as normal procedure. Imagine the feelings of an honest, honorable person in the midst of this! And all this is done under that vapid blanket of a fixed, empty, mealy-mouthed smile; everybody suspecting, hating, and fearing everybody else (as they have to, since the double-cross is the general policy), yet always speaking softly and shaking each other's hands limply. It is not the manner of my kind of brotherly love or benevolence—but the manner of cowards wearing a protective coloration in order not to be hurt: a manner that is automatic, emotionless, lifeless.

Another form of shifting responsibility—when it is not a matter of shifting it to a person—is the scramble for substitutes for thought, for "automatic thinking," for guaranteed security without rational judgment or procedures decision. This is the miserable reliance on precedent and routine, the copying and imitating of anything that was or seemed to be successful, the judgment by any irrelevant side-issues, rather than by rational examination of the evidence. The devotion to routine is everywhere: "I'm doing it this way because so-and-so did it this way successfully in 1910." Business procedures have come down to an incredible, senseless mess of wasted motion, inconvenience, ineffi-ciency—just because it was done that way fifty years ago, and circumstances have changed, but nobody's taken the initiative to notice it and change proce-dures accordingly.

The "judgment by side-issues" is on the pattern of thinking that a movie is good because its particular locale was popular; or because "the theme is timely." Opinion polls [are used] as substitutes for judgment and as guides for action, on all issues, on the most preposterously inapplicable occasions.

Also—the desperate worship of authority (*what* authority and how "authorities" appear is another matter, to be analyzed later). Once somebody is an "authority," everything he says or does is right, without questions or examination, not because it *is* right, but because *he* says or does it. It is never *what* is said, but *who* says it. The strict method of judgment by and from per-sonality. To discredit an idea, one must discredit the speaker or his motives (the smear technique). The attempt to discredit an idea by examining it is treason against the code of the parasite, a breach of the general method of the parasite's world. The examination of an idea can't be done without inde-pendent rational judgment.

The attempts to substitute mechanical devices for judgment (like machines to study audience reactions) are fantastic and extend into the most preposterous spheres. (Like, say, a machine to measure your reactions and tell you whether you really love your wife or not.)

And the first question asked, before any action, is: "*Who* has done it that way?" The statement: "It's never been done before" is pronounced everywhere as the final, unanswerable expression of disapproval, the self-evident defeat of the man who made the proposal, the ultimate damnation, in the same way that we would say: "It's impossible."

The attempts to agree on everything with everyone are sickening. "Why raise an issue?" "Do you have to be disagreeable?" "Do you have to be diffi-cult?" are the constant phrases. A disagreement, of course, implies the need of taking a stand. It's easy to think oneself safe, so long as everybody agrees;

it must be so, since everybody thinks it is and there are no dissenters; but a dissenter brings up the possibility that it may not be so, and *that* brings up the possibility that you may have to decide what is so.

The contradictions and inconsistencies—in speeches, ideas, policies and actions—are unbelievable. They'd rather contradict themselves all over the place than face a contradiction; to face it means that one must resolve it, choose, and make a decision. Nobody says today what he said yesterday. Nobody means what he says—nor says what he means—nor knows what he means when he says it. This, of course, makes all personal relations disgusting. But when this is applied to business matters—the disasters follow. (When they discard the rational faculty, they *have to* live in and for the moment, without connection to the rest of their lives; they break the continuity of an identity—since they have no identity. The power of reason is the identity.)

Nothing and nobody is reliable. There is no way to pin a man down to anything definite, nor to count on him. He has no character—he has no identity, no fixed entity. It is not a world of crooks and dishonesty—crooks have a tangible, definite purpose, robbery, and one could even deal on the basis of *that* as a solid starting point; it is much worse. It is a world in the exact image of a parasite's soul—a gray, shapeless fog. A world with a treacherous quicksand under one's feet—and no defined outlines, no solid shapes, no fixed entities; a heavy, passive, stagnant fog in which something moves, as if trying to form, but dissolves the moment you attempt to focus on or touch it; a world without focus, blurred, not to be reached, never quite in existence. It is something like the spectacle one would see if one's power of central, focused vision were gone and only one's marginal side-vision was left; one would then be in the awful [position] of knowing that one can't function or remain that way, it's an unbearable state, worse than blindness, because one would have to make constant efforts to see clearly, while knowing that it's impossible.

There is only clear attribute of the fog—pain. Suffering. It's not even a specific suffering—how can anything be specific in such a fog?—but a pervading sense of suffering, perhaps more awful for not being defined (if it were defined, one could perhaps combat it). It is as if one heard screams (or sounds approximating screams) among the vague, floating shapes, and whenever these shapes seemed to jell into forms of something for an instant, the forms were those of open wounds. The Hegelian-Marxist process without an object that does the "processing"? There it is.

There is never an event of success, achievement, completion, fulfillment, or happiness in this world. Whenever a definite event emerges from the rotten stagnation, it's a disaster—a failure, a breakdown, destruction, suffering, disappointment, frustration, misery. This—in business life, in public life, in personal life. (Since the parasite functions on the death principle, the positive events are impossible in his world; only the negative ones, the progressive steps to final destruction, can be achieved in reality, the reality he asked for.)

In this world's productive life, nothing is ever done successfully, everything is botched, halfway, doesn't quite come off; but the disasters and failures are clear-cut and definite enough; after each, the productive activity falls a step below the previous level; there is no power of recovery. In personal life, the attempts at happiness are dismal failures—forced, unconvincing, unsatisfying, a pretense at joy rather than real joy—everything is bloodless, in half-tones, in faded, washed-out, blotched pastels—the love affairs, the marriages, the friendships. (Emotions proceed from reason—and where there are no firm rational convictions, there can be no real emotions; their feelings are an exact counterpart of their intellectual state, of the content of their minds.)

The misery of these people is real enough—but not sharp enough to make them stop, scream, rebel and do something about it; that, too, would be a definite emotion. It is more like a chronic state of dull pain, almost as if they had come to take for granted that pain is man's normal state of existence. Occasionally, it becomes unbearable; one of them breaks. And the specific events or results of their personal relationships are all disastrous, each leaving the relationship worse than it was before.

Now, as to their "authorities." It is, of course, part of the basic contradiction of the parasite that he must hate the creator and need him at the same time, that he must destroy the creator and seek him out. So the behavior of men in the parasite's world has both aspects, viciously and ludicrously mixed. First, they try to discard, ignore, hamper, destroy any man of ability and grab his ideas, his property, his position, his prestige. They sense genuine ability, they fear and resent it, and one way of fighting it is the Toohey method of "enshrining mediocrity": while they sneer at heroes and heroism, they practice a maudlin, sickening kind of half-abject, half-sneering hero-worship of their own kind of celebrities, and they eagerly push their mediocrities onto public altars, blow nonentities into giants—while proclaiming their resentment of and the nonexistence of giants. (And don't we see *that* today?) They scramble for the spotlight themselves—and also push *their own kind* into prominence, into the places of the destroyed or missing creators.

The second stage is when the parasites discover what the positions of the creators entail. There is a period of bewildered hesitation and uncertainty. To be "a great man" means to have to take action, make decisions and *bear the responsibility*. This the parasite cannot and will not do; he will run from the mere thought of it. So now there comes the period of the ghostwriter, the front and the patsy. The parasites try to keep their "prestige" and positions, but switch the work and the actual responsibility to someone else. (My story opens just before the beginning of *this* period.) That's the stage equivalent to the Soviet custom of liquidating factory heads for the failure of a five-year plan, the heads who are placed there for that purpose, who have the responsibility of trying to produce under impossible conditions, who never get credit for success (the Commissar does) and get executed for failure. (This is precisely what James Taggart does with his key employees. *There* is one concrete, dramatic issue in human terms.)

The parasites are not concerned with the results, i.e., the actual performance or production that their high position demands. They are concerned only (and fiercely, hysterically) with faking a performance—in the eyes of others and in their own eyes. They maneuver themselves into positions and situations where the responsibility for actual results is not theirs—and they have a plausible alibi for it not being theirs, for their right to put the blame on somebody else, for even being the injured party (on the "I work so hard—and here's what people do to me—I can't help it" pattern).

This is what the parasite has always done in the world of creators—but then he passed the buck to the creators and was able to ride along safely on their energy, on their performance and production. But now he passes the buck to another parasite—and is aghast to find that it won't work. The parasite merely repeats the top parasite's gesture, passing the buck further down. (But there is now no man to stop this chain—to take responsibility and action.)

When this starts with the head of a firm, it spreads on down, in ever widening circles. First, because this is the type of men the parasite would surround himself with, particularly in top positions; he's fired and rejected the creators long ago, the creators "don't belong, they're inharmonious, they're difficult." Second, because the lesser employees (who are actually better men—honest average men—working under the orders of their inferiors, bewildered and embittered under the command of presumptuous, pompous phonies) realize what is expected of them and what is the only way to keep the job they need. They see that the bosses neither want nor understand an actual performance, but are scrambling with one another for the better position from which to fake a performance; they realize that if they attempt to do good honest work it would mean being tagged with the responsibility for somebody else's mistake (and these mistakes are constant, all around them, they see the all-pervading reign of the *mindless*); so they conclude, in excusable self-preservation, that the safe, practical thing to do is not to work, but to fake a show of working and play the game of passing the buck.

(This is excusable for honest average men because they are not creators or initiators, they cannot go into business, start an enterprise, make a living on their own, and they never pretended they could. And it's not possible in their collectivized, frozen, regimented world. They are, by nature, only good employees, and they have no other place to go; the situation, methods, and policy are the same in every enterprise run by the parasites. This is the point at which average men are forced to discard their best and exist by means of their worst—in a society of parasites.)

So these lesser employees start passing the buck to still smaller ones, until only the office boy is certain of his proper job and is performing it (he has no one smaller to use as a front). Then, in a crisis, it is the office boy who gets blamed for the company's ten-million-dollar failure—and it's all proved, explained, alibied, stated in the press, by everybody down the line, in the language of parasites to parasites, in the disgusting, deliberately inexact double-talk that passes for convincing argument. (But then, nobody is convinced of anything anyway, one way or the other, and nobody argues; the explanation, too, is only a show.)

And don't we see *this* today! *This* is the exploitation of the weak by the strong—when strength is [based] not on the intellect, but on plain force; the parasites hold their jobs by compulsion or fraud, not by merit.

(The pretense of an explanation in this case is only a routine remembered from the world of the creators, performed but no longer understood or taken seriously. This is one example of the sickening way in which remnants of a rational world still persist in this insane asylum, in the shape of meaningless hulks, automatic routines gone through for no particular reason, just because no one took the initiative to stop it. It is the letter without the spirit, something like the maintenance of an airport for which there are no longer any planes (they do that, too). There must be many examples of this in the story—in their business and personal lives.)

The third stage is when nobody wants a position of responsibility any longer. Nobody wants a top job. The desperate competition is for *small* jobs, the smaller the safer; it is a scramble for anonymity in a world aimed at and geared to anonymity, the world without a *person*, without identity, without individuality. It has now become dangerous to be important, even important only in show, even to be only an inflated windbag or figurehead. They don't liquidate "the specialists," as in Russia, but the public figures; the big-shot figureheads are beginning to be blamed for the accelerating failures and disasters, for the state of the world (even if no specific personal responsibility can be pinned on any one of them). The big shots *collectively* (didn't they want that?) are beginning to be tagged with a collective blame, there are cries of: *"Something has to be done."* (Nobody knows what to do—everybody knows that it *has to be done*.)

There have been a few cases when top parasites got caught in their own stupidities and criminal negligences, when they weren't able to wriggle out of the responsibility, and were publicly exposed and disgraced, and lost their fortunes, factories, or positions. This has scared the rest of the top parasites. So now there are gaping vacancies in top jobs; the parasites are afraid to take them, the honest average men won't take them, because they know that the job is hopeless, no honest work can be done in this kind of world, particularly not in any responsible executive position. The rules and regulations, which the parasites erected earlier for their own "protection," are now such that no one can untangle them or make a step, or know where he stands— and an honest man cannot accept responsibility when he knows he won't be left free to perform the work for which he is responsible. (Nor will he allow himself to be held responsible for the actions and mistakes of others, whom he can't control, who control him; a slave or a robot cannot be responsible.)

And, of course, the creators are not there to take these top jobs. (They wouldn't, in these conditions, even without a strike—as we see today. It's strange that Soviet Russia has such trouble getting experts and top executives, isn't it?) At this point in the story there must be some important desertions of the few remaining creators to the ranks of the strikers—with disastrous results for the parasites left behind, causing the beginning of the parasites' panic.

The performance of the "authorities" and celebrities begins to be grotesquely ludicrous during this period (which is just a little worse than it is right now). Authorities are picked by mere chance and sheer accident. At first, the parasites were pushing themselves and their friends into celebrity [status]; now they are afraid of it. So the field of fame is open to anyone and everyone, by blind chance; fame without any cause, achievement, or reason (merely because people have to talk about somebody, so somebody's got to be a celebrity). This is fame by default—and another remnant of a better world, the remnant of the conception of greatness, without content. (Something like the way books become best-sellers now, practically without merit, by sheer accident; something's got to sell, one is no better and no worse than another, it actually makes no difference, nobody really cares.)

So any adventurer, ambitious empty-headed bitch, or naive second-hander can leap (or stumble accidentally) into the class of celebrity. Then he or she becomes an "authority"—and people grasp avidly at their opinions or advice, for guidance, never questioning what is said or why the celebrity became a celebrity or whether there is any reason to respect his opinion. The chance remark of almost anybody can convince people that almost anybody else is a reliable authority. Nobody questions who made the first remark nor who started the "authority run." People really don't want to question *that*; it is so much safer to believe that you're dealing with an expert and not to look into his [qualifications] too closely; everybody is eager to rest on somebody else's assertion and to think that the somebody else knew what he was talking about, since no person knows that in regard to his own talk. The pattern is: "Why, sure, Joe Blow is the greatest expert on economics—John Doakes said so and John must have his reasons—so I don't have to look into the reasons, it's perfectly safe to follow the advice of Joe Blow."

This is another example of evasion—and another distorted remnant of a better world: the realization that there are such things as experts, that they must be individuals, not a nameless collective, since any judgment can proceed only from *a mind*, and an expert is a man with trained, self-confident judgment, who knows first-hand what he is talking about. That much of a form is left in people's minds, but an empty form, without content, with no realization of what specifically constitutes an expert on how to recognize him, so that the public attitude is a desperate search for a leader, without any understanding of what he must be or where or how he must lead them. The blind search for a great individual in a world that has discarded the concepts of individualism and greatness. And of the whole crazed herd, the celebrities and authorities are, at this point, the most frightened ones of all.

At this stage, the awful staleness of society is becoming apparent and unbearable to all; this is when they go in for revivals of the past (like the theater now), because nothing new is being produced.

The [fourth] stage is the hysterical compromise, in a growing panic. The parasite begins to see that his principles won't work—but he can't abandon them. He needs the creators—and he can't admit that he needs them. He can't do the work, but it's got to be done—so he wants somebody who'll do it *for him*. He proceeds in his usual twisted, irrational way—his halfway. He wants creators without having to call them creators or give them the conditions they require in order to function. He wants creators as tools—a contradiction in terms; but he thinks it's only a matter of finding some who are *willing* to be tools.

He embarks upon a course compounded of flattery and insults, bribery and threats, incentives and [punishments], all at the same time. He attempts to develop experts and leaders, but to keep them in check, safely harnessed. He fosters a kind of "home-grown substitute for creators," a kind of "ersatz creators." He features individuals too much, offers exorbitant rewards (usually material), names movements and public monuments after them—yet sits guard over them, fiercely and jealously, to see that the "leader" has the proper collectivist spirit, the proper humility, no independence, not too much initiative that could flame into a rebellion; in other words, he wants the performance of a creator with the soul of a parasite, a timid, cowardly soul like his own, a soul that won't demand too much nor develop an actual ego. He wants these alleged creators to function, yet "be kept in their place." And all the rewards and incentives he offers are of a blatantly collectivist, second-handed nature (money, titles, public honors)—he could not venture to offer *personal* rewards, such as freedom, choice, actual authority and responsibility.

Under these conditions, one can imagine what kind of leaders he gets. Those who swim to the top now, those boosted into leadership, are the criminal element—the type of Soviet commissars or G.P.U. agents, the real gangster type, without even the saving grace of a neurosis (if that's a saving grace). These new figures are the reemergence of the savage, the harbingers and symbols of the final retrogression. They have no scruples, principles, or anti-individualist complex; they don't even have a conception of what any of that means; they don't mind carrying out the orders of the parasite and they don't care about his reasons or motives; they know they are not actually carrying out anyone's orders—they are there to loot. They are beasts of prey in the simplest and lowest sense of the word. They are the savages who have no other conception of existence except to grab what they can, where they can, at and for the moment—the exponents of man without a mind, trying to exist through naked brute force. [*This type is represented in the novel by the character of Cuffy Meigs.*]

Their relation to the parasite, who is their official boss and who is now mere window dressing in public top positions of alleged authority, is that of G.P.U. agents to [Communist] Party theoreticians; public strutting and abject fear on the side of the latter, a silent leering contempt on the side of the former; both know who is doing whose dirty work and who is the real boss. (Or, somewhat, the relation of Toohey and Gus Webb.)

And whenever (not often) one of these new leaders turns out to be more naive or a better man than the rest of them, whenever he shows signs of something like real ability, sincerity or popularity, he is promptly liquidated by the parasite. The vicious paradox of the parasite's position is that he must destroy the man who could possibly save him, the moment that man shows signs of such a possibility—and he must leave the field clear to those who are [his own] real destroyers. In an unstated, unadmitted way, the parasite knows this. This is one of the reasons for his growing hysteria, his panic, and his desperate attempts to escape from any thought, from facing any facts. (There must be a concrete incident and relationship like that for James Taggart and some of his last employees.)

Men like these new leaders, with no force to oppose them, would destroy the world quickly, in any stage, at any time. But when it is attempted to have them run the remnants of an industrial civilization, the end comes that much quicker. So this stage does not last long. It is merely a period of accelerated disintegration and destruction.

The [fifth] and final stage is the abject surrender to the creators—without an honest admission or realization of it. The parasite who admits or realizes anything ceases being a parasite. By now, he is not capable of that, if he ever was. But the surrender is there, and the parasite knows it, and his panic at this stage is sheer running from himself, the screaming panic within. The surrender is in the attempts to find Galt, to beg him for help, then to torture him—torture being the last and only resort of the parasite's method: brute force, man expected to act without mind, with pain as sole impetus and motivation. This is the climax, the revelation, the parasite showing his trump card, the thing he has been holding in reserve all this time, his claim upon the world—*this* is the symbol of what he has considered as the source of his right to loot, exploit, rule and devastate the world all these centuries—*this* is his badge, his banner, his essence: torture.

And this is the realization that even James Taggart cannot escape, nor bear. This is the meaning of the scene with the priest. The end of James Taggart is the end of the parasite.

———◇———

*Consider:* since the theme is, in a basic way, that the material comes from the spiritual and the collectivists cannot even feed themselves without the mind—it would be interesting and proper to show the same relationship for sex, as per my note on the "Pattern of the Parasites."

[*AR's grasp of the relation of sex and economics is evidence of her unique capacity for integration; she was expert at identifying the common essence that unites seemingly different facts or areas. The above integration of sex and economics was not only one of the outstanding philosophic achievements in* Atlas Shrugged—*it was also crucial to her development of the plot. After completing the novel, she remarked in an interview:*

> *Rearden, as I first saw him, was the abstraction of the martyred industrialist. He had to be the Atlas who carries the world and receives nothing but torture in payment. But I saw him only as this abstraction, and I could not get anywhere with the idea. I could not get the center of any kind of plot until I changed the conception of Rearden.*
>
> *The [above] note about the issue of sex and its relationship to economics was made before I had thought of the Rearden-Dagny relationship. . . . Then one day it suddenly struck me what type Rearden should be and that the romance between Rearden and Dagny should be the central plot line. And it's from that decision that the rest of the plot fell into place quite easily. That seemed to tie the whole story.*]

———◆———

*To* [*work out*]*:*

The specific, detailed parallel between the methods of a totalitarian economy exploiting a free one and the personal methods of a parasite toward the creators. ([Use as models:] P.H., the girl reader, V.J.—in concrete detail of method, motive, and action.)

The pattern of a dictatorship as the detailed performance of a crumbling world trying hysterically to save itself.

The pattern of Galt versus Taggart in basic terms, from the beginning.

The pattern of disintegration (such as happens to TT) as it would take place in businesses I know—the publishing and the movie industries. Discover the abstract progression of what happens and why—then translate it [for TT's disintegration].

Pick out from "Pattern of the Parasites" the specific points to illustrate in concrete action for James Taggart and his friends.

———◆———

The supposition of man's physical descent from monkeys does not necessarily mean that man's soul, the rational faculty, is only an elaboration of an animal faculty, different from the animal's consciousness only in degree, not in kind. It is possible that there was a sharp break, that the rational faculty was like a spark, added to the animal who was ready for it—and this would be actually like a soul entering a body. Or it might be that there is a metaphysical mistake in considering animals as pure matter. There is, scientifically, a most profound break between the living and the non-living. Now *life* may be the spirit; the animals may be the forms of spirit and matter, in which matter predominates; man may be the highest form, the crown and final goal of the universe, the form of spirit and matter in which the spirit predominates and triumphs. (If there's any value in "feelings" and "hunches"—God! how I feel that *this* is true!)

If it's now added that the next step is pure spirit—I would ask, why? Pure spirit, with no connection to matter, is inconceivable to our consciousness; and what, then, is the sense, purpose or function of matter? That division into spirit and matter as antagonists or opposites, that idea of "setting man free from matter," is untenable, irrational, and vicious (and has led only to man's agony on earth, to rejection of his joy in living—the highest expression of his spirit). The unity of spirit and matter seems unbreakable; the pattern of the universe, then, would be: matter, as the tool of the spirit, the spirit giving meaning and purpose to matter. [. . .]

Also to be noted here: the spiritual is the totally individual, since it is *a consciousness* and a consciousness is an "I." (Whether it's God, man, or an animal, a universal consciousness or the faintest flicker of it—it's an indivisible "I." This is why the Oriental idea of consciousness dissolving into an *impersonal* universal spirit is nonsense, irrational, and a contradiction in terms. Once the indivisible *unity*, *integrity*, *continuity* of an "I" is broken, there's no "consciousness" to speak about.)

———

Men's intellectual capacities have always been so unequal that to the thinkers the majority of their brothers have probably always seemed subhuman. And some men may still be, for all the evidence of rationality, or lack of it, that they give. We may still be in evolution, as a species, and living side by side with some "missing links." [. . .]

We do not know to what extent the majority of men are now rational. (They are certainly far from the perfect rational being, and all the teachings they absorb push them still farther back to the pre-human stage.) But we do know that mankind as a whole and each man as an individual has a *chance* to survive and succeed only to the degree of their general and individual intelligence. That is all that a rational man can deal with, count on or be concerned with. Let him, without wondering about actual numbers or percentages of intelligence in others, act on the basis of "addressing himself to intelligence"—and he will win. And he will find that he does not have to fear stupidity. (Most men now are rational beings, even if not too smart; they are not pre-humans incapable of rational thinking; they can be dealt with only on the basis of free, rational consent.)

If it's asked: what about those who are still pre-human, or near enough to it, and incapable of rationality as a method to guide their lives? What if such do exist among us? The answer is: nothing. Their way of living is not ours; in fact, they have no way of living, no method or means of survival—except through imitating us, who have acquired the human method and means. Leave us to *our* way of living, man's way—freedom, *individual independence*—and we'll carry them along by providing an example and a world of safety and comfort such as they can never quite grasp, let alone achieve.

We *do* this—but even if we didn't, so what? If those creatures incapable of rational existence are sub-human, are we to sacrifice ourselves or be sacrificed to *them*? Are we to descend to their level? Are we to make them the goal of our existence, and service to them our only purpose? If these pre-humans are incapable of rational thinking and of independence, and therefore they need an enslaved, controlled, regimented, "protective" society in order to survive—*we* cannot survive in such a society. By definition, we are then two different species. Their requirements are opposite to ours. They'll perish without us, anyway. *But we will not be sacrificed to them.* We will live in freedom—whether or not others will or can live that way.

**April 27, 1946**

### Specific Instances of Parasite Methods to Be Dramatized
### (For James Taggart, and others like him)

Overall: the escape from the necessity to make an independent rational judgment. (The escape from decision, from responsibility.)

The parasite with a two-cent achievement, who wants to destroy all great achievements, so that his will be tops (and even his achievement is not authentic, not original, but a borrowed composite). On a railroad, this would be a man who makes Taggart reject a great improvement, in order to adopt his silly little one. (Or it can be Taggart himself.)

The parasite who thinks that in order to get a top job he only has to destroy the creator holding it. He succeeds—and merely destroys the job. This can be Taggart himself—if he got his position not through inheritance, but special pull (against Dagny), such as government pressure. (His share of inheritance did not entitle him to be president of the company; he forced his way into that.) If not, then it must be a specific, important case of a parasite who thus destroys a business needed by TT. It is also Taggart forcing a competing, rising new railroad company (which is only a branch so far) out of business through political means—then finding that passengers won't use his substitute, he has merely destroyed the market, and it has cost him more than he could afford (thus weakening TT).

This is also a number of lesser parasites: a critic who forces his way into the place of an honorable one—and finds that people no longer pay attention to reviews. The pseudo-philosopher, who takes the place of the philosopher on strike—and sees his classes shrinking, people losing interest in philosophy, and wonders why it is that he can't be "an influence," as the other man was. The no-melody composer, who takes the place of Gerhardt—and wonders why people don't go to concerts any more, why records of old classics are so popular. The girl-writer's publishers—who see the public reading fewer and fewer books. The automobile manufacturer who sees the public going back to horse-buggies. (This point is eloquent and important, so it can be used in many typical instances, some in detail, some just indicated, as small "bits.")

The parasites who try to "protect" themselves by restricting and destroying competition (by stopping others). [Hence, the] unions with their rules for the performance of useless duties, and quotas of admission, to keep their profession limited. Also, James Taggart and other businessmen like him ganging up on a newcomer in their line, to drive him out (and then TT needs the product he was manufacturing—and the whole damn gang can't deliver it).

James Taggart, in his quest for superiority, goes to great lengths to *beat* some creator, instead of performing some needed achievement of his own. (This might be the railroad which he destroys.)

In his personal relations, the more Taggart gets, the less satisfied he is and the more he demands.

Taggart gives orders for the sheer sake of being obeyed (sometimes even knowing that the order is preposterous—*that* is why he wants to force an abler man to obey it), and he causes untold damage to TT that way. Dagny is fighting that constantly.

[Regarding] Taggart's desire to "influence others": he gives advice to some helpless person (perhaps a poor girl he's trying to have a "romance" with), finds that the advice is wrong and detrimental to her—and insists that she carry it out, just because it's *his* advice and he wants to see *his* influence realized. The actual result of his advice means nothing to him. (Here is the parasite's unreality: the girl asked him to save her, instead he's destroyed her, but he considers *that* beside the point; she took *his advice*, doesn't that make him great and powerful?)

Taggart's nagging jealousy and his insistence on being *first* in the affections of any woman or friend is sickening and becomes unbearable even to the weaklings whom he picks for affection.

Taggart is always surrounded by inferiors—a kind of personal court of fawning moochers. When he brings them into his business (forcing them on TT in the manner of and for exactly the same motive as Caligula and his horse) the results are disastrous. This may be one important incident in the contest between Taggart and Winslow: Taggart forces an offensive mediocrity into the position of Winslow's boss.

Taggart steals someone's invention or idea for TT—then tries to destroy the creator, in order to take the credit (like the designers who steal from Adrian).

Taggart is extremely "touchy" about his "feelings." He believes [subconsciously] that all he has to do is *want* something and he should get it; if he doesn't, then he hates the universe. It never occurs to him that before you can want anything, you must have defined standards, purposes, and reasons; that is, desires proceed from the rational faculty and, therefore, will be (and *must* be) based on reality. The rational man will not want the impossible, the undefined, the self-contradictory; nor will he merely sit and want something, but will know clearly what he wants and how to get it, and will act to get it. But Taggart's attitude is a chronic damning of the universe, because he just *wants* and nothing happens.

Taggart's hatred for the creators is an all-pervading theme-song in his actions. The immediate objects of it are Dagny, Rearden, Winslow. (And in the background, there is always his dread of John Galt.)

An incident when Taggart, after having eliminated a better competitor, stuns Dagny by declaring (she forces this out of him) that he has no desire to improve TT or to make more money now. He wanted to run three trains a day when his competitor ran two, and he wanted to make two million dollars to the competitor's one. But now he is perfectly satisfied to run just one train a day and to make just half a million. It's not the fact that counts, not the actual, objective value—but the relation of beating that other man. (This is toward the end of the story, and Dagny begins to realize the horror of a parasite's nature; she sees a faint hint of an explanation for what's wrong with the world—and she begins to hate her brother.)

Taggart is forever engaged in forming "collaborations," "cooperatives," "agreements," gangs and cliques—and forever running to Washington to have laws passed for "protection." Toward the end, he no longer has any clear sense of what it is that he must be protected from, and his efforts have no practical meaning at all, they are like the convulsions of an animal getting more and more tangled in the thread he has unraveled.

Taggart hates any success or happiness, even of those unrelated to him. Incidents when he double-crosses friends or protégés, just because they seemed happy or had succeeded in something.

Taggart will always sneer and make disparaging remarks whenever anyone is praised in his presence—even if it's only some professor of botany or some prize-cattle farmer. (He likes all the "debunking" biographies, the news and gossip about "feet of clay.")

Taggart's envy—of everything and everyone—is constant, ever-present, and motivates most of his actions.

Taggart loves to talk about and gloat over any misfortune.

Taggart hates Dagny and needs her. He wants to destroy her and to get all he can out of her. One way of doing this is to try to ruin her personal life, make her unhappy, yet permit her to function in business, even hoping that this would make her function better. This is what Taggart does in relation to Stan Winslow.

Taggart's dependence on the material (like the big, luxurious home) reflects his crazy half-notion that his spiritual greatness will come from that. Yet he is extremely stupid about spending money on luxuries (flat, no imagination) and he gets no pleasure from it.

There must also be one of the parasites who will start poor, make a Peter Keating kind of career, and go to pieces when he reaches the top, when he sees that money does not give him what he wanted.

Examples of parasites who don't want to *make* but to "*take over.*"

Taggart always talks about "striving being better than achievement" and "and man's reach should exceed his grasp," etc.

Examples of collectivists that are inordinately concerned with material wealth, and of creators that are calmly indifferent about it—not really indifferent, but self-confident.

Important incident (near the end of the story) showing James Taggart's abject terror of some of his own gangsters.

**April 28, 1946**

*Note for Galt, while he is being tortured:*

He tells them that torture is the only weapon they have—and this is limited by his own will to live. "You can get away with it only so long as I have some desire of my own to remain alive, for the sake of which I will accept your terms. What if I haven't? What if I tell you that I wish to live in my own kind of world, on my own terms—or not at all? This is how you have exploited and tortured us for centuries. Not through *your* power—but through *ours*. Through our own magnificent will to live, which you lack, the will that was great enough to carry on, even through torture and in chains. Now we refuse you that tool—that power of life, and of loving life, within us. The day we understand this—you're finished. Where are your weapons now? Go ahead. Turn on the electric current."

(The electric current was invented by one of the creators—and this is the use parasites put it to, when the creators give it to them.)

———————

Even in Dagny's suffering there is a sense of beauty, strength, and hope. Even in Taggart's joys there is a sense of guilt, shame, and disgust.

Important: dramatize the connection between joy in living and the rational faculty. The reason is clear: the basic sense of joy in living [arises from] the firm realization and conviction that you have the means to satisfy your desires, to achieve joy. Joy is the emotional reaction to a satisfied desire. Reason "produces" the desire and the means to achieve it; joy is the "consumption" of this production. The parasite, who has discarded reason as impotent in his desire to escape reality, is left with the unadmitted, but implicit, conclusion that he has no means to achieve joy—hence his chronic sense of frustration and misery. This primary joy in living is present and shown in all the strikers, but most eloquently in John Galt and Dagny.

———————

For the "reversed process of expansion": just as Henry Ford opened the way (created the chance) for scores of new industries, James Taggart kills the chances of any attempted endeavor that comes in contact with his business. Show lesser, but potentially important, inventions that are killed through his rejection, and more important, through his retrenchment of the particular line where they would be useful. Example: somebody suggests lunch cars on trains; somebody else has a gadget that would make quick, compact lunches possible and could have many uses besides those on trains, could grow into a valuable industry; Taggart declares that there's no reason to give the passengers quick lunches, let them carry lunch boxes, they have no other means of transportation, they'll ride on floors in boxcars if necessary, why should he give them lunches? The gadget and the unborn industry are killed. (This example is not necessarily the one to use, but this is the pattern.)

In clear connection with that, show the method of Hank Rearden, who expands everything he touches (and gets penalized for it in the parasite's world), and [perhaps] have flashbacks to the career of Taggart's great-great-grandfather, founder of TT, who functioned like Henry Ford. *Show the spreading creativeness of the creators—and the contracting destructiveness of the parasites.*

Show instances of the irrational state of the world in retrogression. Progress proceeds logically and new industries grow when and as they are needed, but there can be no logical retrogression. The economy in the parasite's world presents all the senselessness of destruction: [the attempt to maintain] difficult, complex industries, while primary necessities are gone. They're manufacturing—with difficulty and at incredible cost—a few botched tractors a year, when the farmers have no simple plows. They manufacture double-deck observation cars, and have no passenger coaches. There are (botched) television sets for the officials—and no safety pins for the public. It is the spectacle of an erratic, unnatural, irrational shrinking; the signs of the break up, of retrogression. For man, retrogression can only be unnatural; it has to be irrational, because where reason is in control, there is expansion and progress.

Show an instance of penalizing ability: early in the story, Taggart rejects an able employee (the young engineer?) for reasons such as: "He's too good—too brilliant—which will make it difficult for the other employees—there will be no harmony, *no balance*—we'll do better with a lesser, milder man who'll *fit in*." Then show the *specific* results: what the brilliant one would have done, and what the "milder" one does (and the consequences for TT). (In connection with the Tunnel catastrophe.)

Show an instance of an employee (of medium importance) forced to act on his worst, not his best (toward the end of the second stage)—with results disastrous to TT. This, in a higher, more complex sense, also applies as a main line for Stan Winslow.

Show specific, repeated instances when the honest average men (particularly in the later stages) run to the "thinkers" of the period (the pseudo-philosopher, the pseudo-critic, etc.) for spiritual guidance in their growing bewilderment and despair. What they actually need is the basic, profoundly philosophical advice which the thinkers who are on strike could have given them; the advice they get only pushes them into the general horror.

In each instance of creators working with the parasites, show where and how the creators contribute to their own destruction (like Dietrich Gerhardt). The pattern is that of Soviet Russia stealing foreign ideas and inventions, hiring foreign engineers and experts, repudiating loans and debts. The free enterprises must not deal with anyone except free enterprises, otherwise they are working for their own destruction. This means: you cannot work against your own principles, there is no "middle road" or compromise here; if you do, you'll pay for it. Principles *are* absolute. And, applied to the creators on strike: you cannot compromise or work against the basic life principles of the creators.

**April 29, 1946**

*Notes for tomorrow (for detailed thinking out):*

A society of parasites is like a body with hemophilia: the slightest cut can be fatal and lead to bleeding to death; the slightest error, failure of routine, or new circumstance can destroy a whole industry (or society)—there is no power of recovery in the body, no thinking mind.

———◦———

Pat is an example of the penalizing of ability. The conservatives actually reject her for being too good; they prefer [Edgar] Queeny, who is "milder," i.e., less good. Their purpose is to save capitalism. Their result is to [further] the spread of collectivism.

———◦———

Earle Balch [Isabel Paterson's publisher] is an example of the average man who could be good, efficient and productive in a society of creators, but not in a society of parasites. The reasons? Either his disgust, or discouragement, or giving in. Either he's not good, strong and brave enough to buck a society of parasites, or else he swims with the current and delivers just what the society around him requires. This is an example of how a society of producers brings out the best in the average man by rewarding him for his best—while a society of parasites brings out the worst in him by penalizing his best and rewarding his worst. One rewards him for producing, the other for faking. How long can a society go on in that last way? (This is an important point.)

———◆———

The average man doesn't have the strength to do what is right at any cost, against all men. Only the genius can do that. The genius clears the way for the average man. But when the genius goes, the best in the average man goes with him. (John Galt and Stan Winslow?) [*This is AR's last reference to the character of Stan Winslow.*]

The general pattern of the crack-up is this: first, the ground is cut from under all men and all professions; i.e., the primary base—the metaphysical, philosophical, moral, political premises—are undercut. These are discovered, formulated, stated and defended by the thinkers, the geniuses, the creators. They are the necessary first premises for all men, before they can even begin to live and work properly as men. These are destroyed—and the thinkers, who could fight the destruction, do nothing about it, they let their work be destroyed, they offer no other [premises] and no resistance. In the place of the thinkers, there appear the Marxists, the Fadimans [*Clifton Fadiman was book editor of* The New Yorker], and such others. Instead of [reason], individualism, and capitalism men get mysticism, determinism, altruism, and collectivism.

The average man is stopped and destroyed right there. He cannot correct the premises himself—and the genius won't help him. Therefore, the spiritual life of mankind becomes a hopeless, joyless, purposeless, senseless, cynical muddle of bewilderment and helplessness. From then on, [economic events] follow suit; *the material is the expression and consequence of the spiritual.* [This continues] until men can no longer maintain their material existence, i.e., can no longer feed themselves. (And the average man becomes the helpless prey of any parasite—only the genius and the proper principles could protect his human rights, his status as a man.)

In the material realm, the crack-up will embrace the whole [society], every activity. It is only a matter of selecting the key points, of illustrating the most important, the most eloquent, the most representative aspects of it (and showing it progressively, in logical sequence, in order of importance).

————◆————

Here's what I say to the parasites, in effect: "You miserable little bastards! You can't conceive of or value our scale of living—but you think you can get its advantages without its essence, by enslaving and destroying us. You think you can enjoy *our* advantages on *your* level. All right. Try it."

————◆————

When a man destroys a competitor and takes his place, he does not get the place but merely destroys the market. For instance: if a bad writer destroyed all good writers, he would not get their public and market; people would stop reading books. The manufacturer of a bad car, destroying the better manufacturers, would stop people from using cars. (All the parasite can count on is the interim period of disintegration, while people struggle with his bad product, then give up.) This process can be seen now very eloquently in book publishing, the theater and movies. People do not take the trash: they merely stop reading new books, or going to the theaters.

**April 30, 1946**

*Note on the basic theme:* The basic process of a man's life goes like this: his thinking determines his desires, his desires determine his actions. (Thinking, of course, is present all along the line, at every step and stage. His desires are a combination of thought and emotion (the "production" and the "consumption" sides being involved), and all his emotions are determined by his thinking, most particularly by his basic premises.)

So the process is: the right thinking creates the right desires, which create the proper activity. One of the aspects of man's activity must be material production, in order to feed himself and exist. Feeding himself, the economic activity, is just one of the aspects of the fact that he has to give a physical expression or form to his spiritual aims, desires, and needs. This is the basic pattern, or "circle," of man's life on earth: the spirit (thought) through the material activity (production) to the satisfaction of his spiritual desires (emotions). (He must eat in order to think, but he must *first* think in order to eat.)

The wrong thinking leads to the wrong desires, which lead to the wrong activity—and a wrong activity means that man functions improperly in the material realm of production and cannot even feed himself. A spiritual error (wrong thinking) makes it impossible for him to handle the physical world or to preserve his body.

Now, on the general scale of mankind as a whole, here is how the pattern is repeated: the right philosophy leads to the right ethics, which lead to the right politics, which lead to the right economics. The wrong philosophy creates the wrong ethics, which create the wrong politics, which create the wrong economics (they stop production dead).

Therefore, here is what men must be told: if, through improper thinking due to inadequate mental [capacity], you start down the wrong way—you need the creators, the best minds, to correct your errors and show you the right way. If, through inability to do any basic thinking at all, you find yourselves open to scoundrels and parasites who push you toward destruction— you need the creators to save you and show you the right way. If you are one of the scoundrels, those who consciously devise systems of thought as tools of exploitation, you still need the creators. By the nature of your own systems, you can exist only so long as the creators are still there to be fought and looted. The day of your victory will be the day of your own destruction.

### Pattern for James Taggart and TT
### (following the general "Pattern of Disintegration")

*First stage.* An issue at TT in which James Taggart stalls, then hides behind Dagny and another executive, leaving the two decisions to them (particularly objecting to Dagny's decision). Taggart's stalling (and timidity, playing-safe) hampers both lines of endeavor. Dagny wins, the executive fails. Taggart takes credit for Dagny's achievement, and fires the executive, ruining him. The achievement comes out half-botched, due to the interference.

*Second stage.* An issue at TT in which James Taggart discovers the responsibility of being a "great man." He makes an arbitrary decision, then creates a deliberate victim to ruin ("just in case"), and also leans on one of his pet parasites. The new executive, the victim, is in a position where he has to say "yes" to Taggart. But it doesn't work, the buck passing spreads to the bottom. The issue ends in a real disaster (the first major one). Taggart wriggles out of it, ruining the chosen victim and some very minor employee (almost the equivalent of an office boy).

*Third stage.* TT can't get top executives. Lesser disasters are accelerating, like a fabric cracking to pieces. Taggart depends on his suppliers, instead of vice versa. (The dependence on dependents.) An issue at TT in which Taggart's best friend in a contributing business (one of the top parasites, one of these suppliers) gets caught in criminal negligence, is publicly exposed and ruined. His crash is a bad blow to TT. (Here Taggart runs his business *for the sake of his suppliers*—like a publisher who would publish "for critics.")

*Fourth stage.* Taggart brings in a "criminal type" executive to TT. An issue in which the executive aims at nothing but personal looting (blatantly and cynically double-crossing TT). Taggart knows it—and can't fire him.

*Fifth stage.* The issue which destroys TT.

**May 3, 1946**

*Ideas from research:*

If possible, tie Galt to transportation work, i.e., transportation science. (Ragnar Danneskjöld owns a plane designed by Galt, handmade in the valley. Its design attracts Dagny's attention; this is one of the reasons she follows Danneskjöld. The plane could even be called the *John Galt*. The engine could be one that would be extremely valuable if applied to railroad use.) [*This is the first mention of Galt inventing a new type of motor.*]

For Dagny's childhood: she tells Eddie Willers that the rail lines vanishing at the horizon are held in a man's hand, like reins; they come from one man's hand. What man? She doesn't know. No, not her father, not any big man in the office. Someday she wants to meet that man. How will she recognize him? She will.

Use the grass growing between the tracks as a sign of disintegration.

The progressive neglect of maintenance work, the relaxation of vigilance, causes minor defects that lead to major disasters. Here we see James Taggart's (and all the parasites') psychology of living in and for the moment, like a savage or an animal; he is incapable of long-range planning, foresight or continuity, just as he is incapable of integration as a person.

A major flood (like the 1938 one) can be used—only the railroad affected does not recover, and neither do the communities it served. There is no power of recovery in that society.

The examples of following routine and precedent with disastrous results—since every particular problem on a railroad is new and different, to be solved on the basis of the particular, specific case.

[Show] a section of the country killed off when TT closes a branch of their network. Just as new railroads created new sections, brought prosperity to semi-deserted, barren stretches of primitive wilderness—so now we see

the reverse process, the failure and shrinking of railroads kills whole sections, creates abandoned ghost-towns, ghost-ranches, ghost-mines, and
forces the handful of remaining inhabitants in such areas back into primitive
subsistence, poverty, hard [manual] labor—back to savagery, but a desolate
savagery, without hope. There are such dying sections ("blighted areas")
when the story opens; they are taken for granted—they have been spreading
slowly for years. They are the first creepers of the advancing jungle. *But
there must also be a specific plot sequence showing the destruction of such a
section*—through the railroad failures traceable to James Taggart (this will
be one of the turning points of TT's disintegration).

**May 4, 1946**

*Philosophical Notes on the Creative Process*

The creative process is, in a way, the reverse of the learning process.
It's the other part of the circle [that goes] from the concrete to the abstract to
the concrete. Abstractions are derived from the concrete—and then applied
to the concrete in order to achieve one's own purpose. The process of
learning has as its purpose to acquire knowledge. The process of creation is
the process of applying one's knowledge to whatever purpose one wishes to
achieve. Knowledge precedes creation; without knowledge of some sort (no
matter how general) one can't choose and set the purpose one wishes to
accomplish. So the first, basic purpose (a kind of first sub-purpose) preceding every other specific purpose is the purpose of gaining knowledge.
(Before you decide to create, you must know *what* you want to create and
*how* you must [proceed] in order to create it.)

One may stop at the purpose of acquiring knowledge; theoretical
scientists and philosophers do. But it seems to me (I have no clear definitions here as yet) that the complete cycle of a man's life includes the application of his knowledge to his particular goal. Knowledge per se is the base of
all activities; it seems to be only a part of a completed cycle. Yes, the function of the theoretical scientist and the abstract philosopher are more crucially, basically important than that of the applied scientist (inventor) or the
practical moralist; these latter men rest their achievements on those of the
former (and if one man combines both functions, the one of discovering new
knowledge precedes that of applying it). But one cannot quite say that the
discovery of new knowledge is more important than the application of

existing knowledge; "important" here would imply the question: "Important to whom?" and involves a question of values.

Nor can one say that a theoretical scientist is necessarily a man of greater ability than the applied scientist; both functions require a process of new, original thought. One can say only that for any given step in the discovery of new knowledge and its use, the discovery precedes the use; the correct theory precedes the practical application. And also, one can say that the theoretical scientist or the philosopher perform the most obviously first-hand act of thinking, of rational deduction—drawing, from concrete experience, a new abstraction, the statement of new knowledge, never drawn by any other person before.

Still, it seems to me—no matter what great, original first-hand effort of thought is required in these functions—that theoretical science or abstract philosophy are "unfinished" spheres of human endeavor. (I said "*it seems to me*": I may be wrong; this requires more thought and the most careful definitions.) The complete sphere must lead to *man*. It's another completed cycle: from man to abstract knowledge to the satisfaction of man's purposes and desires. Man's essential nature is that of creator—within the reality of an objective universe; before he can act or create, he must study this universe (this is the process of acquiring knowledge); then, he uses his knowledge to set his purpose and to achieve it (this is the process of creation).

In my own case, I seem to be both a theoretical philosopher and a fiction writer. But it is the last that interests me most; the first is only the means to the last; the absolutely necessary means, but only the means; the fiction story is the end. Without an understanding and statement of the right philosophical principle, I cannot create the right story; but the discovery of the principle interests me only as the discovery of the proper knowledge to be used for my life purpose, and my life purpose is the creation of the kind of world (people and events) that I like, i.e., that represents human perfection. Philosophical knowledge is necessary in order to define human perfection, but I do not care to stop at the definition; I want to *use* it, to apply it in my work (in my personal life, too—but the core, center and purpose of my personal life, of my *whole* life, is my work).

This is why, I think, the idea of writing a philosophical non-fiction book bored me; in such a book, the purpose would actually be to teach others, to present my ideas to *them*. In a book of fiction the purpose is to create, for myself, the kind of world I want and to live in it while I am creating it; then, as a secondary consequence, to let others enjoy this world, and to the extent that, they can.

It may be said that the first purpose of a philosophical book is the clarification or statement of your new knowledge to and for yourself; and then, as a secondary step, the offering of your knowledge to others. But here is the difference, as far as I am concerned: I have to acquire and state to myself the new philosophical knowledge or principle I use in order to write a fiction story as its embodiment and illustration; I do not care to write a story with a theme [based on] someone else's philosophy (because those philosophies are wrong); to this extent, I am an abstract philosopher. I want to present the perfect man and his perfect life—and I must also discover my own philosophical statement and definition of this perfection. But when and if I have discovered such new knowledge, I am not interested in stating it in its abstract, general form, i.e., as knowledge; I am interested in applying it, i.e., in stating it in the concrete form of men and events, in the form of a fiction story. *This last* is my final purpose, my end; the philosophical knowledge or discovery is only the means to it. (I state the knowledge to myself, anyway; but I choose the final form of it, the expression, in the completed cycle that leads back to man.)

I wonder to what extent I represent a peculiar phenomenon in this respect; I think I represent the proper integration of a complete human being. Anyway, *this* should be my lead for the character of John Galt; *he*, too, is a combination of an abstract philosopher and a practical inventor; the thinker and the man of action, together.

Now, back to the process of creation. In learning, we draw an abstraction from concrete objects and events. In creating, we make our own concrete objects and events out of the abstraction; we bring the abstraction down and back to its specific meaning, to the concrete; but the abstraction has helped us to make the *kind of concrete we want.* It has helped us to create—to re-shape the world as we wish it to be for our purposes.

Example: I draw the abstraction "individualism" from observing men, their life, society, the universe. I translate that abstraction into a concrete figure, a specific man: Roark. [I do this by] a complex process of making abstractions concrete in details, characteristics, attributes, events; in each step and in the total result the essential process is the same: from the concrete to an abstract principle to the kind of concrete reality I want.

*Thinking, i.e., the rational process,* is involved in both functions: in the activity of acquiring knowledge (getting the abstractions) and in the activity of creating (translating the abstraction back into the concrete).

The same principle (or completed cycle) applies to all of man's activities, not only the specifically creative ones such as art or invention. (I wonder whether this is the point where there is an indication that *every* activity of man is creative, in basic principle and essence. This is to be thought out further.) In order to think at all, man must be able to perform this cycle: he must know how to see an abstraction in the concrete and the concrete in an abstraction, and always relate one to the other. He must be able to derive an abstraction from the concrete (either by his own new discovery, or by knowledge presented to him by others but *rationally* understood and accepted by him), then be able to apply this abstraction both as a guide for his specific actions and as a standard by which to judge the specific ideas or actions of others.

Example: a man who has understood and accepted the abstract principle of unalienable individual rights cannot then go about advocating compulsory labor conscription or nationalization of property. Those who do have not performed either part of the cycle: neither the abstraction nor the translating of the abstraction into the concrete. The cycle *is unbreakable*; no part of it can be of any use, until and unless the cycle is completed (that is, clear in a man's mind, in his rational grasp). (A broken electric circuit does not function in the separate parts; it must be unbroken or there is no current; the parts, in this case, are of no use whatever, of no relevance to the matter of having an electric current.) This is the basic pattern and essence of the process of thinking.

Now, in the basic pattern of man's life as a whole, there might be the indication of a similar cycle: man must think, first and above all, but he must also act. (Keep in mind here that thinking is the base and constant accompaniment or determinant of all action.) By action—in this basic sense—I mean the setting of one's purpose (that's the creation of one's desire) and then the achievement of that purpose (and the satisfaction of that desire). A theoretical scientist (or a philosopher) thinks; his purpose is the gaining of knowledge; when he discovers a new answer, a new step in knowledge, he has achieved his purpose. But the process of gaining knowledge underlies all other activities; so I wonder about the [possibility that] the purely abstract thinker is actually incomplete (since there is no abstract without the concrete, and no concrete (for man) without the abstract).

Incidentally, as an observation: if creative fiction writing is a process of translating an abstraction into the concrete, there are three possible grades of such writing: translating an old abstraction (known theme) through the medium of old fiction means, i.e., through characters, events, or situations used before for that same purpose (this is most of the popular trash); translating an old abstraction through new, original fiction means (this is most of the good literature); or creating a new, original abstraction and translating it through new, original means. This last, as far as I know, is only *me*—my kind of fiction writing. May God forgive me (metaphor!) if this is mistaken conceit! As near as I can now see it, it isn't. (A fourth possibility—translating a new abstraction through old means—is impossible; if the abstraction is new, there can be no means used by anyone else before to translate it.)

# 12

# FINAL PREPARATIONS

*After the notes presented in Chapter 11, AR took a six-week break from writing in her journal. She spent much of the time that spring thinking about the plot while strolling the grounds of her ranch home in California. The present chapter contains the notes she wrote in the summer of 1946, after this break and before beginning to write the novel.*

*AR had thus worked full-time on* Atlas Shrugged *for only five months (April through August, 1946) when she completed her outline and was ready to start writing. This is a remarkably short time; the corresponding period for* The Fountainhead *was two and a half years. There are two main reasons for the difference. First, less research was required—the knowledge of railroads and steel mills needed for* Atlas Shrugged *was much less extensive than the knowledge of architecture needed for* The Fountainhead. *Second, she had far less difficulty in working out the plot.*

*More than 80 percent of her notes from the summer of 1946 are presented here. I have omitted some research notes in which she simply copied factual material from a book,* Economic Geography, *by R. H. Whitbeck and V. C. Finch. I have also omitted a plot outline of the last part of the novel, which merely summarizes events described in earlier notes. Finally, I have omitted several pages of "Notes on Notes," in which AR catalogued the contents of her journal.*

**June 20, 1946**

As the story progresses, the parasites are increasingly concerned with and afraid of natural phenomena and disasters. This is extremely significant and logical—they have lost control over nature. They are returning to the state of being helpless before nature. But man cannot exist at the mercy of nature—his basic essence (his "means of survival") is the fact that he must exist by mastering nature, by controlling it for his purposes.

It was the accumulation of the creators' work that gave mankind protection from nature. (This point is an illustration of: "The creator's concern is the conquest of nature." The creator is concerned with nature and reason—his own will, thinking, actions, and purposes—not with *men*.) When mankind destroys or rejects the creators, when the parasites are in the saddle (those unable to use their independent rational judgment, therefore unable to deal with facts or nature), *nature* takes over once more and becomes an enemy, a menace, instead of a servant. And the world of the parasites has no means of defense. When man is free—man is the master and nature is his servant. When men are enslaved—nature becomes the master.

*Examples:* every variation in natural phenomena and every possible disaster is dreaded, progressively more dreaded throughout the story—and the consequences are worse each time. The creators' civilization had been making men progressively more independent of variations in natural phenomena, prepared against and able to deal with any eventuality. In agriculture, many variable conditions of nature were corrected artificially (fertilizer, irrigation, etc.) and it would take a major and rare disaster (such as extreme drought) to cause real hardships to men (and mankind was moving slowly to counteract even the major natural disasters). In transportation, men could travel and run trains in almost any weather, short of a flood or tornado. In their cities and buildings, men did not have to be concerned with natural variations at all—only in extreme, freak disasters, and then to a limited degree. And when an unusual disaster did strike—men recovered quickly (and the more quickly the more advanced their civilization). (Examples: the rebuilding of a railroad within a few days after a flood; the rebuilding of San Francisco after the earthquake.)

*Now,* in the story, men are returning to fear of and dependence on nature. Their food (agriculture) depends more and more upon weather conditions. Show signs of the return to savage superstitions—prayers and rites, instead of rational action, science, and invention—a sign of sheer despair and helplessness. When a major disaster strikes (flood, earthquake, tornado, etc.) there is no recovery; the town or railroad line or factory has to be abandoned (always "temporarily"—but men begin to see that such "temporary" conditions are permanent). Therefore we see the return of the constant, cringing dread of natural disasters.

(In connection with this—the Taggart Bridge.)

This is the process of "the encroaching jungle"—the signs of the return to savagery in material life, since men have returned to the principles of savagery in their spiritual life.

---

An interesting point to make is the parasite's misunderstanding of the machine. Unthinking men ([including] any second-hander, parasite or collectivist, since they are the men who have rejected, suspended, or left undiscovered the concept of independent rational judgment) see a machine performing many tasks automatically, with perfect logic, which eliminates the need for the machine's operator to think (in certain specific respects *only*). *They then imagine that the machine is a mechanical, automatic substitute for thought;* that the product of reason is a substitute for its source, that it can be preserved and used without its source, and that all one has to do is take over that product; then the unthinking man will become the equivalent of the thinker. (He will not need the thinker any longer, in fact, he must destroy the thinker in order to seize this substitute, the thinker's product, the machine, which will then make him as good as the thinker.) *That* is the crucial mistake of the collectivists. *Show that only intelligence can deal with automatic aids to intelligence.* (They are *only* aids, *not* substitutes.) The greater the intelligence and ingenuity that went into the creation of a machine, the greater is the intelligence required to keep that machine functioning. Destroy the intelligence—and you will not be able to operate or keep the machine. Destroy the source—and you cannot keep its result. Destroy the cause—and you cannot have the effect.

In society as a whole, the machines are not independent entities, finished and cut off from their creators, which will continue functioning by themselves. The machines are products of the creator's energy, which are kept alive, kept functioning by a continuous flow of that energy (or *intelligence*); *that energy is the spiritual fuel which the machines need in order to work, just as they need physical fuel;* cut off the energy (the intelligence, the capacity of independent rational judgment) of the creators—and the machines stop dead; the machines will fall apart and disintegrate in the hands of the parasites, just like a dead body without the energy of life. The machines are extensions of man's intelligence; they are *aids to intelligence*; when that which they were created to aid is gone, they are useless. Then they go, too. They cannot function on their own. They are not independent of intelligence.

It is only the presence of creators that permits a fool to use a machine he does not understand and could not make, creators whose intelligence is free to keep the machines (and the whole world) going for everybody. The creators are the eternal motor, the continuously functioning "fountainhead." When the parasites stop them—everything stops. (And the parasites destroy themselves.)

*This is important.* Be sure to bring it out.

In relation to the story, this is the basic reason and pattern of TT's disintegration.

To use *any* machine—an automobile, a Mixmaster, or a railroad system—one must know *how* to use it and *for what purpose*. The machine will not give you the knowledge or the purpose. The machine is a wonderful slave to take orders. But it cannot give you the orders. The collectivist, like the savage, expects the machine to give *him* orders and set a purpose for him, a purpose for its own function and for his. (Another collectivist reversal.)

James Taggart knows neither how to run a railroad nor for what purpose it should be run. He thinks—"for the public good." But the purpose of the railroad is not "the public good." When the railroad (or any machine) stops serving the specific, individual good (or *purpose*) of any man connected with it (of those who run it and those who use it), it stops having any purpose at all; when there's no purpose or end, there is no way to determine what means to use to achieve it; there is then no standard of means at all, therefore one can't know what to do even at short range (the parasite's range), even at any one given moment (the given moment must be determined by the long-range purpose, by the end, by its relation to the whole). Therefore, the whole system (or machine) stops.

*Stress this "purposelessness" in the progressive steps of TT's destruction.*

———◆———

*A sidelight on the parasite's methods:*

Holding the productive ability of the creator down to the level of the parasite; the holding down of the strongest to the level of the weakest. Such as: union rules to the effect that better workers must not work faster or produce more than incompetent or weaker workers ("unfair competition"); the barber's union that forbade ambitious barbers to keep their shops open on Sunday—it was "unfair" to the barbers who wished to loaf.

This is an eloquent [illustration] of the fool's idea of where wealth and production come from (he *has no* idea—he thinks it's just there, to be "divided up"). The consequences to society as a whole and to the parasites themselves are obvious. *Show specific examples of this and trace the results in concrete steps.*

For the plot construction, consider key activities of mankind (all connected with the railroad): food, clothing, shelter—as represented by *wheat, cotton, lumber*. Connect them with the story of TT.

The three attitudes of the parasites toward the creators are: (1) "We don't need you at all"; (2) "We need you—therefore you must serve us" (the appeal through weakness and pity); (3) "Never mind any reasons, or who's right or wrong—we'll just *force* you to serve us." Show concrete illustrations and examples of all three attitudes.

James Taggart alternates between (1) and (2) [in his attitude] toward Dagny (and everyone else). At the end, James Taggart and the rest of the parasites try to resort to (3) in regard to Galt.

Hank Rearden is a constant victim of (1) and (2) from all his relatives and associates throughout the story.

(You may need more, and more specific, examples and incidents of this.)

Actually, the parasite's attitude is: first, "Help me, because I'm weak and you're strong, I need you so much"; then second, when he got what he wanted: "Don't be so damn conceited, I don't need you at all." Here, the parasite got the effect and forgot the cause. In regard to his appeal, the parasite is humble and begs for charity—so long as the creator will not permit him anything else. The moment the creator is demoralized and disarmed through the creed of altruism, the parasite turns arrogant and demands help as his rightful due, as the creator's duty. "Help me because I need you," then becomes an order, a command—not a plea.

The parasite considers himself defrauded of his personal property—the creator's help. Thus the creator's energy and its products are assumed to be the property of the parasite. *Virtue—strength, intelligence, competence—has no property rights (to itself), but vice—weakness, stupidity, incompetence—* **has** *property rights (to virtue)*. Altruism does this. This is implicit in altruism, logically and consistently. But it is only the creators who make this possible by their acceptance of altruism. The responsibility here is that of the creators; it is up to them to stop the vicious procedure; they are the cause of their own destruction. (This is for Hank Rearden.)

As to attitude (3)—it comes about when (1) and (2) have destroyed all sense, morality and decency in human relations. Then parasites come to (3)—to the belief in plain force, to the bestial arrogance of the criminal moron ("the drooling beast"). Without the groundwork laid and prepared by (1) and (2), the parasites would not think of (3), or would not dare to think of it. The plain criminal types, who exist in any society at any time, would be of no danger or consequence (certainly not *spiritually*), since they would be regarded and treated as what they are: the plain criminal, the anti-rational or sub-human.

*Keep this firmly in mind as a lead:*

By associating with the parasites and a world living on the principles of the parasites, the creators offer themselves up for unspeakable suffering, and achieve, in the net total result, the opposite of that which is their purpose. They suffer in order to be able to do their independent creative work—and only give their enemies the means to torture them and to destroy their work. (Their work survives or is achieved *only* to the extent to which *their* principles of independence are followed, actually or by default. And to have these principles followed even to that extent, the creators purchase that possibility by their own suffering.)

*This* is what the creators must stop. Don't give your enemies the means to destroy you. Don't accept the enemy's terms. *You* are the power. Deliver an ultimatum to the parasites: take *my* terms—or nothing. And *my* terms here mean: individualism, egoism, independence. [This means] the recognition of the primary life principle—the faculty of man's independent rational judgment; the translation of this into concrete morality—the principle that each man exists *only* for his own sake (and can claim nothing from others); the translation of this morality into politics—a society of individualism and capitalism. The creators destroy themselves by any acceptance (complete or partial) of the creed of altruism.

**June 21, 1946**

Civilization (which means everything made by men, not nature—all physical wealth, all ideas and spiritual values) was made by man's intelligence. *It can be used and maintained only by man's intelligence.* (And this applies to any part of it, any product—industry, machines, art, anything.) It has to vanish when intelligence vanishes. But intelligence is an attribute of the individual; it functions individually, it cannot function under compulsion; it cannot be tied to the decisions of others and, therefore, is destroyed in a collectivist society. That is why collectivism cannot produce or survive.

Besides, the intelligent man does not live for others. *The higher the intelligence, the greater the self-sufficiency.* (Your need of others can be used as a measure of your intelligence—in inverse ratio.)

*As a clue to the net effect:* The book could be dedicated "to all those who think that material wealth is produced by material means."

*Minor note:* Since the material is an expression of the spiritual, the physical state of the world in the story (their physical assets, capital goods, means of production, tools, machines, buildings, etc.) must be a reflection of men's spiritual state: incompetent, weak, falling apart, disintegrating, uncertain and senselessly contradictory, maliciously evil, dull, gray, monotonous—above all, decaying.

*Re: looting.* The primitive form of looting is to seize the end products of the work of others, consume them and then look for another victim. This is the pattern of the plain criminal, the most primitive savage tribes, and the early Asiatic nomadic invasions, such as Attila or Genghis Khan. The modern form is to loot the *means of production* and try to carry on (which is only a variation of the same thing, actually more stupid, more vicious, and less practical). This is the pattern of Soviet Russia.

What makes it less practical is the fact that grabbing an industry and expecting it to run without intelligence is like grabbing an automobile and expecting it to run without gas. It rests on a savage's misunderstanding of the nature of production, his ignorance of the fact that *intelligence* is the energy that keeps the tools going, that tools cannot go by themselves, and that intelligence can neither be taken over nor forced.

If the primitive looter left his victims alive, he at least left them alone to start production again—he took over the product, *not* the means of production (the chief of which is *freedom*). The modern collectivist looter takes over the product *and the means.* He enslaves men. He seizes and stops the source. Therefore, after he has consumed the existing accumulated wealth, no more can be produced, neither for him nor for his victims. This is how he destroys the world and himself.

So the pattern of disintegration in the story must be *the increasing consumption of capital assets, without replacements.* (Here the last emergency of taking up old rails fits quite well.)

———◦———

A savage invader also enslaved the conquered population (which is taking over *man* as the means of production); but then he established a slave society, which could just barely exist, in the most primitive way, without intelligence. You cannot enslave intelligence—only brute, physical force, only muscle power. Actual looters, such as the nomadic tribes, grabbed property and departed. Now the modern collectivist is attempting the impossible; he is not a slave master, in the ancient sense of a slave economy, an economy that produced something by means of slaves; he is actually *a perpetual looter,* and what he wants to loot, continuously, is the source of production—man's intelligence. This can't be done.

### The Pattern of the Railroads' Growth

The basic scientific invention: the steam engine.

The application of this invention to transportation: the designing of a steam locomotive.

The parallel growth of two elements (two lines of endeavor, integrated by one purpose): the entrepreneurs who organize railroads, the inventors who improve the technical equipment.

*Main developments here:*

1. *Enterprise:* branching into new territories, laying out new lines, acquiring better equipment, giving better and more service cheaper, planning better organization of the whole system.

2. *Invention:* scientific progress in an immense number of lines, the four main ones being: *track* (rails, ties, grade, tunnels, bridges, terminals), *motive power* (engines: steam, oil, electric, diesel-electric), *rolling stock* (cars, brakes), *signals* (telegraph, radio, semaphores, automatic safety devices).

*Main purposes:* speed, safety, economy, comfort, reliability.

*Results:* the creation of new territories, the birth of new industries and growth of all industries due to rapid transportation permitting exchange of raw materials for production and exchange of produced goods over vast regions, opening up huge new markets.

## The Reverse: The Pattern of Disintegration

As the parasites take over a huge, working system, the first thing to stop is progress. No improvements made, no new lines opened, no new inventions accepted (or made).

Lack of judgment makes Taggart incapable of grasping the needs of the system. Routine makes him keep lines, activities, and procedures no longer necessary; this is a drain on the system and hampers the needed activities.

When the smallest thing goes wrong, he has no idea how to repair it—like a moron operating a dishwasher when he wouldn't know and couldn't think of how to wash dishes by hand; if one small screw falls out, he has no idea how to mend it. Taggart is a moron in relation to TT—a moron with an immense, complex machine. His smallest attempt at "mending" only grows into major destruction of the machine.

Lack of judgment makes Taggart adopt new policies (when forced to by obvious trouble) that are disastrous and only aggravate the trouble (by transferring it to other points and problems).

Unnecessary branches are kept going for irrelevant reasons at great expense and effort. Needed branches curtail their services, dislocating needed industries, while the unneeded ones are artificially kept alive for political and other second-hand reasons.

As needed industries are crippled or dying off, the railroad suffers from lack of the materials and products that it needs.

*The vicious circle: bad railroad service leads to bad industries, bad industries make the railroad service worse—and all go down together, disintegrating.*

In the realm of *enterprise*, the process is: branches being closed off, the system contracting, the service getting worse and more expensive, the organization falling apart with consequent confusion, inefficiency, hit-and-miss policy, a growing chaos.

In the realm of *invention*, the process is: as the technical equipment wears out, it is replaced by older, inferior models of the preceding technical stage, going back to easier, more primitive methods (but not for long, since this can't be done); [there are progressively more] accidents and breakdowns of equipment.

*Track:* rails deteriorate and replacements are made of inferior steel; ties rot and some are not being treated; grades worn by floods and weather conditions are neglected; tunnels collapse and are closed;

bridges collapse and cannot be repaired or replaced; terminals deteriorate—switching causes endless delays, confusion, loss of freight.
*Motive power:* as locomotives wear out, older and weaker ones are
put into service, promptly breaking down, too; locomotives are used
without necessary repairs, or on a shoe-string, with patched-up
"fixing," just to complete one run—with the result that at the end of
the run the locomotive has to be junked, worn out beyond repair
(beyond *their* capacity to repair it, anyway); crucial shortages of
fuel—and inferior fuel that ruins the engines.
*Rolling stock:* the same deterioration and same vain make-shifts as
with engines. Cars for special purposes vanish first—such as refrigerator cars, huge special flat cars, then stock cars, tank cars, grain
cars, until nothing but a few old standard boxcars and flats are left.
Passenger cars get more and more uncomfortable. Diners are eliminated ("economy"), then sleepers (except a few for politicians).
Comforts are eliminated, in reverse order from that in which they
came: first air-conditioning goes, then heating, then water (and toi-
lets), then lighting. Brakes are defective and shaky, causing endless
accidents.
*Signals:* breakdowns, mainly (or at least ostensibly) through inefficient personnel. Breaks in telegraph service leave schedules and
trains in confusion, and cause traffic snarls. Automatic safety devices
are long since gone. Automatic signals are replaced by manual
ones—going back to lanterns and flags—and these wreak total havoc
in the hands of semi-moronic collectivist "lower labor." There are
dreadful accidents—the kind that could have been prevented by
intelligence.

*Main direction of the process:* railroads become slow, dangerous, expensive,
uncomfortable, unreliable.

As they go down to the preceding stage of progress, that stage is *not* like
it was in the past, on the way up, but much worse; it worked then—but it does
not work now, quickly leading only to the next stage below. The contradiction between needs and means grow wider, worse and more destructive; a
freight delivery of two days worked fine for an industry geared to that; it does
not work for an industry that needs goods delivered in two hours; as the
industry collapses, it adds to the growing collapse of the railroad.

On the way up, producers were counting on the intelligence of others
with whom they had to deal. *Now* they have to count on stupidity—so they
are forced to stop.

*Results:* the dying off of whole territories, first the distant, outlying, less developed ones, then coming closer and closer. (Here—the parallel to a weak heart. As the heart grows weaker, first the capillaries (the outlying, smaller districts) atrophy; then the paralysis closes in, growing, in con- tracting circles, closer and closer to the heart and center.) Industries cannot get raw materials and cannot reach a market for their products. Farmers cannot grow raw materials—there is no way to transport them to market. Production becomes hysterically sporadic, like speculation: make so much if you can get the transportation through special (mainly political) pull, take the profit, then run; no planned, continuous, long-range effort is possible. *This brings the worst type, the gambler-speculator type, into momentary industrial leadership;* and the methods of this type cannot run a work- ing industry. (Here is the pure "money" motive—just quick "money," *not* production.)

Insane "deals" are made—so many cars for such-and-such a shipment— for reasons of pull, in total disregard of the needs, rights, and contracts of par- ticular shippers. Rivals destroy each other through "transportation pull" (that is, parasites destroy the few remaining producers) by making senseless deals destroying whole potential trainloads of freight—hurting both the shippers and the railroad. All these "deals" are made for every possible second-hand reason—everything except rational sense and the profit motive. [They give] reasons such as: the public good, help to a needy section, help to a friend, the country *ought to* take this product even if there's no demand for it, so let's *condition* people by delivering sets of "psychological games" when there is no bread, etc.

The result: the cars used for some such fool freight hold up a perishable harvest, the harvest rots, the farmers (who had counted on the railroad) go out of business, and the railroad (who needed the business of this section) finds itself running empty trains at a loss. As industries shrink or vanish, pro- ducers stop counting on railroads altogether. There is less and less transcon- tinental traffic. Production tries to shrink to a local exchange—going back to water transportation, a few old trucks, covered wagons, horses and buggies. But the remaining industries were not geared to be local and cannot go back to that stage. (Just as our house could not exist without electricity; it would be no good for pre-electric living, particularly when no rebuilding can be done.) And no new industries, on a small, local, more primitive scale, can be born—who's going to start them?—the parasites are only trying to run with what they looted and it's falling apart in their hands.

So—in accelerating progression—things stop, industries close, unem- ployment and crime grow, men have neither products nor work, they don't know what to do and can't do it, there is no work for anyone, only the approaching prospect of starvation that becomes obvious to all. There are starvation areas all over the country, epidemics, outbreaks of violence and hysteria (apparently causeless), a growing chaos. The obvious picture? Hunger, disease, rags, ruins. The spiritual picture (as far as the parasites are concerned): all the variations of panic and despair.

---

Choose from these concrete suggestions the key points to illustrate the specific steps of TT's collapse. But remember that what you need is the illustration of the working and results of stupidity (of non-judgment)—not all the details of the specific railroad collapse, only enough of these to make the process and its nature clear.

**June 22, 1946**

*Types of creators who work for their own destruction* (and that of other creators and the world):

> *Frank Lloyd Wright:* The creator who is overly concerned with others for the sake of their admiration. His achievement is authentic and first-hand, he does not let others into this sphere—but he still wants their admiration, afterwards, and it is an important concern to him. By enjoying his role of benefactor and making this role of importance to himself, he sanctions their right to exploit him, to take, to *demand* from him.
>
> He puts himself into the role of the exploited, [conceding] that this is his proper role and function; [he assumes the role of] the giver, the superior one who has riches which others don't have and which they can get only from him, *with the added implication that these riches are there to be taken by these inferior others.* (Taken only by his voluntary gift? That is what he may say. But the others would be justified in saying that once he establishes the principle that these riches, by their essential nature and purpose, are to be given to them, then they are justified in demanding or seizing them when some creator does not give them in the manner they wish, or does not give enough [and is thus] withholding what is theirs. He has established the principle of service to others and exploitation; the form is then only a secondary matter of detail.)

*Prof. Otto Hahn* (as a guess at the type I think he is) [*Otto Hahn was a German physicist who collaborated with the Nazis; AR did not know Hahn personally, but she had done some research on him for the screenplay* Top Secret *(see Chapter 9)*]: A man of ability who despises the lesser men around him, the stupid or less able—and decides that he must seek power (or associate himself with those who seek power, and support them—such as the Nazis) in order to have his way in a stupid world that will never share his intelligence and can only be dealt with by force. In doing this, he destroys the very people with whom he could deal, whose rareness he deplores—the intelligent ones; *they* cannot be ruled by force, they are the first ones destroyed in a dictatorship. And all that is left are the stupid ones, the worst among them, the corrupt and evil, those who will take any order, accept any horror and just obey, like unthinking brutes. And only the worst among *them* would be capable of holding the jobs of rulers in a dictatorship of force, the Gestapo jobs.

So by this kind of reasoning, a man like Hahn would destroy that which he values and needs (intelligence), preserve that which he dreads (corrupt stupidity), and give power (over himself and others) to the worst kind of human element, his own worst enemies.

*Dr.* [*J. Robert*] *Oppenheimer* (my guess about him and his motives): A man extremely conceited about his own intelligence (either honestly conceited—or maliciously so, i.e., with enjoyment of the inferiority of others and of his own superiority by comparison). He decides that he is so sure of what is right and that he is capable of deciding it, while others are not, that he *must* force it on those inferior others, for their own good. In such an attitude, there is the natural impatience of the intelligent man who can't bear to see things done wrong, when they can be done right and he knows how to do it. But this attitude is applied to a crucial error in thinking—that one man can decide what is right (or good) for another, and that the material (as a value) is absolute per se, so that a comfortable house for a ragged bum is "a good" without further consideration or relation to anything.

Man being a rational creature, the only good possible to him is that which he himself has accepted rationally; his primary evil is to do *anything* without his own independent rational acceptance and understanding. A bum forced to accept a house he does not understand, and has not built or earned, is committing an evil if he accepts it "because the leader says it's good," or

if he simply accepts it as an unearned alms; and that house will not do him
any good.

But, more importantly, Oppenheimer is committing the same error as
Hahn: the forcing of his ideas on those who, by his own definition, are inferior and cannot achieve or know what's good for them. [This policy] might
be viewed as merely futile when applied to them; actually, it's worse than
futile—it's a positive evil—putting them into a subhuman position, into the
class of non-rational beings, whereas they can exist or be happy only on the
basis of whatever rationality they possess. They would have to be total
morons or insane to be benefited by forced benefaction—but then, of course,
it can't work and they can't be benefited. This forcing of his ideas on others
is monstrously destructive of the best among them, of the intelligent, of
those he would define as his equals. (Is a possible reason here the fact that
he recognizes no one as his potential equal in this sense? Is it that kind of
conceit?)

The intelligent men cannot be forced—only destroyed. So this attitude,
again, leads to the destruction of that which he values (and of himself as one
among the intelligent), and to the perpetuation of that which he wants to
eliminate or correct (stupidity, incompetence, misery).

If he argues like this: "Well, those lesser people work and struggle on
their own, but stupidly; let them have the benefit of my superior intelligence
and direction; let them be forced to accept my directives whether they agree
or not, whether they understand or not; the result will be to their own
benefit"—the answer is: To accept or obey blindly is the only original sin for
man and the basic source of his destruction. Then a man cannot work well,
not even in his small job. Within *the specific sphere* of his own action, his
job, his life, his active concerns, he must understand what he is doing to the
best of his own intelligence—or he can't do it; his degree of understanding
determines the quality and success or failure of his performance.

If a very stupid type of unskilled laborer takes a job turning a crank in a
factory, without understanding or concern for what the factory is manufacturing or why—*that is quite proper* and safe; there is no obligation on man
to venture beyond the limits of his intelligence; in fact, it is his moral law
and the essence of his nature *not* to touch that which he cannot judge first-
hand, *not to act without intelligence.*

Such a laborer knows his own reasons for taking the job—need of
money, ease of the work, or whatever—and that is his proper and *only possible*
motive. To force him against his wishes or understanding into some wonderful
atomic factory where his limited skill can be used to best advantage (by the

master's decision) will not do him, the factory, or the master any good. It is forcing him into a subhuman state.

And what about this kind of forcing when applied to a better, more intelligent man of high ability, who *can* form his own judgments and conclusions? And how does the master here judge human ability—or whom to force, when, into what, how much, and for what purpose?

The basic mistake here is in judging the nature of man—in not understanding what precisely constitutes a rational being, and how this applies to degrees of human intelligence and ability; in not understanding the nature of *force* and its relation to intelligence; in not understanding the nature and significance of *voluntary* consent; and in assuming that any material good can be objective, i.e., *factually absolute* for all men, without considering the most objective and *factual* part of any "good"—the reaction of the human *mind* involved. ("The good" is a matter of standards; standards are determined by *purpose*. Who, then, sets a man's purpose here? Another creature, a master. By what right? It is the nature of man's intelligence, of survival by means of rationality, to function through purpose. But *he* himself must set the purpose.)

This last, of course, is an error or confusion in the conception of "the good." What is *good* for man? Nothing except that which he finds of value through the independent judgment of his rational mind. He's making an error in judgment? Then he must correct it *rationally*. He can't judge for himself at all? Then nothing can be good for him at all; [in this case], he is either a moron or insane. *And human "good" can be based on nothing except human intelligence. That* is man's basic, determining attribute (his "faculty of survival"). And intelligence is his act of *independent rational judgment*.

————o————

Moral to these men: Concern yourself with virtue, not vice; with intelligence, not stupidity; with strength and ability—not weakness and incompetence.

**June 24, 1946**

How do these last types of men affect my theme?

Are my "creators" (in the story) complete *men* or abstractions of a practical human quality? (They are "men of ability." When they make mistakes, they function on the principles of the parasites. But in the sphere of their work they function on the principles of the creators.)

The parasites in my story are motivated by hatred and exploitation of ability. What is the attitude of the above men [i.e., creators who sometimes function on the principles of parasites] toward ability? (Men of ability are not vicious; parasites are. Men of ability make mistakes; parasites are consciously evil. But it's the mistakes of the men of ability that are most disastrous and pave the way for the evil of the parasites.)

*The two basic qualities of the parasite:* (1) method—refusal to exercise his independent rational judgment, substituting for it the judgment of others; and (2) motive—desire to get the unearned (spiritual values which he doesn't deserve, more material wealth than he can produce).

These men [i.e., the mistaken creators] are not second-handers, but their great, basic error is in considering other men second-handers (or the desire to make them so).

They want others to substitute their (the master's) judgment for their own.
They want others to admire them, without understanding.
They want unearned material wealth from others (taken away by force) for their own purposes (art, research, etc.) Unable to justify this last, they claim: "But I'm working for *your* sake"—*and this is how they enthrone the principle of the exploitation of creators.*

**June 25, 1946**

The progressive steps of TT's destruction must be integrated on three lines: the physical failures and contractions of the railroad must be connected with (come from and lead to) the personal relationships of the characters involved (showing the variations of parasitism) and the progression of their "life lines," their specific, particular fates (such as Dagny moving towards shaking herself free of parasites, James Taggart moving toward spiritual destruction, etc.).

———o———

*Two possible characters for the parasite's side:*

The "traitor creators": the desperate, violent young inventor who accepts force out of despair at stupidity, who thinks that this is the only way to deal with the world—and is destroyed early and violently, unable to stand his own mistake; the more subtle and dangerous professor of physics [Robert Stadler] who wants unearned material wealth for his laboratory, fools himself and others into believing that he works "for the common good," and who supports and makes possible all the brutal police methods of the parasites' government. The professor invents a deadly weapon—and is violently destroyed by the very machinery and the very principles he has created.

---

*For one of TT's disasters:*
    A parallel to [MGM's plans to] build a $3,000,000 studio in England: Taggart spends a small, badly needed fortune to build a new branch through a territory that has been moving to seize his railroad; his reason—"I'll outsmart them by playing with them." He builds the branch—and it is seized, causing great damage to the remaining lines of TT and their operation, [in addition to] the crippling financial loss. (Or should it be a "creator" competitor who does this for Taggart?)

---

    Re: Robert Sherwood writing a biography of Harry Hopkins. This is such a shocking example of a parasite feeding on a parasite (in the intellectual realm) that a parallel must be found and used. [*Robert Sherwood was an American playwright who won the Pulitzer Prize for* Idiot's Delight *(1936); Harry Hopkins was a politician who served as a special assistant to President Roosevelt during World War II.*]

---

    The looter, the man who wants to grab some material wealth and run, living for the profit of the moment (or the man who is *only* after money, not production), wants the effect without the cause—that is why he is doomed to fail, is destructive and acting contrary to nature, his action being *irrational.*
    Reason is the ability to understand the connections of fact and to use them by acting accordingly. Man must act through "final causation" (the choosing of his purpose) and must use "efficient causation" to achieve his purpose. The looter sets his purpose at "getting money" and tries to get it without the necessary steps of the cause that produces the effect of "money"— the cause being productive activity. That is why the looter usually fails himself (though not immediately, and the chain of steps and reasons is not always obvious) and why a society built on the principles of looting, a

society that leaves man no freedom for anything else, will fail and destroy itself.

The productive man wants material wealth or money as the natural, logical, rational, inevitable result of his productive activity—and that is why he won't work without the profit motive; consciously or unconsciously he knows that such work is evil, being unnatural and irrational. Even if he were free to function (which he can't be in a collectivist State without property rights), even if such a situation could be achieved, he would not work without the profit motive—indifferent as he may be to money, his love and interest being in his work, in his creative activity. (Besides, he knows that money, the private ownership of the wealth he has created, is his means to further work.)

The parasite, true to his perverted basic premise and his irrationality, wants the money, with no concern for the productive process, for the work; in fact, with an active hatred for work and those who work—the hatred of dread (and dependence). This is the psychology of the looter-executives in the fourth stage of collapse.

## Specific Steps Toward a Railroad's Destruction

The last one: *a crucial branch is closed to get track for the last, main line.* Without the industries served by the branch, the main line cannot exist for long. (This is "living off capital.")
*The collapse of TT's freight train bridge:* the last break. Most of the other rival lines are gone by then. (This is the "helplessness before nature.")
Disorganization (chaos): *no fuel where fuel was expected* for the Comet's last ride. (This is the plain moron's inability to understand the need of work and action.)
*The "transportation pull" deals:* Major (and fatal) example of it— "help to a needy section which has an industry the country ought to [support]." At a crucial harvest time (when there is a good harvest after several bad years), Taggart unexpectedly refuses trains and cars to the farming section involved and uses these trains for the "preferred" section. Result—hunger for the country, farmers go bankrupt and quit, banks close, endless industries suffer—and TT, returning to its old branch, finds itself running it at a loss, yet unable (and afraid) to close it—"the section must be revived, this is just *temporary.*"
Minor examples of the same method—deals on a smaller scale, involving individual shippers, through which the "gambler-

speculator" industrialists ruin the few remaining producers. Each
time—there is a final loss to TT.

(These are the "second-handers' motives" in action.)

*Incident of the death of a section* (the first one in the story, as part of
the plot): TT closes its branch—one man in the section attempts to
organize a pony express—the collective begins to hamper him with
rules—John Galt tells him to stop—the section dies. (This illustrates
parasite methods and [what happens in] the absence of a creator.)

*Specific incident of an industry closing because of the railroad's
failure:* Loss of crucial, irreplaceable freight in switching yards' tie-
ups and snarls. Later—freight found in some most incongruous
place. (Incompetence.)

*A major traffic snarl:* through break-down of signals or telegraph
service. (Incompetence.)

*The return to flags and lanterns.* (Retrogression.)

*The progressive disappearance of:* diners, sleepers, air-conditioning,
heating, water, lighting. And of: refrigerator cars, stock cars, tank
cars. (Retrogression.)

*The progressive deterioration of motive power:* The use of old locomotives, and locomotives ruined just to make one run. (The parasite's "range of the moment.") The looting chicanery to get
locomotives from other systems—a barely veiled highjacking called
"nationalization," which the looters claim is "temporary, just for the
emergency." [They pass] some law such as that the remaining locomotives belong to the one who can "prove" the biggest "public
good," a grotesque kind of "priorities." (The absence of inventors
and "living off capital.")

In connection with this: *an incident of a locomotive high-jacked
by Dagny (against priorities).* Their own locomotive was taken
through "priorities" by someone else.

*The tunnel collapses*—it cannot be repaired and reopened—
miserable, shaky, make-shift steps to run the railroad around it by
*going back to the rusted remains of an older, pre-tunnel era.* (The
"return of nature.")

*One incident of a disastrous flood* in which a line is destroyed and
cannot be repaired. The section dies. Memories of how such disasters
were repaired in the past. (The "return of nature.")

*One incident of a crucial train run* in which a great deal is at stake
(in the plot), and the failure of the train destroys it. The failure is due
to a cause that seems infinitesimal on the surface (like one loose

screw in the rails), but is really huge as an indication of the cause
behind it, of the second-handers in charge and the bestial idiocy of
their methods. (Incompetence.)

*In connection with lumber industry—the untreated ties and the
result.* (Lack of inventors.)

The "equal rates" introduced by Taggart ("for democracy") that ruin
the more distant farming sections (or a distant but growing and
heathy industry that should have had a future). (Second-handers'
motives.)

*Incident of Taggart deciding that a competitor is ruining him,* that
everything would be all right if it weren't for "unfair competition"—
so he ruins the competitor (with political help) and finds that he can't
run the line and that people won't use it. This one can be connected
with the first death of a section. (Second-handers' envy, and idea that
the job creates the man.)

*Accidents:* one major railroad wreck directly connected to Taggart's
methods, and a few lesser ones (each progressively worse than the
one before). Minor accidents and breakdowns—constantly. (This is
plain, eloquent, screaming destruction—the direct physical expression of the essence, purpose, and final result of the parasite.)

*One incident of a new invention taken over and the inventor kicked
out.* Then the parasites don't know how to use it and have to abandon
it. It can be a young engineer with a new engine as a solution to their
power problems. Or it can even be an invention of Galt's, possibly
an early one—and he has now vanished—and Dagny looks for him,
not knowing his name, she merely wants "the man and the brain who
could do this." (This is "the moron with the dishwasher.")

**June 26, 1946**

*Key Steps (Railroad)*

1. Taggart ruins a competitor—and destroys the line.
2. Taggart introduces the "equal rates"—and the consequences.
3. Invention taken over and young inventor kicked out, with the
invention then failing.
4. Dagny finding Galt's early engine in abandoned factory.

**5.** Factory (needed by TT) closes when irreplaceable freight is lost in switching. Later—freight found in incongruous place.

**6.** The first death of a section and the young man of the pony express.

**7.** The crucial train run that fails (due to an infinitesimal reason [that is a consequence] of the parasites' technique).

**8.** The looting of one another's locomotives—and the incident of Dagny's stolen locomotive.

**9.** The "transportation pull" deal for "preferred" section that kills off a farming section and a branch of TT.

**10.** The tunnel collapse—and the return to an old rusted track.

**11.** The major railroad wreck.

**12.** Last: branch closed, track ripped for main line—and collapse of bridge.

### Key Stages ("Pattern of Disintegration")

*First stage:* Stalling on decisions, evading, routine, destruction of creators. Smaller disasters. Steps 1, 2, and 3.

*Second stage:* Parasites discover responsibility and are scared. Buck-passing, double-cross, parasites leaning on parasites. First serious disasters; parasites alibi themselves. Consequences of steps 1 and 2. Also—step 4.

*Third stage:* Nobody wants top positions of responsibility. Disasters become crashes. Some parasites caught. Almost no creators left. Beginning of parasites' panic. Steps 5, 6, 7, and 8.

*Fourth stage:* The "ersatz-creators"—the emergence of the criminal type as executive, the looter. Now it is plain, accelerating "living off capital." Steps 9 and 10.

*Fifth stage:* Surrender to the creators—the plea to John Galt. Steps 11 and 12.

---

*Incident: the professor,* who stole one of Galt's early inventions (he was Galt's teacher in college). "Who is John Galt?" has become the professor's secret torture (his conscience), growing violently, pathologically unbearable to him as the story progresses. Late in Part I, in a scene with Dagny, the professor talks about this slang-sentence, involuntarily betraying more than he cares to. In answer to Dagny's wonder about the meaning and origin of the phrase, he says that he knew John Galt, but Galt must have died long since. He had a brain such that: "If he had lived, the whole world would be talking of him now." "But the whole world *is* talking of him." This had never occurred to the professor before; he is struck and stunned. "Yes . . ." he whispers softly, terrified. "Why? . . . What is he doing?"

But as Dagny tries to question him, he drops the subject, telling her that it's all preposterous, just a coincidence, the name is common enough, it's a popular piece of slang without significance. He will give her no clue to Galt's identity or profession. She thinks that this is just another one of those occasions when people claim first-hand knowledge of John Galt.

---

*Note:* J.H. as one of the typical parasites. He is mild and friendly to everyone—he admires anything and anyone who makes money (or is popular), indiscriminately, without analysis or understanding or reason— then he acts to destroy the very things and people he wants to use. He feels sad and bewildered about this—but he becomes mean and evil on one point only: any suggestion of the necessity for him to think about it, i.e., for him to assume the responsibility of an independent rational judgment. (His preoc- cupation with "polls" and "trends.") He is truly the "moron with a dish- washer," the savage thrown into civilization—understanding nothing about it, not even that understanding is necessary.

---

*More for the professor:* He stole Galt's invention, early in his career (shortly before Galt vanished) for the following reason: in the growing poverty of the world, there is less and less endowment of science; the professor was pas- sionately devoted to his work, paid little attention to anything else and understood nothing about men, principles or the world; he wanted the gov- ernment to finance his scientific research work and he had sold himself the idea that he was working for "the common good"; the bureaucrats in charge wanted concrete proof of the practical importance of his work; so he stole Galt's idea—justifying this to himself by the notion that he stole it "for the common good," that "science belongs to the people," that he can do so much for mankind if he gets his laboratory, therefore stealing Galt's idea is all right, since it will give him the laboratory, etc. He got the laboratory.

Later he is forced by circumstances to invent the deadly weapon which he did not want to invent. Show the gradual disintegration of his conscience

and of his work (or its direction) in the course of one collectivist compromise after another.

In the end—he betrays and destroys everything he had lived for, everything for which he made his compromises (he thought of them as "sacrifices"):
science, rationality, intelligence. He upholds: brutality, violence, evil, stupidity. (To decide: either circumstances force him to this, i.e., the parasites
[force him] through the very power he has given them; or—his own mind and
convictions, being totally perverted now, bring him to this and lead him to
demand the destruction of John Galt.)

**June 27, 1946**

*Added Points:*

The dreadful state of TT's research laboratory. Routine and second-
handedness: the alleged scientists spend their time proving that new things
"can't be done"—this in order to justify their inactivity and keep their jobs,
which is all they are concerned with. Dagny's constant clashes with this, her
helpless anger and indignation. (This ties to and leads to her interest in
Galt's old engine.)

James Taggart discontinues the research laboratory. The excuse: "Why
look for the new when everybody hasn't got everything of the old? Let's
stop progress until everybody is equal, then we will all go forward together
slowly."

James Taggart tries to have the whole economy frozen and stopped, so
that he will have "security"—a set market, a set amount of traffic, a set routine. ("How can I do anything when things change all the time? I would be a
great executive if only people weren't so unreliable and unpredictable.") The
attempt [to freeze the economy] takes place toward the last third of Part I.

### Galt's Relation to the Other Characters

Here is what Galt represents to them (in specific story terms):
*For Dagny*—the ideal. The answer to her two quests: the man of
genius and the man she loves. The first quest is expressed in her
search for the inventor of the engine. The second—her growing conviction that she will never be in love (and her relations with
Rearden).
*For Rearden*—the friend. The kind of understanding and appreciation
he has always wanted and did not know he wanted (or he thought he

had it—he tried to find it in those around him, to get it from his wife, his mother, brother, and sister).

*For Francisco d'Anconia*—the aristocrat. The only man who represents a challenge and a stimulant—almost the "proper kind" of audience, worthy of stunning for the sheer joy and color of life.

*For Danneskjöld*—the anchor. The only man who represents land and roots to a reckless wanderer, like the goal of a struggle, the port at the end of a fierce sea voyage—the only man he can respect.

*For the composer*—the inspiration and the perfect audience.

*For the philosopher*—the embodiment of his abstractions.

*For Father Amadeus*—the source of his conflict. The uneasy realizations that Galt is the end of his endeavors, the man of virtue, the perfect man—and that his means do not fit this end, that he is destroying his ideal for the sake of those who are evil.

*To James Taggart*—the eternal threat. The secret dread. The reproach. His guilt. He has no specific [connection] with Galt—but he has that constant, causeless, unnamed, hysterical fear. And he recognizes it when he hears Galt's broadcast and when he sees Galt in person for the first time.

*To the professor*—his conscience. The reproach and reminder. The ghost that haunts him through everything he does, without a moment's peace. The [man] that says "*No*" to his whole life.

**June 29, 1946**

*Note on Proper Cooperation (for Dagny's attitude)*

The principle of proper cooperation among men is that no man should be forced to do anything, within the specified province of his job, that he considers wrong [by his own judgment].

The decision here must be his. His superiors must not expect him to obey against his own reason. Of course, they must have the right to decide when they are acting properly or improperly. But if they know they are forcing him (through sheer obedience to an order, not through his rational consent), they are acting improperly (but strictly within their legal rights). His protection—and his proper course, in this last case—is to resign.

Now, this presupposes that in proper cooperation, the specific job of each individual man is clearly and objectively defined. It has to be—and, for success, the definitions must be rationally accepted by all the men involved (rationally accepted—not merely accepted because it's a majority decision, or the boss's decision).

Any boss has the legal right to establish the rules for the organization he heads—and his employees have the choice to work for him on his conditions or not. But the rational definition of jobs is crucially necessary for the success of any organization; the boss (if he is good at *his* job) is the one who has to work out the proper definitions, make them clear to his employees and make it his policy to see that all of them (including himself) act accordingly. The failures, inefficiencies, hard feelings and chicaneries going on in big corporations, particularly the less efficient ones, are probably due to the lack of such definitions, explicitly or implicitly, in the company's policies.

*No work* (neither mental nor physical) can be *done collectively*. All work is done individually. All human energy is individual—generated by and within *one man*: spiritual energy, mental energy, physical energy. A "collective" piece of work is only the sum of the individual work involved. (And "a collective piece of work" is a sloppy, meaningless corruption; what is meant by it is something like an automobile that comes out of a factory where thousands of men have worked and contributed to the production of the automobile. Well, they didn't "blend" or "fuse" their work, their minds, bodies, or energies into a *collective* whole or process; they worked individually as individuals.)

Since all work is done individually, a cooperative work is divided into specific parts, each of which has to be done by an individual; when these parts and the specific individual jobs are not consciously defined by the men involved, inefficiency, friction and trouble follow. An organization is successful to the extent that it functions on such specific division of labor and responsibility, even if unstated and arrived at pragmatically, not consciously and rationally. The extent to which jobs and responsibilities infringe on one another and blend "collectively," with the decisions and judgment of one man interfering with or being forced on another, determines the degree of the organization's inefficiency and failure.

("Division of labor" *must* also be "division of responsibility.")

As example of the absence of such clear definitions, with awful results: the motion picture industry. In their stated theory, the movies have no such definitions; they merely hold the producer as omniscient and omnipotent. In practice, they are forced to observe definitions, sort of by default, "bootleg" definitions—and only to that extent do they or can they function successfully.

As example of proper definition on a railroad: it is the president's job to set the general policy of the road; it is the job of each subordinate to carry out *his* part of the work toward the accomplishment of that policy. A freight agent has no business deciding what the railroad as a whole should do; his job, specifically, is to see that freight is handled in the best manner possible. An engineer on a train must understand and accept the conditions of his job, which is to run the engine of a train. It is *not* his job to decide when the train goes, what it carries, what it charges and to whom. His job is only to make it move, on a certain schedule, from a certain point to another certain point.

If he thinks the conditions imposed on him for the operation of the engine are wrong (in strict relation to his job of running it, and only to that), he should not hold the job; he should quit. For instance, if he thinks the rules of stopping, accelerating, watching signals, etc., are wrong—he must not hold this job, because he cannot hold it successfully. If he does not understand the rules and just obeys automatically, he's no good at the job. If he thinks the rules are wrong, and he is mistaken about it, he still cannot be good at the job by obeying the rules blindly. If he thinks the rules are wrong, and he's *right* about it—he shouldn't keep the job, because the result will be disastrous to him and to the company that enforces the wrong rules. (He is, of course, free to make suggestions to his superiors at any time; but if they disagree and he is convinced that he's right, he should quit.)

How can an average man know whether he's right or wrong? By never attempting a job where, in the *specific* performance of *his* duties, he has to venture beyond the limit of his own capacity of independent rational judgment, and act without understanding. If he understands a problem, he *is* sure of whether he's right or wrong; if he isn't sure, and can't arrive at any certainty with the most careful study, he must leave the problem and the job alone.

Within the province of his job, no man should do anything for a reason such as the desire or opinion of another man, or of a number of other men. Certainly not anything that he himself rationally considers wrong. But more than that: if he has no rational grounds for an action, one way or another, *still* he must *not* do it if the only reason is the desire or order of another man.

Dagny's job (if not by title, then in fact—I must check on that, as far as her official position on TT is concerned) is to run the whole railroad. She accepts the interference of James Taggart and government "regulators" as an unavoidable part of her job, an unavoidable evil. She thinks she can work in spite of that interference, or get around it, or compromise with it, and still make the railroad successful. *That* is her mistake. It can't be done.

By accepting Taggart's decisions, which she knows to be wrong, then by helping him to carry out bad ideas well (such as efficiently delivering the "soybean freight," when it should never have been attempted at all), she only helps him to run the railroad *badly* and thus contradicts and defeats her own purpose, which is to run it well. She postpones the natural consequences of his bad decisions (which would be disastrous) and thus leaves him free and gives him the means to do more damage to the railroad by even worse decisions.

*A bad thing done well is more dangerous and disastrous than a bad thing done badly.* An efficient robbery is worse for the victim than an inefficient one. The fool Republicans who help the New Deal to enforce unworkable regulations destroy their own industries—because unworkable regulations inefficiently enforced would give the industries a better chance to function and survive.

This is Dagny's mistake—based on an imperfect understanding of cooperation with men, of her need of their services in her own aim, and on the difficulty of defining the job of an executive in charge of a huge organization that involves thousands of men. But when she accepts Taggart's stupidities and tries to make them work (for the sake of the railroad, hoping to get around them or counteract their bad effects), she is doing the equivalent of what I would do if I agreed to put something into a book of mine which I considered bad, but which the publishers, critics or public demanded, and if I justified myself by an argument such as: well, they want it, and after all I have to deal with them, etc. I could not say (like all the damn Republican fools) that I would accomplish my purpose in spite of such compromises: if I consider the outside suggestions *bad*, that means they are bad for my book and its purpose, therefore by accepting them I defeat my purpose. (Yet this is just what all men mixed by "social" considerations are doing nowadays. And this, in a more complex form, is what Dagny does.)

———————

The pattern of the proper cooperation among men goes like this:

*First,* the basic premise, without which men cannot deal with one another safely or rationally: that each man lives only for his own sake; therefore, he acts only for his own personal profit, respecting the same right and motive in every other man; therefore, they can act together only if the action is personally profitable to each man involved; and the objective test of that is each man's own free decision and voluntary consent.

*Second,* the objective, general purpose of the organization is understood and accepted by all men involved in it—and it is a "selfish" purpose in the same way as the purpose of each man involved.

*Example:* The purpose of every man working on a railroad should be, generally, to do productive work, which is the proper moral purpose of a human being; more specifically, to do the kind of work he likes or has chosen, and to earn his own living through that work (which means, in effect, to produce and keep the product of one's own work). No man can expect anything from others as a "sacrifice," i.e., as a one-sided advantage, a consideration of his own desires with no *selfish* compensation for or advantage to the other party. (The objective test? Voluntary mutual consent.) No employee can expect ten dollars a day, because *he* needs it, if his boss can get men willing to do the same work for one dollar. No boss can expect an employee to work for one dollar, if the worker can get ten dollars elsewhere. Any forced freezing, or artificial agreements, or the mere confusion of this principle ("no sacrifice of anyone to anyone"), will *not* work. It only leads to hatred, injustice, disaster, and destruction.

The relation of a railroad as a whole to the other industries of the country, to its customers and to the whole nation, is the same as that of each man working on it to each other man; here the railroad may be considered as a unit among other units. The purpose of a railroad is to produce a certain commodity (transportation) and to keep the product of its work (profit). Its purpose is *not* to "serve the nation" nor to "serve its shippers." You do not run a railroad just because sharecroppers need train rides; their need is none of your concern—unless they can pay their fare, i.e., give you something of value in exchange for what you give to them.

And it is not the purpose of the nation or of the shippers to serve the railroad. Men deal with the railroad only when their mutual interests agree and the exchange is to mutual *selfish* advantage. The objective test? The voluntary consent of both parties involved—the railroad and the shippers. But if the railroad is considered and run as a "service" (i.e., service to others being its primary purpose, and profits being ignored), then there is nothing but greed, exploitation, inefficiency, failure, and destruction ahead.

This is so by definition: if a railroad is to be run without regard for *profit*, this means without regard for cost or efficiency; if it serves some project for subnormal charity objects and this service does not pay its cost, someone has to pay for it. The railroad then consumes more than it produces. When all production and all industries are run on such a principle—there is soon nothing left to consume.

Yet the above is precisely what James Taggart tries to do—both in relation to the purpose and policy of TT as a whole ("public service"), and in relation to the duties of employees within the organization ("the strong must serve the weak," "the interest of any employee must be sacrificed to the interest of the railroad," "team-work," etc.). Instead of the growing prosperity that comes from a principle that makes each man profit by cooperating with others, Taggart creates misery and growing poverty by a principle that demands, within, the sacrifice of each man to the organization, and, without, the sacrifice of the organization to other organizations (or collectives, or "the nation"). This is blatantly evident in one simple statement: One system is based on the principle of *profit*, the other—on the principle of *sacrifice*; therefore, one *will* achieve general prosperity, the other—general misery.

This is what Dagny deals with and accepts (if not explicitly, at least implicitly). This is what she hopes to work with and around. *That* is her mistake and her failure. It can't be done.

———⊙———

Here, also, is the difference between Dagny and Roark: Roark had no concern for others, and kept them out of his work (and when they did interfere, he took action against them); Dagny has no concern for others and lets them interfere in her work, accepting the interference. The *proper* concern for others is self-protection—the protection of one's own principles and inalienable rights, and above all, the protection of oneself against being anybody's "servant," the keeping of one's moral principle of living for one's own sake.

———⊙———

Regarding Dagny's determination to function as a creator at all costs: Dagny doesn't understand the difference between the relation of the creator to *nature* and to people. In relation to *nature*, the creator *must* function to shape the world to his wishes—against every obstacle. In relation to *people*, he *must not* allow them (and their rules, stupidity, or force) to come between him and nature—because then he destroys his first function, he makes it impossible, so that he can no longer master nature, but becomes helpless before it, like the parasites.

A creator must function at all costs—but *not* at the cost of his own principles, not at the cost of his independence, because then he makes it impossible for himself to function; he destroys his base and premise.

———⊙———

### Plot Lines for Characters

*(To illustrate, dramatize, and integrate their individual progressions)*

#### John Galt

No progression here (as Roark had none). He is what he is from the beginning—integrated (indivisible) and perfect. No change in him, because *he has no intellectual contradiction and, therefore, no inner conflict.*

His important qualities (to bring out):

*Joy in living*—the peculiar, deeply natural, serene, all-pervading joy in living which he alone possesses so completely in the story (the other strikers have it in lesser degree, almost as reflections of that which, in him, is the source). His joy is all-pervading in the sense that it underlies all his actions and emotions, it is an intrinsic, inseparable part of his nature (like the color of his hair or eyes). It is present *even when* he suffers (particularly in the torture scene)—*that* is when the nature and quality of his joy in living is startling and obvious, it is not resignation or acceptance of suffering, but a denial of it, a triumph over it. (*This* is extremely important to convey—clearly, unmistakably.) And this quality of his is *particularly* what is lacking in the parasites and in their whole world, in the world as it has become. (He laughs, as answer to the crucial question of the torture scene.)

(The worship of joy as against the worship of suffering.)

Self-confidence, self-assurance, the clear-cut, direct, positive action, no doubts or hesitations.

The magnificent innocence—the untroubled purity—a pride which is serene, not aggressive—"the first man of ability who refused to feel guilty."

#### Dagny Taggart

Progression from enthusiastic activity, joy in working, brilliant self-confidence and belief in the triumph of the right (of intelligence and competence)—to a helpless bewilderment in the face of the parasites' behavior and motives—to a teeth-clenched determination to go ahead, ignoring them (end of Part I, beginning of Part II)—to a slow realization of the truth, with a slow anger growing with the steps of this realization.

Her full understanding of the issue and of the parasites is retarded because, as her anger grows, she comes to a stage of bitter contempt for them and refuses to think about them any longer. Her attitude becomes: "To hell with all of them—they are not worth considering or examining—I am not interested in them and never have been—so I will live for and think about my only interest: my work. I will deal with them only as I need them for my work, and I will use them for that. *I* can use them, not vice versa, because I am intelligent and they're not. They'll serve my purposes, not I theirs." And this is true, so long as she does not accept their terms or compromise with their principles anywhere in her work and in her relations with them. When she does—*they* win and *they* use *her*, because they are more consistent in the application of their own principles and because she has placed her intelligence in *their* service, in the furtherance of their aims and principles, and thus she has turned her great and only weapon—her intelligence—against herself.

Thus, it is she who defeats herself—who makes it possible for her enemies to destroy her, to win. This is the pattern of the creators' destruction of themselves through cooperation with parasites. You do *not* cooperate with parasites at any time. When and if you cooperate with a man, you can properly do so only to the degree that he can or is willing to act on the principles and terms of a creator in the particular activity or exchange involved. *And no more than that.* No further. And the terms of a creator are: "Man as an end in himself," therefore every action must have a personal, *selfish* purpose or advantage for every man involved in it, recognized and accepted as such by the others involved in it.

Does this mean that you depend on them, on waiting for their recognition of your rights? No. You don't *have to* deal with them; never *primarily*—only secondarily. So you merely refuse to deal with them, if they do not accept your terms. (Your attitude is: "Take it or leave it.")

Those who can really be of help in the execution of your interests are only those who share your terms (or only to the extent that they do); they are the only ones capable of being of value to you. The others are of no use to you whatever. But *you are* of use to them (on *your* terms). *(Their* mistake is in thinking that they can make you of use to them—on *their* terms.) Hold out—and they will accept your terms to the extent to which they can survive at all. But give in, compromise—and you destroy your work, aims, desires, happiness, and life—you help them to last a while on the terms of evil, you postpone the justice of [reality's] retribution against them, you serve as their shield—and the end is only total destruction for you and for them.

**June 30, 1946**

To illustrate the preceding: Dagny's whole problem is that she cannot find able men to work on the railroad she runs. Her very predicament disproves her idea that she needs others, the stupid or inferior ones, for her purpose, and therefore she must find some way to deal with them, must consider them or compromise with them (she does not really believe it, only wonders about it, is bewildered on this point—but so many others do believe it, particularly the professor). The fact is that she *cannot* do anything with inferiors—the "cooperation" she wants can be achieved only with men of *intelligence* (to the extent of intelligence she needs from them).

Cooperation can be done only on *a level*; if one attempts to do it "down," one fails. If a person's attitude is: "My superior intelligence has a great goal or project in mind, but unfortunately I need dumbbells to carry out my orders, so I must adjust myself to them in some way, scale down my ideas, principles and methods"—that person is doomed to fail. If your project requires the services or cooperation of others, your only chance is to find those equal to the particular task it requires of them; adjusting the great project down to those inferior to their proposed part in it does not raise them, but merely destroys the project.

Dagny needs men with whom she can deal on her own terms, the terms of the creator, the terms of intelligence, capacity and independence—or she can do nothing. What, then, is the proper interrelationship of men working on a project, such as the building of a great skyscraper? They cooperate through and are held together by their various capacities—*not* their inferiorities. The bricklayer *has* contributed his ability—but the architect has contributed a much greater ability: [he has provided] the opportunity for the exercise of the abilities of the others involved, and this must be acknowledged.

What is the message to all men, implied in this? Live honestly and honorably within the limits and to the limits of your own ability—and give thanks to the men whose greater ability has made such a magnificent world possible for you (but remember that *you* were not the great man's goal or motive).

**July 1, 1946**

*Hank Rearden*

Progression: He works fiercely, enthusiastically—then feels guilty about it; he attempts to make up in the altruistic sense; he gives in to every accusation of his family. He loves Dagny and considers this his sin, his guilty passion—while his forced love for his wife he thinks to be virtuous, pure, idealistic.

Part II: his slow awakening to the truth—his understanding of the parasites (his family) and their motives—his understanding of his own value and that his sins had been virtues. His realization that his love for Dagny was his best emotion (after he loses her). His anger against his family then becomes implacable, cold, set, merciless—with the same sense of justice which he had earlier turned against himself. [*This is AR's first note on the romance between Rearden and Dagny.*]

## James Taggart

Progression: from a smug, yet uneasy, satisfaction with his parasitical "top position"—to bewilderment—to malicious restlessness (with people and in business)—to a growing fear (Part II)—to panic, hysteria, and collapse.

## The Professor

Progression: From a righteous (if slightly forced) idealism—to an attempt to drown himself in his work and shut out his uneasiness about the world—to the gradual, growing surrender to the parasites' authority (spiritually and in his work)—to a growing fear of Galt (Part II)—to the cold viciousness of "self-protection," accepting anything to justify his fatal mistake—to disaster.

**July 4, 1946**

### Emotional and Personal Relationships
### Part I

*The love affair of Dagny and Rearden:* first the mutual understanding—then his efforts to avoid her—the affair—his sense of guilt—her simple, natural acceptance—his growing love for her—her growing restlessness.

*Rearden and his wife:* the last of his former love for her, now bewildered and forced. Her subtle campaign of torture, to pull him down. His efforts to atone to her for his love of Dagny.

*Rearden and his family:* mother, sister and younger brother. The torture by the parasites—his constant "atonement."

*The romance of James Taggart:* his former unsatisfactory love life—meeting with Cherryl—the romance and the "Cinderella Girl" campaign—their marriage—Cherryl's hatred and fear of Dagny—the first indication of what the marriage will be.

Dagny and Eddie Willers: the comradeship.

*Dagny and James Taggart:* all the stages of exploitation—deceit, cruelty, hatred on his part, bewilderment and contempt on hers.

Dagny and Francisco d'Anconia: the reluctant friendship.

Taggart and the priest: the spiritual crutch.

Dagny and Gerald Hastings.

Rearden and the parasite whom he builds up (the mines).

Rearden and his secretary.

Taggart's hatred for Rearden, and dislike for Mrs. Rearden, who despises him.

The priest and the professor: a kind of spiritual cooperation.

*The professor's disintegration:* his "forced" idealism at his government laboratory—flashback to how he got laboratory—progression of his work and of his character toward [the support of] totalitarianism.

## Part II

Dagny's break with Rearden (and search for Galt).

Dagny meets Galt—their night together.

Dagny's ultimatum to Galt.

Dagny joins Galt.

(Dagny and the professor.)

(Dagny and d'Anconia.)

(Dagny and Eddie Willers.)

(Dagny and Cherryl.)

Scene where Rearden realizes that Dagny is his real love.

Rearden discovers Mrs. Rearden's affair with James Taggart.

Taggart's gradual destruction of Cherryl—and scene where she realizes his real nature.

The love affair of Taggart and Mrs. Rearden.

(Scene where Taggart confesses affair to priest, who forgives him.)

Scene where professor realizes that Taggart is his master.

Professor's attempt to destroy Dagny.

(Scene where professor curses priest.)

Destruction of the professor.

(Scene: the priest and Galt.)

**July 6, 1946**

*Outline*
*Part II: The Beginning*

The valley—John Galt.

The "transportation pull" deal—TT gives its last grain cars to a soybean project in the south, instead of to the desperately awaited wheat harvest in Minnesota. The deal is arranged by Cuffy Meigs, TT's new executive (the looter), who receives huge, secret rake-off from the head of the project, his friend, one of his own kind. (Chester is involved in this and is behind the project. Its announced aim—"teach people to sacrifice," to live on a lower standard.)

James Taggart, by now, does anything Meigs tells him to. Taggart's growing fear. Cherryl's attempts at self-improvement. Dagny breaks with Rearden; she tells him she loves another man—she does not say who. ("It was my fate to love the impossible.")

Dagny fights desperately, ferociously against the southern deal—but undertakes, personally, to see that the soybean freight is delivered. Here is her crucial mistake—she does it to save the railroad; she contributes to its destruction, instead.

The ride of the soybean freight: the tragic irony of magnificent energy and competence wasted on doing well a worthless and vicious undertaking. (Dagny, her best engineers, Eddie Willers. The weather, the bad track, the last of the rail reserves wasted to fix a useless line.) This is the last run of a train shown in the story—showing a dying system, all the difficulties, impossibilities, inefficiencies involved. The next one—"The Comet"—cannot finish its run.

The disaster resulting from this deal. The collapse of the whole farming district in Minnesota ("the last granary"): the rotting wheat, the bonfires of wheat, the bankrupt farms, the desertions of whole families, trekking away into nowhere, the lines of carts on the roads (like war refugees, but much worse). Rearden loses heavily on the farm machinery—credits he had extended. (He was counting on "help to success," but help was given to failure.) The famine in the rest of the country.

The famine and desertions of workers at the ex-Rearden mine in Michigan.

Parallel developments: Dagny's search for Galt (Francisco d'Anconia, the empty valley).

Rearden and his wife—his realization that Dagny was his real love. His scene with Dagny when he tells her that.

James Taggart crushes Cherryl's attempts to rise—she understands his real nature.

Cherryl's drowning plea to Dagny—the attempt to hang on to a living power.

The circumstances (the result of their mutual problems above) that lead to the affair of James Taggart and Mrs. Rearden. Their ghastly night together—the horror of sex as second-handedness, as hatred, malice, and self-contempt.

Taggart confesses the affair to the priest. The priest forgives him, but feels crushingly uneasy afterwards.

The tunnel collapse. The return to old tracks—the pre-tunnel era. The desperate need of new track. Dagny's worry over the Taggart Bridge.

The professor. Reduction of his laboratory funds. Talk of using his "vibration-ray" against "isolationist" sections. The scene where the professor realizes that Taggart is his master. The professor is demoted—the "determinist" assistant is put in charge of the laboratory.

The rebellion of [Rearden's] secretary against her family—her decision to quit and marry.

Rearden discovers Mrs. Rearden's affair with Taggart. Connected with same event—he sees the real nature of his mother, brother, and sister, and of their attitudes toward him.

Immediately following—the crucial emergency conference: Rearden, Taggart, mine-owner, businessman, bureaucrat. Subject—the new rails for TT. Taggart has raised the rates on the Minnesota line, due to the farm collapse. The mine-owner has raised the price of ore. The bureaucrat does not allow Rearden to raise his prices on rails ("TT can't afford it"). The squeeze-play in the open. Rearden is given an impossible burden—because he is the strongest; it is made impossible for him to function—because they so desperately need him to function. The crucial line (from Taggart): "You'll do something." Now Rearden sees (though not yet in words). He says nothing and walks out of the room.

Rearden in his office—the crushing realization that he will know the truth (which he already knows) at any moment now. His secretary comes in for the promised appointment. She tells him she is quitting—and why. He sees the similarity of their tragedies. He understands everything. . . . He is ready to leave the office, when she tells him about the man waiting to see him. The name in the sealed envelope. "It must be a gag. . . . Send him in, I'll see him. What does he look like?" "Like something made out of a kind of aluminum-copper alloy."

The news that Rearden has quit. The reaction of Dagny and Taggart—

Taggart's terror. He rushes to Lillian Rearden—to make her beg Rearden to remain.

The scene where Lillian Rearden, his mother, brother, and sister beg Rearden to remain. His immovable coldness—they are dead for him, the sense of justice turned against them. He goes away (to the valley).

The scene with his brother and Rearden's superintendent. The superintendent quits, with his staff.

The scene in which a lawyer reads Rearden's deed to the collective: Mrs. Rearden, mother, brother, sister, and the publicity punk. The parasites "with their clothes off"—the naked truth about them. (Mrs. Rearden wishing to sell her share—the predicament of collective ownership.)

The collective hires a friend of Cuffy Meigs as executive. Half the workers have deserted. The executive sells the remaining supplies and crucial machinery, on the side, then vanishes. The collapse of Rearden Steel.

The final emergency to TT—no Rearden rails to come. The small banquet—Dagny, James Taggart, bureaucrat, businessman, Meigs, Mr. Jones. The decision to close the Wisconsin-Michigan ore line. Dagny's desperate, almost screaming protests. Their arguments about "sharing hardships" and "the government needs a transcontinental line." They outvote her. She escapes from the room in horror.

Dagny in the subway. John Galt. She sits crying—and the bum who consoles her ("Oh well, who is John Galt?"). Toward morning, Galt comes back—they go to his room—their night together.

Dagny's challenge to him—his explanation. ("No, there is no conflict—there never can be—as you will learn.")

The closing of the ore line announced—the riots—the fights for the rails—the general panic.

Dagny-Galt: the "enemy romance."(?)

The announced president's broadcast. In radio studio—president, Dagny, Taggart, the professor (perhaps some of the lesser ones, too). The machinery won't function. Then—John Galt's voice. (A gasp and a scream in the studio—the gasp from Dagny, the scream from the professor.) John Galt's broadcast.

Scene in subway with phone booth, afterwards.

The panic—the country falling apart. The professor's hysteria—scene where he demands that the priest curse Galt—the priest refuses.

Government's attempts to negotiate with Galt, by short-wave. His refusal. Secret orders to find him.

The scene: Galt and the priest, in the restaurant. The appeal through pity. His refusal.

Dagny comes to Galt's garret. The appeal through love—his refusal. Then she warns him—he hands her the phone. ("I was waiting to be found—I didn't know it would be you. But it had to be.") She notifies the government.

Dagny returns to Galt's room, with the police, hoping he will be gone. But he is there. The "polite" arrest—the wreck of his laboratory. ("What was in it? You'll never know.")

Galt in a luxurious hotel room. The private bargaining: Galt and Mr. Jones—"What are you after?" Galt's refusal. When Mr. Jones asks is there anything he would like, he answers: yes, he would like to speak to the professor.

The scene: Galt and the professor. "John, I had a good motive!" The boy of eighteen and the sentence about the supremacy of reason. "Why don't you say something?" "You've said it all." The professor escapes from the room, in total spiritual collapse.

The professor tells the others that they cannot let Galt rule, they must destroy him. Professor is placed under "protective custody." He escapes.

Scene: Dagny and Rearden. Rearden is on Galt's side—Dagny confesses to him that she is Galt's mistress.

Scene: Dagny and Eddie Willers, when he leaves for California (by plane) to "save" the Comet. He realizes that he's always loved her.

Galt is ordered to dress in evening clothes and driven to a banquet room. The banquet. The appeal through flattery. The miserable and ludicrous mixture of crawling before him and arrogance in the implication of the value of their admiration. His answer, over the radio: "Get the hell out of my way."

The professor hears the broadcast over his car radio as he speeds toward the laboratory. He realizes that Galt's refusal is more frightening than his acceptance would have been. The "determinist" and Meigs-types of "guards" will not let the professor into the laboratory. He wants the ray to destroy Galt. ("He's won! Don't you understand? He's won, because he's refused!") He screams that Galt is the enemy, because he is the mind. "That's right," says one of the guards. "And what are *you*?" The explosion of the laboratory—the end of the ray and of the professor. (The "thing of screaming pain"—and the greater horror of one spark remaining within it to remember that this had been a great mind.)

The scene is a bare hotel room—Taggart, businessman, bureaucrat, Meigs, Dagny. Galt has been locked back in his room. The "soundless hysteria": the quiet, brief discussion, which has but one meaning, they all know it—the resort to force (with the unstated knowledge that the mere premise of such an attempt is insane). They avoid Dagny—her presence is restraining them, they don't want her to understand. But Dagny is cold, silent, emotion-less—strangely detached. She understands, and much more than they do (she understands what they will understand in the torture scene). She gets up unexpectedly, without a word, and walks out of the room.

Dagny alone in her office in the TT building (night). The emotionless, methodical burning of her papers. The long-distance call from Eddie Willers—trouble for the Comet. She tells him, quietly, to quit. He can't. (But he knew she would: "You, too?")

As she hangs up and proceeds with her burning, an executive rushes in with a report on danger to the Taggart Bridge: a new crack is reported—a storm is rising on the Mississippi—and a crucially awaited heavy freight train is approaching the bridge. Before the man finishes, she leaps to the phone; in the time it takes her to reach her desk, she sees the consequences of the bridge's collapse and the remedy to save it; she sees Nat Taggart and the whole of Taggart Transcontinental. Then, slowly, with a twisted move-ment of her arm, she replaces the receiver. "What are we going to do, Miss Taggart? We don't know what to do!" She thinks: This is it . . . I didn't know it would be so hard. . . . She answers: "I don't, either."

The torture of Galt. The reaction of the parasites—particularly Taggart. Galt laughs at them, pointing out the contradiction of their predicament. Their concern not to kill him (except Taggart: he is passive here—he is seeing the first hints of what he is to discover). The electric engine breaks down. Galt tells them about holding creators through their joy of living. "Go ahead, turn on the electric current." The mechanic cannot repair the machine—he asks for Taggart's instructions. The parasites' answer—"Do something." Galt tells him what to do. The mechanic obeys dazedly—the machine works. The mechanic looks at Galt—at the parasites—then drops his tools and runs away in terror. Galt laughs.

Meigs seizes the engine, to operate it. The businessman whines: "Don't kill him!" Taggart cries suddenly: "Make him scream!" The stunned, embar-rassed silence; they all sense what Taggart sees completely in that moment. Taggart falls back against the wall, white-faced; he is done for. Meigs turns on the current. A man rushes in to announce the collapse of the Taggart Bridge. Galt's moment of involuntary temptation. They stop the torture and rush out, realizing the implications, each to save himself. Taggart has not even heard the news; he is fixed on his discovery.

Taggart and the priest. The confession of total evil and the plea for absolution. "I have nothing to say, James. I'm on strike."

The rescue of Galt by Dagny. (Brute force against mind and force.) He looks up at her, smiling in that complete deliverance which she knows. He says: "We never had to take any of it seriously, did we?" Tears streaming down her face, smiling, she answers: "No, we never had to."

The flight of Galt and Dagny to the valley, over a world where the lights are going out.

The last run of the Comet. Eddie Willers—against the world. The stop in the desert. ("Dagny, in the name of the best within us! . . .") The encroaching nature—the return of the jungle. Eddie Willers sobbing on the tracks, under the motionless ray of the headlight that shoots out to get lost in a dead night.

The music of the composer's "Heroic Symphony" filling the valley and rising out of it to the night sky. Rearden, d'Anconia, Danneskjöld, Hastings at work—the control of nature, the triumph over nature. Talk about future plans, starting everything from the beginning, in a small, *selfish* way. "Galt will run the local railroad from New York to Philadelphia." Galt and Dagny on the rocks above the valley—looking off at the wrecked road and the stubborn fire in the distance. Galt says: "The road is cleared. We're going back."

**July 7, 1946**

*Three Main Lines for Part I*

I. *The gradual disappearance of the creators.*

They are pulled out on strike at crucial moments in the story—in connection with TT's disintegration. Each time, the loss is a specific blow to TT (as in Rearden's quitting). Preferably, each desertion must cause a specific step lower for TT. The men can be TT's big executives, or key suppliers, or key shippers (or one of each). Each time, the loss of one man in a business causes failure for all the others in it. (Probably four instances, at the most— but clear-cut, crucial ones.)

Show Dagny seeing her net of rails breaking and falling apart in her hands. If the strikers are the life blood of the world, then TT is the world's blood system; as the blood goes, the vessels shrink, emptied, and dry off; then the body withers, in growing paralysis. By the time Dagny finds that Galt is a minor employee of hers, she has realized, in despair, that TT is a dying net of vessels without blood. (And Galt is the one who watches the operations of TT and knows when, where, and whom to strike.)

II. *Dagny's quest in connection with Galt's old engine.*

There are two lines of search on her part. First, trying to find someone to understand the importance of the engine, to restore it and make it work. This is futile, except for Rearden (or, every time she has a chance at a good engineer, Taggart ruins it). Second, trying to trace its history and find the man who designed it. Here there is a chance for flashbacks, in strange, half-mysterious hints and conversations, a chance for a gradual movement of Dagny toward Galt. And a chance to show all the variations of the parasites' attitude toward brains and achievement, and toward material property.

III. *"What is wrong with the world?"*

This is the overall, miserably bewildered question in all the minds, but particularly in Dagny's (and, next, in Eddie Willers'). This must be conveyed in small touches, small but tremendously significant in unstated implications. Here there is a chance for such things as: the music, "the cigarette made nowhere" (or some such equivalent, an extremely well-made small gadget that could not have been made in the factories and by the industries which Dagny knows), the girl-writer's book "published nowhere," etc. *The feeling of "Ergitandal"—just exactly that*—first, with the hopeless yearning of an impossible dream—then growing into an ominous reality (ominous in being inexplicably real somewhere)—leading to and climaxed by Dagny in the valley. [*What "Ergitandal" refers to is unknown.*]

———————

Galt as a TT employee. Either: night watchman for TT's research laboratory; or track walker; or switchman on lonely division; or plain laborer in the repair yard, which is connected with the laboratory; or terminal worker in the underground tunnels of the main terminal in New York. (If this last— then their first love scene is in the underground tunnels that vibrate with the motion of the great city above.)

Galt's reason for being an obscure TT employee: he chose TT for the same reason I did, as the crucial blood system that gives him access to the whole economy of the country; by stopping TT and the key industries connected with it, he can stop the world. But while working on TT, he has fallen in love with Dagny Taggart, long before she meets him (he knows all about her activities and her character, and he has seen her in person many times). *That* is his conflict. He knows that he is her worst enemy, in her terms, her secret destroyer—but he knows that he must go on. (This is reflected in his attitude toward her in the valley—but we actually learn it much later, when she does, in Part II.)

*Bits for Part I*

*Chapter II:* "The Theme." Dagny on the train—listening to the "Heroic Concerto." The young porter—his evasive answers. The railroad incident where we learn who she is. When they reach the underground terminal in New York—the sense of exaltation returns to her. As she gets off the train, she is whistling the Concerto. She feels someone looking at her—turns—the younger porter is staring at her tensely.

This music is then used twice again: when Dagny approaches the houses of the valley—and at the very end. (Unless the strikers use it for a code signal.) ([*Note added some time later:*] "The Concerto of Deliverance.")

———

The gold dollar sign placed by Francisco d'Anconia at the entrance to the valley.

———

The oil man whose wells are "nationalized" (directly or indirectly) quits and sets fire to the wells. One gusher—the best—cannot be extinguished. It remains flaming for years, to the end of the story. (The constant reflection of the red glow—the reminder, like the calendar.) At the end—*this* is the stubborn fire which Galt sees in the distance. ("Wyatt's torch.")

**July 9, 1946**

*Notes for Part II* (Tentative)

*Galt and Dagny*

He is the lowest kind of track laborer in the underground tunnels of the Taggart Terminal.

They meet when she is called there because the signal-switch system has broken down; there is no one to repair it—and no one takes the initiative on what to do. (This occurs after a sequence where Dagny was in despair over her inability to find intelligence and competence.)

The love affair in the underground tunnels.

She learns that he has loved her for years—and that he is her worst enemy. (She tries to stop him from "getting" someone—perhaps Rearden.)

The scene where Dagny and important leaders (Mr. Jones) are held up in a train stalled in the Taggart Terminal tunnels. They are discussing important collectivist measures to come. She glances out of the window. Galt is standing by the switch, holding a red lantern.

After the broadcast, Dagny returns to her own office—and finds Galt waiting for her. He tells her that she must leave with him—hell is going to break loose now. She wants to remain. Then, he will remain, too; all the others have left; but he will save her—or go down with her. He tells her she can always find him at his job—and leaves.

After the desperate search for him—Dagny comes to Galt's garret. She begs him to help them, to save TT—the temptation through love. He refuses. She asks him to escape—or she will betray him. He hands her the phone.

**July 10, 1946**

*Notes for Part I: The "Three Main Lines"*

I. *The gradual disappearance of the creators.*
    Galt "gets":

*Railroad men:*

Dagny's Operating (?) Manager (which causes traffic snarl).
Dagny's Freight Manager (which causes loss of crucial freight).
Dagny's Traffic Manager (which causes death of section).
Chief Engineer (loss of tunnel and bridge).
Inventor or young engineer (resorting to old engines).

*Shippers and suppliers:*

Oil man—lack of fuel which [leads to the] end of diesels. (The
burning well—near the future dead section.)
Lumber man—lack of ties, cars, terminal buildings.
Utility man (electricity)—New York loses electricity near the end
(tie with Taggart surrendering power plant to "the city").

III. *"What is wrong with the world?"*

The music ("Heroic Concerto").
The book (part of a book, found by Dagny, "published nowhere").

The flashlight: the small gadget with immense significance. This is a good example of the fact that technical civilization is an end product of intellectual civilization. (Have d'Anconia make some crack about this, such as: "Who made this flashlight? The idea that a table is a table.")

The way the key people quit.

The actions of Francisco d'Anconia.

The incident of Ragnar Danneskjöld's refusal.

The cigarettes.

**July 12, 1946**

Here is the state of TT at beginning of Part II:

*The system has shrunk to little more than a single transcontinental line*—largely useless (because the productive areas on its route have been killed) and unable to pay its own cost.

*The desperate need for Rearden Steel rails*— the track is hopelessly worn out.

Schedules are hopelessly mixed—nobody now expects a train to be on time. Therefore, people (producers and shippers) are not count-ing on trains any longer. (Breakdowns of signals, equipment, and lack of supplies.) Trains are expensive, dangerous, uncomfortable, unreliable.

*Most of TT's main shippers are gone.*

*The Taggart Bridge is in a desperately precarious condition.*

Refrigerator cars and tank cars are gone. Sleepers and heating are eliminated at the end of Part I. Air-conditioning is long since gone. (Water and lighting go in Part II.)

*Diesels are gone*—Old steam locomotives are run with coal—and there is a first return to the use of plain wood (if this is technically feasible).

*The Taggart "research laboratory" is gone.*

*Possible line:*

Dagny is searching desperately for the genius who invented the motor. She is searching also for the mysterious enemy who is destroying TT. When she traps the enemy, to deliver him to those who will destroy

him, she discovers that he is the genius who designed the motor, the man she
wanted.

**July 17, 1946**

### For Part I

The ending: Either the freight car manufacturer has quit, or Dagny is
afraid he will; he is the last good man left in that line and something has just
happened to "put the burden on him." Dagny hurries to stop him. She arrives
too late; she sees his plane taking off at the airport. She follows.

Before that: she hurries by train, but this is "the frozen ride," so she
can't make it. She escapes from the abandoned train, steals or buys someone's plane, and goes on to the small town of the car manufacturer.

The "frozen ride": wrong signals, wrong switches, burned-out brakes—
every kind of lesser sabotage. It ends with the train being abandoned in the
middle of a plain at night. Half an hour or more passes before Dagny finds
out that they are abandoned. Nobody else cares. (This is a complete
example, "in a teaspoon," of a frozen, parasite society.)

The "freeze" [Directive 10–289] is applied because Taggart and the
other parasites cannot find people to take positions of responsibility, and
there is a wave of quitting and pleas for demotion. This happens because of
the double-cross.

The "double-cross" is that Taggart's executive assistant (a deliberately
chosen patsy) and a train engineer are blamed for the tunnel catastrophe and
convicted of manslaughter.

The tunnel catastrophe: a parasite, who is in charge at a station where a
diesel engine breaks down, sends a passenger train into the tunnel with an
old steam engine. The tunnel is in bad condition; its ventilation system
doesn't work. The engine cannot quite handle the grade in the tunnel—the
passengers begin to choke—a fool panics and pulls the brake-cord—the
train cannot get started again. A freight train, loaded with explosives, is
speeding through the tunnel (because of the poor ventilation) and smashes
into the stalled train. The explosion wrecks the tunnel for good. (After this,
Dagny has to organize the "return to pre-tunnel days," using the old track.)

*The oil sequence.* A single successful oil man buys a whole section of
country. (This is a mountain region, not too far from the valley.) He is using,
for shipping, the efficient railroad of Taggart's competitor. Taggart whines

that his branch line would be all right ( it is losing money) if it weren't for the "destructive" competition. Taggart has a law passed (or a railroad association vote) about "duplication" and "seniority." His line is the oldest, so he remains and the competitor is forced out. The oil man goes frantic with Taggart's poor service: endless delays and uncertainty, no cars when needed, lost cars, accidents. (Accidents are always claimed to be "acts of God." Here someone remarks: "Funny how active God's getting to be lately," and is answered: "He always is when man isn't.") The oil man loses a great deal of business (and industries are forced to close) because he cannot deliver the oil on time. (Taggart's poor freight service makes prices rise in the oil town. The workers demand a raise, and the oil man is ordered to grant it, while not being allowed to raise the price of oil. Or—the oil man wants to build his own railroad line, and he is not allowed to, on grounds of "monopoly.") He quits, setting fire to his wells.

Less than a year later, Taggart has to close his branch line because there is no business in this section; the industries supported by and dependent on the oil-field have closed or moved away. This is the "death of a section"— the small farmers, shop owners, and workers are left behind and find themselves without transportation to the outside world. (These are the people who believe that small private property is all right, but big fortunes should be limited.)

The young man who wants to organize a "pony express." He is asked: "So you want to make money on the community misfortune?" The community passes rules: special rates on babies' milk, priorities on food, free rides for the unemployed, etc. That evening, a stranger comes to town. He is present at the town meeting. In the morning, the young man has disappeared with the stranger.

There are earlier references to "dead sections." The first one we see is when Dagny goes to the abandoned motor factory. (So later, in the above sequence, the readers know what is in store for the inhabitants of the town.)

*The iron ore squeeze.* Parasite steel manufacturers [accuse] Rearden of "destructive competition" because he owns his own mine. Mrs. Rearden's pet parasite enlists the help of Taggart—the deal being that the parasite will acquire the mine and give Taggart the ore freight business, instead of shipping it by lake boats (which is much cheaper). Taggart and the others get a law passed that no business can own another business. Rearden has to sell the mine—and Mrs. Rearden pushes him into selling it to the parasite. The parasite has no money (except a government loan for the down payment), so Rearden has to take a time-payment arrangement.

Taggart gets the transportation business from the mine and this destroys the lake shipping. Later, in Part II, close to Rearden's final awakening, there is an emergency when the parasite is making a mess of the mine and it is running at a loss; Mrs. Rearden urges Rearden to "give the man a hand," teach him how to run the mine—"since, after all, you'll lose money if the mine goes bankrupt." This is when Rearden has a fit of fury, his first one against his wife; he realizes that he is asked to make the man a present of the mine that he, Rearden, created, and also teach the bastard how to use his own stolen property. Rearden refuses. This is one of the important steps to his awakening.

Later, when the wheat section is destroyed, Taggart raises freight rates on the ore (there is no lake shipping available)—the parasite raises the price of ore—yet Rearden is not allowed to raise the price of steel. "You'll do something."

*An incident in which Dagny tries to stop an important shipper from quitting—and it is too late.* While she waits in the anteroom, Galt is in the man's office. (We don't know this, of course.) Galt leaves through another door, not through the anteroom. By the time Dagny is admitted into the office, it is too late: the man has decided to quit.

*The Francisco d'Anconia disaster:* D'Anconia has made a big deal with Taggart to build a branch line for his new copper mine in Mexico. Taggart builds it, at great expense, because he is appeasing the Mexican government. The Mexican government nationalizes the line and the mine. D'Anconia loses more than Taggart, but he has made the mine worthless. Dagny realizes that it was done on purpose. (Taggart's motive was the typical one: not any actual facts that d'Anconia presented, but that d'Anconia presented them.) (After that, d'Anconia cannot deliver the copper which TT needs. He uses the weakest shipping company he can find, in order to "help" them—the ships sink. Previously, he had used Hastings' ships.)

Minor possibility: the cigarettes with the dollar sign are used as a code signal among the strikers.

*Possibility:* Galt, who is getting most of his information through Eddie Willers, learns from him about Dagny's affair with Rearden. Eddie is the only one who knows of it—he is jealous, [but] doesn't realize it. He confesses it to Galt—while he, Eddie, is drunk. ("What's that to me—if Dagny Taggart is sleeping with Hank Rearden?")

*Possibility:* Dagny calls on Francisco d'Anconia and Ragnar Danneskjöld to help her save Galt. They have remained in the city, without Galt's knowledge or approval, to stand by him and save him when necessary. When Dagny calls d'Anconia (from a pay booth), he tells her that he expected her call. When he comes to meet her, she makes the sign of the dollar with her fingers, smiling, even though she wants to cry.

### July 18, 1946

The reason that society does not collapse into civil war and violence in my story (as it would have in historical reality) is that even a civil war is caused by some element of independence in men, some active impulse, no matter how misguided. It is the element of decision which makes men revolt, even if blindly, because they realize that conditions are unbearable, cannot be allowed to go on and something must be done. So they resort to violence, in sheer anger and despair—violence being the only resort against the parasites (since reason is what the parasites have discarded, and since they rely on and advocate violence).

So it is still some kind of creator, a man of action or decision to some extent, who is necessary to lead men into revolt and civil war. This is what happens in history when collectivism, the rule of the parasite, becomes unbearable. (Besides, it is the parasites who resort to force when they need more loot and hope to make men produce for them through terror.) Actually, in history, societies are a mixture—no principle is observed consistently, and individualism is allowed to function by default. This is what holds the creators in society, their hope for that accidental chance. But this is no longer true of modern collectivism, such as Russia or Germany.

(A good sidelight here: there are only two possible incentives for human actions: desire for gain, or fear. But fear does not work, except for a while on the most miserable level of subsistence and then only while there is still the production of free men to loot or copy (and it works only on the worst, i.e., useless, types of men). So, actually, there is but *one* incentive for men: gain—*personal desire*.)

In my story, the creators do not try to cooperate with a parasite-ruled society to the point of the unbearable, then revolt, as they do in history. The creators have withdrawn. What is left of humanity without them is capable neither of production nor revolt. Therefore, the end of the world, in my story, is not one of violence, but of slow rot: disintegration, corruption, a dead body falling to pieces (and a society without functioning intelligence *is* a dead body). *It **must** be the rot of stagnation, of hopeless decay, of the gray, the dull, the trite.* (Keep this firmly in mind. Don't have too much emotional violence in Taggart and his kind; even their crises and tragedies are gray rot.) *Without the creators, the world simply stops.*

It is merely indicated that the parasites would like to resort to violence, that it is their natural course, their essence, and their last hope. This is shown in the torture scene, in the sequences relating to the professor's laboratory, and in small, dreadful hints about their intentions, from the Cuffy Meigs types, as well as from "Chester" or "the businessman." But they have nothing to do violence to—the creators have withdrawn beyond their reach and left the parasites to their fate (instead of fighting them in the open), to show them what that fate will be. And what's left of humanity is a miserable, shivering herd, not worth terrorizing, because they are already in terror and will obey without violence; in fact, they ask nothing but to obey; but there's no one there to teach the parasites what orders to give. The remnant herd is not worth ruling—they can produce nothing for the parasites to loot.

*All this must be brought out explicitly.*

———◦———

It is the *abstract* thinkers who go on strike first—since production and all the rest stems from them. Therefore, by the time the story begins, the abstract thinkers are gone already: there are no philosophers and no theoretical scientists. This is shown in the state of the Taggart laboratory, of the professor's State laboratory, and in the prominence of the "Fadiman type" of "philosopher." [*As noted earlier, Clifton Fadiman was book editor of* The New Yorker.]

*Note on Galt* (in connection with above): Make clear that Galt is that rare phenomenon (perhaps, *the rarest*)—a philosopher and inventor at once, both a thinker and a man of action. That is why he is the *perfect* man, the perfectly integrated being. One indication of this—the fact that in college Galt was the star pupil of both the philosopher and the [physics] professor. In fact, Galt was the only student who took such a peculiar (to the college authorities and the time) combination of courses.

**August 24, 1946**

[*AR revised the following chapter outline at some later time. Where the revisions are significant, I present both the original and the revised descriptions. Where the chapter title seems to have been added later, I have marked it with an asterisk.*]

*Final Chapter Outline*
*Part I: The End*
*I. The Calendar*

"Who is John Galt?" Eddie Willers, Taggart Transcontinental, James Taggart. Trouble on the Colorado line. Taggart's evasions.

### II. The Theme

Dagny Taggart on the train—returning from a survey of the Colorado line. The Fifth Concerto. Her carrying the business and the responsibility. Order for Rearden Metal to rebuild the Colorado line. Her young engineer quits.

### III: The Chain

Hank Rearden and Rearden Steel. The mine parasite (Paul Larkin). The bracelet. Rearden and his wife (Lillian), mother, brother (Philip), and sister (Stacey). Larkin's cautious mention of "How is your Washington man?"

### IV: The Top and the Bottom*

[*Original:*] James Taggart's move to force out his Colorado competition and get Rearden's iron ore mine for the parasite. Conference: Taggart, steel parasite (Orren Boyle), mine parasite (Paul Larkin). (Skeptical derision of Rearden Metal—one of the reasons for taking mine away from him: "He'll waste it.") Dagny and the parasite who objects to her use of Rearden Metal—her indifference to advice. Dagny and her staff: Eddie Willers, Gerald Hastings, the young playwright. First mention of Nat Taggart. Issue of parasite in charge of Colorado Division.

[*Revised:*] James Taggart's move to force out his Colorado competition and get Rearden's iron ore mine for the parasite. Conference in the dark barroom: Taggart, steel parasite (Orren Boyle), mine parasite (Paul Larkin), and Wesley Mouch as an obsequious nonentity. (Skeptical derision of Rearden Metal—one of the reasons for taking mine away from him: "He'll waste it.") Dagny: her frustrated romanticism, her sense of life, how she became vice-president. Issue with Taggart about Mexican line, with story of line, San Sebastian, and Francisco d'Anconia. First mention of Nat Taggart. Eddie Willers and his dinner with the worker.

### V: The Anti-Dog-Eat-Dog*

Francisco d'Anconia arrives in New York—[there is a] newspaper scandal about him and some woman. Taggart getting ready for meeting of Board. News that Mexican line was nationalized that morning. The Board meeting—Taggart takes credit for cutting the rolling stock. The Association meeting—Taggart gets vote against competitor (partly on the strength of the Mexican loss). Dagny objects, but even competitor himself accepts it. Dagny and Rearden: plans to hurry [the construction of the] line. [Added later:] Dagny–Ellis Wyatt.

### VI: The Climax of the d'Anconias

Dagny and Francisco d'Anconia. (The Mexican government has found his copper mines to be worthless.) (Dagny's anger at d'Anconia's "Who is John Galt?") [Note that there is no mention yet of a past romance between Dagny and Francisco.]

### VII: The Non-Commercial*

Mrs. Rearden's party: Dagny, James Taggart, Rearden, his family— their interrelationships. D'Anconia is also present. Dagny and Mrs. Rearden: the bracelet. Rearden's antagonism to Dagny and defense of his wife. Rearden's attitude toward women. The cultural phonies (professor of philosophy, musician, writer). The first Galt legend—Atlantis. Rearden's sexual attitude toward his wife—scene in her bedroom.

### VIII: The Materialists*

The law which forces Rearden to sell his mine to the parasite. He accepts this, feeling guilty about his lack of social concern (and, besides, he is too busy with Rearden Metal, his drive and enthusiasm are in that). Dagny and Rearden work together on the new Colorado line. Decision on bridge of Rearden Metal. Incident of Rearden's guilty desire for Dagny. Their heroic effort—the public opposition. (Dr. Stadler comes out against Rearden Metal, through his parasite assistant.) The second Galt legend—"the fountain of youth."

### IX: The John Galt Line*

The triumphant ride of the first freight train over the new Colorado line. Dagny, Rearden, and Ellis Wyatt at their ecstatic celebration. ("To the world as it seems right now!") Dagny's and Rearden's night together (in Wyatt's lonely guest house, in the mountains).

### X: The Sacred and the Profane*

Dagny and Rearden escape for a vacation together. They drive to the abandoned motor factory. They find Galt's engine.

### XI: Wyatt's Torch

The history of the motor, ending on professor in diner advising her to give up the quest. What awaits them on their return: Taggart has given in to the union's demand of no extra speed on the new line. Steel parasites and others concerned have passed a law to force Rearden to sell Rearden Metal "equally." (No pipe-line for Wyatt, no steel for Taggart Bridge, no girders for the coal man.) Dagny hurries to Ellis Wyatt—too late—she sees the flaming oil fields.

### XII: "Why Do You Think You Think?"*

Dagny and Rearden: their secret affair. His sense of guilt, her simple acceptance. (His guilt undermines him in his fight against the parasites, makes him accept them.) Dr. Stadler and Dr. Ferris: the book.

### XIII: The Aristocracy of Pull*

[Original:] Loss of priceless freight needed by Rearden for coal man's order. Dagny and Ragnar Danneskjöld: his refusal [to help her]. When she comes back, coal man quits. (Night of Dagny alone in the office—the shadow of a man outside.)

[Revised:] Taggart marries Cherryl. Rearden and Danagger make illegal deal. The d'Anconia copper stock crash. (Dagny learns that cigarette is "made nowhere.")

### XIV: By Your Guilt*

[Original:] Taggart agrees to get rid of Colorado Division parasite, but Dagny's choice for the position quits; the parasite stays. Taggart marries Cherryl. (Taggart and the priest.) Mrs. Rearden learns of Rearden's infidelity—her enjoyment of it, which Rearden cannot understand. The subtle torture that follows. (Dagny and the young engineer at the employment board.) (The young playwright and Stacey Rearden's peculiar attitude toward his struggle and career.)

[*Revised:*] Eddie tells the TT worker about the importance of the coal man. Mrs. Rearden learns of Rearden's infidelity—her enjoyment of it, which Rearden cannot understand. The subtle torture that follows. Rearden and Dr. Ferris: the attempted blackmail. Danagger quits. Rearden and Francisco: the furnace.

### XV: The Sanction of the Victim*

[*Original:*] The N.Y. utility man—caught between the failures of the oil and coal [industries], and the failures of TT. Dagny comes to see him— too late—he quits. (She waits in anteroom while Galt is in the office.) Taggart is forced to close Colorado line. The death of a section. The young man who quits.

[*Revised:*] Rearden's trial and victory—"the moral sanction." Rearden and Francisco: the loss of d'Anconia copper at sea.

### XVI: Account Overdrawn*

[*This chapter is added in the revised version:*] Taggart is forced to close Colorado line. The death of a section. Lillian discovers Rearden's mistress is Dagny.

### XVII: Miracle Metal*

[*Original:*] The buck passing spreads. The rush of people toward demotion and obscurity. The law freezing the economy. Dagny quits and goes to mountain cabin. (Last Galt legend—the factory.)

[*Revised:*] The law freezing the economy. Dagny quits and goes to mountain cabin. Rearden forced to give away patent [for Rearden Metal].

### XVIII: The Moratorium on Brains*

[*Original:*] Rearden forced to give away patent [for Rearden Metal]. Taggart closes his research laboratory. Taggart overrides Dagny's policies and orders, particularly in regard to locomotives. Eddie Willers and the worker: scene in which Eddie mentions Dagny's hide-out. The tunnel catastrophe.

[*Revised:*] Taggart closes his research laboratory. ("We can save money since we have no fear of competition.") Taggart overrides Dagny's policies and orders, particularly in regard to locomotives. The young man who temporarily replaces Dagny—his idea that his aim is to please Taggart, *not* to do a good job. Eddie Willers and the worker: scene in which Eddie mentions Dagny's hide-out. The tunnel catastrophe.

### XIX: By Our Love*

Dagny in the country—her restlessness. Dagny and Francisco d'Anconia. News of catastrophe over the radio. Dagny goes back. Some parasites have quit. Taggart was considering quitting, but stays when Dagny returns. Dagny's intention to rebuild the line to "pre-tunnel" days. Her appeal to Rearden for all the rails he can deliver. [*In the revised version, the last sentence is crossed out and the following is added:*] Dagny-Rearden-Francisco scene. Dagny hurries after young scientist. Eddie tells worker where she has gone and about her affair with Rearden.

### XX

[*Original:*] Rearden goes to the West Coast to arrange for temporary transportation. Dagny joins him later. The opening night of the playwright's play; Rearden goes with Dagny to the theater. Mrs. Rearden [sees them and] guesses the truth. Sensation of play; the playwright leaves "with some man." That night, after the show, the violent scene between Rearden and his wife. Her ultimatum. He promises to let her know when she returns.

[*This chapter was eliminated in the revised outline.*]

### XXI

[*Original:*] The next morning, the young playwright asks Dagny for his job back, "after a month's vacation." Dagny gets wire from car manufacturer—he can't fill her order. She has to hurry to him at once. At last moment, she gets wire from Rearden, asking her to come as soon as possible. While she is packing, Eddie Willers sees Rearden's dressing-gown in her apartment and guesses the truth. She leaves. Scene of Eddie Willers and the worker in the restaurant, in which Eddie betrays the purpose of Dagny's trip and her affair with Rearden.

[*This chapter was eliminated in the revised outline.*]

### XX: The Sign of the Dollar*

[*Original:*] The "frozen train ride." Dagny and the young playwright. Their walk at night down the track to a telephone. Dagny gives orders to save the train, gets a plane, flies to car manufacturer's town, sees his plane leaving, follows him. The mountains. The crash.

[*Revised:*] The "frozen train ride." Dagny and Owen Kellogg. Their walk at night down the track to a telephone. Dagny gives orders to save the train, gets a plane, flies to young scientist's town, sees his plane leaving, follows him. The mountains. The crash. Her last thought, before she crashed, was burning in her mind, as her mockery of life, as her cry of defiance, the words she hated—the words of hopelessness, of despair, and of a plea for help: "Oh, hell! Who is John Galt?"

*Part II: The Beginning*
*I: Atlantis*

The valley—John Galt.

## *II*

Rearden's decision about Dagny. His looking for her. (His loans to a farm-tool company for the Minnesota harvest.) [*Added later:*] Dr. Stadler and the unveiling of Project X. The open rise of the brute.

## *III*

Dagny's return to New York. Taggart has hired Cuffy Meigs. The freight cars have gone to southern "soybean project." Dagny's break with Rearden—she tells him she loves another man. [*Added later:*] He tells her that he loves her. Dagny and Lillian; Dagny's broadcast.

## *IV*

The disaster resulting from the "transportation pull deal." The collapse of the farming district of Minnesota. Rearden's heavy losses on his credits. Mrs. Rearden's attempt to make him help mine parasite—his first anger at her.

## *V*

Taggart's married life—he crushes Cherryl's efforts to rise. Cherryl's "drowning plea" to Dagny. ([*Added later:*] Cherryl's suicide.) [*The next two sentences were crossed out:*] Rearden realizes that Dagny is his real love— he tells her so. Dagny's search for Galt; Francisco d'Anconia, the empty valley.

## VI

*[Original:]* The affair: Taggart and Mrs. Rearden. Taggart confesses it to the priest. The priest forgives him. The rebellion of Rearden's secretary against her family—her decision to quit and marry.

*[Revised:]* The affair: Taggart and Mrs. Rearden. Francisco saves Rearden in a situation where Rearden sees, at last, who is on whose side. The "wet nurse." [*This is the* only *reference to the "wet nurse" in AR's journals, and it was added to the outline years later. After completing the novel, AR described the "wet nurse" as "an exception in my writing career, a character that started without my intention and wrote himself."*]

### VII: Atlas Shrugged*

The scheming of Taggart and the mine parasite to save themselves. Rearden discovers Mrs. Rearden's affair with Taggart. He sees the real nature of his family. The emergency conference: Rearden, Taggart, mine parasite, Wesley Mouch. The rise in TT's freight rates for ore and in the price of ore; Rearden is not allowed to raise prices, yet rails for TT are expected of him. The squeeze play. "You'll do something." Rearden walks out of office—the scene with his secretary in his office—he sees the similarity of their tragedy. "A man waiting to see him."

## VIII

News that Rearden has quit. His wife begs him to stay—his implacable coldness. He goes away (to the valley). Scene where lawyer reads Rearden's deed to "the collective"—their panic. Rearden's brother and factory superintendent. Superintendent quits—and half the workers are gone. "The collective" hires a friend of Cuffy Meigs, who promptly loots the place. The collapse of Rearden Steel.

## IX

The final emergency of TT—the decision to close the Michigan line, against Dagny's violent protest. When Dagny returns to the office, she is called to the terminal tunnels—the breakdown of the signal system. John Galt. Dagny escapes, sits sobbing in the terminal waiting room. (The bum who consoles her: "Oh well, who is John Galt?") Hours later, she returns to the tunnels. Galt was expecting her to return. The affair underground. Then he tells her of his past love. She breaks with him, declaring that they *are* enemies. (She learns that Galt is both the ideal, the man she wanted—

and her worst enemy; that he loves her—and that he is destroying her railroad.)

## X

The closing of the ore line is announced: the riots, the general panic. The announced broadcast of Mr. Thompson.

### XI: This Is John Galt Speaking

The broadcast (Mr. Thompson, Dagny, James Taggart, and others in the studio). John Galt's speech.

## XII

When Dagny returns to her office, Galt is waiting for her there. He offers her a last chance—she refuses. He tells her he will stand by and gives her his address. The panic—the country is falling apart. The government attempts to negotiate with Galt by radio—he refuses. The search for him. ("We do not recognize your right to negotiate"—or—desperate blind appeals into space, and no answer.)

## XIII

Galt and the priest in the restaurant. The appeal through pity. Dagny comes to his garret. The appeal through love. He refuses. She warns him— he hands her the phone. When she comes back with officials, he is still there. [*Later, the preceding two sentences were crossed out and replaced by the sentence:*] The officials had followed Dagny—they come in. The search and destruction of his laboratory. His "polite" arrest.

## XIV

Galt in a luxurious hotel room. The attempted bargaining by Mr. Thompson—he refuses. Dr. Stadler. Dagny and Rearden: she tells him that she loves Galt and that she betrayed him. The banquet: the appeal through flattery. "Get the hell out of my way."

## XV

Dr. Stadler and the explosion of Project X, collapse of the Taggart Bridge. The scene in a bare hotel room: Taggart, the mine parasite, Wesley Mouch, Cuffy Meigs, Dagny. The "quiet hysteria." Dagny understands and walks out. She goes to her office, starts destroying papers. (Call from Eddie Willers; she tells him to give up, but he can't.) A man rushes in with news about Taggart Bridge. Her moment of temptation—then: "We don't know what to do!" and her answer: "I don't either." She leaves the office, calls Francisco d'Anconia, meets him and Ragnar Danneskjöld on a street corner.

### XVI: The Generator

The torture of Galt. The broken generator—the escape of the mechanic. A man rushes in [and announces that] the Taggart Bridge has collapsed. Galt's single moment of temptation—but he keeps silent. They all escape, leaving him tied.

### XVII

Taggart and the priest. The confession of total evil. "I have nothing to say, James. I'm on strike." The rescue of Galt by Dagny, d'Anconia, and Danneskjöld. (Brute force against mind and force.) "We never had to take any of it seriously, did we?" "No, we never had to."

### XVIII: In the Name of the Best Within Us

The flight to the valley—Galt, Dagny, d'Anconia, Danneskjöld, New York City without electrical power. The sight of a world in ruins. Eddie Willers and the last ride of the Comet. The music of the Concerto filling the valley. The strikers talk of future plans—a new beginning. (Rearden says: "John will run the railroad from New York to Philadelphia.") Galt and Dagny on the rocks above the valley, looking at the wrecked road and the stubborn fire of Wyatt's torch in the distance. Galt says: "The road is cleared. We are going back." The sign of the dollar.

[The above outline contains AR's last references to the priest. Years after completing the novel, she explained the meaning of the character and why she decided to eliminate him.]

I wanted to illustrate the evil of the morality of forgiveness. Also, I wanted to illustrate that the power of religion consists of the power of morality, the power of setting values and ideals, and that is what holds people to religion—and that this is what belongs to philosophy, not to religion. As a type, I wanted [the priest] to be my most glamorized projection of a Thomist philosopher, of a man who thought he could combine reason with religion. Through his relationship with James Taggart I wanted to show the way in which he realized that he was sanctioning evil. And the drama of him refusing to sanction Taggart at the end appealed to me very much.

But it did not take me very long to realize that it would be an impossible confusion. Since all the other strikers in the story can be taken literally, [since] they are all representatives of rational, valuable professions, to include a priest among them would be to sanction religion.]

**August 26, 1946**

### Questions

Trouble for stalled locomotive, for Dagny to correct?
Who would be in charge of the tunnel and the bridge?
What would be the specific position of the young engineer who quits?
What is the usual period of time before the placing of a new steel alloy on the market and the actual orders for it, particularly by railroads? Is there any special procedure about this?
Specific troubles that would cripple ore mines?
What would happen (to track and equipment) in a case such as Taggart taking over Colorado competitor?
Problems of rebuilding new Colorado line?
*The wage rates* (in connection with Colorado line issue)?
Possible cause of freight snarl and loss of freight?
Vital item which could have been lost?
Who appoints division heads and similar regional executives?
Ask details about automatic signal systems?
If branch line is closed, how soon after decision do trains stop running?
Would "pre-tunnel days" rails be rotted by time of the story? (What is the time element for such rails?)
Are telephones on poles? Whom would Dagny call?
Time element for [the order] of Rearden rails?
Breakdown of N.Y. terminal signal system?
The kind of generator for torture scene? And what goes wrong with it?

What goes wrong with locomotive on the Comet's last ride?
What would be Dagny's official title at TT? Also—Taggart's title?
Sizes and duties of division, districts, and regions?


**1946**

[*AR prepared the following questions for an interview with Lee Lyles,
assistant to the president of the Atchison, Topeka, and Santa Fe Railway
system.*]

*Who are the key men, the spark-plugs, of a railroad company?*
*What are the actual, concrete, specific duties and problems of a rail-
road president?*
Who actually owns a railroad and appoints president?
*What would be specific duties and problems of "Vice-President in
charge of Operations"?*
What would be Galt's job at TT? (Lowest job in terminal tunnels.)
Who makes decision about building a new line or re-building an old
one? How far in advance of starting?
Who orders rails? How far in advance of need are orders placed?
How long does it take to get them? In what quantity are they usually
ordered? In the case of a new metal or experimental rail, who makes
the decision to use it?
How long does it take to get rolling stock and locomotives? (Pas-
senger cars—6 months; freight cars—3 months.)
Would saving the locomotives and rolling stock be of any finan-
cial consequence in the case of the nationalized Mexican line? *Yes.*
What is the most important position for an engineer? (Superintendent
of Transportation, Mechanical man.)
Who appoints division heads and other regional executives? (If it's
Dagny, would Taggart interfere?)
Who are the main shippers? Agriculture—etc., auto-parts for
assembly line, oil, ore.
If branch line is closed, how soon after decision do trains stop running?
*Any specific points about a railroad's deterioration? What would
crack first? When brains are gone, where would the result show first,
and how?*
How much in advance would freight cars be promised to "soybean
project"? When would they be sent there? When would they have
been sent to Minnesota farmers?

Details and chief causes of bridge deterioration and collapse? How many years at the least?

Do railroads own their own electric power plant—such as for N.Y. terminal?

**August 28, 1946**

### *Extra Touches*

Possible lesser incident (for destruction of main transcontinental line): a big shipper, who is a parasite (inherited), goes bankrupt through parasites' methods, and his failure is a bad blow to TT. His father was one of TT's most important and reliable shippers, one of their mainstays. (This can be lumber, cotton, or some other basic commodity.)

Possibility—the "crucial train run," which fails for reasons of parasites' technique, may precede and motivate either Wyatt's quitting or the closing of the oil line.

Don't forget to stress (near the middle of Part I) that Dagny begins to suspect the existence of an enemy who is destroying TT. Dagny and the "feeling of Ergitandal."

Have brief, eloquent ("condensed") flashbacks or references to Galt's past, giving picture of his life and of his essential character. (Mainly in Part II—possibly some, without naming him, in Part I.)

**August 31, 1946**

### *Notes for Railroad Business*

*James Taggart: President*—head of Executive Department under alleged authority of Board of Directors (which is really concerned with corporate, not railroad matters).

One of [Taggart's] chief-assistants, or vice-presidents, is the Public Relations man (extra-parasite) ("not to do, but to give the impression of doing").

*Dagny Taggart:* Vice-President in charge of *Operating Department.* (*Traffic* involves selling the service; *operating* involves producing the service.)

*Three main jobs of railroads:* Maintenance of way, maintenance of equipment, transportation.

*Divisions, districts*, and *regions* have the same three departments.

---

### Philosophical Points

The people in the story are functioning, in their human moments, on old premises and principles, i.e., on the principles left over from the creators' world, the principles of the strikers—to the extent to which they exist and function as human beings at all. They do not realize it, of course. Their avowed principles are those of collectivism and altruism. But whenever they have to act upon, or rely upon, or appeal to, decency or sense—they are implying the principles of the creators. This has a desperate quality—particularly when someone points it out to them; they are counting on the ideas they have denounced and discarded. (Example: any appeal to honesty, honor, integrity, rational sense—or personal profit. Along these lines: Francisco d'Anconia pointing out the mistake of assuming that he wishes to make money.)

---

Unions and trade-associations are not directed against employers or the public *but against the best among their own members.* (Stress this explicitly—in the railroad association's vote against Taggart's better competitor; in the steel association's actions against Rearden and his patent; in the union's policy regarding the new oil line and its speed.) This is one of the most obvious demonstrations of the fact that collectivism does not aim at any kind of "justice" or "fair play" or protection of the weak [man] against any actual infringement of his rights by the strong—*but simply at stopping the strong for the sake of the weak*—stopping ability for the sake of incompetence—not just robbing the production of the able, but stopping him from producing—not raising the weak in any way whatever, but simply forcing the strong down to the level of the moron. (Of course, if you do that, you destroy the world—weak and strong both. And the weak do not profit by this—not even for the moment.)

---

*Regarding controlled economies:* Man will not produce if all the essential elements involved are not under his rational control, i.e., if they are not understandable to him, and, therefore, predictable, so that he can set his purpose and plan of action, his end and means, accordingly. Nature is under his control—"other men" are not. If his productive activity has to depend upon the arbitrary decision or whim of some human agency, against whom he has no recourse and no choice (such as the government)—he will not produce.

This is why men can deal with a private utility company; they have an objective, mutual element to count upon—private profit, for both; both have something the other needs. But if electric power were nationalized, its best users, the biggest industrialists (and particularly new ventures that need electricity), would stop. A great industrialist is not going to venture into a huge undertaking when the ground can be cut from under him at any moment—when the sole source of electric power, which he needs, can be cut off arbitrarily by some punk bureaucrat. Never mind the fact that the bureaucrat won't cut it off, in most likely practice; the fact that he *can* is enough; he knows it and the industrialist knows it—and the bureaucrat has the power of blackmail, the power to demand anything he wishes, without the necessity of making a threat. Yes, second-rate businessmen, of the second-hand kind, would accept such an arrangement and even love it; they'd get special advantages or rates for themselves, they'd be glad to pay off the bureaucrat, they'd consider him their tool. But a real industrialist will not do it. He knows who holds the power in such a set-up.

Also: man will not produce if the essential motivation to consider is not his own profit. In a free economy, no one can ask him to work at a loss; this is only the economic aspect of a much more important fact—nobody can ask him to work for his own detriment or to struggle toward his own suffering or pain. In a collectivist economy, he must do just that; he must work without reward—and, when the collective wishes, toward his own destruction. The motivation is not profit—but *self-sacrifice*.

---

Rearden realizes that his mistake (about himself and his view of life) was due to the "strike" of the philosopher.

Scene of "common man" crying: "Why are they doing this to us? We thought our leaders *knew* what they were doing!"—and someone answering: "Those abstract, theoretical philosophers, whom you have always considered useless, are the only ones who can give men that knowledge."

———◦———

*The prevalence of "Oriental" philosophies* in the parasites' world: These are the kind of ideas the parasites would love (and even originate). Show the despair these ideas create in them and in their world. "Nothing is anything"— "We can't be sure of anything"—*"Why do you think you think?"*—"Obey, since you can't think"—"Feel, don't think"—"Act spontaneously, don't think"— " 'Immediate' perception, not thinking or reason"—"The present moment, not any long-range view"—"You are nothing anyway, so why worry about anything?"—"You are low and vile anyway, so why worry about virtue?"— "Sacrifice and suffering are a Universal Law"—"The individual is an illusion"—"Total annihilation (Nirvana) is the supreme ideal."

(Show the influence of this on: Taggart's wife, Mrs. Rearden, Stacey, Rearden's brother, the secretary, Eddie Willers, Taggart and his parasite friends. Also show how the professor comes to this [philosophy].)

———◦———

The arrogance of the "common man": he expects "to be convinced," with no mental effort on his own part. When confronted with the most lucid and explicit speech, idea, statement, or book—he simply declares that "he is not convinced," and this saves him from the necessity of taking a stand, of pronouncing an independent rational judgment. It saves him even from recognizing that the argument is unanswerable, so he must do something about it; he tells himself that since he's "not convinced," there must be something wrong with the argument, it's not absolute, he doesn't have to do anything about it. (So, of course, he will never let himself be convinced. Actually, he simply does not think at all and does not give the argument any sort of rational consideration.)

He wants mental food to be pre-digested and automatic. Also—he is firmly convinced that the main job of the thinkers (perhaps, the *only* job) is to convince *him*, to educate him. If asked how one could go about educating him (or making him understand anything), his answer would be: "*I* don't know. That's *your* job. You've got to educate me—both give me the right ideas and invent a way to convince me that they are the right ideas. I'm the aim of all society and all existence, ain't I? You're the strong, intellectually—I'm the weak. Your moral duty and only goal in life is to help me. Well, help me." (This is the "Adrian attitude.")

———◦———

An *extremely important point of the parasite's philosophy*: the desire to exploit the creators and also make them take the blame for the moral evil of such a situation.

This is more prevalent and more vicious than I suspected. I have mentioned one aspect of it: the parasite's demand that the creator, whom he exploits, must not admit that it's exploitation; to protect the parasite's feelings, the creator must fake reality. There are others. The parasite who accepts an unearned favor tries invariably to fake things so as to make it look as if it's his benefactor who is accepting favors. This is always the case when a person moves into someone's house, starts doing housework, then yells that the host exploits him (Monica). The parasite cannot accept a favor as a favor—simply and gratefully, as would happen between equals. The parasite resents the favor because he knows his own motive; it is not a plain favor, or a single incident, or a temporary condition—but his permanent way of living, which he knows to be exploitation. He does not help his host as a return courtesy; he does it to fool himself in his own mind, and to reverse the tables—to claim that the host is indebted to him.

The desire here is not to return a courtesy, but to make the benefactor evil or guilty; the motive is not gratitude, but malice. And it is not even a desire to gain self-respect, except most indirectly and viciously: not through raising himself, but through debasing the host.

In a wider, philosophical sense, this vicious reversal is shown in all the collectivist patter about the great men and geniuses being only the product (or voices, or plagiarizers) of the people (or the nation, or the era, or the race, or humanity). This makes the "common men" the creators or source of everything (in some manner which is never stated, explained, or defined), while the genius is only their creature, their mouthpiece—the robot directed by their power, fed by their "spirit." Now, in fact, the exact opposite is true: the "common men" move and live on the ideas, discoveries, and mental energy of the creators, the originators, the geniuses.

(Perhaps the parasites, the collectivists, are conscious of this—perhaps they actually know and recognize the theme of my story—and those vicious theories of reversal are their answer, their protection. Perhaps John Galt's accusation—and the awakening of the strikers—is what they dread most.)

This parasites' psychology leads to the attitude which *I must blast* above all: *"It is not only your duty to serve the world, but also to suffer for doing it, to be tortured by those you serve, for the privilege of serving them."*

This is what the parasite offers to the creator as the sublime virtue. "Virtue is all you'll have, since you're a hero, aren't you? I'll have everything else."

Translated into the parasite's morality, this is what it amounts to: "I need you, because you're my superior. For that same reason, I hate you. If I can have the satisfaction of torturing you for the advantages you give me, I'll have both satisfactions, the spiritual and the material; I'll be happy—and you'll be truly altruistic. You'll let me exploit you—and absolve me of the moral blame. Evil must be paid for by suffering—so you'll pay for my sin. You'll do the suffering. In permitting me to hate you and torture you, you will save me from the painful knowledge of your greatness and my smallness, of your virtue and my depravity. You will feed both my body and my spirit—at the expense of yours. I am incapable of your kind of happiness and I cannot bear the sight of it, since it is a reproach to me—so you will renounce it for my sake. You are a creature of joy—and I, a creature of suffering. So you will choose suffering—for the sake of letting me have *my kind* of joy, the joy of seeing you in agony. *That* is the true self-sacrifice to an inferior. *That* is real pity. *That* is altruism."

This is *most* important and requires special handling, in dramatized events, not just in implication. (Probably for Galt and "the man of pity.")

*Note on style:* Nothing must be over-detailed; I want it extreme, simplified, stylized, impressionistic—in main, abstract outlines only—like the drawing of a skyline in forms, without details. (Remember the picture of a stylized sky with long, straight bands of clouds.)

# 13

# NOTES WHILE WRITING: 1947–1952

*AR began writing* Atlas Shrugged *on September 2, 1946. This chapter presents the notes she made while writing the novel up to John Galt's speech.*

*I have included about two-thirds of the material from this period. Most of the omitted notes simply outline events in individual chapters, describing what the reader of the novel already knows. I have also omitted repetitive notes and some research on a book,* This Fascinating Railroad Business, *by Robert S. Henry.*

**January 18, 1947**

*Note for last chapter* (philosophical conclusion): The strikers have won, not because the parasites have learned anything or because the parasites have collapsed physically, but because the last of the strikers (Rearden and Dagny) have learned the lesson that Galt wanted to teach the best brains of the world—the lesson of not supporting their own destroyers, and of the creators' nature, function, and proper code. From now on, the exploitation of the best by the worst will never again be permitted by the best.

**January 20, 1947**

*An important point to stress:* blast the fool idea that material production is some sort of low activity, the result of a base "materialistic" impulse—as opposed to the "spiritual realm" (whatever they think *that* is), which consists of some sort of vague, passive contemplation of something or other. Show that material production is the result of and comes from the highest and noblest aspect of man, from his creative mind, from his independent rational judgment—which is his highest attribute and the sole base of his morality.

To exercise one's own independent rational judgment is the essence of man's morality, his highest action, his sole moral commandment that embraces all his virtues. Material production comes from *that*—it requires the *noblest* moral action (independent thought) as its source. It is the result of the highest morality, of the noblest courage, *of the best within man.* (Remember this for the last chapter.)

Never mind the weak little second-handers, of all degrees and variations, who coast on the thinking of the few geniuses, who make a great busy show of a "grossly materialistic" pursuit of *money*, who manage to amass fortunes through the "human," rather than the creative angle, through the Peter Keating–second-hander's–politician's method of using and exploiting *men*, not originating ideas. They are only the scum on the surface, the free riders on the flow of the genius's energy. Who originates the ideas, methods, discoveries which they exploit? They are not the representatives of the essence of material production. They are not its sources. The genius is.

Material production is the result of the *highest spiritual quality* and activity. That the second-handers ride on it, push themselves to the forefront and often grab all the profit, is due to the geniuses permitting it, [which in turn is due to] the acceptance of the moral theory of altruism and the blindness of the geniuses to their own nature and function, to the actual principles of their own existence.

And, in degree, in regard to each particular man involved in material production, he succeeds only to the extent to which he functions on the principles of the creators, on his independent rational judgment; to the extent to which he uses the "social" method and functions on the principles of a second-hander, he fails. (In a free society, he fails personally. As society begins to get collectivized (controlled), he has a chance of succeeding in the narrow sense of keeping his graft, loot or profit—but then, and to the extent of his success in this, he destroys society and the whole economy. Material production is *not* the product of the second-hander and cannot be kept going on his methods and principles.)

Show that the real sources, the spark-plugs of material production (the inventors and industrialists), are creators in the same sense, with the same heroic virtues, of the same high *spiritual* order, as the men usually thought of as creators—the artists. Show that *any* original rational idea, in any sphere of man's activity, is an act of creation. *Vindicate* the industrialist—the author of material production (John Galt, Hank Rearden, Dagny Taggart).

Of course, that cheap snobbery about material production is based on a deeper philosophical error—on the vicious idea of "matter as sin" and spirit as its antagonist. And it's logical that if one accepts that idea (which represents the debasement of man and of the earth), then one considers the activity of preserving man's survival (material production) as low and evil. To be high, one must then starve to death—that's "liberating the spirit."

Tie this to the clear exposition of the fact (as *clear* as you can make it) that the material is only the expression of the spiritual; that it can be neither created *nor used* without the spiritual (thought); that it has no meaning without the spiritual, that it is only the means to a spiritual end—and, therefore, any new achievement in the realm of material production is an act of *high spirituality*, a great triumph and expression of man's spirit. And show that those who despise "the material" are those who despise man and whose basic premises are aimed at man's destruction.

For anyone who gets confused by the spectacle of second-handers "placing the material first"—show that these second-handers are not the creators, but the destroyers of material production. Show that to conquer, control, and create in the material realm requires the highest kind of spiritual activity and the highest type of "spiritual" man.

And, to go to the roots of the whole vicious error, *blast* the separation of man into "body" and "soul," the opposition of "matter" and "spirit." Man is an indivisible entity, possessing both elements—but not to be split into them, since they can be considered separately only for purposes of discussion, not in actual fact. In actual fact, man is an indivisible, integrated entity—and his place is here, on earth. His "spirit" is his mind—his control over the earth.

Incidentally, note that the good industrialists (such as I've met) are high types of men—whereas the artists (allegedly the "spiritual" men) are neurotic or depraved weaklings. The material producers deal in, with and through reason (they have to)—and look at the successes they have achieved. The alleged "men of the spirit" deal in emotionalism and mysticism, in the irrational (by having accepted the irrational or "inspirational" premise)—and look at the sickening state and centuries-long stagnation of men's spiritual life (their philosophies, their morality, their state of misery, futility, and confusion). The industrialists are moral *because* they function on the basis of reason. The artists are the depraved types. (There's the tie of reason and morality.)

**January 22, 1947**

In connection with above: d'Anconia's dollar sign is a symbol of this, and also of the sanctity of the profit motive, of the morality of egoism.

———◇———

For the banker (Mulligan?): he quit because of the squeeze; he was ordered (by law) to give unsound credit to some group of the needy (investment as charity, not on the ground of production, but on the ground of *need*)—and then he would be blamed as a vicious capitalist for the collapse of the bank, for the wiping out of the savings of "the little people, widows and orphans, etc."

**1947**

### Dagny and [Dan] Conway

His acceptance and resigned indifference.

Her indignation—this is worse than Taggart's attitude.

He thinks the decision was right, but on the basis of such morality he has no desire to go on. He says "it's right," but there is no life left in him.

His reasons: The world is in a terrible state and if men can't get together, how will they solve it? The majority's got to decide, it's the only fair way, he had agreed to abide by the decision of the majority, they had a right to do it, but . . .

He could fight nature, but he can't fight this. (She knew that it wasn't James Taggart who had beaten him.)

Her attitude: "Such a wrong cannot be right." "One cannot be penalized for ability." "We can't live in that kind of a world."

It is his honorable attitude, "keeping his word," that makes the outrage possible for the parasites.

This is the good average man up against the morality of altruism. And this is a "real life" example of going on strike.

**February 11, 1947**

[*The following are AR's first notes on the romantic relationship between Dagny and Francisco.*]

Their relationship—like two people on a desert island. Sex as their celebration of life. The complete innocence. They are both incapable of the conception that joy is sin. They exhaust each other—"Isn't it wonderful that our bodies can give us so much pleasure?" His ingenuity at it. She never wore anything but slacks and plain dresses, but she had never been so feminine.

He comes to meet her secretly in New York that winter, once in a while.

The complete secrecy of their affair. Nobody suspects it, not even Eddie. Dagny's reason for the secrecy—her hatred for people's view of sex. Furious indignation that anyone should dare presume to lay down rules about it for her. Contempt for those who consider it sin—no desire to fight them ([or even] grant them the right to discourse about it), only to keep away, not even to brush against them, because she senses something monstrously unclean about them.

**February 15, 1947**

*Note: Creators never act with **pain** as their motive.* This is illustrated by Dagny and Rearden. This is the principle behind the parasite's accusation that people like Dagny and Rearden "have no feelings." *They feel*—and much more profoundly than any lesser person or whining parasite (the parasites neither think *nor* feel)—but they are not run by their feelings, and they are not afraid of pain. Nothing they do is ever motivated by a desire to avoid pain or to be protected against it; they act on the motive of *happiness*, on the desire to get what they want, at any cost, even if pain is part of the cost.

They suffer more than any parasite could ever bear or imagine (except that it's a different form of suffering, it's clean, it doesn't go all the way down nor damn the universe), but they know how to stand pain, and they don't care too much about it, they don't actually give it any thought, they don't include it in their calculations or consideration of cost, they just meet it when it comes, stand it, brush it aside and then go on—*and they win*. They win over all pain, to the happiness which they want and which *they are*.

The parasites *are* motivated by pain. They are the motors and the embodiments of pain. The parasites, in effect, say to the creators as an accusation, as a statement of damning sin and guilt: "But you don't suffer—you're not unhappy—you've never been unhappy."

This is the difference between considering suffering an accident, a temporary exception—and suffering as a basic principle, a major concern, a main motive, suffering as the norm and the nature of the universe.

**March 8, 1947**

*The progression of a man's mental (and psychological) development.*
(The progression of a man's consciousness.)

**1.** He acquires factual knowledge of objects around him, of events,
and therefore concludes that a universe exists and that he exists
(through the evidence given to him by his senses, grasped and put in
order by his reasoning mind). Here he gets the materials to grasp two
things: objective reality and himself, consciousness and self-
consciousness.

**2.** He discovers that he has the capacity of choice. First, he grasps
objects, entities—then that these entities *act*, i.e., move or change. (It
may seem to be almost simultaneous, but actually he must grasp
"entity" before he can grasp "acting entity.") The same [applies to]
himself: first he gains self-consciousness, then he learns that this self
can act (*or must act*) and that he must do it through choice. (Such as:
if he is hungry, he must ask for food, or cry for it, or go and get it,
but he must *do* something, choose what to do, and choose to do it.)
Why does he get the conception of the necessity to act? *That* is his
nature as man—he must preserve his life through his own action and
that action is not automatic; he must preserve his life through *conscious choice*.

The basis of his choice will be self-preservation; this will form
his first standard of values, and give him his first conception of such
things as "*value*" and "a *standard* of value." This is his first conception of "good" and "evil." His physical entity will give him the first
evidence and the start toward it—through physical pain and pleasure.
He feels pain when he is hungry; he has no choice about this; but he
discovers that he must exercise choice if he wants the pain to stop—
he must get food; the food isn't given to him automatically. If he
finds pleasure in eating, he learns that he must choose to act in order
to get that pleasure, and *choose right*.

This is the basic pattern, and as he grows and discovers other
fields of activity, the same holds true: he learns that he must choose
and act on his choice; he forms desires according to the standards of
value he has established (his own pleasure, satisfaction or happiness—this grows in complexity as his mind, experience, and knowledge grow) and he acts to [satisfy] these desires according to these
values.

His first desires are given to him by nature; they are the ones that he needs directly for his body, such as food, warmth, etc. Only these desires are provided by nature and they teach him the concept of desire. Everything else from then on proceeds from his mind, from the standards and conclusions accepted by his mind and it goes to satisfy his *mind*—for example, his first toys. (Perhaps sex is the one field that unites the needs of mind and body, with the mind determining the desire and the body providing the means of expressing it. But the sex act itself is only that—an *expression*. The essence is mental, or spiritual.)

Essentially, and most basically, his standard of value will always be *pleasure* or *pain*, ie., *happiness* or *suffering*, and these, essentially, are: that which contributes to *the preservation or the destruction* of his life. (This applies to his most complex, abstract desires later on.)

(Note: "life" and "self-preservation" are actually synonyms, in the sense that the last is implied in the first. Life is a process, an activity, which the living thing must perform—that is what makes it a living thing. Man must do it consciously—the essence and tool of his life is his mind.)

This stage, then, is the discovery of *choice and values*, i.e., of *free will* and *morality*.

**3.** Now that he knows that he can choose (and must choose), can have desires and can achieve them—he is ready to start forming his conscious convictions about the universe, about himself and about what he intends to do. (These convictions, or basic principles, are already implied in the above process. But now he must state them.)

---

These three steps are the essence of the process. But now man must remain convinced consciously of the validity of what he's learned in that process. It implies: *free will, self-confidence* (confidence in one's own judgment), *self-respect* (the conviction that the preservation of his life and the achievement of his happiness are values, are *good*), and a *benevolent universe* in which he can achieve happiness (if he remains realistic, that is, true to reality observed by his *reason*). If his desires are derived from and based on reality correctly observed—they *will be achievable* in this universe. All his desires come from reality, but the wrong ones are due to his mistakes in judgment; if he realizes the mistake, a contradiction or an inherent impossibility, he will *not* continue to desire these objects; he won't damn the universe for not giving him the irrational or impossible.

Here it must be noted that his self-respect starts as a general axiom, but specifically must be achieved by him. This is in accordance with the nature of man: that part where value is possible, the field of choice, the field of morality, is open to him. First, he must value himself as a man; then his self-respect must be based on living up to the standards of value, the morality, proper to man.

Another interesting point to be noted here: man is given his entity as clay to be shaped, he is given his body, his tool (the mind) and the mechanism of consciousness (emotions, subconscious, memory) through which his mind will work. But the rest depends on him. His *spirit*, that is, his own essential character, must be created by him. (In this sense, it is almost as if he were born as an abstraction, with the essence and rules of that abstraction (man) to serve as his guide and standard—but he must make himself *concrete* by his own effort, *he must create himself.*) Specifically, he is born as an entity: man. But his field of action and emotion is open to his choice. He must survive, preserve himself and achieve happiness through choice, and the choice must be made by his reason, i.e., by his reason learning about and judging objective reality (both the world around him and himself). So he must have a code of values by which he must choose (he cannot choose without values, and he cannot have values where no choice is involved or possible).

The basic standard by which he establishes his code of values is man's survival and happiness. This means man's survival as man, i.e., in a way proper to man, which is the only way he can actually survive or be happy; mere physical, animal survival, at the price of his standards, will give him misery. Happiness, essentially, is the emotion naturally accompanying man's *proper* survival.

Thus man develops his moral code—with the Ideal Man, man at his highest possibility, as the final goal of the code. *Then he will base his self-respect, his valuation of himself, on how well he lives up to that code.*

And that is how he creates his spiritual entity, his character—by the convictions he's made. If they're honest, but mistaken convictions (or, rather, limited), he will be an average good man. If they're honest and correct—he will be a great man. His reason is the tool and the creator of his character. (Here, the degree of his intelligence might affect his stature as a man. But *not* his moral value—that, in proportion to his abilities, is the same for all men.)

But now is where the danger starts. The above are the *basic, essentially needed* convictions. If he loses any one of them, he's done for—he ceases acting according to his nature as a man, he starts going against himself, which means, toward self-destruction. He must not lose the conviction of free will—if he does, he loses the capacity to desire, i.e., to choose a purpose, to act purposefully as a man must. He must not lose self-confidence—if he does, he becomes incapable of thought, judgment or action. He must not lose self-respect—if he does, he becomes incapable of morality, of the desire to be *good*, because he has lost the only possible base of man's proper morality: self-preservation in the most essential sense of the word. (Here, altruism helps to ruin him.) He must not lose the conviction of a benevolent universe—if he does, none of the rest will make any sense.

*And above all, above absolutely all,* he must not lose the commitment to reason—because if he does, *everything crashes.* If he does, he is a screaming pain in the midst of terror and chaos. His essence, as a being, is his consciousness—not his body, because the body without consciousness is just inanimate matter. Whether he has a soul or is a material being with the attribute of consciousness, in either case his *distinctive*, essential attribute is consciousness, *not* matter. *And his consciousness is his reason.* When he renounces that, he has renounced himself, his essence, his nature—and the result can be nothing but horror and self-destruction.

Of course, he cannot renounce reason completely. If he did, he would have to go insane or simply perish. The tricky secret (and *key*) of man's nature is that he can be nothing except reasonable, but he cannot be reasonable automatically, i.e., unconsciously. *He has to be reasonable by a conscious decision or effort of his reason* (and that effort has to be exercised continuously throughout his life—in general, as basic conviction, and specifically, as applied to each concrete instance, moment, event or action of his life).

This is the turning point, the decisive point in a man's spiritual development. This is the point where most men fail. Yes, this mistake is always open to man's correction in later life, since he remains essentially rational, but is merely acting against his nature, therefore he can retrace his steps and go back to the proper conviction. But the correction becomes harder and harder each year, because the further he goes along the road of irrationalism, the more harm he has done to himself and his thinking capacity, the more suffering he has endured, and the more painful and frightening an attitude of honest rationality becomes to him. (He is then afraid of having to damn himself factually, irrevocably, of having to pronounce himself evil without evasions or loopholes.)

The joke of it is that his only essential evil is the irrationalist attitude, and that no crime which he has committed in the past and which he is afraid to consciously acknowledge is as evil as his persisting in irrationalism. It's irrationalism that made his original guilt possible—the guilt and the crime were the consequence of it, but the *irrationalism* was the root and the cause, *the only basic evil*.

The manner in which man remains "irrationally rational" is that he gets caught in his emotional mechanism. *His emotions proceed from his reason*, i.e., from his convictions (and these convictions were made consciously at some time, but may have been forgotten or deliberately evaded), and they proceed logically, following all the implications of his convictions. ([The process is] subconscious and automatic. *The conscious* is the field of free choice, *the subconscious* is automatic; but it is *the conscious* that determines the content of *the subconscious*, the premises which a man has accepted.) So the irrationalist is at the mercy of his emotions, with all the errors, contradictions, conflicts, evil that are contained in them, since they come *logically* (consistently) from mistaken premises.

But the irrationalist holds his emotions (or "instincts," "hunches," "revelations," "extra-sensory perceptions," etc.) above his reason; he fights his reason with them. And of course, he's done for. Whatever he does, he will achieve nothing but suffering, in one form or another, he will always be frustrated and fail in whatever it is specifically that he thinks he wants in his own twisted, self-contradictory manner. His whole trend will be toward suffering and self-destruction, since he is acting against himself, against his own nature.

He will survive, achieve his purposes and achieve happiness only to the extent to which he continues to act rationally, even against his own stated and accepted premise of irrationalism (and he *must* remain rational to some extent or cease to exist altogether). To the extent to which he indulges in the irrational, he is working toward his own misery and moving toward his own destruction. *That* is the contradiction and civil war within him.

The net, total result is still basic misery—because *one cannot be part-rational or unintentionally, unconsciously rational. Here is an issue that demands perfection. No basic or long-range happiness is possible except to a man who is totally, completely, absolutely, consciously committed to reason.*

What most irrationalists do consciously is, of course, to "limit" reason; they don't deny it outright, or at least not often, even in their conscious convictions and statements. But that "limit" or "part-time" is enough to do the damage of basic and complete misery for them (with just a few moments of joy as guilty, uncertain points of relief from the chronic misery). You cannot be "part-insane," just as you cannot be part-pregnant, or part-cancerous, or part-honest, or part-dead. *These are examples of absolutes.*

Without going into greater detail now, I must mention only that the real cause of a man going into irrationalism (and then on to mysticism, altruism, the malevolent universe, second-handedness and all the other spiritual diseases) is *always an act of self-condemnation*, that is, of judging oneself evil by one's own standard of values. The accusation of others will not do it, it might make a man hate others or the universe, but not himself—and that is not so disastrous or dangerous to his future. The teachings or values of others will be only details or contributing factors, but *not* decisive. The decisive act of catastrophe is a man's self-condemnation, i.e., his realization that he has done something which he himself has defined as evil by his own standards of value; therefore he then considers himself as evil.

How can he do that at all, since no man will do that which he actually and completely believes to be evil? *He can do it only by suspending his reason, his conscious rational judgment,* at the time of and for the issue when he commits the action which he later judges as evil. *This* is the essence of the only evil act man can really do—that act of shutting off his conscious rational judgment, which *is not automatic*. (This is a point which I must state in greater detail—but *that's* the heart of the problem of man's morality.)

After this act of original, initial evil, a man [may] proceed to perpetuate that evil, to become an irrationalist—in order not to face his own judgment on himself, since no man can pronounce himself absolutely and irrevocably evil, and continue to exist. Is the way to morality and self-respect open to him? Yes—always—so long as he is alive and sane. But the *only* way is return to a *conscious [policy] of rationality*, to his own essence and nature as man, *to himself.*

### March 22, 1947

*Note* (be sure and use this): the parasites' conception of equality is actually not "to make even," but "*to get even with*"—that is, to get even with a man for the fact of his ability.

### March 29, 1947

*Make use of:* "Clearance," "*Right* of Way," "Stop, Look, Listen" signs. Note that men *must* run to destruction if they ignore the danger signals along the way. One of the obvious danger signals of a civilization's collapse is the falling off of production, of wealth, a falling standard of living, a growing poverty (since the material *does* come from the spiritual and *is* its expression). But men ignore that because, in their spiritual confusion and growing depravity, they begin to take poverty, discomfort and self-denial as *signs of virtue*, as signs of strength or courage or future success (as England is blabbering now). This is quite logical—since the morality of altruism is the morality of death and has to lead to self-destruction.

**April 29, 1947**

The tunnels of TT are like the catacombs of the early Christians in Rome—the power of the spirit hiding from the world that is destroying it while being fed by it, the power of the trains and of the mind that made them, the power of John Galt who has to hide as the lowest, most despised kind of worker there. And the sign of the dollar is like the sign of the cross— the secret symbol of the heroes and martyrs.

**May 31, 1947**

*The strikers' oath:* "I swear by my life and my love of it that I shall never live for the sake of another man or ask another man to live for mine."

**1947**

*Notes for Rewrite of* [ *"The Climax of the d'Anconias"* ]
*Main Problems:*

*Dagny-Francisco romance*—its actual nature and meaning, the build-up to it, the four years when she is his mistress. The nature of her feeling for him, what he means to her—and of his feeling for her.

*Francisco's genius and purposefulness*—incidents to show what he was and where he is going—show him as the kind of man who could not become a playboy—show his religious zeal for d'Anconia Copper—show his worship of purpose and his contempt for drifters. (Particularly, show the period when he is manager of the New York office of d'Anconia Copper, at [age] 20–23. He is as swift and efficient at a business desk as he was at ballgames or tennis. He drives his business as he drove a car.)

Francisco would despise the conventional, the established, the safe, the routine—and look for the new, the difficult, the different, the unusual.

He would despise repeating and memorizing—he would want to think, discover, create. He wants the *created*, not the repeated—he would write an essay on his own ideas, rather than a report on somebody else's thinking, such as an analysis of some classic. It is the accepted, ready-made, arbitrary *standards* that he won't accept. He'll make his own standards.

With all his wealth, he is not interested in ready-made playthings such as gadgets, cars, etc. He wants to *make* things. He wants the *self-made*, not the *ready-made*.

### The two main lines for Dagny-Francisco past:

*For Francisco:* A brilliant, ambitious, violently active, impatient, religiously purposeful, self-willed boy—who *could not* become a drifter.

*For Dagny:* What he represents in her life is the entity of pure joy—the joy of ability.

[*There are few notes on Francisco's character. The explanation seems to be given in a comment that AR made in 1961: "Francisco, more than anyone else, seems to have been Minerva in my mind—he came in ready made."*]

**1947**

[*AR made the following notes for the party scene in which Francisco introduces himself to Rearden.*]

### For Rearden-Francisco:

The essential issue of the strike.

Francisco's approach—the key questions.

Rearden's failure.

*The essential issue is: you* support the parasites, you make it possible for them to destroy you and the world, you are responsible for their actions because you grant them a virtue they don't possess, you don't realize your own importance and their impotence, you act on their terms, not being completely clear about your own.

*Rearden's failure is: his generosity,* he wants to protect lesser people, he grants them virtue—*his over-confidence*, he thinks he can win and produce under any and all conditions—*his vitality*, he wants to live, work, function, ignoring everything around him, thus not seeing that he is his own destroyer. [. . .]

*Possibility:* Dagny sees Francisco as the personification of the kind of gaiety the party could have been. He sees her as truly feminine—what the others can't see. (What *she* wants Rearden to see. Rearden does, of course.)


**July 1, 1947**

For Galt's speech: "What is the objective test of whether a man is a parasite or not, who determines that? Each man himself. If you think that it is proper (or possible) to work under compulsion, to take orders from others, and you feel you would be willing to do it—you are a parasite. If you think that there are no achievements, no distinctions, no ability or genius among men, that one man's work is as good as another's, that all men are interchangeable—you are a parasite who knows nothing about the nature of work. (And you have merely described yourself—and classified yourself thereby.)"


**July 3, 1947**


### Note on Rearden

Incident when his mother wants Rearden to give Philip a job at the mills. Rearden refuses with implacable, icy anger—his mills come first, he will never do *this* for his family. That is precisely what they hate him for. His attitude is that he would give Philip a job only if he deserved it; the fact that Philip is a relative has nothing to do with it. His mother's attitude is that that is what makes him cruel and heartless: if he loved his brother, he'd give him a job the brother didn't deserve, *that* is what she would consider true affection, generosity and brotherhood. If the brother *deserves* the job, there is no virtue in giving it to him—that's just selfishness. *Virtue is to give the undeserved.*


### For Chapter VIII: The Materialists

While Dagny and Rearden battle alone against tremendous public opposition, staking everything they own on their judgment, with rational truth as their only motive—the "writer" (who has talked about the artist's pure, "non-commercial" search for truth, about the artist's spiritual concerns and scorn for the material) is having fits of panic over the future public reception of his latest book, is grabbing every opinion and adjusting the book accordingly, is wondering whether he should make his thesis and ending the exact opposite of what they are now—which would go over better?—and is sniveling about the thousand dollar authentic Mandarin coat now selling for a bathrobe, which he wants.

**1947**

[*AR made the following notes on the scene in which Dagny speaks to Dr. Stadler about the State Science Institute's condemnation of Rearden Metal.*]

### Dr. Stadler

The great mind—and the great conceit; not showoffishness, but the actual conviction that practically everyone else is some sort of vicious, helpless animal. His attitude is: "I could teach them to live so much better than they do. . . . Persuade them? How can I? They have no mind and are not open to reason. There's nothing anyone can do except force them. That's all they understand." ("But I know that I'm right—and I've seen so much stupidity in my life!")

His contempt for industrialists—"Oh, yes, the men who make gadgets and are interested in nothing but the dollar." Contempt for applied science and material production. Yet—he wants unlimited funds and multi-million-dollar cyclotrons. His cynicism: "Oh, no, you can't expect industrialists to support science." ("Who is supporting you now?" "Society.")

He is completely indifferent to the "practical" side of the [State Science] Institute. He is very satisfied with his "abstract" isolation. Dr. Ferris "takes care" of everything—and he prizes Ferris for this reason. (He thinks Ferris is his servant—he doesn't know that it's the other way around.) The Institute was established for Dr. Stadler, on his endorsement and agreement, on the glory of his name. But it is Dr. Ferris who established it, who "put it through" the legislature. Ferris is the "Washington man" of the Institute. ("Washington" leaves Dr. Stadler strictly alone—and kowtows to him as to an idol. So he doesn't think that politicians are "difficult" or "a problem." Does he like dealing with them at all? "Oh, dear me, no—but what can one do in this world? One has to accept some sort of ugliness." (He [prefers] politicians to businessmen.)

He is uneasy with Dagny—he wants to enjoy her visit, to be the brilliant man to an appreciative audience, as he used to be with her—but he can't. There are a few sharp little touches of annoyance, impatience, evasion in his manner. [. . .]

**August 12, 1947**

*Philosophical Note*

If man forms his own character through the basic premises he accepts (his character being the result and consequence of the premises), does this mean that he has no permanent character at all, no fixed entity, since it is subject to and open to constant change? No. *Here* is the permanence of man's entity: those of his basic premises which are *true* cannot change (since premises come from convictions about observed reality); it is only the mistaken premises which are open to change, are constantly challenged by reality and should be changed. The "fluidity" or impermanence of his character corresponds to the number of mistaken premises he holds; to the extent of such mistakes, he lacks "*entity*" or is *not* a complete, perfect, integrated entity, therefore, does not actually *exist* completely. His permanence, his full reality, his *existence* depend upon his *right* premises. The *perfect* man would hold nothing but the *right premises*.

This process is the key to the secret of man's character and of the incompleteness of his existence. This is the process of man creating himself, becoming man—the illustration of: "Being a man is given to him, remaining a man is not." ("Everything is something." Everything that exists *must* be an entity. Physical objects are set as entities by nature. *Only man* has to create himself; his body is only the means; his essential entity is his soul—and that he must create himself. *There* is the god-like aspect of man. What is his starting point, his tool for creating himself? The rational mind. All the rest is only a development of it, a matter of remaining true to his rational mind.)

When I say that a man holds a *true* premise, I mean that he holds it with complete rational conviction, as far as his knowledge goes. Therefore, such a premise cannot be changed in his mind; further knowledge would only amplify it—it cannot contradict or destroy it. The case of a man who had a right premise, then dropped it because of some erroneous new conclusion, is not relevant here: such a case merely means that the man did not hold or understand the right premise, or any part of it, in the first place. My statement here applies only to *actual*, full, rational conviction about a basic premise—not to a psychological illusion of conviction, nor to any sort of "faith," nor to any partially, provisionally accepted hypothesis.

An important point here: the "acting on the most likely hypothesis" rule applies to and is proper only in relation to the specific and the concrete, such as any one person, event or course of action, *but not to basic premises*. In regard to basic premises, no halfway is possible; *anything short of absolute conviction is worthless,* is no conviction at all. (In connection with this, I must define the nature and content of basic premises.)

### Note for Rearden

Both Lillian and Stacey want Rearden to succumb to an affair with a mistress. Their motives and attitudes are basically identical, both being expressions of the parasite, but they are two different variations of the same theme, about equally vicious.

*Lillian* wants to see Rearden's strict moral purity broken, so that she can torture him through his own guilt, so that she can feel the satisfaction of seeing a great man degraded, and so that she can assume moral superiority over him, thus becoming the representative of morality. Therefore, Lillian's game includes an over-stressed, over-grim recognition of morality—in order to hold Rearden through his guilt at having betrayed the moral code.

*Stacey* wants to see Rearden abandoning morality so that she and he can be united like gangsters or criminal conspirators against the moral world, a kind of relationship expressed by a wise wink at each other. She wants him to become immoral in her way, to hold morality as a convenient hypocrisy with which to fool others, but to acknowledge that he and she know better, are wiser than that—in fact, are rotters and satisfied with it. This, in effect, would also hold him through guilt—the guilt of being self-confessedly and boastfully evil. Thus Stacey's scheme includes morality only as the thing to defy; she and Rearden would be bound together, not within and by morality, but *against it.*

Of the two women, Lillian is smarter: she knows that Rearden is essentially great and pure, that his essence cannot be changed, that she can merely make him suffer through his recognition of his own sin. Stacey thinks that sensual indulgence can actually turn Rearden into a rotter, become his essence and make him pleased with, not tortured by, depravity, in the same way that she is.

*It is important to stress* and make clear how wrong both women are: on their malevolent, parasite's premise, they can expect a man's happiness (as represented by sex, its highest expression) to become the means of his degradation, of evil, of torture and of their acquiring power over him. The truth is that happiness (in the real sense of the word) cannot do this and cannot be used in this way. It is and does the opposite: it is both the means and the expression of man's elevation, of his good, his joy, his freedom, *and his independence.*

That is what Rearden learns from his affair with Dagny. Any suffering involved for him in that affair (and only superficially, never tragically or essentially) came only from the fact of his own error about the nature of the relationship and his right to it; it came only from his own ignorance and mistake—*not* from anything done by Lillain or Stacey. Only *he* made his suffering possible—they, the parasites, *could not* make him suffer—and he set himself free of the suffering, when he understood the truth.

*This* *is a very important point*—an important illustration of the theme, of the fact that any evil done to a good man is done only because, and to the extent to which, he permits it. (Rearden permitted it by accepting the parasite's view of morality, happiness, and sex.)

---

*Regarding Rearden and Lillian:* In their sex life, she held her impotence as virtue, his desire as vice. *This is impotence held as superior to life energy.*

**1947**

[*AR prepared the following list of questions prior to visiting three steel companies. Short answers to some of the questions were added after her interviews.*]

### Questions Re: Steel

Regarding Rearden Metal: What qualities would be most valuable in a new metal alloy, besides: tougher, cheaper and longer lasting than steel? Heat resisting.

What would Dagny have to see besides "Rearden's formula and the tests he showed her"?

General description of Rearden Steel mills. Watch for characteristic details.

What sort of tests and research would be done to achieve Rearden Metal (in a general way)?

"Today, the first *heat* of the first *order* of Rearden Metal had been poured." (Do they call it *heat*? Yes. Do they call it *order*? Yes.) Do they pour alloys—is the procedure approximately the same as for making steel, or is it entirely, basically different—and how much leeway do I have on this? Yes, [they pour alloys.]

Difference between mill, foundry and scrap business? (Who manufactures what?) (Mill: sheet steel and plate steel.)

Could the bracelet be made from that poured metal *that same day*? Yes.

Would Rearden Ore be referred to as a "mining company"?

"Rearden's *started rolling the rails*." Yes. "The first *shipment* of rail will get to the site in a few weeks, the *last in six months*." (?) (Time element of order okay.)

Is it *machine tools* they need and lack to make Diesels?

The time schedule for the Rearden rails order: seven months for the whole order—first delivery in two months, second in another two months, last in three months after that. Dagny has him cut last five months to three. (?) (About 300 miles for line up to Wyatt Oil, more for whole line, though not all of track is being replaced.)

What is the proper extra price per ton that Rearden would charge for the rush? (*10%*) What is the price of the best ton of rail now? What would be a steep extra for rush? What has been the increase in cost of steel rail per each decade?

What is the longest credit Rearden would give Dagny on the rail order?

What kind of crane would load rails on flat cars? Would it have a jaw that snaps open and drops the rails? Or a hook, with the rails tied in bunches by chains? Or are rails loaded singly? Overhead crane, rails are tied with chains.

**September, 1947**

[*AR made the following notes on an interview with Carleton B. Tibbets, CEO of Los Angeles Steel Casting Company.*]

The key men in a steel mill are: general manager; superintendent; rolling superintendent. (Superintendent coordinates the melting department.)

U.S. Steel employs 15,000 men in the largest plant; 300,000 men in all their plants.

Rearden's plant would employ about 5,000 to 6,000. Plant would disintegrate in about a month after Rearden leaves.

Example of destructive inefficiency: somebody taps steel too soon, which is known as "taps a cold heat." Examples of looting: selling

cranes, selling rolling equipment. Example of inefficient management: steel is insufficiently purified; this causes "progressive frac-
ture"—steel breaks.

*Oil Pipe Line:*

Would be ordered from steel mills up to size of 12 inches. If larger, it
has to be ordered from a special foundry. Wyatt's pipe line would be
ready in about six months normally, one or two years in present circumstances.

*Suggestions for Rearden Metal:*

Main interest of steel makers at present is heat-resisting steel. Have
Rearden metal be able to stand temperatures up to 3000° (this is
almost the melting point of steel). Present limit is 1800°. Have metal
hold its strength and ductility at the same time. This type of metal
would revolutionize the manufacture of internal-combustion engines.
Elements to use in Rearden metal: molybdenum or vanadium. Both
are rare elements, particularly vanadium. It can be obtained from
only one company in this country. Molybdenum is now used in the
amount of .4 to .6 percent of steel mixture, or 8 to 12 pounds per ton
of steel. Vanadium is now used in the amount of .2 percent of steel
mixture, or 4 pounds per ton of steel.

Main customers of steel mills are railroads, oil companies, building
industries, and a huge number of manufacturing companies such as agricul-
tural implements, automobiles, etc.

**October, 1947**

### Notes on Visit to Kaiser Steel Plant

Site of steel mill [in Fontana, California]: 13,000 acres or about ³/₄
square mile.

Plant was completed in 13 months. First coke ovens were in operation in six months.

Cost of plant: $123,000,000 in wartime. Present value or normal
cost: $35,000,000 to $40,000,000.

Geneva plant built in wartime by government. Cost $200,000,000.
U.S. Steel bought it from the Government for $40,000,000 (about 20

percent of original value). Defense Corporation's return on all its war plants which were sold averages about 17 percent.

Price of steel in East is $50–$55 per ton. Eastern steel costs about $15 per ton more in the West, the difference being the cost of transportation. The Kaiser Company owns an iron ore mine and a limestone quarry in California. It leases a coal mine in Utah and operates it.

*Miscellaneous Information:*

Blast furnaces are usually named after women. The one at Kaiser's is named "Bess" after Mrs. Kaiser and is referred to by the workers as "Old Bess."

The big pipe around the belly of the blast furnace is referred to by the workers as the "Bustle" pipe.

*Possible Technical Trouble:*

Gas explosions—caused by combustible gases, air or oxygen in a confined space and high enough temperature to set it off.

Heat going through the floor of the furnace—this is known as a "breakout." It can happen either to the blast or open-hearth furnaces. It is usually caused by closing the tap-hole improperly.

*Possibilities for Inefficient Management:*

Buying strip coal instead of coking coal—the blast furnace will go cold.

Foreman stops charging coke for six hours—furnace will freeze up.

Foreman feeds nothing but limestone for a whole turn—furnace will become lime-set.

*Possibilities for Looting:*

Selling raw materials; selling pig iron and scrap; selling turning rolls from rolling mills; selling spare tuyeres on blast furnace.

*The Essential Staff of a Steel Mill:*

About 12 percent of the total employees (Kaiser Plant employs 3300 people). The essential jobs are: vice-president in charge of operations; general superintendent; assistant superintendent; department superintendents; department assistant superintendents; general foreman; turn foreman; blower; open hearth melter. There are about 100 men in Metallurgical Department.

**October–November, 1947**

*[AR made brief notes in a memo book while on a train trip from California to New York and back to Cheyenne, Wyoming. On this trip, she*

*interviewed employees of the New York Central Railroad and visited facili-ties of Inland Steel.*]

### Trip to New York

The hood of a black car looks like a mirror and reflects objects ahead and the sky.

The effect of rocks at sunset—a dark gray, flat silhouette of rocks against shadows of mountains which are dark gray and barely suggested.

The mountains. The approach to a small town. The train and sparks at night. The fireflies.

*The mountains in Wyoming.* A base of rock, rising from a green slope, with brush, pines and a smooth green cover that looks like moss rising up on the rock. The moss and brush vanish gradually, and the pines go on struggling up, in thinning strands, till only a few drops of single trees are left, going up. At the top, there is a naked rock, with snow in the crevices. The snow looks as if a handful had been thrown violently into a crevice and had splattered up the sides, in single rays.

The mountain peaks look very close, as if rising a very short distance from the road—until one sees the tiny size of the pine trees near the top.

*A small town* is seen in the distance, rising from the plain, as a solid line of bushy green trees, with roof tops among them—and, rising above trees and roofs, a few round, silver water-tanks that look like huge pearls. The water tanks compete in height with the church spires. The water tanks win.

*A train* moving at night looks like a solid streak of lighted glass—the band of the windows—and a streak of sparks flying above them in the opposite direction.

*The fireflies* rise from the grass at dusk like slow sparks, moving at floating angles, just a bit slower than sparks of fire, and paler—they have a cold, white, metallic sparkle.

*New York skyscrapers* look like solid structures of lighted glass, in the evening, when all the windows are lighted. As it gets later, the buildings assume black shapes again, with only a few lighted windows scattered among them, and an occasional row of vertical lights, like a row of buttons—the lights of a stairwell.

New York skyscrapers in the fog look as if the closest ones can be seen in every detail, but behind a thin blue smoke; in the next row, the details are blurred, simplified to essentials; farther on, the buildings are simplified to mere shapes; and beyond that, they become blue shadows, in faint silhouettes.

*A plain and town,* seen from the height, with the unusual effect of long, straight, thick bands of clouds low in the sky above them, at twilight, so that it looks as if part of the sky were a lake beyond the town, and the clouds were the strip of the other shore.

### Trip back

*The steel mills.* When a heat is being poured, the smoke is semi-transparent, like waves of heat, and the outlines of smokestacks behind it look as if they were shimmering.

There is red smoke, orange-yellow smoke, blue smoke—and thick, rich, satin-lustrous coils of smoke rising out of smokestacks, that look like mother-of-pearl.

There is a great abundance of power lines in steel mills, long, many-stranded bands of wire.

The silhouette of the steel mills in Lorain, Ohio, standing against the sky.

The rust colored water of the river at the steel mills in Johnstown, Pennsylvania.

The odor of sulfur and the constant metallic clatter, like the sound of grinding wheels.

*The approach to Pittsburgh* (on the way east): From the parkways, to the old, vertical houses on steep hillsides, to the slums, with narrow, cobblestone streets—then the sudden view of the river and the blurred silhouettes of skyscrapers—the rise to the triumphant goal and spirit of the place, of the great effort that made it.

*Pennsylvania*—green mountains, some plains, many hills.

*Ohio*—hills and some plains. (The Patrick Henry University should be on a bluff over Lake Erie.)

*Indiana*—flat plains, dull.

*Illinois*—flat plains.

*Wisconsin*—hills in the eastern part, more plains in the west. Wisconsin has a great many *pines*; also some birch trees. The road goes up and down, more than in curves. The road going up a hill rises straight up, almost vertically, before the driver, then lowers as one

approaches, almost as if folding over and lying down like a bridge
being lowered before you.

*Minnesota*—hills in the eastern part, flat, dull plains in the west.

*South Dakota*—flat plains and terribly dull up to the Missouri.
Desert-like hills and plains west of the Missouri. The hills gather,
tighten and grow as one approaches the Black Hills region. Here—
rock and pines. The view from near the Wild Cat Cave—a huge
spread of mountains, green and filled with pines. The pines look
small as weeds. The mountains are slashed in places, in straight, vertical cuts, as if cut to show the layers of rock under the smooth green
cloth covering them.

The view of a lake at sunset: straight, thin, black shafts of trees with
a spread of gold beyond and above them—the sky and the water of
the same glowing yellow color.

(For Galt and Dagny: When he carries her to the town in the
valley, he does not hold her in the impersonal, wholesome manner of
a man carrying a wounded woman. It is an embrace—even though
nothing in his manner suggests it and his face shows no emotion. It is
merely the fact that his whole body is aware of holding hers.)

A line of telephone poles at each side of a straight road going off into
the distance: the poles grow shorter and the spaces between them
narrower, until they become like a picket fence in the distance.

Clouds at sunset, covering the sun: only the edges of the clouds are
like bright fire—against a clear blue sky, with the clouds faintly
grayer, deeper blue; the edges are like a net of thin neon tubes—
or like a map of winding rivers (or a map of railroads) traced in
silver fire.

**November, 1947**

[*AR prepared the following questions for her interviews with personnel
of the New York Central Railroad.*]

How long would it take to lay rails through the Colorado section? How
long from Cheyenne to El Paso?

How much would the San Sebastian Line cost (300 miles)?

Key men of railroad company? Of Operating Department?

Day of operating vice-president?

Who assigns freight cars?

Who supervises the construction of a new line?

**November 22, 1947**

*[The following notes are from an interview with A. H. Wright, vice-president of operation and maintenance for the New York Central Railroad. Describing this interview later, AR remarked: "[Mr. Wright] was seventy years old and retiring, and I remember thinking how shocked he would be if he knew that he would become a thirty-four-year-old woman in my novel."]*

*[Previous jobs:]*
> Yard clerk during the day, filling in as brakeman at night.
> Trained crews and examined men on operating rules in office of train master.
> Assistant train master in largest freight yard (Syracuse, N.Y.).
> Train master on another division.
> Assistant superintendent, then superintendent of N.Y. water and marine operations.
> Assistant general manager of eastern lines.
> General manager.

*Key men:*
> Division superintendents: operating costs and service to the public.
> General manager: coordinates work of division superintendents.
> Engineer of maintenance of ways: maintenance of tracks, buildings and *bridges*.
> General superintendent of motive power and rolling stock.
> Signal engineer: construction and maintenance of all signals.

*Day:* Requests for expenditures and additional help, and matters of discipline of employees. (Half of time on line, the rest in office.)
*Coal*—very crucial. (Burn 600 cars of coal a day.)
[Railroad] ties good for 20 years.
Rails good for 10–12 years.
Rails are moved from high speed track to yard track.
Steel bridges—keep them painted to avoid corrosion—members replaced when corroded or obsolete (in regard to weight of locomotives and trains). Abutments must be watched.
Lay rails: 6–8 months.
Main line—automatic signals.
Side lines—manual signals.

If they went back to manual system, could operate only 10% of
present traffic.
Radio communication between engineering and yard masters,
between engineers and signal men, between front and rear of train.
American Association of Railroads can give arbitrary orders for cars.
Five miles of side-track to reach a mine: $300,000.
(San Sebastian Line should be about $50,000,000.)

---

[*The following notes are from an interview with K. A. Borntrager, manager of freight traffic for the New York Central Railroad.*]

A union proposal to put an engineer and fireman in each unit of a
Diesel.
130,000 employees working for New York Central Railroad, about
1–3% are appointive positions. This small group *are the brains*.
About 5,000 men are under Mr. Borntrager; only about 100–150 are
appointive.
Car Service Department: 300 people, only six to eight appointive
positions. If these men were gone, there would be chaos in two or
three weeks.
Somebody has to coordinate all the machine records—unless somebody can do it, a machine economy *cannot function*.
*For construction:*

Cannot get drilling steel, explosives. Steel came—they put in
wooden stringers for missing pieces. They have rocks to blast—
heavy equipment wears out very fast, many replacements are
needed—they have no drills—equipment wore out—they have to
resort to chipping, hand-work. The brains saved money, now it will
cost much more. Have rails, but have no specialists to build frogs
and switches.

(Unions are always trying to encroach on appointive positions—constant, silent battle. [Management] has the right to appoint
the station agents (freight and passenger); unions claim that positions
are not big enough, an ordinary man from the ranks could do it on
seniority basis. Mr. Borntrager would run a railroad better if he could
appoint twice as many people. Would like to take young man and
raise him from position to position (from the ranks), but he cannot
do it.)

*Signals* are very intricate mechanisms; couldn't get *copper*—so they use steel wire; signals fail. Spend a horrible amount of money—and get a makeshift thing when you get through.

**November 25, 1947**

*Notes on Visit to Inland Steel [In Chicago, IL]*

Railroad rails are shipped in gondolas. They are picked up by an overhead crane (magnetic), six to ten at a time, and deposited on cars inside a building. Walls of building can be open.

*Process of rail making* (approximately): Iron from blast furnace (*"caste"*)—steel from open hearth furnace (*"heat"*)—steel is poured into ingot molds—ingots go to blooming mill and are rolled into billets (for rails and structural shapes) or slabs (for sheet, plate, etc.). Final shape of rails is done by three sets of rolls (mills). (The shape is the rolls themselves.)

*Steel heat:* the metal is *white*, not red or orange. It has no suggestion of flame, only of a blinding white liquid. There is a violent red glow in the rising smoke—a shower of white sparks—and bits of metal that fall on the floor and start flaming. When the ladle is full, you see nothing but black and white, a blinding white liquid boiling and running over, spilling with a kind of wasteful, arrogant prodigality. The white rivulets on the side of the ladle turn to a glowing brown, then to black metal, like icicles, and start crumbling off. The slag in the slag-ladle on the side starts crusting over in thick, uneven, brown ridges, like the earth's crust. Small flames appear in the cracks. As the crust thickens, two or three craters appear, with white liquid metal boiling slowly.

A steel mill *rolls* steel; a foundry *casts* it (in sand molds).

*Coke ovens.* The coke is pushed out like slices of toast. It crumbles like red-hot walls, in layers and in sudden cracks.

———◇———

*From Mr. Fred Gillies (general manager):* The attempted embargo on freight cars for deliveries to steel plants—by the government. Excuse—they do not empty cars fast enough. Reason—bureaucrats

want freight cars to ship coal to Europe. (Stopping the country's production for the sake of looting.)

A plant was built by the government during the war, at a cost of
25 million dollars. Twice the capacity that was ever needed or used
(six open hearth furnaces—only three were used). Company that
wanted to buy another such plant was refused permission by government (anti-trust law), so they did not bid on this one. No one has bid
on plant. It is now used by the government as a warehouse for war
surplus—clothes, candy, etc. (!)

Diesel freight engine with four motor units weighs 464 tons.
Tractive force when starting—220,000 pounds.
Average load of boxcars—27 tons. (Weight of boxcar—20 tons.)
One-hundred-car trains would weigh about 5,000 tons.
*Bridge:* 1,650 feet—38,000 tons of steel.

### December 19, 1947

Have instance of rotten, inherited capitalist who *wants* to be nationalized—with payment, of course. He doesn't want the responsibility of running his business, he wants to make a profit on the government paying him
off at more than the business is worth, and he uses political pull to get that.

———

The kind of knowledge, judgment and intellectual initiative which is
needed for production (the article on oil in the Texaco magazine)—and the
bureaucrats' method of evasion, double-talk, avoidance of the responsibility
of the clear-cut and the specific. *Show how and why production cannot be
achieved by such method.*

### January 5, 1948

*Notes for Labor Rules*

Unions forbid their members to run more than a certain number of
miles per month. Why? To keep jobs for more men than is necessary?
To whose advantage is that, except the union bosses who get extra dues? At
whose expense is this done? At the expense of the abler men of the union,

who have no right to advance, no right to work as long and make as much as they otherwise would have.

If we suppose that all the members are equally able—still, some are extraneous and should go into other work. This system only has the effect of collective, organized mediocrity—it provides that no man in the profession is going to work harder than the others, so that all will be kept at a certain level of effort and income—I suppose on the assumption that it makes them less subject to the dangers of change of job with the growth of progress and the need of fewer men in their profession. This is organized stoppage of progress—as is any case where effort and ability are artificially stopped or limited. Also—this keeps the better, abler, more ambitious men out of the profession.

Does this really protect them in their jobs, even the mediocre men? Or does it create artificial dangers of protracted unemployment? And, of course, it holds their living standard down, by stopping general progress. Actually, industrial progress which cuts jobs in one old line, creates more of them in several new lines. The readjustment or transition should not be difficult or involve periods of unemployment—*in a free economy* (because it is *gradual*). [Union policies are] instances of the savage or animal "range of the moment" psychology in an industrial civilization that functions on the *long range* principle of the intellect.

*Unions are organized **against** the better members of their own profession.*

(For pay rates of railroad labor, see *This Fascinating Railroad Business* [by Robert S. Henry], pp. 405–407.)

### For Labor Troubles (Chapter XI)

Pat Logan and other good engineers do not get any advantage out of the John Galt Line—the higher speed only reduces their working time and they have to loaf the rest of the month, while unemployed engineers from the closing railroads flock to get part of this work, part of the new, fast runs.

The unions immediately raise the costs of the operation of the John Galt Line, when the economy of operation is so desperately needed.

With the shortage of engines and cars—*they demand to limit the length of trains,* thus requiring more engines and cars, without making full use of the ones available.

Management and inventors do everything in their power to exercise their genius to *raise the productivity* of employees. The employees do everything in their power to hamper and prevent this—yet demand raised pay.

Union's demand for engineer and conductor for the "guest" line in case of emergency when train is routed over tracks of another line.

*Demand for extra men on each Diesel unit.*

Extra *day's* pay for breaking a train in half and taking the two sections over a hill individually—in mountainous country.

Union's excuse for limiting train length—*the caboose jerks*!! In the case of passenger train—the "poor conductor" has too much work!!

(See the "Railway Progress" article for quotes of union leaders' attitude toward "*those locomotive giants*" and for examples of paying employees twice for work not done.)

The added expense cuts the slim profits of the stockholders who need their own money desperately—show this concretely, as one of the results of what happens when the John Galt Line does not pay. (This leads to the ruin of the Colorado stockholders—the first pressure is on Ellis Wyatt.) (*Ted Nielsen*—no Diesels.)

———

The "*limitation of ability*": Rearden is forbidden to produce more than Orren Boyle is able to produce. The reason: "Rearden is destroying Boyle's market and chance at a livelihood." (Same principle—Pat Logan and the bums who cannot run a big train, but Logan's opportunity to run more trains is stopped.)

At the same time—the "Fair Share Law": Rearden has to supply everybody, while he is not allowed to produce. Here—the rise of Mouch, who shrugs when the contradiction is pointed out to him: "Everything is a contradiction—we act on the expediency of the moment." Mouch *wants* Rearden to fail, so that all business can be nationalized.

**January 17, 1948**

The judge on strike in the valley: "I was supposed to be the guardian of justice. But the laws they asked me to enforce made of me the executor of the vilest injustice ever perpetrated on earth."

———

The legend of Prometheus who took the fire back, until men called off their vultures. (It is probably Francisco who tells [Dagny] this.)

**January 30, 1948**

*For Chapter IX: The John Galt Line*

The reaction of the public as it watches the progress of the John Galt Line: *those who sympathize and admire; those who are honestly neutral* and watch with a growing sense of sympathy, not knowing its real reason and not knowing anything about the business or technical part of it; *those who hate it and want it to fail,* in interested malice, like Orren Boyle, or in the pointless malice of the men of destruction, like James Taggart, Bertram Scudder, Philip Rearden; but *the most vicious ones* (?), the truly evil, are *those who watch with cautious interest, the safe-players and middle-of-the-roaders*, who want somebody else to take the risks, then get ready to grab the benefits.

*James Taggart's attitude* must be shown clearly: when things go well, he is not happy about it, he is insidiously sarcastic; when things go badly, he is scared, but there is a strange undertone of gloating pleasure in him at the same time. This last, without his conscious admission to himself, is his gratification of his real desire—the wish for destruction.

*Philip Rearden's attitude* must be shown: he is not involved like Taggart, but his essential attitude is the same. In his case, it is the plain joy of seeing Rearden fail—then he is not the only failure, his great brother can fail, too, the great brother isn't as great as he thinks, etc.

**February 8, 1948**

*Note for Galt's Speech*

The whole issue in the world is between the men who want to work under compulsion and the men who don't. Well, those of us who don't work as slaves leave the rest of you free to do it; go right ahead, organize any kind of slavery for yourselves among yourselves. But *don't* try to impose it on us and don't expect us to accept it. We don't need you. We don't seek to force you—we rest on the principle of voluntary relations among men. But *you*—by your very premise—admit that you need us, since you find it necessary to use force against us. Well, it can't be done.

And as for those who wish to rule, who think they don't want to work under compulsion, but want to exercise compulsion upon others to make them work—the same applies to them. If they think work can be done under compulsion, they know nothing about the nature of work. If they find it necessary to use compulsion on others, it means that they need something from those others. Well—*we* refuse it to them. They think they want to force their inferiors. What about us—the men of ability, their equals or superiors? Do they think they can force us? And as to those they think are inferiors, what is the standard when force is involved? If they believe that they cannot deal with a man's intelligence, because he hasn't any, force will not give it to him. If, by their own definition, *they* are the men of intelligence, what do they need from the stupid ones and what do they fear?

*Chapter IX: The John Galt Line*
*The Ride*

*The sense of movement—and the achievement it represents.*
*Dagny's feeling—the sense of achievement and triumph.*
The overall mood—the real kind of joy. ("It is so easy—and so right!")
The philosophical meaning—life is motion, the essence of man's life is the achievement of a purpose he has chosen, and any purpose of man can be achieved only through his reason.
Dagny thinks of Nat Taggart and the initials on the first train ever to cross the continent. This is the first new Taggart Line or venture in many generations.
*The people gathered to watch the train* (on hills, on city station platforms)—as in the old days.
*The guard of honor along the way.*
*Dagny and Rearden:* The physical sensation is the same as that of the ride: the ride is physical, but its only meaning is spiritual, the physical sensation of pleasure in the flying speed through space is given only by the spiritual knowledge of what made it possible, of one's achievement. The feeling of: "*I* am flying here—and *I* made it."
Dagny feels tense—and easy in tension, like the work of Pat Logan. She feels suspended over life as the engine is over the rails.
Dagny and Rearden in the motor units. Dagny thinks of the intelligence these motors represent—again, the physical as the shape of the spiritual. The feeling of: "Don't let it go!" She wonders why she feels that *this* is threatened.
The flight across the bridge.
The arrival at Wyatt station.

[*The following notes were made for the scene in which James Taggart and Cherryl Brooks meet for the first time. The scene immediately follows the success of the John Galt Line, and conveys Taggart's attitude toward this success.*]

### For: James Taggart and Cherryl Brooks

Show that Taggart's attitude is a total dead-end, the hatred of that which he himself needs for survival, the hatred of his own gain or advantage—the *real paradox*. This has to be the advance notice of his final scene, of the full revelation that the parasite functions on the principle of death.

*Cherryl's* attitude in this scene is trust and naive admiration; she feels encouraged, uplifted that a man like Taggart finds her of interest or value; she thinks he sees something good in her. *Taggart's* attitude toward her is contempt—contempt for a person so low as to admire *him*; yet he wants the admiration—and he knows that it can come only from someone who is low; he would fear any better sort of person. That is why he hates Cherryl's later attempt to rise.

The paradox is that he wants her admiration to be sincere—that is what attracts him to Cherryl—he would not want the flattery and pretense of a designing gold-digger, and he would recognize that as a lie. He wants the good (sincerity) from and for an evil (from stupidity, for his rottenness)—and *there* is the "moral blackmail" or exploitation of the good against itself: he wants the advantage of a real virtue (sincerity) for the satisfaction of his rottenness, he wants good in the service of evil, he wants to use and hurt Cherryl by means of nothing but her own virtue, not by means of any of her bad qualities (hurt her—because it is deceit and fraud that he is putting over on her). He wants the satisfaction of a *real* admiration for virtues which he does not possess—he wants a spiritual reward, unearned—he wants the spiritual, moral "something for nothing"—and the "something" in this case has to be real, while nothing about him is.

That is why their relationship leads to tragedy. Good cannot come from evil; Cherryl's [admiration comes] not from stupidity, but from ignorance, so Taggart's scheme could not work; she had to begin to see the truth. Her horror is the discovery that he has a desire to keep her low, to have her rotten, not to let her improve or rise—that he loved her, not for her value, but for her rottenness, that *that* is what he saw and sought in her. She sees the horror of "love as an answer to evil," instead of "love as an answer to value"—which is the whole essence of man's need of love. In their marriage, what pleased him was her inferiority, which made him superior and magnanimous by comparison. He lost his interest in her when she lost her inferiority. She realizes that he wanted his "love" for her to be alms—he did not want her to deserve it, to *earn* it. (*There's* another perverted "balance"—real "disinterested," "rewardless" altruism—he wanted something unearned from her, and he wanted her to get something unearned from him. The reality of something *earned*, of a real virtue or a *real value* and "spiritual payment or exchange," was intolerable to him, it smashed his whole fraudulent structure of emotions and relationships. And here is an example of Taggart's "death principle"—he cannot tolerate any *value*; but the basis of life is search for and achievement of *values*.)

In contrast to the relationship of Dagny and Rearden, James Taggart's [feeling for] Cherryl is not love as an answer to and reward for value, but the ghastly perversion which is love as alms—love as a "looking down"—love, not for value, but for its absence—the essential pattern of any unearned love, such as "love of humanity," love as pity, as mercy, as anything but *justice*. (Love as justice is essentially admiration—*and nothing else*.)

---

In their subsequent meetings, James Taggart takes pleasure in stressing his unhappiness, in whining—because he knows that Cherryl cares and feels concern. She is the first person who has ever really cared about what he feels, who doesn't want to see him suffer—so he enjoys making her suffer when he whines and complains. His motive here is an ugly, twisted mixture of sadism and, at the same time, appeal for her pity. His own feeling for her is based, in a sense, on pity—since he looks down upon her; yet, at the same time, he wants her to feel pity for him, for his suffering—which means, in effect, to look down upon him.

### July 5, 1948

Have an example (later) of how Taggart uses his "Washington" power—what it consists of. Some ghastly little bureaucrat has the crucial power to decide some tremendous issue (the power is his accidentally, not intentionally, through the sheer complex stupidity of the laws and the set-up)—and he decides it in Taggart's favor for some such consideration as a thousand dollars and a dinner at a nightclub with "important people." The results of his decision involve billions [of dollars] of other people's wealth, are disastrous to Rearden and to the economy of the whole country. (This may be used with regard to the moratorium on brains.)

**October 18, 1948**

[*The following deals with Rearden's anniversary party.*]

### Main Point of Party Scene

*The guilt of the creators* is that they don't claim moral value, moral superiority, and moral sanction.

*One of the causes of it*—generosity: the reluctance to rub it in, to remind the weaker ones of their weakness; the belief that the weaker ones know it anyway and are grateful; the benevolence of over-abundance, the pleasure of helping others to enjoy life; the belief that the weaker ones do enjoy life and *are* on the moral standard of loving life, ability and greatness; the living power of strength, which respects living human beings and leaps in to eliminate suffering anywhere, almost automatically.

*The result*—the creators are the ones who suffer, who permit the parasites to become their torturers, who make it possible for the parasites to destroy everything sacred to the creators, to hamper the creators' work and function, to block the creators' way, to destroy all the things the creators live for, to spread and commit evil, and finally to destroy the creators themselves. This is the "penalizing of virtue" and the "torture of the best by means of the best within them." The parasites have no weapon—except the creator's own moral virtue turned against him. May God damn every man who uses another man's virtue to his detriment, as a means of *harming* the victim.

*The proper course*—not to support or tolerate any man who is not on the creators' moral standard. To define that standard and then follow it ruthlessly, with total consistency, in every aspect of one's life. To make no allowances and permit oneself no pity. To give nothing *unearned* to anyone, in any form—not physical and most particularly *not spiritual*. Neither financial alms nor *undeserved* affection. *Self-interest* must be present in one's every action.

(If Rearden has no selfish interest in Lillian, he *must* leave her; never mind what she feels or why. If Rearden does not approve of Philip's way of living, he *must not* support him. Even if Philip were struggling to work, Rearden must not give him loans or help, *unless* it is on a real business basis, that is, unless Rearden can actually get a profit from the loan. Then it would help them both. *Not* otherwise. *Not* if Rearden does it *only* for Philip's sake. This is the crime of *selflessness*. And here is the outline of the *"trader principle."*)

Since the basis of the creators' morality is the principle of *living*, they commit the greatest moral sin possible to them when they become "their own executioners," i.e., when they furnish the means for their destroyers to destroy them.

The creators must understand the basic difference between themselves and the parasites: the creators are on the life principle, the parasites are on the principle of death. The creators' final, overall purpose is the continuation of human life (one's own, and, as secondary consequence, *all* human life, since there is no conflict or contradiction here); the parasite's final, overall purpose is destruction and death (*not* a "pitiful, inept attempt to live," which would deserve the stronger man's help—but *actually* the intention to destroy oneself and others, to destroy everything that constitutes life, every form of pleasure and happiness first of all, and, as close second, every form of virtue, value, competence, greatness).

———◇———

When the bastards preach that "virtue suffers in this world," they *do* mean it, though not in the way it sounds. In *their* world, virtue *does* suffer and is meant to suffer—the *real* virtue, the virtue of competence; while their phony altruist virtue, of course, fails and suffers in relation to physical success—and this gives them ground for damning this earth, for considering it evil. So the result is that the truly virtuous, competent man is made to feel guilty, to feel that his success is evil, to suffer spiritually and morally—while the altruist makes a glory of his own failure and appropriates moral satisfaction (which he can't enjoy, just the same).

———◇———

[*The following dialogue between a businessman and Francisco was cut from an early draft of the party scene.*]

"I mean, is it necessary to hurt anybody's feelings? There's some truth to whatever it is you said. On the other hand, there's some truth to what Jim Taggart says. Jim's got a pretty decent record of public spirit and service. What I say is, do we have to go to extremes?"

"To extremes of what?"

"Of anything."

"No, we don't have to. They'll come to us."

"Who?"

"The extremes."

He walked off, leaving the businessman staring after him.


**October 30, 1948**

*To think over:*

Ragnar Danneskjöld—doesn't he impede plot? Is he useless to plot—or can he be integrated better?

*Direct line from beginning to—destruction of Ellis Wyatt— destruction of Ken Danagger—destruction of Rearden.*

Will the "rations on Rearden Metal" and the "Miracle Metal" law clash—as repetitions? [*Added later:*] No.

Will the closing of the John Galt Line clash with the closing of the Minnesota Line? [*Added later:*] No.

*Make economic outline of story line.* (Plot key points of destruction—key figures vanishing and the effect it has.)

Decide on new role for Ragnar Danneskjöld. [*Note added the next day:*] The Robin Hood who robs the humanitarians and gives to the rich.


**January 11, 1949**

*Key Points of Personal Story*
*Part I*

*Dagny-Rearden romance.* His discovery of the nature of sex, the relation between body and spirit.

*Rearden-Lillian* (and *Rearden-parasites*): his helplessness without a sense of moral sanction, his vulnerability when he accepts any part of the parasites' code.

The rise of Wesley Mouch.

Francisco's speech on "money is the root of all good." (Rearden-Francisco)

*The finding of Galt's engine—Dagny's quest—Hugh Akston* in the diner and the dollar-sign cigarette.

Dagny sees the flaming oil fields as *Wyatt quits.*

Dagny waits in anteroom while "some man" is in Ken Danagger's office. *Danagger quits*—his talk about excursion trip around Manhattan Island.

The actions of Ragnar Danneskjöld.

Colorado division parasite (later responsible for tunnel catastrophe) getting position as result of minor Taggart-Boyle-Mouch deal—*after* good superintendent quits.

Another major loss by d'Anconia Copper.

*Lillian Rearden learns of Rearden's infidelity*—the subtle torture that follows.

Francisco learns of Dagny-Rearden romance.

*Dagny quits* [because of] "moratorium on brains" and escapes to the country.

Dr. Stadler and Dr. Floyd Ferris.

*Rearden and "Miracle Metal."*

The scene with [Rearden and] Francisco at night—saving the furnace.

Dan Conway (when Dagny needs him).

Rearden–Ragnar Danneskjöld.

Eddie Willers and the worker: Eddie mentions Dagny's hide-out.

Dagny-Francisco in the country, news of tunnel catastrophe. (Tie reasons for rush of train to the parasites—their "deals" and their inability to take the initiative on anything, their evasion of responsibility and following of routine.)

Rearden-Francisco: the slap in the face.

Dagny's last attempts to save TT—news of car manufacturer quitting—she has to go after him.

Rearden–Mrs. Rearden when she discovers his affair with Dagny.

Dagny packing; Eddie sees Rearden's dressing-gown.

Eddie and the worker: Eddie betrays the purpose of Dagny's trip and her affair with Rearden.

The "frozen train ride"—Dagny and Owen Kellogg—her flight after car manufacturer—the crash.

## Part II

The valley. Dagny and Galt. Dagny and Hugh Akston, Richard Halley, Midas Mulligan, the judge, and all the others.

Dagny's break with Rearden.

Dagny's search for Galt—the empty valley. (?)

The blackmail of Rearden by the bureaucrats—Dagny discovers it.
The affair: James Taggart–Lillian Rearden. Cherryl's suicide.
Francisco loses the last of the d'Anconia fortune.
Rearden-parasites, Rearden-family. He quits.
Dagny–John Galt in the terminal tunnels.
The broadcast—Galt's speech.
The temptation of Galt: through love—Dagny. She betrays him, his arrest. Further temptations: through pity—(Eddie Willers?); through fear—Dr. Stadler; through "ambition"—Mr. Thompson; through vanity—the banquet.
Dagny quits—joins Francisco on street corner, then Ragnar Danneskjöld; plan to save Galt.
The torture of Galt. Taggart's realization.
The collapse of the Taggart Bridge. (And the death of Dr. Stadler.)
The rescue of Galt, the flight over New York as the lights go out, the world in ruins.
Eddie Willers and the last ride of The Comet.
The valley—the rebirth—"We're going back."


### Key Points of Destruction (Economic outline)
### Part I

Destruction of Ellis Wyatt. (No transportation. Dagny limited on trains and speed. Rearden limited on production—and ordered to "give a fair share to everybody." No pipe line for Wyatt—and no other railroad.)
Destruction of Ken Danagger. (No oil for his power plants. No Rearden Metal girders.)
Destruction of N.Y. utility man—no coal, oil, or copper wires.
Another d'Anconia disaster.
Death of Colorado and closing of John Galt Line.
The moratorium on brains ("Miracle Metal" and Slave Labor law).
Total controls and enslavement of ability. (Rearden Metal is taken over because "Rearden was not able to supply everybody's need.")
The tunnel catastrophe.
Car manufacturer quits.
(Show, each time before a key figure quits, that the burden of impossible conditions is switched to *him*.)

## Part II

Freights cars sent to "soybean project" (Cuffy Meigs and Wesley Mouch). "Transportation pull."

[*Added later:*] Project X.

Destruction of Minnesota farmers; Rearden's losses.

The end of d'Anconia Copper (indirectly caused by Rearden?).

Destruction of Rearden. (Rearden is asked to sell steel as cheaply as Boyle does—and Boyle has government subsidy. The squeeze—and he quits.)

(After Rearden quits—"temporary nationalization" of everything, for "emergency.")

Decision to close Michigan Line—panic—riots.

The broadcast—John Galt's speech. (Here—proof of why "planning" won't work with "good" men—*good* men don't work that way.)

Galt's arrest and torture—and liberation.

The collapse of the Taggart Bridge.

The end of New York.

The last ride of The Comet.

The valley—and the rebirth.


### Additional Notes

*Things to integrate into the main story:*

The romance and marriage of Taggart and shop girl (later, her suicide).

The progression of *Dr. Stadler* toward the destruction of the mind. (And the climax of Dr. Stadler's course.)

*Ragnar Danneskjöld* ("I do not accept your morality, nor loan you parts of mine.")

The rise of *Wesley Mouch*—then of *Cuffy Meigs*.

More participation of *Francisco d'Anconia* in the events of destruction.

The absence of *Hugh Akston* and its effect on the despair of good men like Eddie Willers—the gray, stagnant, flameless mood of people—the confusion and hopelessness. (Specific illustration.)


**January 13, 1949**

*From Chapter XI:* Rearden cannot deal successfully with the parasites—he is disarmed by his guilt. He thinks: "They're evil—but so am I. Who am I to cast the first stone? . . . Don't think of it. Just work. Work harder. Don't look around you." (If he were certain of their total, inexcusable evil—and of his own righteousness—he would have smashed them, or died in the attempt; and he would have won.)

**February 21, 1949**

*Dagny-Rearden Vacation*

They stop at small hotels or sleep in the woods. They talk little. But they drive in silence and can talk to each other in the middle of a train of thought—"gloating" about the John Galt Line, or plans for the future. They are enjoying, "assimilating" their achievement—and "getting charged" for new journeys ("because joy is one's fuel"). Rearden's self-centered enjoyment: the way he carries her across a stream, the way he breaks a branch out of their path, the way he makes a fire. The emphasis is not on the views they see, but on *their* seeing it. The point is their active estimate of value; if a tourist sees something without a judgment of value and an emotional reaction of his own—what's the point of gazing at things? People are willing to be mirrors or blotters; but not Rearden—*he* is a ray of light, bringing things into sight and meaning. His manner of comment is always what can be done—or what one can learn from what has been done—always the *active*, purposeful reaction.

They sleep together in a ravine, under the remnant of a trestle. She thinks that this is an *underground* honeymoon, and wonders why it has to be "underground." No, it is not an accident of his being a married man, of his having first chosen the wrong woman—she senses dimly some connection between their secret wandering and the desolation of the country around them.

The slovenly auto court landlady—who sneers at them because she knows that they enjoy sex (that they are held together by nothing but pleasure) and because they have a good, expensive car. The denunciation of sex, of pleasure, of *self*-indulgence—and of the rich and the industrialists at the same time. Both have a common root.

Dagny realizes (in indifferent wonder) that she and Rearden are expected to feel guilty. People look at them as at enemies.

**March 10, 1949**

*History of the "Twentieth Century Motor Corporation"*

The purpose of every step of this history is to show the futility of men possessing material means, if they do not have the mind to know how to use them.

(This is the answer to the whining attitude of: "If I only had the money, or the factory, or the movie studio, etc." or "It isn't fair that one guy inherits a factory—nobody gave *me* a factory . . . etc.")

The parasites (the second-handers incapable of independent judgment, of new rational connections) own an inexhaustible means of wealth in the Motor Company—*Galt's motor*—but they do not know what to do with it, and so it doesn't do them any good. With the means—property and equipment—of the best motor company in existence, the parasites can achieve nothing but ruin. This answers the fools who think that they'd do wonders if only somebody would hand them the tools of achievement. It is not the *tools* that achieve. And the man with the mind capable of using the tools will *earn* his own tools.

While showing the above, in the history of the motor company, show also the kind of motives, morals, ideas, and human characters who make the "something-for-nothing, give-me-a-chance" attitude (and actions) possible.

*Also:* show the savage, "range-of-the-moment" irresponsiblity of those who think that making money is a matter of speculation, of putting something over on somebody, of exchange without production—the parasites who think that wealth is a matter of grabbing a material possession and palming it off on somebody fast, not realizing that the profit they thus make (on the re-sale of the factory, for instance) is made possible only by someone being a *producer*. When there are no producers, the material wealth is worthless. The "short-range" savage may think: what the hell, *he* got away with it—but did he? And can we have a society geared to giving a chance to these parasites? Will such a society remain productive long? (In a *free* economy, the Reardens sweep these types out, just as productive citizens eliminate criminals who are then only "marginal"; a controlled economy eliminates the Reardens and breeds the "short-range" savages or speculators of the moment.)

(A proper trader is one who performs a real service of distribution of goods, a service *needed by the producers* of the goods. Such a trader takes intelligent risks [based on] his knowledge and long-range judgment. A speculator functions on the confusion or trouble of the moment, without plan. No, they cannot be differentiated by any law. The objective reality of their performance, in a free economy, builds up the first and destroys the second. The trader creates his own function where his services are needed, where no one else is doing this particular job. A speculator functions when proper exchange and proper traders are restricted by force. As example: a blockade-runner is a trader; a black-marketeer who pays off the bureaucrats, who is their representative or partner, is a speculator.)

**March 25, 1949**

### Notes Regarding the Welfare State

(For the scene with Dagny and the old worker from the Twentieth Century Motor Corporation, and for the general theme.)

Under capitalism, the motive and basic principle throughout the whole system is *the positive good*, and human ability. A worker works so that he himself will make a profit, the boss will make a profit, and the customers who have earned the price of the product will buy it. The motive throughout is reward (satisfaction), an *earned* reward, and the standard of value is *ability*.

Under a collectivist system, the basic principle is suffering and incompetence. A worker works to *contribute* something to the collective—not for his own profit, reward, or satisfaction. His boss is not supposed to make a profit. The customer is not supposed to be the man who has earned the price of the product, but the incompetent or disabled who *needs* it. The purpose of the whole society is to work for and be inspired by the incompetent and the disabled. If the goods produced are supposed to be a value—then it is suffering and incompetence (the "death qualities") which are rewarded, not success and ability, not the "life qualities." It's not only that the "life qualities" are penalized; it's that the "death qualities" are made the inspiration, goal, and motivation of the whole society.

Also, every man in such a society is a beggar, whether he earns or doesn't earn his "share." A worker simply gives his effort—as alms to society. Whatever he gets in return is alms given to him by society (by other workers), since he has no claim or *right* to a reward; he does not *sell* his product, he *gives* it. It is not even supposed to be his to give; he has no property rights to his product or to himself, and therefore the payment he receives is not *his* in the proper sense of a salary earned, it is a gift, a *charity* from society. (His *production* gives him no right, but his *need* does. He may demand that others take care of him, but he may not take care of himself. Failure, misery, incompetence are to his advantage and give him a claim; effort and ability give him nothing.)

*Re: "From each according to his ability, to each according to his need."* In a *normal* human being, *need and ability are exactly balanced.* A normal man has the capacity to produce everything he needs—if he does not copy or borrow his desires from others, but stays within the bounds of his own mind, i.e., if he is not a second-hander who defines his needs or *desires* by envying (or wishing to impress) the men of greater ability who can produce more than he can—and if he lives in a free, capitalistic economy. (Besides, in a free, capitalistic economy the better minds help him to produce more than his own ability could produce if he were left entirely to his own devices.)

The only instance when a man's needs exceed his ability to satisfy them is the state of illness—the sick, disabled, or insane; i.e., the abnormal.

*Can society be geared to and ruled by the standards of the abnormal?* Should normal men exist for the sake of the abnormal? Should the abnormal be the goal, inspiration and *first concern* of the normal? Can healthy men live on the regime of a hospital?

(Children, of course, cannot satisfy their needs either. But *that* is what constitutes being a child, what distinguishes a child from an adult. Childhood is growth into, preparation for, adulthood—for the state of independence, i.e., a state in which one *can* satisfy one's needs. Should society be geared to and ruled by the standards of the incomplete, the unformed, the not-yet-fully-human?)

A system which penalizes honesty and rewards dishonesty is vicious. This is what happens in the "needs" society. Assuming that the goods produced are a value (and they are, since everybody's goal is to produce them), and assuming that all the citizens have accepted the "needs" principle as their moral code—then an honest man, trying to be an altruist-collectivist, will have to minimize his needs, demand as little as possible from society and thus be penalized, i.e., get less value; whereas a dishonest man, preaching but not practicing the general moral creed, will exaggerate his needs in every way he can, demand as much as possible from society and thus be rewarded, getting greater value the more he was able to cheat (since every "selfish" demand is cheating, i.e., is breaking the altruist principle). The better you observe this moral code, the more you suffer; the greater your break of the code, the more you are rewarded.

Now, if the person himself is not allowed to present his demands and define his own needs—*who does it*? The vote of the collective? By what standard does the collective then decide and define it? What is a "need"—beyond a cave, a bearskin and a bone to chew? And can even these be determined by others? What kind of bone, for instance?

A man with no right to demand any payment and no right to define his own needs is in a lower position than a slave or a charity ward in a poorhouse, and certainly lower than an animal.

In a capitalist system, a man is not asked to sacrifice himself or penalize himself. It is *honesty* that brings rewards—the honest exercise of one's best ability, the honest production of valuable goods. Production has to be honest—when there are no *controls* or force involved to help one man to defraud others, no way to gain anything except through demonstrated ability, voluntarily accepted by others as a *value*. The man fully living up to the principle of personal ambition, personal responsibility, and independence is the man who wins, who gets the most value. There is no foothold or loophole for the dishonest. The man who cheats, who doesn't produce or tries to be a parasite in any manner, is defeated by the system itself.

---

*Note for Dagny and the old worker* (who tells her about the beginning of the strike): He tells her about the terrible state of working in the "needs" system—when you hate your own effort, when you lose your self-respect by the constant pressure of the incentive to do less and less, the incentive *not to do your best*. You begin to hate all your brothers [because you] worry which one of them is going to develop new needs that will become your responsibility, your burden. You begin to hate them for every pleasure they may enjoy, you begin to meddle into their private lives, because if they break a leg it's you who'll suffer, who'll have to work and pay for it; you begin to meddle into their sex lives, because if they produce more babies, it's you who'll have to carry the burden. You can plan nothing, count on nothing, you have no future, since you don't know when or where someone's need will claim your whole effort, regardless of what plans or ambition you may have had for *your own* future.

And since you do not approve of their desires or needs, you lose the incentive to work; you cannot work if the concrete result or aim of your effort is repugnant to you. And you have the nasty doubt of whether those brothers of yours *will* take care of you, in case *you* need something; you begin to suspect them and to hate them for this, too. Dependence breeds hatred—and you're doubly dependent on them: in your aim and in your needs, in both your production and your consumption.

(If this cannot be told by the same worker, have Dagny meet some other ex-worker, who tells her this, *earlier*.) (I think this last, another worker, will be better—somewhere along her quest for the motor, but *not* in Chapter XI.)

*More for above point:* How can you judge the *needs* of your brothers and approve or disapprove? By what standard? You would have to take the attitude that you approve without standards, merely because *this is what they want*. But by your common moral code, *they* have no moral right to want or ask anything, they cannot define their needs either. Who does it, then? The elite super mind, of course. The dictator of the collective who is "the voice of the people," who "exists only to serve and knows what is good for them." *This* illustrates the real motive and appeal of collectivism. This is the secret ambition of all the collectivist professors.

----

Altruism seeks to patch the wounds of the sick by cutting off pieces of the bodies of the healthy.

**April 26, 1949**

*Emotional Main Line:*

Rearden hears Franciso's speech on "money is the root of all good."
The next step of their friendship—but then Francisco tells of another [impending] crash of d'Anconia Copper.
On the evening of Ken Danagger quitting: Rearden and Francisco—the furnace.
Rearden comes to Francisco—the mutual loneliness. Rearden tells him about ordering *his* copper—Francisco's moment of tragedy, when he leaps to the phone, but he doesn't call.
Rearden learns of sinking ship, loss of copper.
Dagny and Francisco in the country, when she has quit.
Blackmail of Rearden—[he gives in] for Dagny's sake.
Dagny-Francisco-Rearden. Francisco comes to Dagny's apartment, to stop her—Rearden enters with key—Francisco learns the truth—Rearden slaps his face. After Francisco leaves, Dagny tells Rearden

the truth. Their love scene—he does not say it, but we know that he knows he loves her.

## Questions

*Integrate ending—after tunnel catastrophe.* After whom does Dagny fly? (Would like something better than car manufacturer, more important to plot, main character rather than bit, if possible.)
Last Dagny-Rearden scene of this part?
How does Lillian discover truth?
*The death of Colorado*—specific events to cause it, and to bring about closing of the John Galt Line.
*Tunnel catastrophe*—integrate the parasites' actions to main line of parasites' activity.
*Ken Danagger quits*—specific hints leading up to it.
*Ragnar Danneskjöld*—?

**April 27, 1949**

The main line of this whole part should be centered on Dagny-Rearden-Francisco. The events of economic ruin should be subordinated to their personal conflict, should be merely indicated, not presented in detail. From now on, the steps of destruction are accelerated, and also the signs of the strike, the steps of the clarification of the strikers' purpose, motive, and philosophy.

**May 7, 1949**

Stress the *reason of everybody's fudging and cowardice*: people know that they now have to exist by *favor*, not by independent work and merit. Therefore, they must not offend anyone or criticize anything, they must not make enemies, they must try to make friends of everybody, they can't tell on whose favor they may have to depend or when, they can't tell at whose mercy they may be in the future. They *do* know one thing: that they are now in a world of arbitrary power and undefined values, that reason, justice, merit are gone—and therefore it is dangerous to be moral, it is useless to be honest, it is more important to have "friends" than to have virtue; this is a world where *morality* is being penalized.

**May 10, 1949**

*For Galt's speech:*

"So you want to know who is John Galt? I am the first man of ability who refused to feel guilty about it. I am the first man who would not do penance for my virtues nor allow them to be used as the tools of my own destruction. I am the first man who would not suffer martyrdom at the hands of those who were kept alive by my energy, yet who wished me to bear punishment for the privilege of saving their lives. I am the first man who did not accept—neither in weakness nor in generosity—the miserable little enticement of affection offered by liars and beggars in exchange for my lifeblood. I am the first man who told them that I did not need them—and until they learned to deal with me as traders, giving value for value, they would have to exist without me, as I would exist without *them*; then I would let them learn whose is the need and whose the power—and if mankind's survival is the standard, whose terms would set the way to survive."

**May 14, 1949**

*For Francisco's Speech on Money*

Another proof of the noble nature of money is that people are able to keep it only so long as they keep their virtues—and no longer. When men become corrupt, when they compromise, when they lose their self-respect and their courage—swarms of looters rise at once to seize their wealth, and the men are unable to defend it. When their money is unearned, when they do not have the proud, virtuous knowledge of their right to it—they are unable to hold it.

A man without self-respect cannot defend himself. A man without respect for his wealth cannot defend his wealth. But respect is an emotion which cannot be given or received as alms, which cannot be unearned and causeless. Respect is an emotion possible only to the trader—an emotion as ruthlessly just as the laws of gaining a profit. To respect his wealth, a man must know that he has earned it. To respect himself, a man must know that he has the capacity to earn and that he has translated this capacity into reality by producing a [value]. This is where the root of human virtues is tied to the root of human wealth.

**May 16, 1949**

*For Dagny-Lillian*

Lillian makes a crack about Dagny being successful in business because she doesn't care for "power over men," because she is sexless, men are not attracted to her. Then Lillian wants the bracelet back—Dagny refuses.

Lillian says: "Do you know what your wearing that bracelet should mean?"

Dagny answers that it *should* mean that she is sleeping with Rearden— sex as admiration, as an answer to one's highest values.

"Then any woman should want to sleep with my husband?"

"Any woman who values herself highly enough."

"Then what do you feel for me as his wife?"

"I am answering your exact words, Mrs. Rearden: the most profound respect. You are, of course, the only one to judge whether that respect is rightly yours." [*This last sentence was crossed out.*]

**May 19, 1949**

*Note on Morality*

Man exists for his own happiness, and the definition of happiness proper to a human being is: *a man's happiness must be based on his moral values.* It must be the highest expression of his moral values possible to him.

This is the difference between my morality and hedonism. The standard is *not*: "that is good which gives me pleasure, just because it gives me pleasure" (which is the standard of the dipsomaniac or the sex-chaser)—but "that is good which is the expression of my moral values, and *that* gives me pleasure." Since the proper moral code is based on man's nature and his survival, and since joy *is* the expression of his survival, this form of happiness can have no contradiction in it, it is both "short range" and "long range" (as all of man's life has to be), and it leads to the furtherance of his life, not to his destruction.

The form of happiness which involves "a price" to be paid for it afterwards ("a price," not in the sense of the means and effort to achieve it, but in the sense of a consequence which is evil to him by his own standards, such as the hangover the morning after a drunken orgy) is an improper form of happiness by that very fact, a sign that the man who finds enjoyment in it holds a destructive premise that must be corrected.

A man must, above all, be *proud* of his happiness, of the things in which he finds enjoyment and of the nature of his enjoyment. *This* is the difference between James Taggart and the strikers. The strikers find their joy in self-exaltation, in achievement. James Taggart finds *his* joy in evil—in cruelty, fraud, degradation of others to his own level. (For example, he takes pleasure in the fact that people are disgraced by paying homage to him, and he enjoys bringing them to this degradation.) His happiness is based on that which, by his own standards, is evil; his happiness *requires* evil. Man's proper happiness *must not* depend upon or be derived from anything which is evil, low, contemptible, undesirable by his own standards.

The evil man is not the one who mistakenly believes that bad things are good and acts accordingly; this is only an error of knowledge, not a sin, not a moral flaw. The evil man is the one who loves evil *for being evil*. (The poor fool who indulges in sex while semi-believing that it is evil according to his church morality, is not wholly bad because he does not really believe that sex is evil. But this *does* destroy his self-respect and creates all kinds of miserable conflicts for him. The evil man is the one who, knowing that sex is good, takes pleasure in forbidding it and thus causing men to suffer.)

Man *does* exist for happiness; he *has* the right to seek that which makes him happy. But he is a being of free will, therefore a being who cannot exist without a moral standard (a standard of values). If he attempts to drop his own essence—*reason*—and to seek happiness in the irrational and the contradictory, if he evades his responsibility for his own emotions, if he lets his emotions rule him without thought as to where these emotions came from, permitting himself to be determined by his own feelings, which means by his own *stale* thinking, by his *arrested reason—that* is where he destroys himself and is unable to achieve any sort of happiness.

This is the key to the pattern of how men "suspend" their reason.

*Another aspect: a man's happiness must not include any evil as its essential element.* This is the point which disqualifies the alleged happiness of an altruist. His happiness depends, by definition, on somebody else's suffering; he considers this suffering an evil, since he finds it so important to relieve and eliminate it, since he makes that the paramount aim of his life. Therefore, his happiness is based on an evil, and requires that evil to exist. In a world of happy men, he could not be happy (which, of course, is one of the reasons why collectivists achieve horrors).

If it is said that suffering exists in the world anyway, permanently and essentially, therefore it's noble to combat it—then *that* is the malevolent universe. *Man does not exist for suffering.* Suffering is an accidental, "marginal" part of his existence, which he must fight in order to be free to exist in happiness; [a part] which he must overcome as quickly as possible—and *not* spend his life seeking, thus making it the aim of his life. The suffering which threatens men from physical nature is negligible compared to the suffering he brings upon himself and others. If man functioned properly in the field open to him and determined by him—the field of his choice, his free will, his thinking and actions—he would eliminate most, and perhaps even all, of the suffering caused by the accidents of his physical nature.

The essence of suffering is destruction. By acting on the premises of self-destruction, man brings about suffering, his own and that of others. And he acts on a premise of self-destruction when he places *others* above self. He acts against his own nature and theirs. The suffering of others *cannot* be made one's concern. It is not within our power of action. It is not within the function of our nature.

Help to others can, at best, be only an incidental activity and then only on a "trader's" basis—such as help to a loved one, where one has a specific, selfish, personal reason for wishing to help. Just as one cannot conduct one's own life on the basis of trying to avoid pain and holding that to be a final goal, just as one must live *for one's happiness* and fight one's suffering as an incidental on the way, so one cannot live for the relief of the suffering of others, as a goal—only this last is infinitely more improper.

And neither can one live for the happiness of others—because that involves one's own suffering as an essential, since one's happiness is not automatic, but has to be achieved by one's own effort, and that effort *is* the chief duty of one's life (essentially, the *sole* duty). One's own happiness *is* within one's own power, and one's whole nature is tied to the necessity of achieving it; the happiness of others is not. *This* is the point involving and illustrating man's essential independence.

---

*Note in regard to Christian morality:* The Christian moralists would accept the first paragraph of my statement here—but then, of course, the difference lies in the definition of the moral code involved. And *that* is where they would not accept the second part of my statement—the fact that one's happiness must not include evil as its essential part. The Christian morality includes the most vicious evil as the most essential part of the happiness it advocates: *self-sacrifice*. This leads to all the vicious paradoxes of "be happy because you're not happy," "find happiness in suffering," etc.

*There is no conflict and no sacrifice* necessary when a man functions on his proper moral standards. Giving up a party in order to write a novel *is not* a sacrifice, but plain common sense, an acknowledgment of the impossibility of "having your cake and eating it, too" or of doing two things at the same time. *A rational man does not desire the impossible*—and, therefore, feels no pain in not having it, and commits no sacrifice. The sense of sacrifice is possible only to the emotion-ruled man, who *wants* or *feels* without thinking. The happiness of man's proper morality does not require his own suffering.

The essential test of any moral code or teaching is the presence or absence of *the paradox*. A paradox cannot exist. It is only the result and sign of man's errors in thinking. If one accepts a paradox as an essential part of one's moral code—*right there* is the sign that one has accepted a code untrue to reality, that one is in the realm of the irrational, and, therefore, one has accepted destruction as a principle, and as a goal of one's conduct. (Besides, a code based on a paradox *cannot* be practiced; so this leads to the "lip-service morality" of preaching what one cannot practice.) Destruction *is* the result of a departure from reality. Man's destruction is a result of his suspending his means of survival and his tie with reality—*his reason*. By accepting any sort of paradox, he destroys reality in his own eyes, he destroys his control over reality, his means of knowledge, he destroys his mind—and his destruction can be the only result.

A point requiring a great deal of detailed consideration is that *the paradox is the chief symptom and the chief weapon of all the destroyers of man*.

**May 29, 1949**

*For "Money is the root of all good"*

"So you think that money is the root of all evil? Have you ever looked at the root of money?"

The root of money—production. The root of production—the mind.

Money is the material form of a spiritual achievement.

To *make* money requires the highest spiritual values. (America is the first nation that ever spoke of "making" money.)

Money is the tool of a society of free men—men as equals—money as the guarantee that the product of your effort will be exchanged for the product of the effort of others, that you are dealing with producers—not with parasites or looters. Money is the symbol of your dealing with men whom you can trust.

Money is the tool of freedom—it gives you choice of everything being produced.

Money is the tool of your values—the means to exercise your values.

Money will buy happiness—if you understand both money and happiness. Money is your tool of achievement and enjoyment. It will give you the enjoyment that you create; but it will not buy you the second-hand kind of enjoyment, the source of which is in others. Money is your passkey to the services of other men—your means of dealing with them, not through force, fear, or suffering, but through the good—through offering them a value, a means to the achievement of *their* desires, in exchange for what you want from them.

But money will *not* become a tool of evil. Money destroys those who attempt to [make it such a tool].

Money destroys those who defy its root. Money will not buy intelligence for the fool. It will not buy the admiration and respect of men who understand these terms—for the man who doesn't deserve them. It stands as the best guard of man's virtues—the virtues needed for "making" money. Money always remains an effect—and refuses to become a cause. It will not give the parasite what he wants most—its own source—the *unearned, undeserved* virtues of the man who *makes* money.

Money is the hardest test of a man—look at the heirs who are wrecked by it. No man may be smaller than his money. Money is the barometer of a man's character—if he claims to despise it, he's making it dishonestly; if he is proud of it, he's earned it and deserves it. [*This paragraph was added later.*]

In the hands of the producer, money is the means of security. In the hands of the looter, money is the agent of his destruction (as in the case of the criminal). Whenever a society establishes criminals-by-right, whenever the looter is permitted to rob legally—his money is the attraction for other looters, who will get it from him as he got it, achieving nothing but general destruction and slaughter.

Money is the barometer of a society's virtue.

Whenever money is in the wrong hands, in the hands of those who have not earned it, in the hands of grafters and looters (whenever one can get richer by dishonesty than by honesty)—it is the sure sign that that society is evil, that it is corrupt and in the process of destruction.

[*Note added later:*] Paper money—a check on an account which the bureaucrat does not own.

Money is the symbol of virtue. It cannot be made by nor will it stay in unclean hands. The highest virtues are required to make money—or to keep it. Men without courage, without pride, without the highest moral sense of and for their money (the men who apologize for their money)—are not able to keep it. They are the natural prey of looters.

Now, in the first real country of money in history—the country of production and achievement—men have come to regard money as the savages did. Throughout history, money was made by the producers and seized by the looters. Men have continued, in every different form, to exploit and despise the producers and exalt the looters. Now the one country of money is proclaiming the looter's standards; its men of honor are the looter, the moocher and the beggar. Unless and until it accepts money as its highest, noblest standard—it is doomed to the destruction it is asking for and deserves.

Tears, whips and guns—or dollars. Take your choice, there is no other.

(When money ceases to be the tool—then men become the tools of the looters.)

("You damn money and you all want it. So you damn yourselves.")

("When you denounce money, it's always the heir-parasite or the crook that you denounce. What about the man who made the money? You denounce the parasite of the unearned—and, as cure, you wish everybody to become parasites of the unearned.")

### Outline of Money Speech

The nature of money:

    The root of money—production, mind, virtue.

    The money in your wallet as a symbol of trust—not of moochers and looters.

    Definition of money—guardian of rights, independence, freedom, benevolence, brotherhood, integrity; the tool of your values.

    Money as a scourge of the "reversers of cause and effect." The things which money won't do: buy happiness, intelligence, etc.

    The heirs of great fortunes.

    What happens when you acquire money by contemptible means—this is the root of the hatred of money. (The lovers of money are willing to work for it. Run from the haters.)

Sociology:

    The apologizing rich won't stay rich for long.

    The looters-by-law: the rule of brutality. (The society of death.)

    Money as a barometer of a society's virtue.

    The destruction of gold—paper money.

    The consequences—the demoralization of men.

    Answers to all the smears against money: made by the strong at the expense of the weak—your neighbors don't pay you a just reward—charity, instead of competence.

    The denunciations of the parasite and the criminal, the silence about the producer—what you are really after.

    The industrialist and the scientist—the real benefactor.

History:

    The history of glorifying looters and despising producers (and the source of the quote about the evil of money).

    America—the country of money. The self-made man. "To make money."

    The rise of the looters' standards here. The warning.

**August 28, 1949**

### Note Regarding Art vs. Entertainment

The idea that "art" and "entertainment" are opposites—that art is serious and dull, while entertainment is empty and stupid, but enjoyable—is the result of the non-human, altruistic morality. That which is *good* must be unpleasant. That which is enjoyable is sinful. Pleasure is an indulgence of a low order, to be apologized for. The serious is the performance of a duty, unpleasant and, therefore, uplifting. If a work of art examines life seriously, it must necessarily be unpleasant and unexciting, because such is the nature of life for man. An entertaining, enjoyable play cannot possibly be true to the deeper essence of life, it *must* be superficial, since life is not to be enjoyed. (Why can't a man like Graham Greene, for instance, write an "art" story which is also entertaining? Because his philosophical premises are false to life and could not be expressed *in action*, in plot, which means: *in reality*.)

Such is the credo of all the modern intellectuals who divide literature into "art" and "entertainment." This school of thought will have two kinds of representatives in practice, both equally disgusting: the intellectual who will be bored by the best kind of plot story because "if it has suspense, it can't be serious"; and the intellectual who will reject any element of seriousness in a story as "high-brow," declaring ostentatiously: "Me—I don't believe in 'messages,' I'm for *entertainment*" and hold that the burlesque theater is the highest form of art. These [two types] are, basically, the "saint" (of altruism) and the cynic who takes pride in wishing "to go to hell," to be daringly evil.

Why does this school of thought always fail at the box office? Why doesn't the public agree with these intellectuals? Because the public has not been corrupted by any serious acceptance of the essence of the altruist morality; the public thinks of altruism as some sort of innocent form of good will and charity to one's fellow men. *The public does not believe that enjoyment is evil.* The public has never accepted the depravity of "if I enjoy this, it's no good" and "if I enjoy anything, I'm no good."

Incidentally, the intellectual *does not* enjoy anything; the dutiful form of boredom he [feels for] his chosen "art" works is certainly not enjoyment, but a kind of masochistic satisfaction in liking it because he's supposed to like it, a form of quest for self-esteem on the pattern of: "*There*, I'm virtuous if I approve of this dull mess I'm supposed to like; I can't *really* like it, but my trying to is my step toward virtue." (Contrast the public enthusiasm for a hit play in the old days with the "sophisticated," "we-don't-go-to-extremes" attitude of "smart" New Yorkers today.)

Test: do you enjoy a book or play for its own sake?—or do you "enjoy" it as a means to an end, the end being that self-conscious sense of acquiring some virtue from it? *Joy is an end in itself.* My pattern of enjoyment is: *I'm good,* and if this thing has given me enjoyment, then *it* is good. Their pattern is: I'm no good and if this thing has made me better, then it is good.

My pattern holds joy as its own end, man's end. Their pattern holds joy and man as a means to an end—the end being God or the supernatural, since they hold that man exists "for God" (or for others, or for the universe, or for anything but himself). Any man's enjoyment *is* based on his standard of values. I can enjoy an entertaining story because my standard of values holds man as a noble being and joy as his proper aim in life. *They* cannot enjoy an entertaining story because *their* standard of values holds man as depraved and joy as evil; therefore, they get to the paradox of *enjoying only the unenjoyable. There's* another example of the use of the paradox. Man cannot escape from joy, as the altruists and mystics want him to; he can only pervert it into horror and sadomasochism.

This is an illustration of the morality of altruism in practice. So they preach that joy is evil? Well, they do achieve this much: their disciples lose the capacity of enjoyment altogether. And since joy is the means, the advancer and protector of life, the joyless creatures are ready for destruction; they have, in fact, destroyed themselves and their capacity for life. *There's* altruism and its ultimate goal—destruction.

**October 4, 1949**

### For Rearden and Dagny

*He told her that:* he feels contempt for her; she is a bitch, as vile an animal as he is; he wants no pretense about love, devotion, or respect, no shred of honor to hide behind; he will have her at the price of his self-respect.

*Show him learning the opposite:* that his admiration and respect for her are the source of his sexual desire; that his desire is for the possession of the highest woman he knows and is the expression of his greatest self-respect; that he loves her, i.e., she is the most important and precious person to him, as *a person*, not only as "a lay"; that instead of abasement, their affair gives him a feeling of elevation, it raises his self-respect, not destroys it; that he feels love, respect, devotion, admiration for her, all the real moral emotions, the ones expressing recognition of value.

*His other sensual capacities:* love of good clothes, good cars, good furniture (as in his office), good jewelry for Dagny, other "self-indulgent" luxuries for both of them, the jade vase in his office.

Jealousy of the other man in her life.

(So far, I have shown: that he makes her wear the bracelet of Rearden Metal; that he wants to leave his "official" life and go away with her and is happy with her; their understanding and respect for each other; that he turns against Lillian when she indirectly calls Dagny a gutter bitch; that he turns against Mayor Bascom when he insults Dagny; that he takes pleasure in Dagny's greatness, that *that* arouses his sexual desire; that he takes pleasure in the thought of Dagny and another man, which is an unconscious acknowledgment that sex, as such, is great and beautiful, not evil and degrading.)

———◦———

The *incident of the ruby pendant:* he learns that enjoyment of material luxury is an expression of spiritual values—the pendant would be meaningless to him on another woman (it would be meaningless on the most beautiful naked woman, if she were only a beautiful body); it would be meaningless if he had not earned it, if it had been given to him or if he had inherited it. It is not only that he wants her to have the pendant—he wants her to have it as a gift *from him.* Would it mean the same to him if she just happened to have the pendant? No. Would he enjoy giving it to some woman who craved it desperately, but who meant nothing to him? Hell, no.

---

He looks at her as a painting, but he wants the "painting," and all it implies, in *real* life: the hopeless yearning versus the man of reality and action.

*Tie their scene to his groping for the moral issue*—to the nature of mistaken morality, of wrong moral values. And tie his feeling for her to his feeling for his work.

---

He tells Dagny he would like her to be his kept woman; she laughs, saying that she'd like it for a month or two, but asks: would he like her, just as she is, if she were nothing but a kept woman? "You couldn't be!" "No, I couldn't. But if I were, would you like it?" "I'd be bored to death." He stops short, understanding the implications.

---

*Rearden's problem about sex is:* he was bitterly disillusioned in his early experiences, and he resented the fact that he felt a violent physical desire that seemed to be independent of and in contradiction to his rational will and spiritual code of values. He concluded that sex is purely physical, and as such he hated it—it was a surrender of his will, a degrading necessity that held such an immense power over him, created such a violent desire, yet had no spiritual meaning.

He learns that the *capacity* of sex is physical, a mechanism for the use and expression of his spirit, the means of expressing in physical form one's greatest celebration of life, of joy, of one's highest self-exaltation and one's highest moral values in regard to man—that is, in regard to himself and the woman of his choice. He learns that sex is the means and form of translating spiritual admiration for a human being into physical action—just as productive activity is the translation of spiritual values into physical form, just as all life is a process of conceiving a spiritual purpose, based on one's spiritual code of values, then giving it a material form—which is the proper, moral, and *complete* cycle for man's existence, for the relation of man's spirit to physical matter. The spirit sets the purpose and uses matter as its tool, as *material*; the spirit gives form to matter. Just as pure "spirituality," divorced from physical action, is evil hypocrisy—so is the materialism which attempts to have matter give man purpose, value, and satisfaction. Just as "Platonic love" is evil hypocrisy—so is purely physical sex, which is an evil destruction of one's values.

He thinks that his guilt is that while admiring Dagny as the highest woman, he wants to degrade her by making her a tool for the satisfaction of his physical need. He thinks it's evil that his response to the highest is sexual desire. He learns that *that* is precisely the high, moral quality of his desire for her. His desire is a response to his highest values. He learns that evil consists of the attitude of other men who are attracted, not by the highest, but by the lowest they know—by a mere body, with no regard for a woman's character, or by a woman they consciously despise, this giving them a sense of their own elevation by contrast; the rotten self-fraud of men with an inferiority complex, men who try to acquire self-esteem by triumph over a woman they have estimated as worthless.

---

The wrap of blue fox, and the roadside restaurant in winter.

The conversation about the "kept woman": the realization that *they* are much more capable of enjoying this than the drunken "playboy" at the next table. Dagny remembers the "reversal" at her first ball. He remembers her words at his party.

The flowers.

The cup carved of chalcedony.

The crystal glasses—and the way he holds the glass when she serves him the drink.

---

In contrast to his love of luxury: the way he enjoys nature, a sensual enjoyment, his body stretched on the ground in slacks and short-sleeved shirt. It is, of course, *not* a contrast, but the same thing—spiritual enjoyment of material nature.

Rearden as the man who *is* the master of physical nature, whose *spirit* is the master of matter—in factory, countryside, or luxury.

———◦———

The evening when, on his way to her apartment, he feels loathing for the whole world, the shrinking feeling that he doesn't want to touch anything: he has no sexual desire, no trace of it; then the sight of her against the city brings back *his* feeling of the world, the world in which he *wants* to act and work, and with that his sexual desire returns. It is an act of celebration— and he feels consciously that it is a great achievement of hers, a value, not a degrading sin, when he feels her experiencing pleasure and knows that she is capable of it, that she is celebrating life as he is.

———◦———

The incident when he has an affair with her in her office—the deliberate contrast and "impropriety" of it.

His "sadistic" touches of this kind.

The way he runs his fingertips down the skin of her arm—here an example of the fact that he never indulges in the physical as such, i.e., merely as contact—the purely physical in this sense is meaningless to both of them—it is not the contact that arouses pleasure in them, it is the contact *when* it is an expression of their spiritual attitude toward each other at that particular moment. (Such as: their first affair as result of the train ride and the triumph which it represents; the way he takes her the next morning; their first scene in her apartment, the broken shoulder-strap.)

**October 6, 1949**

### Philosophy of Sex and Morality

*Note:* The reason why people consider sexual desire insulting to a woman is, in the deepest sense, the fact that to most people sex is an evil, low, degrading aspect of man's life. Since most people, in their philosophical premises, have damned themselves and life on earth, their sex desires and actions *are* an expression of evil (this is clearest in the case of desire for a woman consciously estimated as one's inferior). On such a premise, sexual desire *is* insulting to the woman who is the object of it. Conventionally, the man is supposed to redeem this insult by the so-called higher, *spiritual* implications of marriage; but, if marriage is not involved, sexual desire is supposed to be insulting.

The twisted element of truth here is that sex has to have a high spiritual base and source, and that without this it is an evil perversion. But the actual relation of sex and spirit is *not* the way they believe: they believe that sex is evil as such, and that the spiritual aspects of marriage serve to redeem or excuse it, or make it a pardonable weakness which has no tie with and is opposed to the spiritual elements of the relationship. They do not suspect the *essential*, unbreakable tie between sex and spirit—which is the tie between body and soul.

On the *right* philosophical premise about sex, on *my* premise, it is a great compliment to a woman if a man wants her. It is an expression of his highest values, not of his contempt. In this sense, a husband would feel honored if another man wanted his wife; he would not let the other man have her—his exclusive possession *is* the material form of her love for him—but he would feel that the other man's desire was a natural and proper expression of the man's admiration for his wife, for the values which she represents and which he saw in her.

It is on the above ground that *Galt* feels no jealousy and no resentment of Francisco and Rearden in Dagny's past. His reaction when he hears about Dagny's affair with Rearden is simple, non-malicious envy—merely the shock of learning that another man has what he himself so desperately wants. It is also the shock of the possibility, which he has kept in mind all these years, that Dagny *may* love another man and he, Galt, may never have her, not even after she joins the strike. But it is not the conventional fury against the thought that another man degrades Dagny by possessing her.

---

Note how dreadful the general attitude on sex is: since all [the accepted] philosophies damn man, his life, and the earth—men's attitude on sex is a degrading, ugly, corrupting evil, in all the many variations. And this is another proof that sex *is* the expression of one's entire philosophy and attitude toward life. Since most people's philosophy is a hodgepodge of contradictory bits, so is their attitude on sex. But man *cannot* exist without a basic philosophy, from which all his actions, emotions and desires will come.

The cheap little schools of "free love" attempt to glorify sex on a silly sort of materialistic basis—simply glorifying physical joy, considering themselves "vital as animals." They are unable to discover a *moral*, spiritual premise to justify sex—so they try to enjoy it without any morality, and, of course, it doesn't work, it doesn't bring them any sort of spiritual happiness, and not even much satisfaction.

This is the same mistake as that of the materialists who—in protest against mystical morality—declare that existence on earth has nothing to do with and requires no morality. This attitude merely drives people back to church, to mystical morality—and people drag themselves back to it regretfully, reluctantly, knowing that it is unsatisfactory, that it cannot work—but knowing also that they cannot exist without some form of morality, some code of values. This is another example of the vicious cutting of man in two—and setting his spirit against his body.

My most important job is the formulation of *a rational morality of and for man, of and for his life, of and for this earth.*

(No wonder the advocates of religion are so insistent that "there can be no morality without religion." They seem to know their danger point. *There's* my main job.)

The basic issue, of course, is the standard of values. Good and evil—why? By what standard? Their standard is an arbitrary, "revealed," unprovable "categorical imperative"—as they jolly well have to admit—and it rests on *their* conception of God, and is then translated into indefensible nonsense in regard to conduct on this earth. (For instance, *why* should charity please God as the highest virtue? Why should *He* be that unjust?) The standard supposedly is in another dimension, opposite and contradictory in nature to ours—yet we are supposed to live by it on earth, in *this* dimension. A rational morality starts with a standard of values (of good and evil) based on man, his life, and the earth; it starts with the fact that values are possible and necessary *only* to a being of free will who has to function through choice and purpose.

————◦————

If any school of morality considers morality a *social*, not an individual, matter—i.e., a code for the relation of man to man, and not for man's own conduct in regard to himself—then, of course, it will necessarily be a collectivist [theory] and it will not work. This is true of any religious morality or of any attempt at a "social" morality, like communism.

Both above schools of "morality" have this in common: that they begin by placing the standard of their code of values outside of man: God is the standard in one case, "society" in the other. But since *man* is the *entity*, the unit under discussion for whom the code of morality is being proposed, the proper standard of values has to begin with *him*.

Most blatantly obvious, in theory and in observable practice, is the fact that man's moral code has to apply primarily to his own private conduct in relation to himself and his life—and that only on the basis of the right code toward himself will he or can he observe any sort of moral code toward others. Conventionally, it is thought that a man on a desert island needs no moral code. *That* is where he would need it the most. The proper code, of course, is: *rational control* of himself and his actions, a rational view of reality (identifying facts for what they are, to the best of his knowledge and capacity, *being true to truth*), the rational choice of his purpose and the action to achieve it.

Conventionally, both the religious and the social schools of morality make it appear that moral behavior is an obligation which man owes to others, but not to himself—that he has no *selfish interest* in morality—in fact, that his selfish interests are actually opposed to his moral code, but he must observe it as a sacrifice for and to others. Thus he is a sacrificial animal to God or to society—sacrifice, suffering, renunciation of happiness on earth are made [the essence] of his moral code. He must *live for* God, or society, or humanity, or the poor, or whatever; he is always taken as a means to some end—but he is never taken as an end in himself.

But we can see all around us that the men who are immoral toward others are first of all and more profoundly immoral toward themselves. The criminal or fraud or con-man is the irresponsible man who exists without a purpose, wastes his life and hurts himself more than he harms others. The liar is not "honest with himself, but dishonest with others"—he does not fake reality for others, while having a clear, honest grasp of it for himself; *he* is the one who fakes reality for himself, in his own mind, much more dreadfully and disastrously than he can ever fake it for others; *he* is the man who has renounced the rational identification of facts, the "being true to truth"— *he* is the neurotic full of complexes and in dread of ever facing reality.

Incidentally, if morality *were* merely a social matter, a code for the relation of man to man, then a plausible case could be made for taking "society" (or the collective) as the basis of moral values, for letting "society" choose the terms of the code, for the precept that "the good is whatever is good for society," or for the idea that society itself needs no moral code—that the majority may do anything it pleases, since it physically *can* do it—that whatever the majority decrees, *that* is moral.

A good example here as to *why* a society or a man needs a moral code is the difference between what a man *can* do or *may* do. A man *can* cut his own throat—but he *may not* do it, if his purpose is to live. Society *can* become collectivist and destroy itself—but it *may not* do it, if its purpose is to exist, or prosper, or achieve happiness for *any* of its members. (Here again—the relation of morality and purpose is clear.)

Incidentally, it is debatable whether a majority *can* do anything it pleases, even in the crudest physical terms. Those who think it, think simply of a wild mob overrunning an individual or a small, opposing minority— simply in terms of physical numbers and physical force. But even this is not true: one man with a machine gun can defeat a mob. This is an example of "force" versus "mind and force." Man *cannot do anything* by sheer physical force—his muscles have to be guided by his mind, his mind has to set the purpose of his actions—and *right there* is the illustration of why a majority is actually *helpless* as such, if its physical numbers are the only criterion of its strength. If it's asked: but what about a numerical majority with a vicious leader or with a vicious idea?—then the answer is: on those terms, the question of the *mind* is involved, and then the man with the right idea will win, regardless of numbers; he will win, even if his following is much smaller than that of the evil leader—and he will also win even in the minds of the enemy's following, to the extent of their intelligence.

### Note for Francisco and Rearden

It is Francisco who tells Rearden what people's attitude on sex is: the quest for self-esteem, when sex should be an expression of self-esteem.

This is the scene when, after their unfinished conversation at the mills, Rearden comes to Francisco's suite at the Wayne-Falkland. Rearden asks how a man of Francisco's intelligence can find any sort of satisfaction in the life of a playboy, in running after countless cheap women who have nothing but beauty. Francisco tells him that he has never touched any of those women—why the women keep up the pretense—and that he has loved only one woman in his life and still loves her.

**October 26, 1949**

### "Being True-to-Truth"

*Logic is the art of non-contradictory identification.*

The essence of consciousness *is* identification. Our senses give us information about physical reality. Our mind grasps it, organizes it, identifies it, establishes conceptions—*ideas*. Our ideas about reality establish our emo-

tions, desires, purposes, motives. The "spiritual" duty of our mind is to identify our ideas and all their consequences, all the functions and aspects of our
consciousness as strictly as we identify the facts of physical reality. Here,
too, our first and foremost (and probably only) duty is: non-contradictory
identification. *This* establishes our moral character as a person—this is
probably the whole essence of morality. ("A broken person is one who dares
not admit to himself the nature of what he is doing.")

Since existence *cannot* be contradictory, this rule of consciousness *is*
the rule of morality—the life-serving principle. A *contradiction*, being
impossible, has to lead to destruction—therefore, a philosophy containing
paradoxes (particularly the intentional, conscious acceptance of paradoxes)
has to have destruction as its ultimate result. (This is an important clue for
the distinction between the "life" and "death" philosophies.)

***

*To think over in this connection:* the example of the certainty of a sleep-
walker. Define the exact relation of *how* to set your abstractions in such a
way that the concrete action follows *automatically* and *correctly*. This is
both for general thinking and particularly for *the process of writing*.

**November 5, 1949**

*For Speech on Money*

There are only two possible societies: where men work for *reward* or
where men work from *fear*—*the incentive of joy* or *the incentive of suffering*.
These are basic, because man has, essentially, only the two sensations: pleasure and pain. Now, which of these two societies do you want?

If man is to work, not for *his own* pleasure, but for the pleasure of
others, then others have to take care of him, of providing *his* pleasure. Then
man in relation to his brothers is simultaneously a sucker and a beggar. Is
*that* what you consider good? Is that the rule of a moral society? *That*—as
against a society where the relationship of men is that of self-respecting,
self-supporting, responsible equals.

Money is the tool of intelligence and of freedom. It requires *judgment*,
in order to be produced and to be spent. When a man pays you in money, he
leaves to you the choice of how to spend it. *You* are the judge of what you

want to get in exchange for your effort. What would you prefer—that your employer decide what you should have and what he will give you?

The men who hate their work "because they have to work for money" are immoral. The fault is theirs—they are the kind who hate work or the kind who want others to support them in a work for which those others get nothing.

**December 13, 1949**

### Main Points of Galt's Cause

Man exists for his own happiness; he is an end in himself and does not exist for the sake of others.

If any man is asked to sacrifice himself for others, it means that he has something of value, some virtue, which they lack. Therefore, it means that the worthless is given a claim of priority over the valuable, the unvirtuous over the virtuous, the miserable over the happy. It means—whatever the standard of values, since it is only a *value* that can be sacrificed—that the good must be sacrificed to the evil.

Men of virtue, do you value your virtues as little as that? Are you willing to make them serve, feed and preserve those who are evil? Are you willing to support your own enemies? *You* are your own destroyers.

If the inferiors base their entire claim on the fact that they need the superior—then how can they enforce their claim and their exploitation, unless it's the superior who permits it, accepts it, and works for his own destruction? It is the superior who makes possible his own torture, enslavement, exploitation, and ruin.

If they need *you*, while you do not need them—it is *you* who must dictate the terms. (There is no question of sacrifice between equals, or between any two men who have something to offer to each other; there is only a trade—a just, honorable exchange. Whenever sacrifice is [demanded], it means that one party wants something from the other but has nothing to offer in return.)

The great, primary error of the superior men has been the fact that they have accepted the *morality* of their own exploiters.

What morality is and why it is the cardinal need of man's existence: man is a being of free will, he has to survive by conscious choice and effort, he has to choose his purpose and the means to achieve it. The choice of the means depends on the purpose, and the choice of the purpose depends on his code of values. A being of free will cannot choose, act, or exist without a standard of values. His standard must be himself—*man's nature*. His basic, primary, essential purpose must be to live. He can live only in the manner proper to his nature—proper to man. He must understand his nature, define it—and *that* will give him his standard of values.

Man's essence and sole means of survival is his mind—his capacity to think—his rational [faculty]. Any departure from it or denial of it is a destruction of his consciousness. A morality or standard of values not based on his reason is impossible for him to practice and can lead only to his destruction. He cannot live against and in contradiction to his consciousness. He cannot be good, if the "good" is that which is contrary to his nature, that which is impossible to him. Nor can he exist if he accepts himself as essentially evil: then his life, too, is evil—and he can have no desire to struggle for the continuation of the evil existence of an evil being. It is thus that he is set against himself.

The cardinal crime in morality has been the placing of the standard of values outside and beyond man. This was done by chopping man into two contradictory parts, set to war against each other: body and soul. Then the standard of values was placed in the alleged realm of this alleged soul, as an enemy of the realm of his body. This left man's existence on earth without any morality; man had no code of values for this earth; in fact, to exist at all, he had to be immoral.

Man's consciousness is not material—but neither is it an element *opposed* to matter. It is the element by which man *controls* matter—but the two are part of one entity and one universe—man cannot *change* matter, he can control it only by understanding it and shaping it to his purpose. (The distinction between "entity" and "action"—between noun and verb. The essence of *being*.)

Man's soul or spirit is *his consciousness*—here, now, on earth. The ruling element, the control, the free-will element of his consciousness is his *reason*. The rest—his emotions, his memory, his desires, his instincts—*all* are determined by his thinking, by the kind of conclusions he has made and the kind of premises he has accepted.

*The man of spirit is the man of the mind. He* is the man who is not the slave, but the ruler of matter. *He* is the man who makes it possible for mankind to survive. *He* is the creative man.

The morality of the mind—to be true to truth. The great courage, integrity and responsibility that it requires. The only cardinal sin is the denial or suspension of one's reason—the refusal to face reality, identify it and make rational connections. No man can go against his own mind—and that is why he cannot submit to force. The greatest field where this morality is needed and expressed is the field of material production.

All material production is an achievement of the spirit—of the mind. Every human creation has to start in the mind and be given form in matter—whether it's a work of art or a commercial gadget. Every spiritual value of man has to be expressed in material form or action. What is a virtue, if man does not practice it or act upon it? The great courage and virtue of the producers.

The hatred for the producers is the hatred for man, for life and for this earth. Those who despise material producers are motivated by the desire for man's destruction. They are the men of death.

The desire for the unearned in matter is only a consequence and an expression of a deeper, more vicious aim: the desire for the unearned in spirit. Those who want to seize the material wealth produced by others actually want the virtues of the producers, and they want to obtain them unearned and undeserved: unearned respect, unearned love, unearned admiration. They hope to obtain it by reversing man's standard of values, by regarding all the virtues of life and of this earth as sins, and their opposites—the qualities based on and leading to death—as virtues.

The victims—the producers, the men of this earth—have accepted this monstrously evil reversal for too long. It has always been supported by force—the brute force of the organized destroyers—but the producers have submitted and obeyed, because they were disarmed morally; they had accepted the destroyers' morality and never found their own.

The power of the "moral sanction." It is not enough to be neutral about one's productive talent; one must hold it as one's highest, proudest virtue.

The free enterprise system—the system based on the morality of the producers—is now being destroyed because the producers have never [identified] their proper morality.

America versus India: which country [represents] the triumph of spirit over matter?

The present struggle is a conspiracy against the mind, a conspiracy against ability.

The men of production must set themselves free of the *guilt* which has been attached to them for centuries. Do not accept the destroyers' morality. Do not submit to force. You do not need your exploiters. They need *you*. Let them try to get along without you. Do not give them that which they cannot force out of you, which they cannot obtain without your consent: your living power—the power of your love for life—your mind. Put an end to the use of your virtues for your own torture—and of your love of life as a tool of destruction and death. We are on strike against the morality of death. We are fighting for the morality of man, of life and of this earth.

**December 19, 1949**

[*AR seems to have prepared the following for a conversation with Earl Reynolds, an employee of Kaiser Steel. She notes down some of his answers.*]

### Questions Regarding Furnace Accident

**1.** The exact nature, cause, appearance and progression of accident? "Charge hangs up" in a blast furnace (can be from wrong ore).

**2.** The exact action needed to prevent disaster and the danger to the rescuers?

**3.** When alarm rings—who is supposed to answer it? Who should have taken care of accident, instead of Rearden?

**4.** Would coke ovens be operated late in the evening—about 8 p.m.? Yes. Do you call it a "door"? Yes.

**5.** Is it "structural shapes" that Danagger would get for his coal mines? If so, how much? Or is there a more essential thing which he could get direct from Rearden?

**6.** Is 500 tons of Rearden Metal (equivalent to 1,000 tons of steel) about right for the "quota"?

**7.** *For Mr. Ward's harvesters:* how many would a modest sized plant put out in a year? How much steel would he need? 2,000–3,000 harvesters at about 1–2 tons per unit.

**8.** Is it "Purchasing Manager" of steel mills? Is line correct: "We'll make it up on *volume*"? Tonnage.

**January 28, 1950**

### Notes for Rearden's Trial

The overall point: the sanction of the victim.

The looters try (e.g., through Bertram Scudder) to use the trial to discredit Rearden in the eyes of the public, to destroy his popularity, which is due to Rearden Metal. The looters are worried over the fact that the public,

in gloomy silence, realizes the value and the productivity of the industrialists—as exemplified in the history of Rearden Metal.

The looters have tried to counteract it by a barrage of screaming about
"greed, selfishness, the profit motive." It has not worked. The public attitude
is a glum, impassive silence. People say obediently: "Yeah, Rearden was
after nothing but his own profit"—but there is no condemnation in it, no
anger or indignation; they say it without conviction—they have begun to
doubt that that's evil—they have no conviction about anything, neither in
approval nor disapproval—they feel nothing but a gray, hopeless apathy.
This worries the looters. They try—by means of the trial—to whip up hatred
for the industrialists, for the rich, to make men like Rearden the goats and
blame the national emergency on them—"they prevent the national plans
from working, they break the regulations and thus stand in the way of the
prosperity that the plans would certainly have given us otherwise."

It does not work. Rearden's attitude blows it up completely. They want
Rearden's admission that the "planning" and the controls are good, but that
he selfishly ignored them. They want him to apologize for his action. He
doesn't. They wanted an industrialist's endorsement of the public value of
controls. They wanted it to be a debate over the "public good." If he claimed
that his action was for the "public good"—they would have had him,
because nobody would believe it. They would have had the moral sanction.
This is what he doesn't do.

———◦———

Dagny says: "Hank, that we should have come to do business like
criminals!" He answers: "The real evil is our accepting it as being criminal.
Ask yourself why plain highwaymen and robbers have never been a grave
problem to mankind, but legal looters have made the whole of human history into a tragedy and a procession of horrors."

———◦———

[AR copied the following quote from Will Cuppy, critic and humorist
for the New York Herald Tribune:] "If the insects do win and set up a government, how will they manage, without us to raise crops for them? Do they
intend to exterminate mankind or will they let a few of us remain in some
minor capacity, such as planting apple trees for the Codling Moth and cotton
for the Boll Weevil?"

*For Rearden:* He is asked to contribute Rearden Metal for a slum playground. He asks: "What is more important—to give the slum a playground or to give Ellis Wyatt his pipeline?"

**February 16, 1950**

### Notes for Government Encroachments on Railroads

Regulations are imposed in the name of safety "for passengers and employees." First, the miserable condition of the equipment—which is due to lack of money, rising costs and wages, no permission to raise rates, low profits—causes accidents. Then, the accidents are used as an excuse for "safety" controls.

*The purpose of controls is to eliminate the necessity of judgment* (!) and to eliminate the competition, for the parasites, of the men capable of judgment. (The *"freezing"* of judgment. *This* is for "the moratorium on brains.")

*For the tunnel catastrophe:* Government Board reinstates employees (with back pay!) who have been discharged for serious infractions of basic safety rules. (See p. 9 of Union Pacific Pamphlet.) Here—the pull of the labor leader who keeps "his men," in exchange for control of union's votes, etc.

**April 24, 1950**

[*AR made the following notes for the scene in which the parasites discuss Directive 10-289.*]

### Elements for Parasites' Scene

Stress the fact that the parasites lean on need, weakness, incompetence as the base and justification for all of their schemes. Show the "death principle" in practical application. [. . .]

*Above all*—show the hatred of ability and of the mind. The conspiracy against ability. The attempt to eliminate the necessity of judgment. The "freezing" of judgment. The attempt to substitute a mechanical security, an automatic routine, for the risk and responsibility of exercising one's own judgment. The attempt to seize "the motions" of the able, to copy them, and to forbid the able to advance, forbid them to make any new "motions" which would destroy the "security" of the aping robots.

The directive is known as "Directive No. 289." It requires Mr. Thompson to declare a state of total emergency—in the name of "total stability."

In the scene: Mr. Thompson, Wesley Mouch, Eugene Lawson, Mr. Weatherby, James Taggart, Orren Boyle, Dr. Ferris, and the labor leader (Fred Kinnan).

### Main points of "Moratorium on Brains":

**1.** Everybody is attached to their jobs—cannot quit or be fired. (Freedom from worry.)

**2.** The industrialists are forbidden to quit—if they do, their property will be nationalized. (Freedom from risk.)

**3.** No more inventions and new products for the duration of the emergency. (Freedom from speculation.)

**4.** All patents and copyrights are taken over—to be used equally by everybody "for the public good." Patents and copyrights are to be signed over to the nation "voluntarily" as a patriotic emergency gift. (Freedom from greed.)

**5.** Everybody is to produce the same amount as in the "basic year"—no more and no less. Over- or under-production is to be fined. (Freedom from exploitation.)

**6.** Everybody has to spend as much as they did in the "basic year." (Freedom from privation.)

**7.** All wages, prices, dividends and interest rates are frozen as in the "basic year." (Freedom from future.)

Their main cry is to "end instability"—to "achieve security."

This will end "wasteful competition"—"we'll close all research departments, we won't have to worry about new inventions upsetting the market, we won't have to waste money just to keep up with over-ambitious competitors."

Their attitude is, in effect: things are getting worse and worse, to hell with progress if we can only remain as we are; we can exist now, but we won't be able to if things continue going down, so let's hold still. They are rolling down the slope of an abyss—and want to [stop] themselves by hanging on to a branch on the way.

Wesley Mouch acts like a cornered rat—his sole recourse is to get angry, with the petulant anger of an offended tyrant, as if the country's troubles are an affront to him and people better do something, since he's angry. He's become used to the fact that people seeking favors are afraid of his anger—and he's beginning to feel that his anger is the solution to everything, his anger is omnipotent, all he has to do is get angry. But the basic element in his anger is a rat's fear. He keeps screaming "I've got to have wider powers! . . . I've got to have *power*!" like an injured party, as if the guilt for everything is on those who haven't given him the power. Wesley Mouch is the zero at the meeting point of opposing forces. (He is resentful of Mr. Thompson—he knows that Thompson has the power to kick him out, but won't because Mouch has balanced the forces skillfully and Thompson is too dumb and too busy to break through the mesh.)

The white obelisk monument in the window. When they decide to pass the "emergency directive," Taggart rises and pulls the blinds down over the white obelisk.

This is the scene of "nothing is anything—there are no absolutes—there are no principles—we must act pragmatically on the emergency of the moment." Men without mind or morals running amuck on power—since what logic, morality or justice is possible under the unlimited rule of the "public good"?

*The overall mood of the scene:* **fear.** Fear of the public, of their own victims. "Can we get away with it?" This is where we see the power of the moral sanction—which these bastards know and dread, without acknowledging it in so many words. The public could have thrown them all off like lice—by moral means, by refusing to accept their actions as just. It is the victims who are making their own destruction possible.

**July 16, 1950**

### Note for Tunnel Catastrophe

The disaster is made possible by the illusion of the old morality, on which people rely, even though it is not there any longer, they count on it after they have destroyed it. The old morality, which created discipline and confidence among the employees of a railroad, was the principle of rationality and of self-interest based on reason and rights: every man knew that the purpose of the railroad and of everyone connected with it was to run trains well, that this was in their common interest, that every man could expect a good performance from every other man, and that objective truth was the criterion and standard of justice.

If anyone tried to be a vicious exception and to pass the buck, he would be exposed and penalized, because the principle of objective truth was the standard, and the objective fate of the railroad enforced this standard upon the owners. Therefore, trusting this principle, everyone still trusts his superiors and carries out their orders; and the passengers do not even imagine that the railroad employees can have any motive other than to move them safely; they take this motive and safety for granted—with no thought of what it is based on.

But *now*, the purpose of the railroad is *not* the objective success of an objective performance—as it is not the purpose of the whole society and of its present economic system. *Now*, one lives, not by the objective result of one's effort, but by means of and at the expense of other men. Therefore, every man on the railroad has only one interest: to gain an advantage over others, to protect the *appearance* of his performance in the eyes of authority, to be *judged* right, *not* to *be* right, and this at the expense of others. Therefore, every man has to fear and distrust all the others. Their interests now clash: one man's loss is another man's gain. The fate of the passengers means nothing to the railroad men, since it is not by the fate of the passengers, not by the performance of the train, that they are to be judged (and rewarded).

This is how, functioning on the dead hulk of a morality which they have destroyed, counting upon it when they have made it impossible, men come to the spectacle of a great physical machinery (the railroad)—built for safety [on the basis of] a moral principle (individualism)—becoming the tool of a dreadful destruction, instead. This is what the material shell will do, when its soul has been destroyed. This is all the good that the seizure of material wealth, without the mind, will do for the looters.

**July 18, 1950**

[*AR continues her notes on the Taggart Tunnel catastrophe.*]

*The passengers "who weren't guilty":*

The last one must be the most vicious insult to businessmen, applying unmistakably to Ellis Wyatt.

The man who said: "Why should Rearden be the only one permitted to manufacture Rearden Metal?"

The man who said that man exists for the good of society and has no other right or justification for existence.

The man who said that majority will is law—"society can do anything it pleases."

The man who said that an individual's conscience doesn't matter; an individual has no right to any conscience, it's just a luxury for prosperous times, not for emergencies—"In an emergency, society hasn't time to bother about individual consciences."

The man who said that there is no individual achievement, that individual effort does not count nor matter, that everything is done collectively.

The man who said that men are vicious morons unfit for freedom, that their natural instincts, if left alone, are to lie and murder—therefore, lies and murder are the only proper means to rule them and keep them in order.

The man who said that rewards and persuasion do not work, but punishments and fear do.

The man who saw no difference between the power of money and the power of a gun.

The man who believed that it is proper and moral to use compulsion "for a good purpose," who believed that he had the right to use force upon others for the sake of his own idea of a "good purpose," which did not even have to be an idea, only a "feeling," not even knowledge, only a "good intention."

The man who said that "poverty is so horrible that I don't care if we use force, compulsion or murder so long as it's for the poor."

The man who said that the able must be penalized in favor of the parasite.

The man who said: "Me? I'll find a way to get along under any political system."

The man who said that there is no mind, there is no logic and men do not live by reason.

The man who said that there are no principles, no rights, no morality, no absolutes—and the practical way to live is to act on the expediency of the moment.

The man who "could not take sides" because he had to think of his children.

The man who was against Directive [10–289], but would not "be quoted" publicly.

The man who wanted controls to stifle a competitor.

The man who wanted the government to guarantee him a job.

The man who wrote sniveling little obscenities about the evil of businessmen.

The man who belonged to "The Friends of Progress" because it was fashionable.

**July 19, 1950**

### For the passengers:

Main philosophic points:

> *Collectivism.* (School teacher: "Unlimited majority rule.")
> *Anti-ability.* (Professor of sociology: "There is no individual achieve-
> ment and there are no great men." Humanitarian: "The able must be
> penalized.")
> *The malevolent universe.* (Newspaper publisher: "Men are vicious
> and must be ruled by force.")
> *Power lust.* (Journalist: "It is all right to use force for a good
> purpose.")
> *Anti-reason.* (Professor of philosophy: "There is no mind or logic"
> and "There are no principles, rights, morality or absolutes.")
> *Materialism.* (Professor of economics: "The mind doesn't count, it's
> only a matter of seizing the machinery.")
> *Anti-business.*

Personal types:

> The rotter who "can get along under any system."
> The man who "has to think of his children."
> The man who wanted to control a business competitor.
> The worker who wanted a guaranteed job.

**July 31, 1950**

### Note on Morality

Figure out (define the principle and the standard of moral guilt) who is
more evil: Lillian or Ferris? Ferris or Toohey?

Lillian has two elements of truth in her: knowledge of Rearden's greatness and evaluation of it as great. Then she acts against both.

Ferris has only one element of truth: knowledge of Rearden's greatness.
He does not evaluate this greatness as valuable or important. He acts against
only one element of truth in him.

Toohey knows many more elements of truth than Lillian or Ferris, and
acts against all of them.

Yet I have the impression that Lillian is more vicious than Toohey, and Ferris is more vicious than Lillian. *Why?*

There are two aspects involved here: one, the element of truth in a person, in the sense of correct perception; in this sense, Toohey is the best of the three. The second aspect is the acting against one's own knowledge of the good, the doing of evil consciously; in this sense, Toohey is morally the guiltiest of the three.

Obviously, the issue here is between faults of knowledge and moral faults. By knowledge here I mean knowledge of fundamentals that would affect a person's essential character, such as Lillian's reaction to Rearden. I do not mean plain factual information or errors of information or lack of factual knowledge, such as is acquired in schools; I mean a fundamental perception. *Define this* and get at the principle and standard of evaluation involved here. *It is important.*

In connection with it: the capacity for enjoyment is a virtue, the result of truth, of right premises. Toohey, Lillian, Ferris, Taggart, and Mouch are all incapable of any sort of enjoyment. They have no terms in which they could actually enjoy anything. Toohey's power lust gives him no enjoyment—neither does Lillian's sense of power nor her malice—neither does Taggart's pleasure in any failure of Dagny's or Rearden's. Orren Boyle is, perhaps, capable of some enjoyment, in the momentary form of some crude orgy. The others cannot even do that. *Why?* It is not merely a matter of intelligence; Orren Boyle *is* dumber than the others, but Mouch is even dumber than Boyle—yet Mouch is totally devoid of any capacity for or sense of enjoyment. *Define* the exact principle involved here.

*Note:* this line of thought started with the idea that a former friend who admires me will act more viciously toward me, if he goes bad, than would a person indifferent toward me in the first place, one who sees no special value in me. This is an example of the inability of eliminating a truth once a person has seen it—and with the growth of an evil trait, this truth can take a terrible form, become corrupted into a greater evil, in action, than if the person had never seen it in the first place. This is an example to analyze carefully in relation to the difference between truth (or virtue) as a trait of character (as the *created* personality), and the truth or virtue of an action (as a moral or immoral action, particularly in relation to the essence of immorality: the doing of conscious evil).

The reason why people who start out with many virtues and a few flaws grow progressively worse, with the flaws winning, is the fact that an evil cannot remain stationary: it must either be eliminated entirely or it will grow (like "a few" controls in a free economy). The question I ask myself here is:

but what, then, happens to the virtues, which I consider indestructible (in the sense that a truth, once perceived, cannot be eliminated and replaced by an error)? *Define this.*

The difference between an error of knowledge and a moral error is that in the first case, a man does not suspend his consciousness (his reason), he is exercising it fully and he merely lacks all the necessary information; in the second case, he acts *against* his reason, he *does not want* to know and, therefore, he is guilty of the basic, cardinal sin (which, perhaps, is the one essential sin that embraces and contains all the others): the sin of suspending his consciousness, which amounts to suspending life or destroying the essence of life. In the first case, a man remains open to new knowledge, open to the possibility of correcting his error. In the second case, the man has closed the door to knowledge, therefore closed it to correction, and therefore his error (and his evil) will grow worse and worse.

**August 27, 1950**

*[The following is from an early draft of the scene in which Francisco finds Dagny in her country home, after she has quit.]*

[Francisco:] "If you had left TT then [twelve years ago], what would have become of it?"

[Dagny:] "Some botched form of existence, if any. Someone else would have been willing to bear the torture in order to keep it running."

"Why were you willing to bear that torture?"

"Because I loved the railroad, I loved my work—and the torture was the price I had to pay for it."

"Dagny, suffering is evil. One must never make terms with suffering. One must not accept it as normal. Suffering is the call to action, the call to fight it and destroy it—not to bear it.

"Why should love be tied to pain, as its permanent price? Why should the virtue of your ability, your competence, your intelligence, your great, living fire, be paid for by pain? Isn't there some terrible evil in that, which you have accepted? The one evil, the root and source, which we must fight? The immortalization of pain? The damning of life as a chronic state of suffering?

"Dagny, by the nature and essence of existence, no paradox can exist. Pain is destruction—the sign of the evil, the wrong, the improper, the contradictory. Pain *cannot* be the natural accompaniment of talent, of creative work, of living activity. The essence of man's life—creative action—cannot be the cause which has pain as its effect. If this is what you see around you, throughout man's existence—then what sort of code are men acting on? Who caused that? Whose idea are you acting on and what sort of an idea is it? Do you realize that *that* is pure, naked evil—the idea of death? Virtue cannot and may not be tied to pain. When it is, then it is evil that we are serving. . . .

"Have you ever wondered why the peddlers of the cannibal morality lay such a stress on imperfection? They are careful to make men think that the mere desire for perfection is evil, that it is a sin, the sin of pride. Why? Because this holds the whole secret of their moral code. It is the code of destruction—which *cannot* be practiced fully, or mankind would perish. But in that ghastly agony of the just-about, the approximation, through which they have dragged mankind for centuries, lies the only advantage they hope to achieve. If the man of virtue does not expect perfection, he will put up with undeserved pain. If the evil man does not expect perfection, he will escape the full punishment which he deserves, he will get the unearned, he will get—in spirit and in matter, in moral honor and in physical wealth—the rewards of the man of virtue, while that man of virtue will bear the evil-doer's punishment. *That is the whole heart of the 'morality of imperfection.'*

"*That* is what we've borne for centuries. Dagny! That's the evil we have to end, once and for all. No part of our virtue, no work or product of it, must go into the service of evil. No part of it must be left unrewarded and unpaid for. No moment of our suffering must be spent for the sake of providing unearned joy to the looters. One hour of undeserved pain which we accept is an hour given to the looters, the hour when we make evil possible—the only hour that makes it possible—the act of feeding and supporting evil. *That* is what we have to refuse them. Nothing unrewarded and undeserved, neither in matter nor in spirit, neither in escaped punishment nor in uncollected reward. The code of the traders, Dagny. The code of justice."

[*AR commented later on the problems she faced in writing some of the philosophical scenes with Francisco: "It was enormously difficult to decide how much could be given away and where—and what should be saved for Galt's speech." The above passages were probably cut because Francisco comes too close to identifying death as the standard of the parasites' moral code—a point that AR had to save for Galt.*]

**January 5, 1951**

*Notes for Part II*

As illustration of "Laws are made to be broken"—the state of the country now is such that one cannot survive (or get rich, which is the same) except as a criminal: by breaking the looters' laws, by paying for pull, by paying for the right to exist. The "death principle" is now almost blatantly obvious; you have to *pay* for the right to live—existence is now a *crime*.

Make use of Danneskjöld's gold given to Rearden. If possible, have it become the only money left to Rearden, his only means of escape.

Make issue of the copper shortage (in connection with or leading up to the final, total crash of d'Anconia Copper).

Make issue of Danneskjöld's blockade against the production of Rearden Metal by the looters.

*To consider* (as a possibility): the importance of California (or the West Coast) to the final disintegration and to Project X (the rule of brute force)—this was why Mouch wanted Kip Chalmers to control California. This could also be why parasites have to hold the main line of TT, rather than the Minnesota Line—thus sacrificing production to political power. They would rather have more semi-starving people to loot than to have more production—they cannot *permit* production.

**March 20, 1951**

### Note for Galt's Speech

*"Live and let live* is our moral code. The code of our enemies, the code of evil, is the code of death. It will work out to its logical conclusion and it will destroy them; but *we* will not save them, will not give life to their evil, will not make it work. Thus, toward them, our code is: *live and let die.* Anyone who desires be an irrationalist—let *him* perish by his own ideas, but do not help him to destroy the world and yourself. You cannot hold mercy above morality. To make terms with that which *you* consider evil, to be an accomplice of evil, to betray your own moral standards, in the name of 'mercy'—and to hold this as moral—is the lowest corruption ever devised by men."

**March 21, 1951**

### Key economic events for Part II:

"Unification" of railroads.
"Unification" of steel.

Crash of d'Anconia Copper.

"Soybean project"—freight cars—collapse of Minnesota.

Closing of Minnesota Line.

End of Rearden Steel.

Collapse of Taggart Bridge (which is end of TT and of New York).

---

This is the rule of the brute—the economics of gangsters, the mixture of production and guns, the "expediency of the moment," the plain, crude attempt to seize whatever's still available, with no pretense of any plan or thought of the future.

**March 24, 1951**

*Chapter I: Atlantis*

Dagny–John Galt.

The music of Halley's Fifth Concerto.

The sign of the dollar.

The car coming to meet them—Hugh Akston, Midas Mulligan. ("You're in the arms of the inventor of the motor.")

Ellis Wyatt passing them on the street.

Galt's house—the famous surgeon—the breakfast.

Quentin Daniels.

The industries of the valley.

The restaurant and the shop.

The Mulligan Bank.

The power plant (Galt's motor). (Mind and body.)

The grocery store and general store.

Dwight Sanders undertakes to fix her plane.

The dinner at Mulligan's house: Galt, Akston, Mulligan, Richard Halley, Ellis Wyatt, Ken Danagger, Quentin Daniels, Judge Narragansett, Dr. Hendricks. Her feeling about heaven and meeting all the great men. Galt's explanation: "We're on strike."

Galt drives her back to his house. She asks, on the way: "What do you call this place?" "I call it Mulligan's Valley. The others call it Galt's Gulch." "I'd call it—" but she doesn't finish.

He takes her into his guest bedroom. Hands her the gun. "Have you forgotten that you wanted to shoot me on sight?" (The contradiction in her premises, which she will have to resolve.)

She notices the inscriptions on the wall: "You'll get over it—Ellis Wyatt." "It will be all right by morning—Ken Danagger." "It's worth it— Roger Holt." She asks him about it, he explains and adds: "This is the room you were never intended to see. . . . Good night, Miss Taggart."

---

### Chapter II: The Utopia of Greed

The next morning: Galt is called out, she is fixing breakfast, when the blond stranger rushes in. "Oh, have *you* joined us?" "No, I'm a scab." Galt comes in, introduces them—Ragnar Danneskjöld. Explanation about her account.

She becomes Galt's paid cook and servant—for a month.

The arrival of Owen Kellogg. He tells her about the Comet's trip, he has arranged a job for Jeff Allen with the Taggart man at Laurel, she is thought to be lost in plane crash, he has spoken on the phone to Rearden. She asks Galt to let Rearden know—he answers: No, there is no communication with the outside world for a month.

Francisco's arrival. The scene between them.

The progression of the Galt-Dagny romance. The scene where she has to make her choice. He tells her about the universal longing for the ideal: "It's real. It's possible. Here it is—and it's yours—but at the price of dropping every delusion of mankind's vicious past, every error of the centuries of self-immolation, including the willingness to suffer unnecessary pain and to endure injustice." Her reasons: her last hope for the power of rationality and of man's self-interest, which will make her win over the looters. He tells her she will have to discover whether those men really *want* reason or life.

He flies her out of the valley. "Don't look for me. You won't find me until you really want me—with no contradictions and for what I really am. And when you'll want me, I'll be the easiest man to find."

July 6, 1951

### For Mulligan's Dinner

1) Richard Halley (new symphony)
2) Judge Narragansett (book on the philosophy of law)

**3)** Dr. Hendricks (medical research—disinfectant)
**4)** Ellis Wyatt (shale-oil research)
**5)** Ken Dannager (mine prospecting)
**6)** Midas Mulligan
**7)** Hugh Akston (book on the philosophy of reason—"the single absolute")
Quentin Daniels
John Galt (his laboratory is in N.Y.)
Dagny Taggart

———❖———

"Gentlemen—Taggart Transcontinental."
Mulligan's house—selection, not accumulation.
"We don't make assertions"—Akston.
Daniels on the floor—Galt apart, on the arm of Akston's chair—Akston's gesture—the abnormality of it all being so natural.
*Galt:* "We're on strike." The only group of men that has never struck before—who can't get along without whom—the penalizing of ability—the penalizing of virtue for being virtue—the torture of the best by means of the best within them.

———❖———

**1)** *Akston:* he quit in protest against intellectuals who teach that there is no intellect; he did not want to make that possible for them; let them try to exist without the intellect.
**2)** *Mulligan:* he quit because, when he saw money handed to need, he saw the bright faces and eyes of men like young Rearden being tied and bleeding on altars at the feet of Lee Hunsacker.
**3)** *Judge Narragansett:* he quit because he could not accept the opposite of the function he had chosen: he could not accept the position of a *judge* dispensing *injustice*—the vilest injustice conceivable to his judicial mind.
**4)** *Richard Halley:* he quit because he would not be a martyr to those whom he benefited. He had been willing to accept anything and give them anything; if they had said: "Sorry to be so late—thank you for waiting," he would have asked nothing else. But it was the smug cannibals who claimed that it was his duty to accept the torture inflicted on him by their stupidity, for *their* sake—the cannibals who

make a virtue of spiritual impotence, just as they make a virtue of
material impotence—the cannibals who demanded the unearned in
spirit, just as they demand it in money—that made him quit.

**5)** *Dr. Hendricks:* "Do you know what it takes to perform a brain
operation?"—the kind of skill and devotion required—he quit
because he could not let *that* be at the mercy, command and disposal
of men whose sole qualification and right to rule him rest on their
cowardly, evasive brutality. In all the discussions of socialized medicine, men discussed everything, except the wishes, will, and choice
of the doctors. Men considered nothing but the "*welfare*" of the
patients. Well, let them cure themselves and exist without him.

**6)** *Ellis Wyatt:* he quit because he knew that it was his blood—his
carcass—they needed in order to survive.

**7)** *Ken Danagger:* he quit because he did not need them.

**8)** *Quentin Daniels:* he quit because he could not deal with
unreason. The scientist who deals with unreason is the guiltiest man
of all.

**9)** *Galt:* he abandoned the motor, because he knew that it would do
men no good without a mind able to understand it.

*The history of the valley:* first, just Mulligan's private retreat, then Judge
Narragansett joined him, then Richard Halley. The others stayed outside,
[living by] their rule: do not work in your true profession, do not exercise
your ability, do not give men the use of your mind. Their assignment outside: to watch men of ability, to approach them when they're ready and to
pull them out. They all went on working at their professions, but sharing
nothing with men, giving nothing. The yearly vacation—one month to rest
and to live in a human world, in *society* as it should be.

Then, particularly since the destruction of Colorado, they began to join
Mulligan and settle in the valley, because they had to hide. They converted
their wealth into gold or machines. The valley is not a state, not an organization of any kind; it is a voluntary association held together by nothing but
every man's self-interest. Mulligan owns the valley and leases the land to
the others. Judge Narragansett is the arbiter, in case of disagreements; there
haven't been many. (This code of principles is the Constitution of the
United States, without the contradictions: the code of inalienable individual
rights.)

The valley is now almost self-supporting, so that most of them can live
there full-time and earn their living (Dr. Akston, Owen Kellogg, the young
porter). Mulligan takes care of dealing with the outside world for the

purchase of goods that they cannot produce in the valley; he has a special agent for that (Ragnar Danneskjöld). Soon they will all have to live in the valley exclusively—because the world is falling apart so fast that the outside will be starving; but they will be able to support themselves here. (The frozen trains, etc., are *not* part of the strike—they're the natural response of whatever rational element is left in people, the same kind of protest, the natural, inevitable break-up.)

[The strikers] had started with no time limit in view, but now they think that they will see, and soon, the day of their triumph and their return. When? When the road is clear, when the looters have collapsed. Let the looters collapse without the mind—let them get out of the way—then Galt will call off the strike and they will return to the world.

They speak of their professions which they are still pursuing, each naming his particular work.

Galt points to the roads of the valley—"the most expensive roads in the world." The men who could do *only* physical labor or road-building are now starving for lack of jobs which they cannot originate—while the men who could have provided jobs, factories, automobiles, radios, if they were free and their time were released, have, instead, been building roads. "We can survive without them. They can't survive without us."

**June 30, 1951**

### Notes on Emotions

*All emotions are [responses to] judgments of value.*

The fundamental division is: *pleasure and pain.* This applies to physical sensations and to emotions; the emotional equivalent of pleasure and pain is *joy and sorrow.*

### Classification of Emotions

I. *Emotions toward oneself*
  *Positive:* Self-respect, pride, confidence, assurance
  *Negative:* Self-contempt, shame, guilt, self-doubt

II. *Emotions toward objective reality (toward events)*
  *Positive:* Joy, hope (?), interest (?)
  *Negative:* Sorrow, fear, disappointment, frustration, boredom (?)

III. *Emotions toward other people*
   *Positive:* Admiration, respect, affection, love
   *Negative:* Contempt, anger, hatred (Fear—? Fear is felt toward an event or
   an *action* of the person, not toward the person)

*The single emotion toward an objective to be reached—desire.*
   Compassion—don't know where to classify. (?)
   Analyze which are primary, which are combined emotions—and define
the *kind of valuations* that are involved in the primary emotions. This could
be a basic chart for the specific provisions of a code of ethics.
   *Question to analyze:* since all valuations pertain to a realm of choice
and are acts of choice, perhaps emotions can be felt *only* toward actions, not
toward static entities. This may clarify the exact connection between one's
emotions and one's actions. Emotions toward people are toward the *entity* of
a person—but they come from one's estimate of that person's *actions*. We
feel the emotion toward that quality of a person's character which was
responsible for the action. The same applies to emotions toward oneself.
Emotions toward objective reality are *all* estimates of *events*, past, present or
future, which [are] means of *actions*. The emotion of *desire* (to reach an
objective) is toward *action*. (The one exception seems to be esthetic pleasure—which is admiration for an attribute of a static entity: physical
beauty.)

**December 11, 1951**

*Elements of Chapter II*

*Three main lines:* Galt-Dagny, Francisco-Galt, and Dagny–the valley.

*Scenes:*

   **(1)** Dagny–Richard Halley.
   **(2)** Dagny–Kay Ludlow, after the theater performance.
   **(3)** Galt's lectures.
   **(4)** Dagny–young mother.
   Dagny—plan of railroad.
   **(5)** *Dr. Akston, his three pupils, and Dagny.*
        (Akston on emotions as the philosophical "summary" of a man.
   The essence of *being*: identification—the joke on the body and soul

preachers—the "bottling up" of the soul in a jail—why his three pupils have accomplished everything.) [*This paragraph is crossed out.*]

**(6)** "From where have you watched me all these years?" "What is your job in the world? Don't tell me that you're a second-assistant bookkeeper!" "No, I'm not."

The "sensual" pleasure of cooking for Galt, the relationship of being his servant. ("You could hold me here." "I know it.")

**(7)** *Rearden's plane.*

**(8)** *Scene where Francisco guesses Galt-Dagny romance.* (Francisco asks Dagny to move to his house; Galt refuses.) (Scene where Francisco passes by Galt's house.) [*The last sentence was crossed out.*]

**(9)** *Scene where Dagny decides to go back.*

**January 4, 1952**

*Scenes for Chapter II (Tentative)*

*Scene where Dagny decides to go back* (two days before last, June 28): here the dialogue between Dagny and Galt is about love, but never directly. It is their declaration that they love each other—they both understand, but nothing is said openly. In her mind, interspersed with the things she says aloud, are the lines of her speech of dedication: "You whom I have always loved and never found . . ." He tells her that the ideal is here, it's real, it's possible, but . . .

(Write the two themes in counterpoint, so that his words underscore and answer the words in her mind—so that the whole is clear and is a declaration of love, but only as a whole, not in what either of them says aloud.)

*Scene where Francisco discovers Galt-Dagny romance* (toward end of month). "And you said that I was the one who took the hardest beating! . . . I should have known it. I should have known it twelve years ago, before you ever saw her. I have stated it myself. You were everything that he was seeking, everything he told us to live for or die, if necessary."

[*Added later:*] Galt had said to Francisco, in sending him to Dagny: "If you want your chance, take it. You've earned it." Francisco says: "Take it. You've earned it—and it wasn't chance."

Here, too, the counterpoint dialogue. Nothing is said openly—everything is said through their mutual understanding. *Francisco's attitude:* I understand,

I approve, it's as it ought and had to be. *Galt's attitude:* I'd give anything not to hurt you—anything but this, because this, as you know, is beyond sacrifice. *Dagny's attitude:* It's true, but I'll only hurt him as I've hurt you, and my price for it is that I'm hurting myself right now as much as both of you have suffered—but it is a price that I have to pay. Yet, through this, simultaneously, she feels "the sense of enormous rightness" and a sense of joy—for all three of them, for being alive. (It's Galt who expresses this last, who gives voice for all three of them to the sense of joy, to *their* sense of existence.)

*Scene of the "non-sacrifice."* Elements for it: Francisco tells Dagny about Galt sending him to her in the country. Galt refuses to let Dagny move to Francisco's house. Dagny is set free of the fear of sacrifice—she sees what ugliness this would have been if they had acted on the moral standards of the outside world.

———◦———

[*Note on the writer who was a fishwife in the valley:*] Galt tells Dagny that the girl is in love with him—and mentions the contemptible paradox of the outside world's attitude toward unrequited love: men hold love to be a supreme virtue, yet a woman who loves a man without answer is supposed to be ridiculous, she is supposed to hide her feeling as some sort of disgrace or shame, in order to protect her "pride," or else she makes a claim and a burden upon the man out of her unrequited feeling and pursues him, half as a begger, half as a sheriff. But *here*, love is [held to be] what it actually is by its nature: a recognition of values and the greatest tribute one human being can give another, gratefully to be accepted, whether one returns it or not.

*Scene of Rearden's plane.* This comes after some scene where Dagny is violently happy about her relationship with Galt—after some clear indication of his love for her and of her happiness with him. The plane serves as the climax or last incident of the contest among the three men in her mind. It is Galt who wins—the scene must end on some indication of this.

*Scene of Dr. Akston, his three pupils, and Dagny.* (For philosophical theme—"emotions as the philosophical summary of a man.") [*This last sentence was crossed out.*] For personal theme—Akston's reminiscences about Galt, Francisco, and Danneskjöld in college. This will show us what sort of men they were and how they faced their future. Francisco—the richest heir in the world; Danneskjöld—the European aristocrat, without money, but with the sternest tradition of honor and nobility; Galt—a wholly self-made man, out of nowhere, penniless, family-less, tie-less, son of a factory worker in Ohio, left his home at the age of twelve and has been on his own ever since. (Akston refers to him as "Minerva, the goddess of wisdom, who was born ready and whole out of Jupiter's brain.") Akston mentions their choice of physics and philosophy as their major subjects—and their reasons: the union of mind and body.

(This might be the place to state their attitude on religion—the atheism of all four of them. "Do you believe in God, Miss Taggart?" "God, no!" "That's about all that one needs to say on the subject. We are here concerned with reason. It is a big enough job—enough for the life of any man.")

Show Akston's love for his three pupils, his paternal devotion to them—past and present. For present, such touches as: "Don't sit on the ground, Francisco. It's getting chilly. You've always been careless about taking chances." Akston calls Dagny "Miss Taggart"—then, after a specific reference to the three men as his sons (and after some hint of the Dagny-Galt relationship), he suddenly addresses her as "Dagny" and she sees him looking at Galt. This is Akston's acceptance of Dagny as his daughter—as Galt's wife.

*Scene of temptation.* The night when Galt and Dagny almost surrender to an unendurable desire for each other. She sees the look and the torture of desire in his face. ("Do you wish to hold me here?" "More than anything else in the world." "You could hold me." "I know it." Then: "It's your acceptance of this place that I wish. What good would it do me to have your physical presence without any meaning? That is the sort of fraud on reality which people cheat themselves by. I'm incapable of it.") He is first to leave—to go to his bedroom. She lies in bed, tortured, unable to sleep. She wonders whether Galt is tortured in the same manner. She hears no sound, sees no light in his room. Then she hears the sound of a step and the click of a cigarette lighter. (Then—she hears the steps outside and hears Francisco speaking to Galt. She learns that Galt had been sitting on the sill of his open window, smoking a cigarette. Francisco is on his way home from Richard Halley's house. They speak for a few moments, then Francisco walks on. She realizes that Francisco has no suspicion of any attraction between her and Galt—and now Francisco can be certain that they do not sleep with each other.) [*This last parenthetical passage was crossed out.*]

*Scene of Galt telling her about his first sight of her.* This must come in some context such as the one at the power house, so that when she asks: "When did you see me for the first time?"—the question actually is: how long have you been in love with me? He tells her that he saw her ten years ago, one night, on the underground platform of the Taggart Terminal. She was wearing an evening dress, a light, flowing, ice-blue gown, like the tunic of a Greek goddess, with the short hair and imperious profile of an American girl. She had a fur cape, half sliding off her body, he saw her naked back, shoulders and profile, it looked for an instant as if the cape would slide further and she would stand naked. She looked preposterously out of place on a railroad platform—it was not of a railroad that he was thinking, and yet it *was*, she *did* belong here, she was the real spirit and meaning of it, luxury and competence combined, energy and its reward. She did not seem to be aware of her clothes, she was giving orders to three men, her voice clear, swift, confident, she was intent on nothing but her work. He came close enough to hear two sentences: "Who said so?" asked one of the men. "I did," she answered evenly. That was all. That was enough. He knew that this was Dagny Taggart—and he knew, then, that he was in love with her. She wonders which one among the streams of passengers that she ignored had been Galt—she wonders how close she had then come and had missed. "Why didn't you speak to me, then or later?" she asks. He says: "Do you remember what you were doing in the terminal that night?" She remembers vaguely that she had been called from a party she was attending, because the new terminal manager had caused some mess—the old one had quit a week earlier. He says: "It was I who made him quit."

Before that night, Galt had heard about Dagny from Francisco, but very little: Francisco had told him that she was one of them, that she was the sole hope and future of Taggart Transcontinental, but that TT would be hard to destroy, because she would be their most dangerous enemy, she would be very hard to win for their strike, she had too much endurance and devotion to her work. Francisco had spoken briefly, dryly, non-commitally, as if merely reporting on a future striker. Galt knew that they had been childhood friends, that was all. After Galt had seen her, he began to question Francisco about her whenever he could. He noticed that Francisco was eager to talk about her, in spite of himself. He realized what Francisco's past with her had been, that she had been Francisco's mistress, that Francisco had given her up for the strike and was still desperately in love with her. But Galt never let him guess the nature and reason of his own interest in her. It sounded merely as if he were questioning Francisco about an important future striker. The scene ends on

Dagny wondering whether Galt intends to sacrifice his own love for the sake of Francisco.

*Smaller, preliminary scenes:* (1) Scene where *Dagny asks Galt* from where he had been watching her and what job he holds in the world; he refuses to answer both questions. (2) *Dagny and Francisco in his house.* (The two silver goblets—he's never used them; they're all he wants to save, everything else will go, in a few months.) His design of a copper smelter, his talk about his first d'Anconia Copper mine, here, in the valley; instead of the doubled production he had dreamed about, he might produce only a single pound of copper at the end of his life, but he will be richer than with all the tons produced by his ancestors, because that pound will be wholly his, with no part of it feeding the looters. (The start of d'Anconia Copper—and of the world—has to be in the U.S.) In this scene, there is a touch of possibility of her love for Francisco. (3) *Scenes of Dagny and the valley:* Galt's lectures; Dagny–Richard Halley; Dagny–Kay Ludlow; Dagny–young mother. (4) *Dagny and the plan for the railroad* (then—"what for?") (5) *Scene where they discuss Dagny's departure:* Dagny, Galt, Francisco, Mulligan, Akston. Here they beg Galt to remain in the valley, he has no further reason to stay outside; but he says that he has not yet decided, he might stay outside—for "the one thing he wants for himself" (though not in any collaboration or compromise with the looters—nor with the "scabs," this is not *for* Dagny, but *for him*).

---

*Think over:* whether to indicate the economic future of the world when the strikers return—and Judge Narragansett's proposed amendment to the Constitution.

**January 5, 1952**

### Decisions to Make for Key Scenes

[*The answers to these questions seem to have been added later.*]

**1.** Scene of Galt telling Dagny about the past: *Where* does scene take place? In his house. What form of temptation leads to her questions? He finds her asleep, waiting for him.

**2.** *Rearden's plane:* In what context? What precedes and follows her sight of the plane?

**3.** *Temptation scene:* What leads to it? (Combine with 1.)

**4.** *"Non-sacrifice":* In what context? In context of: "If you want your chance, take it." Where does scene take place?

**5.** *Francisco's discovery:* Where does scene take place? In his house. What gives him his final clue? Galt's decision to go back to job.

### Tentative order of scenes (Chapter II):

**1.** *Scene of Galt telling Dagny how he saw her for the first time.* (Preceded by her question about how he watched her and what is his job in the outside world.) (He finds her asleep. The story is followed by the temptation scene.)

**2.** *Dagny–Francisco, in his house.*

**3.** *Dagny–the valley* (Galt's lectures, Richard Halley, Kay Ludlow, young mother).

**4.** *Dagny–plan of railroad.* ("I won't ask you—you'll tell me when you've decided.")

**5.** *Dr. Akston and his three pupils.*

**6.** *Rearden's plane.*

**7.** *Scene of "no-sacrifice."*

**8.** *Discussion of Dagny's departure.* (Talk of danger to Galt, of break-down and Taggart bridge, makes her decide to go back.)

**9.** *Francisco discovers Galt-Dagny romance.* (They walk home together and stop at Francisco's house. Question of Galt going back to his job. The two silver goblets. "Take it. You've earned it.")

**10.** *The flight by plane, and their parting.*

**January 6, 1952**

### Note on Paradoxes

The essential paradox, which is the root of all philosophical errors, is as follows: to substitute for an abstraction one of the concrete applications of that abstraction, and at the same time make that concrete contradict and invalidate the abstraction. Example: when a man decides that thought is not valid, that he will not think, but will instead obey the orders of a dictator, it is an act and decision of thought; he substitutes specific "political thought" for the general abstraction of "thought," declares thought to be invalid and holds this as a justification for the thinking which led him to decide to stop thinking about politics and to obey political orders.

**June 7, 1952**

### For Taggart and Cherryl

Taggart's desire for the unearned spiritually—he does not want Cherryl to rise, *he wants his "love" for her to be alms* and he wants her admiration for him to be sincere, but unearned; her torture under an impossible paradox. *Her horror when she realizes that his love was in answer to flaws*, rather than in answer to values (the exact opposite of the Rearden-Dagny romance). Taggart's hold on her through her pity; he stops her doubts by means of his whining and her generosity—until she sees the truth. She thinks that suffering is still a sign of the good in him, of his struggling for something—*until she realizes what the nature of his suffering is: his frustrated desire for destruction.* (Her struggle with "culture"—her boredom with the Eubank kind of art, her bewilderment at the revivals of classics, Taggart's anger at her questions about it. Here—parallel to the last-stage economic looting.)

**June 9, 1952**

### Taggart and Cherryl

Taggart wishes to celebrate the deal which has given a loan to the People's State of Chile in exchange for the promise that the d'Anconia Copper mines will be nationalized on September 2, then turned over on "operation lease" to an "international group" consisting of Orren Boyle, an equivalent of Cuffy Meigs, and others of that sort. No word has been said publicly about Dagny's broadcast, but Bertram Scudder has been made the goat: his program is abolished. He has to keep silent if he doesn't want to be framed and jailed or [punished as] the authorities please.

Taggart's sudden realization that nothing gives him pleasure. Taggart and Cherryl, their "formal" dinner. Her poise and silence, his attempts to get her sanction.

Flashback to highlights of their marriage and of her growing realization.

Her bewilderment about their wedding party—and her determination to understand, and to be worthy of him.

Her attempts at self-improvement, and his vicious attitude toward it.

She begins to suspect his position on the railroad (faith versus truth); she decides to investigate. The evasiveness of the railroad officials; the common workers tell her the truth; Eddie Willers tells her the whole truth.

Taggart's fury about her "ingratitude," then his play for pity and "understanding"—her tortured fairness and patience. (Her disappointment in "culture"—his incomprehensible anger about it.)

Now, at dinner, his attempt at "celebration" fails—he talks about "causeless" love—she will not grant him sanction. ("What I feel is fear." "Of me?" "No, not exactly. Not of what you can do, but of what you are.")

Cherryl goes to see Dagny. Cherryl's apology and despair; Dagny cannot fully reassure her.

Lillian comes to see Taggart about stopping the divorce. He can't help her, but they both share the enjoyment over Francisco's coming ruin and over Rearden's crushing burdens. *This* is the celebration Taggart wanted. Their affair.

Cherryl comes home to find that Taggart is in the bedroom with some woman. Cherryl does not walk in, she hides in her own study and waits, then comes out and confronts Taggart when he is alone. His vicious admissions, his boast that the woman was Lillian Rearden, his laughter when Cherryl offers to give him a divorce—her horror at the full realization of the meaning of his love, the love "in answer to flaws." She almost names the death principle—he slaps her.

She runs out of the house, wanders through the streets, the city—as her symbol of greatness, but now she is in total terror that she has no way of knowing the good from the evil. (The traffic lights.) Her suicide—she leaps into the river.

**August 26, 1952**

*Note for Galt's Speech*

[In regard to] the "death principle" and James Taggart: Taggart wanted Cherryl to be vicious—and moral—at the same time. This means that he wants good people to "weaken" occasionally and thus give him both the benefit of their virtue and the license for his evil. It is their "weaknesses," their evil, that would make it possible for him to exploit their virtues. (Example: Rearden's sex guilt and the gift certificate.) It is the "middle-of-the-road" morality—the theory that "there's something bad in the best of us"—that is the most immoral theory possible, because it is the only theory that makes it possible for evil to exist. Pure evil is impotent, it is destruction and nonexistence; it is only by feeding on and penalizing virtue that evil can act and have power in the world.

**October 1, 1952**

### *[Part III, Chapter V:] "Their Brothers' Keepers"*

**1.** The complete chaos, the blind, random chance, the arbitrary senselessness, the total lack of logic and reason in *production*—and the steady, inexhaustible logic in the progression of *destruction*. (Men are still achieving their ideas—hold the premises of destruction and you'll get it.)

**2.** The futile and horrible rushing to save the needy at the expense of the able—the last of the country's wealth is going to support the incompetent in the emergency of the moment. The incompetent perish and the wealth goes down the drain with them, while the competent, who could have survived, are immolated the minute before, i.e., their chance of survival is destroyed to let the incompetent last that one minute longer—the range of the moment, which keeps getting shorter and shorter. The revolting obscenity of acting on the cult of need, of taking need as claim and motive. The "brothers' keepers" see themselves being eaten alive, with the "brothers" making their work impossible and making more demands at the same time—the final, naked insolence of the cannibalistic parasite who yells that "you're morally evil because I starve, look at my misery, it is your moral failure and sin—do something!—how do I know what?—it's your problem and responsibility, you've got the mind, I haven't, you're my keeper, I have the right of misery, incompetence and helplessness!" (Give examples of this along the whole range—both public and private, both for industries and for personal, family relations.)

**3.** The grotesque preposterousness of the "world planners"—such as the "soybean project," the power-hungry incompetents, each with a plan of his own to rule the economy of the nation, each getting a little bit of his plan into action, at a devastating cost. Here we have soybeans, TV sets, etc. manufactured for the pleasure of the masters and the planners—while the country is starving. Here material goods follow the pattern of the men who are still left—the senseless and non-essential goods are manufactured, the essential ones vanish. The motives here are an almost inextricable mixture of corruption and humanitarianism—some projects are undertaken for pure Cuffy Meigs–like looting, others for a Eugene Lawson–like vicious hysteria of giving away and saving the needy of the immediate split-second. (Show that the motive makes no difference.)

# NOTES WHILE WRITING GALT'S SPEECH

In a 1961 interview, AR recalled her thoughts as she approached writing John Galt's speech: "I knew it was going to be the hardest chapter in the book.... I underestimated. I thought, with a feeling of dread, that it would take at least three months. Well, it took two years." AR began her outline on July 29, 1953; she finished the speech on October 13, 1955.

Her difficulty was not primarily with philosophical content. By 1953, she was clear on nearly all of the ideas. The only fundamental that she discovered during the writing was the relationship of the concept "value" to the concept "life." The other problems of content were in formulating the ideas with the total precision she demanded.

It was the literary requirements of the speech—it had to be a dramatic, emotion-charged statement serving as the strikers' ultimatum to the world—that gave AR the most difficulty, particularly in regard to the order of presentation. She explained in a 1961 interview:

I started by making an outline of the issues to be covered. First as a general listing of material, then in approximate order of presentation. But I couldn't stick to that outline; it had to be redone many times. I originally began the theoretical presentation with metaphysics, starting with existence exists, going from metaphysics to epistemology, then planning to go to morality. After writing quite a few pages, I had to stop because I knew it was absolutely wrong. That is the logical order in non-fiction, but you can't do it in fiction. The speech had to start by presenting the morality, which is the real theme of the book, and where Galt would have to begin his explanation to the world. So I had to rewrite the whole thing.

*The brief notes presented here are apparently all that she kept from her two years of work on Galt's speech; regrettably, the early draft and revised outlines that she refers to are not among her notes.*

**July 29, 1953**

### Main Subjects of Galt's Speech

*Metaphysics:* Existence exists—A is A.
*Epistemology:* Reason—thinking is volitional, not automatic.
*Morality:* The need of morality for a being of free will. The Morality of Life: Life as the standard of value—thinking as the only basic virtue, from which all others proceed—non-thinking as the only basic vice—the recognition of reality or the non-recognition. Force. Mysticism. *The morality of death:* all the forms of the attempt to fake reality; destruction as the only result. Basic premises. Emotions and reason.
*Economics:* The unearned. The *gift* of inventors.
*Politics:* Rights.

### Outline of Galt's Speech (Philosophical Content)

*Metaphysics*
Existence exists. A is A.

*Epistemology*
Mind and body. The nature of reason—the evidence of the senses, integrated by his mind according to the rules of logic. *Logic is the art of non-contradictory identification.* The nature of abstractions. *Thinking is volitional*—it is not an automatic process. The root of "free will"—you have no choice about what reality *is*, but you have the choice of *knowing* what it is or not. The mind is man's tool of survival. Life is given to you, survival is not. To survive, you must think; you must discover the means and methods of survival proper to man; you have no arbitrary freedom about it—you cannot survive "at random," you must learn what is necessary for your survival as man.

July 29, 1953

V Main subjects of Galt's speech

Metaphysics — Existence exists — A is A

Epistemology — Reason — Thinking is volitional, not automatic

Morality —
The need of morality for a being of free will. Life as the standard of value — thinking as the only basic virtue, from which all others proceed — non-thinking as the only basic vice — (the recognition of reality or the non-recognition) Force, Mysticism. The morality of death: all the forms of the attempt to fake reality, destruction is the only result. Basic premises. Emotions and reason.

Economics (the unearned)
Politics (the gift of inches)
(Rights)

## Morality

The need of morality for a being of free will—a being who must survive by means of choice—a rational being who must think and must *choose* to think. The process of reason is: Yes or No? Right or Wrong? This is the process of thinking and of every action a man takes as a result of his thinking. Truth (perception of reality) is the standard of value for his thinking. He needs a standard of value to guide the actions he'll take as a result of his knowledge, to estimate the choices he'll make: *his existence as man is his standard of value*—as man, because he can exist in no other way, yet he has to maintain his status as man and his existence by his own will and choice.

### The Morality of Life

Thinking as the only basic virtue, from which all others proceed; non-thinking as the only basic vice. The recognition of reality or the non-recognition; existence or non-existence; life or non-life; entity or zero. The responsibility of saying "It *is*." Joy and pain as the barometer of life or death. The function of pain in one's body—the pain in one's spirit. Emotions proceed from reason. Emotions as the summary of a man's philosophy. Emotions are based on your estimates, and your estimates on your basic premises, on your moral code.

Joy is the purpose of the Life Morality. When man's life is the standard and reason the judge, no contradictions are possible, no "destructive" joy, no "hangovers"—and no desire "to have your cake and eat it, too," *no desire for the irrational*. Life is the value, pursuit of happiness is the goal; man exists for his own sake and for his own happiness. The same code applies to all men: there is no clash of interests if no man expects another to live for him, if no man expects the unearned. There is no sacrifice in human relationships—only the pattern of *traders*. Men trade value for value, in matter and *in spirit*.

*The virtues of the Life Morality: thinking*—therefore rationality, the refusal to go against your own consciousness and judgment, the refusal to fake reality; *independence*—the refusal to submit to the authority of others, to place another's judgment above your own; *honesty*—which is only another name for rationality, the loyalty to reality, the "being true to truth"; *purposefulness* (productiveness)—the choice of your life purpose and the achievement of it; *happiness*—which is possible only as the result of virtue, as the full integration of your reason and action; *self-esteem*—which means pride, self-value—which means the conscious practice of your moral code, the living up to your values, the creation of your own character. (Errors of knowledge versus moral errors; in the realm of morality, nothing counts but *perfection*.) (Man's need of an ideal.)

*The vices of the Life Morality: non-thinking*—which means the evasion of knowledge, the placing of anything whatever above your own mind, any form of mysticism, of faith, or denial of reality; *dependence*—the placing of others above yourself in any manner whatever, either as authority or as love; *aimlessness*—the non-integrated life; *pain*—the submission to it or acceptance of it; *humility*—the acceptance of one's moral imperfection, the willingness to be imperfect, which means: the indifference to moral values and to yourself, i.e., self-abnegation; *the initiation of force*—as the destruction of the mind, as the method contrary to man's form of survival, as the anti-man and anti-life.

### The Morality of Death

Such moralities place the standard of value outside of man and of reality, e.g., God, the hereafter, the needs of the soul as opposed to the body. By definition, they are impossible to man; the "good" is the opposite of life. The result is such evils as the opposition of soul and body, of theory and practice, of the moral and the practical. All of it is a rebellion against reality. You cannot fake reality. The desire for a non-stable reality is the desire for non-existence (A is A).

The morality of sacrifice: the sacrificing of virtue to vice, of the good to the evil, of value to non-value, of a positive to a negative, of achievement to need, of ability to inability—the lack, the flaw, the absence, the zero as the consistent standard and the ultimate goal. Life is a sin, under this morality, because everything required by life is a sin. Joy is a sin, pain is a virtue. The death principle throughout it all. *The creed of the unearned.*

*The worship of emotions*—but emotions are only your "stale thinking." The demand for unearned love—they do not expect causeless fear, but they do demand causeless love.

The "strong" and the "weak"—so you expect men to survive while being irrational?

*The conspiracy against life, ability and the mind.* The paradox of the defenders of freedom resting their case on mysticism, while the destroyers of the mind claim to represent reason—the paradox of all absolutes being mystical or non-existent; the absolute of reason is denied by all. Which is the triumph of spirit over matter: India or New York?

*Politics*

Man's rights—inherent in the need of his survival as man. No initiation of force. No sacrifice of man to man. No compulsion. No subordination of one man's mind to that of another. Voluntary transactions. The trader principle. The proper function of government—retaliation by force against those who initiate force, *and nothing else.*

*Economics*

Man's right to his own property, to the product of his labor, rests on the law of cause and effect. You cannot have the result, if you destroy the source. You cannot have the product of a man's mind, except on *his* terms. How free enterprise worked—the benefit given to others by inventors and innovators, the inestimable benefit of an idea. The relationship of the "weak" and the "strong": the strong (intellectually strong, which is the only strength possible in a free, non-force economy) raise the value of the weak's time by delegating to them the tasks already known and thus being free to pursue new discoveries. Proper mutual trade to mutual advantage. The interests of the mind are one, no matter what the degree of intelligence, provided nobody seeks the unearned.

---

*The address to the men of the mind:* do not accept the morality of your own destroyers. It is *you* who have made them possible. Set your own terms and code. Put an end to the use of your virtues for your own torture. Learn to understand the nature of your enemies: they do seek death and universal destruction. Yours is the code of Life. Fight for it. There is no other.

**July 30, 1953**

[*The following seems to be a revision of the above outline, beginning with morality.*]

*Outline of Galt's Speech*

You have achieved your moral ideal. It is your morality that has destroyed the world.

*What is morality?* Man—reason—need of a code—man's only choice: to think or not to think—the essence of thinking: A is A—the

standard of value: man's survival as man, *life* as the value. It is on a
desert island that you would need morality most.

*What is your morality?* The morality of death—the anti-man,
anti-mind, anti-existence. Mysticism and force—mind and body.
Whatever your code, reason is your common enemy. The conspiracy
against the mind. We have withdrawn. (I have merely done by design
what has been done throughout history by default.) Now look at your
morality and your world.

*The Morality of Death.* The standard of value outside of man; *original sin*; life as guilt, the mind as guilt, every virtue needed to support life as guilt, the moral versus the practical, *joy* as guilt.

*Sacrifice:* the total immorality of its meaning—the *zero* as the
consistent standard of value.

*The consequences of the contradiction* (personal): the botched, half-living creatures scared to think—all the consequences of the morality
of death—the worship of emotions—"wishes" versus reality.

*Man's need of self-esteem:* his chronic fear, his knowledge that he *is*
his own destroyer—all his virtues are called vices, all his vices are
called virtues—the dread that *evil* is practical (since *life* is evil).

*The creed of the unearned:* the real purpose of all mystics: the
unearned in spirit; the rebellion against a stable reality, against the
*absolute* of reality; the anti-cause-and-effect; the desire to reverse
cause and effect. But the escape from reality, in any form whatever,
is the desire for non-existence.

*The consequences of the contradiction* (social): the defenders of
freedom are now mystics, and the destroyers of the mind claim to
represent reason; the idea that morality and absolutes *must* be mystical; the attitude toward "desires" and man's psychology which savages had toward physical nature. *The constant oppositions:* mind and
body, the moral and the practical, theory and practice, reason and
emotions, security and freedom, yourself and others, selfishness and
charity, private interests and public interests, the "having and eating
your cake" principle. A "social" or mystical morality is self-defeating by definition, it *has to* make man immoral—but try to consider all those concepts with reason as the standard and you'll see
that there are no contradictions where no element of mysticism, of
the irrational, has been introduced.

*The constant demands for the impossible:* the desire to have men survive while being irrational. "Public welfare": who is the public?—
failure as [conferring] the right to the title of "public."

*The destruction of America:* the country of reason; what has been done to it? America's self-sacrifice to the vilest savages—which is the triumph of spirit over matter: India or New York?—why America could not survive on the morality of altruism.

*The Morality of Life:* Life as the standard—thinking as the only basic virtue—joy as the purpose—man existing for his own sake and for the pursuit of his own happiness—no duty, no temptation—evil as non-practical—the pattern of traders—justice, not mercy—no sacrifice, no initiation of force, no obedience to force.

*Politics:* Man's rights. The proper function of government regarding force.

*Economics:* Property (the profit-motive, the dollar-sign). How free enterprise worked: the spiritual benefit given by the inventors. The separation of State and economics.

(I have merely done by design what has been done throughout history by default. What I have done, too, is merely an act of identification. The extent to which you have lived and found joy is the extent to which you have acted on my morality.)

*The address to the men of the mind:* To the best within you. Do not accept the morality of your own destroyers. Set your own terms. Yours is the code of life. Fight for it. There is no other. When Life is once more the value—*then*, we'll return. The strikers' oath.



**September 28, 1953**

When we say that nobody actually believes in God, it is true, if by "belief" we mean the equivalent of a rational conviction. But the trick, the psychological "gimmick," of mystics is the fact that they do not *"believe"* in reality, either. What we mean by a rational conviction has no equivalent in their consciousness. No, they do not "believe" in God in the same way as they "believe" in food, money or their material existence—but their material existence has no full reality for them, either—and *that* is some special state of consciousness, that is the root of the faking, the pretense, the going through an act, the unreality which I sense about most people and which I hate more than anything else, that is the form of their Death Premise, as if they do not merely wish to destroy existence, but have never even permitted existence to exist.

**January 9, 1954**

### The Morality of Death

*Metaphysics:* the worship of the zero; the rebellion against a stable reality, against absolutes, which is the wish for non-existence.

*Epistemology:* the "sixth sense," the definitions by means of the negative, the modern mystics and relativists, the "stolen concepts," the worship of emotions, the mixture of existence and consciousness, the anti-cause-and-effect, the creed of the unearned.

*Morality:* mind and body; the placing of the standard of value outside of man; original sin; life, mind and joy as guilt; the opposition of the moral and the practical; *sacrifice*: the total immorality of its meaning, the *zero* as the standard of value. (It is evil to produce, it is good to mooch.)

*The purpose of that morality:* the sacrifice of the good to the evil, the conspiracy against ability and the mind—what the strikers are on strike against. (You need us? It is the generosity of the good that makes the evil possible.)

### The Consequences of the Morality of Death

*Personal:*

   Man's need of self-esteem: life or death. Their sense of guilt and fear: the knowledge of their non-thinking. Fear—because they have abandoned their tool of survival. Guilt—because they know that they have done it volitionally. They are their own destroyers. (Their search for "themselves"—the *self* is the mind.)

   They have given up reason—then complain that the universe is a mystery.

   The conflict of the practical and the moral.

   The fear that evil is practical—since *life* is evil.

   ("It's only logic." The fortune-teller and the fortune-maker.)

*Social:*

   The defenders of freedom are mystics, while its enemies claim to represent reason.

   The contradictions between: soul and body, mind and heart, the moral and the practical, yourself and others, security and freedom, public interest and private interest, human rights and property rights.

   The principle of expropriation throughout society—*every* man is rewarded in proportion to his flaws, and penalized in proportion to his virtues.

*The evil of the "middle-of-the-roaders":* they place their best in the service of their worst, and destroy their best in the same way as they destroy the best men in society. (The cost of their compromises: the death of their children as result of their government subsidy.)

What the men of the mind had given them—the pyramid of ability.

What they must do: stand on the judgment of your mind—you don't know much?—don't discard that which you know. Reason is an absolute.

Errors of knowledge versus moral errors. Perfection. ("Benefit of the doubt.")

Traders—help to others on the basis of values, not flaws, not *need*.

The single axiom: *the evil of force.* Good men will not work under compulsion. The obscenity of using force "for their own good."

"Some of you will never know who is John Galt."

The moments when they do know who is John Galt.

The damnation of Stadler. (The man who places his mind in the service of evil, while he is *able* to know better, but does not care.)


**Undated**

[*The following note critiques the Kantian idea that "things in themselves" are unknowable. AR cut this topic from Galt's speech. Later, she covered it in the title essay of* For the New Intellectual.]


### Notes for [Galt's] Speech

*Metaphysics: "Things in Themselves"*

Walk into any college classroom and you will hear your professors teaching your children that knowledge is impossible to man and that his consciousness has no validity whatever. A savage does not know the nature of his means of perception; your teachers go him one better: they know and they disqualify man's consciousness on the ground that its means are specific and knowable.

You can know nothing, they tell you, because you perceive only that which your senses can perceive; your sight is made possible by light rays, your hearing is made possible by sound waves—therefore, your knowledge is not valid, since your consciousness works through these means and no others, since it is itself and can be nothing else, since it cannot step outside itself to verify its knowledge. Your knowledge is not valid, they tell you, because your perceptions are not *causeless.* You cannot know, they tell you, whether the things you perceive are real, because you have no consciousness other than your own and do not know what some other sort of consciousness might see. No matter how much you learn, they tell you, you will always be limited by the fact that you can learn only that which you can learn; you will never be able to know that unlimited zero—the things defined as *"not* that which you can know" seen by a consciousness defined as *"not* yours."

You listen to them and you blank out the fact that this argument denies the validity of any form of consciousness whatever: if you were the omniscient God of their invention, you would still know only that which your means of knowledge perceived, whatever such means would be, unless—and this is the core of their mystic inventions—God were not "limited" by being an entity and his means of perception were *causeless*. God's knowledge would be valid, they tell you, because it would be unaccountable, God would know everything, because he would know it by means of nothing, while you can know nothing, because you know it by means of something. You are blind, they tell you, because you have eyes, and deaf, because you have ears; true sight and true hearing would have neither.

You are blind, they tell you, because you can never know *"things in themselves"* or *"things as they are,"* which means: "things as they are *not* perceived by you," things as they are apart from your consciousness and apart from *any* consciousness. By this concept, reality is that which no one perceives, the moment it is perceived it ceases to be real—existence is outside the bounds of any consciousness, to know it you must know it without consciousness, the moment you're conscious, it ceases to exist, the moment you're conscious, you are unconscious. Knowledge is impossible to you, they tell you, because the moment you are A, you're no longer able to be non-A, the moment you are an entity, you are no longer able to be a zero—and the *zero* is the only thing that's certain, omniscient, omnipotent and *real*.

Do you wonder what is left of a young mind after an intellectual training of this sort? Do you wonder why your childen leave college as neurotic *nonentities*, ready for any witch doctor to knock over?

Since, in fact, no consciousness can hold on to a zero, there is a specific purpose in all of this mystical claptrap: the nearest thing to "causeless knowledge" is an *irrational wish*—and your teachers' revolt against causal perception is the desire to place above reality and reason those nameless wishes of theirs which they know to be contrary to both.

The closest approach, in practice, to the theory of "things in themselves" is as follows: if you steal your neighbor's wallet, your action *in itself* and *as it is* is a crime; but since you *wanted* his wallet and held your wish as superior to reason, you blank out the nature of your action and continue to regard yourself as honest, by telling yourself and others that there's no such thing as *objective* reality and you would not be able to know it if there were.

[*The following are some topics covered in an early draft of Galt's speech. AR identifies the number of handwritten pages on each topic.*]

### The Epistemology of Evil

Definition of two kinds of mystics: 1 page.

Their "sixth sense": 1 page.

Identifications by means of the zero: 2 pages.

Their "superior" world and "somehow": 1 page.

Their secret—the *wish*: 1 page.

Escape from the law of identity: 3 pages.

Reversing existence and consciousness; mechanics of "the wish": 6 pages.

Escape from the law of causality: 5 pages.

Who pays for the orgy?—under both mystics: 8 pages.

Modern mystics; the blank-out ("motion" and "change"—the industrialist and the law of identity—"proof" of existence—axioms—montage of examples): 9 pages.

The savage and the baby (sensory perception): 7 pages.

The modern attack on the senses—"things in themselves": 8 pages.

Summary: the destruction of knowledge ("faith" and "the collective"): 5 pages.

Return to pre-language and blank-outs about the mind: 5 pages.

The present economic "grabbing" and blank-outs: 5 pages.

Power lust: 9 pages.

The mystic psychology of a dictator: 19 pages.

The conspiracy against life and man: 9 pages.

[*The following passages were cut from Galt's speech. AR put them in a folder marked: "Discards from* Atlas Shrugged *(which I like)."*]

You have heard it said that this is a time of moral crisis. You have mouthed the words yourself. You have wailed against evil and at each of its triumphs you have cried for more victims as your token of virtue. Listen, you, the symbol of whose morality is a sacrificial oven, you who feel bored by what you profess to be good, and tempted by what you profess to be evil, you who claim that virtue is its own reward and spend your life running from such rewarding, you who resent and despise those you hold to be saints, and envy those you hold to be sinners, you who proclaim that one must die for virtue, but dread having to live for it—listen—I am the first man who has ever loved virtue with the whole of my mind and being, the man who never sought another love, knowing that no other love is possible, and thus the man who rose to put an end to your obscenity of sacrificing good to evil.

<hr />

Only the man who is morally fit to live on a desert island is morally fit to live in society—the man who knows that man's life depends on production and production depends on man's mind, that he must live by his own effort and think through his own brain, that if he chooses to live by means of force or fraud, by mooching, extorting or plundering the products of the minds of others, he is choosing to abandon his human status—to exist as something other than a man, yet to let his life depend on those who choose the existence of rational beings; he is trying to switch to them the death which would have been his on that island, he is living by the mind of his victims, by the virtue of those whom he destroys—he is choosing *death* as his standard of value, and he will reach it through an agony sure as, but more ugly than, starvation on a desert island. Yet your code of morality was designed to foster this breed of the subhuman, to destroy the men who think and to turn the earth into that desert island. You have succeeded.

<hr />

If you preach that man must hold the pursuit of his own happiness as evil and must seek self-sacrifice as his moral goal, you are asking that he twist himself into a monstrosity that takes pleasure in his own pain and finds pain in his own pleasure, that enjoys his suffering and despises his joy, that strives for his own frustration, that holds desires only to renounce them, fights battles only to lose, seeks wounds as victories and sores as medals, [like] a machine set in reverse, with its gauges switched from life to death, with death as its goal and its standard of value—a monstrosity that fights against itself and crashes in a final, bloody heap, leaving a trail of destruction behind it.

*That* as a moral ideal? *That* as a code of love for man?

―――――◇―――――

The mystics, who preach self-sacrifice, who preach that the highest virtue man can practice is to hold his own life as of no value, who claim that they despise the body and worship the spirit—do not grant to man's spirit the importance they grant to his body. They know that if a human body were to reject the function of maintaining its existence, it would cease to live and would turn into a mass of corruption, carrying the poison of death to those who did not avoid its contact. Yet they do not expect a life-rejecting human spirit to become an agent of infection—and they let it loose upon the world as the death-carrier which it has been through all the ages. Do you preach that the purpose of morality is to curb man's instinct of self-preservation? It is for the purpose of self-preservation that man needs a code of morality.

―――――◇―――――

Do you think they are taking you back to the dark ages? They are taking you back to darker ages than any your history has known. Their goal is the era of the pre-human. Consider what feat of intelligence was performed by the nameless genius who was first to identify the fact that man possesses a *mind.* Consider what tremendous mental power was spent on the invention of language, what span of centuries had to be traveled from the first inarticulate sounds that named immediate objects to the words that conveyed abstractions. The greatest achievement in communication was not the wireless telegraphy nor transatlantic radio, but the feat of the genius who grasped and taught to others the concept of identifying reality in words of objective meaning. These are the achievements which your teachers now seek to negate and to destroy, by refusing to identify them and pretending that neither mind nor words have ever been discovered. Their goal is to take you back, not to the age of pre-science, but the age of pre-language.

―――――◇―――――

A man of self-confidence knows the nature of knowledge; he knows that existence exists, that reality cannot be faked, that a mind cannot be forced. He knows that nothing can be accomplished by ruling a herd one has reduced to the level of morons and liars. He is unable to fool himself about the loathsome spectacle of men who have to act under compulsion; he is unable to regard the role of a ruler as anything but personal infamy. It takes a mystic to reach so low a stage of self-deception as to derive any value or pleasure from the extorted motions faked by others—extorted by and faked under the threat of a gun.

———◇———

You accept the morality of selflessness—but observe that you are unable to live except by taking *yourself* as the standard of value—a depraved, irrational, contradictory self, blindly seeking its own pleasure, struggling by corrupted means to comply with the law of existence. You profess to damn matter, but you lie and cheat to get rich; you profess to value chastity, but seek pleasure from whores; you profess to hold an altruist as your moral ideal, yet make no move to reach his rank, though it is in your power—but the man of ambition, of selfish achievement, is the man you envy, and you scramble to obtain his rank without earning it, though you profess to consider him immoral.

———◇———

You believe that your heart is superior to reason, that man must live by his feelings, not his mind—as if hatred, fear and envy were not feelings, as if a man of unbridled emotions would become a paragon of virtue—as if the dope fiend who robs a store, the woman who murders in a fit of jealous rage, the sadist who indulges his craving for torture were exponents of coldly impersonal logic, while the surgeon who performs a brain operation were a man directed by his feelings.

You believe that security is superior to freedom—as if a livelihood earned by your effort voluntarily traded for the effort of others, with your body and property protected from seizure, were a state of precarious uncertainty—but the state of being bound, gagged and fed by the mercy of an arbitrary ruler, who possesses the power to cut off your food, to rob, to torture, to murder you at whim, were a state of peaceful security.

———◇———

A mystical morality makes it impossible for you to pass moral judgment. *You cannot judge by an incomprehensible standard,* be it God or society or anything outside reason. When you are told: "Do not try to understand what is good, *believe it*," you become unable to estimate any value, action, person or event, or to make any firm choice.

If you cannot judge, you will not think. The aim of every action, mental or physical, is to achieve a value, to further your life. Why think, if you cannot reach any conclusion, if you cannot appraise the value of any choice? *Every thought implies a value judgment.* If you cannot value, you cannot think. You may know that giving poison to a man will kill him, but why consider it, if you cannot know whether it is right or wrong to kill him?

If you cannot think, you will act on the spur of the emotions of the moment. The creed of expediency is the worship of emotions. Emotions, in fact, are the summary of your philosophical premises—and destruction will follow from the contradictions in your premises if you act blindly on your emotions. All emotions are appraisals, inexorably based on the rule of "What's in it for me?" but you have no way of judging what *should* be in it for you, what *is* your self-interest—and your destruction follows from such blind choices.

Your morality disarms you and protects itself from your mind *by making a virtue of imperfection*: humility is a virtue, pride is a sin. It gives you a blank check on evil and forces you to give a blank check to others. If you cannot be proud of yourself, you cannot condemn any depravity. The man who is unable to praise himself is unable to blame anything on anyone.

———————

You create your character or destroy it by the same means which create or destroy all your values: by the act of thinking or non-thinking. Your *self* is your *mind*, and its constant choice is the act of self-affirmation or self-denial, of perceiving or refusing to perceive, the act of *being* or *non-being* by which your mind, like a pilot-light within you, goes on or off. This act is your primary choice, it is your *will*, the only will you have, your only choice, from which all other choices proceed.

———————

Just as you possess a pair of legs, but must learn to use them, and the ability to walk becomes automatic, but the decision to walk does not, and you will not walk without a decision to cross the room, the street or the world—so you possess a brain, but must learn to use it, and the ability to think becomes automatic, but the decision to think does not.

It is not values that you have to renounce, but only your fakes and pretenses: the prestige which you don't possess, the respect which no one grants you, the love which you do not feel, the faith which you don't believe. Get out of your snarl of deceit which has deceived no one but yourself. Get out of the dank prison of your emotions into the hard, clean sunlight of the mind. And if, in exchange for your scrap heap of borrowed slogans and undigested commandments, you are able to reach by the work of your mind no more than the first-hand conviction that water is wet and fire is hot, you will still be incomparably richer than you were and you will know the meaning of self-esteem.

Only a man of integrity can possess the virtue of honesty, since only the faking of one's consciousness can permit the faking of existence.

You believe you got away with your evasions? Look again and check the addition that sums up your soul and your life. You had cheated in business, but you see no connection between that and the fact that your wife has deserted you? You had paid off a bureaucrat to destroy your competitor, but you see no connection between that and the fact that your market has vanished and your business has crashed? You extorted high wages by means of directives, but you see no connection between that and the fact that you're now condemned to jobless starvation? You had preached ideas you hated, in exchange for the favor of men you despised, but you see no connection between that and the fact that you've now become an alcoholic? You had prospered on government subsidies, but you see no connection between that and the fact that your son has been killed in a war to bring prosperity to the natives of some jungle People's State? You had set every part of you to betray every other, you believed that your career bears no relation to your sex life, that your politics bear no relation to the choice of your friends, that your values bear no relation to your pleasures, and your heart bears no relation to your brain—you had chopped yourself into pieces which you struggled never to connect—but you see no reason why your life is in ruins and why you've lost the desire to live?

———◆———

Like the criminal who plays it short range, who believes that he gets away with the unearned and does not see why his loot disappears into the pockets of any blackmailer and any criminal more ruthless than himself—so you believed that you could exist as half-producer, half-thief, and did not see what parasites you paid in exchange for your little snatch of the unearned. Every time you cheated the honest, it is the dishonest you had to pay off. Every time you resorted to force—passing a law—to destroy your superiors, it is to your inferiors that you handed the weapon by which they destroyed you in your turn. Whether you were a businessman or a worker, your blank-out consisted of believing that you were fighting and looting each other—and what you did not dare to identify was that you were looting the better men of your own profession, that any kind of collectivist action is intended to milk the better members of the collective—and as you destroyed your abler competitor or your abler fellow-worker, ten incompetents were ready to pounce upon you and to drain you dry in turn. So you're reaping a profit you did not deserve and wonder why bureaucrats are devouring your profit. So you've gained security where the boss cannot fire you and no other newcomer can compete for your job—and you wonder why your wages are buying less and less, and why you live in terror of your union leaders, whose whim can condemn you to starve.

———◆———

You believed that compromise was practical, that you could not succeed on merit, that some shortcuts were needed to help you to rise, that your sins were assisting your virtues. But there is no compromise between good and evil, between reason and force, between production and looting. Your vices have devoured your virtues, your intelligence was spent on protecting your evasions, your ability on paying for your frauds, your energy on enriching the parasites who bled you—while you were gaining a penny of graft in exchange for a dollar of your own honest profit.

When you established the right of the unearned and accepted need, the zero, as a claim, you did not see—you blindest of fools, the businessman or laborer of the compromise economy—that any man on any level who continued working, was losing in proportion to his effort and his work, and that those who gained, were gaining in proportion to their having accomplished nothing. You had connived to destroy your superior and had hoped to step into his shoes, but you did not step into his fortune, you stepped into his place under the social squeezer which *you* had set in motion—and when you are squeezed dry in your turn, you will find that the ultimate winner is the looter who made no compromise with working, but stuck to the absolute of robbery and murder, the "practical" hero of the short-cut, who will perish on the carcass of the last compromiser.

<hr />

## Mind and Body

Man is an entity of mind and body, an indivisible union of two elements: of consciousness and matter. Matter is that which one perceives, consciousness is that which perceives it; your fundamental act of perception is an indivisible whole consisting of both; to deny, to [separate] or to equate them is to contradict the nature of your perception, to contradict the axiom of existence, to contradict your basic definitions and to invalidate whatever concepts you might attempt to hold thereafter.

Your consciousness is that which you know—and are alone to know—by direct perception. It is that indivisible unit where knowledge and being are one, it is your "I," it is the self which distinguishes you from all else in the universe. No consciousness can perceive another consciousness, only the results of its actions in material form, since only matter is an object of perception, and consciousness is the subject, perceivable by its nature only to itself. To perceive the consciousness, the "I," of another would mean to become that other "I"—a contradiction in terms; to speak of souls perceiving one another is a denial of your "I," of perception, of consciousness, of matter. The "I" is the irreducible unit of life.

Just as life is the integrating element which organizes matter into a living cell, the element which distinguishes an organism from the unstructured mass of inorganic matter—so consciousness, an attribute of life, directs the actions of the organism to use, to shape, to realign matter for the purpose of maintaining its existence.

That which you call your soul or spirit is your consciousness, the life-keeper of your body. Your body is a machine, your consciousness—your *mind*—is its driver; and that which you call your emotions is the union of the two, the product of the integrating mechanism by which your mind controls your body.

Man has wrested existence from the mystic demons, but not consciousness—material reality, but not his mind. Men still look at consciousness as savages looked at material nature. Men have progressed in material production, but have not progressed in spirit—because the first was the province of reason, but the second is still the province of faith and emotions. There has been no *moral* progress, because the tool of all progress—the mind—was banished from morality.

## PART 5

# FINAL YEARS

# NOTES: 1955–1977

---

*This chapter presents a miscellany of notes written from 1955 to 1977. AR's notes for two books, also made during this period, are saved for the last chapter.*

*The following material begins with notes on psychology written in the same year that AR completed Galt's speech. These notes are unrelated to the speech; AR kept them in a separate folder. They contain the build-up to and her first discussion of "psycho-epistemology," a concept she originated; she later defined it as "the study of man's cognitive processes from the aspect of the interaction between the conscious and the automatic functions of the subconscious" (see The Romantic Manifesto). She begins by referring to a man's conscious premises and subconscious processes as the "super-structure" and the "sub-basement" of the mind, without giving explicit definitions of these terms. Later, she writes: "Super-structure is the realm of philosophy, of premises, ideas, convictions, etc.—that is, the content of a person's mind; sub-basement is the realm of psychology—the method by which a mind acquires and handles its content."*

*Almost a third of AR's notes on psychology are presented here—those in which AR is writing as a philosopher about the foundations of psychology. The rest of the material, which I have omitted, pertains to topics outside the realm of philosophy, such as particular neuroses. Her motive in writing the latter notes was to understand the people she knew, many of whom baffled her. However, she was not interested in psychology as a subject, and never made a systematic study of it. So the omitted notes are of less interest.*

*The rest of the material in this chapter is from the post–Atlas Shrugged period, when AR was writing prolifically on philosophy. Considering the complexity of the issues she dealt with in this period, it may be surprising that she made so few notes. But she found non-fiction writing much easier than fiction. Typically, she wrote from brief outlines, which are omitted here because they merely list the main ideas in the published articles.*

**May 13, 1955**

[*In her 1955 notes on psychology, AR used the term "rationalist" to refer to "an exponent of reason." Since this term is associated with the rationalist-empiricist dichotomy in philosophy, which she rejected, I have eliminated it in favor of "rational man."*]

*Psychological "Epistemology"*

The three metaphysical fundamentals with which a human consciousness has to deal are: existence, consciousness—and the consciousness of other people.

The crucial decision that a man makes is: in which category does he place the consciousness of others—in external existence or in his own consciousness? The first is the proper process of a rational man. The second means that the consciousness of others becomes a factor in the mind's process of judgment; it becomes, not an external fact, but an $x$ factor by means of which facts are to be judged; not that which the mind perceives, but that by means of which it does the perceiving. This is the root of the "epistemological" corruption of a human consciousness.

Example: A rational man thinks: "Two plus two equals four." A second-hander thinks: "Two plus two plus $x$ equals four—maybe, the $x$ permitting." The $x$ stands for the unknown and unknowable decision of the consciousness of others.

*Question to investigate:* These three fundamentals are probably the three premises which determine a man's psychological "epistemology." *Is there a special method of thinking that a man will employ according to the premises he has formed about these three fundamentals?* And, as sub-category: in relation to his own consciousness, is there a crucial premise formed by a man about *his thinking and his emotions?* Is this premise another determining factor in the thinking method that a man will employ? [. . .]

*Next assignment:* Define more fully and specifically what we know so far about methods of thinking.

What is the exact role of the conscious mind (of the "spark") as driver and as spectator of the material provided by the subconscious?

What is the exact nature of the subconscious as the repository of stored knowledge—and as the automatic creator of emotions?

What is the exact role of emotions in a process of thinking? (Are they selectors, integrators, blockers—or all of these, according to one's premises?)

What is the exact nature of the process of integration?

What is the nature of the state which a man takes as certainty? How does he know that he knows? (Or is certainty possible only to a rational man? If so, what takes its place in a corrupted consciousness?)

Is the question of "*certainty*" related to the question of "*values*"? My lead here is the fact that when I attempt to calculate a chess game my mind gives up on a very violent feeling of "What's the use?" [. . .] (Later question: Does [a man] become immoral (non-valuing) because he has formed the premise of a fluid reality—or does he form the premise of a fluid reality because he has rejected his value-setting power? I suspect that it is the first. I also suspect that one's concepts of *reality* and of *values* are inseparable corollaries. This, I think, is the point at which the independent mind and the sovereign value-setter are united.)

*In relation to emotions:* The two fundamentals are pleasure and pain. In psychological motives they become: love or fear (love for values, ambition for pleasure, i.e., happiness—or—fear of pain, escape from pain). (This leads to: activity or passivity, achievement of the positive or escape from the negative.) An important *moral* lead is the question: Is a man motivated by fear in any part of his psychology? He is immoral to the extent of his fear motivations—immoral in the primary sense of morality: fear leads to the refusal to think, to perceive reality. (Fear as an "epistemological" factor.)

**May 25, 1955**

The first two metaphysical fundamentals which a human consciousness has to grasp and deal with are: *existence* and *consciousness*. Within each of these two, there are two fundamentals which a man grasps with his earliest concepts: *existence* is divided into *facts* (reality) and *people* (other people's views of reality)—*consciousness* is divided into *mind* and *emotions* (thinking and feeling).

If a man is unable to integrate these four concepts (reality, people, thinking, feeling) in a proper, rational manner, if he finds himself torn by conflicts among these four—*then* what he sacrifices and what he chooses to preserve determines his basic character, his metaphysics and his epistemology. [. . .]

The proper pattern of a rational man in regard to the four fundamentals is as follows: Mind above emotions (but not in the sense of emotional suppression, only in the sense of knowing that the mind is the source of emotions)—and *reality* [above people] (a single, indivisible reality to be perceived and judged by one's own mind). The specific distinction of a rational man is the fact that the consciousness of others *as an epistemological factor* does not exist for him, that he holds no such concept, that a conflict such as *his* view of reality versus the view of *others* has never occurred to him epistemologically and has never been an issue within his own processes of thought. A rational man regards others and their views as [external] facts of existence, to be judged by his mind—and *not* as an inner fact, to be part of his judgment. A man of *unbreached consciousness* is one who has never allowed the opinions of others to become an epistemological issue, that is, to shake his confidence in the validity of his own perceptions and of his own rational judgment.

**May 27, 1955**

*Assignment:* The next and most urgent step in this inquiry should be a full, exact and objective definition of:

1. What these four fundamentals are, what realm they cover, in what form they exist within a consciousness, by what objective signs one can detect them.
2. The exact influence of the sub-basement on the super-structure.
3. The manner in which sub-basement premises are formed (since they are not formed as a conscious, philosophical conviction).

**May 28, 1955**

### The Four Fundamentals and the Issue of Values

The crucial error of the man who chooses "emotions above mind" in the sub-basement consists of acquiring an "epistemology" that makes emotions part of his thinking process in the specific role of a *judge of values* and, later, almost the judge of truth and facts (or *the meaning* of facts) and, therefore, the judge of certainty in any given thought process. While to a rational man the answer to a problem is a factual identification or explanation of reality—to a sub-basement emotionalist the answer to a problem is the achievement of a happy or positive emotion.

The formula for this crucial difference is as follows:

An emotionalist's identification of values is: *"The good is that which will make me happy."*

A rational man's identification of values is: *"I will be made happy by that which is good."*

Thereafter, the rational man will be incapable of emotional response without knowing the nature of that to which he is responding. In complex situations, he might need time to identify *all* the elements of his particular emotional response (since an emotional sum is calculated by the subconscious much faster than a conscious process of thought could do it), but the identification will always be available to him, open to his conscious mind, and his emotions will always correspond to his conscious standard of values. He might be mistaken in any given situation about his conscious identification of the facts involved—but he will never be off his standard of values, there will never be a contradiction between his emotional response and his conscious, rational, stated standard of values. He will never be in love with a person whom he consciously despises, nor be resentful of a person whom he consciously admires.

The emotionalist will be open to all the above kind of conflicts. Only the strength of his rational super-structure will guarantee whether he responds to the right values or not, according to his conscious standard or not. He will experience an emotion *ahead* of his full rational knowledge of that to which he is responding. He will do so by means of a "package deal": since emotions are sums, he will respond to his first, vague, *generalized* perception of an object or to some particular "highlight" of an object. He will respond to the *total* of an object, person or event—without breaking it up into its parts or attributes. In his "emotional epistemology," he will be in a position similar to that of a child who perceives entities, but has not yet learned to identify them by means of their attributes.

When his emotional response clashes with his later, rational identification of a given object, the emotionalist is left in an insoluble conflict: (1) He does not know how to untangle the emotional from the rational in his own mental processes; (2) He feels a tremendous reluctance against analyzing his emotions or their object, against breaking up the "package deal"; such an analysis is contrary to his basic metaphysics and his basic concept of himself; he feels as if he were doing violence to himself and his universe; (3) Even if he succeeds, by a painful, forced process of "old-fashioned will power," in analyzing the object of his emotions, the conclusion made by his mind lacks full conviction to him, lacks the fire and certainty of conviction—because *the emotion, not the facts*, is his final judge of the value of reality, which does mean: *his final judge of reality.*

The emotionalist is the man who says that "the cold hand of reason destroys emotions." To a rational man, such a statement is incomprehensible.

*Sub-basement premises remain in an adult consciousness in the form of "psychological epistemology"*—in the method of thinking ("front seat" or "back seat," directed or contemplative), in the place which emotions occupy in a process of thought (reason as the active director, emotions as the passive result—or—emotions as the active judge, reason as the passive result) and in the nature of the emotional response (specifically particularized—or—vague and generalized).

*Sub-basement premises are the methods of functioning of a consciousness*—they are specifically the field of *psychology* (as distinguished from philosophy)—they are the *workings* of a soul's mechanism, not the content of its ideas.

*Sub-basement premises* are *not* premises in the sense in which we use the concept philosophically. A rational adult with an emotionalist premise in his sub-basement *does not* hold somewhere deep in his subconscious the conviction that "emotions are superior to reason." What he holds is an epistemological *method* which, if translated into a philosophical premise, would amount to "emotions are superior to reason." He did not choose it in terms of a conscious conviction; he chose it in terms of an inner method of reacting which, by the time he is old enough to identify it, has become automatic, appears to be an irreducible primary and is extremely difficult for his own consciousness to identify.

The same is true of the other crucial sub-basement fundamental: reality versus people. There may be other fundamentals pertaining to the sub-basement, which will need to be identified. At present, I am tracing only the influence of the two metaphysical fundamentals with which I started these notes: existence and consciousness. It remains to be seen (to be examined separately) whether these two cover the whole sub-basement or not. What I am certain of at present is:

1. I have found the key to the pattern of how metaphysical fundamentals are translated into psychological fundamentals.

2. What we called "sub-basement premises" *are* methods of functioning or what we called "psychological epistemology."

3. What we called "super-structure" *is* the realm of philosophy, of premises, ideas, convictions, etc.—that is, the *content* of a person's mind; "sub-basement" is the realm of psychology—the *method* by which a mind acquires and handles its content. But since the method *was* determined by implied (if not conscious) philosophical ideas formed by a person's mind—it is philosophical ideas that can correct the method, provided the psychologist is able to identify them for the patient.

4. The role of psychology is "*the science of epistemological retraining.*" A patient needs, not just a correct philosophy, but *a new method* of thinking and feeling. A psychologist must first communicate the essentials of a correct philosophy, then start the patient on a

course of "epistemological retraining"—as soon as the psychologist has grasped the specific nature of the patient's errors (from the patient's conscious and subconscious premises). This eliminates the need of constant analyzing of particular, concrete troubles, confusions and relapses. (This answers my own particular bewilderment at the fact that our best and most intelligent converts were not always able to derive from our philosophical abstractions the concrete applications which, to me, seemed self-evident.)

*(Note to Nathan [Nathaniel Branden, psychologist and associate of AR's until 1968]:* I know that the above is very vague and generalized, but my stomach (and brain) is screaming that *this* is the right track. The "epistemological" methods that we have discovered so far (such as "back-seat driving," etc.) are not the whole story—but I am sure that the role of psychology is to discover, identify and then be able to cure *all the essential* "epistemological" errors possible to a human consciousness. We will know that we have discovered them all when we are able to explain every basic aberration of a human consciousness. In the past, we have been identifying and detecting specific, individual bad premises in a patient's mind, some of them fundamental, others fairly superficial, with no general plan of procedure, no systematic view of a cure. What I am glimpsing now is at least the first key to establishing the mileposts of a systematic road to analysis and cure; the mileposts themselves are still to be identified; this is only the first of them.)

### 1955

[*In the following note, AR is discussing those who refuse to judge right and wrong because of their fear of opposing others.*]

Isn't this the "Rose Wohl issue"? [*An unknown reference.*] She said she did not want to think that others were so wrong. I thought she meant that she would find it horrifying to live among evil creatures and, therefore, prefers not to know that they are evil; I took her motive to be: (*a*) a kind of good will, which makes her resist the necessity of hating and loathing others, a mistaken form of desire for a benevolent universe, which she thinks she can achieve by evasion; (*b*) a practical sort of cowardice, which makes her resist the idea that she might be living among monsters and in constant danger, and makes her prefer not to know it, on some grounds such as "what you don't know won't hurt you"—again on the principle of plain ("wholesome"?!) evasion, such as the evasion of a man who refuses to see a doctor in order not to find out whether he has a deadly disease.

What I see now is that she meant she does not *dare* think that others are wrong, she does not dare oppose them even in her own mind; they would *punish* her for *holding* such an opinion; it is dangerous not only to *act* against them, but even to *think* against them. (!!!) This amounts to a *voluntary brain-washing* as a basic policy of life. (Good God!)

This issue is the reason why of any depravity, the one I've always loathed most is the slogan "If you can't beat them, join them." But again, I thought of it in semi-rational terms, i.e., I thought it meant the advice to fake the terms of others *in action* and beat them at their own game. But here I think I had a "stomach-sense" of the truth, because this slogan made me much more indignant and horrified than any rational interpretation warranted; I sensed something much more evil in it. Now I see that it means the surrender of one's consciousness, in the sense of: "If you can't beat them, *don't think*"—it is meant to apply, not to *action*, but to *thought*, not to the realm of existence, but to the realm of consciousness, not in the sense of accepting values you do not really believe for the sake of some "practical" advantage, but in a sense unspeakably worse: in the sense of discarding your capacity to agree and replacing it by uncritical *obedience*—thus making obedience take metaphysical and epistemological primacy over acceptance or rejection, truth or falsehood, which means: over one's judgment.


**Undated**

### Memory-Storing Epistemology

The "emotional" epistemology of the "perceptual" level [mentality] works as follows: instead of storing conceptual conclusions and evaluations in his subconscious, a man stores concrete memories plus an emotional estimate. Example: instead of conceptual conclusions in the form of political principles, he stores specific memories of concrete events of his own experience, with the memory that these things or events were "bad" ("painful"). Thereafter, when he has to consider any new political event, his epistemology works as follows: first, a strong negative emotion—then, the emotion, acting as selector, revives or brings out of his subconscious a lightning-like montage of memories of other political events, all of them painful—then his conclusion is that the new event is and/or will be painful, hopeless, and generally negative.

Any specific judgment that he utters, in such cases, is completely accidental or irrelevant: it is dictated, not by a rational conclusion, but by random or chance association and is, in fact, intended by him only as an approximation (though not consciously). Any conceptual conclusions, principles, or sentences he may have accumulated through the years on that particular subject are stored as loose concretes along with his memories of events, almost as accidental, undifferentiated rubble or barnacles clinging to the events. In effect, the ideas are also stored as concrete facts, as memories of something he has heard, read, or thought, not as ideas or concepts. Therefore, he does not exercise any selectivity or discrimination when he utters a comment.

His comment is approximate, because it is intended to stand for the total montage, the "gestalt," that his emotion brings out of his subconscious. The only thing he really intends to communicate, his actual judgment, is: "This is painful." Translated into words, his judgment would be: "This is painful, because of all the similar events I remember as painful." Thus his memories serve as the proof or the validation of his judgment, performing, in his consciousness, the function performed by logical, conceptual evidence in a rational consciousness. This is the process by which emotion takes precedence over logic; in fact, it does not take precedence—it substitutes for logic. (Logic is a conceptual tool—it cannot operate by means of percepts, it cannot deal with unanalyzed, undifferentiated, "irreducible" concretes.)

This method, of course, is as near to a perceptual level of epistemology as a conceptual, human consciousness can come. It consists of treating memories as percepts, as "package-deal" irreducible primaries, and of forming value judgments by a primitive, animal-like standard of "pleasurable" or "painful," these two standing for "good" or "bad," without any further analysis or understanding, without any knowledge of why something is good or bad, why something was pleasurable or painful. This is exactly what an animal's "pleasure-pain mechanism" would do. In the case of an animal, this mechanism works as an immediate response to immediate concretes and is assisted by memory. An animal's memory is purely associational, and thus an animal can be trained by a repetition of pleasurable or painful experiences, of rewards or punishments (the repetition makes the animal memorize or associate).

In the case of a man, this method becomes the issue of "stale thinking." When a man claims that he cannot separate his emotion from his perception of the event to which he is responding, that he feels as if the two come simultaneously (which means that he evaluates something before he has grasped what it is, yet he is epistemologically unable to take time to perceive the event fully), his consciousness, in fact, is reacting to past events, to memories called out of his subconscious by his first glimpse of some accidental resemblance or association between the present perception and the events of his past. (It is in this sense that he does not actually perceive the present event and cannot identify it or think about it; and it is somewhat inaccurate to call his memories "stale thinking"—they are not his old conclusions or conscious value-estimates, they are merely unanalyzed "gestalts" of concrete events and automatic emotional reactions.)

A man whose epistemology functions in this manner, by accidental associations of "pleasure" or "pain," has no way of knowing whether his judgment (his emotional response) is or is not relevant to the present event or the facts confronting him or the immediate reality with which he is dealing, but which he has not actually perceived. He has no way of knowing whether his judgment (his substitute for judgment) is right or wrong, true or false, nor why.

The terrible consequence of this method for a human consciousness is the fact that it does make a full perception of reality impossible, that it does make a man epistemologically unable to take time to perceive. Since man needs a system of symbols to deal with the enormous complexity of his experiences, since he has to condense and simplify every new event by means of its essentials, since he cannot treat every new event as if it were an undifferentiated, unprecedented first in a baby's blank consciousness, but must integrate (or at least relate) it to the context of his past knowledge, this method substitutes an emotion for the perception and selection of an essential.

Thus, a rational man, considering a specific political event, will call on his conceptual knowledge to identify the event by means of its essence. He will observe, for instance, that a given law establishes government controls and he will estimate it as evil, by means of his previously reached conviction that government controls are evil. He will not need to examine every concrete detail of the law or ponder over all its future consequences; his conceptual grasp of the essential element involved will contain and cover all those concretes.

But a man with an "emotional-perceptual" epistemology is helpless and lost before the complexity of the same law. His only method of condensing the meaning of that law is his emotion, backed by the context of his memories, which are loosely stored by resemblance, similarity, or chance association. He has no way of determining what is essential in that law, and thus his emotion becomes the essential—and, without examining or analyzing that law (which he cannot begin to do and would not know how), he concludes that the law is "bad" or "good" according to whatever aspect of it has the strongest emotional meaning for him, the strongest emotional associations or connotations. This is the reason why such men jump to conclusions rashly, on the mere hint of some isolated aspect of an issue, and miss the most important, essential, or relevant points, regardless of their intelligence and perceptiveness. This is why such men are always context-dropping; this is why they see the whole issue only when some advocate of reason points it out, and then they wonder: "Why didn't I think of this before? Why didn't I see it by myself?" This is how that epistemology can paralyze and negate the best mind.

Notes for cure: The difficulty in correcting this epistemology is the fact that a man's emotion has become his only selector. Without it, he would feel totally lost in a maze of incomprehensible complexities (which no mind could hold), he wouldn't know where to begin, he would literally feel something resembling the disintegration of his consciousness. (His emotional "yes" or "no" is the only integrator of his consciousness, that is: of his memories.) Therefore, one cannot simply forbid him to use his emotion as selector, one cannot remove it without providing him with a substitute. So the first step to take is as follows: while building up his conceptual files by a constant process of verbalizing and defining, teach him to analyze his emotional selector when he catches it in action. Thus, if he feels that politics is "bad," make him ask himself: "Why do I feel this?" and name as many reasons as he can find. The reasons do not have to be exhaustive immediately; the purpose is to train him to the process of identifying the causes of his emotions—and, gradually, he will learn to discover deeper and deeper reasons, to remove more "onion skins," and ultimately to reduce his emotional premises down to their philosophical, primary base. (Do not rush this process—let him do it—don't let him memorize formulas and dogmas which he does not fully understand.)

[*AR's notes on psychology end here.*]

[*Several years later, AR noted some ideas for short stories.*]

A "horror story" about mechanics in charge of an H-bomb. The crime of the concrete-bound people—or of those who think only "down to a certain point."

A savage with a computer, who perishes because he does not know how to operate it. This is the relationship of man to the automatic integrations of his consciousness, i.e., to his emotions. (Add the fact that the computer is operating constantly and that the savage thinks it's a deity he must obey.)

—◦—

"The Inside Story." A dramatization of an inner conflict, with different actors presenting different, clashing premises—and the existential result.

**May 27, 1959**

### The Inside Story

Tom.

The well-groomed man (social metaphysics). ("What would people say?") [*"Social metaphysics" refers to the neurosis resulting from automatized second-handedness, i.e., the type of psycho-epistemology that is focused primarily on the views of others, not on reality.*]

The shabby man (malevolent universe). ("It's too dangerous!")

The temperamental man (whim-worship). ("But I want it!")

The fat man (anti-effort). ("Why bother?")

The joker (death premise). (Laughter at values.)

The wife: Edna.

The doctor: Dr. Clark.

The temperamental man on the phone—screaming irrational denials. ("She knows, but can't prove it.")

Tom on the phone—assuring her of his love. (Her advice to him.)

The well-groomed man on the phone—"What would people say?" (Her ultimatum.)

The shabby man on the phone—the slap in the face—Edna walks out.

The panic over Dr. Clark.

Fight—the joker dominating—the knife—the windows are closed—the scream—the phone ringing.

Last scene—(three pages).

**Undated**

[*This series of philosophic notes was paper-clipped together.*]

Values set the psycho-epistemological rhythm (or tempo) of cognition. They make one hold a given percept or concept in mind long enough to integrate; integration is what makes a thing or issue "real."

Thus non-attention or non-retention is a matter of lack of values. And values have to be connected to action.

An "out of focus" state may be a state of rushing past everything (psycho-epistemologically), while focus requires slowness. (?)

*Think this over;* it has many implications. (Such as the relationship of mental action to existential action.)

———

The reification of "forces" of nature is the rebellion against (or ignorance of) the law of identity: it separates entities from actions, implying that actions are not caused by the nature of the entities that act, but are caused by some outside power. For example: "Death takes a holiday" implies that death is not inherent in the nature of living entities. Or: "Spring brings flowers"—implying that the growth of flowers is not inherent in nature. This is an example of the inability to grasp that *existence exists*.

The process of reifying abstractions is proper only in the *moral* realm, i.e., *only* in regard to human character. Here, it is not a metaphor, a fantasy, or contradiction of reality—it is possible in fact, it is a *model*.

———

The "determinism" to look for in human psychology is *logic*. The logic of a man's basic premises determines his motivation and actions. (This is in regard to [the view] that the science of psychology cannot exist unless man is subject to determinism.)

———

Possible article: "The Vested Interest in Self-Abasement."

Fear of unearned flaws and/or the desire to indulge real flaws.

The desire to be "safe" rather than happy.

Fear of one's own emotions—and lack of knowledge of their source and meaning.

The "plausibility" of the notion of original sin.

In algebra, the relation of $x$ (the unknown) to the other (known) elements of an equation determines its nature because $x$ is the only variable, while the other elements are fixed and stable. This is the relationship of consciousness to existence: the content of consciousness is variable; the facts of existence are constant. Only on this basis can consciousness determine the nature of any given fact or problem that it is investigating.

**February, 1960**

### For Yale lecture (random philosophical notes)

*Religion is "canned philosophy":* you don't have to know what's in it or how it's cooked, no effort is required of you, just swallow it—and if it poisons you, it was your own fault, the cooks will tell you, you didn't have enough "faith."

The phenomenon of "wanting to have your cake and eat it, too"—the primacy of consciousness—is a luxury of a high civilization, of parasites who "feel safe." *There are no whim-worshippers on a desert island.* (?) (The "primacy of consciousness" is the primacy of *wishes*.)

The "stolen concept."

Attila and the Witch Doctor. [*AR's analysis of these two archetypes—the man of force and the man of faith—is presented in* For the New Intellectual.]

The contradiction of wanting "democracy," "collective living and cooperation," the "will of the people," etc.—*and* the abolition of reason. *Reason* is the only means of collective communication.

The worship of suffering. (Observe that the whim-worshippers are always malevolent universers.)

*The new obscurantism:* if it's knowledge, it's untrue—if it's an absolute, it's wrong (if it's indeterminate, it's true).

The meaning of the "anti-system-building premise": anti-integration. (Philosophers as "garage mechanics.") (Non-objective law.) (Treating symptoms and [attacking] anyone who looks for a cause.)

*Epistemological advice:* do not take the blame for "failure to understand" [the stuff you are taught], the others do not understand it, either. Do not think: "It can't mean what it seems to mean;" it *does* mean just that (the technique of the "Big Lie").

Reason as "perception of reality"—the "new intellectual."

The symptoms of today's decadence: "I *feel*" and "It seems to me."

(The strangeness of my position in addressing a modern audience is the fact that I have to speak of what everybody knows, and be shocking and new, for that very reason—that I am not addressing ignorance, but evasion—that I am not answering a desire to know, but a desire *not* to know—that the prevalent premises are "don't dare identify what I am struggling so hard not to admit" and "don't dare say that anything you say can make a difference, which means: that knowledge matters." Well, that *is* what I am going to say. I am here to identify what you all know by the modern method of knowledge: by feeling.) [*This paragraph was crossed out.*]

Is the H-bomb to be [launched] by "faith"?

Do you want to know the H-bomb as it "*really* is"?—as a "thing in itself"? Do you want to grasp it by "direct perception," without the effort of the "cold hand of reason"? Or to grasp it "with your whole person"?

**1960**

[*The following passages were cut from the title essay in* For the New Intellectual.]

The abdication of philosophy is all but complete. To understand the extent of the collapse, one must remember that the task of integrating abstractions into wider abstractions, of integrating knowledge into theories and principles, of integrating theories and principles to their practical applications, of maintaining a constant unifying process between broad concepts and their concrete, perceptual roots, thus achieving and preserving a noncontradictory sum and frame of reference—is not an automatic task nor an easy one; it requires the highest, most demanding level of conceptual psycho-epistemology. It is the specific task of philosophy, which cannot be performed by any other profession. Philosophers, by the *proper* requirement of their task, are the guardians of man's knowledge *and of his capacity to know*.

———————

Every society of men—from the most primitive tribe of savages to present-day America—has a certain cultural atmosphere which is determined by the kind of ideas that underlie the actions, *the mode of living*, within that society. Whether the majority actually believes these ideas or merely accepts them by default, no society and no men can exist without certain basic ideas to direct their actions, so long as they *do* have to act, that is: to deal with reality, with physical nature and with one another. Most men accept their ideas, not because they have judged them to be true, but merely because they believe that these ideas seem to be accepted by others. The unstated premise behind such acceptance is the desire to escape the responsibility of independent judgment and to "play it safe" by means of the evader's basic formula of: "Who am I to know? Others know best."

It never occurs to such evaders that most of those others accept their ideas in precisely the same manner, with no more thought, judgment or knowledge than their own. When men attempt to evade the responsibility of thinking, they become the victims of an enormous self-made hoax, each man believing that his neighbor *knows* that the ideas they share are true, even if he himself does not know it, and the neighbor believing that *his* neighbor knows it, even if *he* doesn't, and so forth. Where, then, do these ideas come from? Who sets the terms and the direction of a culture? The answer is: *any man who cares to.*

For good or evil, whether such a man is a profound thinker or an ambitious demagogue, an idealistic hero or a corrupt, man-hating destroyer— those who choose to deal with ideas determine the course of human history. Those who formulate men's thinking determine their fate. The makers of trends, the creators of cultures, the actual leaders of mankind are the *philosophers.*

If you study history, you will be shocked to discover how few—how very few—of these philosophers were profound thinkers or idealistic heroes. But this should not be astonishing: when men attempt to escape the responsibility of thinking, it is not the thinker or the hero that they will attract to the role of their intellectual leader.

The old slogan of con men "You can't cheat an honest man" is nowhere as applicable as in the field of the intellect. An honest mind may make errors, but will not be taken in. The trickiest sophistries of the con men of philosophy are impotent against a mind honestly concerned with the pursuit of knowledge. Such a mind will accept nothing until his own independent, *rational* judgment has weighed it and found it to be true. But the pretentious, half-conscious zombie, who wants to be intellectual without effort and who mouths fashionable formulas, with no idea of their meaning, source, or implications, feeling safe in the belief that some omniscient, infallible authority somewhere has proved them to be true and saved him the bother— is sure to be the victim of those whose purpose is to destroy the mind he has abandoned. An intellectual leader such as Aristotle does not seek blind believers and formula-reciters; a leader such as Immanuel Kant does.

———·———

There is one paragraph of Hume's, a single short paragraph, which has been working like a paralysis-ray on the brains of ethical theorists up to the present time, and which I should like to quote:

In every system of morality which I have hitherto met with I have always remarked that the author proceeds for some time in the ordinary way of reasoning, and establishes the being of a God, or makes observations concerning human affairs; when of a sudden I am surprised to find, that instead of the usual copulations of propositions, *is* and *is not*, I meet with no proposition that is not connected with an *ought*, or an *ought not*. This change is imperceptible; but it is, however, of the last consequence. For as this *ought* or *ought not* expresses some new relation or affirmation, it is necessary that it should be observed and explained; and at the same time that a reason should be given for what seems altogether inconceivable, how this new relation can be a deduction from others that are entirely different from it. [*Quoted from* A Treatise of Human Nature.]

This, in terms of modern philosophy, is the issue of the "*is*" versus the "*ought*." It purports to mean that *ethical* propositions cannot be derived from *factual* propositions—or that knowledge of that which *is* cannot logically give man any knowledge of what he *ought* to do. And wider: it means that knowledge of reality is irrelevant to the actions of a living entity and that any relation between the two is "inconceivable."

**May 21, 1961**

[*AR made the following notes while attending a conference on "Methods in Philosophy and the Sciences" at The New School in New York City.*]

[*Speaker: Noam Chomsky, "Some Observations on Linguistic Structure."*]

*Noam Chomsky* (an expert social-metaphysical-elite witch doctor): "Studies" should not be multiplied beyond necessity.

Simple trees [*i.e., diagrams used in modern symbolic logic*]: is the manner of presentation always in mid-stream, assuming previous knowledge?

*Pure* Rube Goldberg. [*Goldberg was an American cartoonist who drew absurdly complex mechanical devices.*]

How many trees would I need to build in order to understand *Atlas Shrugged*—and in how many volumes?

Is Chomsky trying to systematize all conceptual relationships in language?

———◈———

[*Speaker: Paul Ziff, "About Grammaticalness."*]
*Paul Ziff* (a social-metaphysical hatchet-man):
"If a sentence is ungrammatical, then native speakers balk." [This] as a test and criterion of grammaticalness!!! (Stolen concept!!)
"[There are] 7029 or possibly 7023 grammatical categories."(!!!)
*What* is the method?

———◈———

[*Speaker: Nelson Goodman, "Commentary." This talk addresses the goal of linguistic analysis.*]
*Nelson Goodman* (a nervous, old-fashioned professor):
The whole damn thing is an attempt to escape from or by-pass the issue of *context* and *integration*.

———◈———

[*Speaker: Yehoshua Bar-Hillel, "Mechanical Recognition of Sentence Structure."*]
*Yehoshua Bar-Hillel* (a conscientious scholar):
I think the hierarchical structure of concepts is what they need for their problem—if I understand him at all.
All this is obviously a substitute for epistemology—or an attempt to fill the vacuum left by the destruction of epistemology; linguistic analysis had to lead to this.
[Bar-Hillel concludes that] it is impossible, by present knowledge, to arrive at a unique interpretation of syntactic structures for use in computers. His reasons: readers use "context" ("they are not tabula rasa"). "The hope for a complete automatization of syntactic analysis is close to utopian." They had the hope of substituting "redundancy" for context.
He *seems* to be good.

———◈———

[*Speaker: Hans Herzberger, "Kernalization."*]

*Hans Herzberger* (a voodoo or medieval witch-doctor):

To "kernalize" a sentence is to break it into simpler "kernal" sentences. Arbitrary BS.

A batch of undefined terms related to nothing—practically a total divorce of thought and language from reality.

The time it would take to do all that would eliminate the need for a computer—it would take less time to solve the problem by one's own non-mechanical thinking.

**May 20, 1962**

[*AR attended the same conference the next year.*]

[*Speaker: George Simpson, "Explanation of the Evolution of Life as a Sequence of Unique Events."*]

*Prof. Simpson:*

There are no laws in evolution (or in biology); everything is unique. After stating that no explanation is possible, since everything is unique, he states that we all have an "intuitive, instinctive feeling" that explanation and prediction are connected "in some way."

After all the modern BS, he goes right back to abstraction, via such things as "anterior and consequent configuration."

———◦———

[*Speaker: Colin Pittendrigh, "Evolution and the Explanation of Organization."*]

*Prof. Pittendrigh:*

"Organization in biology is end-directed."

"It can trap the improbable and make it common." This is a sample of the approach, of the method of speaking.

"Organization is strongly history-dependent."(!!)

There could have been more than two ways of respiration—but only two exist, the "possibilities" being limited by "history." Good God, by what standard? What do they mean by possibility of other ways?

———◦———

[*Speaker: Ernest Nagel, "Commentary."*]

Regarding syllogisms: you will not draw any conclusion unless the necessary terms were "smuggled into" the premises. Example: You can't deduce the age of the captain from the position of the ship. (Good God!!!)

"Whether something is explicable or not depends on the assumptions which you are making." (Boy, oh boy!)

All of this is an escape from—or ignorance of—abstractions. God, what is left of epistemology?!

They all substitute metaphors for concepts—like savages.

None of them know what they are talking about and all of them are going through the motions. *Anyone* can set the terms and the direction.


**Undated**

### Note for "Self-Esteem" (and Morality)

The "able to live" and the "worthy to live" issue can be called "Darwinism" as applied to man: only the man who has made himself *able* to live is *worthy* to live—which means: the man *fit* to survive, *can* survive—which means: the intellectual (and moral) "survival of the fittest." But observe the meaning of this, as against the "Spencerian" kind of Darwinism: (*a*) other species survive by "*destruction*" of lesser species (incidentally, *not* by the destruction of their own species, there is no such thing as "dog-eat-dog")—man survives by *production* (not by fighting over the given in nature); (*b*) the human "survival of the fittest" benefits every human being (the "pyramid of ability"), except the parasites.

All altruist societies create the metaphysical contradiction of: the man *fit* to survive finds himself *unable* to survive—because of conditions geared to the non-thinking parasite and because of the principle of penalizing virtue for being virtue. (This is the [key] for explaining the altruist's package-deal about "compassion" and concern for the "unfit"—the *unable* or the *unwilling*?—their *real* concern is: "Let me survive out of focus at *your* expense.")


**Undated**

[*AR made the following notes while planning an article on "The Unsacrificed Self."*]

### Issues

The sacrifice of material goods is only the last, and superficial, result of altruism. The basic demand of altruism is the sacrifice of one's mind.

To sacrifice material goods means to sacrifice one's values—which means, to sacrifice one's judgment—which means, to sacrifice one's mind. (Give clear examples.)

(Power-lust is the attribute of the irrationalist. A rational man wants to know the truth, to perceive reality, and has no vested interest in the subversion or submission of another man's mind.)

The basic motive of altruism: parasitic survival or the destruction of the mind? Both—since it is the same issue. Existentially, it is not so much parasitic survival (and, sometimes, not at all) as the "sense of life," "pseudo-self-esteem" kind of search for metaphysical-epistemological vindication or "pseudo-efficacy"—for the reassurance that if one can destroy man's reason, one can get away with surviving by one's corrupt, irrational psycho-epistemology. It is the constant urge to *get away with* irrationality—in order to escape the anxiety of knowing that one is unfit to exist. In this sense—the "*non-venal*" lust for power ("obedience for the sake of obedience").

The dominance of anti-mind in world religions: Lucifer, Adam, Prometheus, Phaethon, Icarus, the Tower of Babel. Pride as a sin is always the *pride of the mind*, that is, *reason*. (Which means: the absolutism of one's own rational judgment, the reliance on one's own "unaided" intellect.) Superficially, people think that pride is some sort of *moral* conceit, the boast "I am good," usually unearned. But it does not pertain to *morality*—it pertains to *epistemology*, as intended by the altruists. For mystic altruists—it is "the pride of the mind"; for collectivist-altruists—it is "the pride (or the evil) of independence." (Observe how the second brings out the intention of the first, by bringing the issue down to earth. This is an instance of the mystics of muscle being the product and heirs of the mystics of spirit.)

The need of all power-lusters for a "higher authority" to sanction their doctrines, either God or Society—the ultimate reason is that no man could get away with demanding the sacrifice of *your* mind to *his*; he *has to* be the spokesman of a "higher power."

"*Under altruism, no moral calculations are possible.*" All altruistic-collectivist systems are guilty of the "fallacy of the stolen concept" in regard to individualism: they intend to preserve the values of individualism while destroying their base.

(America's subordination to the "underdeveloped nations" in the U.N. is the national counterpart of what altruism demands of the individual: the sacrifice of the power of judgment.)

Non-objectivity—as revolt against the independent mind. The "tyranny of reality."

People do not want total irrationality or dependence. What they want is much worse: an independent mind who, in case of conflict, accepts their judgment above his own. (This is impossible, therefore the result is neurotics with switching metaphysics; also—the men who reserve their independence for their professions, but surrender their mind in everything else. Examples: Einstein, Frank Lloyd Wright.)

The ultimate political-social result and expression of the sacrifice of the mind: unlimited majority rule, "democracy," numbers (or the collective) as the standard of morality and truth. (Current examples: Kennedy, the Saskatchewan doctors.)

The "frozen absolute" attitude toward altruism-collectivism: "What will you do about the poor?"

Altruism is destructive of the mind of the giver and also of the *receiver*. ("It's for your own good"—white lies, etc. Example: the universal tragedy of "self-sacrificial" parents.)

**November 4, 1964**

[*AR was interviewed by the* New York Times *on the day after the 1964 Goldwater-Johnson presidential election.*]

### Told on the Phone to the N.Y. Times

"*I am not* a 'conservative,' but an advocate of laissez-faire capitalism. I think that this campaign was conducted very badly, that this is the end of old-fashioned, anti-intellectual 'conservatism'—and that the advocates of capitalism have to start from scratch, not in practical politics, but as a cultural-philosophical movement, to lay an intellectual foundation for future political movements. It is *earlier* than you think. The *status quo* of today is a mixed economy with a fascist, rather than socialist, trend—and [Lyndon] Johnson is the conservative in the exact sense of that word. Today, the advocates of laissez-faire capitalism, which Sen. [Barry] Goldwater is not, are and have to be radical innovators."

**February 20, 1966**

### Possible Themes for Articles

"*The Short-Range View of Reason*": The people who claim that "man cannot live by reason alone" are concrete-bound, range-of-the-moment nonthinkers who have no idea of principles, wide integrations, fundamental issues, philosophy—and, therefore, who use their mind only moment by moment, on immediate, concrete problems. They have no inkling of a phenomenon such as a sense of life and no idea of the way in which mind determines emotions. These are the people who say that *reason* can deal only with the *means* to achieve values, but not with the ends—that the choice of values is subjective, mystical or arbitrary—that morality is not the province of reason, and there can be no rational morality. (If a man like [Ludwig von Mises] advocates this last, it is a sign of some enormous repression (or second-handedness) in the realm of values—since he is certainly *not* concrete-bound in his *professional* psycho-epistemology; if anything, he is "rationalistic" (Kantian) and inclined to floating abstractions. This is an interesting psychological lead.)

———

*"Sense of Life and the Primacy of Consciousness":* Man *needs* a state of psychological integration—of inner unity and, therefore, *full certainty*. Uncertainty is a dangerous state for man existentially, and unsupportable psychologically. The truly unbearable uncertainty is uncertainty about the validity of one's own consciousness. And since man never learned how to live with a volitional consciousness, how to possess certainty and knowledge without infallibility and omniscience—his most urgent need is the *validation* of his own consciousness. Therefore, in the absence of a *rational epistemology* (which is the only solution to this problem) man takes his consciousness as an absolute (uncritically) and fakes reality to fit it—in order not to face the horror of an impotent consciousness; hence, Platonism and other such philosophies. (This is the distorted element of truth in such systems—or the psycho-epistemological need which makes them possible. A great deal of conscious evil and faking for evil motives is involved in the authors of such philosophies, as, for instance, in Hume or Kant.)

**March 6, 1966**

### Themes for Articles

*Psychological selfishness:* the kind of selfishness that consists of constant focusing on: "What does it show about me?" (Which implies psycho-epistemological passivity, determinism, the taking of emotions as causeless primaries, emotion-motivation, whim-worship, the primacy of consciousness.)

The "games" of double-meaning dialogue, focused on "beating" somebody—the focus on "impressing" somebody or "proving" something about oneself, rather than on facts and reality. In regard to art: the focusing, not on whether one enjoys a given work of art, but on: "What will it prove about me if I enjoy it or not?" (The paradox: enormous and irrational concern with one's *moral status*—by a person who has given up values and moral sovereignty.) The irrationality of altruism on this issue: the advice to "come out of yourself" and "concern yourself with the 'wider' world," which is equated with "concern with others"—as if the objective *meant* the collective, as if "others" had a stake in reality, but one did not, as if the withdrawal from reality into one's own feelings were actually to one's own interest.

(This is actually the issue of "self-doubt-centeredness.") [*AR regarded the term "self-centered" as a pejorative, meaning, roughly, "neurotically concerned with one's own worth," i.e., "centered on self-doubt." In her view, the virtue of selfishness requires that one be "reality-centered."*]

———————

*The issue of men's unidentified best:* The reversal of the idea that men pretend to be good in public, but are monsters in private (like *Peyton Place*). The exact opposite is true: men (I suspect, predominantly) repress and hide their best (their values, their honest or profound thoughts, their *serious* concerns), and put on an act of cautious, empty superficiality (and, often, moral treason) in public. The "lynching" spirit: the worst in men is encouraged by a mob feeling (and I doubt whether the best ever is—such instances as "public" courage are not courage).

(The springboard for this article: The fact that men use the right epistemology in the physical sciences, to the extent that they do succeed, but have never identified it.)

**1966–1967**

[*The following passages were cut from* Introduction to Objectivist Epistemology.

*The first is from the conclusion to Chapter 5, "Definitions."*]

It is as if man were still screaming in terror before the mystery of his own consciousness, unable to grasp the fact that human cognition is not to be achieved automatically, neither by passive absorption nor by active distortion of perceptual data, and that knowledge can be acquired only by a specific method whose terms are set irrevocably by the nature of man's consciousness and of reality, and are not open to man's choice, only to his discovery and practice—a rigorous method, to be practiced volitionally, whose reward is *objective* knowledge.

―――――――

[*From Chapter 6, "Axiomatic Concepts":*]
The disintegration of a human consciousness means the attempted descent to an animal's perceptual level of awareness, but with this difference: an animal, being unable to question reality, is unable to fake it and acts, moment by moment, in accordance with such facts as his limited awareness entitles him to perceive. Man, possessing the power to expand his consciousness, does not possess the power to shrink it; he cannot escape the integrating power of his brain and restrict himself to snatches of moment-by-moment awareness. If he rejects the task of conscious integration, his subconscious does the job for him, and the result is not *cognitive* integration, but a blind, nightmare mixture of the part-grasped, part-evaded, part-felt, part-wished and whole terror, the state of a creature unfit to perceive reality on any level of awareness, and unable to survive—samples of which may be observed in any psychiatrist's office or in the ranks of any irrationalist movement.

―――――――

[*From Chapter 7, "The Cognitive Role of Concepts":*]
The growth of language follows the growth of knowledge, guided by the principle of unit-economy. Every new branch of science creates a vocabulary of its own (which should be, but today is not, translatable without contradiction into the general language). The advent of every new industry creates new words, i.e., new concepts. (If Plato's theory of universals needed any modern refutations, test it by asking yourself whether the archetypes of "monkey wrench," "spark plug" and "television" had to wait two and a half thousand years in another dimension to be finally recalled by man.)
[*After crossing out the above, AR wrote:*]
The growth of language follows the growth of knowledge and the expansion of human activities. It is a vast, anonymous process, with many variations (in the optional area), many changes, false starts and short-lived attempts. Yet certain basic principles can be observed, demonstrating, not the arbitrary character, but the *objectivity* of that process.
In secular practice (i.e., omitting the concepts of mysticism, which have

no referents), a word survives and gains general usage only when and if it designates an actual category of existents that need conceptual designation—with the principle of unit-economy determining that need. Slang is a major source of new words in the general language. Many slang terms are coined every year, by one group or another; some of them become fashionable, enjoy a brief, artificial popularity of random mouthing (intended to designate the fact that one is in with the right group, rather than any category of existents) and vanish, like the stale debris of some noisy party. But a few slang expressions survive and become part of formal language—the apt, incisive ones that designate some aspect of reality for which no formal term had previously existed (such as the verb "to kid" or the nouns "bum" or "stuffed shirt").

*[From Chapter 8, "Consciousness and Identity":]*
Such knowledge as mankind has acquired and such progress as it has made were achieved in spite of and in a constant struggle against its dominant theories of epistemology. Cognitive *objectivity* has existed in the world as a kind of unofficial, unrecognized underground, in isolated instances and sporadic snatches, fed by such partial leads as could be found in Aristotle's far from perfect system. Objectivity has never had a full statement, a consistent theory or a firm epistemological foundation; and, even though it represented the *implicit* method practiced in every scientific achievement, particularly in the spectacular progress of the physical sciences, it was not identified nor acknowledged by its practitioners, which is an eloquent illustration of the ultimate futility of practice without theory, of man's helplessness when he lacks an explicit statement of his merely implicit knowledge. Those who sought cognitive objectivity were helplessly vulnerable to the theoretical onslaughts of both mystics and skeptics—they had no answer to the flood of equivocations, merely sensing that something was very wrong in those arguments, but unable to discover why—and they lost the battle again and again, as they have lost it today, when we witness the spectacle of nuclear missiles on one hand and, on the other, a unanimous chorus proclaiming that knowledge is impossible to man (and, presumably, that a process of cognition based on conceptual "family resemblances" [*a reference to Wittgenstein*] will determine when those missiles are to be used).

**May, 1968**

[*The following was cut from AR's introduction to the twenty-fifth-anniversary edition of* The Fountainhead.]

I have been asked whether I have learned anything from the history of *The Fountainhead* and its readers. I have—and it was not an attractive discovery. I learned, at least in part, what makes those stillborn men extinguish the unrepeatable fact of being alive.

Without apology to Dostoevsky, this part of my discussion may be entitled "Notes from the Underground."

It took me some time to identify and confirm the nature of that particular underground. I shall list the key points of the evidence, as I observed it.

Of the twelve publishers who rejected *The Fountainhead*, the most shocking rejection, to me, was by a house whose editor told me that their editorial board had evaluated my novel as: "a work of almost genius— 'genius' in the power of its expression—'almost' in the sense of its enormous bitterness," but that they rejected it because they were certain it would not sell. (Incidentally, what they took for "bitterness" was the unforgiving tone of moral indignation.) The phenomenon of men acting on wrong standards of value did not puzzle me; but the phenomenon of men rejecting that which they regarded as a value by their own standards and judgment was, to me, psychologically inconceivable. I felt that I was sensing some profound evil which I would have to learn to identify someday.

After the publication of *The Fountainhead*, I met a woman, by chance, in a beauty parlor. She heard my name and she approached me to tell me how much she admired my novel. She was not gushing; she spoke quietly, intently and, to the best of my judgment, sincerely. It was the sincerity that made me take notice when she complimented me on my courage and added, with the faintest note of despair in her voice, referring to the spirit of my book: "Many of us feel that way, but we don't have the courage to say it. We're afraid." "Afraid of what?" I asked. She could not answer; she merely sighed and spread her hands out in a gesture of hopelessness, as if she were thinking of something intangible, too vast to identify. I tried to question her, but got no further clue. I truly did not know what she was talking about. I never saw her again. But the incident remained in my mind because I felt it was a clue to something either evil or very, very wrong, which I had to understand.

A brilliant young man [Leonard Peikoff] whom I met when he was seventeen (and who since has become one of my best friends), asked me, on our first meeting: "Is Howard Roark moral or is he practical? He seems to be both—yet I have always been told that it's one or the other." This choice was deeply disturbing to him, because he took moral issues seriously and because the same people urged him—at different times—to choose alternate sides of this dichotomy. It did not take me long to convince him that this was a false dichotomy, caused by the irrationality and impracticality of the mystic-altruist ethics, and that this was one example of why man needs a rational code of ethics. But I wondered—as I had wondered often, before and since—about the psychological state of those who maintain that dichotomy. What are moral values divorced from practice? And what is it that one chooses to practice, if it is divorced from moral values? [*This paragraph was crossed out.*]

In the early days of *The Fountainhead*'s history, when its success was still uncertain, I noticed the peculiar attitude of an editor of my acquaintance: his conviction that my novel was a great value and his emotional commitment to it were unquestionable, he had demonstrated it, in action, on many occasions—and yet, whenever I consulted him on any action to be taken on its behalf, his answers were vague, almost forced and singularly half-hearted. Then, one day, I asked him: "Tell me, you believe that *The Fountainhead* is great and, precisely for that reason, you believe that it is doomed, don't you?" He answered in a low, unhappy voice: "Yes."

The instances of men who paid me extravagant, unsolicited compliments at private gatherings, but never stated it in print or on public occasions, are too numerous to count. I do not mean the usual sort of gushers. Those men were prominent literary or professional figures who had no reason to flatter me; in many cases, they did not even say it to me, but to others, without knowing that I would ever hear about it. If such were their views, they had no reason to be afraid of expressing them publicly. Yet they kept silent.

The final clue was provided by a very perceptive friend of mine. He said he had observed a strange quality in many people's enthusiasm for *The Fountainhead*: it was a furtive, secretive, subjective quality, almost like the reluctant confession of a guilty love. "They talk as an unhappily married man would talk about his secret mistress," he said. "Their marriage is to the Establishment, to conventional values and the 'accepted' intellectual positions. But *The Fountainhead* is their passion."

What I felt was something like a cold shudder.

What I grasped was that this was deeper and worse than simple cowardice or conformity. For whatever complexity of reasons—whether out of fear, or bewilderment, or discouragement, or repression, or years of conditioning by altruism's vicious dichotomy between the moral and the practical, with the consequent feeling that the good is impractical, and the practical has no place for values—those men were consigning their values, the things they loved or admired or enjoyed, to the airless dungeon of subjectivism, as private fantasies or fragile, private treasures unfit for the sunlight of reality.

**circa 1977**

[*The following daily schedule was undated. It was written after AR stopped writing* The Ayn Rand Letter *in February 1976, and before the death of her husband in November 1979.*]

*Tentative Schedule*

Get up at 7:30 a.m.
7:30 a.m.–8:30 a.m.: Wake up and dress.
8:30 a.m.–1 p.m.: Main work (and Frank's breakfast).
1 p.m.–2 p.m.: Lunch, house cleaning, order groceries.
2 p.m.–3 p.m.: Mail.
3 p.m.–4 p.m.: Algebra.
4 p.m.–5 p.m.: Reading lesson.
5 p.m.–6 p.m.: Reading.
6 p.m.–8 p.m.: Cooking, dinner, wash dishes.
8 p.m.–11 p.m.: Reading.
11 p.m.–1 a.m.: TV.
1 a.m.: Go to bed.

———

At present, main work should be "Philosophic Revolution Plan." The reading period from 5 p.m. to 6 p.m. should be given to order—cleaning up the organization of the house. The period after dinner should be elastic—including dates or talks with Frank. Once a week (Monday) should include attending to hair and wardrobe, or shopping (also—health). Sunday should be totally free—"whim-worshipping." Saturday—should have secretary for mail.

———

*Overall assignments:* Time schedule—"pleasure epistemology"—learning to read—algebra—diet.

*Elements of action:*

> Business (literary contracts, lectures).
> Contacts (social dates, contacts for possible magazine).
> Correspondence (fan-mail, personal) and bills.
> Clothes (shopping, mending).
> Order (papers, files, drawers, closets—house in general).
> Health (dentist, etc.).
> Meals.

*Elements of creative action:*

> Reading.
> Time to think about psychology.
> Time to think about myself and specific plan.

# TWO POSSIBLE BOOKS

*In the decade after* Atlas Shrugged, *AR made notes for a non-fiction book on Objectivism and for a novel entitled* To Lorne Dieterling. *She did not get far in planning either book; the notes here represent in total a few days of work on each, spread over a period of years—what AR referred to as "work in small glances."*

**June 8, 1958**

### Objectivism
*A Philosophy for Living on Earth*

#### Preface

I apologize for the subtitle of this book: it is the intellectual corruption of our age that made it necessary. If men were taught how to speak, it would be obvious that the word "living" refers to man; that man lives on earth; that "philosophy," being the science of the nature of existence, is concerned with discovering the knowledge man requires for living; and, therefore, that the only words necessary are: "A philosophy."

But since "philosophy" is the one concept which, today, has been all but destroyed, there are reasons why modern men cannot achieve a state of conceptual precision prior to acquiring the knowledge here to be presented. The purpose of this book is to make its subtitle redundant.

**June 19, 1958**

*"Cosmology" has to be thrown out of philosophy.* When this is done, the conflict between "rationalism" and "empiricism" will be wiped out—or, rather, the error that permitted the nonsense of such a conflict will be wiped out.

What, apparently, has never been challenged and what I took as a self-evident challenge (which it isn't) is Thales' approach to philosophy, namely: the idea that philosophy has to discover the *nature* of the universe in cosmological terms. If Thales thought that everything is water, and the other pre-Socratics fought over whether it's water and earth and fire, etc., then the empiricists were right in declaring that they would go by the evidence of observation, not by "rational" deduction—only then, of course, the whole issue and all its terms are [thoroughly confused]. The crux of the error here is in the word *"nature."* I took Thales' attempt to mean only the first attempt at, or groping toward, a unified view of knowledge and reality, i.e., *an epistemological, not a metaphysical,* attempt to establish the fact that things have natures.

Now I think that he meant, and all subsequent philosophers took it to mean, a *metaphysical* attempt to establish the *literal* nature of reality and to prove by philosophical means that everything is literally and physically made of water or that water is a kind of universal "stuff." If so, then philosophy is worse than a useless science, because it usurps the domain of physics and proposes to solve the problems of physics by some non-scientific, and therefore mystical, means. On this kind of view of philosophy, it is logical that philosophy has dangled on the strings of physics ever since the Renaissance and that every new discovery of physics has blasted philosophy sky-high, such as, for instance, the discovery of the nature of color giving a traumatic shock to philosophers, from which they have not yet recovered. [*AR is referring to the discovery that our perception of color depends on the nature of the light and the human visual system as well as on nature of the object, which led many philosophers to conclude that perception is subjective.*]

In fact, this kind of view merely means: rationalizing from an arrested state of knowledge. Thus, if in Thales' time the whole extent of physical knowledge consisted of distinguishing water from air and fire, he took this knowledge to be a final omniscience and decided on its basis that water was the primary metaphysical element. On this premise, every new step in physics has to mean a new metaphysics. The subsequent nonsense was not that empiricists rejected Thales' approach, but that they took him (and Plato) to be "rationalists," i.e., men who derived knowledge by deduction from some sort of "innate ideas," and therefore the empiricists declared themselves to be anti-rationalists. They did not realize that the Thales-Plato school was merely a case of "arrested empiricists," that is, men who "rationalized" on the ground of taking partial knowledge as omniscience.

Aristotle established the right metaphysics by establishing the law of identity—which was all that was necessary (plus the identification of the fact that only concretes exist). But he destroyed his metaphysics by his cosmology—by the whole nonsense of the "moving spheres," "the immovable mover," teleology, etc.

The real crux of this issue is that *philosophy is primarily epistemology*— the science of the means, the rules, and the methods of human knowledge. Epistemology is the base of all other sciences and one necessary for man because man is a being of volitional consciousness—a being who has to discover, not only the content of his knowledge, but also the means by which he is to acquire knowledge. Observe that all philosophers (except Aristotle) have been projecting their epistemologies into their metaphysics (or that their metaphysics were merely epistemological and psychological confessions). All the fantastic irrationalities of philosophical metaphysics have been the result of epistemological errors, fallacies or corruptions. "Existence exists" (or identity plus causality) is all there is to metaphysics. *All the rest is epistemology.*

Paraphrasing myself: Philosophy tell us only *that* things have natures, but *what* these natures are is the job of specific sciences. The rest of philosophy's task is to tell us the rules by which to discover the specific natures.

### June 20, 1958

The philosophy which I now will have to present is, in essence, the "rules of thinking" which children should be taught in the proper society (which the Wet Nurse needed). It is fundamental epistemology—plus psychological "epistemology." All the evils of philosophy have always been achieved via epistemology—by means of the "How do you know that you know?" Consider the fact that the first and greatest destroyer, Plato, did it by means of the issue of "universals vs. particulars." Mankind as a whole seems to be caught in the trap of the nature of its own epistemology: men cannot think until they have acquired the power of abstractions and language, but having done so, they do not know how they got there and are vulnerable to any attack on their means of knowledge. Like the discovery of "A is A," their epistemology is implicit in their thinking, but unidentified. This will be the main part of my job: my theory of universals—the hierarchical nature of concepts—the "stolen concept" fallacy—the "context-dropping" and the "blank-out" (the *refusal* to identify)—the "Rand's razor" ("state your irreducible primaries")—the rules of induction (and definitions)—the "integration into the total sum of your knowledge"—the proof that "that which is empirically impossible is also logically impossible (or false)"—etc.

This will be the issue of "teaching the world my particular kind of epistemology" (which I took to be self-evident and known). This is also why I always thought of philosophy as a static, "finite" base, like logic, i.e., as a closed discipline which has to be learned in order then to proceed to live, with "life" beginning above this base. This, probably, is the root of what Leonard [Peikoff] had in mind when he called the present state of the world "the age of pre-reason." It will help me to think of my job as *"Philosophy for Hank Rearden."*

### Notes for "Objectivism"

[*Most of the remaining notes for the book deal with AR's theory of concepts, which she later published in* Introduction to Objectivist Epistemology.]

A *unit* is a *concrete entity* considered apart from the other entities which are subsumed under the *same abstraction.*

Thus, an *inch* is a concrete entity of the abstraction *"length"* and is a *unit of measurement* for any other length which is conceptualized by means of its relationships to the chosen unit; thus a yard is so many inches, a mile is so many yards, etc.

*Number is the abstraction of the process of abstraction.* It stands for the relationship of an entity to other entities, all of which have to be absolute and immutable *in their defining characteristic*, in that which permits them to be regarded as *units* subsumed under *a single concept.* Number is the concept that identifies the transition from *"entity"* to *"unit,"* the mental transformation of a *concrete, perceptual entity* into the material to be integrated by a *concept.* Mathematics is the pattern (the blue print) of the conceptual level of man's consciousness—the abstract pattern of the process of concept-formation, in the sense that it isolates and identifies the process which man's mind has to perform in regard to every abstraction, every concept it reaches, regardless of the concretes involved—that is: the abstraction of "number" stands for *any* concrete entities regarded as "units" to be integrated into a concept which then becomes a new, *single unit.* (The concept "ten" is a single unit denoting a certain number of "ones"; the abstraction "man" is a single unit denoting "*n* number" of concrete men, that is: denoting a mathematical series to be extended into infinity, to subsume *any* number of men.)

(*Next step:* The relationship of every concept to the "open-ended" mathematical series.)

*"Measurement"* is the establishment of a *relationship*—the relationship between a concrete unit, which serves as the standard of measure, and other concretes belonging to the same abstraction (length, weight, etc.). A *"concept"* is also the establishment of a *relationship*—the relationship between a concrete unit and other concretes belonging to the same abstraction; the standard of measure here is the defining characteristic.

*Fallacies:*

"Stolen Concept" (connected with "irreducible primaries").
"Context-dropping."
"Reification of the Zero."
"Stepping into Limbo."
"Non-differentiation between Existence and Consciousness."
(A *"unit"* is the concept of *identity*. If you take "a group" as a start and proceed to define a "unit" by breaking up the group—you have committed the fallacy of the "stolen concept": you have already accepted the *group* as a *unit*.)

Regarding *"context-dropping"*: a variant or corollary fallacy is the idea that considering a thing *in context* is a *"relativistic"* premise, thus: if values are selected by man, they are "relative" to man. This is an example of the "whose whim" fallacy: either values are *intrinsic* (arbitrarily set by the whim of God or nature)—or they are *subjective* ("relative" to or set by the whim of man); the concept of objectivism (of an immutable *nature* of things) is missing. The reasoning behind it goes like this: if a thing has to be considered in a context, then it is not an absolute, then anything goes. The error is: the substitution of infinity for a given, *known* context. Example: [a philosophy professor] claiming that the airplane invalidates the absolutism of the law of gravitation.

**April 9, 1959**

*Notes for Epistemology*
*(Re: Mathematics of Consciousness)*

The basic and most universal concepts in the functioning of a human consciousness are: existence—identity—entity—unit.

The first two pertain to metaphysics, the second two to epistemology.

To grasp existence is to grasp that existence is identity—that a thing is what it is.

To grasp that is to grasp the concept of entity—a *thing*.

To continue the process of consciousness is to transform the concept of entity into the concept of a unit, thus: a *"unit"* is an entity which is independent of any other entity of its own kind—or, a unit is any part of an entity *considered* independently of the rest of its own kind, such as an inch of string considered as an independent length of string while it is part of a ten-inch string. *This* is the start of the process of *measurement*.

All measurement is integration, by means of a basic unit, that is: the bringing of a vast or complex whole into conceptual form by relating it *mathematically* to a basic unit. Example: a *mile* is so many *feet*.

All abstractions (all concepts) are the identifications of a basic unit of measurement, with the specific measurements of the particular concretes omitted. For example, *length* is the abstraction of spatial extension, which omits the specific spatial extension of any given entity, but defines the kind of unit by means of which this entity is to be measured in regard to its attribute of spatial extension.

The unit of measurement for all concepts pertaining to consciousness is their *content*. Since consciousness is a "representation" or "reflection" (a more exact term is here needed) of existence, the concepts pertaining to consciousness are ultimately reducible to the *existents* which they "reflect" or "represent." Examples: a "thought" is differentiated from another thought by means of its subject (of what the thought is about); an "emotion" is differentiated from another emotion by means of the value judgment it represents, and a value judgment is a thought (a thought dealing with the realm of action in existence).

In establishing a unit of measurement one has to observe two rules: the unit has to be a tool of both division and integration, it must give one the conceptual possibility of breaking an entity into such units and of integrating it back again, as well as integrating it with other entities of the same kind into groups or sums. Example: if an "inch" is taken as the unit to measure *length*, one must be able to break up a longer string into inches, then add them up to get a concept of the string in terms of an *integrated sum of inches*. (This requires a great deal more careful thinking and more precise definitions. But this is a lead to the process of forming concepts or abstractions.) [. . .]

My hypothesis is that all consciousness is a mathematical process (or, rather, the *function* of any consciousness is a mathematical process). To prove this I would have to identify the basic principles common to perception and mathematics. (By perception I mean here the total process of human awareness, from sensations to perceptions to conceptions.) I would have to identify the wider abstractions underlying the processes of concept-formation and of mathematics. And I would have to integrate them with neurology on the one hand (with the physiological part of the integration of sensations into perceptions)—and with metaphysics on the other.

If my hypothesis is true, then algebra might give me the clue to the *objective* rules of induction—to a kind of "Organon of Induction." [*Aristotle's works on logic are called the "Organon," Greek for "instrument."*]

## June 18, 1959

*(Hurried notes, which require hours and hours of further thinking.)*

Arithmetical numbers are *taken* as entities in any arithmetical calculation, which means: an arithmetical calculation is an action by which the relationship of certain entities leads to the discovery of a final entity, which is the goal *and the stop* of the action. A series of arithmetical equations involving action is incomplete until it has reached the stopping point of a specific arithmetical entity, e.g., a *number*.

But the numbers themselves are composites. The only *primary* entity here is the *unit*—the concept of *one (1)*. Every other number is an abstraction which replaces a certain repetition of ones by a single concept meant to stand for that repetition (*1 1 1 1* means *4*).

This is the epistemological method of the first level of abstractions—that is, the abstractions (or conceptions) derived directly from perceptions and constituting "ostensive definitions," e.g., the abstractions of immediately perceived objects, such as: chair, table, man, red, green, color, living being, etc. (Note the mixture of levels, such as "red" and "color.") [*AR seems to be correcting herself here—"color" and "living being" are not "first-level" abstractions.*] (Perceptions here mean that which a human consciousness *automatically* integrates out of sensations.) The next (and *volitional*) level are the abstractions from abstractions—which is the epistemological method of algebra (the discovery of unknown quantities by means of their relationship to the known quantities).

*Notes for "Objectivism"*

Re: *fallacies.* The two most important fallacies which I must define thoroughly are, in effect, *extensions* of two of the fallacies defined by Aristotle: *"context-dropping"* is really the wider (and more modern) name for Aristotle's "ignoratio elenchi"; and *"the stolen concept"* is the other side, the reverse, of "petitio principii." If this last is "begging the question" or "assuming that which you are attempting to prove," then "the stolen concept" is "begging the answer" or "assuming that which you are attempting to disprove." (Many instances of "the stolen concept" are, in fact, instances of "petitio principii," such as [Bertrand] Russell's attempt to derive the concept "unit" from [the concept] "group," which, throughout the whole reasoning, presupposes knowledge of the concept "unit." But such instances are merely fraudulent attempts to *prove* something; the most important part of "the stolen concept" is its application to the fraudulent attempts to *disprove* something, particularly to disprove basic axioms. This is the worst of the fallacies in modern philosophy.)

[*The notes for* Objectivism: A Philosophy for Living on Earth *end here.*]

———◆———

[*During an interview in 1961, AR remarked:*

I don't know whether I will ever write fiction again. The difficulty is that *Atlas Shrugged* was the climax and completion of the goal I had set for myself at the age of nine. It expressed everything that I wanted of fiction writing. Above everything else, it presented my ideal man fully. I can never surpass Galt. More than that, I now have four variants: Roark, Galt, Rearden, and Francisco. There is no point in multiplying them. What worries me about my future in fiction is that the motor of my interest—the presentation of the ideal man and the ideal way of life—is gone. It's completed, fulfilled. . . .

*If and when I see an aspect of my sense of life that I have not covered, then I will write another novel. One can't exhaust the sense of life; it is not like philosophical problems.*

*At the time, AR had already made a few notes for* To Lorne Dieterling. *In* Atlas Shrugged, *the focus was on the whole of society, and the*

November 30, 1957                                    (1)

First notes for:

"To ~~Vivre Dickling~~ ~~Hidden~~ ~~Lansing~~"

Basic theme: The story of a woman who is ~~totally~~ motivated by love for values — and how one maintains such a state when alone in an enemy world.

Next step of theme: The whole issue of values and of happiness. The role of values in human psychology, in the relationships among men and in ~~the~~ the events of their lives. What it means to "live for one's own sake" — ~~not as~~ (shown) a social-political (scale) but in men's (on) (moral lives). ~~As a~~ consequence — show the manner in which men betray their values, and show the results. Select, for the characters of the story, the key versions of men's attitudes toward values.

*philosophic issues were dealt with explicitly. In* To Lorne Dieterling, *the focus is on the heroine, Hella, and her sense of life.*]

---

**November 30, 1957**

First notes for: *To Lorne Dieterling.*

*Basic theme:* The story of a woman who is totally motivated by love for values—and how one maintains such a state when alone in an enemy world.

*Next step of theme:* The whole issue of values and of happiness. The role of values in human psychology, in the relationships among men and in the events of their lives. What it means to "live for one's own sake"—shown not on a social-political scale, but in men's personal lives.

As a consequence, show the manner in which men betray their values, and show the results. Select, for the characters of the story, the key versions of men's attitudes toward values.

The hidden, basic issue here will be: effort or non-effort, or *happiness versus non-effort. The issue "to think or not to think" takes actual form, existentially and psychologically, as the issue: "To value or to conform."* It is not the independent thinker as such that people actually resent, but the independent value—which means: the person who feels intensely about his values. (This point will require long, detailed analysis here.)

*The set-up of characters, at present:*

Hella: the fully rational valuer.
Lorne Dieterling: the repressor (a rational man who goes off the rails on the question of action—who, starting with the absolute that he will not let people stop him, finds himself placing action above ideas).
The "practical man."
The "glamorizer."
The "idealist."
Gloria Thornton: the "energy without effort" type.

The above are *pro-life people.* Hella and Lorne are rational; the rest are the better types of social-metaphysicians.

On the "below-zero" side are the *pro-death* people—the actual haters of life and values.

> The "Uncle Ed" type: the power-luster, who wants power for the sake of power; actually, he is after nothing at all.
> The sneerer: the professional cynic, whose sole motive is to sneer at everything; specifically, at *any kind of values* (the *New Yorker* magazine type).
> *The humanitarian:* the type whose motive is to penalize values for being values, to make men feel guilty about their intelligence, or ability, or beauty, or success, or wealth.

*The story must show:* that the death-premisers are actually after nothing, that they achieve nothing but a senseless, meaningless vacuum, that their horror is their mediocrity; and that *they* are the value-setters of a society of social-metaphysicians. (The rational men do not "take care" of other men; the thinkers require thinking men. It is only the most profoundly dependent social-metaphysicians, the power-lusters, who will undertake to "think for others." As a consequence, the value-betrayers in the story—the men who gave up values for the sake of "safety," on the ground that "others know best"—find, in the end, that their treason and all of their torture were for no better purpose than to have the world obey "Uncle Ed's" opinion on cigarettes. Or, as another example: the girl who renounces the man she loves, because of her mother's objections—finds that her mother's ultimate purpose was to stay in bed an hour later than usual "on whim.")

*The story must also show:* that the value-betrayers end up by achieving the exact opposite of the goals they sought to achieve by social-metaphysical means.

Here there are two separate aspects to consider: Whether these men have some semi-rationally selected goal and believe (emotionally) that social-metaphysics is the means—or whether in their very selection of goals, they chose the socially prescribed, chose it uncritically, as a self-evident, irreducible primary. (I believe it is more this second. As an example: the "practical man" who chooses wealth and material success without any thought of "why?" or "what for?," simply on some such feeling as "it's *good* to be successful, everybody wants to be successful, how can that be doubted?"—which amounts to the feeling: "one is *supposed* to be successful." Another example: the woman who has children without ever questioning whether she wants to have them—simply on the feeling that "one is supposed to have children.")

The "practical man" goes bankrupt.

The "glamorizer" is viciously betrayed by his "best friend" (or wife) and suffers a terrible tragedy.

The "idealist" becomes the particular "cat's paw" of the villains in their attempted destruction of ideals.

Gloria Thornton—whose "ego-value" was her competence in the achievement of any values prescribed by society, who obeyed, adjusted and conformed in the expectation that "others" (or "reality") would reward her with happiness—finds herself empty, exhausted, enjoying nothing and reaching a state of chronic panic.

*Examples of value-betraying* (these are random examples of the things I hate most):

The man who, in middle-life, finds the woman he could be truly in love with, and passes her up because "it would upset his whole life."

In the same category as above: the man who avoids any serious emotional commitment, who runs from anything that he could feel strongly about—for reasons such as: "I would be afraid to lose it" or: "It would hurt me too much to lose it," etc.—the man who deliberately chooses the second-rate and second-best, the man who *seeks* dullness and mediocrity.

The man who says: "I don't want to be happy, I just want to be contented—happiness is too demanding, exaltation is too difficult to bear."

The man who says: "Don't take anything too seriously," and, later and more accurately: "I don't take myself seriously."

The man who says: "There is no black and white. All men are gray." (With the result that he then proceeds to a mawkish, hysterical defense of any depravity as "not wholly black"—and to a malicious resentment against any man who is wholly white, and more: against any *claim* that any man *can* be wholly white.)

The man who excuses (and sanctions and accepts) another man's evil action by claiming that the actor's motives or intentions were good.

The man who believes that ideals are "too good for this earth." His variants are: "If it's good, it's doomed," or: "If it's successful, it can't be good," or: "If *I* want it, it's impossible."

Any believer in any sort of compromise.

Any man who believes that mankind is essentially, metaphysically evil—and proceeds to make terms with the evil. (Any "appeaser.")

*Key points of the original "unrequited love" story:*

Hella's dedication to the "curse" of always seeing things "as they ought to be." ("The Archer" prologue.)

The Hella-Lorne romance—and breach.

Hella learning of Lorne's engagement to Gloria at Gloria's birthday party; Lorne following Hella to her home and their scene. ("It is only *my* pain—and I can take care of it.")

Hella's work on her book—the excruciating loneliness—the discovery of "her own world," her "dates" with Lorne "as they should have been."

The publication of the book—the general fury against her—the torture scene. ("This is our wedding-night, even if such is the only form of it that I can have.")

The walk through the woods. ("To keep moving, just to keep moving . . . just to take the next step . . .") The collapse—the enraptured rededication. ("No, I don't regret it. . . ."—the "all right, even this" answer to every past torture.) Lorne joins her. ("I have not asked you to forgive me." "To forgive you? For what?")

———————

[*On January 1, 1963, AR attached the following comment to these notes:*]

The above notes are *totally wrong* for this story. The approach in them is too broad and transforms the story into a wide-scale, *social* novel (by presenting the stories of all the other types, of all the variants). This turns it into a novel about *men's attitude toward values*—and *not* the story of *one valuer*. These notes may be used only as source material for the lesser characters of the supporting cast. This is *not* the right statement of the theme. [*After twelve years of work on* Atlas Shrugged, *AR, it seems, had automatized the approach to a wide-scale, social novel.*]

**February 10, 1959**

*New statement of theme:* the art of psychological survival in a malevolent world; the art of spiritual self-sufficiency.

*To think over:* the principles (and definitions) of how one knows what depends on oneself, and how one reacts to existential events which are not wholly dependent on oneself; what one aims to achieve as rewards; the preservation of action and goals in the world without dependence on others (without the torture of hope) and *without subjectivism.*

*Hella as a dancer* (projecting her view of man and of his relationship to existence, the stylized and benevolent universe).

The *real essence* of the story is to be the universe of my "tiddlywink" music, of the "Traviata Overture" and "Simple Confession," of *my* sense of life. [*"Tiddlywink" music was AR's name for her favorite lighthearted popular tunes from the turn of the century.*]

Use the incident of *Good Copy* as a psychological key. [*The "incident" occurred when* Good Copy *was read in a 1958 fiction-writing seminar given by AR. Some of the students regarded the story as philosophically superficial or meaningless* because *it was lighthearted and cheerful; AR explained that such a criticism was based on the malevolent universe premise (see* The Early Ayn Rand).]

Lorne as the man who sacrifices values for the sake of "living on earth"—for the sake of action, motivated by a passionate pro-life premise, an unbreached ("Narcissus"-like) self-esteem, but thrown off by the wrong premise of taking action as a primary.

*The "above zero" types of value-betrayers:*

> *The idealist-aspirer:* the subjectivist who holds his values only as a private dream, only in his own consciousness, and betrays Hella because he comes to feel resentment against the *possibility* of values being achieved in reality. Starting with a "Who am I to act?" attitude, he ends up with the premise (or feeling) that "if it is in reality, it is *not* a value."
>
> *The "Byronic" idealist* who builds pain into his "despair-universe" and ends up with the premise that "if no pain is involved, it is not a value nor an ideal; if it's cheerful, it's vulgar, superficial and inconsequential." He ends up as a real "pain-worshipper."
>
> *The "glamorizer"* who dares not admit to himself the existence of pain or evil in the world, who goes on pretending to himself that everything is good, because he wants the good so desperately— and ends up by letting the good perish rather than discover that evil is evil.

The *"below-zero"* types who set the values to which all the "value-betrayers" surrender:

> *The cynic* who hates values for being values, and whose sole pleasure is in destruction.

*The Babbitt:* the human "ballast" who has no values and doesn't give a damn.

*The "Uncle Ed" type:* the power-luster, who wants power for the sake of power; actually, he is after nothing at all.

*The "top-average" type:* the presumptuous mediocrity who wants the unearned.

### Temporary Outline

Lorne's note—Hella on her way to the hotel—the flashback:

Hella's love for Lorne—his conflict between Hella and Gloria—Hella's conflict with the world (her "curse" of "seeing things as they ought to be").

Love scene between Hella and Lorne—his best "passion for life."

The missed date—Gloria's party—the announcement of Gloria's engagement to Lorne. Hella's walk home—Lorne follows her, their scene. ("It is only *my* pain—and I can take care of it.")

Hella's struggle—the senseless dance-engagements—her excruciating loneliness—Lorne's marriage.

Hella's practice and saving for her debut—the discovery of "her own world," her "dates" with Lorne "as they should have been."

Lorne's struggle with his precarious empire—the deterioration of his relationship with Gloria and of their marriage.

Hella dancing in the dive. The stranger, who is Lorne's uncle—their friendship.

Hella's debut—total disaster, except for the presence of Lorne and of the uncle.

The uncle's death—the conditions of his will.

Lorne's trap—his conversation with the lawyer, his decision.

Back to the present: the scene in the hotel room (which is the "torture scene").

*Lorne's final choice* (probably in court, in connection with the will)—his reunion with Hella, their unobstructed future.

**February 11, 1959**

Approximate text of the note:

Hella,

I have to see you. It is crucially urgent. If you ever loved me, you'll come. There is nothing to fear. No one will know. I will be waiting for you at the_____Hotel—room 503 tonight, 10:30.

Lorne

**December 25, 1959**

*To Lorne Dieterling*

The music to be used (dance numbers):

La Traviata Overture [by Giuseppe Verdi]—theme song, build the whole novel on it, in scale. First time—for the first meeting of Hella and Lorne. Then—for walk through the forest.
"Will o' the Wisp"—for dance in the dive.
"Reconciliation Polka."
"Marionetta at Midnight."
"Eva Overture" [by Franz Lehar] or "Simple Confession."
"Anima."
Possibly use "In the Shadows" and "Polichinelle" (from "La Source").

**March 21, 1963**

The story of Atlas who did *not* go on strike. (The issue of "pronouncing moral judgment," of *not* sanctioning evil. Or: "how to lead a rational life in an irrational society.")

What would happen if a few key people or cultural leaders maintained a "moral tone"—instead of today's scared, social-metaphysical, cowardly surrender to any *immoral* assertiveness (which is the policy of letting evil set the moral terms). Why are people more afraid of me than of communism? Is it that they know I demand immediate, moral-epistemological action from them, and a long-range stand—while communism is a threat they can evade and make unreal in their own minds? Is it the issue of their guilt and lack of self-esteem, which makes physical terror or disaster more "acceptable" to them than psycho-epistemological terror, than the immediate threat to their (pseudo) self-esteem?

—◦—

(On re-reading the above:) I think it's obvious that the issue here is: Does one want a world and a life geared to one's best—or to one's worst? Today's people prefer to protect their own vices and weaknesses rather than fight for their virtues. This makes one point obvious: the "gray" people are the guiltiest and rottenest of all; *they* make evil possible. There is no such thing as a "mixed" moral position—it is *only* the evil that can profit by and win in a "mixed psychology" (or "mixed morality")—just as in a "mixed economy."

What causes that? Lack of self-esteem and, therefore, of self-confidence. What is the cause of that lack? Lack of moral knowledge—but only in part; more fundamentally, it is the indulgence of emotions at the expense of reason: a basic, *volitional* psycho-epistemological issue which does not depend on the content of one's knowledge.

**January 2, 1964**

### To Lorne Dieterling

*Theme:* Loyalty to values, *as a sense of life.*

My earlier notes are all wrong. The approach I projected is too intellectual—too explicit. The novel has to deal with the generalized terms of a "sense of life"—i.e., with *emotional metaphysics.* The nature of the assignment (and the trick) is to *concretize the story, while keeping it abstract.*

This is why Hella has to be a dancer. Convey the meaning of music and dancing as the esthetic expression of a "sense of life."

### Key points of the story:

Hella's love for Lorne.

His engagement party to Gloria—and the scene between Hella and Lorne on her way home.

Her "private universe."

His betrayal of her (and of his values).

Her career disaster.

Her walk—and her triumph.

*Tentative Outline*

[*The first part of the outline, through the deterioration of Lorne's marriage to Gloria, has been omitted here because it is the same as earlier.*]

Gloria and the "playboy." Lorne's request. The "playboy's" murder. Hella as witness (or suspected witness).

The scene between Gloria and Lorne: her demand. Hella receives Lorne's note.

Back to the present: the scene in the hotel room.

Hella's dismissal from the University (a kind of "trial scene"). Her debut—dancing for a single man in the audience. Her walk home—Lorne follows her, their final reunion.

**April 28, 1965**

*To Lorne Dieterling ("Sense of Life")*

*Emotional abstractions.* An emotional abstraction consists of all those things which have the power to make one experience a certain emotion. For instance: a heroic man, the New York skyline, flying in a plane, a sunlit "stylized" landscape, ecstatic music, an achievement of which one is proud. (These same things will give an emotion of terror and guilt to a man with the wrong premises; all except the last, which is impossible to him.) An opposite example: a humble or depraved man, an old village or ruins, "walking on the moors," a desolate landscape, folk songs or atonal music, the failure of someone else's achievement or ambition.

(The root and common denominator in all these things is self-esteem or lack of it; pro-man or anti-man; pro-life or anti-life.)

**January 1, 1966**

*To Lorne Dieterling*

The two basic "sense of life" music numbers are: "Will o' the Wisp" (as the triumph, the *achieved* sense of life) and "La Traviata Overture" (as the way there).

*To be used as dance numbers:*

"*La Traviata Overture*": the first dance described—the dance of
rising, without ever moving from one spot—done by means of her
arms and body—ending on "Dominique's statue" posture, as "higher
than raised arms," as the achieved, as the total surrender to a vision
and, simultaneously, "This is I." (The open, the naked, the "without
armor.") (Possibly, her first meeting with him.)

"*Will o' the Wisp*": *the* triumph—the tap dance and ballet combined—
*my* total sense of life. (Probably, danced in a low-grade dive, with
Lorne present. Possibly, projected as a dance, with him, much earlier,
as *his* sense of life, too; thus, a crucial turning point in his realization
of the way he is going, the wrong distance he has traveled.)

"*Destiny Valse*": done at the worst time of her break with him—
danced alone, *projecting his presence.*

**January 2, 1966**

*To Lorne Dieterling*

Hella Maris
Lorne Dieterling
Gloria Thornton
Aurelius Taylor (the professor, the spiritual "intellectual")
Bruce Beasely (the businessman, the plain brute)
Frieda Baker (the flat-foot dancer)
The traitor
The playboy
The town—Athens, Maine.

———◆———

*The notes end here.*

*This story has obvious features in common with AR's early fiction. The
protagonist is a woman, as was almost always the case prior to* The Fountainhead. *Further, the heroine's romantic love is unrequited, as in* The Husband I Bought *(see* The Early Ayn Rand*). And, as in* The Little Street *or the
screenplay* Ideal, *the protagonist faces an "enemy world" in which most
people betray their values.*

*So AR has come full circle. She returned at the end to a problem that
had concerned her from the beginning: how does one maintain a view of life*

*as it could be and ought to be, while living in a culture that is predominantly hostile to rational values? At this stage, however, she knows the solution, and serenity has replaced her earlier bitterness. Despite the tragic aspects of* To Lorne Dieterling, *the novel was to have an uplifting theme. AR's purpose was to show that Hella, as a profoundly independent person, can be affected "only down to a certain point." Though she suffers as a result of the moral treason of others, she is ultimately able to preserve the exalted sense of life that is so eloquently expressed in AR's favorite music.*

*AR regarded philosophy as a means to the achievement of a unique goal: the lighthearted, joyous state of existence that she had envisioned— and experienced—from the time of her youth. It is fitting, therefore, that her last fiction notes are about a woman like herself, who maintains such a view of life to the end, even while those around her do not.*

# INDEX